**8th EDITION**

# the TOOLS & TECHNIQUES of

## EMPLOYEE BENEFIT AND RETIREMENT PLANNING

### STEPHAN R. LEIMBERG and JOHN J. McFADDEN

The
**NATIONAL UNDERWRITER** Company
PROFESSIONAL PUBLISHING GROUP

P.O. Box 14367 • Cincinnati, Ohio 45250-0367
1-800-543-0874 • www.nationalunderwriter.com

ISBN 0-87218-634-2

Library of Congress Control Number: 2003107217

**THE NATIONAL UNDERWRITER COMPANY**

Copyright © 1989, 1990, 1993, 1995, 1997, 1999, 2001, 2003
The National Underwriter Company
P.O. Box 14367
Cincinnati, Ohio 45250-0367


Eighth Edition


Third Printing

Printed in the United States of America

# DEDICATION

## Stephan R. Leimberg

*To Dan Hoellering, my friend
who always found the time to
do so much for so many*

## John J. McFadden

*To Rhoda, Susanna, and Diana*

# ABOUT THE AUTHORS

## Stephan R. Leimberg

Stephan R. Leimberg is CEO of LISI, an e-mail commentary and tax law news service, CEO of Leimberg and LeClair, Inc., an estate and financial planning software company, and President of Leimberg Associates, Inc., a publishing and software company in Bryn Mawr, Pennsylvania. He is a lecturer-in-law in the Masters of Taxation Program of Villanova University School of Law, holds a B.A. from Temple University, and a J.D. from Temple University School of Law.

Leimberg is the author of numerous books on estate, financial, and employee benefit and retirement planning and a nationally known speaker. Leimberg is the creator and principal author of the five-book *Tools and Techniques* series including *The Tools and Techniques of Estate Planning, The Tools and Techniques of Financial Planning, The Tools and Techniques of Employee Benefit and Retirement Planning, The Tools and Techniques of Life Insurance Planning*, and *The Tools and Techniques of Charitable Planning*. Leimberg is co-author of *Tax Planning with Life Insurance* with noted attorney Howard Zaritsky, *The New Book of Trusts - Post '97 Tax Law* with attorneys Charles K. Plotnick and Daniel Evans, and *How to Settle an Estate* with Charles K. Plotnick.

Leimberg is co-creator of many software packages for the financial services professional including *NumberCruncher* (estate and financial planning), *Business QuickView* (business valuation, projection, and analysis), *IRS Factors Calculator* (actuarial computations), and *Financial Analyzer II*. His most recent software packages are *Estate Planning Quickview* (Estate Planning Flow Charts), *Gifts That Give, Gifts That Give Back, Long-term Care*, and *Toward a Zero Estate Tax* (PowerPoint Client Seminars).

A nationally known speaker, Professor Leimberg has addressed the Miami Tax Institute, the NYU Tax Institute, the Notre Dame Law School and Duke University Law School's Estate Planning Conference, the National Association of Estate Planners and Councils, and the AICPA's National Estate Planning Forum. Leimberg has also spoken to the Federal Bureau of Investigation, and the National Aeronautics and Space Administration.

Leimberg was awarded the Excellence in Writing Award of the American Bar Association's Probate and Property Section. He has been honored as Estate Planner of the Year by the Montgomery County Estate Planning Council and as Distinguished Estate Planner by the Philadelphia Estate Planning Council. He is also a recipient of the President's Cup of the Philadelphia Life Underwriters, a two time Boris Todorovitch Lecturer, and the First Ben Feldman Lecturer.

Leimberg was named 1998 Edward N. Polisher Lecturer of the Dickinson School of Law.

## John J. McFadden

John J. McFadden is Professor of Taxation at The American College in Bryn Mawr, PA. His undergraduate degree is from Lehigh University, with a master's degree from the University of Rochester, and a J.D. from Harvard Law School. He has been admitted to the Pennsylvania Bar and the United States Tax Court.

At the American College Mr. McFadden, a tax and compensation planning specialist, is responsible for the College's graduate courses in Advanced Pension and Retirement Planning and Executive Compensation. He is editor of the College's current guidebook, *Financial Services 2000*.

Mr. McFadden is the author of articles in tax and professional journals on such subjects as professional corporations, accumulated earnings, retirement plan distributions, and nonqualified deferred compensation. He is author of *Retirement Plans for Employees* and co-author of *Employee Benefits*, 6th edition, published by Dearborn Financial Publishing, Inc. in 2000.

Mr. McFadden also speaks and consults on tax and compensation planning matters and conducts seminars for financial planners active in those areas.

# PREFACE

*The Tools and Techniques of Employee Benefit and Retirement Planning*, 8th edition, is intended to serve as an easily accessible, up-to-date guide to creative employee benefit and retirement planning for use by practicing financial planners, insurance agents, accountants, attorneys and other financial services professionals, as well as company managers, personnel departments, and law and graduate school students. It is designed to meet these professionals' needs for timely and accurate introductory, overview, or review information in this area. Such needs are increasing for two reasons. First, the high direct and indirect expenses involved with recruiting, retaining and ultimately retiring employees mandates a careful search for the benefit and compensation package that will accomplish an employer's objectives in the most cost effective way. Second, in recent years, there has been a tremendous growth in federal legislation and regulatory activity in the compensation area; this increases the difficulty of designing benefit packages and also the cost (in taxes and penalties to employer and employee) of mistakes in benefit planning.

This book covers all major types of employee benefit arrangements. Although special consideration is given to employee benefit arrangements as applied to smaller, closely held businesses, most of the benefits described here are used by both small and large companies, and the same tax and other rules apply to both.

As is the case with our companion books, *The Tools and Techniques of Estate Planning*, 12th edition, *The Tools and Techniques of Financial Planning*, 6th edition, and *The Tools and Techniques of Life Insurance Planning*, 2nd edition, in this book each individual tool or technique of benefit or retirement planning is discussed in an easy-to-use format that is aimed at answering the planner's major questions:

WHAT IS IT? provides a brief description of the benefit planning tool or technique.

WHEN IS IT INDICATED? summarizes the client situations where the particular technique is most often beneficial.

ADVANTAGES and DISADVANTAGES provides a summary of the advantages and disadvantages of each technique.

DESIGN FEATURES summarizes the characteristic features of the technique and the planning options that are available.

TAX IMPLICATIONS describes the federal income, estate and payroll tax implications of the technique to both employer and employee; some state tax aspects are also noted where appropriate.

ERISA AND OTHER IMPLICATIONS summarizes the ERISA reporting and disclosure, funding, and other non-tax federal regulatory requirements.

HOW TO INSTALL THE PLAN provides a summary of the steps that must be taken for an employer to adopt and implement the plan.

WHERE CAN I FIND OUT MORE ABOUT IT? provides a list of references for further study and information.

QUESTIONS AND ANSWERS discusses some specific problems (and their solutions) that are often encountered by planners in connection with the benefit plan.

Where appropriate, some chapters may deviate somewhat from this format in order to provide the best approach to understanding the material.

The authors wish to acknowledge many members of the benefit planning community for discussions and critiques that over the years have contributed to the perspective taken in this book. Also, in particular, the authors are fortunate to have received substantial technical copy editing assistance from the following editors: Deborah A. Miner, J.D., CLU, ChFC; April K. Caudill, J.D., CLU, ChFC; William J. Wagner, J.D., LL.M., CLU; Joseph F. Stenken, J.D., Sonya E. King, J.D., LL.M., and John H. Fenton, J.D., M.S.B.A.

# CONTENTS

# Contents

# Appendices

# Chapter 1

# THE PROCESS OF EMPLOYEE BENEFIT PLANNING

The tools and techniques of employee benefit and retirement planning described in this book are aimed at and should be used to solve both general and specific financial planning problems for employers and their employees. This chapter explains the broad *process* by which the employer-client's needs are determined and "matched-up" with the appropriate benefit arrangements.

## WHAT BENEFIT PLANS CAN DO

As with any kind of financial planning, the starting point must be a full appreciation of what the tools and techniques at hand can actually accomplish for clients. In the case of employee benefit plans, two fundamental results can be achieved:

1. *Help employees meet needs that otherwise cannot be met.* This is the fundamental reason for employee benefit plans, and planners should always keep it in focus. Employee benefits have primarily been developed to help employees meet fundamental needs. For example—

   • health care costs for a serious illness are too great for people other than the very wealthy to meet "out of pocket." Insurance is a necessity—and the least expensive and simplest form of health insurance or health plan is usually a group plan provided by an employer for a group of employees.

   • retirement saving is difficult for most people; employer-sponsored plans not only promote retirement saving but provide tax "leverage" for such saving that the employee cannot obtain personally.

   • family protection in the event of an employee's untimely death can be promoted by employer-sponsored plans that are an attractive supplement to private life insurance—and for some employees, are the *only* form of life insurance reasonably available.

2. *Provide unique tax benefits.* Even if an employee is able to meet health care, retirement and other needs

without the employer's help—which is a rare situation, there's a dollars-and-cents reason why an employee benefit plan is the best way to provide for these needs. In many benefit plans, the employer's dollar is "leveraged" by what amounts to an additional contribution by the U.S. Treasury through tax benefits provided for employee benefit plans. This makes the employer's benefit dollar go further than a dollar expended for cash compensation. Specifically:

   • for qualified retirement plans, employers get an up front deduction for funding the plan, but employees do not pay taxes on the benefits until they receive them. This tax *deferral* available under an employer plan substantially increases the benefits available at retirement, compared with equal amounts of non tax-deferred private savings by the employee.

   • employer costs for employee health care plans are fully deductible *and* the benefits are *completely tax-free* to employees, regardless of amount. Without the employer plan, employees would have to pay for insurance or health care with after-tax dollars, with a tax deduction available only if (1) the taxpayer itemizes deductions and (2) the medical expense for the year exceeds the substantial "floor" for medical expense deductions.

   • other plans with substantial tax benefits include group-term life insurance plans, dependent care assistance plans, flexible spending accounts, incentive stock options, disability plans, and others discussed in this book.

## STEPS IN THE PLANNING PROCESS

The process of employee benefit planning can be broken down into six identifiable steps:

1. *Meet the client and gather data.*

2. *Identify the employer's objectives; quantify and prioritize them.*

3. *Analyze existing plans to identify weaknesses and needs for revision.*

4. *Formulate a new overall employee compensation plan.*

5. *Communicate the new plan effectively.*

6. *Develop a program for periodic review of the plan's effectiveness.*

*STEP 1: Meet the client and gather data.*

The planning process begins with fact finding. Only a thorough knowledge of the client's personal and business financial picture can provide the right analysis of benefit plan needs.

Some of the most important information will include:

- an employee census; this should include a list of all current employees with their ages, current compensation levels (both anticipated total (Form W-2) income as well as stated salaries), employment status (full or part time), ownership in the business if any, and dates of employment. Data for the current year is mandatory. Similar data for at least five prior years and the employer's projections for the future are extremely useful to the planner.

- financial information about the employer. Current balance sheets and income statements are mandatory, as well as historical data to give an indication of what level of expenditure the business can sustain for compensation programs.

- full information about all existing employee plans—their coverage, funding costs, contract expiration dates, and the like.

- if executive benefit planning for top executives or business owners is a significant consideration—and it usually is—the planner needs information about the executives' individual financial and estate planning situations and needs.

Benefit planners should develop a "fact finder" to record and document the data gathering process. Appendix C contains a data gathering form developed by The American College for its courses in Advanced Pension Planning; this form should help give some idea of documentation needs.

Planners should remember that formalizing the data gathering process in a fact finder not only provides the

information for current planning, but it also documents the *fact* that the planner went through this process of "due diligence" should any question about the design process ever arise in the future.

*STEP 2: Identify the employer's objectives; quantify and prioritize them.*

Clients may have conflicting objectives for their benefit plans, unrealistic expectations as to what the plans can accomplish, or an inaccurate idea of the cost of achieving certain objectives. The planner must formulate realistic objectives for the client's compensation planning and must establish an order of priorities. Realistic, achievable goals then become the basis for plan design.

Some benefit plan objectives that clients may formulate include:

- meeting employee needs for health care, retirement income, and protection against disability and premature death

- maintaining a program that complements (without duplicating) Social Security and each employee's own efforts in providing for health care, retirement income, and other needs

- meeting the "4-R" needs of the employer: recruiting, retaining, rewarding, and ultimately retiring employees

- maintaining a program that helps resist unionization or matches benefits for nonunion employees with those of union employees

- providing employee benefits that are comparable to those of other employers in the industry or in the same geographical area

- meeting cost targets; providing the most effective benefit package within cost limitations

- compensating key employees competitively while minimizing costs for non-key employees

- maximizing benefits for shareholder or owner-employees

*STEP 3: Analyze existing plans to identify weaknesses or needs for revision.*

To what extent do existing plans fail to meet client needs? Here's a checklist:

- Who is covered under the existing plan?

- What benefits are provided?

- What documentation exists? What documentation have employees received—that is, what have they been promised?

- What are the plan's annual costs and in what direction are these costs headed?

- How is the plan funded or financed?

- Who administers the plan—the employer or a third party?

- What are the expiration dates of existing plan contracts?

*STEP 4: Formulate a new overall employee compensation plan.*

A planner does not necessarily have to overhaul an employer's entire compensation package in order to serve the employer well, but it is important that whatever the planner recommends, it should be based on a comprehensive view of the employer's compensation planning needs, and should contribute to the employer's overall goals.

Individual chapters of this book provide detailed information about the advantages and disadvantages of each individual type of benefit plan, with an indication of situations in which that benefit plan will be most useful. But there is no simple formula by which the right "mix" of benefit plans can be designed to meet an employer's goals. That is an area where the planner's diligence and judgment will make a difference.

*STEP 5: Communicate the new plan effectively.*

From the earlier discussion of employer objectives, note that a large part of an employer's goals in instituting employee benefit programs depend on the employees' *subjective reaction* to the plan—how it improves morale, helps recruit and retain employees, complements employee efforts, and the like. Also, from other chapters in this book the planner will note that many types of benefit plans require informed choices by employees in order to be effective.

No matter how well the plan is designed, it will *fail* to meet those types of goals if it is not *communicated* effectively to employees. Thus effective communication is a

great deal more than a "soft" aspect of plan design; it is just as much a hard, dollars-and-cents matter as drafting documents correctly.

In today's benefit climate, communication with employees is a sophisticated process. First, although employers and planners should try to simplify benefit provisions as much as possible, government regulation and the complexity of the financial environment for benefit plans often make the plans very complicated. (See Appendix A for specific ERISA disclosure requirements.) Second, employees invariably have some degree of skepticism about the value of employer-instituted programs that must be overcome by appropriate types of communication. Finally, the often-noted decline in reading, writing, and speaking skills among the public in general means that planners can no longer assume that normal means of communicating information within a business will be adequate. Special efforts must be made.

Employers traditionally have provided a "benefits booklet" for employees that they can keep for reference concerning benefit plan provisions; however, under ERISA, "summary plan descriptions" are mandatory for many types of plans (see Appendix A). Employers should not view this as purely a paperwork requirement. On the contrary, a special effort should be made to provide summary plan descriptions that are part of a "benefits booklet" approach. The booklet should not only meet legal requirements but should also provide information about the employer's benefit plans that is clear and really useful to employees.

Another ERISA requirement that can be turned to advantage is the requirement to provide an "individual benefit statement" to employees on request. Again, instead of providing only the minimum individual information required by law, the statement can be used as a way for the employer to show the employee the full value of the employer's benefit program. Surveys by consulting firms almost invariably show that employees substantially underestimate the value of their benefit plans. Many employers provide individual benefit statements annually, whether or not the employee requests one. An example of such a benefit statement is included at the end of this chapter.

*STEP 6: Develop a program for periodic review of the plan's effectiveness.*

Benefit plans exist in a dynamic business and government regulatory climate. A business can change drastically in a short time due to new ownership or external or internal business changes. Benefit plans are heavily affected by federal tax laws and Congress, driven by revenue needs, changes the tax laws all too frequently. Thus, no tool or technique of benefit planning is likely to be effective indefinitely without revision.

As part of the planning process, a schedule should be established for reviewing and monitoring plan effectiveness and plan costs. Revision procedures must be developed to assure continuing achievement of the client's objectives.

**Figure 1.1**

## INDIVIDUAL BENEFITS STATEMENT

This Individual Benefit Statement lists the benefits that both protect you and your family now and provide security for your future. We know you will find this statement informative, and we hope it will be useful in your personal planning.

■ **HEALTH-CARE BENEFITS**

You have elected coverage for   ❐ yourself.      ❐ your family.      ❐ You have not elected coverage.

The highlights of your Comprehensive Medical Plan are summarized in the following table. See your employee handbook for further details.

| *In-Hospital Benefits* | *Out-of-Hospital Benefits* | *Special Benefits* |
|---|---|---|
| $100 deductible per person each calendar year (3-deductible maximum per family) | | 100% of outpatient emergency treatment of accidental injury (no deductible). |
| 100% of covered expenses, including maternity care, after the deductible is met. | 80% of first $3,000 of covered expenses, then 100% of remaining covered expenses. 50% of psychiatric treatment up to $1,000 a year ($20-a-visit maximum benefit). | 80% of diagnostic X-ray and laboratory tests (deductible applies). |
| OVERALL PLAN MAXIMUM: $1 million per person | | |

■ **DISABILITY INCOME BENEFITS**

*Salary Continuation Plan*

- Your full salary continues for _____ weeks, then 3/4 of your salary continues for _____ weeks.

*Long-term Disability Income Plan*

- If disabled over 26 weeks, you will receive _____ a month. This is 60% of your base pay and includes benefits under the corporation's plan and any Social Security benefits, other than family benefits, for which you are eligible.

- If you have eligible dependents you can receive additional family benefits under Social Security up to _____ a month.

- If total long-term disability income from the above sources exceeds 80% of your base pay, disability benefits under the corporation's plan will be reduced to bring the total to the 70% level.

■ **SURVIVOR'S BENEFITS**

*Group Life Insurance*

- If you die from any cause your survivors will receive _____ from the corporation's group life insurance plan.

*Supplemental Life Insurance*

- If you participate in the corporation's supplemental life insurance plan, your survivors will receive an additional _____ upon your death from any cause.

*Travel Accident Insurance*

- An additional benefit of _____ will be paid to your survivors if your death results from an accident while traveling on corporate business.

*Social Security*

- Social Security will provide a monthly income of up to _____ a month if you have an eligible spouse with 2 or more children.

*Medical Coverage*

- Dependent's coverage can continue on a contributory basis.

**Figure 1.1 (continued)**

---

■ **RETIREMENT BENEFITS**

*Normal Retirement*

- At age 65, you will receive an estimated _____ a month from the corporation's retirement plan and Social Security. Additional social security benefits are payable for an eligible spouse age 62 or older.

- Your spouse will receive an estimated _____ a month from the corporation's retirement plan and Social Security if your spouse is age 65 or older at your death.

- If you leave the corporation before retirement, you will be eligible to receive a pension amounting to the vested portion of your accrued benefit. The pension is payable at age 65, but reduced benefits are available as early as age 55. Your current accrued benefit is approximately _____ a month. Your vested benefit is _____ a month.

*Early Retirement*

- You may retire as early as age 55 with five years' service and receive a reduced benefit. For example at age 62, your retirement income from the corporation's plan and Social Security would be approximately _____.

*Other Retirement Benefits*

- Medical coverage continues after retirement and is coordinated with Medicare.

- Group life insurance coverage continues in the amount of $5,000.

### BENEFIT STATEMENT REVIEW FOR

_____

Many of us forget that there is more to our paycheck than the amount we take home. The following are the "extras" that were provided in _____ (year) and their value as determined by the cost to your employer.

| | Annual Value | Value per Hour |
|---|---|---|
| (1) Social Security (employer's contribution) | $_____ | $_____ |
| (2) Workers' Compensation Insurance Premium | _____ | _____ |
| (3) State Unemployment Insurance Premium | _____ | _____ |
| (4) Paid Holidays | _____ | _____ |
| (5) Vacation Days | _____ | _____ |
| (6) Pension | _____ | _____ |
| (7) Salary Continuation | _____ | _____ |
| (8) Long-Term Disability Income Insurance | _____ | _____ |
| (9) Life Insurance | _____ | _____ |
| (10) Medical Expense Insurance (employer's contribution) | _____ | _____ |
| (11) Others | _____ | _____ |
| _____ | _____ | _____ |
| _____ | _____ | _____ |

The $_____ value of those sometimes forgotten benefits is equal to _____% of the $_____ you received as salary or wages in ____ (year). These benefits are provided to protect you and your family from certain financial risks and help provide for your future retirement.

# Chapter 2

# DESIGNING THE RIGHT PENSION PLAN

This chapter is an overview of the process of designing a pension plan for a business client. It is intended to provide a framework for the detailed discussions of *each* type of plan provided in Part A of this book, "Pensions and Deferred Compensation."

Designing the "right" pension plan for a business can be divided into three broad steps:

*Step 1: Gather the relevant facts.* The most important factual information is (1) an employee census (i.e., a list of all employees with their compensation levels, ages, and years of service for the employer); and (2) information about existing and past pension programs, if any, that the employer has maintained. These are essential; but many other details about an employer's business may be important in various cases. Appendix C of this book contains a detailed Fact Finder developed by The American College for its Advanced Pension Planning courses.

*Step 2: Identify employer objectives.* In addition to factual information, the planner must develop with the client a list of objectives (objectives that can be promoted by a pension plan) and their priorities with the employer.

*Step 3: Choose plan features that promote the employer objectives.* This chapter is a preliminary guide to matching objectives with plan design features. Once the design process has zeroed-in on specific plans or design features, later chapters will provide the necessary details.

## WHAT CAN A PENSION PLAN DO FOR THE EMPLOYER?

The pension planner must begin with an overall idea of what employer objectives can be promoted by a pension plan. A pension plan—in the broad sense of retirement, deferred compensation, or savings plan of any type—can, if properly designed and implemented, promote many employer and employee objectives, the most important of which are listed here. While not every one of these objectives can be met with a single plan—in fact, some are conflicting—it is useful to begin this chapter by noting what pension plans *can* do.

1. *Help Employees With Retirement Saving.* This is the most fundamental reason for pension plans and it should not be overlooked. Most employees, even highly compensated employees, find personal savings difficult. It is difficult not merely for psychological reasons, but also because our tax system and economy are oriented toward consumption rather than savings.

   For example, the federal income tax system imposes tax on income from savings (even if it is not used for consumption) with only three major exceptions: (1) deferral of tax on capital gains until realized; (2) exclusion of gain on the sale of a personal residence; and (3) deferral of tax and other benefits for qualified retirement plans and IRAs. In other words, a qualified retirement plan or IRA is one of only three ways our government encourages savings through the tax system, and the benefits of a retirement plan are available only if an employer adopts the plan.

2. *Tax Deferral for Owners and Highly Compensated Employees.* While many employees in all compensation categories can benefit from pension plans, owners and other key employees typically have more money available for saving, have higher compensation, have longer service with the employer, and often are older than other employees; thus, they can benefit more from pension plans. When designing a plan for a business owner, a typical objective is to maximize the benefits for the owner (or, in some cases, to minimize the discrimination *against* the highly compensated that is built into some of the qualified pension plan rules.)

3. *Help Recruit, Reward, Retain, and Retire Employees.* These "four R's" of compensation policy are an important objective in designing pension plans. The plan can help *recruit* employees by matching or bettering pension benefit packages offered by competing employers; it can *reward* employees by tying

benefits to compensation; it can help *retain* employees by tying maximum pension benefits to long service; and it can help *retire* employees by allowing them to retire with dignity—without a drastic drop in living standard—when their productivity has begun to decline and the organization needs new members.

4. *Encourage Productivity.* Certain types of plan design can act as employee incentives; this is particularly true of plans whose contributions are profit-based or those providing employee accounts invested in stock of the employer.

5. *Discourage Collective Bargaining.* An attractive pension package—as good as or better than labor union-sponsored plans in the area—can help to keep employees from organizing into a collective bargaining unit. Collective bargaining often poses major business problems for some employers.

## QUALIFIED VERSUS NONQUALIFIED PENSION PLANS

All pension plans involve deferral of part of an employee's compensation for performing services for the employer. Deferred compensation is compensation that is not paid currently—in the year services are performed or shortly thereafter.[1] Retirement plans are either *qualified* or *nonqualified*. Qualified plans receive more favorable tax benefits, but are subject to very stringent government regulation.

The chart in Figure 2.1, which is taken from The American College's Executive Compensation graduate course, summarizes differences between qualified and nonqualified plans.

*When is a Nonqualified Plan Indicated?* Chapter 15 discusses in detail when and how nonqualified plans are used. Some highlights:

- nonqualified plans can be designed for key employees without the sometimes prohibitive cost of covering a broader group of employees.

- nonqualified plans can provide benefits to executives beyond the limits allowed in qualified plans.

- nonqualified plans can provide "customized" retirement or savings benefits for selected executives.

## QUALIFIED PLANS—WHAT THEY ARE AND WHAT THEY CAN DO

A qualified plan receives tax benefits that are not available for a nonqualified plan. These tax benefits are:

- Amounts paid into the plan—employer contributions and also employee salary reduction contributions—are deductible by the employer (or tax-excludable by the employee) in the year for which they are paid.

- Employees are not taxed in the year that the employer contributes to the plan, even if they are fully vested in their plan benefits at that time.

- The plan itself is a tax-exempt fund. Earnings on plan investments accumulate tax free in the plan and are not taxed currently to the employer or the employee. This significantly increases the effective investment return on plan assets.

- Certain lump-sum benefits may be eligible for a special 10-year averaging tax computation (available to certain employees born before 1936) that may reduce tax rates on the benefit.

These tax benefits add up to a substantial, quantifiable amount of tax "leverage," as will be shown later in this chapter.

### Types of Qualified Plans

Qualified plans are either defined contribution or defined benefit plans. As the names imply, this depends on whether the plan specifies an employer contribution rate on the one hand, or guarantees a specified benefit level on the other.

### Defined Contribution Plans

In a defined contribution plan, the employer establishes and maintains an individual account for each plan participant. When the participant becomes eligible to receive benefit payments—usually at retirement or termination of employment—the benefit is based on the total amount in the participant's account. The account balance includes employer contributions, employee contributions in some cases, and earnings on the account over all the years of deferral.

**Figure 2.1**

| | Item | Qualified Retirement Plan | Unfunded Nonqualified Deferred Compensation Plan |
|---|---|---|---|
| **COMPARISON OF VARIOUS ITEMS OF QUALIFIED RETIREMENT PLANS WITH UNFUNDED NONQUALIFIED DEFERRED COMPENSATION PLANS** | | | |
| a. | Timing of corporation's income tax deduction | Corporation receives a deduction when contributions are made to the plan. | Corporation receives a deduction when benefits are received by employees. |
| b. | Who must be covered by plan | 70 percent of nonhighly compensated employees, or alternative test under Code section 410. | Corporation free to discriminate as it sees fit if plan covers only independent contractors or members of management or highly compensated employees. |
| c. | Extent to which benefits may be forfeitable | Must meet 5-year or 3-to-7-year vesting test; faster vesting for top-heavy plans, and for matching contributions after 2001. | The qualified plan vesting rules apply only if plan covers rank-and-file employees. If plan covers only independent contractors or a select group of management or highly compensated employees, benefits may be forfeitable in full at all times. |
| d. | Tax treatment of earnings on amount set aside to fund plan | These earnings accumulate tax free but will be taxable to employee along with other plan assets when distributed to employee; no income tax deduction for employer. | These earnings will be taxed currently to the employer and will be taxable to the employee when distributed as benefits; however, employer will be entitled to an income tax deduction at that time. |
| e. | Coverage of independent contractors and directors | Only employees are eligible for coverage. | Independent contractors and directors may be covered in the same manner as an employee. |
| f. | Balance sheet impact | Satisfactory if plan is not underfunded. | Can be adverse (see Appendix E). |

The employer does not guarantee the amount of the benefit a participant will ultimately receive in a defined contribution plan. Instead, the employer must make contributions under a formula specified in the plan. There are two principal types of defined contribution plan formulas:

- *Money purchase pension plan.* Under a money purchase plan, the employer must contribute each year to each participant's account a stated percentage of the participant's compensation. This percentage is usually about 10%, although percentages up to 25 are possible. The money purchase plan is probably the simplest of all types of plans.

- *Profit sharing plan.* A profit sharing plan is a defined contribution plan under which the employer determines the amount of the contribution each year, rather than having a stated contribution obligation. In a profit sharing plan, the employer can decide not to contribute to the plan at all in certain cases. Typically, plan contributions are based on the employer's profits in some manner. If a contribution is made, the total amount must be allocated to each participant's account using a nondiscriminatory formula. Such formulas are usually based on compensation, but service can be taken into account. The allocation formula can also be weighted in favor of plan participants who entered the plan at older ages—using an "age-weighted profit sharing plan" or a "cross-tested (new comparability) plan," as explained later in this chapter.

Profit sharing plans often feature employee contributions, typically with an employer match. For example, the plan could provide that employees may contribute to the plan up to 6% of their compensation, with the employer contributing 50 cents for every $1 of employee contribution. This type of plan is referred to as a *thrift* or *savings* plan. (A SIMPLE IRA uses this type of design, with certain additional requirements; see Chapter 20.)

Another variation on the profit-sharing plan design is the *cash or deferred* or *Section 401(k)* plan. Under this type of plan, employees can make tax deferred contributions by electing salary reductions. For 2003, contributions of up to $12,000 annually per employee are permitted. In addition, catch-up contributions of up to $2,000 in 2003 are permitted for certain employees over age 50. Employers often match employee salary reductions in order to encourage employee participation in these plans.

All these types of plans are discussed in more detail in separate chapters of this book.

### Defined Benefit Plans

Defined benefit plans provide a specific amount of benefit to the employee at normal retirement age. There are many different types of formulas for determining this benefit, as discussed in Chapter 9 of this book. These formulas are typically based on the employee's earnings averaged over a number of years of service. The formula also can be based on the employee's service.

These plans are funded actuarially, which means that, for a given benefit level, the annual funding amount is greater for employees who are older at entry into the plan, since the time to fund the benefit is less in the case of an older entrant. This makes defined benefit plans attractive to professionals and closely held business owners; they tend to adopt retirement plans for their businesses when they are relatively older than their regular employees. A large percentage of the total cost for a defined benefit plan in this situation funds these key employees' benefits, as discussed further in Chapter 9.

## WHY A QUALIFIED PLAN IS—OR IS NOT— BETTER THAN CASH

The tax advantages of qualified plans mean that an employer's dollar spent on qualified plan benefits is "bigger" than a dollar spent on cash compensation. This is because while the employer gets a current deduction for the cost of the plan, benefits are not taxable to employees until paid. The taxes that are not paid currently can be thought of as an "interest free loan" from the U.S. Treasury. The time value of money "leverages" the value of each employer dollar; the income earned on deferred taxes directly benefits the employee but costs the employer nothing extra.

So why doesn't every employer immediately maximize the qualified plan benefits for every employee, since qualified plan benefits are "cheaper" than cash compensation? The problem is that not every employee *perceives* the same value for qualified plan benefits.

Employees who value retirement benefits most highly include:

- older employees nearing retirement

- long-term employees with substantial vested benefits

- highly compensated employees who can afford to forego substantial cash compensation for retirement benefits

- employees who do not depend on their compensation for basic living expenses—for example, the "supplemental" earner in a two-income family

Employees not in these four categories often do not value and do not want deferred plan benefits—they would rather have immediate cash:

- younger employees view retirement as a distant prospect and therefore psychologically "discount" the value of retirement benefits

- transitory employees do not expect to stay with an employer long enough to fully vest or accrue substantial benefits

- low-paid employees cannot afford to forego any substantial amount of cash compensation in return for retirement benefits.

**Figure 2.2**

| WORStructure | | |
|---|---|---|

### WORKSHEET
### Qualified Plan vs. Private Savings

for <u>Dr. Leberkrank, P.C.</u>

**Inputs and assumptions**

| | | |
|---|---|---|
| 1. | Assumed pre-tax rate of return | 8% |
| 2. | Annual plan contribution for owner | $40,000 |
| 3. | Cost for employees if plan provides line 2 contribution for owner | $ 3,000 |
| 4. | Total cost (line 2 plus line 3) | $43,000 |
| 5. | Pre-retirement tax rate | 35% |
| 6. | Assumed post-retirement tax rate | 33% |
| 7. | Years until retirement | 24 |
| 8. | Desired number of years of annuity payout (generally no more than single/joint life expectancy at retirement) | 20 |

| Calculations | Qualified Plan | Private Savings |
|---|---|---|
| 9. Accumulation at retirement (future value (FV) of [line 7] years of payments) | $2,670,590 <br> • Annual payment = line 2 <br> • Interest rate = line 1 | $1,161,457 <br> • Annual payment = line 4 - (line 5)% of line 4 <br> • Interest rate = line 1 - (line 5)% of line 1 |
| 10. Annual annuity available (amortization [PMT] of line 9 over [line 8] years) | $272,006 <br> • Principal = line 9 <br> • Interest = line 1 | $105,620 <br> • Principal = line 9 <br> • Interest = line 1 - (line 6)% of line 1 |
| 11. Income tax on annuity payment | $89,762 <br> (line 6)% of line 10 | -0- |
| 12. Net annuity (line 10 - line 11) | $182,244 | $105,620 |

In other words, pension plan design for most employers requires more sophistication than simply "loading up" on benefits. Money spent on plan benefits for employees who do not value these benefits is, in effect, a "pure cost" of the plan. Such costs must not outweigh the value of benefits for those who do want them; otherwise the employer's compensation policy is inefficient and may even be counterproductive.

In designing the plan, a designer must attempt to both (1) maximize the benefits for those who want them and (2) choose a plan design that will be perceived as valuable by the maximum number of employees.

*Is a qualified plan cost-effective? An example:* For a given client, the threshold question raised by the issues just discussed must be: "Does *any* qualified plan make any sense at all in the client's business?"

To illustrate, let's look at what might be viewed as a "worst case" scenario—the small professional corporation. It is a worst-case situation because the owner or owners are generally much older and higher paid than the rest of the employees; and there is often high turnover among the younger employees. So, the owners want the maximum pension benefits but the rest of the employees probably do not value these benefits much. Thus, the cost of benefits for nonowner employees is about as close to a "pure cost" of providing the owners' benefits as the planner commonly runs into.

Suppose your client, Doctor Leberkrank, age 41, and two office employees are the only employees of the doctor's professional corporation. The doctor wants to establish a qualified profit sharing plan that will enable him to contribute the $40,000 annual maximum (as indexed for 2003). A preliminary plan design analysis indicates that in order to do this, a total of $3,000 will have to be contributed annually on behalf of the two office employees, in order to meet the qualified plan nondiscrimination rules. Thus, the doctor's choice is between $40,000 annually of private savings outside the plan or a $43,000 annual contribution to the plan with its accompanying tax deferral benefits.

Let's use the worksheet in Figure 2.2 (from The American College's Advanced Pension Planning courses). The worksheet records these facts and other inputs and assumptions necessary to make a preliminary calculation.

The worksheet shows that, based on these facts and assumptions, the qualified plan will provide more financial security for the client than a private savings program. The plan will provide an annual net income at retirement of $182,244, as compared with only $105,620 under the private savings program.

Note that the monetary advantage of the qualified plan depends to a considerable extent on minimizing contributions on behalf of nonowner employees. Obviously, this will be difficult where there are many employees in the business. In this example, the qualified plan worked out well, but it might not have, had the required contribution for office employees been higher.

High required contributions for nonowner employees do not necessarily mean that the plan is not viable. The next step for the planner is then to consider refinements and alternatives:

- Contributions for employees are not really "wasted"—they're a valuable form of additional compensation for employees. The planner should try to design a plan where these contributions have a maximum perceived value for the employees and, thus, contribute positively to the employer's "recruiting, retaining, rewarding, and retiring" goals.

- The plan can be redesigned to maximize contributions for the owners and minimize contributions for other employees.

Planning options that can achieve these results are discussed in the next section.

## MATCHING EMPLOYER OBJECTIVES WITH THE RIGHT PLAN DESIGN

Each type of qualified plan meets some planning objectives better than others. Plan design consists of finding the right match between employer objectives and the qualified plan "menu." Some common employer objectives, and the matching plan design features that are available for customizing the plan to the employer's objectives, will be summarized here.

OBJECTIVE: *Maximize the proportion of plan costs that benefit highly-compensated employees.*

Many employers, particularly small, closely held companies, view retirement plans as worthwhile only if they provide substantial, tax-sheltered retirement benefits for key employees. The following are the commonly used techniques for doing this:

1.  *Defined benefit plans.* Defined benefit plans typically provide the maximum possible proportionate benefits for key employees when key employees, as a group, are older than rank and file employees. This age distribution exists in the majority of small businesses.

    A defined contribution plan allows a contribution of no more than $40,000 (in 2003) annually for an employee—but for a defined benefit plan there is *no* dollar limit on the amount of contributions. Instead, the projected *benefit* (not the contribution) is subject to a limit of the lesser of 100% of high three-year average compensation or $160,000 annually (in 2003). Funding the maximum annual benefit for a younger employee generally requires a deductible employer contribution that is less than $40,000 annually, while for an employee who enters the plan at an age greater than approximately 45, the deductible contribution for the maximum benefit is considerably more than $40,000 annually. For a given set of actuarial assumptions, there is a "crossover" age at which the defined benefit plan is more favorable to adopt.[3] (See Figure 2.3.)

    Defined benefit plans can be made even more favorable to key employees by appropriate choices of actuarial assumptions, retirement age and late retirement provisions, form of benefits, and level of Social Security integration. All of these design aspects of defined benefit plans are discussed further in Chapter 9.

2.  *Service-based contribution or benefit formulas.* A plan's contribution or benefit formula can be based on an employee's years of service with the employer. This generally benefits the owners and key employees who typically have longer service. Such formulas can be used in defined contribution plans, but are

**Figure 2.3**

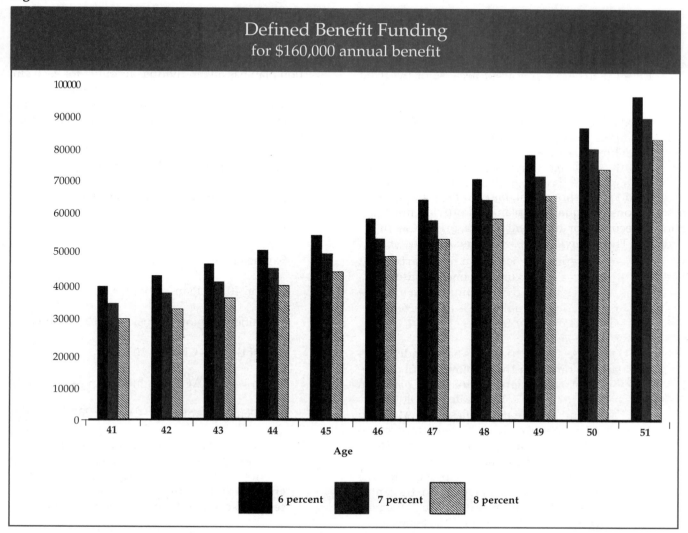

## Defined Benefit Funding
### for $160,000 annual benefit

Age

6 percent  7 percent  8 percent

even more effective in defined benefit plans. Defined benefit plans can even provide benefits for *past* service—service prior to establishment of the plan. Of course, the Code's nondiscrimination requirements discussed in Chapter 25 must be satisfied.

3. *Age-weighting and cross-testing.* The age-weighting aspect of a defined benefit plan, which provides favorable funding of benefits for older plan entrants, can also be provided in a defined contribution plan. Where the employer wants to avoid the complexity of the defined benefit approach, age-weighted defined contribution plans should be considered.

There are two types of defined contribution plans that tend to favor older employees in this manner: the cross-tested plan, and the fixed formula age-weighted plan. These are described in Chapter 22.

The cross-tested plan, which is the most commonly used, provides a flat percentage allocation (5% of compensation or more) to most rank-and-file employees and the maximum allocation (generally the $40,000 (in 2003) maximum under the annual additions limit) for key employees and owners. By projecting contributions to each employee's retirement age and computing the equivalent benefit for this projected accumulation, the benefit structure can generally be shown to be nondiscriminatory under the tax regulations, so long as most of the rank-and-file employees are younger than the highly compensated employees.

The alternative is to use a fixed age-weighted formula, under which the percentage of compensation contributed for each employee is based actuarially on the employee's age on entering the plan (higher for older employees). This type of plan can be either a profit sharing plan (where employer contributions each year are discretionary) or a pension plan (which requires annual employer contributions). The latter type of fixed-formula age-weighted plan (pension plan) is called a target plan. Target plans are rarely used because of the fixed contribution requirement.

4. *Combinations of defined benefit and defined contribution plans.* Is it possible to contribute the maximum limits for an employee under *both* a defined benefit plan *and* a defined contribution plan? Under ERISA as originally enacted in 1974, the answer was no. However, the "combined plan formula" originally set forth in ERISA and Code Section 415(e) was repealed, effective after 1999.[5] It is thus possible to have a defined contribution plan and a defined benefit plan for a participant that provides the maximum benefit under both plans, subject to an overall limitation on employer deductions equal to 25% of covered payroll, with certain exceptions.

5. *401(k) plans.* Section 401(k) plans have tended to be popular with rank-and-file employees, but designers should not overlook the fact that these plans can be favorable to highly compensated employees as well. The nondiscrimination rules—the ADP and ACP tests[6]—inherently allow a higher rate of contribution for highly compensated employees. However, these rules require maximum participation from nonhighly compensated employees for the highly compensated to fully enjoy the extra contribution levels, so the employer must "sell" the plan to employees in order to maximize the benefits of a 401(k) plan to the owners. In the alternative, a SIMPLE or safe harbor 401(k) plan design could be used (see Chapter 19). These special plan designs allow employers who are willing to meet certain funding and other requirements to *avoid* ADP/ACP testing, as well as to maximize benefits to the highly compensated employees without regard to the participation levels of nonhighly compensated employees.

6. *Social Security integration.* Employers are allowed to "integrate" certain qualified plans with Social Security benefits. The rules for this are very complicated,[7] but in effect they allow a higher rate of qualified plan contributions or benefits for each employee with compensation above a specified level. This reduces employer costs for the qualified plan benefits for lower-paid employees and correspondingly allows greater benefits or contributions for higher-paid employees.

OBJECTIVE: *Provide a savings medium that employees perceive as valuable.*

1. *Defined contribution plans.* Every defined contribution plan has an "individual account" for each employee who participates. As a result, the employee knows exactly how much his or her personal benefit is worth from year to year. Defined contribution plans include:

   ESOP/Stock Bonus Plan—Chapter 10

   Money Purchase Pension Plan—Chapter 14

   Profit Sharing Plan—Chapter 16

   Savings Plan—Chapter 18

   Section 401(k) Plan—Chapter 19

   Simplified Employee Pension (SEP)—Chapter 21[8]

   SIMPLE IRA—Chapter 20[9]

   Cross Tested/Age Weighted Plan—Chapter 22

   Tax Deferred Annuity—Chapter 23[10]

   The "savings account" feature of defined contribution plans is often popular with younger employees, who may not expect to stay with the employer until retirement—which in any event seems like a remote contingency to them.

2. *Cash balance plans.* These plans are a type of defined benefit plan that operates very much like a defined contribution plan of the money purchase type. The employer guarantees the principal and interest rate, so the employee assumes no investment risk. However, cash balance plans tend to provide greater benefits to younger employees and those with shorter service, as compared to other defined benefit plans.[11]

3. *Plans with employee participation.* Qualified "savings" plans can allow employees to make after-tax contributions and a Section 401(k) plan[12] permits *before-tax* salary reductions. Such a plan looks to the employee very much like a tax-favored savings account sponsored by the employer.

   Figure 2.4 is a chart comparing the advantages and disadvantages of different types of retirement savings alternatives that provide for employee participation.

Figure 2.4

| A COMPARISON OF RETIREMENT SAVINGS ALTERNATIVES | | |
|---|---|---|
| **Savings Alternative** | **Major Advantages** | **Major Disadvantages** |
| • After-tax Savings | 1. No employer action necessary<br>2. Complete flexibility for employee | No tax benefits |
| • Traditional IRA | 1. No employer action necessary<br>2. Contribution tax-deductible | 1. Limitation if covered under qualified plan<br>2. 10% penalty for withdrawal before age 59½; no loans<br>3. $3,000/year maximum($2,000 in 2001)<br>4. No 10-year averaging on distribution<br>5. Cannot invest in life insurance |
| • Roth IRA | 1. No employer action necessary<br>2. Withdrawals completely tax-free after waiting period | 1. Limitation if covered under qualified plan<br>2. Waiting period for withdrawals<br>3. No tax deductions for contribution<br>4. $3,000/year maximum(in 2002)<br>5. No 10-year averaging on distribution |
| • SIMPLE (Savings Incentive Match Plan for Employees) IRA plan | 1. Employee can choose amount of saving<br>2. Amounts contributed are non-taxable to employee<br>3. Tax-free accumulation<br>4. Easy for employer to adopt | 1. Less flexibility for employer than qualified plan<br>2. $7,000 limit (in 2002, $6,500 as indexed for 2001) on salary reduction<br>3. Relatively complex administration<br>4. No forfeitures available for reallocation to long-term employees<br>5. No loans permitted<br>6. 25% penalty for pre-age 59½ withdrawal during 1st two years of participation; 10% thereafter<br>7. Employer must make matching or nonelective contributions<br>8. Cannot invest in life insurance |
| • Thrift (Savings) Plan | 1. Employee can choose amount of saving<br>2. Employer contribution non-taxable to employee<br>3. Tax-free accumulation<br>4. Employer matching is attractive incentive feature<br>5. Liberal loan and withdrawal provisions<br>6. 10-year averaging in some cases | 1. Qualified plan cost and complexity<br>2. Employer has fixed, nondiscretionary contribution obligation<br>3. Ten percent penalty on pre-age 59½ withdrawal<br>4. Must meet Section 401(m) tests |
| • Section 401(k) Profit-Sharing Plan | 1. Employee can choose amount of savings<br>2. All or part of contributions can be salary reduction<br>3. Amounts contributed are non-taxable to employee<br>4. Tax-free accumulation<br>5. Hardship withdrawals and loans available<br>6. 10-year averaging in some cases<br>7. Employer deduction increases to 25% of payroll after 2001, 15% before 2002 | 1. Qualified plan cost and complexity<br>2. $11,000 (in 2002; $10,500 as indexed for 2001) annual limit on salary reductions<br>3. 401(k) provisions add administrative costs<br>4. No forfeitures available for reallocation to long-term employees<br>5. In-service withdrawals limited to hardship and loans<br>6. Ten percent penalty on pre-age 59½ withdrawal |

OBJECTIVE: *Provide adequate replacement income for each employee's retirement.*

An employer may wish to adopt a plan that provides an adequate "replacement ratio"—the ratio of postretirement income to that received just before retirement. What is an adequate replacement ratio? Generally speaking, no plan attempts to provide 100% of preretirement income, because, apart from the high cost of such a plan (1) an employee's income needs are generally somewhat reduced after retirement and (2) personal savings are deemed to contribute part of the employee's income needs. A higher replacement ratio is necessary for lower-paid employees than for the higher-paid, since fixed costs dominate at lower income levels.

Most early studies indicated that replacement ratios of about 50% to 70% were adequate. More recent thinking suggests that higher replacement ratios are desirable. Figure 2.5 gives results of some studies analyzed by the American Society of Pension Actuaries (ASPA). The ASPA study proposes that the results can be quantified into a formula or "algorithm" under which the pension target for an individual is 85% of final pay not exceeding three times the poverty level ($6,810 was the figure used in the ASPA study), plus 70% of any additional final pay.

If adequate replacement income is an employer's objective, a defined benefit plan is the best vehicle for the following reasons:

- A defined benefit plan can provide a benefit based on final average compensation, regardless of the employee's years of service (or a full benefit can be earned after only limited service such as 25 years). Defined contribution plans provide benefits that are directly related to service, and a short service employee cannot accumulate a substantial retirement account.

- There is no investment risk taken by the employee in a defined benefit plan—the employer guarantees the benefit (and there is also a limited federal government guarantee of benefits through the Pension Benefit Guaranty Corporation).

- Employer funding of the benefit is mandatory, subject to underfunding penalties, even if the employer's profits drop.

- Maximum life insurance can be provided through a defined benefit plan, providing the fullest protection for beneficiaries even if the employee dies after only a few years of service.

**Figure 2.5**

| | REPLACEMENT RATIOS | | | | |
|---|---|---|---|---|---|
| Preretirement Earnings | 1981 PCPP Study (married couples) | Georgia State (1987 study) | Georgia State (1991 study) | Colin England Study | Algorithm |
| $ 6,500 | 86% | — | — | 88% | 85% |
| 10,000 | 78% | — | — | 85% | 85% |
| 15,000 | 71% | 82% | 90% | 78% | 85% |
| 20,000 | 66% | 75% | 85% | 74% | 85% |
| 25,000 | — | 71% | 82% | — | 82% |
| 30,000 | 60% | — | — | 68% | 80% |
| 40,000 | — | 68% | 77% | — | 78% |
| 50,000 | 50% | 66% | 73% | 73% | 76% |
| 60,000 | — | 66% | 71% | — | 75% |
| 70,000 | — | 66% | 70% | — | 74% |
| 75,000 | — | — | — | 74% | 74% |
| 80,000 | — | 68% | 68% | — | 74% |
| 90,000 | — | 68% | 66% | — | 73% |
| 100,000 | — | — | — | 74% | 73% |

Source: Executive Summary, "National Retirement Income Policy," American Society of Pension Actuaries, 1993.

OBJECTIVE: *Create an incentive for employees to maximize performance.*

1. *Profit sharing plan.* Although a "profit sharing" plan is not technically required to make contributions out of profits, most plans are designed to do so. The profit sharing element provides extra, bonus compensation to participating employees when the business does well, and that acts as an incentive.

2. *ESOP/stock bonus plan.* A plan providing that the employee's account balance is partially or totally invested in stock of the employer has substantial incentive features, paralleling the "equity-based" compensation arrangements often used for executives. The participant's account goes up and down in value with company stock. So, its value depends almost entirely on good performance by the business. If the employee believes that his or her performance has an effect on business results, the plan can be a powerful performance incentive.

3. *Any other defined contribution plan or cash balance plan.* In these plans, employees have an account that begins to grow as soon as they enter the plan. Because of this high visibility, these plans tend to have a better psychological incentive value than defined benefit plans.

OBJECTIVE: *Minimize turnover.*

1. *Defined benefit plan.* In defined benefit plans, employees are encouraged to stay until retirement because (1) benefits can be based on years of service; and (2) benefits are generally based on the employee's highest annual compensation. However, defined contribution benefits also continue to grow with each year of service. In many cases, there is no clear type of plan that minimizes turnover, and other features of the compensation and work environment may be dominant.

2. *Graduated vesting.* Plans are often designed with graduated vesting schedules—that is, an employee is not entitled to the full benefit earned until a minimum period of service has passed. Under current law, the longest wait permitted for full vesting is seven years (under the graduated 3- to 7-year vesting schedule; however, the schedule is 2-6 years for matching contributions).[13] Thus, vesting has only limited effect on employee turnover, and should probably be better viewed as a way for the employer to minimize the cost of covering short-service employees.

OBJECTIVE: *Encourage retirement.*

Any retirement plan acts as an incentive to retirement to some degree, since it makes it possible for the employee to support himself and his dependents after retirement.

However, a defined benefit plan works best to encourage retirement because:

- The plan can be designed to allow full benefits to accrue after a specified period such as 25 years, with no further benefits accruing thereafter. Thus, no further benefits can be earned by working for more years thereafter.

- It is relatively easy to design a "subsidized" early retirement benefit in a defined benefit plan by providing a benefit at age 62 (or other early retirement age) that is more than the actuarial equivalent of what the retiree would get at age 65. This provides an economic incentive to retire early.

- A defined benefit plan makes it relatively easy to design a "window" plan to encourage early retirement. A window plan provides additional retirement benefits, often in the form of deemed additional years of service, that provide additional benefit accruals. These benefits are available to specified employees who retire early during a specified "window" period. Window arrangements are also possible with defined contribution plans, but they generally can take the form only of additional cash bonuses or severance pay. Defined benefit plans are much more flexible in this regard.

OBJECTIVE: *Maximize employer contribution flexibility.*

The most flexible plans from a contribution standpoint are qualified profit sharing plans and SEPs. In these plans, the amount contributed each year can be entirely at the employer's discretion. Contributions can be omitted entirely for a given year without affecting the plan's qualified status. (However, for a profit sharing plan, contributions must be "substantial and recurring" or the IRS may claim that the plan has been terminated.)

Other types of plans are inflexible to one degree or another:

1. Defined benefit plans are subject to the minimum funding requirements of the Internal Revenue Code,

and the required annual minimum contribution must be made or the employer is subject to penalty.

However, if the employer is in economic distress it may request from the IRS *in advance* a waiver from the minimum funding rules. It should also be noted that the rules for actuarial funding of qualified plans permit some year-to-year variation in the amount that the employer can or must contribute. Thus, in a good year, the employer may contribute the maximum deductible amount, which may tend to reduce the minimum amount that has to be contributed in later years.

2. Defined contribution pension plans (money purchase and target) must have fixed contribution formulas that require a contribution each year based on a percentage of payroll. Failure to make this contribution subjects the employer to minimum funding penalties. The only relief for this is to apply to the IRS for a minimum funding waiver, or to make a timely amendment to the plan to reduce the contribution level.

3. "Matching" plans (e.g., 401(k), savings, and 403(b) plans, as well as SIMPLE IRAs) that require the employer to match employee contributions involve a legally binding commitment by the employer to make the promised matching contributions. Thus, the employer's costs are dependent on employee decisions and out of the employer's control. In addition, matching contributions in certain plans are subject to a faster vesting schedule (20% after two years, increasing by 20% each year to 100% after six years).[14]

## FOOTNOTES

1. For tax purposes, compensation is considered current when it is paid no later than 2½ months after the year in which it is earned. Any compensation paid later than this is considered *deferred*, which means that the employer's tax deduction is deferred also unless the plan is a qualified plan. For a *controlling* employee—one who owns more than 50% of the employer—even the 2½ month rule does not apply (i.e., the compensation must be paid within the year earned for the employer to get a tax deduction for that year).

2. IRC Section 415(b), as amended by EGTRRA 2001.

3. This is discussed further in the "Question and Answers" for Chapter 9.

4. Treas. Reg. §1.401(a)(4)-9(c).

5. IRC Section 415(e), prior to amendment by SBJPA '99. See Chapter 25 of this book.

6. IRC Section 401(k)(3). See Chapter 19 of this book.

7. IRC Section 401(l). See Chapter 25 of this book.

8. A SEP is not technically a qualified defined contribution plan, but from the employee perspective it works the same way.

9. A SIMPLE IRA plan is not technically a qualified defined contribution plan, but from the employee perspective it works the same way. A SIMPLE 401(k) plan, by contrast, is a qualified defined contribution plan—see Chapter 19.

10. A tax deferred annuity is not technically a qualified defined contribution plan, but from the employee perspective it works the same way.

11. See Chapter 8. The fact that a cash balance plan is technically a defined benefit plan has no bearing on the planning objectives discussed here.

12. Tax-exempt employers have the option of adopting either a Section 401(k) plan or a Section 403(b) annuity, which provides many of the same advantages. Governmental organizations may not adopt 401(k) plans, but public schools can adopt 403(b) plans.

13. The vesting rules are covered in Chapter 25.

14. IRC Section 411(a)(12).

## Chapter 3

# DESIGNING THE RIGHT LIFE INSURANCE PLAN

Life insurance planning for executives ranks in importance with retirement and health benefit planning. This chapter summarizes the steps in designing a life insurance plan for executives that will meet identified employer and employee objectives. The design of plans for selected executives, rather than broad groups of employees, is stressed here. For the broad employee group, insurance planning generally emphasizes the group-term plans discussed in Chapter 38.

## STEP 1: IDENTIFY INSURANCE/CAPITAL ACCUMULATION NEEDS

Do executives have specific identifiable needs for death benefits or capital accumulation programs that can be financed with life insurance? The business's dollars for executive benefits should be focused toward actual and perceived needs.

Insurance and capital accumulation needs are widespread; the two most common situations involve:

- needs for family protection for the younger executive to cover family support needs in the event of premature death

- needs for accumulation of liquid funds in the executive's estate to cover taxes and expenses, or to carry out the transfer of a closely held business interest.

## STEP 2: ANALYZE EXISTING PLANS

The employer's existing plans must be analyzed to determine whether and to what extent these plans meet the needs identified. To the extent possible, it is also advisable to take the executive's personally-owned insurance into consideration.

Employer plans that can provide death benefits or capital accumulation include:

- group-term life insurance.

- pension, profit sharing and other qualified plans. These plans almost always provide some form of death benefit, even if there is no specific life insurance benefit in the plan. Benefits from these plans are discussed in Chapter 26. Specific life insurance benefits from qualified plans are discussed generally in Chapter 13.

- nonqualified deferred compensation plans. What benefits are provided if the employee dies—before or after retirement? How is the plan financed? Are specific assets set aside to meet the employer's obligation?

- other insurance plans of the employer such as split dollar, death benefit only, or other similar arrangements.

## STEP 3: IDENTIFY OBJECTIVES

What are the employee and the employer intending to accomplish with the plan—and how are the objectives prioritized? Some common objectives in designing life insurance plans include:

- provide life insurance protection at the lowest possible cost;

- provide the maximum feasible death benefits;

- design a plan with the lowest tax cost (or the maximum tax "leverage");

- maximize the employee's federal estate tax marital deduction;

- enhance cost effectiveness of the plan by giving the employer (or in some cases the employee) control of policy cash values; and

- portability or nonportability. The executive generally wants maximum portability, while the employer might want to use the plan as a way of tying a key person to the company—the "golden handcuffs" concept.

### STEP 4: DESIGN THE PLAN

When needs and objectives have been analyzed, the planner can then match these needs and objectives with the right type of plan(s). This book covers the major tools of life insurance planning in detail:

- Bonus or "Section 162" life insurance—Chapter 28

- Split dollar life insurance—Chapter 52

- Insurance financing of nonqualified deferred compensation plans—Chapter 15

- Death benefit only plans—Chapter 32

- Life insurance in qualified plans—Chapter 13

The following chart compares some major characteristics of these plans.

**Figure 3.1**

| | Split Dollar* | Bonus Insurance | Insurance in Qualified Plan | Insurance Financing of Nonqualified Deferred Compensation Plan | DBO |
|---|---|---|---|---|---|
| Tax deduction for employer outlay | None | Yes (deductible compensation) | Yes (within "incidental" limits) | Deduction deferred to year paid** | Deduction deferred to year paid** |
| Current taxable income to employee | Term cost*** less employee contribution | Bonus amount fully taxable | Term cost*** less employee contribution | None | None |
| Recovery of employer outlay | Yes | No | No | No | No |
| Amount of death benefit for employee | Amount at risk (standard plan) | Full death proceeds | Full death proceeds | Full death proceeds "leveraged" by employer's tax deduction | Full death proceeds "leveraged" by employer's tax deduction |
| Income taxation of death benefit to employee's beneficiary | Tax free | Tax free | Amount at risk is tax free | Fully taxable as received | Fully taxable as received |
| Federal estate tax treatment | Includible to extent of incidents of ownership | Includible to extent of incidents of ownership | May be excluded by subtrust technique | Value of deferred comp. benefits included | Excluded (noncontrol employee) |

* For information on the treatment of split dollar life insurance under proposed regulations, see Chapter 52.

** Note, however, that the deduction is based, not on what the employer paid into the plan, but on the much larger amount the employer pays out.

*** Table 2001 rates (P.S. 58 rates may be used for certain split dollar arrangements entered into before January 28, 2002) or one year term cost if lower. Vested cash values in a split dollar plan may also be currently income taxable; see Chapter 52.

# Chapter 4

# DESIGNING THE RIGHT HEALTH BENEFIT PLAN

Health care plans are among the most popular and important employee benefits, and are expected to remain so, particularly in view of the aging of the population as the new century begins. However, the design of these plans is in a state of great change, if not crisis. Employers are faced with problems associated with both the rising costs of medical procedures and an aging work force.

The purpose of this chapter is to provide a broad outline for the design of an appropriate health care plan, based on the planning tools discussed in detail in later chapters.

## 1. WHAT HEALTH BENEFITS DO EMPLOYEES WANT?

The first step in adopting a new benefit design or changing an existing design is to make a preliminary determination of the types of health benefits that will be most valued by employees. In smaller firms, this can often be done by personal interviews and management's personal knowledge of the company's employees. Larger firms often use questionnaires designed by benefit consultants.

The make-up of the employee group may provide some typical responses. For example, a younger work force will typically want to maximize benefits for childbirth and pediatric care, while an older work force will want adequate coverage for major medical expenses. However, employers should not simply accept generalizations, but should make an effort to determine what employees actually want.

Where there is a wide variety in the health care needs perceived by the employees, designers should consider making use of two major tools that allow employees to choose the benefits provided by the employer's dollars:

- Cafeteria Plans—Chapter 29

- Flexible Spending Accounts—Chapter 35

## 2. PLAN DESIGN FEATURES

In designing a health insurance plan to provide appropriate benefits, three aspects are vitally important:

- Efficient *delivery* of the benefits.

- Meeting the employer's *cost* constraints.

- Positive employee *perception* of the plan.

Employers should consider plans designed along the lines of traditional health insurance, as discussed in Chapter 39, as well as alternatives, such as Health Maintenance Organizations, which are addressed in Chapter 40. But modern benefit design requires consideration of a much broader range of options.

For many years, health care costs increased faster than the rate of inflation. Although the rate of increase has slowed somewhat recently, it is expected that this trend will continue. While employees expect health care coverage as a standard employee benefit, they are naturally resistant to accepting less cash compensation in return for health benefits. Thus, employers are coming under increasing cost pressures in this area. Employee resistance may be diminished by education in health care economics and tax policy. This is illustrated by the success of premium conversion plans (discussed in Chapter 29).

Traditional health insurance plans (discussed in Chapter 39) are *postpaid* plans—plans that reimburse (or pay directly) *after* the employee has independently chosen a physician or other provider and undergone the medical or other procedure. Although there are methods for designing cost controls into such plans, with traditional health insurance, the fundamental "levers" of cost control are outside the employer's control.

In the past decade, the concept of managed health care has become an accepted and familiar option in the design of health care plans. Managed health care is a broad concept, aimed at getting the basic cost management into the hands of employers—the people who pay for the product. Managed health care includes the use of "prepaid" health care plans, such as HMOs (discussed in Chapter 40). But the concept is a broader one that can utilize a variety of delivery methods for health care services.

In designing health care plans, employers and benefit specialists must consider managed health care concepts. There is no one type of plan that can be described as a "managed health care plan." Managed health care is a set of tools and techniques that can be used to design a health care plan to meet employer—and also employee—needs and cost requirements.

## Managed Health Care— Tools and Techniques

Designers of modern health care plans for employers should consider one or more of the following recognized health care management tools and techniques:

1. *Prospective pricing.* A prospective price for health care services is one that is negotiated by the employer (or by a provider or consultant on behalf of the employer) *before* the year in which the health services will be provided to covered employees.

    An HMO is an example of this type of pricing. However, prospective pricing can be used in other types of health care arrangements, such as a Preferred Provider Organization (PPO). A PPO is a group of providers with whom an employer negotiates per-unit charges for various types of health services. Employees covered under the employer's health plan are "channeled" or "steered" toward these providers, usually by providing a lower employee share of the cost if the employee uses the PPO members.

    Why would a health care provider be willing to agree to prospective pricing? Apart from cost pressures that are causing consumers to increasingly demand such arrangements, there is a potential benefit to the doctor, hospital, medical group, or other provider in prospective pricing. While prospective pricing requires the health care provider to assume the risk of cost overruns, the provider also gets the benefit of cost savings not anticipated. And since prospective pricing creates incentives to keep costs down, it can contribute to reducing or slowing health care cost inflation in the long run.

2. *Negotiated discounts.* As either a supplement or an alternative to prospective pricing, employers can negotiate to obtain health services at discounted prices. For example, a hospital might agree to charge the covered employees 75% of the hospital's "usual and customary" rate for hospitalization. However, if the hospital raises its usual and customary rates over the period of the agreement, the amount charged under the plan also goes up, with the discount in effect, so costs are not absolutely controlled.

3. *Channeling.* In order to maximize the benefit of negotiated and prepaid rates, employees must be encouraged, as much as possible, to utilize providers who operate under these rate agreements. HMOs and PPOs are examples of health care delivery systems that involve channeling. Channeling can also be provided in plan design by providing more favorable cost sharing for utilization of the preferred providers.

4. *Bundling of services.* If a health plan agrees to a per-diem room and board rate with a hospital and the hospital becomes dissatisfied with its revenues during the term of the agreement, there is an incentive for the hospital to try to make up its losses on room charges by increasing pharmacy, laboratory, and other ancillary charges. *Bundling* is a concept designed to avoid this type of "end run" around a pricing agreement. The price negotiated with a provider for a given type of services is arranged to cover the broadest possible range of services connected with a hospital stay or other covered medical event. For example, the agreement would provide a specified price for all hospital charges for a patient whose gall bladder is removed.

5. *Capitation payment.* Under traditional contracts, health care providers have a built-in incentive to maximize utilization, since they get paid only when a procedure is actually done. One cost-saving answer is a *capitation* payment—a flat monthly or periodic fee to the provider per plan participant, regardless of the number of procedures the provider actually performs. This helps remove the financial incentive to order tests and procedures that are of relatively little benefit to the patient. Moreover, a simple capitation payment agreement can eliminate the need for complicated fee negotiations in many situations.

6. *Peer review.* Peer review is a concept under which a decision to perform medical or surgical procedures on a patient is reviewed by professional colleagues of the physician or provider who first sees the

patient. Peer review is built into group practice systems, such as HMOs and clinics. Its importance in health benefit plan design lies in the recognition that a large number of medical and surgical procedures currently being performed are unnecessary—unnecessary, that is, in the view of the medical profession itself. Peer review helps to avoid unnecessary procedures, and thus plays an important role in controlling costs.

7. *Utilization review.* Utilization review is similar to peer review, but is more specifically targeted. An example of utilization review is a requirement in an employer's health benefit plan that covered employees must obtain a second surgeon's opinion in order to be covered for (or to receive full coverage for) specified surgical procedures. These specified procedures are typically those most likely to be recommended unnecessarily.

8. *Quality review.* The quality review concept attempts to insure that health services provided to employees meet minimum quality levels, and thus do not simply lead to further medical costs. With quality review, the employer's health plan provides full coverage only for facilities that meet minimum requirements, professional groups with minimum credentials, or procedures that follow established medical norms.

9. *Cost sharing.* Cost sharing by requiring deductibles and copayment is a familiar method of holding down an employer's health insurance costs. Currently, good plan design involves creative use of these devices to actually *encourage* employees to use alternative, lower cost methods of providing equivalent health care. For example, the plan should provide an equal or higher employer share for outpatient services than for equivalent inpatient hospital services, so that the plan does not discourage utilization of less costly outpatient alternatives.

10. *Lifestyle management.* The employer should develop programs that encourage employees to stay healthy—an obvious way to reduce health care costs. Exercise programs, weight-loss, and no-smoking programs, in addition to many others, can be considered.

### "Defined Contribution" Health Plans

An emerging trend in health care plans is the "defined contribution" health plan. The term defined con-tribution is used to describe various health plan models. What they all have in common, however, is that they shift the payment and selection functions from employers to employees. Most of these defined contribution models could be provided within the existing employer-provided health insurance system, through the use of cafeteria plans or otherwise. But they could also be structured to allow employees to purchase health insurance directly from carriers, and some have suggested that they may even result in new forms of risk pooling for health care services. Employers are attracted to defined contribution health plan models because they are perceived as permitting employers to avoid future legislation, regulations, and litigation, which is expected to result from the public's growing disenchantment with managed care, and thus enable the employer to control health care cost increases. These models also dovetail nicely with the trend of giving workers more control over their benefits, as illustrated by the growth in 401(k) plans.

## 3. HEALTH BENEFITS FOR EXECUTIVES

Does the employer want to provide health benefits for selected executives over and above benefits provided for employees in general? Congress has indicated its intention to impose "nondiscrimination" rules that would limit special executive benefits in this area. But its first attempt to impose these rules—Section 89, enacted in 1986—proved unworkable and was repealed in 1989. Current law is relatively flexible. The options for executive health plans are discussed in Chapter 47, Health Reimbursement Arrangements.

## 4. THE PROCESS OF DESIGN AND MAINTENANCE

Designing and maintaining a health benefit plan has the following components:

- Plan design

- Communication with employees

- Financing the plan

- Claims administration

- Claims payment

- Periodic plan review and updating

- Compliance with federal and state regulatory requirements

There are many ways to split responsibilities for these various plan components. A very large corporation may perform all of these responsibilities itself, while at the other extreme, an employer might delegate all of them to a traditional health insurer.

Increasingly, however, specialized organizations have become available to carry out specific responsibilities in the most cost-effective manner. For example, there are many independent firms that contract to do claims administration for employers or insurers. Similarly, plan design is often done by specialized benefit consulting firms that do not take on any of the other responsibilities, although often they recommend organizations for this purpose.

For the employer, finding the right people and organizations for these responsibilities can be as important to the cost-effective delivery and positive perception of benefits as plan design itself.

# Chapter 5

# BENEFIT PLANS FOR PROPRIETORSHIPS, PARTNERSHIPS AND S CORPORATIONS

For benefit plan purposes, proprietorships and partnerships have one significant difference from corporations—the owners of these businesses are not technically *employees* of the business. By contrast, in a corporation an owner, even a 100% shareholder, who works in the business is technically an employee of the corporation. For S corporations, the Internal Revenue Code requires that shareholder employees (those holding more than two percent of the S corporation's stock) be treated as partners for employee benefit purposes.[1]

Proprietorships, partnerships, and S corporations can have benefit plans for their employees that are exactly the same as those of regular or "C" corporations. Deductibility of benefit costs is the same, and tax treatment to these regular employees is also the same.

But—when the plan attempts to cover the business owners, some differences arise that are covered in this chapter and throughout the book. Many sections of the Code providing favorable tax treatment of employee benefits apply only to employees. Thus, the benefit package for these organizations involves less favorable benefits for owners than if the organization was incorporated. If the situation is seriously adverse to the owners, the planner might even consider incorporating the organization (or, in the case of an S corporation, terminating the S corporation election).

Qualified retirement plans are a very significant exception to the unfavorable treatment of business owners in these organizations. Qualified plans can cover owners of unincorporated businesses or S corporations on much the same basis as regular employees. The differences are discussed in Chapter 12—HR 10 (Keogh) Plans. These differences are so small that it seldom pays to incorporate a business or terminate an S corporation election for qualified plan benefits alone.

## PARTNERSHIPS AND PROPRIETORSHIPS

For federal income tax purposes, a proprietorship—an unincorporated business with one owner—is consid-ered simply an extension of the owner. The proprietorship's profit or loss is computed on Schedule C of the owner's federal income tax return. The net income or loss from the business is added to the owner's adjusted gross income from other sources. As a result, business profits are added to other income, while losses are subtracted directly from other income.

This treatment allows all business expenses to be deducted "off the top" so they are available regardless of whether the taxpayer itemizes deductions. Proprietorship expense deductions are also available without any "floor" requirement that may be applicable to itemized deductions. For example, a proprietor can deduct all expenses for business use of an automobile, while an employee must itemize deductions and is subject to a two percent of adjusted gross income floor for employee business expenses.

The tax rates applicable to the business profits of a proprietorship are the same as those applicable to any other kind of individual income, and the income is taxed only once. By comparison, business income of a corporation is taxed at corporate rates, which are different from individual rates. Corporate income is taxed at the corporate level and then again at the shareholder level when it is paid out as dividends, although certain dividends may be taxed at capital gains rates.

With the exception of contributions to qualified plans, benefits and compensation paid to a proprietor are *not* deductible business expenses. Put another way, expenditures for employee benefits of a proprietor are treated the same as cash taken out by the proprietor. For example, health insurance premiums, life insurance premiums, direct medical reimbursements, or any other form of benefit provided to the proprietor is nondeductible to the business and thus appears directly as income on the proprietor's Schedule C. The owner's benefits are nondeductible even if the business maintains the benefit plan for other, nonowner employees of the business as well as for the owner.

Partnerships, in principle, are treated for tax purposes the same as proprietorships. That is, the partners, not the partnership, are the taxable entities. However, because more than one taxpayer is involved, the tax rules for partnerships are complicated. In fact, they are among the most complex provisions of the tax law, but fortunately for benefit purposes most of the complexities can be overlooked.

A partnership typically pays no federal income taxes. All the taxes on the partnership's income are paid by the partners. However, a partnership must file a federal income tax return; the return is an information return that reports the partners' shares of income, losses, and other tax items.

Each partner must report and pay taxes on his "distributive share" of the partnership's income for the taxable year. A partner's distributive share is the amount of income that he is entitled to receive under the partnership agreement, even if it is not actually distributed to him during the taxable year. If the partnership has losses, each partner may deduct his share of the losses on his own tax return, subject to various limitations on "passive loss" deductions designed to deter "tax shelter" partnerships.

Employee benefits for partners are treated as follows:

- For qualified retirement plans (1) contributions for partners are deductible by the partnership along with those for regular employees, and (2) partners are taxed on qualified plan contributions and benefits much the same as regular employees. (See Chapter 12.)

- Costs for fringe benefits of any other type are deductible by the partnership in computing its taxable income—they are deductible under Section 162 as "guaranteed payments" to partners as defined in Code section 707(c). (This is the same way that guaranteed "salary" payments to partners are treated.) Alternatively, the partnership can treat the premium payment or other fringe benefit cost as a reduction in cash distributions to the partner.[2]

- Partners must then report as taxable income the value of all fringe benefits (other than qualified plans) provided for them by the partnership.[3]

## S CORPORATIONS

The S corporation is a corporation that has elected (under Subchapter S of the Internal Revenue Code) to be taxed like a partnership for federal income tax purposes. (Most state income tax laws also recognize S corporations). "Like a partnership" is an oversimplification, of course—this will not come as any surprise to students of federal tax law. However, for fringe benefit purposes it is generally a close enough description.

In order to elect S corporation status, the corporation must comply with certain "don'ts"—it must *not*:[4]

- have more than 75 shareholders

- have a shareholder that is not an individual, an estate, or a certain type of trust

- be organized in a foreign country or have a nonresident alien shareholder

- have more than one "class of stock" (some differences in voting rights are allowed)

- be one of several specified ineligible types of corporation.

Qualified plans under Code section 401(a) and certain charitable organizations (Code section 501(c)(3)) may be S corporation shareholders.[5] An individual retirement account (IRA) is not a qualified shareholder for this purpose. An employee stock ownership plan (ESOP) may hold S corporation stock.[6]

Some of these restrictions can have relevance in benefit planning that involves the use of employer stock. Such plans cannot violate the 75-shareholder rule, or use a nonindividual as a shareholder. Qualified plans and charitable organizations are treated as one shareholder for purposes of the 75-shareholder rule. Also, benefit plans using stock must be designed so as not to violate the "one class of stock" requirement.[7]

The Code provides that if an employee of an S corporation owns more than two percent of the stock (an MTTPSE—*more-than-two-percent shareholder-employee*—for purposes of this chapter), the MTTPSE is treated as a partner for fringe benefit purposes.[8] The Congressional committee reports on this provision[9] include the following specific fringe benefits (1) the tax exclusion for *benefits* under a health and accident plan, Section 105; (2) the tax exclusion for *coverage* under a health and accident plan, Section 106; (3) the tax benefits for group-term life insurance, Section 79; and (4) the exclusion for meals and lodging furnished for the convenience of the employer, Section 119. Qualified retirement plans are *not* covered by this provision; MTTPSEs are treated much like regular employees for qualified plan purposes.

Fringe benefits provided to MTTPSEs are treated as follows for tax purposes:

- The S corporation can deduct the cost of fringe benefits for MTTPSEs in determining its taxable income.[10]

- MTTPSEs must report—as compensation income—the value of any fringe benefits provided to them. These items must be included on the Form W-2 provided by the employer to the MTTPSE. Note that in the case of health and accident premiums, the amount of the premium is includable in full, but the MTTPSE is eligible for a deduction as set out in Code section 162(l). See Chapter 39.

- For FICA (social security) purposes, these fringe benefit amounts may or may not be includable, depending on the FICA rules for the type of plan involved. For example, health and accident premiums are not includable in the FICA tax base if there is a "plan or system" of health benefits for employees and dependents generally, or a class of employees. However, if the premiums are paid for a single employee or a few executives, the amounts may be includable in the FICA base.[11]

- Qualified retirement plans for MTTPSEs present some additional technical problems that are discussed in Chapter 12. The principal issue is, "What constitutes the MTTPSE's compensation for plan purposes?"

## SPECIFIC FRINGE BENEFITS

The chart in Figure 5.1 summarizes the treatment of specific fringe benefits for proprietors, partners, and MTTPSEs.

A "yes" in the chart indicates that the plan can be provided for these people with full tax benefits. A "no" indicates that the plan will provide no tax benefits for these key people. Note that some fringe benefit provisions of the Code such as dependent care (Section 129) do provide tax benefits for proprietors, partners, and MTTPSEs, despite the provisions discussed in this chapter.

Finally, in reviewing this chart, note that it reflects the treatment only of partners, proprietors, and MTTPSEs. All business organizations can adopt benefit plans providing full tax benefits for rank and file employees.

## FOOTNOTES

1. IRC Section 1372.
2. Rev. Rul. 91-26, 1991-1 CB 184.
3. Under IRC Section 61(a), all fringe benefits are currently taxable unless there is a specific provision of the Code that exempts or defers taxation of the benefit. Since most benefit exemptions or deferrals in the Code apply only to employees, partners are currently taxable on virtually all fringe benefits.
4. IRC Section 1361.
5. IRC Sec. 1361(c)(6).
6. *General Explanation of Tax Legislation Enacted in the 104th Congress* (JCT-12-96) pp. 130-131 (the Blue Book).
7. IRC Section 1361(b)(1)(D).
8. IRC Section 1372.
9. Committee Reports, Subchapter S Revision Act of 1982, P.L. 97-354, enacted October 19, 1982.
10. Rev. Rul. 91-26, 1991-1 CB 184.
11. Announcement 92-16, 1992-5 IRB 53.

**Figure 5.1**

| Comparison of Fringe Benefits by Entity Type | | | | |
| --- | --- | --- | --- | --- |
| **Benefit** | **Sole Prop.** | **Partnership** | **S Corp** | **C Corp** |
| Qualified plan | Yes | Yes | Yes | Yes |
| Deferred compensation | No | No | No | Yes |
| Salary continuation | No | Yes | Yes | Yes |
| Group life | No | No | No | Yes |
| Group health | Yes | Yes | Yes | Yes |
| Group disability | No | No | No | Yes |
| Medical reimb. plans | No | No | No | Yes |
| Accidental death | No | No | No | Yes |
| Disability income plan | No | No | No | Yes |
| Employee death benefit | | | | |
|   -Employer provided | No | No | No | Yes |
|   -Qualified plan | Yes | Yes | Yes | Yes |
| Educ. assistance plan | Yes | Yes | Yes | Yes |
| Dependent care | Yes | Yes | Yes | Yes |
| Meals & lodging | No | Yes | Yes | Yes |
| Cafeteria plan | No | No | No | Yes |

Source: Adapted from Jenkins, Gary E., "The Impact of Choice of Entity Selection upon Compensation and Fringe Benefit Planning after Tax Reform," *Journal of American Society of CLU and ChFC*, March 1988. See also Eule and Mustone, "Some Fringes are Still Free to S Corporation Owner-Employees," *Taxation for Lawers*, April, 1992 and Trinz, "Which Tax-Free and Tax-Favored fringe benefits are pass through owners entitled to?" *RIA Pension and Benefits Week*, August 5, 2002. With regard to self-funded benefit plans, the correct treatment is unclear. See Eggertsen *et al*, "Guidence on Partner Health Leaves Self-Funding Questions Unanswered," *Journal of Taxation*, January, 1992. Revised 2003.

# Chapter 6

# THE RETIREMENT PLANNING PROCESS

Retirement planning is an increasingly important part of the financial services industry. With the baby boomers ranging from middle age to early retirement age, the number of individuals with significant savings and retirement planning needs is increasing dramatically. At the same time, the economic and tax complexity of all types of retirement-related financial planning has also increased.

Retirement planning is "interdisciplinary." It combines the skills of the traditional estate planner, the financial planner, and the benefit/compensation planner. The broad range of issues that must be addressed makes this one of the most challenging of the financial services disciplines now emerging.

Retirement planning is also multifaceted because of the broad range of clients that must be served. For example it encompasses advice to clients many years in advance of retirement, as well as to clients just at retirement and thereafter. Clients may also range from business owners who are able to use their businesses to help provide retirement benefits, to key executives who can bargain effectively with their employers regarding retirement benefits, to employees who have no significant say in their employee benefit package. All these different types of clients may have needs for retirement planning as well as sufficient assets to enable the payment of adequate fees or commissions to the planner.

Perhaps no single individual should attempt to handle all aspects of retirement planning. Any person giving advice in these situations should know when it is appropriate to call in an employee benefits expert, a lawyer specializing in estate planning, an expert portfolio manager, or whatever other specialist is required. However, all financial planners should understand the basics of retirement planning—the broad general approaches, the tools and techniques—and where they fit in.

This chapter is designed to provide the beginnings of an understanding of the *process* of retirement planning—some broad guidelines with an indication of where individual financial planning tools and techniques fit into this process. In particular, the employee benefit aspects covered in this book will be highlighted here.

## I. THE RETIREMENT PLANNING PROCESS— LONG RANGE

Serious retirement planning should begin well in advance of actual retirement. Nobody would expect a person in their twenties to make firm financial plans for retirement, other than very general plans such as establishing the basics of a savings and investment program and participating in employer retirement plans such as 401(k) plans. However, beginning 15 to 20 years in advance of retirement, clients become aware that they should begin definite and detailed plans.

While detailed planning is appropriate at this point, planners and clients should not expect exactness in the financial planning targets. There are too many imponderables—future investment return rates, future tax rates, the client's life expectancy. Nevertheless, the targets for retirement planning are near enough at this point to try to quantify plans and make sure they are systematically carried out.

*Step 1: Where is the client now?*

As with estate planning, a worthwhile retirement plan cannot be provided unless the planner has detailed and precise financial information about the client. In fact, "due diligence" in retirement planning *requires* the planner to make every effort to obtain accurate and complete financial information. The planner should be wary of clients who are reluctant to provide such information. (See Appendix H, Malpractice.)

Retirement planning practitioners should develop a "fact finder" for clients that will systematize this process. Some key elements:

A. *Benefit plan information.* Retirement planning requires complete information about all employee benefit plans in which the client *and* the client's spouse are currently participating *or have ever participated.* Not only retirement plans (qualified or nonqualified) but other benefit plans such as health insurance, life insurance, or even such fringe benefits as membership in company athletic or health clubs after retirement may be significant in the retirement planning process.

In addition to private employer benefit plans, government benefits also should be estimated—Social Security, veterans' benefits, and the like.

In order to accurately forecast the level of employee benefits available, the planner needs to see actual benefit plan documents; it is not enough to rely simply on the client's informal impression of what his benefit programs provide. Generally, if a plan provides a Summary Plan Description (SPD), as do most ERISA-affected plans (see Appendix A), the SPD should be sufficient. For qualified plans, employers are required also to provide an individual benefit statement at least once annually. In some cases, the planner might wish to look at the actual underlying plan documents, which under ERISA the client has the right to do. (Companies can charge a reasonable copying fee for providing copies.)

For non-ERISA plans, there often are no formal documentation requirements, so it may be difficult to obtain adequate written information about such benefits. However, most companies provide a "benefits manual" or other literature covering these benefits.

In general, in examining benefit plans, focus on

- What vested benefits at retirement does the plan *now* provide—that is, even if the employee terminated employment today?

- What will the plan provide at retirement, if the employee continues working? If the benefits are based on salary, what is a reasonable salary forecast?

- How solid are predictions of future benefits? For example, health benefit plans are currently in constant flux. Can a planner have any confidence that health benefit plans available at retirement 15 years from now will have any resemblance to current benefits? The employer's financial stability also has a bearing on this issue.

- To what extent can the employee control the employee benefits available at retirement? Do employer plans have options available to the employee to change or increase benefits, possibly on a contributory basis? (See the chapters on FSAs (Chapter 35) and Cafeteria Plans (Chapter 29), for example.) Can the employee individually negotiate better or different benefits? At the ex-

treme, an owner or majority shareholder can—and generally should—arrange the company's benefit plans to be consistent with his own individual retirement planning.

B. *Detailed current asset information.* The planner must have detailed information about the client's current assets and sources of income. Completeness is a must—it is not optional. Develop asset fact finders; a sample Retirement Planning Asset Worksheet (see Figure 6.1) is included at the end of this chapter.

Assets must be valued—book value is of little use in developing a financial or retirement plan. Some assets are easy to value; others may be impossible to value with certainty. Asset valuation is discussed in *The Tools and Techniques of Estate Planning.*

Owners of closely held businesses are in a special category. It is difficult to value an interest in a small business, of course. But retirement planning requires more than this. The important factor about a small business interest is not what it is worth now, but what will happen to it in the future—how (and if) it will continue as a source of income in retirement. In other words, retirement planning for closely held business owners is inextricable from planning for business succession through buy-sell agreements, gifts or sales to successors, or whatever mechanism is set up for continuation of the business or retrieving its value for the owner's benefit.

In obtaining asset information, do not overlook *liability* information. This includes not only traditional debts outstanding, but also legal obligations such as future alimony or child support that involves a recurring obligation, property settlement payments that are outstanding, state or federal tax liabilities outstanding, or fines or judgments not yet fully paid. Many of these are things that clients understandably would rather not think about and they may not be volunteered.

C. *Other information.* As with estate and financial planning, retirement planning requires the development of a complete profile of the client's financial status. For example, does the client have major financial needs coming up *before* retirement—perhaps a child's college or graduate school expenses, or long term care for a dependent? Or, on the plus side, does the client expect a future windfall—an inheritance, for example? These contingencies can be very difficult to value. In extreme cases they can render a financial or retirement plan virtually worthless. The planner must deal with these issues as well as possible, but must also be willing to "caveat" the ultimate retirement plan—that is, state clearly that the plan *does not* take into account certain contingencies that potentially exist but are impossible to predict.

*Step 2—Determine Retirement Needs*

Although a client far from retirement cannot foresee what his or her life will actually be like after retirement, a good approximation of retirement needs—at least a good starting point—is to make an estimate of what it costs *now* for a standard of living that the client considers acceptable. By adjusting these amounts for inflation, a reasonable estimate of the total capital needs—the lump sum amount needed at retirement—can be made.

A Retirement Needs Worksheet outlining the steps in this process is included at the end of this chapter (see Figure 6.2). As an illustration of this worksheet, suppose that your client provides information for lines 1 through 9 that indicates he will need $60,000 annually (in current dollars). If the client is 10 years from retirement, assuming a 4 percent rate of inflation, this translates to a need for $88,814 (line 14) at retirement 10 years from now. Assuming continued 4% inflation, a 20-year payout after retirement, and after-tax investment return of 7%, this requires a total capital at retirement (line 21) of $1,374,059.

This worksheet converts everything to a capital equivalent. For example, if the client in the preceding paragraph expects to receive a monthly pension benefit at retirement, it should be converted to its then lump-sum equivalent. If the benefit is worth $300,000, for example, then the client's capital need is reduced to $1,074,059 ($1,374,059 less $300,000).

*Step 3—Getting there.*

The retirement planner's critical contribution is, after identifying the needs and the current assets, to develop a plan for reaching the client's targeted capital needs. All the tools and techniques of financial planning for capital accumulation should be brought to bear on this problem.

Planning requires not only reaching the capital needs targets, but also making sure that the capital is translated appropriately into living expense needs. For example, a client's personal residence may have a considerable market value on paper, but how will this value contribute to living standards in retirement? Questions like this emphasize the need for planning for liquidity and diversification—here as in all investment planning, but with a focus on retirement needs.

## II. PLANNING AT OR NEAR RETIREMENT

As retirement approaches, the focus changes from accumulation planning toward the need to make the right decisions about assets the client already has. These issues include:

- Housing—what should be done with the client's primary residence? What are the client's long range plans for housing?

- Health care—What options are available under the client's employee health plans? (See Chapter 39.) What private insurance is necessary to supplement employee benefits and government benefits?

- Pensions and Social Security—Here there are often many possible choices and options; issues include:

  1. How much current income does the client need?

  2. Does the client want to maximize current income or provide for beneficiaries after his (or his and his spouse's) death?

  3. What options are available under the client's benefit plans?

  4. What are the tax consequences of different distribution options—federal income tax, and federal estate and gift taxes, as well as state taxes?

  5. Does the client want to explore possibilities of moving money out of current qualified plans (through a rollover or other option) and investing it in another way—annuities, life insurance, or other investments?

Issues concerning distributions from qualified plans, tax deferred annuities, and IRAs are discussed in Chapter 26 in greater detail. See also Appendix J for retirement and estate planning issues. For a discussion of work after retirement and the extent to which it may result in a reduction of Social Security, see *The Social Security Manual* (published annually), National Underwriter Company, Cincinnati, Ohio.

**Figure 6.1**

## RETIREMENT PLANNING ASSET WORKSHEET

DATE: _____

Client's Name: _____

Address: _____

Telephone: (home) _____ (office) _____

Business Address: _____

Spouse's Name: _____

Business Address: _____ Telephone: _____

**Figure 6.1 (continued)**

## RETIREMENT PLANNING ASSET WORKSHEET

### ASSETS
Valuation as of data prepared unless otherwise indicated.

*1. Cash and cash equivalents*

| | Value | Current Return (pretax) |
|---|---|---|
| a. checking accounts | _____ | _____ |
| b. saving accounts | _____ | _____ |
| c. money market accounts | _____ | _____ |
| d. life insurance cash values | _____ | _____ |
| **Total Cash/Cash Equivalents** | _____ | _____ |

*2. Retirement Plans*
(Do not include defined benefit plans)

| | Current balance | Current Return (pretax) |
|---|---|---|
| a. IRA | _____ | _____ |
| b. Keogh | _____ | _____ |
| c. Section 401(k) | _____ | _____ |
| d. Section 403(b) | _____ | _____ |
| e. Other defined contribution | _____ | _____ |
| **Total Retirement Plans** | _____ | _____ |

**Figure 6.1 (continued)**

3. *Investments*

(Do not include amounts included in 2 above)

| | Fair Market Value | Adjusted Basis | Current Return (pretax) |
|---|---|---|---|
| a. Portfolio Investments | | | |
|   (1) *money market instruments* | | | |
|     certificate of deposit | _____ | _____ | _____ |
|     T bills | _____ | _____ | _____ |
|     commercial paper | _____ | _____ | _____ |
|   (2) *fixed-income securities* | | | |
|     U.S. government | _____ | _____ | _____ |
|     U.S. agencies | _____ | _____ | _____ |
|     municipal bonds | _____ | _____ | _____ |
|     preferred stock | _____ | _____ | _____ |
|     corporate bonds | _____ | _____ | _____ |
|     notes receivable | _____ | _____ | _____ |
|   (3) *common stocks* | | | |
|     listed | _____ | _____ | _____ |
|     OTC | _____ | _____ | _____ |
|     restricted stock | _____ | _____ | _____ |
|   (4) *other portfolio Investments* | | | |
|     options | _____ | _____ | _____ |
|     mutual funds | _____ | _____ | _____ |
|     physical assets (collectibles) | _____ | _____ | _____ |
| b. Passsive Investments | | | |
|   (1) direct participation investments | _____ | _____ | _____ |
|   (2) real estate (passive) | _____ | _____ | _____ |
| c. Active Businesses | | | |
|   (1) value of business owned and operated | _____ | _____ | _____ |
|   (2) real estate (active participation) | _____ | _____ | _____ |
| **Total Investments** | _____ | _____ | _____ |

**Figure 6.1 (continued)**

### 4. *Personal Assets*

| | Fair Market Value | Adjusted Basis |
|---|---|---|
| a. primary residence | _____ | _____ |
| b. other real estate | _____ | _____ |
| c. household contents | _____ | _____ |
| d. automobiles | _____ | _____ |
| e. other | _____ | _____ |
| **Total Personal Assets** | _____ | _____ |

## LIABILITIES

### 1. *Short-Term Liabilities*

(12 months or less)

| | Balance Outstanding | Interest Rate | Monthly Payment | Maturity Date |
|---|---|---|---|---|
| Consumer credit (credit card & open charge accounts) | _____ | _____ | _____ | _____ |
| Personal notes payable | _____ | _____ | _____ | _____ |
| Loans from life insurance policies | _____ | _____ | _____ | _____ |
| Notes guaranteed | _____ | _____ | _____ | _____ |
| Other | _____ | _____ | _____ | _____ |
| **Total** | _____ | _____ | _____ | _____ |

### 2. *Long-Term Liabilities*

| | Balance Outstanding | Interest Rate | Monthly Payment | Maturity Date |
|---|---|---|---|---|
| Mortgages on personal residences | _____ | _____ | _____ | _____ |
| Loans against investment assets | _____ | _____ | _____ | _____ |
| Loans against personal residences | _____ | _____ | _____ | _____ |
| **Total** | _____ | | | |

**Figure 6.1 (continued)**

*3. Other*

Deferred taxes _____  _____  _____  _____

Alimony, child support, etc.. _____  _____  _____  _____

Judgements, etc.. _____  _____  _____  _____

| **Total** | _____ |

### SUMMARY

*Assets (fair market value)*

Total cash and cash equivalents _____

Total retirement plans _____

Total investments _____

Total personal assets _____

| **Total Assets** | _____ |

*Liabilities (outstanding balances)*

Short-term _____

Long-term _____

Other _____

| **Total Liabilities** | _____ |

**Figure 6.2**

## RETIREMENT NEEDS WORKSHEET

### Estimated Retirement Living Expenses and Required Capital (in current dollars)

| | Per Month x 12 = | Per Year |
|---|---|---|
| 1. *Food* | | |
| 2. *Housing:* | | |
| a. Rent/mortgage payment | | |
| b. Insurance (if not included in a.) | | |
| c. Property taxes (if not included in a.) | | |
| d. Utilities | | |
| e. Maintenance (if you own) | | |
| f. Management fee (if a condominium) | | |
| 3. *Clothing and Personal Care:* | | |
| a. Wife | | |
| b. Husband | | |
| c. Dependents | | |
| 4. *Medical Expenses:* | | |
| a. Doctor | | |
| b. Dentist | | |
| c. Medicines | | |
| d. Medical insurance to supplement Medicare | | |
| 5. *Transportation:* | | |
| a. Car payments | | |
| b. Gas | | |
| c. Insurance | | |
| d. License | | |
| e. Car maintenance (tires and repairs) | | |
| f. Other transportation | | |
| 6. *Recurring Expenses:* | | |
| a. Entertainment | | |
| b. Travel | | |
| c. Hobbies | | |
| d. Club fees and dues | | |
| e. Other | | |
| 7. *Insurance* | | |
| 8. *Gifts and Contributions* | | |
| 9. *Income Taxes (if any)* | | |

**Figure 6.2 (continued)**

| | Per Month x 12 = | Per Year |
|---|---|---|
| 10. Total Annual Expenses (current dollars) | _____ | $ _____ |
| 11. Inflation Rate until Retirement (I) | _____ | |
| 12. Total Years until Retirement (N) | _____ | |
| 13. Inflation Adjustment Factor $(1 + I)^N$ | | x _____ |
| 14. Total Annual Expenses (future dollars) | | = _____ |
| 15. Inflation Rate Postretirement (i) | _____ | |
| 16. Aftertax Rate of Return (r) | _____ | |
| 17. Anticipated Duration of Retirement (n) | _____ | |
| 18. Inflation-Adjusted Discount Factor $$a = \frac{1 + i}{1 + r}$$ | | _____ |
| 19. Capital Required at Retirement to Fund Retirement Living Expenses $$\text{Amt line 14 x } \frac{1 - a^n}{1 - a}$$ | | $ _____ |
| 20. One-Time Expenses | | +$ _____ |
| 21. Total Capital Need at Retirement | | =$ _____ |

Source: Robert J. Doyle, Jr., *Retirement Planning Handbook*, The American College, Bryn Mawr, PA.

# Chapter 7

# KNOWING THE RULES: GOVERNMENT REGULATIONS AND HOW TO FIND THEM

An employer can pay its top executives as much as it wants to; the federal government does not regulate this except for a very general "reasonableness" limit on the amount of salary payments that can be deducted and, recently, a maximum cap of $1,000,000 on deductible compensation for certain executives. By contrast, federal tax law specifically limits the maximum pension benefit that an employer can provide to an employee.

There are innumerable other detailed federal laws and regulations effective in the employee benefits area; just to pick another one at random, the government specifies, to the day, when an employer must allow an employee to begin participating in the employer's pension plan.

Why does the federal government "micromanage" an employer's benefit programs? What is the impact of this extensive regulation on the employee benefit planner, and how can the planner keep up with the rules? That's the subject of this chapter.

## WHY THE RULES EXIST

Maintaining income of individuals when they cannot support themselves has been a major governmental concern. Governments are not always happy at being handed this responsibility but usually end up with it if it is not picked up somewhere else in society. So, governments have always tried to encourage private organizations to act in this area. This is one reason why charitable institutions are exempt from tax.

When the American economy started to become mainly industrial around the beginning of the 20th century, the need for retirement plans increased, since the industrial economy tended to break up the traditional supportive, extended farm family, and industry provided less work for the aged than farming. The government became involved in retirement plans in a twofold way.

First, in the 1920s the federal government began encouraging private, employer-sponsored retirement plans by providing two kinds of tax benefits: (1) pension funds were made tax exempt[1] and (2) employer contributions to plan funds were made currently deductible even though benefits were not paid until later years.[2] The second big federal initiative in the retirement plan area was, of course, the adoption of the Social Security system in the 1930s at a time when private pension plans were in great decline.

Since the 1940s, private pension plans have revived to an enormous degree; assets in these plans now amount to more than 3 *trillion* dollars—a pot of money constituting as much as 10 percent of the nation's *total capital.*

However, something else has grown as fast or faster than the dollars in pension funds: the words, paragraphs, pages, and volumes of federal statutes, court cases, rulings, and regulations based on the simple, original 1920s tax benefit arrangements for private pension plans. How does the government justify the sometimes almost unbelievable complexity of this regulatory scheme? Three reasons are generally given; two are respectable, while the third is questionable:

- The government loses substantial revenue by providing tax benefits for retirement and other benefit plans. So, it has to make sure that benefits go where they are most needed so that the tax "expenditure" is cost effective.

- Private saving for retirement should be encouraged so that individuals do not become dependent on the government. But such saving should not fail to help those who really need the retirement benefit. There have to be rules so that plans do not simply benefit highly compensated employees who have other sources of retirement income.

- The government can gain a lot of tax revenue— without the political pain of "raising taxes"—by fine-tuning the employee benefit law to reduce tax benefits for certain plan participants. Fine-tuning adds page after page to federal laws and regulations, year after year. Last year's fine-tuning scheme is seldom repealed—it's just added to or amended.

What's the significance of all this history and government policy to the benefit planner? Just two points have to be made:

- It is a lot easier to understand the rules if you know where they come from. For example, can you adopt a plan provision that gives extra benefits to one or more employees who are not "highly compensated"? You can search the federal law until doomsday and you will not find the answer to this in so many words. But if you understand what the law is trying to do, you will understand immediately that this kind of provision usually will not violate the law.

- If you know what kinds of concerns motivate our Congress, you can give your clients useful advice about potential future changes in the law. While nobody can predict tax law changes in detail, it's pretty safe to say, for example, that prohibiting discrimination in favor of highly compensated employees will continue to be an important policy consideration.

## THE RULES

Planners need to understand where the employee benefit plan rules are and how to find them. They also must understand the significance of the rules; for example, some rules are binding on everybody, while certain other authorities are merely sources of information about the government's position on a certain issue in case the issue should get into court.

Government regulation is expressed through the following, in order of importance: (1) the statutory law; (2) the law as expressed in court cases; (3) regulations of government agencies; (4) rulings and other information issued by government agencies.

*The law (statutory).*

The "law" as expressed by statutes passed by the U.S. Congress is the highest level of authority and is the basis of all regulation; the court cases, rulings, and regulations are simply interpretations of the statute. If the statute was detailed enough to cover every possible case, there theoretically would not be any need for anything else. But despite the best efforts of Congres-

sional drafting staffs, the statutes cannot cover every situation.

Benefit planners should become as familiar as possible with the statutory law since it is the basis for all other rules, regulations, and court cases. One of the main causes for confusion among non-experts is a lack of understanding of the relative status of sources of information. That is, while a rule found in the Internal Revenue Code is controlling, a statement in an IRS ruling or instructions to IRS forms may be merely a matter of interpretation that is relatively easy to "plan around."

In the benefits area, the sources of statutory law are:

- *Internal Revenue Code (the Code).* The tax laws governing the deductibility and taxation of pension and employee benefit programs are controlling. These are found primarily in Code sections 401-424, with important provisions also in Sections 72, 83, and other sections.

- *Employee Retirement Income Security Act of 1974 (ERISA), as amended, and other labor law provisions.* Labor law provisions such as ERISA govern the non-tax aspects of federal regulation. These involve plan participation requirements, notice to participants, reporting to the federal government, and a variety of rules designed to safeguard any funds that are set aside to pay benefits in the future. There is some overlap between ERISA and the Code in the areas of plan participation, vesting, prohibited transactions, and others.

- *Pension Benefit Guaranty Corporation (PBGC).* The PBGC is a government corporation set up under ERISA in 1974 to provide termination insurance for participants in qualified defined benefit plans up to certain limits. In carrying out this responsibility, the PBGC regulates plan terminations and imposes certain reporting requirements on covered plans that are in financial difficulty or in a state of contraction.

- *Securities laws.* The federal securities laws are designed to protect investors. Benefit plans may involve an element of investing the employee's money. While qualified plans are generally exempt from the full impact of the securities laws, if the plan holds employer stock, a federal registration statement may be required and certain securities regulations may apply.

- *Civil Rights laws.* Benefit plans are part of an employer's compensation policies, and these plans are therefore subject to the Civil Rights Act of 1964 prohibiting employment discrimination on the basis of race, religion, sex, or national origin.

- *Age Discrimination.* The Age Discrimination in Employment Act of 1967, as amended, has specific provisions aimed at benefit plans.

- *Disabled Employees.* The Americans with Disabilities Act of 1990 generally prohibits an employer from discriminating against a person on the basis of the person's disability in the areas of employment, public services and transportation, public accommodations and telecommunication services.

- *State legislation.* ERISA contains a broad "preemption" provision under which the provisions of ERISA supersede any state laws relating to employee benefit plans. If ERISA does not deal with a particular issue, however, there may be room for state legislation. For example, there is considerable state legislation and regulation governing the types of group-term life insurance contracts that can be offered as part of an employer plan. There are also certain areas where states continue to assert authority even though ERISA also has an impact—for example in the area of creditors' rights to pension fund assets.

*Court cases.*

The courts enter this picture primarily when a specific taxpayer decides to appeal a tax assessment made by the IRS. The courts do not act on their own to resolve tax or other legal issues. Consequently, the law as expressed in court cases is a crazy-quilt affair that offers some answers but often raises more questions than it answers. However, after statutes, court cases are the most authoritative source of law. Courts can and do overturn regulations and rulings of the IRS and other regulatory agencies.

A taxpayer wishing to contest a tax assessment has three choices: (1) the Federal District Court in the taxpayer's district; (2) the United States Tax Court; or (3) the United States Court of Federal Claims.[3] So, tax law can be found in decisions of any of these three courts.

All three courts are equally authoritative. Most tax cases, however, are decided by the U.S. Tax Court,

because it offers a powerful advantage: the taxpayer can bring the case before the Tax Court without paying the disputed tax. The other courts require payment of the tax followed by a suit for refund.

Decisions of the Federal District Court and the United States Tax Court are appealed to the Federal Circuit Court of Appeals for the applicable federal "judicial circuit"—the U.S. is divided into eleven of these circuits. Decisions of the United States Court of Federal Claims are appealed to the Court of Appeals for the Federal Circuit. The circuit courts sometimes differ on certain points of tax law; as a result, tax and benefit planning may depend on what judicial circuit the taxpayer is located in. Where these differences exist, one or more taxpayers will eventually appeal a decision by the Court of Appeals to the United States Supreme Court to resolve differences of interpretation among various judicial circuits. However, this process takes many years and the Supreme Court may ultimately choose not to hear the case. Congress also sometimes amends the Code or other statute to resolve these interpretive differences.

*Regulations.*

Regulations are interpretations of statutory law that are published by a government agency; in the benefits area, the most significant regulations are those published by the Treasury Department (the parent of the IRS), the Labor Department, and the PBGC.

Regulations are structured as abstract rules, like the statutory law itself. They are not related to a particular factual situation, although they often contain useful examples that illustrate the application of the rules. Treasury regulations currently are often issued in question-and-answer form.

The numbering system for regulations is supposed to make them more accessible by including an internal reference to the underlying statutory provision. For example, Treasury Regulation Section 1.401(k)-2 is a regulation relating to Section 401(k) of the Internal Revenue Code. Labor Regulation Section 2550.408b-3 relates to Section 408(b) of ERISA.

Issuance of regulations follows a prescribed procedure involving an initial issuance of *proposed regulations,* followed by hearings and public comment, then *final regulations.* The process often takes years. Where taxpayers have an urgent need to know answers, the agency will issue *regulations* that are both *temporary* and proposed. Technically, temporary regulations are binding while regulations issued only in proposed form are not. However, if a taxpayer takes a position contrary to such a proposed regulation, the taxpayer is taking the risk that the regulation will ultimately be finalized and be enforced against him.

*Rulings and other information.*

*IRS Rulings.* IRS rulings are responses by the IRS to requests by taxpayers to interpret the law in light of their particular fact situations. A *Technical Advice Memorandum (TAM)* is similar to a ruling except that the request for clarification and guidance is initiated from an IRS agent in the field during a taxpayer audit, rather than directly from the taxpayer.

There are two types of IRS rulings—*Revenue Rulings,* which are published by the IRS as general guidance to all taxpayers, and *Private Letter Rulings (Let. Ruls.),* which are addressed only to the specific taxpayers who requested the rulings. The IRS publishes its Revenue Rulings in IRS Bulletins (collected in Cumulative Bulletins—CB—each year). Revenue rulings are binding on IRS personnel on the issues covered in them, but often IRS agents will try to make a distinction between a taxpayer's factual situation and a similar one covered in a ruling if the ruling appears to favor the taxpayer.

Private letter rulings are not published by the IRS, but are available to the public with taxpayer identification deleted. These "anonymous" letter rulings are published for tax professionals by various private publishers. They are not binding interpretations of tax law except for the taxpayer who requested the ruling, and even then they apply only to the exact situation described in the ruling request and do not apply to even a slightly different fact pattern involving the same taxpayer. Nevertheless, letter rulings are very important in research since they are often the only source of information about the IRS position on various issues.

A *General Counsel Memorandum (GCM)* is an internal IRS document prepared by the General Counsel of the Service for its own staff's guidance in administering the Code. GCMs also give an indication of the probable approach the Service will take in a particular area.

A *Field Service Advice (FSA)* is an IRS document prepared for internal use within the IRS. Until 1998, these documents were not released to the public and, therefore, depending on when a particular FSA was written, may contain candid analysis of the issues involved. As a result of Freedom of Information Act litigation and subsequent legislation, FSAs issued after 1985 are required to be released to the public.[4] While FSAs are not binding even to the person to whom they are written, they do provide insight into the thinking of the IRS at the time they are written.

Because of frequent changes in the tax law, the IRS has been unable to promulgate regulations and rulings on a timely basis, and has increasingly used less formal approaches to inform taxpayers of its position. These include various types of published *Notices* and even speeches by IRS personnel. Finally, many important IRS positions are found only in *IRS Publications* (pamphlets available free to taxpayers) and *instructions* for filling out IRS forms. The IRS also maintains telephone question-answering services, but the value of these for information on complicated issues is minimal.

*Other rulings.* The Department of Labor and the PBGC issue some rulings in areas of employee benefit regulation under their jurisdiction. DOL rulings include the *Prohibited Transaction Exemptions (PTEs)* which rule on types of transactions that can avoid the prohibited transaction penalties—for example, sale of life insurance contracts to qualified plans.

## HOW TO FIND THE ANSWERS

Tax experts find it difficult to get answers to employee benefit tax questions, so non-experts should not be surprised if they also have trouble. The following approach is used by many successful financial planning professionals:

1. Investigate secondary sources, choose several that you find helpful, and keep them handy. Secondary sources are overviews of the law that give you a general understanding and direct you toward more detailed information. The *Tools and Techniques* series of books are examples of secondary sources of information that provide rapid access to an overview and general explanation of the law.

2. When a tax or other benefit issue arises, review the secondary sources to get a general idea of the law in that area and where additional information can be found.

3. Review the statutory provisions and regulations (if any) relating to the issue—particularly the Internal Revenue Code and ERISA and the related regulations.

4. Review court cases and rulings dealing with the issue and compare their factual situations with the one you are dealing with.

At this point, non-lawyer professionals must confront the problem of *unauthorized practice of law*. While the concept of "practice of law" is too complex to define here, in general a non-lawyer may not express an opinion to a client as to the specific law applicable to, and the legal implications of, the client's factual situation. A professional can, however, discuss the legal background of the client's situation in general and can advise the client to obtain an opinion of counsel as to the law's specific impact on the client. That should be the non-lawyer professional's role in a benefit planning situation involving complex or unsettled legal issues. See Appendix F.

## WHAT HAPPENS IF THE LAW IS NOT FOLLOWED?

There are both *criminal* and civil penalties that can apply if a taxpayer fails to abide by the tax law by taking too large a deduction or under-reporting items of income. Criminal penalties are those that can result in imprisonment.[5] Nothing will be said further here about criminal penalties except this: if a client discovers that the IRS is considering criminal tax sanctions against him, that client is in very serious trouble and needs immediate legal help from an expert in criminal tax law.

Most IRS audits that end unfavorably to the taxpayer do not result in penalties; the taxpayer merely has to pay back taxes plus interest—which can be substantial. However, certain penalties can also be assessed. These include penalties for:

- failure to file return or pay the tax indicated on the return. *Penalty*—5% of the underpayment per month, up to 25%.[6]

- substantial understatement of income tax (understatement of the greater of $5,000 or 10% of tax). *Penalty*—20% of the understatement.[7]

- negligence, imposed if a taxpayer fails to make a reasonable attempt to comply with the tax law. *Penalty*—20% of the underpayment.[8]

- fraud. *Penalty*—75% of the underpayment.[9]

- substantial valuation overstatement (for example, an overstatement of pension liabilities to inflate pension plan deductions). *Penalty*—20 to 40% of the underpayment.[10]

*Legal opinion letters.* Can a taxpayer rely on a legal opinion as to the tax consequences of a transaction— that is, will the taxpayer at least avoid the negligence or fraud penalties by doing so? Yes, generally speaking; however, there are some things the client should watch for:

- Many legal opinion letters avoid expressing an opinion on certain aspects of a transaction, so the client must read the opinion letter carefully.

- The client should be sure the legal opinion applies to the taxpayer and transaction in question, and is not aimed at some other, similar transaction or is simply a generic opinion relating to a group of potential taxpayers. A "borrowed" opinion letter may provide useful information but taxpayer reliance on it is risky since the author of the opinion did not focus on the facts of the actual situation.

- If the transaction involves a "tax shelter," which is broadly defined, the substantial underpayment penalty can be avoided only if the taxpayer reasonably believes that his tax treatment was "more likely than not" the proper treatment.[11] Therefore, the opinion letter should provide a basis for the "more likely than not" standard in these cases.

## FOOTNOTES

1. Revenue Acts of 1921 and 1926.
2. Revenue Act of 1928.
3. Prior to October 30, 1992, the U.S. Court of Federal Claims was known as the U.S. Claims Court.
4. *Tax Analysts v. Internal Revenue Service*, 117 F.3d 607 (D.C. Cir. 1997); IRS Restructuring and Reform Act Section 3509.
5. A complete discussion of both criminal and civil penalties is contained in Saltzman, *IRS Practice and Procedure*: Warren, Gorham and Lamont, 2nd ed., 1990.
6. IRC Section 6651.
7. IRC Sections 6662(b)(2), 6662(d).
8. IRC Sections 6662(b)(1), 6662(c).
9. IRC Section 6663.
10. IRC Sections 6662(b)(4), 6662(f), 6662(h).
11. IRC Section 6662(d)(2)(C).

# Chapter 8

# CASH BALANCE PENSION PLAN

## WHAT IS IT?

A cash balance pension plan is a qualified defined benefit plan that provides for annual employer contributions at a specified rate to hypothetical individual accounts that are set up for each plan participant. The employer guarantees not only the contribution level but also a minimum rate of return on each participant's account. A cash balance plan works somewhat like a money purchase pension plan discussed in Chapter 14, but money purchase plans do not involve employer guarantees of rate of return.

## WHEN IS IT INDICATED?

1. When the employees are relatively young and have substantial time to accumulate retirement savings.

2. When employees are concerned with security of retirement income.

3. When the work force is large and the bulk of the employees are middle-income. (Banks and similar financial institutions find this type of plan particularly appealing.)

4. When the employer is able to spread administrative costs over a relatively large group of plan participants.

5. When the employer has an existing defined benefit plan and wishes to convert to a plan that provides a more attractive benefit for younger employees and may lower costs for older employees.

## ADVANTAGES

1. As with all qualified plans, the cash balance plan provides a tax-deferred savings medium for employees.

2. Lump sum distributions from a cash balance plan may be eligible for the special 10-year averaging (for certain employees born before 1936) tax computation available for qualified plans.

3. The employer guarantee removes investment risk from the employee.

4. Plan benefits are guaranteed (within limits) by the federal Pension Benefit Guaranty Corporation (PBGC).

5. The benefits of the plan are easily communicated to and appreciated by employees.

## DISADVANTAGES

1. The retirement benefit may be inadequate for older plan entrants—see Figures 8.1 and 8.2.

2. Because of the need for actuarial services, the minimum funding requirements, and the PBGC guarantee, the plan is more complex administratively than qualified defined contribution plans.

3. The shift of investment risk to the employer increases employer costs.

## DESIGN FEATURES OF THESE PLANS

A cash balance plan provides a hypothetical individual account for each participant. These hypothetical accounts are credited by the employer at least once a year with two types of credit—the "pay credit" and the "interest credit."

The pay credit uses a formula based on compensation. For example, the plan might require the employer to credit each employee's account annually with a pay credit of 6% of compensation. The pay credit formula may also be "integrated" with Social Security. With Social Security integration, compensation below a level specified in the plan—the "integration level"—receives a lesser credit than compensation above the integration level. This reflects the fact that the employer pays Social Security taxes to provide retirement benefits through Social Security. Social Security integration for qualified plans is discussed in Chapter 25 of this book.[1]

**Figure 8.1**

## CASH BALANCE PLAN ACCUMULATIONS

Pay credit: 10 percent of compensation
Interest credit: 7 percent annually guaranteed rate

| Age at plan entry | Annual compensation | Account balance at age 65 |
|---|---|---|
| 25 | $30,000 | $640,827 |
| 30 | 30,000 | 443,739 |
| 40 | 30,000 | 203,028 |
| 50 | 30,000 | 80,664 |
| 55 | 30,000 | 44,349 |
| 60 | 30,000 | 18,459 |

**Figure 8.2**

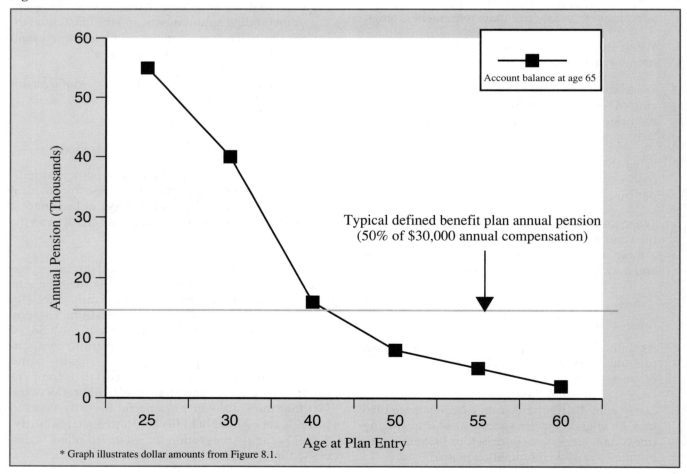

* Graph illustrates dollar amounts from Figure 8.1.

The interest credit is an amount of employer-guaranteed investment earnings that is credited annually to each employee's account. The interest credit must follow a formula in the plan and cannot merely be discretionary on the employer's part. For example, the interest credit formula in the plan might provide for each employee's account to be credited annually with a rate of earnings defined as the lesser of (a) the increase in the Consumer Price Index over the preceding year or (b) the one-year rate for U.S. Treasury securities. The plan can allow the employer to credit accounts with actual plan earnings, if these are higher.

In a cash balance plan there are no actual individual accounts, as there are in defined contribution plans. All amounts are pooled in a single fund. Any plan participant has a legal claim on the entire fund to satisfy his or her claim to plan benefits.

The employer's annual cost for the plan is determined on an actuarial basis because of the employer guarantee feature. Investment risk lies with the employer; if actual plan earnings fall below total interest credits for the year, the employer must make up the difference. Employer costs can be controlled primarily by choosing the right kind of formula for the interest credit, one that does not risk uncontrollable and unforeseeable employer obligations. However, the interest credit formula should not be excessively conservative—if actual plan earnings year after year are more than interest credits, plan participants may resent the employer's enrichment and the positive employee relations value of the plan may be lost.

Investment discretion by participants (earmarking) is not available in a cash balance plan, because the plan is not technically an individual account plan under ERISA section 404(c). Loans from the plan can be made available, but most employers will not want a loan provision because of the administrative problems resulting from the plan's status as a defined benefit plan without separate participant accounts. Life insurance can be purchased by the plan as an incidental benefit to participants or as a plan investment, under the limitations discussed in Chapter 13.

*Modification of Existing Defined Benefit Formula.* Some employers that have a traditional defined benefit plan (see Chapter 9) become dissatisfied with the plan because it does not provide an attractive benefit for younger employees, but imposes substantial costs for employees nearing retirement. Termination of the defined benefit plan and substitution of a defined contribution plan would require that most or all existing plan assets would have to be immediately credited to vested participants. However, a less costly alternative might be to revise the existing plan's formula into a cash balance formula.

A conversion can result in a reduction in the accrual rate for an employee's benefit; in fact this is often a factor in the employer's decision to make the conversion—to save money on older employees' retirement benefits. However, under regulations proposed in 2002, the conversion will not violate IRC Section 411(b)(1)(H) (dealing with age discrimination in defined benefit plans) if the converted plan satisfies one of two alternative rules:

- The converted plan determines each participant's benefit as not less than the sum of the participant's benefits accrued under the defined benefit plan and the cash balance account; or

- The converted plan establishes the participant's opening account balance as an amount not less than the actuarial present value of the participant's prior accrued benefit using reasonable actuarial assumptions. The interest rate assumption could not increase, directly or indirectly, as a result of the participant's attaining any age.[2]

The second alternative could result in a "wear-away" period—that is, a period following the conversion when no benefits would accrue to the participant since the participant's opening account balance is greater than the cash balance amount that would have resulted if the cash balance plan had been in existence when the participant first entered the employer's defined benefit plan. Nevertheless, the proposed regulations take the position that there is no age discrimination under these circumstances.

If an employer amends a defined benefit plan (or any other plan subject to the Code Section 412 funding standards) to adopt a cash balance formula, or makes any other change resulting in a reduction in the rate of future benefit accrual, the plan administrator must provide a prescribed written notice to affected plan participants and beneficiaries. Failure to provide the notice results in a $100/day penalty.[3] The provision allows for regulations exempting certain plans with fewer than 100 participants under certain circumstances.

## TAX IMPLICATIONS

1. Employer contributions to the plan are deductible when made.[4]

2.  Internal Revenue Code section 415(b) limits the benefits provided under the plan to the lesser of $160,000 annually (in 2003, as indexed[5]) or 100% of the participant's high 3-year average compensation.[6] This is the *defined benefit* plan limit. This limit may be more or less favorable than the defined contribution limit applicable to a comparable money purchase plan.

3.  Taxation of the employee on employer contributions is deferred.[7] Both contributions and earnings on plan assets are nontaxable to plan participants until withdrawn, assuming the plan remains "qualified." A plan is qualified if it meets the eligibility, vesting, funding and other requirements explained in Chapter 25.

4.  Distributions from the plan must follow the rules for qualified plan distributions. Certain premature distributions are subject to penalties. These distribution rules are discussed in Chapter 25.

5.  Lump sum distributions may be eligible for the special 10-year averaging (for certain employees born before 1936) tax computation available for qualified plans. Not all distributions are eligible; see Chapter 26 for coverage of these rules.

6.  The plan is subject to the minimum funding rules of section 412 of the Internal Revenue Code.[8] This requires minimum contributions, subject to a penalty if less than the minimum amount is contributed

**Figure 8.3**

| | Cash Balance Plan | Typical defined contribution plan | Typical defined benefit plan |
|---|---|---|---|
| **CASH BALANCE vs. CONVENTIONAL PLANS** | | | |
| Contribution rate | percentage of salary (with actuarial aspects) | percentage of salary | actuarially determined |
| Investment risk | employer | employee | employer |
| Investment earmarking | not available | available | not available |
| Social Security integration | available | available | available |
| PBGC cost/ coverage | yes | no | yes |
| 401(k) feature | not available | available in profit-sharing plan | not available |
| Adequate benefit for older entrants | no | no | yes |
| Administrative cost | higher | lower (unless 401(k) or earmarking) | higher |

in any year. If the plan is not fully funded, the subsequent year's contributions must be made on at least an estimated quarterly basis.[9]

7. Since a cash balance plan is a type of defined benefit plan, it is subject to mandatory insurance coverage by the Pension Benefit Guaranty Corporation (PBGC). The PBGC is a government corporation funded through a mandatory premium paid by employer-sponsors of covered plans. The premium is a flat rate is $19 annually per participant;[10] however, an additional annual premium may be required, depending on the amount of the plan's unfunded vested benefit.[11] If the plan is terminated by the employer, PBGC termination procedures must be followed.

8. Certain employers adopting a plan may be eligible for a business tax credit of up to $500 for "qualified startup costs." See Chapter 27 for details.

9. A plan may permit employees to make voluntary contributions to a "deemed IRA" established under the plan. Amounts so contributed reduce the limit for other traditional or Roth IRA contributions. See Chapter 13 for details.

10. The plan is subject to the additional ERISA reporting and disclosure rules outlined in Appendix A.

## ALTERNATIVES

1. Money purchase pension plans and profit sharing plans build up similar qualified retirement accounts for employees, but without the employer guaranteed minimum investment return. (See the comparison chart in Figure 8.3.)

2. Traditional defined benefit plans provide guaranteed benefits for employees, but are more complex in design and administration. (See the comparison chart in Figure 8.3.)

3. Individual retirement saving is always an alternative or supplement to any qualified plan, but there is no tax deferral except in the case of certain IRAs.

## HOW TO INSTALL A CASH BALANCE PLAN

A cash balance plan follows the qualified plan installation procedure discussed in Chapter 27 of this book.

## WHERE CAN I FIND OUT MORE ABOUT THESE PLANS?

1. Graduate course: Advanced Pension and Retirement Planning II (GS 843), The American College, Bryn Mawr, PA.

## FOOTNOTES

1. Prop. Treas. Reg. §1.411(b)-2(b)(2)(iii)(D), (E).

2. A safe harbor provided for cash balance plans in nondiscrimination regulations under Section 401(a) permits a cash balance plan to satisfy the permitted disparity rules on the basis of the defined contribution rules. See Reg. §1.401(a)(4)-8(c)(3).

3. IRC Section 4980F. Note that all provisions of EGTRRA 2001 are scheduled to sunset, or expire, after December 31, 2010.

4. IRC Section 404(a).

5. Notice 2002-71, 2002-45 IRB 830.

6. IRC Section 415(b). This limit is subject to indexing for inflation after 2002, in increments of $5,000. IRC Section 415(d)(4)(A).

7. IRC Section 402(a).

8. Actuaries differ as to the correct approach in applying the minimum funding rules. For discussion, see Grubbs, "The Cash Balance Plan—A Closer Look," *Journal of Pension Planning and Compliance*, Vol. 15, No. 3 (1989).

9. IRC Section 412(m).

10. ERISA Section 4006(a)(3)(A)(i).

11. ERISA Section 4006(a)(3)(E). This extra premium was formerly "capped" at a maximum of $53 per participant, but after June 30, 1996 there is no cap. URAA '94, Section 774(a).

## Chapter 9

# DEFINED BENEFIT PENSION PLAN

### WHAT IS IT?

A defined benefit pension plan is a qualified employer pension plan that guarantees a specified benefit level at retirement.

### WHEN IS IT INDICATED?

1. When the employer's plan design objective is to provide an adequate level of retirement income to employees regardless of their age at plan entry.

2. When the employer wants to allocate plan costs to the maximum extent to older employees—often key or controlling employees in a closely held business.

3. When an older controlling employee in a small business—for example a doctor or dentist in a professional corporation—wants to maximize tax-deferred retirement savings.

### ADVANTAGES

1. As with all qualified plans, employees obtain a tax-deferred retirement savings medium.

2. Retirement benefits at adequate levels can be provided for all employees regardless of age at plan entry.

3. Benefit levels are guaranteed both by the employer and by the Pension Benefit Guaranty Corporation (PBGC).

4. For an older highly compensated employee, a defined benefit plan generally will allow the maximum amount of tax-deferred retirement saving.

### DISADVANTAGES

1. Actuarial and PBGC aspects of defined benefit plans result in higher installation and administration costs than for defined contribution plans.

2. Defined benefit plans are complex to design and difficult to explain to employees.

3. Employees who leave before retirement may receive relatively little benefit from the plan.

4. The employer is subject to a recurring annual funding obligation (that must be paid in quarterly or more frequent installments) regardless of whether, in a given year, it has made a profit or incurred a loss.

5. The employer assumes the risk of bad investment results in the plan fund.

### DESIGN FEATURES

Defined benefit plans provide a specified amount of benefit to the plan participant at the plan's specified retirement age—the "normal retirement age."

There are many types of formulas for determining this benefit. The most common formulas can be summarized as the "flat amount," the "flat percentage" and the "unit credit" types. (See Chapter 2 for a discussion of appropriate income replacement percentages in retirement.)

*Flat amount formula.* A flat amount formula provides simply a stated dollar amount to each plan participant. For example, the plan might provide a pension of $500 per month for life, beginning at age 65, for each plan participant. Such a plan might require some minimum service to obtain the full amount—perhaps 10 or 15 years of service with the employer—with the benefit scaled back for fewer years of service.

A flat amount formula does not differentiate among employees with different compensation levels, so it would be appropriate only when there is relatively little difference in compensation among the group of employees covered under the plan.

*Flat percentage formula.* Flat percentage formulas are very common; they provide a retirement benefit that is a percentage of the employee's average earnings. For example, the formula might provide a retirement benefit at age 65 equal to 50% of the employee's average earnings prior to retirement. Under this formula, a participant whose average annual pay was $100,000 prior to retirement would receive an annual pension of $50,000.

Typically a plan will require certain minimum service—such as 10 or 15 years—to obtain the full percentage benefit, with the percentage scaled back for fewer years of service. For example, if the plan provides a benefit of 50% of average compensation for an employee who retires with at least 10 years of service, it might provide a benefit of only 25% of average compensation for an employee who retires at age 65 with only five years of service for the employer.

*Unit credit formula.* A unit credit formula is based on the employee's service with the employer. For example, the formula might provide 1.5% of earnings for each of the employee's years of service, with the total percentage applied to the employee's average earnings. Under this formula, a participant with average annual compensation of $100,000 who retired after 30 years of service would receive an annual pension of $45,000 (that is, 1.5 times 30, or 45% of $100,000).

There are two methods generally used to compute average earnings for these formulas, the "career-average" and the "final average" methods.

Under the *career average* method, the formula uses earnings averaged over the employee's entire career with the employer. The career-average method takes early and often low-earning years into account, and thus the total benefit may not fully reflect the employee's earning power at retirement.

Under the *final average* method, earnings are averaged over a number of years—usually the three to five years immediately prior to retirement. The final average method usually produces a retirement benefit that is better matched to the employee's income just prior to retirement.

In either a career average or final average formula, only the first $200,000 (in 2003, as indexed) of each employee's compensation is taken into account.[1] In other words, an employee earning $275,000 in 2003 is treated as if compensation were $200,000.

In many plans, these formulas are further modified by "integrating" them with Social Security benefits. Integrating the formula gives the employer some credit for paying the cost of employee Social Security benefits. It helps to provide a reasonable level of retirement income for all employees by taking Social Security benefits into account. The rules for integrating defined benefit formulas are very complex; they are discussed in more detail in Chapter 25.

Employers must fund defined benefit plans with periodic deposits determined actuarially to insure that the plan fund will be sufficient to pay the promised benefit as each participant retires. The objective is to accumulate a fund at the employee's retirement age that is sufficient to "buy an annuity" equal to the retirement benefit. (In some plans, annuities are actually purchased at retirement age, but this is not required.)

---

*Example:* Suppose the actuary hired by the employer estimates that a pension of $50,000 per year beginning at age 65 is equivalent to a lump sum of $475,000 at age 65. In other words, for a given interest rate and other assumptions, the amount of $475,000 deposited at age 65 will produce an annuity of $50,000 per year for the life of an individual aged 65. For a participant aged 45 at plan entry, the employer has 20 years to fund this benefit—that is, to build up a fund totaling $475,000 at age 65.

The actuary will use various methods and assumptions to determine how much must be deposited periodically. As an illustration, a "level annual premium" method (equal annual payment method) with a 6% interest assumption would require the employer to deposit $12,180 annually for 20 years in order to build up a fund of $475,000. This shows how investment returns work for the benefit of the employer; the 20 deposits of $12,180 total only $243,600, but at age 65 the fund will actually total $475,000 if all annual deposits are made and the fund actually earns a 6% investment return annually.

---

Actuarial methods and assumptions are chosen to provide the desired pattern for spreading the plan's cost over the years it will be in effect. The actuarial method and assumptions often have to be adjusted over the years to make sure that the fund is adequate. It is even possible for a defined benefit plan to become overfunded, in which case employer contributions must be suspended for a period of time.

The actuarial funding approach for defined benefit plans means that, for a given benefit level, the annual funding amount is greater for employees who are older at entry into the plan (see table below), since the time to fund the benefit is less in the case of an older entrant.

### AGE/CONTRIBUTION LEVEL FOR DEFINED BENEFIT PLAN

| Age at Plan Entry | Annual Benefit at Age 65 | Years to fund | Annual Employer Contribution |
|---|---|---|---|
| 30 | $25,000 | 35 | $ 1,971 |
| 40 | 25,000 | 25 | 4,309 |
| 50 | 25,000 | 15 | 10,847 |

This set of calculations assumes (1) that money deposited before retirement will earn a 7% investment return (2) no mortality (i.e., no discount for the possibility that some plan participants may die before retirement) and (3) a unisex annuity purchase rate of $1,400 per $10 monthly at age 65 (i.e., it will take a deposit of $1,400 at age 65 to purchase a lifetime annuity of $10 per month beginning at age 65, for any plan participant, male or female).

This makes defined benefit plans attractive to professionals and closely held business owners; they tend to adopt retirement plans for their businesses when they are relatively older than their regular employees. A large percentage of the total cost for a defined benefit plan in this situation goes to fund these key employees' benefits.

---

*Example*: Doctor Retractor, aged 48, is a sole practitioner with two office employees, a nurse aged 35 and a receptionist aged 25. The doctor earns $250,000 annually (of which only $200,000 (in 2003) can be taken into account in the plan formula) and the nurse and receptionist earn $30,000 and $20,000 respectively.

The doctor wants to adopt a new qualified plan for his medical practice. Compare the initial cost allocation below for a maximum (i.e., maximum benefit for the doctor) defined benefit plan with that for a maximum defined contribution plan.

The maximum defined contribution plan provides 20% of compensation for each employee. The contribution for the doctor is 20% of $200,000 (the compensation limit under IRC section 401(a)(17), as indexed for 2003), which equals $40,000, the maximum Section 415 amount for the doctor (in 2003, as indexed).

Assume that the doctor adopts a defined benefit plan that uses the safe harbor for fractional accrual plans (see the Questions and Answers at the end of this chapter). The maximum benefit for the doctor under such a plan is limited because he has only 18 years remaining until his retirement age of 66 (see item three under "Tax Implications" below). Regulations under Section 401(a)(4) require 25 years of service for a highly compensated participant to accrue the full benefit. Under the fractional accrual safe harbor, the doctor could accrue 18/25 of the benefit provided to nonhighly compensated participants. Thus, the doctor could receive 18/25, or 72% of compensation, provided the nonhighly compensated participants receive a benefit of 100% of compensation. The doctor's benefit is 72% of his compensation (as limited) of $200,000 (as indexed for 2003), or $144,000.

The cost comparison is as follows:

| | Annual cost for Defined Benefit Plan | Annual cost for Defined Contribution Plan |
|---|---|---|
| Doctor | $44,758 | $40,000 |
| Nurse | 2,876 | 6,000 |
| Receptionist | 916 | 4,000 |
| Total | $48,550 | $50,000 |
| Percent for Doctor | 92% | 80% |

Assumptions for defined benefit calculation: 7% pre-retirement investment return, no pre-retirement mortality, lump sum required at age 65 for each $10,000 of annual benefit: $112,959. Results will vary for different assumptions.

---

To back up the employer's funding obligation and safeguard employees, defined benefit plans are insured by the federal Pension Benefit Guaranty Corporation (PBGC) up to specified limits. The employer must pay annual premiums to the PBGC to fund this insurance. Furthermore, the employer is liable for reimbursement to the PBGC for any guaranteed payments the PBGC must make to employees.

## TAX IMPLICATIONS

1. Employer contributions to the plan are deductible when made.[2]

2. Taxation of the employee on employer contributions is deferred. Contributions and earnings on plan assets are nontaxable to plan participants until withdrawn, assuming the plan remains "qualified."[3] A plan is qualified if it meets the eligibility, vesting, funding and other requirements explained in Chapter 25.

3. Under Code section 415, there is a maximum limit on the projected annual benefit that the plan can provide. For a benefit beginning at age 65, the maximum life annuity or joint and survivor benefit is the lesser of (a) $160,000 (in 2003, as indexed)[4], or (b) 100% of the participant's compensation averaged over his three highest-earning consecutive years.

---

*Example:* If Foxx retires in 2003 at age 65, and his high three-year average compensation was $60,000, his employer's defined benefit plan cannot provide a life or joint and survivor annuity of more than $60,000 per year. For employee Sharp, who retires in 2003 at age 65 with high 3-year average compensation of $250,000, the limit is $160,000 annually.

---

4. Distributions from the plan must follow the rules for qualified plan distributions. Certain premature distributions may be subject to penalty taxes. The distribution rules and reporting forms are discussed in Chapter 26.

5. The plan is subject to the "minimum funding" rules of Code section 412. This requires minimum periodic contributions by the employer, with a penalty if less than the minimum amount is contributed. If a plan is not fully funded, in subsequent years, the employer must make plan contributions at least quarterly until full funding is achieved.[5] Chapter 25 explains the minimum funding rules.

6. A defined benefit plan is subject to mandatory insurance coverage by the Pension Benefit Guaranty Corporation (PBGC). The PBGC is a government corporation funded through a mandatory premium paid by employer-sponsors of covered plans. The premium consists of a flat rate of $19 annually per participant, plus an extra amount calculated on the basis of the plan's unfunded vested benefits, if any.[6] If the employer wants to terminate the plan, the PBGC must be notified in advance and must approve any distribution of plan assets to participants.[7]

7. Certain employers adopting a new plan may be eligible for a business tax credit of up to $500 for "qualified startup costs." See Chapter 27 for details.

8. A plan may permit employees to make voluntary contributions to a "deemed IRA" established under the plan. Amounts so contributed reduce the limit for other traditional or Roth IRA contributions. See Chapter 13 for details.

## ERISA REQUIREMENTS

The plan is subject to all the ERISA requirements for qualified plans (participation, funding, vesting, etc.) described in Chapter 25 and the ERISA reporting and disclosure requirements outlined in Appendix A.

## ALTERNATIVES

1. Money purchase pension plans provide retirement benefits, but without employer guarantees of benefit levels, and with adequate benefits only for younger plan entrants.

2. Target benefit pension plans may provide adequate benefits to older entrants, but without an employer guarantee of the benefit level.

3. Cash balance pension plans provide an employer guarantee of principal and investment earnings on the plan fund, but provide adequate benefits only to younger plan entrants.

4. Profit sharing plans, simplified employee pensions (SEPs), stock bonus plans, and ESOPs provide a qualified, tax-deferred retirement savings medium, but the benefit adequacy is tied closely to the financial success of the employer.

5. Section 401(k) plans, savings plans and SIMPLE IRAs provide a qualified, tax-deferred savings medium in which the amount saved is subject to some control by employees themselves.

6. Private retirement saving outside a qualified plan does not provide the same tax benefits as saving within a qualified plan, except in the case of certain IRAs.

See Chapter 2 for a further discussion of planning alternatives.

## HOW TO INSTALL A PLAN

Defined benefit plans are installed according to the qualified plan installation procedure outlined in Chapter 27.

## WHERE CAN I FIND OUT MORE ABOUT IT?

1. Scott, Elaine A., *Simple Defined Benefit Plans: Methods of Actuarial Funding*, Homewood, IL: Dow Jones-Irwin, 1989.

2. Graduate Course: Defined Benefit Plans (GS 843), The American College, Bryn Mawr, PA.

3. CLU/ChFC/CFP Course: Planning for Retirement Needs (HS 326), The American College, Bryn Mawr, PA.

4. CFP Course: Retirement Planning and Employee Benefits (CFP IV), College for Financial Planning, Denver, CO.

## QUESTIONS AND ANSWERS

**Question** — At what age is a defined benefit plan more advantageous than a defined contribution plan for tax-deferring the maximum amount of retirement savings?

*Answer* — Somewhere between age 45 and 50 approximately, depending on the actuarial method and assumptions used in the defined benefit plan.

---

*Example:* Suppose a doctor, a sole practitioner, aged 42, wants to adopt a plan providing the maximum deductible contributions. Under Code section 415, the maximum contribution to a defined contribution plan is the lesser of $40,000 annually (in 2003), or 100% of compensation. Can the doctor put more into a defined benefit plan with the maximum benefit allowed by Section 415 ($160,000 in 2003)? That depends on the actuarial assumptions. For example, the following table (which is illustrated graphically in Chapter 2) shows the annual contribution level for a maximum defined benefit plan for a given set of actuarial assumptions and method, varying only the assumed investment return.

| Age at Entry | Level funding amount at | | |
|---|---|---|---|
| | 6% | 7% | 8% |
| 41 | $36,734 | $32,086 | $27,959 |
| 42 | 39,720 | 34,933 | 30,655 |
| 43 | 43,018 | 38,091 | 33,660 |
| 44 | 46,675 | 41,606 | 37,020 |
| 45 | 50,745 | 45,533 | 40,791 |

Assumptions: $160,000 annual benefit at age 65, equivalent to lump sum at age 65 of $1,866,666; no mortality assumption. These figures can be converted to their post-2003 values by multiplying them by

$$\frac{\text{Current Section 415 dollar limit}}{\$160,000}$$

This indicates that at age 43, based on the assumptions in this table, a defined benefit plan would allow a larger contribution, using an investment return assumption of 6%. Of course, this example is oversimplified; in actual cases a careful study of all the possible actuarial methods and assumptions should be made.

---

**Question** — Can an employee be covered under both a defined benefit plan and a defined contribution plan of the same employer?

*Answer* — Under ERISA, as originally enacted in 1974, there was a required cutback for one or both plans through a complex "combined plan formula," if either plan approached the maximum limits. However, the combined plan formula was repealed, effective after 1999.[8] Consequently, it is possible to have a defined contribution plan and a defined benefit plan for a participant that provide the maximum benefit under both plans. However, this possibility will continue to be limited by Code section 404(a)(7), which imposes a 25% of payroll limit (or the required funding for the defined benefit plan, if greater) on total annual employer deductions for the two plans. This limit does not apply if the only contributions under the defined contribution plan are elective deferrals.

**Question** — If the retirement age is less than 65 in a defined benefit plan, can the annual funding level be increased because of the shorter time left to fund the benefit?

*Answer* — Yes. However, the tax benefits of this for highly compensated employees are limited by the fact that the maximum Section 415 limitation on benefits is cut back for retirement earlier than 62.[9] This cutback (to be determined under forthcoming regulations) limits the deductible annual funding and thus the amount of extra tax deferral available through an accelerated retirement age.

Another factor that has to be taken into account, if acceleration of funding is desired, is that the maximum benefit limit is also cut back proportionately if a participant has participated in the plan for less than 10 years.[10] For example, suppose Dr. Drill, a self-employed dentist, aged 57 wants to start a defined benefit plan. If the retirement age is 65 in the plan, Dr. Drill will have only eight years of participation at retirement. Assuming that the maximum benefit would be $160,000 for 10 years of participation, the benefit for Dr. Drill will be cut back to 8/10 of that amount, or $128,000 annually.

**Question** — Suppose an employer can afford to make substantial contributions to a defined benefit plan. Can a plan be designed with a very low actuarial interest assumptions so that the annual deductible contributions will be maximized?

*Answer* — In designing a plan for a "cash rich" employer an actuary will generally use the lowest reasonable actuarial interest assumption in order to maximize deductible contributions in the early years of the plan, thus maximizing tax deferral. However, Congress and the IRS have restricted the discretion of actuaries to choose relatively low interest assumptions.

The Code requires that all actuarial assumptions be reasonable, including a requirement that in combination, they offer the actuary's best estimate of anticipated experience under the plan.[11] An actuary cannot justify an aggressively low interest rate on the ground that other actuarial assumptions are less aggressive. In years when market rates were higher, the IRS challenged interest rate assumptions lower than 8% and retirement ages lower than 65; however, it was repeatedly defeated in the courts and eventually conceded defeat.[12]

A possible alternative for the "cash rich" employer is to use *fully insured* funding for the defined benefit plan. A fully insured plan, also known as a "412(i) plan," is not subject to many of the restrictions on deductible funding and may permit larger plan contributions in the initial years of the plan. Fully insured plans are discussed further in Chapter 13 (Life Insurance in a Qualified Plan).

**Question** — What is the impact of the nondiscrimination regulations on defined benefit design, particularly for older owner-employees of closely held businesses?

*Answer* — The regulations under Code section 401(a)(4) impose rules, with respect to nondiscrimination in benefits, that restrict the design possibilities for defined benefit plans, particularly for business owners who are less than 25 years from retirement.

Under the regulations, there is a *general* test for nondiscrimination, with three "safe harbors" available if the plan does not meet the general test.[13]

*General test.* Although the general test is complex, essentially the effect of it is to require that highly compensated employees covered under the plan not accrue benefits faster than nonhighly compensated employees. For example, suppose a plan is adopted for an employer with two employees: one is aged 55 and is highly compensated and the other, nonhighly compensated employee is aged 30. If the plan provides both participants with a benefit equal to 50% of final average compensation, it will not satisfy the general test because the older, highly compensated employee will accrue full benefits in ten years (at age 65) whereas it will take the younger employee 35 years to accrue the same benefit.

It should be noted that the general test for nondiscrimination in benefits requires extensive record keeping and actuarial services and, thus, may not be cost effective as compared to the safe harbors, particularly for plans of smaller employers.

*Safe harbors.* Three safe harbor exceptions are available for defined benefit plans. Generally, if the benefit formula is uniform and one of the following is satisfied, the plan will be deemed to be nondiscriminatory:

1.  *Unit credit plan*: a unit credit plan calculates benefits for each year of service as a percentage of compensation or a fixed dollar amount per year. Generally, the annual accrual rate for any year of service must not be more than 133⅓% of the accrual rate for any prior year of service.[14]

2. *Fractional accrual plan*: Under this second safe harbor, a plan must satisfy the "fractional accrual" rule as well as certain other requirements. Under the fractional accrual rule, each employee's accrued benefit under the plan as of any plan year before normal retirement age must be determined by multiplying the employee's fractional rule benefit by a fraction: the numerator is the employee's years of service as of the plan year, and the denominator is the employee's projected years of service as of normal retirement age.[15]

---

*Example*: If an employee enters the plan at age 40, with 25 years to retirement, his benefit after 10 years of service cannot be more than 10/25 of the total under the fractional rule.

---

As the "Doctor Refractor" example earlier in this chapter suggests, the use of this safe harbor limits, but does not eliminate, the favorable aspects of defined benefit plans for older business owners.

3. *Fully insured plan*: The third safe harbor applies to a fully insured insurance contract plan under Code section 412(i) (discussed above) that meets certain benefit accrual requirements.[16]

## FOOTNOTES

1. IRC Section 401(a)(17). Note that all provisions of EGTRRA 2001 are scheduled to sunset, or expire, after December 31, 2010.
2. IRC Section 404(a).
3. IRC Sections 402(a), 403(a).
4. IRC Section 415(d).
5. IRC Section 412(m).
6. See ERISA Sections 4006(a)(3)(A)(i) and 4006(a)(3)(E) for an explanation of the calculation of these amounts. The extra premium was formerly "capped" at a maximum of $53 per participant, but after June 30, 1996 there was no cap. See URAA '94, Section 774(a).
7. ERISA Section 4041.
8. IRC Section 415(e).
9. IRC Section 415(b)(2)(C). The age 62 limited cutback is effective for plan years ending after 2001. For prior years, the cutback applied to retirement ages earlier than 65.
10. IRC Section 415(b)(5).
11. IRC Section 412(c)(3). Under pre-1988 law, actuarial assumptions had to be reasonable only in the aggregate.
12. See IR-95-43. For taxpayer victories over the IRS' assault on low interest rate and retirement age assumptions, see *Vinson & Elkins v. Comm.*, 93-2 USTC ¶50,632 (5th Cir. 1993); *Rhoades, McKee & Boer v. U.S.*, 93-2 USTC ¶50,425 (W.D.MI 1993); *Wachtell, Lipton, Rosen & Katz v. Comm.*, TC Memo 1992-392, aff'd 94-1 USTC ¶50,272 (2d Cir. 1994).
13. Treas. Reg. §1.401(a)(4)-3.
14. Treas. Reg. §1.401(a)(4)-3(b)(3).
15. Treas. Reg. §1.401(a)(4)-3(b)(4).
16. Treas. Reg. §1.401(a)(4)-3(b)(5).

# Chapter 10

# ESOP/STOCK BONUS PLAN

## WHAT IS IT?

A stock bonus plan is a qualified employer plan—similar to a profit sharing plan—in which participants' accounts are invested in stock of the employer company. An ESOP is a stock bonus plan that the employer can use as a conduit for borrowing money from a bank or other financial institution.

## WHEN IS IT INDICATED?

1. To provide a tax-advantaged means for employees to acquire company stock at low cost to the employer.

2. When estate and financial planning for shareholders would benefit from the additional market for company stock created by a stock bonus plan or ESOP. Moreover, an ESOP not only creates a market but provides the opportunity for estate tax benefits for sale of stock to the ESOP.

3. To provide an advantageous vehicle for the company to borrow money for business needs.

4. When a company wants to broaden its ownership—for example, to help prevent a hostile takeover of the company.

5. When the business is a corporation. Partnerships do not have stock and thus are ineligible to establish an ESOP or stock bonus plan. S corporations are permitted to establish an ESOP or stock bonus plan; however, they are not eligible for all the tax benefits provided to C corporation ESOPs.[1]

6. When the employee group as a whole is not clustered in the older ages (see the Question and Answer section below regarding the put requirement).

## ADVANTAGES

1. Employees receive an ownership interest in the employer company, which may provide a performance incentive.

2. A market is created for employer stock, which helps improve liquidity of existing shareholders' assets or estates and helps in business continuity planning.

3. Employees are not taxed until shares are distributed. Furthermore, unrealized appreciation of stock held in the plan might not be taxed to employees at receipt of distributions from the plan. Taxation of the unrealized appreciation can generally be deferred until shares are sold by the employee.

4. The employer receives a deduction either for a cash contribution to the plan or a noncash plan contribution in the form of shares of stock.

5. The overall cost of corporate borrowing can be reduced by using an ESOP.

6. A shareholder can obtain tax benefits by selling stock to the plan.

## DISADVANTAGES

1. Since the plan is qualified, all the qualified plan requirements apply—coverage, vesting, funding, reporting and disclosure, and others.

2. Issuing shares of stock to employees "dilutes" (reduces the relative value of) existing shareholders' stock and their control of the company.

3. Company stock may be a very speculative investment. This can create employee ill will either because the plan is not considered very valuable by employees or because employees expect too much from the plan.

## DESIGN FEATURES

ESOPs and stock bonus plans are qualified defined contribution plans similar to profit sharing plans. However, participants' accounts are stated in terms of shares of employer stock. Benefits are generally distributable in the form of employer stock.[2] Dividends on shares can be used to increase participants' accounts or can be paid directly in cash to participants. If dividends are paid directly in cash, the employer gets a tax deduction (see below) and the dividends are currently taxable to the employees.

Employer contributions are either shares of stock, or cash that the plan uses to buy stock.

Plan allocation formulas must not discriminate in favor of highly compensated employees and are typically based on employee compensation. For example, if total payroll of participating employees is $500,000 and the employer contributes stock worth $50,000, an employee earning $10,000 would be allocated $1,000 worth of stock under a compensation-based allocation formula. As with all qualified plans, only the first $200,000 of compensation (in 2003, as indexed) can be used in the plan's allocation formula.[3] The formula for a stock bonus plan can be integrated with Social Security, but this is rarely done. An ESOP formula cannot be integrated.[4]

If shares of the employer company are closely held—that is, not publicly traded on an established securities market—and more than 10% of the plan's assets are invested in securities of the employer, then plan participants must be given the right to vote on certain specific corporate issues: (a) approval or disapproval of any corporate merger or consolidation, recapitalization, reclassification, liquidation, or dissolution; (b) sale of substantially all assets of the trade or business; or (c) a similar transaction as prescribed in IRS regulations.[5]

If employer stock is publicly traded, plan participants must be allowed to vote the stock on all issues.[6]

Distributions from stock bonus plans and ESOPs are subject to the same rules applicable to all qualified plans, as described in Chapter 26. For example, distributions prior to age 59½, death, or disability are subject to a 10% penalty, with some exceptions. Note, however, that a stock bonus plan or ESOP is generally not required to provide a joint and survivor annuity or other spousal death benefit.[7]

Participants can demand that distributions from a stock bonus plan or ESOP be made in the form of employer stock (except in the case of certain S corporation plans). However, if the participant receives stock that is not traded on an established market, the participant has a right to require the employer to repurchase the stock under a fair valuation formula. This requirement is referred to as the "put option."[8]

To protect employees against unrealistic expectations of stock value, if the stock or securities used in the plan are not traded on an established market, stock valuations used for all plan purposes must be made by an independent appraiser.[9]

Another protective feature is a requirement that participants in ESOPs who have reached age 55 and who have at least 10 years of participation in the plan be entitled to an annual election to diversify investments in their accounts. For a 6-year period after becoming eligible for this election, the participant can elect annually to diversify a total of up to 25% of the account balance. In the last year, diversification of 50% of the account balance can be elected. (A plan may offer higher percentages of diversification, if desired.) The plan must offer at least three options other than employer stock for diversification.[10]

## ESOP Loans

An ESOP is distinguished from a regular stock bonus plan primarily by the "leveraging" feature of an ESOP that enables the employer company to borrow money on a favorable basis.[11] The transaction works like this (see Figure 10.1):

(a) The ESOP trustee borrows money from a lending institution such as a bank (with the loan guaranteed by the employer corporation).

(b) The trustee uses the loan proceeds to purchase stock of the employer from the employer corporation (or from principal shareholders of the corporation).

(c) The employer makes tax deductible contributions to the ESOP in amounts sufficient to enable the trustee to pay off the principal and interest of the loan to the bank or other lender.

The net effect of this is that the corporation receives the loan proceeds and repays the loan, both principal and interest, with tax deductible dollars.[12]

## TAX IMPLICATIONS

1. Employer contributions to the plan are deductible when made, up to an annual limit. The limit for a stock bonus plan or an S corporation ESOP is 25% of payroll of employees covered under the plan.[13] For a C corporation ESOP, a higher limit is available— up to 25% of covered payroll for amounts used to

**Figure 10.1**

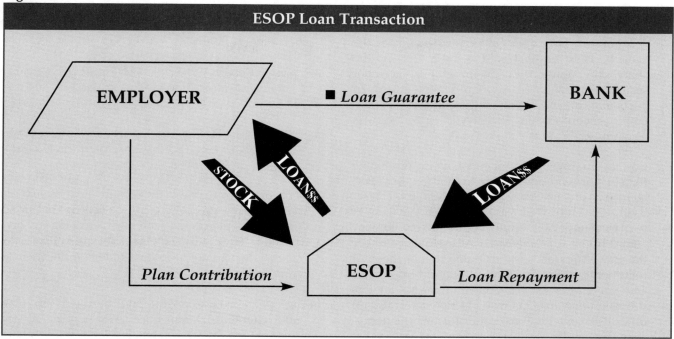

**ESOP Loan Transaction**

EMPLOYER — ■ *Loan Guarantee* → BANK

*STOCK* — *LOAN$$*

*LOAN$$*

*Plan Contribution* → ESOP ← *Loan Repayment*

repay loan principal, with no limit on amounts used to pay interest.[14]

2. The regular annual additions limit for defined contribution plans applies to ESOPs and stock bonus plans: the annual addition to each participant's account cannot exceed the lesser of (a) 100% of the participant's compensation or (b) $40,000 (in 2003, as indexed).[15] For a C corporation ESOP, deductible employer contributions applied by the plan to the payment of interest on certain loans incurred to acquire employer stock, as well as forfeitures of employer stock acquired with such loans, are excluded from this limit if no more than one-third of the employer contributions applied to the repayment of such loans are allocated to highly compensated employees. This provision is unavailable to S corporation ESOPs.[16]

3. Within certain limitations, a C corporation can deduct dividends paid on stock acquired with an ESOP loan. The dividends must be (a) paid in cash to plan participants or beneficiaries, (b) paid to the plan and distributed within 90 days to plan participants or beneficiaries, (c) payable as described under (a) or (b) at the election of participants or beneficiaries or (d) used to make payments on certain loans incurred to acquire employer stock. Furthermore, the dividends must be nonforfeitable, under the vesting provisions of IRC Section 411. It is important to note that dividends deducted under these

provisions are *not* subject to the special lower tax rates that apply to certain other dividends under JGTRRA 2003.[17]

4. Taxation to the employee on employer contributions is deferred, as with any qualified plan.[18] An additional tax benefit to employees with a stock bonus plan or ESOP is deferral of tax on unrealized appreciation of stock received in a lump sum distribution.[19] For example, suppose an ESOP buys stock for $1,000 and allocates it to participant Farley's account. At retirement 20 years later, the stock is worth $5,000. If Farley receives this stock in a lump sum distribution from the plan, he pays tax only on $1,000. The $4,000 of unrealized appreciation is not taxed until Farley sells the stock. Farley could, however, elect out of this deferred treatment.

The taxable amount of any lump sum distribution from a stock bonus plan or ESOP may be eligible for the special 10-year averaging (for certain employees born before 1936) tax treatment for qualified plans.[20]

5. The plan is subject to the eligibility and vesting rules applicable to all qualified plans (see Chapter 25).

6. Shareholders of nonpublicly traded C corporations do not have to recognize gain for income tax purposes when they sell shares to an ESOP.[21] To qualify for this treatment, the shareholder must use the

proceeds from the sale to purchase "replacement securities"—that is, stock or securities of another corporation. The replacement securities take the same basis as the stock sold to the ESOP, and the shareholder does not pay tax until the replacement securities are sold. Many requirements apply; in particular, the ESOP must own at least 30% of the employer corporation. Special holding period rules also apply.[22]

7. Certain employers adopting a plan may be eligible for a business tax credit of up to $500 for "qualified startup costs." See Chapter 27 for details.

8. A plan may permit employees to make voluntary contributions to a "deemed IRA" established under the plan. Amounts so contributed reduce the limit for other traditional or Roth IRA contributions. See Chapter 13 for details. Contributions under this provision may also (as with elective deferrals and other IRA contributions) count toward the nonrefundable credit for lower-income taxpayers, explained in Chapter 13.

## ERISA AND OTHER REGULATORY REQUIREMENTS

The plan is subject to the usual ERISA eligibility, vesting, and funding requirements for qualified plans discussed in Chapter 25 and the reporting and disclosure requirements summarized in Appendix A.

Certain directors and policy-making officers with ESOP or stock bonus accounts may be subject to "insider trading" restrictions under federal securities laws.[23]

## HOW TO INSTALL THE PLAN

Plan installation follows the qualified plan installation procedure described in Chapter 27. In addition, if the employer's stock is subject to securities regulation requirements and the employer issues new stock for the plan, a registration statement may have to be filed with federal or state securities regulatory agencies.

## WHERE CAN I FIND OUT MORE ABOUT IT?

1. Leimberg, Stephan R., et al., *Tools and Techniques of Estate Planning*, 12th ed. Cincinnati, OH: The National Underwriter Company, 2003.

2. Kalish, Gerald, *ESOPs, The Handbook of Employee Stock Ownership Plans*, Probus Publishing Company, Chicago, IL, 1989.

3. Frisch, Robert A., *ESOP: The Ultimate Instrument of Corporate Finance*, Margate Associates, Los Angeles, CA, 1990.

4. Blasi, Joseph R., *Employee Ownership*, Ballinger Publishing Company (a subsidiary of Harper & Row Publishers, NY), 1988.

## QUESTIONS AND ANSWERS

**Question** — How is an ESOP or stock bonus plan used for estate planning for shareholders of closely held businesses?

*Answer* — The existence of the ESOP or stock bonus plan as a potential buyer for stock can be very valuable in planning the estate of a shareholder of a closely held business. Such estates are often illiquid because of a lack of a market for the stock, while at the same time the estate may be liable for substantial death taxes because of the inherent value of the stock. EGTRRA 2001 repeals the estate tax for one year in 2010.

The estate planning and related planning opportunities using ESOPs and stock bonus plans for closely held businesses are best illustrated by looking at three typical scenarios: (1) purchase of stock at death; (2) business continuation planning opportunities; and (3) simply using the plan as a source of cash.

*(1) Purchase of stock at death.*

In most small companies, owners typically expect the company to buy stock from their estate at the shareholder's death. However, for a number of reasons this plan may be difficult to carry out:

(a) Accumulation of corporate funds can be difficult. Funds to purchase stock must be accumulated by the corporation out of after-tax income, which can be particularly burdensome since corporate tax rates may be higher than individual rates.

(b) The corporation can purchase life insurance to provide assured funding, but the premiums are not deductible to the corporation, so this is also an accumulation from after-tax income.

(c) An accumulation of funds at the corporate level may result in exposure to the accumulated earnings tax, particularly if the shareholder is a majority shareholder.

(d) Receipt by the corporation of otherwise income-tax-free life insurance proceeds may trigger the corporate alternative minimum tax (AMT).

(e) If insurance is owned by the corporation to fund a buyout, corporate value is increased, which in turn increases the federal estate tax.

Use of an ESOP or stock bonus plan as the purchaser avoids these problems. The corporation gets a deduction for amounts contributed to the plan, and the plan is a tax-exempt entity so its income is not taxed. Thus, funds accumulate in the plan on a before-tax basis. Also, the plan is not subject to the accumulated earnings tax or the alternative minimum tax. Furthermore, life insurance held in the ESOP will not increase corporate value for purposes of the federal estate tax.

While it may be difficult to accumulate a large amount of cash in the plan, particularly in a short time, the plan can purchase insurance on the shareholder's life as an investment that will provide funds to purchase stock from a shareholder at the shareholder's death.

Should there be a formal plan to carry out this type of stock purchase? Probably not. A shareholder can give the ESOP or stock bonus plan an option to buy his or her shares, but requiring the plan to do so would probably violate the ERISA fiduciary requirements.

One potentially serious tax problem with this type of plan should be noted—the possibility that the IRS will treat the sale of stock as a dividend paid to the estate by the corporation rather than a sale to the ESOP. Taxwise, this could greatly increase the cost of the transaction. As a sale, little or no capital gain would be realized by the estate because its basis for the stock would be stepped up to the date of death value. (However, EGTRRA 2001 replaces a stepped-up basis with a modified carryover basis for decedents dying in 2010. Thus, some gain could be realized if death were to occur in 2010.) But proceeds from the sale might all be taxable if treated as a dividend. Amendments by the Jobs and Growth Tax Relief Reconciliation Act of 2003 reduced (and, in some cases, will eliminate) income taxes on cer-

tain dividends and capital gains. However, the special treatment does not apply to dividends that have been deducted under IRC Section 404(k) (i.e., the deduction for dividends paid on certain employer securities).[24] In the absence of this special treatment, all the proceeds from the sale would be taxable.

In any event, dividend treatment on a sale of stock to an ESOP is not a potential issue unless the decedent was a major shareholder. However, the IRS will probably consider all stock held by the decedent and related family members together in determining whether the decedent was a controlling shareholder. In such cases, despite the apparent policy of Congress to encourage stock sales to ESOPs, the IRS may ignore the ESOP and treat the transaction as a dividend paid directly from the corporation to the shareholder, the decedent's estate.

It may be advisable, in doubtful situations, to apply to the IRS for a ruling that the transaction is not a dividend. However, the IRS has announced that it will not issue such a ruling unless the combined beneficial interest of the selling shareholder and all related persons in the stock held in the plan does not exceed 20% and certain other representations are made.[25] It may be possible to meet this condition in certain cases by amending the ESOP or stock bonus plan to reduce the stock in the selling stockholder's account below this 20% limit.

A final and important incentive for the use of ESOPs in estate planning relates to the tax benefit provided for sales of stock to these plans (see the following section).

*(2) Business continuation.*

In some circumstances, ESOPs and stock bonus plans can be used to help solve business continuation problems, along with the related estate planning problems. For example, suppose Monty Bank owns 100% of Knab, Inc., a closely held business with 10 employees. Monty's children are not interested in continuing the business.

One way of providing business continuity and a means of selling the stock is to establish an ESOP for Knab, Inc.'s 10 regular employees, excluding Monty. This will meet the nondiscrimination requirement for qualified plans, since the plan is permitted to discriminate against a highly compensated employee (Monty). Monty sells 49% of the shares of

Knab, Inc. to the ESOP, using the proceeds of an ESOP loan. Since Monty retains 51%, he remains in control of the business.

Since this sale presumably meets the requirements described in paragraph (6) of Tax Implications, above, Monty recognizes no gain on the sale, but he must reinvest in other securities (generally not a problem) and the replacement securities take the basis of the stock sold to the ESOP. If Monty holds these replacement securities until his death, they receive a stepped-up basis and the gain on the sale to the ESOP will avoid income taxation altogether. However EGTRRA 2001 replaces a stepped-up basis with a modified carryover basis for decedents dying in 2010. Thus, some gain on the sale to the ESOP could be taxed if Monty were to die in 2010.

In the years following the sale, shares sold to the ESOP will be allocated to the accounts of the 10 employees, with the highest paid employees receiving the most shares. At Monty's death, Monty's heirs will receive his 51% share, but they will likely be able to sell these shares to the Knab employees (through the ESOP) at that time since the employees will want to retain control of the business to protect their existing investment in Knab.

*(3) Source of cash.*

If the more elaborate plans described above do not apply, a shareholder may be able to establish an ESOP or stock bonus plan simply as a way of turning shares into cash as needed in a lifetime sale.

The issues discussed under (1) above, with respect to dividend treatment (particularly after JGTRRA 2003) apply to a lifetime sale of stock to an ESOP as well. If the shareholder's stock has a low basis—as is often the case in closely held companies—then the capital gain under a "sale" treatment will generate almost as much gain as dividend treatment would. For example, if a shareholder sells stock with a basis of $20,000 to an ESOP for $500,000, the taxable capital gain is $480,000, while dividend treatment could result in taxable dividends of $500,000. Lower tax rates (i.e., 15%/5%) generally apply to most long-term capital gains and dividends under JGTRRA 2003; however, certain exceptions apply.[26]

**Question** — Does the "put option" impose special obligations on the employer, and if so, how can that obligation be financed?

*Answer* — The put requirement obliges the employer, not the plan, to repurchase the employee's stock if the employee so demands. An employer must anticipate this need and as part of prudent plan administration insure that liquid funds are available as required. Some methods of financing this requirement are:

- An asset reserve or sinking fund can be maintained by the employer. Such a fund may be unreliable since the employer may be forced to use it in the business during hard times.

- Life insurance can be owned by the employer. Life insurance contracts on plan participants, held by the employer as key-person insurance (owned, paid for, and payable to the employer) can provide funds either in the form of cash values accessible at the employee's retirement, or funds available at the employee's death to reimburse the employer for its outlays.

- Plan assets can be used to repurchase the stock from the employer (if in fact the plan has significant assets other than employer stock).

- Stock can be sold by the employer on the market, if such a market exists.

If the employee group as a whole is relatively old when the plan is adopted, financing the put requirement may be difficult, and consequently the adoption of an employer-stock plan may be imprudent in such a situation. The problem here is somewhat similar to the difficulty in funding an age-weighted or defined-benefit plan for an older group.

**Question** — Can any type of stock or securities be used in an ESOP?

*Answer* — Stock used in an ESOP must be either (a) common stock traded regularly on an established market or (b) common stock having a combination of voting power and dividend rights equal to or greater than that of the employer's class of common stock having the greatest voting rights and the class of stock having the greatest dividend rates.[27] If there is only one class of stock, as is often the case with closely held companies, the second test is met.

**Question** — Can any type of business organization have an ESOP or stock bonus plan?

*Answer* — Currently, S corporations may adopt ESOPs. However, S corporation ESOPs may be subject to a special penalty if allocations of stock are made to persons owning (or deemed to own) more than 50% of the shares in the corporation.[28]

Unincorporated businesses—partnerships or proprietorships—cannot have ESOPs or stock bonus plans because they have no stock.

Finally, a professional corporation may not be able to establish an ESOP or stock bonus plan because state corporate law may require all shareholders of a professional corporation to be licensed professionals.

**Question** — How can an ESOP or stock bonus plan be used to carry out a corporate buy-sell agreement among shareholders?

*Answer* — For illustration, take a very simple situation with only two major shareholders, Alf and Ben, each owning about half of the corporation's stock, with a relatively small amount held in a stock bonus plan for participants other than Alf and Ben.

The simplest type of arrangement is for the plan trustee to purchase insurance on the lives of Alf and Ben. This insurance is held as key person insurance, since the trust has an insurable interest in the lives of the two business principals. On the death of one shareholder—suppose it is Alf—the trustee collects the insurance proceeds and uses that money to purchase stock from Alf's estate. The stock is reallocated to plan participants. Ben's account will probably receive most of this stock eventually and Ben will retain majority ownership. However, some stock may also be allocated to other participants.

Another arrangement, slightly more formal, makes use of "participant investment direction" or "earmarking," which is permitted under ERISA. With participant investment direction in a qualified plan, a participant is given the right to direct the trustee to invest his or her plan account in specified property. In this case, Alf directs the trustee to invest in insurance on Ben's life, and Ben directs a similar investment in insurance on Alf's life. The insurance proceeds on the death of one owner are therefore used to purchase stock directly for the account of the other owner, with no allocation of stock to other plan participants.

**Question** — Can a stock bonus plan or ESOP hold life insurance or investments other than employer stock?

*Answer* — A stock bonus plan is apparently flexible in its investments and can hold the same types and diversity of investments as a regular profit sharing plan.

An ESOP, however, must meet a requirement that it be invested "primarily in employer securities."[29] Neither the IRS nor the Labor Department has issued an official interpretation of this "primarily" requirement, so investments other than employer securities should be very limited. However, some practitioners argue that this requirement means merely more than 50% of the assets.

Stock bonus plans and ESOPs can invest in insurance contracts, within the limitations discussed here. However, if the plan participant has the right to name the beneficiary of the death benefit, the amount of insurance is subject to the same "incidental" limitations that apply to qualified profit sharing plans (see Chapter 13).

## FOOTNOTES

1. See IRC Section 1361(b)(1)(B). Special rules enacted by EGTRRA 2001 are designed to discourage the use of S corporation ESOPs to primarily benefit a small number of highly compensated employees. It should be noted that all provisions of EGTRRA 2001 are scheduled to sunset (expire) after December 31, 2010.

2. Treas. Regs. §§1.401-1(a)(2)(iii); 1.401-1(b)(1)(iii). See also, IRC Section 409(h).

3. IRC Section 401(a)(17); Notice 2002-71, 2002-45 IRB 830.

4. Treas. Regs. §§1.401(l)-1(a)(4)(ii), 54.4975-11(a)(7)(ii).

5. IRC Sections 401(a)(22), 409(e)(3).

6. IRC Section 409(e)(2).

7. IRC Section 401(a)(11)(c).

8. IRC Sections 401(a)(23), 409(h).

9. IRC Section 401(a)(28)(C).

10. IRC Section 401(a)(28)(B).

11. The prohibited transaction exemption required for ESOP loans is in IRC Sections 4975(d)(3), 4975(e)(7) and 4975(e)(8).

12. Prior to 1996 legislation, the Code allowed an additional advantage in the form of an exclusion for the lending institution of 50% of the interest income from a loan to an ESOP used to acquire employer securities (provided the ESOP owned more than 50% of the outstanding stock of the employer corporation). This exclusion was repealed, generally effective for loans made after August 20, 1996. IRC Section 133, prior to repeal by SBJPA '96. However, certain refinancings (of the principal amount immediately before the refinancing) and loans pursuant to a written

contract in effect on June 10, 1996 are treated as having been made prior to the effective date of the repeal. SBJPA '96, Sec. 1602(c).

13. IRC Section 404(a)(3); IRC Section 404(a)(9)(C).

14. IRC Section 404(a)(9).

15. IRC Section 415(c); Notice 2002-71, 2002-45 IRB 830.

16. IRC Sections 415(c)(6), 404(a)(9)(B).

17. IRC Sections 404(k)(2)(A), 404(k)(7), as amended by JCWAA 2002. See IRC Section 1(h)(11)(B)(ii)(III), as added by JGTRRA 2003.

18. IRC Sections 402(a), 403(a).

19. IRC Section 402(e)(4). If employer securities are distributed in other than a lump sum distribution, the net unrealized appreciation is excludable only to the extent attributable to nondeductible employee contributions. IRC Section 402(e)(4)(A).

20. IRC Section 402(d)(4), prior to repeal after 1999 by SBJPA '96.

21. IRC Section 1042.

22. IRC Sections 1042(b)(4), 4978(b)(1).

23. See Blair, "Insider Reporting and Short Swing Trading Rules for Qualified Defined Contribution Plans," *Benefits Quarterly*, 1st Quarter 1992.

24. See IRC Sec. 1(h)(11), as added by JGTRRA 2003.

25. See Rev. Proc. 87-22, 1987-1 CB 718.

26. See IRC Sec. 1(h)(11), as amended by JGTRRA 2003.

27. IRC Sections 4975(e)(8), 409(l).

28. See IRC Sections 409(p), 4975A. These provisions generally are effective for plan years beginning after 2004, but in the case of ESOPs established after March 14, 2001 and ESOPs holding stock in a corporation that made an S election after March 14, 2001, the rules are effective for plan years ending after March 14, 2001.

29. IRC Section 4975(e)(7)(A).

# Chapter 11

# GOVERNMENTAL AND TAX–EXEMPT EMPLOYER DEFERRED COMPENSATION (SECTION 457) PLANS

## WHAT IS IT?

Code section 457 provides rules governing all nonqualified deferred compensation plans of governmental units, governmental agencies, and also non-church controlled tax-exempt organizations. A plan designed to comply with these rules is referred to as a Section 457 plan.

## WHEN IS IT INDICATED?

Any nonqualified deferred compensation plan adopted by an employer that is an affected organization generally must comply with the rules discussed here.

## DESIGN FEATURES

### What Employers Are Covered by Section 457?

Section 457 applies to nonqualified deferred compensation plans of:

1. A state, a political subdivision of a state (such as a city, township, etc.), and any agency or instrumentality of a state or political subdivision of a state (for example, a school district or a sewage authority); and

2. Any organization exempt from federal income tax, except for a church or synagogue or an organization controlled by a church or synagogue.[1]

### Limit on Amount Deferred

Under Section 457, plans that include limits on the amounts deferred are subject to favorable tax treatment; these are generally referred to as *eligible* Section 457 plans. Plans providing greater deferral, generally designed for executives, are referred to as *ineligible plans*;

these are discussed in the "Questions and Answers" below.

*Basic limit*. For an eligible plan, the amount deferred annually by the participant cannot exceed the lesser of (1) 100% of the participant's compensation or (2) an applicable dollar amount, as follows:[2]

| | |
|---|---|
| 2003 | 12,000 |
| 2004 | 13,000 |
| 2005 | 14,000 |
| 2006 | 15,000 |
| After 2006 | Index in 500 increments |

*For 2001, the deferral limit is the lesser of $8,500 or ⅓ of the participant's compensation.

In determining these limits, all Section 457 plans in which an individual participates must be aggregated.

---

*Example*: Sam, age 45, works for 2 governmental employers, Municipal Salt Works and also Municipal School District, earning a $30,000 salary from each. Both employers maintain a Section 457 plan. Sam participates in both plans, but for 2003 Sam's total contribution to both plans is limited to $12,000. This amount can be allocated between the plans in any manner consistent with the plans' provisions.

---

However, Section 457 salary reduction contributions do not reduce contributions to another type of salary reduction plan such as a Section 403(b) or Section 401(k) plan. This presents an opportunity for a "double dip."

---

*Example*: Municipal School District maintains both a 457 plan and a 403(b) plan. Max, aged 40, works for Municipal School District and earns $40,000. For 2003 Max can contribute $12,000 to the School District's 457 plan and also contribute $12,000 to the School District's 403(b) plan, a total salary eduction contribution of $24,000.[3]

---

The "100% of compensation" limit applies to gross compensation before salary reductions. For example, Max in the example in the preceding paragraph is considered to have $40,000 of compensation for purposes of the 100% limit (not $40,000 less salary reductions). Obviously, this rule increases the available salary reduction contribution considerably in certain situations like this one.[4]

*50-or-over catchup contributions.* All participants in a plan of a governmental employer (but not a private tax-exempt organization) who are aged 50 or over are eligible for additional salary reduction contributions, as follows:[5]

| Taxable year beginning in | Additional deferral permitted |
|---|---|
| 2003 | 2,000 |
| 2004 | 3,000 |
| 2005 | 4,000 |
| 2006 | 5,000 |
| After 2006 | Indexed |

Notwithstanding the amount in the table, the 50-or-over catchup can't exceed the excess of the participant's compensation over all regular elective deferrals.

---

*Example:* If a participant over age 50 in 2003 has compensation of $13,000 and has regular salary reductions of $12,000, the catchup for 2003 can't exceed $1,000.

---

However, the Section 415 limitation (annual additions to participant's accounts can't exceed the lesser of $40,000 (2003) or 100% of compensation) does not limit the use of the 50-or-over catchup.

---

*Example:* A participant over age 50 in 2003 with annual compensation of $100,000 has regular annual additions of $40,000 to various defined contribution plans of the employer. The participant is nevertheless eligible for the full $2,000 catchup (2003) in addition.

---

To complicate matters a bit further, there is an "old" 3-year catchup provision for 457 plans that still applies, as discussed below. The 50-or-over catchup provision is not available for a participant who is eligible for a higher catchup under the old 3-year provision.[7]

*Old 3-year catchup provision for 457 plan participants.* The 3-year catchup provision applies during the participant's last three years prior to the plan's normal retirement age.[8]

During those years, the limit on deferrals is increased to the lesser of (1) twice the amount of the regularly applicable dollar limit; or (2) the sum of: (a) the otherwise applicable limit for the year, plus (b) the amount by which the applicable limit in preceding years exceeded the participant's actual deferral for those years.[9] The old 3-year catch-up rule applies to all eligible 457 plans, not just eligible 457 governmental plans. Thus, during the last three years prior to the plan's normal retirement age, an eligible participant in an eligible 457 governmental plan may defer the greater of (1) the regular applicable dollar amount plus the catch-up amount permitted under IRC Section 414(v); or (2) the amount permitted under the 3-year catch-up provisions of IRC Section 457(b)(3).[10] Catch-up contributions made under IRC Section 414(v) by participants age 50 (or over) are not subject to any otherwise-applicable limitation of IRC Section 457(b)(2) (determined without regard to the special catch-up rule of IRC Section 457(b)(3)).[11]

## Timing of Salary Reduction Elections

Employee elections to defer compensation monthly under Section 457 must generally be made under an agreement entered into before the beginning of the month.[12]

## Distribution Requirements

Plan distributions cannot be made before:[13]

1. The calendar year in which the participant attains age 70½;

2. Severance from employment;[14] or

3. An "unforeseeable emergency," as defined in regulations. The definition of unforeseeable emergency is discussed in the "Questions and Answers," below.

A participant can elect to receive an involuntary cashout up to $5,000 from his account under a tax-exempt nongovernmental organization's plan, if no amount has been deferred by the participant for two years, and there has been no prior distribution. A cashout distribution in excess of $1,000 (and, by definition, less than or equal to $5,000) must be automatically transferred to an individual retirement plan unless the participant affirmatively elects to have the distribution transferred to another eligible retirement plan or to take the distribution in cash.[15] However, the automatic rollover rule does not apply to any distribution until final safe harbor regulations are issued by the Department of Labor.[16]

A participant may make a one-time election, after amounts are available and before commencement of distributions, to defer commencement of distributions.[17]

Minimum distributions must be made under the rules of Section 401(a)(9),[18] which apply to qualified plans as well; the minimum distribution rules are discussed in Chapter 26.

The qualified plan rules of Section 414(p) regarding Qualified Domestic Relations Orders (QDROs) apply to Section 457 plans.[19]

### Coverage and Eligibility

There are no specific coverage requirements for Section 457 plans. For a governmental organization, the plan can be offered to all employees, or to any group of employees, even to a single employee.

However, most private non-governmental tax-exempt organizations are subject to ERISA. Therefore, the ERISA eligibility rules may apply to the Section 457 plan of the tax-exempt organization. The eligibility requirements would be the same as those applicable to a nonqualified deferred compensation plan for a taxable employer, as discussed in Chapter 15. Such plans can avoid the ERISA rules if they are structured to take advantage of specific ERISA exemptions, such as the exemption for unfunded plans covering only a select group of management or highly compensated employees—the "top-hat" group.[20]

### Funding

*Nongovernmental tax-exempt organizations.* A Section 457 plan for such organizations may not be funded. However, "financing" the plan with insurance or annuity contracts is allowed and is almost always appropriate, as discussed in the "Questions and Answers."

For the plan of a tax-exempt organization that is subject to ERISA, the "no funding" requirement of Section 457 may conflict directly with certain ERISA requirements, such as the funding and exclusive pur-

pose requirements; this issue has not yet been resolved.[21] One way to eliminate the conflict is to limit participation in the plan to a select group of management or highly compensated employees—the "top-hat" group.

*Governmental organizations.* Governmental plans *must* be funded—that is, they must hold plan assets in trusts or custodial accounts.[22]

### TAX IMPLICATIONS

1. Since the employer sponsoring a Section 457 plan does not pay federal income taxes, deductibility is not an issue.

2. A limited nonrefundable tax credit is available to certain lower income taxpayers who make salary deferrals to an eligible Section 457 governmental plan. (see "Questions and Answers," below).

3. A plan may permit employees to make voluntary contributions to a "deemed IRA" established under the plan. Amounts so contributed reduce the limit for other traditional or Roth IRA contributions. See Chapter 24. Contributions under this provision may also (as with elective deferrals and other IRA contributions) count toward the nonrefundable credit for lower-income taxpayers, explained in the Questions and Answers below.

4. Employees (or their beneficiaries) include Section 457 *governmental* plan distributions in income when they are paid. Employees (or their beneficiaries) include Section 457 non-governmental, tax-exempt plan distribution in income when they are actually paid or otherwise made available.[23] Even if life insurance financing is used, benefits are taxable; see "Questions and Answers," below.

   However, if a nonqualified deferred compensation plan of a governmental or tax-exempt employer does not comply with Section 457, compensation deferred is included in the employee's income in the first taxable year in which there is no substantial risk of forfeiture of the rights to the compensation. Any distributions from an ineligible plan are treated in the same manner as annuity distributions under Section 72.[24] The implications of this are discussed in the "Questions and Answers," below.

5. Section 457 plan distributions are not eligible for the favorable lump sum 10-year averaging treatment available for qualified plans.[25]

6. Plan participants may exclude from income amounts directly transferred (i.e., from trustee to trustee) from a Section 457 plan to a governmental defined benefit plan and used to purchase permissive service credits. Likewise, a participant may use such directly transferred amounts to repay contributions or earnings that were previously refunded because of a forfeiture of service credit, under either the transferee plan or another Section 457 plan maintained by a governmental employer in the same state.[26]

7. Participants in an eligible Section 457 plan of a governmental employer may rollover distributions to an IRA or other eligible plan, under the same rules that apply to rollovers from qualified plans—see Chapter 26.[27] The "direct rollover" (direct trustee-to-trustee) provisions applicable to qualified plans also apply to governmental Section 457 plans.[28] In addition, participants in any eligible plan (including those of tax-exempt nongovernmental organizations) can roll over a Section 457 plan distribution to another Section 457 plan without incurring income tax on the amount rolled over.[29]

## ERISA REQUIREMENTS

Governmental employers and church-related organizations are not subject to ERISA. However, tax-exempt private employers will encounter the ERISA compliance problems discussed above.

## ALTERNATIVES

Tax-exempt employers can adopt qualified pension and profit sharing plans for employees. In addition, certain tax-exempt organizations can adopt Section 403(b) plans that provide as good or better benefits for employees as a Section 457 plan (see Chapter 23, Tax Deferred Annuity). Tax-exempt organizations (but not governmental entities) can adopt 401(k) plans (see Chapter 19).[30] Also, tax-exempt employers and governmental entities are permitted to maintain SIMPLE IRA plans,[31] and tax-exempt organizations (but not governmental entities) are permitted to maintain SIMPLE 401(k) plans.[32] (See Chapter 20).

Governmental employers can also adopt governmental pension plans similar to qualified private plans. However, since the Section 403(b) type of plan is not available to governmental employers (except state and local governments with respect to employees perform-

ing services for public schools), such employers are more likely to use Section 457 plans to supplement a pension plan (see Chapter 23, Tax Deferred Annuity).

The design of nonqualified deferred compensation plans for top management employees of governmental and tax-exempt employers is discussed in the "Questions and Answers," below.

## HOW TO INSTALL A PLAN

A written plan containing the provisions described above should be adopted. Also, forms must be furnished to employees to carry out any salary reduction elections. For tax-exempt private employers subject to ERISA, the same ERISA requirements applicable to nonqualified deferred compensation will apply. These are discussed in Chapter 15.

## WHERE CAN I FIND OUT MORE ABOUT IT?

1. *Fundamentals of Employee Benefit Programs*, 3rd ed. Washington, DC: Employee Benefit Research Institute, 1987.

2. *Tax Facts 1*, Cincinnati, OH: The National Underwriter Company, (revised annually).

3. O'Meara and Anderson, "Section 457 Plans," *Journal of Pension Planning and Compliance*, 1992.

## QUESTIONS AND ANSWERS

**Question** — How can a governmental or tax-exempt employer provide a substantial deferred compensation benefit for an executive or key employee for whom the annual dollar limit would be inadequate?

*Answer* — The following statutory provisions would allow deferred compensation beyond the annual dollar limit, and planners should investigate these where executive compensation plans are desired.

*Grandfathered plans.* Grandfather provisions applicable to Section 457 may preserve some existing deferred compensation plans. These grandfather provisions apply to nonelective and elective plans. In the case of *governmental employers*, Section 457 does not apply to nonelective deferred compensation that was deferred before July 14, 1988, or to amounts deferred on or after that date under a written agreement in effect on July 14, 1988 that provided for deferral of a fixed amount or under a fixed formula. For nonelective plans of *nongovernmental tax-exempt employers*, the effective date is apparently January 1, 1988.[33]

*Nonemployee plans.* Nonelective deferred compensation plans for nonemployees—for example, doctors working for hospitals as independent contractors—are not subject to Section 457. However, for this exception to apply, all such nonemployees (other than those who have not satisfied any applicable initial service requirement) must be treated the same under the plan, with no individual variations.[34]

*"Ineligible" or Forfeitable plans.* The most general provision that allows escape from the annual dollar limit is Section 457(f). Under this section, if an employee defers more than the annual dollar limit, the deferred amount is not necessarily taxed immediately; it is taxed in the first taxable year in which there is *no substantial risk of forfeiture*. Thus, if a deferred compensation plan has forfeiture provisions, amounts greater than the annual dollar limit can be deferred until the year in which the forfeiture provision lapses.

An extension of the forfeiture provision agreed to before it expires may be acceptable to extend deferral of taxation.[35] However, the IRS probably would not accept a plan with a "rolling" forfeiture—that is, a provision designed for regular annual extensions.

---

*Example:* An employer subject to Section 457 might provide supplemental deferred compensation to selected executives, in amounts greater than the annual dollar limit, with a provision that the amount deferred would not be payable unless the executive served a full term under a multi-year contract. Taxation on the amount deferred would not occur until the year in which each executive served the full term and the deferred amounts became nonforfeitable.

---

The IRS has approved forfeitable deferred compensation plans of this type for employers subject to Section 457,[36] and this should be considered an appropriate technique of executive compensation for governmental and nonprofit employers.

A major problem in designing such plans is to develop forfeiture provisions that are substantial enough to defer taxes (see Chapter 15), but are nevertheless acceptable to the executive. Another major design problem occurs at retirement. In general, it is very difficult to design a bona fide, substantial forfeiture provision that extends past the executive's retirement. Consequently, Section 457(f) amounts generally are taxable in full no later than the year of the executive's retirement. If deferral past retirement is essential, other techniques, such as equity-type split dollar plans, might be investigated.

*Severance pay plans.* A bona fide severance pay arrangement is not subject to the Section 457 limits.[37] See Chapter 50.

**Question** — What constitutes an "unforeseeable emergency" that would permit distributions from a Section 457 plan?

*Answer* — The current regulations under Section 457 define unforeseeable emergency as severe financial hardship to the participant resulting from a sudden and unexpected illness or accident of the participant or a dependent, a loss of property due to casualty, or other similar extraordinary and unforeseeable circumstances arising as a result of events beyond the control of the participant.[38]

The regulations specifically mention that the purchase of a residence or college education of children is not considered an unforeseeable emergency. Any amount distributed from the plan as the result of an emergency cannot exceed the amount reasonably needed to satisfy the emergency.

**Question** — How is a Section 457 plan informally funded or "financed" through the purchase of insurance or annuities?

*Answer* — *Nongovernmental tax-exempt employer.* Although a Section 457 plan cannot be funded in the same sense as a qualified plan (that is, with an irrevocable trust fund for the exclusive benefit of employees), the employer can, and in most cases should, finance its obligations under the plan by setting aside assets in advance of the time when payments will be made. Life insurance or annuity contracts are often used for this purpose.

If the employer purchases life insurance contracts to finance the plan, there is no current life insurance cost to employees, as long as the employer retains all incidents of ownership in the policies, is the sole beneficiary under the policies, and is under no obligation to transfer the policies or pass through the proceeds of the policies. This favorable result applies even if the contracts are purchased at the option of participants.[39] However, as with all deferred compensation plans, benefits to participants and their beneficiaries, including death benefits, are not excludable as life insurance proceeds, even if life insurance is used to finance the plan.[40]

*Governmental employer.* Governmental plans must hold assets in trust funds or custodial accounts. If such plans hold life insurance contracts for participants, by analogy with the rules for qualified plans, employees should pay income tax on the value of current life insurance protection,[41] and the death proceeds from the life insurance contracts should be free of income tax to their beneficiaries. (See Chapter 13). However, as of this writing, neither the IRS nor Congress has clarified this issue.

**Question** — Who is eligible to claim a nonrefundable credit for salary contributions to an eligible Section 457 governmental plan?

*Answer* — Certain lower-income taxpayers may claim a temporary, nonrefundable credit for "qualified retirement savings contributions" in taxable years beginning after 2001 and before 2007.[42] "Qualified retirement savings contributions" include salary contributions to an eligible Section 457 governmental plan, as well as elective deferrals to other plans and contributions to Roth or traditional IRAs. (However, the total is reduced by certain distributions received by the taxpayer or his spouse during the prior two taxable years and the current taxable year for which the credit is claimed, including the period up to the due date (plus extensions) for filing the federal income tax return for the current taxable year.)

The credit is allowed against the sum of the regular tax and the alternative minimum tax (minus certain other credits) and is allowed in addition to any other deduction or exclusion that would otherwise apply. In addition, to be eligible, the taxpayer must be at least 18 as of the end of the tax year and must not be claimed as a dependent by someone else or be a full-time student.

The amount of the credit is limited to an "applicable percentage" of IRA contributions and elective deferrals up to $2,000. The "applicable percentages" are as follows:

### ADJUSTED GROSS INCOME

| Joint return | | Head of a household | | All other cases | | Applicable percentage |
|---|---|---|---|---|---|---|
| Over | Not over | Over | Not over | Over | Not over | |
| 0 | $30,000 | 0 | $22,500 | 0 | $15,000 | 50% |
| 30,000 | 32,500 | 22,500 | 24,375 | 15,000 | 16,250 | 20% |
| 32,500 | 50,000 | 24,375 | 37,500 | 16,250 | 25,000 | 10% |
| 50,000 | | 37,500 | | 25,000 | | 0% |

*Example:* Max and Erma together have adjusted gross income of $31,000 for 2003. Their government employers sponsor an eligible Section 457 governmental plan and they each elected to make a salary reduction contribution of $2,000 to the plan. Neither has received any distributions in the current or two preceding taxable years. Max and Erma will be able to exclude their salary reduction contributions as well as each being eligible to claim a credit of $400 (20% x $2,000) on their federal income tax return ($800 if married filing jointly) for 2003.

## FOOTNOTES

1. IRC Sections 457(e)(1), 457(e)(13).
2. IRC Section 457(e)(15).
3. IRC Section 402(g)(3)(D).
4. IRC Section 457(e)(5).
5. IRC Section 414(v)(2)(B)(i).
6. IRC Section 414(v)(2)(C).
7. IRC Section 414(v)(6)(C).
8. IRC Section 457(b)(3).
9. IRC Section 457(b)(3), as amended by EGTRRA 2001.
10. IRC Section 457(e)(18), as added by JCWAA 2002.
11. IRC Section 414(v)(3)(A), as amended by JCWAA 2002.
12. IRC Section 457(b)(4); Treas. Reg. §1.457-2(g).
13. IRC Sections 457(b)(5), 457(d)(1).
14. After December 31, 2001, distributions may be made upon "severance from employment," rather than upon "separation from service." IRC Sec. 457(d)(1)(A)(ii), as amended by EGTRRA 2001 Section 646. Under prior law, a Section 457 plan (like a 401(k) plan) could not make amounts available before the earliest of: (1) the calendar year in which the participant attains age 70 1/2; (2) the date when the participant separates from service; or (3) the date when the participant is faced with "an unforeseeable emergency." The "same desk rule" (which is also applicable to 401(k) plans) provides that an employee is not considered to have separated from service when he continues on the same job for a different employer as a result of a liquidation, merger, consolidation, or similar event involving his former employer. A severance from employment occurs when a participant ceases to be employed by the employer sponsoring the plan. An employee may experience a severance of employment without experiencing a separation from service.
15. IRC Section 401(a)(31)(B), as added by EGTRRA 2001.

16. EGTRRA 2001 Section 657(d).

17. IRC Section 457(e)(9).

18. IRC Sections 457(b)(5), 457(d)(1)(B), 457(d)(2), as amended by EGTRRA 2001. For distributions prior to 2002, Section 457 plans are also subject to special distribution rules under IRC Section 457(d)(2), prior to amendment by EGTRRA 2001.

19. The qualified plan rules regarding QDROs under Section 414(p) apply to Section 457 plans for years beginning after December 31, 2001, so that a Section 457 plan will not violate the restrictions on distributions under Section 457(d) by making a QDRO distribution. IRC Section 414(p), as amended by EGTRRA 2001. Under prior law, such distributions were not permitted.

20. See DOL News Release 86-527, [September 1985 — December 1987 transfer binder] Pens. Plan. Guide (CCH) ¶23,720C.

21. The IRS has recognized this "catch 22"—that a plan subject to Title I of ERISA will not be able to satisfy the Code's requirement that the plan be unfunded. See Notice 87-13, 1987-1 CB 432, at 444, Q&A-25; Let. Rul. 8950056. Section 457 plans for nongovernmental tax-exempt organizations are generally subject to Title I of ERISA unless they are structured to take advantage of specific exemptions from ERISA coverage. DOL News Release 86-527, [September 1985 — December 1987 transfer binder] Pens. Plan. Guide (CCH) ¶23,720C. The most significant exemptions are for (1) top-hat plans (i.e., unfunded plans maintained primarily for the purpose of providing deferred compensation for a select group of management or highly compensated employees); and for (2) unfunded excess benefit plans (i.e., unfunded plans maintained solely for the purpose of providing benefits for certain employees in excess of the limitations imposed by Code section 415). See ERISA Sections 3(36), 4(b)(5), 201(2), 301(a)(3), 401(a)(1), 503. Unless a Section 457 plan for a nongovernmental tax-exempt organization is structured to take advantage of an ERISA exemption, it will be subject to ERISA and will probably be unable to satisfy the Code's requirement that the plan be unfunded.

22. IRC Section 457(g).

23. IRC Section 457(a), as amended by EGTRRA 2001. For distributions made before 2002, a participant or beneficiary in any eligible Section 457 plan must include deferred compensation (and income thereon) in gross income for the tax year in which it is paid or otherwise made available. IRC Section 457(a), prior to amendment by EGTRRA 2001.

24. IRC Section 457(f).

25. IRC Section 402(e)(4)(D)(i).

26. This rule is effective for transfers made after December 31, 2001, IRC Section 457(e)(17), as amended EGTRRA 2001.

27. IRC Section 457(e)(16), as added by EGTRRA 2001.

28. IRC Section 457(d)(1)(C), as amended by EGTRRA 2001.

29. IRC 457(e)(10).

30. IRC Section 401(k)(4)(B).

31. IRC Section 408(p); see also Notice 98-4, 1998-2 IRB 25.

32. IRC Section 401(k)(4)(B); IRC Section 408(p).

33. Section 1107 of the Tax Reform Act of 1986 extended Section 457 to apply to nongovernmental tax-exempt organizations effective after 1986, but in Section 1107(c)(3)(B), a grandfather provision exempted nonelective plans that were in writing on August 16, 1986, so long as they remain unmodified. Section 6064(d)(3) of the Technical and Miscellaneous Revenue Act of 1988 extended the grandfather provision to plans of governmental organizations, with an effective date of July 14, 1988. Letter Ruling 9629022 appears to indicate that the IRS's position is that the grandfathering date is January 1, 1988 for nonelective plans of nongovernmental tax-exempt organizations. See also Notice 88-8, indicating that the IRS would not enforce Section 457 for nonelective deferred compensation plans for taxable years of employees beginning before January 1, 1988. Since the Letter Ruling applies only to the taxpayer on whose behalf the ruling was issued and because it addressed only *nonelective* plans, a cautious practitioner must remain mindful of the August 16, 1986 date for elective plans of nongovernmental, tax-exempt clients.

34. IRC Section 457(e)(12).

35. Compare Let. Rul. 9431021 (postponing vesting date of restricted stock would not trigger taxation of stock as long as future services required of employee were and would continue to be substantial). This ruling has generated some controversy. See, e.g., the comments of Thomas A. Brisendine, Branch 2 Chief of the Office of Associate Counsel, Employee Benefits/Exempt Organizations in 22 Pens. & Ben. Rep. (BNA) 1099-1100 (1995).

36. See, e.g., Let. Ruls. 9429007, 9008059, 8831022. Letter Ruling 9008059 involved a nonprofit (Section 501(c)) employer that had *two* Section 457 plans, both maintained only for a select group of management and highly compensated employees (the top hat group). Plan One provided benefits within the $7,500 limits (and had graduated vesting) while Plan Two provided supplemental additional benefits that were forfeited if employment was terminated prior to normal retirement age for reasons other than death or disability.

37. IRC Section 457(e)(11).

38. Treas. Reg. §1.457-2(h)(4).

39. Let. Rul. 9008043.

40. See Treas. Reg. §1.457-1(c).

41. For taxable years ending after December 31, 2001, the Internal Revenue Service has stated that it will no longer treat or accept the P.S. 58 rates as a proper measure of current life insurance protection for federal tax purposes. Instead, under interim guidance, taxpayers may use Table 2001 (see Chapter 13) to determine the value of current life insurance protection on a single life provided under a qualified retirement plan. Notice 2001-10, 2001-5 IRB 1.

42. IRC Section 25B, as amended by EGTRRA 2001.

# Chapter 12

# HR 10 (KEOGH) PLAN

## WHAT IS IT?

A Keogh plan, sometimes referred to as an HR 10 plan, is a qualified retirement plan that covers one or more self-employed individuals. A self-employed individual is a sole proprietor or partner who works in his or her unincorporated business. Like all qualified plans, a Keogh plan enables those covered under the plan to accumulate a private retirement fund that will supplement their other pension and Social Security benefits.

A Keogh plan works much like any qualified plan; the details of the various types of qualified plans such as defined benefit or profit sharing plans are discussed in separate chapters of this book. This chapter focuses on the special features of a qualified plan that covers self-employed individuals.

## WHEN IS IT INDICATED?

1. When long-term capital accumulation, particularly for retirement purposes, is an important objective of a self-employed business owner.

2. When an owner of an unincorporated business wishes to adopt a plan providing retirement benefits for regular employees as an incentive and employee benefit, as well as retirement savings for the business owner.

3. When a self-employed person has a need to shelter some current earnings from federal income tax.

4. When an employee has self-employment income as well as income from employment, and wishes to invest as much as possible of the self-employment income and defer taxes on it.

## ADVANTAGES

1. Keogh contributions are deducted from gross income, and tax is deferred until funds are withdrawn from the plan at a later date.

2. Income generated by the investments in a Keogh plan is also tax-deferred until it is withdrawn from the plan. This reinvestment of income and build-up of tax deferred earnings is one of the main features that make Keogh plans attractive.

For example, the following table shows the results of investing $7,500 annually in a Keogh plan where the rate of return is 8%, compounded daily:

| Number of Years | Total Contribution | Tax Deferred Interest | Total Value |
|---|---|---|---|
| 5 | $ 37,500 | $ 10,645 | $ 48,145 |
| 10 | 75,000 | 45,365 | 120,365 |
| 15 | 112,500 | 116,201 | 228,701 |
| 20 | 150,000 | 241,213 | 391,213 |
| 25 | 187,500 | 447,490 | 634,990 |

As can be seen, the tax-deferred earnings portion of the program will eventually exceed the amount of personal annual contributions. This is a strong incentive to start early and continue to make the largest possible contribution to such a plan.

3. Under current law, plan loans to owner-employees are subject to the same rules as are applied to regular employees (generally up to $50,000 or half the vested benefit).[1]

4. Certain lump-sum benefits may be eligible for a special 10-year averaging tax computation (available to certain employees born before 1936) that may reduce tax rates on the benefit.

5. The limits on Keogh plan contributions, as for all qualified plans, are more liberal than those applied to IRAs (individual retirement accounts). IRAs are subject to the following annual contribution limits: $3,000 in 2002 through 2004 ($6,000 for an individual and spouse). In contrast, the maximum contribution under a defined contribution Keogh plan is $40,000 (2003 figure as indexed). (See the discussion under "Types of Keogh Plans" below regarding how to take advantage of the full $40,000 limit). Thus, a self-employed person may be eligible to

contribute over 13 times as much to a Keogh plan as to an IRA. In addition, deductions for IRA contributions may be limited if the individual (or his spouse) is an active participant in a qualified retirement plan (see Chapter 17).

6. From the viewpoint of an employee of an unincorporated business, Keogh plans are advantageous because employees of the business must participate in the plan (within the limits of the coverage requirements for qualified plans described in Chapter 25).

7. Certain employers adopting a plan may be eligible for a business tax credit of up to $500 for "qualified startup costs." See Chapter 27 for details.

## DISADVANTAGES

1. Keogh plans involve all the costs and complexity associated with qualified plans. However, for a small plan, particularly one covering only one self-employed individual, it is relatively easy to minimize these factors by using prototype plans offered by insurance companies, mutual funds, banks, and other financial institutions.

2. If a self-employed person has a significant number of employees, the qualified plan coverage requirements, which require nondiscriminatory plan coverage (see Chapter 25), may increase the cost of the plan substantially.

3. As with all qualified plans, there is a 10% penalty, in addition to regular federal income tax, for withdrawal of plan funds generally before age 59½, death, or disability (see Chapter 26).

4. Again as with regular qualified plans, benefit payments from the plan generally must begin by April 1 of the later of (a) the year after the plan participant attains age 70½, or (b) the year the participant retires; however, in the case of a more-than-5% owner, payments must begin by April 1 of the year after attainment of age 70½, regardless of whether the participant has retired. There is a penalty for noncompliance (see Chapter 26). Thus, Keogh plans, like all qualified plans, cannot be viewed as a means of avoiding income tax, or passing assets to succeeding generations tax free.

5. Life insurance in a qualified plan for a self-employed person, described below, is treated somewhat less favorably than for regular employees.

## TYPES OF KEOGH PLANS

In general, any type of qualified plan can be designed to cover self-employed persons. However, the typical Keogh plan covering one self-employed person, and possibly the spouse of the self-employed person, as well as a few employees, is usually designed as a defined contribution plan without a fixed contribution formula (profit sharing type of plan).

In a *defined contribution plan*, an annual contribution of any amount up to 25% of the total payroll of plan participants is generally deductible.[2] If the plan is the profit-sharing type, plan contributions can even be omitted entirely in a bad year. However, the IRS requires "substantial and recurring" contributions, or the plan may be deemed to have been terminated.[3] This contribution flexibility is very advantageous for a small business, the income of which may fluctuate substantially from year to year.

As with all qualified plans, the compensation base is limited to $200,000 (in 2003, as indexed).[4] This imposes a limit on Keogh profit sharing plans for self-employed persons with earned income of $200,000 or more—an income level that is not unusual for a successful professional. Although the 25% deduction limit would produce a deductible contribution of $50,000, the annual additions limit (see Chapter 25) effectively limits profit sharing plan contributions to $40,000.[5]

A partnership or proprietorship may also establish a 401(k) plan (see Chapter 19). Matching contributions made to a 401(k) Keogh plan on behalf of a self-employed person are not treated as elective employer contributions, thus they are not subject to the $12,000 (in 2003) annual limit.[6]

A *money purchase plan* contains a fixed annual contribution formula of up to 25% of earned income, for self-employed persons (25% of compensation for any regular employees covered under the plan).[7] However, a money purchase plan is subject to the Code's minimum funding requirements (see Chapter 25). These require the employer to make contributions to each employee's and self-employed person's account each year equal to the percentage of compensation stated in the plan. Such contributions are mandatory, regardless of good or bad business results for the year.

A partnership or proprietorship can adopt other types of qualified plans as well. A *defined benefit* plan (see Chapter 9) is attractive to the older self-employed person who is just starting a plan, because the actuarial funding approach allows a greater relative contribution for older plan participants. Often, considerably more can be contributed annually to a defined benefit plan than the $40,000 maximum (in 2003, as indexed) for defined contribution plans.

Partnerships and proprietorships can also adopt cross-tested or other age-weighted plans (see Chapter 22) with self-employed persons as participants. These plans, like defined benefit plans, allow contributions to be weighted (that is, provide contributions equal to a higher percentage of compensation) for older plan entrants, who tend to be the owners of the business.

## HOW ARE KEOGHS DIFFERENT FROM OTHER QUALIFIED PLANS?

The unique feature of a Keogh plan, as compared with qualified plans adopted by corporations, is that the Keogh plan covers self-employed individuals, who are not technically considered "employees." This leads to some significant special rules for self-employed individuals covered under the plan.

### Earned Income

The most important special rule is the definition of earned income. For a self-employed individual, "earned income" takes the place of "compensation" in applying the qualified plan rules. Earned income is defined as the self-employed individual's net income from the business after all deductions, *including the deduction for Keogh plan contributions.*[8] In addition, the IRS has ruled that the self-employment tax must be computed and a deduction of one-half of the self-employment tax must be taken *before* determining the Keogh deduction.[9]

To resolve the potential complexity of this computation, *IRS Publication 560* specifies the following steps in determining the Keogh deduction:

(1) determine net income from Schedule C income;

(2) subtract one-half of the actual amount of the self-employment tax; and

(3) multiply the result by the "net" contribution rate from the rate table below.

---

*Example*: Len earns $100,000 of Schedule C income in 2003. His self-employment tax is $13,466.15. (The net income amount of $100,000 is first reduced by 7.65%, leaving $92,350 net earnings subject to the self-employment tax—$87,000 x 12.4% (OASDI) + $92,350 x 2.9% (HI) = $13,466.15.) The deduction for one-half of the self-employment tax then is $6,733.08 ($13,466.15 ÷ 2). The Keogh contribution base is thus $100,000 less $6,733.08, or $93,266.93. If the nominal plan contribution rate is 25%, the net contribution rate is 20%. This rate is applied to the Keogh contribution base and results in a contribution of $18,653.39. (Note that this amount is 20% of "earned income," which is equal to $74,613.54 (i.e., the Keogh contribution base of $93,266.93 less the Keogh contribution of $18,653.39).)

---

The IRS table of "net" contribution rates is as follows:

### Self-Employed Person's Rate Table

| Column A<br>If the Plan Contribution Rate is:<br>(shown as a %) | Column B<br>The Self-Employed Person's Rate is:<br>(shown as a decimal) |
|---|---|
| 1 | .009901 |
| 2 | .019608 |
| 3 | .029126 |
| 4 | .038462 |
| 5 | .047619 |
| 6 | .056604 |
| 7 | .065421 |
| 8 | .074074 |
| 9 | .082569 |
| 10 | .090909 |
| 11 | .099099 |
| 12 | .107143 |
| 13 | .115044 |
| 14 | .122807 |
| 15 | .130435 |
| 16 | .137931 |
| 17 | .145299 |
| 18 | .152542 |
| 19 | .159664 |
| 20 | .166667 |
| 21 | .173554 |
| 22 | .180328 |
| 23 | .186992 |
| 24 | .193548 |
| 25 | .200000 |

### Life Insurance

Life insurance can be used as an incidental benefit in a plan covering self-employed individuals, but the tax treatment for the self-employed individuals is different from that applicable to regular employees in a qualified plan.

The entire cost of life insurance for regular employees is deductible as a plan contribution. Employees then pick up the value of the pure life insurance element as extra taxable compensation valued under Table 2001 (generally for use after 2000), which replaced the P.S. 58 table (generally used for years ending before 2002).[10] For details, see Chapter 13.

By contrast, for a self-employed individual, the pure life insurance element of an insurance premium is *not* deductible.[11] Only the portion of the premium that exceeds the pure protection value of the insurance is deductible. The pure protection value of the insurance is determined using Table 2001 (generally for use after 2000) or the P.S. 58 table (permitted for years ending before 2002). Since all income and deductions flow automatically to the owners in an unincorporated business, the nondeductible life insurance element in effect becomes additional taxable income to the self-employed individual.

---

*Example:* Leo, a self-employed individual, has a Keogh plan providing incidental insurance through a cash value life insurance contract. This year's premium is $3,000, of which $1,200 is for pure life insurance protection and the remainder is used to increase the cash value. Leo can deduct $1,800 of the premium as a plan contribution. The remaining $1,200 is nondeductible. Leo therefore must pay tax on the $1,200 used for pure life insurance protection.

---

Another difference in the treatment of life insurance arises when benefits are paid from the plan. Regular employees have a "cost basis" (a nontaxable recovery element) in a plan equal to any Table 2001 (formerly P.S. 58) costs they have included in income in the past, so long as the plan distribution is made from the same life insurance contract on which the costs were paid (see Chapter 13). For a self-employed individual, however, Table 2001 costs, while effectively included in income since they were nondeductible, are not includable in cost basis.[12]

## Loans

Qualified plans can make loans to both regular employees and to self-employed participants, within a $50,000 maximum and certain other limits (see Chapter 26).[13]

## TAX AND ERISA IMPLICATIONS

Except for the differences described just above, Keogh plans generally have the same tax and ERISA implications as regular qualified plans. For example, see Chapter 16 for the tax treatment of profit sharing plans.

The annual reporting requirement for qualified plans is simplified for many Keogh plans and other small plans. If a plan covers only the business owner or partners, or the owner or partners and their spouses, the reporting requirement is satisfied by filing Form 5500-EZ. A sample Form 5500-EZ is included at the end of this chapter.

## ALTERNATIVES

1.  The disadvantages, if any, of Keogh status of any qualified plan can be eliminated if the business owner incorporates the business and adopts a corporate plan. The owner is then a shareholder and employee of the corporation. Generally, under current law, it is not advantageous to incorporate a business simply to obtain corporate treatment for qualified plans. Incorporation may result in higher taxes overall and the advantages of corporate plans over Keogh plans are minimal in most cases.

2.  A simplified employee pension (SEP) or SIMPLE IRA may be even simpler to adopt than a Keogh plan, particularly if only one self-employed individual is covered. In addition, SEPs can be adopted as late as the individual's tax return filing date, when it is too late to adopt a new Keogh plan. See Chapter 21 for more discussion of SEPs, and Chapter 20 for an explanation of SIMPLE IRAs.

3.  Tax deductible IRA contributions may be available up to $3,000/$6,000 annually (in 2002 through 2004) if the individual (or his spouse) is not an active participant in a qualified plan. The deduction is subject to cutbacks based on adjusted gross income if the individual (or his spouse) is an active participant in a qualified plan (see Chapter 17). Roth IRAs are also subject to the same limits (see Chapter 24). Because of these limitations, a Keogh plan often permits much greater levels of tax-deferred savings.

## HOW TO INSTALL A PLAN

A Keogh plan follows the installation procedure for qualified plans described in Chapter 27. However, in adopting a Keogh plan, it is common to use a "prototype" plan designed by a bank, insurance company, mutual fund, or other financial institution. With a prototype, the sponsoring institution does most of the paperwork involved in installing the plan, at low or nominal cost to the self-employed individual. In return, the self-employed individual must keep most or all of the plan funds invested with that institution.

## WHERE CAN I FIND OUT MORE ABOUT IT?

1.  Banks, insurance companies, and other financial institutions actively market Keogh plans and will usually provide extensive information about their services.

2.  IRS Publication 560, *Self-Employed Retirement Plans*, covers Keogh plans in detail. It is revised annually and available free from the IRS.

3.  *Tax Facts 1*, Cincinnati, OH, The National Underwriter Co. (revised annually).

## QUESTIONS AND ANSWERS

**Question** — Who can establish a Keogh retirement plan?

*Answer* — Any sole proprietor or partnership, whether or not the business has employees—for example, doctors, lawyers, accountants, writers, etc. Generally, employees of the business must be included as participants in the plan on the same general basis as the key employees.

**Question** — Can I collect benefits if I become disabled?

*Answer* — In the event that any participant in the plan becomes so disabled as to render him or her unable to engage in any substantial gainful activity, all contributed amounts plus earnings may be paid immediately without being subject to a premature distribution penalty.

**Question** — What happens to my plan if I die?

*Answer* — In the event that any participant dies, all contributed amounts plus earnings may be immediately paid to the participant's designated beneficiary or estate.

**Question** — May I set up a Keogh plan in addition to an IRA?

*Answer* — Yes. If you are eligible to set up a Keogh plan you may also create a traditional or Roth IRA as well. However, because you are an active participant in the Keogh plan, traditional IRA contributions will not be tax deductible if your income is above certain limits (see Chapter 17).

Beginning after 2002, a plan may permit employees to make voluntary contributions to a "deemed IRA" established under the plan. Amounts so contributed reduce the limit for other traditional or Roth IRA contributions. See Chapter 13 for details.

**Question** — Can a Keogh plan be established if the self-employed person is covered under a corporate retirement plan of an employer?

*Answer* — Yes. An individual who works for a regular employer, and is covered under that employer's qualified plan, can establish a separate Keogh plan for an additional business carried on separately as a self-employed individual. For example, an engineering professor at a university may have additional income earned as a consulting engineer for outside clients. A Keogh plan will shelter some of that income from taxation and provide increased retirement savings on a tax-favored basis. The deduction limits for Keogh contributions are not affected unless the individual also controls or owns the regular employer.

For example, suppose an engineer earns $60,000 this year from his university position and is covered under the university's qualified pension plan. The engineer earns an additional $40,000 in consulting fees from outside clients. If he adopts a Keogh money purchase plan for this year, he can contribute and deduct up to 25% of *earned income* (see discussion above) to the Keogh plan.

**Question** — Can a Keogh plan fund be reached by the owner's creditors?

*Answer* — In general, assets in a qualified pension plan may have protection under federal law against diversion for any purpose other than providing benefits for the plan participant and his or her beneficiary, including an ERISA prohibition against "assignment or alienation" of benefits.[14] This can protect pension assets from creditors,[15] and even spouses have only the limited rights provided under the QDRO provisions (see Chapter 26).

## FOOTNOTES

1. See IRC Section 4975(f)(6).

2. IRC Section 404(a)(3)(A).

3. Treas. Reg. §1.401(b)(2).

4. IRC Section 401(a)(17).

5. IRC Section 415(c)(1).

6. IRC Section 402(g)(8).

7. IRC Section 404(a)(3)(A)(v) was amended by EGTRRA 2001 to clarify that a money purchase plan will be treated in the same manner as a profit sharing plan for purposes of the deduction limit.

8. IRC Section 401(c)(2).

9. GCM 39807.

10. Notice 2002-8, 2002-1 CB 398 .

11. IRC Section 404(e); Treas. Reg. §1.404(e)-1A(g).

12. Treas. Reg. §1.72-16(b)(4).

13. IRC Section 401(c)(3).

14. IRC Sections 401(a)(1), 401(a)(13); ERISA Section 206(d)(1).

15. The U.S. Supreme Court held that assets in a plan that is qualified under section 401(a) of the Internal Revenue Code and subject to Title I of ERISA (including the anti-alienation requirements of Section 206(d)(1)) are protected in bankruptcy. *Patterson v. Shumate*, 112 S. Ct. 1662 (1992). However, it is important to note that Keogh plans that cover only sole owners or partners (and their spouses) are not considered to cover "employees" within the meaning of Title I of ERISA (see Labor Reg. §2510.3-3) and, thus, are not subject to Title I of ERISA. A line of cases holds that such "plans without employees" are not protected by *Patterson*. See, e.g., *In the Matter of Branch*, 1994 U.S. App. Lexis 2870 (7th Cir. 1994) (unpublished opinion); *In re Hall*, 151 Bankr. 412 (Bankr. W.D. Mich. 1993); *In re Witwer*, 148 Bankr. 930 (Bankr. C.D. Cal. 1992), *aff'd without opinion*, 163 Bankr. 614 (9th Cir. BAP 1994); *In re Lane*, 149 Bankr. 760 (Bankr. E.D.N.Y. 1993).

Form **5500-EZ**

Department of the Treasury
Internal Revenue Service

## Annual Return of One-Participant
## (Owners and Their Spouses) Retirement Plan

This form is required to be filed under
section 6058(a) of the Internal Revenue Code.

▶ **Complete all entries in accordance with
the instructions to the Form 5500-EZ.**

Official Use Only

OMB No. 1545-0956

This Form is Open to
Public Inspection.

---

**Part I**   **Annual Return Identification Information**

For the calendar plan year 2002
or fiscal plan year beginning    MM / DD / YYYY    **and ending**    MM / DD / YYYY

**A**   This return is:   **(1)** ☐   the first return filed for the plan;   **(3)** ☐   the final return filed for the plan;

**(2)** ☐   an amended return;   **(4)** ☐   a short plan year return
(less than 12 months).

**B**   If filing under an extension of time, check box and attach required information. (see instructions) ............................................. ▶ ☐

---

**Part II**   **Basic Plan Information** -- enter all requested information.

**1a**   Name of plan

**1b**   Three-digit plan number (PN) ▶    **1c**   Date plan first
became effective    MM / DD / YYYY

**Caution:** *A penalty for the late or incomplete filing of this return will be assessed unless reasonable cause is established.*

Under penalties of perjury and other penalties set forth in the instructions, I declare that I have examined this return, including accompanying schedules, statements and attachments, as well as the electronic version of this return if it is being filed electronically, and to the best of my knowledge and belief, it is true, correct and complete.

**Signature of employer or plan administrator**

**SIGN HERE** ▶    Date    MM / DD / YYYY

Type or print name of individual signing as employer or plan administrator

For Paperwork Reduction Act Notice, see the instructions for Form 5500-EZ.    Cat. No. 63263R    Form **5500-EZ** (2002)

0 3 0 2 0 0 0 0 1 0 6

v5.0

# HR 10 (KEOGH) Plan

Official Use Only

**2a** Employer's name and address (Address should include room or suite no.)

1) Name

Name Continued

2) C / O

3) Street

4) City

5) State    Zip Code

6) Foreign Routing Code

7) Foreign Country

8) D/B/A

9) Location Address if different than Street

Location Address if different than 4) or 5)

**2b** Employer Identification Number (EIN)
(Do not enter your Social Security Number)

**2c** Employer's telephone number

**2d** Business code (see instructions)

**3a** Plan administrator's name and address (If same as employer, enter "Same")

1) Name

Name Continued

2) C / O

3) Street

4) City

5) State    Zip Code

6) Foreign Routing Code

7) Foreign Country

**3b** Administrator's EIN

**3c** Administrator's telephone number

**4** If the name and/or EIN of the employer has changed since the last return filed for this plan, enter the name, EIN and the plan number from the last return below:

**a** Employer's name

**b** EIN  ‑

**c** PN

0 3 0 2 0 0 0 2 0 7

# HR 10 (KEOGH) Plan

Official Use Only

**5**   Preparer information (optional)

**a**   Name (including firm name, if applicable) and address

**1)**   Name

         Name Continued

**2)**   Street

**3)**   City                                                           **b**   EIN

**4)**   State    Zip Code

**5)**   Foreign Routing Code                                           **c**   Telephone number

**6)**   Foreign Country

**6**   Type of plan:   **(a)** ☐   Defined benefit pension plan (other than a plan    **(d)** ☐   Profit-sharing plan
                                    described in Code section 412(i))

                        **(b)** ☐   Defined benefit pension plan described in          **(e)** ☐   Stock bonus plan
                                    Code section 412(i)

                        **(c)** ☐   Money purchase pension plan (see instructions)     **(f)** ☐   ESOP plan (attach Schedule E (Form 5500))

**7a**  If this is a master/prototype, or regional prototype plan, enter the opinion/notification letter number .......... ▶

   **b**  Check if this plan covers:

        **(1)** ☐   Self-employed individuals,   **(2)** ☐   Partner(s) in a partnership, or   **(3)** ☐   100% owner of corporation

**8a**  Enter the number of qualified pension benefit plans maintained by the employer (including this plan) ..................... ▶

   **b**  Check here if you have more than one plan and the total assets of all plans are more than $100,000 (see instructions) ......... ▶ ☐

|                                                                                                                              | Number |
|------------------------------------------------------------------------------------------------------------------------------|--------|
| **9**   Enter the number of participants in each category listed below:                                                       |        |
| **a**  Under age 59 1/2 at the end of the plan year ............................................................................ |        |
| **b**  Age 59 1/2 or older at the end of the plan year, but under age 70 1/2 at the beginning of the plan year ................ |        |
| **c**  Age 70 1/2 or older at the beginning of the plan year ................................................................... |        |

0 3 0 2 0 0 0 3 0 8

# HR 10 (KEOGH) Plan

Official Use Only

**10a** *(1)* Is this a fully insured pension plan which is funded entirely by insurance or annuity contracts? ▶ ☐ Yes    ☐ No

If "Yes," complete lines 10a*(2)* through 10f and skip lines 10g through 13d.

*(2)* If 10a*(1)* is "Yes," are the insurance contracts held: ............................................ ▶ **(1)** ☐ under a trust    **(2)** ☐ with no trust

**b** Cash contributions received by the plan for this plan year ......................................... [        ].00

**c** Noncash contributions received by the plan for this plan year .................................... [        ].00

**d** Total plan distributions to participants or beneficiaries (see instructions) ................. [        ].00

**e** Total nontaxable plan distributions to participants or beneficiaries ........................... [        ].00

**f** Transfers to other plans ................................................................................. [        ].00

**g** Amounts received by the plan other than from contributions .................................... [        ].00

**h** Plan expenses other than distributions ............................................................... [        ].00

|  | **(a)** Beginning of Year | **(b)** End of Year |
|---|---|---|
| **11a** Total plan assets ........ | [        ].00 | [        ].00 |
| **b** Total plan liabilities ..... | [        ].00 | [        ].00 |

**12** **Specific Assets:** If the plan held assets at any time during the plan year in any of the following categories, check "Yes" and enter the current value of any assets remaining in the plan as of the end of the plan year. Otherwise, check "No."

|  | Yes | No | Amount |
|---|---|---|---|
| **a** Partnership/joint venture interests ................................. | ☐ | ☐ | [        ].00 |
| **b** Employer real property ............................................... | ☐ | ☐ | [        ].00 |
| **c** Real estate (other than employer real property) ............ | ☐ | ☐ | [        ].00 |

03020000409

Form 5500-EZ (2002)          Page **5**

Official Use Only

| | | Yes | No | Amount |
|---|---|---|---|---|
| **d** | Employer securities ............................................................. | ☐ | ☐ | ⬜⬜⬜⬜⬜⬜⬜⬜⬜⬜ .00 |
| **e** | Participant loans (see instructions) ................................. | ☐ | ☐ | ⬜⬜⬜⬜⬜⬜⬜⬜⬜⬜ .00 |
| **f** | Loans (other than to participants) ................................... | ☐ | ☐ | ⬜⬜⬜⬜⬜⬜⬜⬜⬜⬜ .00 |
| **g** | Tangible personal property ................................................. | ☐ | ☐ | ⬜⬜⬜⬜⬜⬜⬜⬜⬜⬜ .00 |

**13** Check "Yes" and enter amount involved if any of the following transactions took place between the plan and a disqualified person during this plan year. Otherwise, check "No."

| | | Yes | No | Amount |
|---|---|---|---|---|
| **a** | Sale, exchange, or lease of property ............................... | ☐ | ☐ | ⬜⬜⬜⬜⬜⬜⬜⬜⬜⬜ .00 |
| **b** | Payment by the plan for services ..................................... | ☐ | ☐ | ⬜⬜⬜⬜⬜⬜⬜⬜⬜⬜ .00 |
| **c** | Acquisition or holding of employer securities ................. | ☐ | ☐ | ⬜⬜⬜⬜⬜⬜⬜⬜⬜⬜ .00 |
| **d** | Loan or extension of credit ............................................... | ☐ | ☐ | ⬜⬜⬜⬜⬜⬜⬜⬜⬜⬜ .00 |

| | | | Yes | No |
|---|---|---|---|---|
| **14a** | Does your business have any employees other than you and your spouse (and your partners and their spouses)? ........................................................................ ▶ | | ☐ | ☐ |
| | If 14a is "No," do not complete line 14b or line 14c. See the specific instructions for line 14b and line 14c. | | | |
| **b** | Total number of employees (including you and your spouse and your partners and their spouses) ........................... ▶ | | ⬜⬜⬜⬜ | |
| **c** | Does this plan meet the coverage requirements of Code section 410(b)? ........................... ▶ | | ☐ | ☐ |
| **15a** | Did the plan distribute any annuity contracts this plan year? ................................................................. ▶ | | ☐ | ☐ |
| **b** | During this plan year, did the plan make distributions to a married participant in a form other than a qualified joint and survivor annuity or were any distributions on account of the death of a married participant made to beneficiaries other than the spouse of that participant? ........................... ▶ | | ☐ | ☐ |
| **c** | During this plan year, did the plan make loans to married participants? ........................... ▶ | | ☐ | ☐ |

0 3 0 2 0 0 0 5 0 A

# Chapter 13

# LIFE INSURANCE IN A QUALIFIED PLAN

## WHAT IS IT?

Life insurance for employees covered under a qualified plan can often be provided favorably by having the insurance purchased and owned by the plan, using deductible employer contributions to the plan as a source of funds. This chapter deals with the advantages and methods of doing this, as well as the limitations.

## WHEN IS IT INDICATED?

1. When a substantial number of employees covered under a qualified plan have an otherwise unmet life insurance need, either for family protection or estate liquidity.

2. When there are gaps and limitations in other company plans providing death benefits, such as Section 79 group-term life insurance plans, nonqualified deferred compensation plans, and split dollar plans. Planners should consider using life insurance in a qualified plan to fill those gaps or supplement those plans.

3. When a qualified plan for a closely held business or professional corporation is overfunded or close to the full funding limitation for regular trusteed plans, the addition of an incidental life insurance benefit, or a change to fully insured funding, may permit future deductible contributions at a higher rate than before.

4. When highly compensated plan participants are potentially subject to substantial estate taxes on death benefits.

   • Insured plan death benefits can (potentially) be structured to avoid estate taxes.

   • Life insurance in a plan can provide funds to pay estate taxes if any, thereby enhancing the ability of plan proceeds to provide financial security for the participant's survivors.

5. When life insurance would be attractive to plan participants as an additional option for investing their plan accounts. This technique is most often used in a profit sharing or 401(k) plan, but can be used in other types of defined contribution plans as well.

6. When an employer wants an extremely secure funding vehicle for a plan, with the best available guarantees as to future plan costs and benefits.

## ADVANTAGES

1. The tax treatment of life insurance in a qualified plan, as discussed below, usually provides an overall cost advantage, as compared with individual life policies provided by the employer outside the qualified plan or those personally owned by plan participants.

2. Life insurance provides one of the safest available investments for a qualified plan.

3. The use of appropriate life insurance products for funding a qualified plan can provide extremely predictable plan costs for the employer.

4. Life insurance products in a qualified plan can provide employees with retirement benefits guaranteed by an insurance company as well as by the employer.

5. The "pure insurance" portion of a qualified plan death benefit (basically, the death proceeds less any policy cash values) is not subject to income tax. This makes it an effective means of transferring wealth.

6. Some authorities believe that insured plan death benefits can be structured to keep them out of the plan participant's estate for federal estate tax purposes. (See "Questions and Answers," below.)

7. A fully insured plan (one holding only life insurance policies or annuity contracts) is exempt from the minimum funding standards and the actuarial certification requirement of Code section 412. This can reduce the administrative cost and complexity

of a defined benefit plan. A fully insured plan can also allow a higher initial level of deductible plan contributions than a regular trusteed plan.

8. Some life insurance companies provide low cost installation and administrative services for plans using their investment products. This also reduces the employer's cost for the plan.

## DISADVANTAGES

1. Some life insurance policies may provide a rate of return on their cash values which, as compared with alternative plan investments, may be relatively low. However, rates of return should be compared on investments of similar risk.

2. Policy expenses and commissions on life insurance products may be greater than for comparable investments.

## HOW IS IT USED?

### Insurance Coverage

Insurance coverage should be provided for all plan participants under a nondiscriminatory formula related to the retirement benefit or plan contribution formula. For example, the amount of insurance for each employee might be specified as 100 times the expected monthly pension under the plan.

Insurance coverage can be conditioned on taking a medical exam if this does not result in discrimination in favor of highly compensated employees. For employees who do not "pass" the medical exam, insurance is typically limited to the amount, if any, that can be purchased for them using the amount of premium dollars that would be available if they were insurable. For example, if the plan's insurance formula provides insurance of 100 times the monthly benefit for standard risks (employees who pass the medical exam), the insurance provided for a medically "rated" employee might be only 50 times the monthly benefit, since a 50 times benefit for that employee would cost as much to provide as a 100 times benefit for a standard risk.

Turnover costs involved in buying cash value insurance policies can be minimized by having a longer waiting period for insurance than the plan's waiting period for entry. In the interim period, the death benefit for participants not covered by cash value policies can be provided by term insurance. In the past, many plans did not provide insurance for employees who were beyond a specified cutoff age; under current age discrimination law, this probably is disallowed. (See Appendix I.)

### How Much Insurance—The "Incidental" Test

Life insurance can be used to provide an "incidental" death benefit to participants in a qualified retirement plan, either a defined contribution or defined benefit plan. The IRS considers any nonretirement benefit in a qualified plan to be incidental so long as the cost of that benefit is less than 25% of the total cost of the plan. Since this standard by itself is difficult to apply, the IRS has developed two practical tests for life insurance in a qualified plan.[1] If the amount of insurance meets either of the following tests, it is considered incidental:

1. The participant's insured death benefit must be no more than 100 times the expected monthly benefit, or

2. The aggregate premiums paid (premiums paid over the entire life of the plan) for a participant's insured death benefit are at all times less than the following percentages of the plan cost for that participant:

| | |
|---|---|
| "ordinary life" insurance | 50% |
| term insurance | 25% |
| universal life | 25% |

Traditionally, defined contribution plans such as profit sharing plans have used the "percentage limits" in determining how much insurance to provide. Defined benefit plans have typically used the "100 times" limit. However, any type of plan can use either limit. It is becoming more common for defined benefit plans to use the percentage limits since the necessary calculations are easily computerized.

### Life Insurance in Defined Benefit Plans

Life insurance is particularly advantageous in defined benefit plans because it *adds to* the limit on deductible contributions. This add-on feature allows greater tax-deferred funding of the plan. That is, a defined benefit plan can be funded to provide the maximum tax-deductible contribution for retirement benefits for each participant. The cost for life insurance can then be added to this amount and deducted.

By comparison, in a defined contribution plan, the costs of the life insurance must be part of the contributions to each participant's account. Using life insurance does not increase the Section 415 annual additions limit for participants' accounts in defined contribution plans. That limit is the lesser of (a) 100% of compensation or (b) $40,000 (in 2003, as indexed; for details, see Chapter 25). This limit applies whether or not life insurance is provided.

Life insurance can be used in defined benefit plans in many ways. Three common approaches will be discussed here: the "combination plan," the "envelope funding" approach, and the fully insured plan.

## Combination Plan

In a combination plan, retirement benefits are funded with a combination of (1) whole life policies and (2) assets in a separate trust fund called the "side fund" or "conversion fund." At each participant's retirement, the policies for that participant are cashed in. The participant's retirement benefit is then funded through a combination of the policy cash values and an amount withdrawn from the side fund. (Since whole life policies have a relatively slow cash value buildup, the cash values alone are not usually adequate at age 65 to fund the retirement benefit; this is the reason for the side fund.)

This type of funding combines the advantages of (1) an insured death benefit and the investment security of policy cash values, together with (2) an opportunity to invest more aggressively using side fund assets.

Combination plans are very appropriate for funding smaller pension plans—fewer than about 25 employees—but can be administratively costly for larger plans due to the number of insurance policies necessary for funding.

The amount of death benefit provided for each employee is usually determined using the 100-to-1 test. The annual cost for the plan each year then consists of the insurance premiums required, plus an amount deposited in the side fund that is determined on an actuarial basis. Actuarial methods and assumptions for the side fund can be varied within reasonable limits, providing some flexibility in funding.

The following example shows how a combination plan works and how it differs from an uninsured plan providing the same retirement benefit:

---

*Example:* Dr. X, a sole practitioner physician, adopts a pension plan at age 45. His annual compensation is $200,000.

| | Insured Plan | Uninsured Plan |
|---|---|---|
| Monthly pension at age 65 | $ 7,500 | $ 7,500 |
| Insured death benefit | 750,000 | 0 |
| Amount required at age 65 | 900,000 | 900,000 |
| Less: cash value at age 65 | 258,750 | 0 |
| Side fund at 65 | 641,250 | 900,000 |

---

| | Insured Plan | Uninsured Plan |
|---|---|---|
| Level annual deposit at 6% from age 45 to age 65 | 16,446 | 23,082 |
| Life insurance premium (not considering dividends) | 16,343 | 0 |
| Total annual contribution | 32,789 | 23,082 |

Note: Future dividends on the life insurance contract can be applied to reduce the annual premium, and typically will reduce it substantially after a number of years.

---

## Envelope Funding

At the opposite pole from the combination plan, where the entire plan is structured around the insurance policies, is the envelope funding approach, where insurance policies are simply considered as plan assets like any other asset. In funding, the actuary determines total annual contributions to the plan to provide both retirement and death benefits provided under the plan. The employer makes the contributions as determined by the actuary. Assets, including insurance policies, are purchased by the plan trustee to fund the costs of both the death benefits and the retirement benefits.

The amount of insured death benefit in this approach is kept within the incidental limits either by providing a death benefit of no more than 100 times each participant's projected monthly pension, or by keeping the amount of insurance premiums within the appropriate percentage limits (50% of aggregate costs for whole life insurance, 25% for term insurance, and so on).

The envelope funding approach tends to require lower initial contributions to the plan than a combination plan approach, since the actuary's assumptions are usually less conservative than the assumptions used to determine life insurance premiums. Long-term costs, however, will depend on actual investment results, policy dividends, and benefit and administrative costs of the plan.

## Fully Insured Pension Plans

A fully insured pension plan is one that is funded exclusively by life insurance or annuity contracts (and meets other requirements discussed below). There is no trusteed side fund. Such plans were once common, but the high interest rates of the late 1970s lured many pension investors away from traditional insured pension products. Today, however, the advantages of fully insured plans are coming into their own, and life insurance agents and pension sponsors should take another look at these products. The immediate reason is that changes in the pension law have made many noninsured plans "overfunded," and fully insured plans may offer a solution to this widespread problem. But even where the overfunding problem is not a factor, the fully insured plan may offer advantages.

## The Overfunding Problem

Qualified defined benefit plans are subject to minimum funding standards requiring a minimum annual employer contribution, with penalties for noncompliance. The minimum funding amount is determined actuarially, and there is a "full funding limitation" which, when reached, prevents further deductible contributions.[2]

For some defined benefit plans, the funding limitations can result in a reduction or outright elimination of plan contributions:

1.  The full funding limitation of Code section 412(c) and ERISA section 302(c) imposes a funding "lid."

2.  In addition, the law limits interest rates that can be used in determining plan liabilities. Code section 412(b)(5) requires that the interest rate in general must be within 10% of the

average rate for 30-year Treasury bonds for the prior 4-year period. This rule frequently requires interest rates considerably higher than actuaries used in the past. For example, for plan years beginning in May 2003, the weighted average interest rate was 5.43%, and the permissible range of interest rates was 4.89% to 6.52%.[3] Many actuaries used interest rates as low or lower than these in prior years to maximize current contributions.

## A Solution—Fully Insured Plans

"Fully insured plans" (also known as IRC Section 412(i) plans) have always been exempt from the minimum funding rules.[4] Furthermore, exemption from the minimum funding rules in effect exempts fully insured plans from the impact of the unfavorable changes discussed above, since they are part of the minimum funding rules.

A plan is considered fully insured for the plan year if it meets the following requirements:

*   the plan is funded exclusively by the purchase of individual insurance contracts. Under the regulations, such contracts can be either individual or group, and can be life insurance or annuity contracts or a combination of both.[5]

*   the contracts provide for level annual (or more frequent) premiums extending to retirement age for each individual. However, the employer's cost need not be level, since the regulations permit experience gains and dividends to reduce premiums.[6]

*   plan benefits are equal to the contract benefits and are guaranteed by a licensed insurance company.

*   premiums have been paid without lapse (or the policy has been reinstated after a lapse).

*   no rights under the contracts have been subject to a security interest during the plan year.

*   no policy loans are outstanding at any time during the plan year.

The nondiscrimination regulations provide a safe harbor for fully insured plans meeting certain requirements; the benefit formulas of plans satisfying the safe harbor and specified uniformity requirements will be considered to be nondiscriminatory.[7]

## Other Advantages

In addition to exemption from minimum funding, a fully insured plan is eligible for a simplification of the ERISA reporting requirements (Form 5500 series). An insured plan need not file Schedule B, Actuarial Information, with its Form 5500 (or 5500-EZ) and thus does not need a certification by an enrolled actuary.[8] This reduces the cost and complexity of plan administration to some degree. Finally, a fully insured plan is exempt from the requirement of quarterly pension deposits[9] since that is also tied together with the minimum funding requirements. Fully insured plans are, however, subject to Pension Benefit Guaranty (PBGC) coverage and annual premium requirements.

## How Does It Work?

Fully insured funding can be used either with a new plan or an existing plan.[10] The employer can be a corporation or an unincorporated business. Typically, a group type of contract is used, with individual accounts for each participant. All benefits are guaranteed by the insurance company. The premium is based on the guaranteed interest and annuity rates, which are typically conservative, resulting in larger initial annual deposits than in a typical uninsured plan. (See Figure 13.1.) However, excess earnings beyond the guaranteed level are used to reduce future premiums.

Using excess earnings to reduce future premiums results in a funding pattern that is the opposite of that found in a trusteed (uninsured) plan. In the insured plan, (for a given group of plan participants) the funding level is higher at the beginning of the plan (or the fully insured funding arrangements) and drops as participants move toward retirement. This allows maximization of the overall tax deduction by allowing more of it to be taken earlier. It also often permits deductions for an existing plan that has reached the full funding limitation with uninsured funding. By comparison, a traditional trusteed plan starts with a relatively low level of funding, which increases as each participant nears retirement.

## Life Insurance in Defined Contribution Plans

In defined contribution plans, a part of each participant's account is used to purchase insurance on the participant's life. This plan can provide (a) that insurance purchases are voluntary by participants (using a *directed account* or *earmarking* provision[11]), (b) that the insurance is provided automatically as a plan benefit, or (c) that insurance is provided at the plan administrator's option (on a nondiscriminatory basis).

The amount of insurance must be kept within the incidental limits already discussed. Usually, defined contribution plans rely on the percentage limits applicable to the type of insurance purchased. For example, if whole life insurance is purchased, aggregate premiums paid from each participant's account must be kept below 50% of aggregate contributions to that account. It

**Figure 13.1**

| Current Age | Age 65 Annual Benefit | Self-Admin. Plan Cost | Split-Fund. Plan Cost | Fully Insured Plan Cost** |
|---|---|---|---|---|
| **EFFECT OF INCIDENTAL LIFE INSURANCE BENEFIT ON ANNUAL CONTRIBUTION** | | | | |
| 35 | $91,524 | $11,596 | $14,705* | $ 26,023 |
| 45 | 91,524 | 26,716 | 31,747* | 49,168 |
| 55 | 98,064 | 73,437* | 73,437* | 134,913 |

\* Full funding limitation
\*\* Full funding limitation does not apply to fully insured plans

*Source:* Lecture by Henry A. Deppe, CLU, inaugurating the Henry Deppe Lecture Series sponsored by The American College. A tape and script of this lecture are available from The American College, Bryn Mawr, PA 19010.

may be inadvisable to lock the plan into an arrangement requiring premium payments up to the full 50% limit. This limits both investment flexibility and employer ability to reduce contributions in lean years. A whole-life premium of about one-third of plan contributions is a conservative guideline.

If a plan has been in existence for a number of years, it may be possible to purchase a considerable amount of insurance in a later year, because the tests are computed in the aggregate.

For example, suppose a money purchase pension plan has existed for ten years and the employer has contributed $10,000 annually to employee Clyde's account. In the eleventh year, suppose the employer contributes another $10,000 to Clyde's account in the plan. In that eleventh year, an insurance premium amounting to just under $55,000 (50% of aggregate contributions of $110,000) can be paid out of Clyde's account to purchase whole life insurance. In some cases, such large purchases of insurance may be justified for planning purposes. The planner must be sure, however, that application of the percentage limits in the future will not prevent the deductible payment of required periodic premiums under the policy.

Profit sharing plans have an additional feature that may allow large insurance purchases. Since profit sharing plans potentially allow in-service cash distributions prior to termination of employment (see Chapter 16), the amount available for an in-service distribution can be used without limit to purchase life insurance. Based on IRS rulings,[12] this means that any employer contribution that has been in the profit sharing plan for at least two years can be used up to 100% for insurance purchases of any type as long as the plan specifies that the insurance will be purchased only with such funds.

## TAX IMPLICATIONS

1.  Employer contributions to the plan, including those used to purchase life insurance, are deductible if the amount of life insurance is within the incidental limits discussed earlier.

2.  The economic value of pure life insurance coverage on a participant's life is taxed annually to the participant at levels specified by the IRS. Generally, the value is taxed at the lower of (a) the IRS "Table 2001" costs (see Figure 13.2) or (b) the life insurance company's actual term rates for standard risks.[13] For years ending before 2002, the "Table P.S. 58" rates

issued in earlier guidance by the IRS were used instead of the Table 2001 costs, for purposes of this rule.[14] For periods after 2003, the ability to use an insurer's published rates is much more limited.

Any amount actually contributed to the plan by the participant is subtracted from this amount. (If the participant is an owner-employee in a "Keogh" plan, the taxation is slightly different, as discussed in Chapter 12.)

_Example:_ Participant Lemm, aged 45, is covered under a defined benefit plan that provides an insured death benefit in addition to retirement benefits. The death benefit is provided under a whole life policy with a face amount of $100,000. At the end of 2002 the policy's cash value is $40,000. The plan is noncontributory (that is, Lemm does not contribute to the plan).

For 2002 Lemm must report an additional $92 of taxable income on his tax returns (60 times the Table 2001 rate of $1.53 per thousand for a participant aged 45, to reflect the amount of pure insurance coverage in 2002). The employer is required to report the insurance coverage on Lemm's Form W-2 for the year.

This computation is shown in more detail in the NumberCruncher software illustration in Figure 13.3.

3.  Taxation of an insured death benefit received by a beneficiary can be summarized in the following points:

    -   The pure insurance element of an insured plan death benefit (the death benefit less any cash value) is income tax free to a participant's beneficiary.[15]

    -   The total of all Table 2001 (or, if applicable, P.S. 58) costs paid by the participant can be recovered tax free from the plan death benefit (if it is paid from the same insurance contracts that gave rise to the costs).[16]

    -   The remainder of the distribution is taxed as a qualified plan distribution.[17] If the decedent participated in the plan before 1987, there may also be some favorable "grandfather" tax provisions for a lump sum distribution that may apply.

**Figure 13.2**

## TABLE 2001
## ONE-YEAR TERM PREMIUMS
## FOR $1,000 OF LIFE INSURANCE PROTECTION

| Attained Age | Premium | Attained Age | Premium | Attained Age | Premium |
|---|---|---|---|---|---|
| 0 | $0.70 | 34 | $0.98 | 67 | $15.20 |
| 1 | $0.41 | 35 | $0.99 | 68 | $16.92 |
| 2 | $0.27 | 36 | $1.01 | 69 | $18.70 |
| 3 | $0.19 | 37 | $1.04 | 70 | $20.62 |
| 4 | $0.13 | 38 | $1.06 | 71 | $22.72 |
| 5 | $0.13 | 39 | $1.07 | 72 | $25.07 |
| 6 | $0.14 | 40 | $1.10 | 73 | $27.57 |
| 7 | $0.15 | 41 | $1.13 | 74 | $30.18 |
| 8 | $0.16 | 42 | $1.20 | 75 | $33.05 |
| 9 | $0.16 | 43 | $1.29 | 76 | $36.33 |
| 10 | $0.16 | 44 | $1.40 | 77 | $40.17 |
| 11 | $0.19 | 45 | $1.53 | 78 | $44.33 |
| 12 | $0.24 | 46 | $1.67 | 79 | $49.23 |
| 13 | $0.28 | 47 | $1.83 | 80 | $54.56 |
| 14 | $0.33 | 48 | $1.98 | 81 | $60.51 |
| 15 | $0.38 | 49 | $2.13 | 82 | $66.74 |
| 16 | $0.52 | 50 | $2.30 | 83 | $73.07 |
| 17 | $0.57 | 51 | $2.52 | 84 | $80.35 |
| 18 | $0.59 | 52 | $2.81 | 85 | $88.76 |
| 19 | $0.61 | 53 | $3.20 | 86 | $99.16 |
| 20 | $0.62 | 54 | $3.65 | 87 | $110.40 |
| 21 | $0.62 | 55 | $4.15 | 88 | $121.85 |
| 22 | $0.64 | 56 | $4.68 | 89 | $133.40 |
| 23 | $0.66 | 57 | $5.20 | 90 | $144.30 |
| 24 | $0.68 | 58 | $5.66 | 91 | $155.80 |
| 25 | $0.71 | 59 | $6.06 | 92 | $168.75 |
| 26 | $0.73 | 60 | $6.51 | 93 | $186.44 |
| 27 | $0.76 | 61 | $7.11 | 94 | $206.70 |
| 28 | $0.80 | 62 | $7.96 | 95 | $228.35 |
| 29 | $0.83 | 63 | $9.08 | 96 | $250.01 |
| 30 | $0.87 | 64 | $10.41 | 97 | $265.09 |
| 31 | $0.90 | 65 | $11.90 | 98 | $270.11 |
| 32 | $0.93 | 66 | $13.51 | 99 | $281.05 |
| 33 | $0.96 | | | | |

Chapter 26 contains a detailed discussion of the tax treatment and planning options available for an insured death benefit from a qualified plan.

4. As compared with the tax treatment of life insurance personally owned or provided by the employer outside the plan, there is usually an economic advantage to insurance in the plan, all other things being equal. Insurance outside the plan is paid for entirely with after-tax dollars, so there is no tax deferral. The death benefit of non-plan insurance may be entirely instead of partially tax-free; however, the deferral of tax with plan-provided insurance potentially results in a measurable net tax benefit.

5. Qualified plan death benefits are, in general, included in a decedent's estate for federal estate tax purposes. However, it may be possible to exclude the insured portion of the death benefit if the dece-

**Figure 13.3**

| TABLE 2001 COMPUTATION* | |
|---|---|

**PART A**

| | | |
|---|---|---:|
| INPUT: | Employee's Age | 45 |
| INPUT: | Face Amount of Death Benefit | $100,000 |
| INPUT: | Cash Value to Employer | -$40,000 |
| | Net Amount at Risk | $60,000 |
| | Table 2001 Charge | $1.53 |
| | Gross Amount Includible | $92.00 |
| INPUT: | Employee's Contribution | $.00 |

**PART B**

| | | |
|---|---|---:|
| INPUT: | Amount of Dividend Paid in Cash to Employee | $.00 |
| INPUT: | Amount of Dividend Used to Reduce Amount of Dividend Premium Contribution | $.00 |
| INPUT: | Amount of Dividend Held at Interest for Employee | $.00 |
| INPUT: | Amount of Dividend — If Cash Value & Death Benefit of Paid Up Additions Are Controlled by Employee | $.00 |
| INPUT: | Amount of Dividend — If Dividends Were Used to Buy One Year Term Insurance for the Employee | $.00 |
| INPUT: | Table 2001 Cost or, If Lower, Published Yearly Renewable Term Cost — If Employer Gets Cash Value of Paid Up Additional Insurance and Employee's Beneficiary Receives Any Balance | $.00 |
| | Reportable Table 2001 Cost | $92.00 |

(Insert Co's standard individual 1 year term rates at B1 if lower.)

*Illustration Courtesy of NumberCruncher Software, Leimberg and LeClair, Inc., P.O. Box 1332, Bryn Mawr, PA 19010.*

dent had no "incidents of ownership" in the policy. This planning technique is discussed further in the "Questions and Answers," below.

## ALTERNATIVES

1. Personally-owned life insurance

2. Group-term life insurance

3. Life insurance financing in a nonqualified deferred compensation plan

4. Split dollar life insurance

## QUESTIONS AND ANSWERS

**Question** — Can life insurance be used in a Keogh (HR 10) plan?

*Answer* — A Keogh plan is a qualified plan covering a proprietor or one or more partners of an unincorporated business. Life insurance can be used to provide a death benefit for regular employees covered under the plan, subject to the rules discussed in this chapter. Life insurance can also be provided under the plan for a proprietor or partners. However, slightly less favorable rules apply; these are discussed in detail in Chapter 12.

**Question** — Can life insurance be used in a Section 403(b) tax deferred annuity plan?

*Answer* — Life insurance can be provided as an incidental benefit under a tax deferred annuity plan. It is provided on much the same basis as in a qualified profit sharing plan. Covered employees will have Table 2001 (or P.S. 58) costs to report as taxable income, as in a regular qualified plan.

**Question** — Can universal life insurance be used to provide an insured death benefit under a qualified plan?

*Answer* — Universal life and similar products may be used. However, even though universal life has an investment element like that in a whole life policy, the IRS has taken the view that the "incidental" limits applicable to universal life premiums are the same as those that apply to term insurance. So, if the percentage test is used, aggregate universal life premiums must be less than 25% of aggregate plan contributions. This appears to be an overly conservative rule, and may eventually be subject to a court challenge.

**Question** — Is it possible for an insured death benefit to be excluded from the decedent participant's estate for federal estate tax purposes?

*Answer* — Although there have not yet been any decisive court cases or IRS rulings on the issue, some planners believe that an insured death benefit in a qualified plan is governed by the estate tax rules relating to insurance policies (IRC Section 2042) and, therefore, can be kept out of a participant's estate by avoiding "incidents of ownership" in the policies.

For insurance in a qualified plan, this probably requires at least the following steps: (1) having life insurance policies owned by separate "subtrusts" under the plan; (2) appointing the subtrustee and successors (who should be independent parties such as a bank) irrevocably; (3) having all incidents of ownership exercised by the subtrustee, including owning the policy, receiving the proceeds, and selecting the beneficiary; and (4) designing plan provisions so that the participant has no lifetime right to receive policy cash values (policy cash values can be assigned to fund the required spousal survivor annuity).

**Question** — If a plan participant is uninsurable but already owns insurance policies, can these policies be sold to the plan to fund the plan death benefit?

*Answer* — Yes. Although the sale of property from a participant to a qualified plan would ordinarily be a prohibited transaction, the Department of Labor has issued an exemption that allows such sales for this purpose.[18] The opportunity to sell personally owned insurance to the plan must be offered to all participants on a nondiscriminatory basis in order to use this exemption.

**Question** — How can insurance coverage be continued by a qualified plan after a plan participant has retired or accrued the maximum benefit under the plan?

*Answer* — If a plan participant's full retirement benefit has accrued, the employer can no longer make deductible contributions to the plan. Several alternatives are available for continuing insurance coverage: (1) the policy can be put on a reduced, paid-up basis; (2) the policy can be sold to the participant for its cash surrender value (possibly financed using a policy loan);[19] (3) the participant can continue to pay premiums (they are nondeductible); or (4) the plan trustee can continue to pay premiums out of fund earnings (Table 2001 or P.S. 58 costs to the participant continue under this alternative).

**Question** — What types of employers should consider using fully insured plans?

*Answer* — Fully insured plans should be considered if contributions to an employer's existing, conventionally funded defined benefit plan have been severely reduced by the restrictions on actuarial assumptions or by the full funding limitation. Also, consider fully insured plans for an employer that wants to maximize its initial rate of contribution to a new defined benefit plan, because of particularly good current financial conditions, or because substantial early funding is preferable for any reason, including maximum current tax sheltering.

One caution: if any of the conditions under Section 412(i) that are listed above is not met for a plan year, the plan ceases to be a fully insured plan and must meet the minimum funding requirements for that year. In particular, a failure to make a regular premium payment will terminate fully insured status. Therefore, a fully insured plan is not appropriate for an employer if there is any doubt about its financial ability to make regular premium payments now and in the foreseeable future. A stable business, rather than a boom and bust enterprise, is the best prospect for fully insured funding.

**Question** — What are the considerations in determining whether fully insured funding is advisable from an economic, investment point of view?

*Answer* — Employers are likely to wonder if the accelerated tax deduction permitted under fully insured plans is outweighed by an increased overall cost for the plan over the years in which it is in effect. This is not an easy question to answer. In theory, the excess earnings credited to the employer under the contract could provide as good a return on investment as the employer might obtain in a trusteed plan. However, there is no reliable method to predict future earnings, either under the contract or in a trust. Selling a fully insured plan requires "selling the company" so that the employer has confidence that the rate of return will be reasonable. The guarantee features of the contract must be paid for, which implies a lower rate of return in the contract. However, these features are valuable to the employer, since they reduce the downside risk of large losses. Lower administrative costs for fully insured plans must also be factored into the analysis.

**Question** — Can a participant in a qualified plan have the plan purchase life insurance on the life of another person—a spouse or a business partner, for example?

*Answer* — Yes; some of the applications of this technique are (1) the purchase of life insurance on a co-shareholder to help fund a buy-sell agreement; or (2) to provide for a beneficiary and avoid estate taxes on the death of the employee-participant.

These "third-party" insurance techniques are primarily used in qualified profit sharing or stock bonus plans because of the need for an "earmarked" or "directed investment" account, as well as rulings prohibiting pension plans from providing third-party insurance.[20] They are discussed further in Chapter 10 and Chapter 16.

A profit sharing plan can also hold "second-to-die" life insurance on the lives of the participant and his or her spouse. This technique is also discussed in the questions and answers in Chapter 16.

**Question** — Can a qualified plan trustee borrow against the cash value of life insurance policies held in the plan?

*Answer* — Yes, but borrowing by the plan creates "unrelated business taxable income" from any reinvestment of the loan proceeds. For example, if the loan proceeds are reinvested in certificates of deposit, the plan must pay tax on interest income from those certificates.[21]

## FOOTNOTES

1. See e.g., Rev. Rul. 68-453, 1968-2 CB 163; Rev. Rul. 74-307, 1974-2 CB 126.
2. IRC Section 412(h). In addition, note Code section 6662(f) imposes a *penalty* for the substantial overstatement of pension liabilities.
3. Notice 2003-32, 2003-21 IRB 949.
4. IRC Sections 412(h), 412(i).
5. Treas. Regs. §§1.412(i)-1(b), 1.412(i)-1(c).
6. Treas. Reg. §1.412(i)-1(b)(2)(ii).
7. Treas. Reg. §1.401(a)(4)-3(b).
8. Labor Reg. §2520.104-44; Instructions for Schedule B (Form 5500).
9. IRC Section 412(c)(10).
10. See Rev. Rul. 81-196, 1981-2 CB 107, which allowed an existing split-funded plan to be converted into a fully insured plan. See also Rev. Rul. 94-75, 1994-2 CB 59, imposing certain requirements for uninsured plans that are converted to Section 412(i) plans. The most significant new requirement in this ruling was that the plan must continue to accrue benefits after conversion. Existing plan liabilities must be fully funded in order to make the conversion.
11. ERISA Section 404(c).
12. See e.g., Rev. Rul. 61-164, 1961-2 CB 99; Rev. Rul. 66-143, 1966-1 CB 79. See also Rev. Rul. 94-76, 1994-2 CB 46 (funds rolled over to profit sharing plan from money purchase plan).
13. Notice 2002-8, 2002-1 CB 398.
14. IRC Section 72(m)(3); Treas. Reg. §1.72-16(b).
15. Treas. Reg. §1.72-16(c)(4).
16. Ibid; see also, Let. Rul. 8539066.
17. IRC Section 72(m)(3); Treas. Reg. §1.72-16(c).
18. PTE 92-6, 57 FR 5189, revising and extending prior PTE 77-8, 1977-2 CB 425, to include self-employed persons and shareholder-employees in S corporations.
19. "Springing" cash values — cash values that increase greatly *after* the policy has been distributed — are subject to IRS scrutiny. Announcement 92-182, Audit Guidelines.
20. Rev. Rul. 69-523, 1969-2 CB 90.
21. TAM 8445006, citing *Dean v. Simpson*, 35 TC 1038 (1961).

# Chapter 14

# MONEY PURCHASE PENSION PLAN

## WHAT IS IT?

A money purchase plan is a qualified employer retirement plan that is, in many ways, the simplest of all qualified plans:

- Each employee has an individual account in the plan. The employer makes annual contributions to each employee's account under a nondiscriminatory contribution formula. Usually the formula requires a contribution of a specified percentage (up to 25%) of each employee's annual compensation. Annual contributions to the employee's account generally cannot be more than $40,000 (in 2003, as indexed).

- Plan benefits consist of the amount accumulated in each participant's account at retirement or termination of employment. This is the total of employer contributions, interest or other investment return on plan assets, and capital gains realized by the plan on sales of assets in the employee's account.

- The plan may provide that the employee's account balance is payable in one or more forms of annuities equivalent in value to the account balance.

## WHEN IS IT INDICATED?

1. When an employer wants to install a qualified retirement plan that is simple to administer and explain to employees.

2. When employees are relatively young and have substantial time to accumulate retirement savings.

3. When employees are willing to accept a degree of investment risk in their plan accounts, in return for the potential benefits of good investment results.

4. When some degree of retirement income security in the plan is desired. (While accounts are not guaranteed, annual employer contributions are required. This provides a degree of retirement security that is intermediate between a defined benefit plan and a profit sharing plan.)

5. When an employer seeks to reward long-term employee relationships.

## ADVANTAGES

1. As with all qualified plans, a money purchase plan provides a tax-deferred retirement savings medium for employees.

2. The plan is relatively simple and inexpensive to design, administer, and explain to employees.

3. The plan formula can provide a deductible annual employer contribution of up to the lesser of (a) 100% of the employee's compensation or (b) $40,000 (in 2003). However, the employee's deduction is limited to 25% of covered payroll. Therefore, a money purchase plan typically provides a formula of up to 25% of each employee's compensation, not to exceed $40,000.[1]

4. Plan distributions may be eligible for the 10-year special averaging computation available for certain lump sum distributions from qualified plans.

5. Individual participant accounts allow participants to benefit from good investment results in the plan fund.

## DISADVANTAGES

1. Retirement benefits may be inadequate for employees who enter the plan at older ages. For example, if an employer contributes 10% of compensation annually to each employee's account, the accumulation at age 65 for employees with varying entry ages will be as follows, assuming the plan fund earns an average return of 9%:

| Age at plan entry | Annual compensation | Account balance at age 65 |
|---|---|---|
| 25 | $35,000 | $1,289,022 |
| 30 | 35,000 | 822,937 |
| 40 | 35,000 | 323,134 |
| 50 | 35,000 | 112,012 |
| 55 | 35,000 | 57,961 |
| 60 | 35,000 | 22,832 |

This illustration shows that the "time factor" works rapidly to increase account balances. If a closely held corporation that has been in business for many years adopts a money purchase plan, key employees often will be among the older plan entrants. The money purchase plan's failure to provide adequately for such employees, even with their high compensation levels, can be a serious disadvantage.

However, this is not the whole story—there's another factor in realistic situations that reduces the apparent disparity between long-service and short-service employees. Because salaries increase over time, the long service/short service disparity in the annual pension from a money-purchase plan—as a percentage of final average compensation—is much less than if salaries do not increase. Figure 14.1 shows that, if all salaries increase at 7% annually, a 15-year employee receives a pension of 19% of final average salary while the 35-year employee gets 48% of final average salary. This is much less than the disparity resulting if salaries increase at only 3% annually, or do not increase at all. In short, in actual practice a money purchase plan may not be as disadvantageous to shorter service employees as might appear.

2.  The annual addition to each employee's account in a money purchase plan is limited to the lesser of (a) $40,000 (in 2003, as indexed), or (b) 100% of compen-

**Figure 14.1**

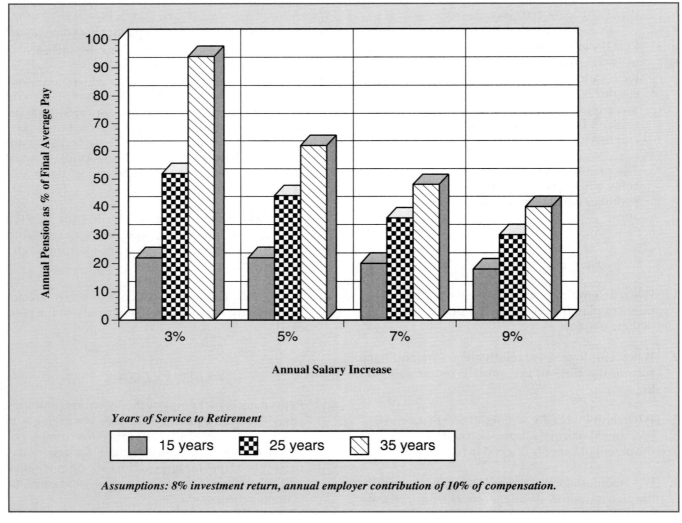

Years of Service to Retirement: 15 years, 25 years, 35 years

Assumptions: 8% investment return, annual employer contribution of 10% of compensation.

sation.[2] This, plus the $200,000 cap on compensation (in 2003, as indexed), limits the relative amount of funding available for highly compensated employees. For example, if an employee earns $300,000 in 2003, no more than $40,000 annually can be contributed for that employee; but that $40,000 is only 20% of the $200,000 of the employee's compensation that is allowed to be taken into account.

3.  Employees bear investment risk under the plan. The ultimate amount that can be accumulated under a money purchase plan is very sensitive to investment return, even for an employee who entered the plan at an early age. Figure 14.2 shows this by comparing the ultimate account balance resulting from $1,000 of annual contribution at two different return rates.

    While bearing investment risk is a potential disadvantage to employees, it does tend to reduce employer costs as compared with a defined benefit plan.

4.  The plan is subject to the Internal Revenue Code's minimum funding requirements. Employers are obligated to make the plan contribution each year or be subject to minimum funding penalties. Under current law, a qualified profit sharing plan (see Chapter 16) permits the same level of deduction to the employer (i.e., 25% of payroll), without the requirement of mandated minimum annual contributions.

## DESIGN FEATURES

Most money purchase plans use a benefit formula requiring an employer contribution that is a flat percentage of each employee's compensation. Percentages up to 25% may be used. Only the first $200,000 (in 2003, as indexed) of each employee's compensation can be taken into account in the plan formula.[3]

Some money purchase formulas also use a factor related to the employee's service. Service-related factors generally favor owners and key employees. In small, closely held businesses or professional corporations, the use of a service-related factor might result in prohibited discrimination in favor of highly compensated employees. Plan designers generally avoid service-related contribution formulas in these situations.

**Figure 14.2**

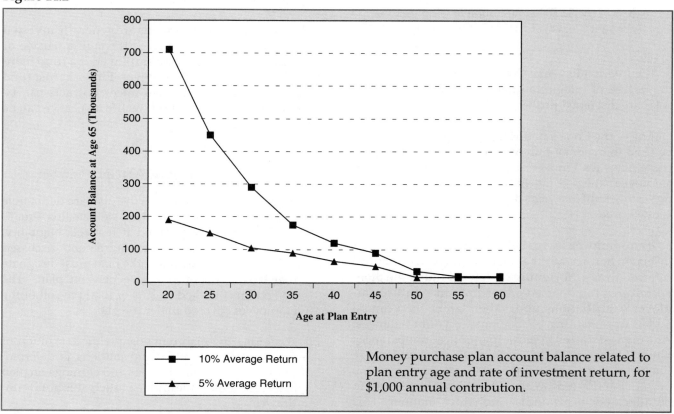

Money purchase plan account balance related to plan entry age and rate of investment return, for $1,000 annual contribution.

Nondiscrimination regulations under IRC Section 401(a)(4) provide safe harbors for money purchase plans with uniform allocation formulas; alternative methods for satisfying nondiscrimination requirements include satisfying a general nondiscrimination test, restructuring, or cross-testing (testing defined contribution plans on the basis of benefits see Chapter 22).[4]

A plan benefit formula can be "integrated" with Social Security (integration is also referred to as "permitted disparity"). This avoids duplicating Social Security benefits already provided to the employee and reduces employer costs for the plan. An integrated formula defines a level of compensation known as the "integration level." The plan then provides a higher rate of employer contributions for compensation above that integration level than the rate for compensation below that integration level.

---

*Example:* A money purchase plan specifies an integration level of $20,000 and provides for employer contributions of 14% of compensation above the $20,000 integration level and 10% below the $20,000 integration level. Employee Art Rambo earns $30,000 this year. The employer contribution to Art's account this year totals $3,400—14% of $10,000 (Art's compensation in excess of the $20,000 integration level) plus 10% of the first $20,000 of Art's compensation.

---

The Internal Revenue Code and regulations specify the degree of integration permitted in a plan. These rules are discussed further in Chapter 25.

Any of the Code's permitted vesting provisions can be used in a money purchase plan. Since money purchase plans tend to be oriented toward longer service employees, the 5-year "cliff vesting" provision (that is, no vesting until five years of service, then 100% vesting) is often used.

If an employee leaves before becoming fully vested in his or her account balance, an unvested amount referred to as a "forfeiture" is left behind in the plan. Forfeitures can be used either to reduce future employer contributions under the plan or they can be added to remaining participants' account balances. Adding forfeitures to participants' account balances tends to be favorable to key employees, since they are likely to participate in the plan over a long time period. For this reason, the IRS requires forfeitures to be allocated in a nondiscriminatory manner. This usually requires forfeiture allocation in proportion to participants' compensation, rather than in proportion to their existing account balances.

Benefits in a money purchase plan are usually payable at termination of employment or at the plan's stated normal retirement age. Money purchase plans traditionally provide that the participant's account balance is converted to an equivalent annuity at retirement, based on annuity rates provided in the plan. This is the origin of the term "money purchase." It has become more common to provide for a lump sum or installment payment from the plan as an alternative to an annuity. However, a money purchase plan, as a condition of qualification, must provide a joint and survivor annuity as the automatic form of benefit. The participant, with the consent of the spouse, may elect a different benefit option. This is discussed further in Chapter 26.

The IRS generally does not allow money purchase plans to provide for "in-service distributions"—that is, benefits payable before termination of employment. Distributions of employer contributions or earnings from pension plans are not permitted prior to death, retirement, disability, severance of employment or termination of the plan.[5] However, plan loan provisions are allowable, although relatively uncommon.

Money purchase plan funds are generally invested in a pooled account managed (through a trustee or insurance company) by the employer or a fund manager designated by the employer. Either a trust fund or group or individual insurance contracts can be used. Chapter 13 discusses how life insurance can be used in the plan.

## TAX IMPLICATIONS

1. Employer contributions to the plan are deductible when made, so long as the plan remains "qualified."[6] A plan is qualified if it meets eligibility, vesting, funding and other requirements discussed in Chapter 25. In addition, the plan must designate that it is a money purchase pension plan.[7] The deduction is limited to 25% of total payroll of the employees covered under the plan.[8]

2. Assuming the plan remains qualified, taxation of the employee on plan contributions is deferred. Both employer contributions and earnings on plan assets are nontaxable to plan participants until withdrawn.[9]

3. Under IRC Section 415, annual additions to each participant's account are limited to the lesser of (a) 100% of the participant's compensation, or (b) $40,000 (in 2003, as indexed).[10] Annual additions include: (1) employer contributions to the participant's account; (2) forfeitures from other participants' accounts; and (3) employee contributions to the account.[11]

4. Distributions from the plan must follow the rules for qualified plan distributions. Certain premature distributions are subject to penalties. The distribution rules are discussed in Chapter 26.

5. Lump sum distributions made after age 59½ may be eligible for a special 10-year averaging tax computation (available to certain employees born before 1936) that may reduce tax rates on the benefit. Not all distributions are eligible for these calculations. Chapter 26 covers these rules, including IRS forms.

6. The plan is subject to the minimum funding rules of IRC Section 412.[12] This requires minimum annual contributions, subject to a penalty imposed on the employer if less than the minimum amount is contributed.[13] For a money purchase plan, the minimum contribution is generally the amount required under the plan's contribution formula. For example, if the plan formula requires a contribution of 20% of each participant's compensation, this is generally the amount required to meet the minimum funding rules. Chapter 25 discusses these rules further.

7. Certain employers adopting a new plan may be eligible for a business tax credit of up to $500 for "qualified startup costs." See Chapter 27 for details.

8. Beginning after 2002, a plan may permit employees to make voluntary contributions to a "deemed IRA" established under the plan. Amounts so contributed reduce the limit for other traditional or Roth IRA contributions. See Chapter 17 and Chapter 24 for details.

9. The plan is subject to the ERISA reporting and disclosure rules outlined in Appendix D.

## ALTERNATIVES

1. Target benefit plans are much like money purchase plans, but the employer contribution percentage can be based on age at plan entry—higher for older entrants. Such a plan may be more favorable where the employer wants to provide adequate benefits for older employees.

2. Profit sharing plans provide more employer flexibility in contributions but less security for participants. The limit on deductible contributions to a profit sharing plan was 15% of payroll before 2002, but increased to 25% of payroll for years beginning after 2001.

3. Defined benefit plans provide more security of retirement benefits and proportionately greater contributions for older plan entrants, but are much more complex to design and administer.

4. Nonqualified deferred compensation plans can be provided exclusively for selected executives, but the employer's tax deduction is generally deferred until benefit payments are made. This can be as much as 20 or 30 years after the employer's contribution is made.

5. Individual retirement saving is available as an alternative or supplement to an employer plan, but except for certain IRAs, there is no tax deferral.

See also the discussion in Chapter 2, "Designing the Right Pension Plan."

## HOW TO INSTALL A PLAN

Installation of a money purchase plan follows the qualified plan installation procedure described in Chapter 27.

## WHERE CAN I FIND OUT MORE ABOUT IT?

1. Graduate Course: Advanced Pension and Retirement Planning I (GS 814), The American College, Bryn Mawr, PA.

## QUESTIONS AND ANSWERS

**Question**—Can a self-employed person adopt a money purchase plan?

*Answer* — A self-employed person can adopt a money purchase plan covering not only his or her regular employees, if any, but also covering the self-employed person(s). Such plans are sometimes referred to as "Keogh" or "HR 10" plans. The self-employed person is treated much the same as the regular employees covered, but there are some special rules and planning considerations that are covered in Chapter 12 of this book.

**Question** — What special issues are involved in money purchase plans covering shareholder-employees in an S corporation?

*Answer* — S corporations can have money purchase plans that cover shareholder-employees as well as regular employees. However, the plan contribution formula generally cannot provide an employer contribution for all of the shareholder-employee's income from the corporation. The employer contribution formula can be based only on the shareholder's compensation for services rendered to the corporation. Any portion of the shareholder's income that represents dividends must be excluded from the plan formula.

**Question** — Can an employer fund a money purchase plan using employee salary reductions?

*Answer* — Salary reductions by employees allowing employee contributions on a before-tax basis are allowed only in (1) a profit sharing (Section 401(k) type) plan, (2) a salary reduction SEP (simplified employee pension), which had to be adopted before 1997—see Chapter 21, (3) a SIMPLE IRA, see Chapter 20, or (4) a Section 403(b) tax deferred annuity plan (tax-exempt employers only). Thus, this kind of funding for a money purchase plan is not available except for a plan "grandfathered" under pre-1974 law.

However, money purchase plans can allow after-tax contributions by employees to increase account balances (permitting greater tax-sheltered investment accumulation) and ultimate retirement benefits. Such after-tax contribution provisions must meet the administratively complex nondiscrimination rules of Code section 401(m). (These are discussed in Chapter 18.) As a result of these rules, after-tax contribution provisions in money purchase plans are less common than in the past.

## FOOTNOTES

1. The employer's deduction to a money purchase pension plan cannot exceed the Section 415 annual additions limit for a defined contribution plan. IRC Section 404(j)(1). For years beginning in 2003, this 415 limit is the lesser of (a) $40,000, or (b) 100% of compensation. IRC Section 415(c).
2. IRC Sec. 415(c).
3. IRC Section 401(a)(17).
4. See Treas. Reg. §1.401(a)(4)-2.
5. See Rev. Rul. 69-277, 1969-1 CB 116; Rev. Rul. 74-417, 1974-2 CB 131. If money purchase plan assets are "spun-off" to a profit sharing plan, the accounts in the new plan must retain the money purchase restrictions on in-service distributions. However, if the money purchase accounts are "rolled over" to a profit sharing plan, the money purchase plan in-service restrictions no longer apply. Rev. Rul. 94-76, 1994-2 CB 46.
6. IRC Section 404(a).
7. IRC Section 401(a)(27)(B).
8. IRC Section 404(a)(3)(A)(v).
9. IRC Section 402(a).
10. See IRC Sec. 415(c); Notice 2002-71, 2002-45 IRB 830.
11. IRC Section 415(c)(2).
12. IRC Sections 412(a), 412(h).
13. IRC Section 4971.

# Chapter 15

# NONQUALIFIED DEFERRED COMPENSATION

## WHAT IS IT?

A nonqualified deferred compensation plan is any employer retirement, savings, or deferred compensation plan for employees that does not meet the tax and labor law (ERISA) requirements applicable to qualified pension and profit sharing plans.

Nonqualified plans are usually used to provide retirement benefits to a select group of executives, or to provide such a select group with supplemental benefits beyond those provided in the employer's qualified retirement plans.

Nonqualified plans do not provide the same type of tax benefit as qualified plans, because, in the nonqualified plan, the employer's income tax deduction generally cannot be taken "up front." The employer must wait until the year in which the employee reports income from the deferred compensation plan to take its deduction. However, a nonqualified plan can provide tax deferral for the employee, as well as meet employer and employee compensation and financial planning objectives. Informal financing of the plan through life insurance or some other type of employer-held asset reserve can increase the security of the plan to the employee almost to the level of a qualified plan.

## WHEN IS IT INDICATED?

1. When an employer wants to provide a deferred compensation benefit to an executive or group of executives, but the cost of a qualified plan would be prohibitive because of the large number of non-executive employees who would have to be covered. A nonqualified plan is ideal for many companies that do not have or cannot afford qualified plans but want to provide key employees with retirement income.

2. When an employer wants to provide additional deferred compensation benefits to an executive who is already receiving the maximum benefits or contributions under the employer's qualified retirement plan.

3. When the business wants to provide certain key employees with tax deferred compensation under terms or conditions different from those applicable to other employees.

4. When an executive or key employee wants to use the employer to, in essence, create a forced, automatic, and relatively painless investment program that uses the employer's tax savings to "leverage" the future benefits. Since amounts paid by the employer in the future will be tax deductible, the after-tax cost of the deferred compensation will be favorable. For example, if the employer is in a combined federal and state tax bracket of 40%, it can pay $50,000 to a retired executive at a net after-tax cost of only $30,000, because its tax deduction saves it $20,000 (40% of $50,000).

5. When an employer needs to solve the "4R" (recruit, retain, reward, or retire) problem. These plans are a fundamental tool in designing executive compensation to meet these issues.

6. When a closely-held corporation wants to attract and hold nonshareholder employees. For such employees, an attractive deferred compensation package can be a substitute for the equity-based compensation packages—company stock and stock options—that these employees would expect to receive if they were employed by a publicly-held company.

## ADVANTAGES

1. The design of nonqualified plans is much more flexible than that of qualified plans. A nonqualified plan:

   - allows coverage of any group of employees or even a single employee, without any nondiscrimination requirements

   - can provide an unlimited benefit to any one employee (subject to the "reasonable compensation" requirement for deductibility)

- allows the employer to provide different benefit amounts for different employees, on different terms and conditions

2.  A nonqualified plan involves minimal IRS, ERISA, and other governmental regulatory requirements, such as reporting and disclosure, fiduciary, and funding requirements.

3.  A nonqualified plan can provide deferral of taxes to employees (but the employer's deduction is also deferred). The advantage of deferral is always debated when income tax rates are relatively low and there is some expectation of higher rates in the future. However, if dollars otherwise paid currently in taxes can be put to work over the period of deferral, planners can show advantages in nonqualified plans, even if future tax rates are higher.

4.  Historically, the tradeoff in current federal corporate rate and individual rates for the highest income levels has favored deferred compensation, since the marginal individual rate (38.6% in 2002)[1] was greater the that marginal corporate rate (35%). For example, if an individual paid a $10,000 annual premium for personally owned life insurance, the before-tax cost to that individual was $16,287 ($10,000 multiplied by $1/(1-.386)$). If the corporation paid that premium (for example, in a nonqualified deferred compensation plan financed by corporate-owned life insurance) for the same individual, the before-tax cost was $15,385 ($10,000 multiplied by $1/(1-.35)$). While not every situation works out exactly this way, these marginal rates favored corporate financing of deferred compensation, rather than cash bonuses.

5.  A nonqualified plan can be used by an employer as a form of "golden handcuffs" that help to bind the employee to the company. Since the qualified plan vesting rules do not apply if the plan is properly designed (as discussed below), the plan can provide forfeiture of benefits according to almost any vesting schedule the employer desires and for almost any contingency, such as terminating employment before retirement, misconduct, or going to work for a competitor.

6.  Although the plan generally involves only the employer's unsecured promise to pay benefits, security to the executive can be provided through informal financing arrangements, such as corporate-owned life insurance (COLI) or a "rabbi trust" (defined below).

7.  Assets set aside in some types of informal financing arrangements are available to use for corporate purposes at all times.

## DISADVANTAGES

1.  The employer's tax deduction is generally not available for the year in which compensation is earned; it must be deferred until the year in which income is taxable to the employee. This can be a substantial period of time—10, 20, or even 30 or more years in the future.

2.  From the executive's point of view, the principal problem is lack of security as a result of depending only on the employer's unsecured promise to pay. In addition, most of the protections of federal tax and labor law (ERISA) that apply to qualified plans—for example the vesting, fiduciary, and funding requirements—are not applicable to the typical nonqualified plan.

3.  While accounting treatment is not entirely clear (see Appendix E), some disclosure of executive nonqualified plans on financial statements may be required. This would reduce the confidentiality of the arrangement, which could be considered undesirable by both employer and employee.

4.  Not all employers are equally suited to take advantage of nonqualified plans.

    - Because of their pass-through tax structure, S corporations and partnerships cannot take full advantage of nonqualified plans.

    - The employer must be one that is likely to last long enough to make the payments promised under the plan. Although funds can be set aside to provide payments even if the employer disappears, the full tax benefits of the plan cannot be provided unless the employer exists at the time of payment, so it can take its tax deduction. Many closely-held businesses, family businesses, and professional corporations do not meet this criterion.

    - Special problems exist when tax-exempt or governmental organizations enter into nonqualified plans. See Chapter 11.

## OBJECTIVES IN PLAN DESIGN

Through its considerable flexibility, a nonqualified deferred compensation plan can help both the employer and the employee achieve their planning objectives. The plan should be designed to achieve these objectives to the maximum extent possible. Figure 15.1 provides a design worksheet that can be used to illustrate the design process.

### Employer Objectives

Employers usually adopt nonqualified deferred compensation plans to provide an incentive to hire key employees, to keep key employees, and to provide performance incentives—in other words, the typical employer compensation policy objectives that apply to other forms of compensation planning.

Plans reflecting employer objectives will typically consider the following types of design:

- Eligibility will be confined to key executives or technical employees that the employer wants to recruit and keep.

- Plan eligibility can be part of a predetermined company policy or the plan can simply be adopted for specific individuals as the need arises.

- Performance incentive features will be included. The features may include benefits or contributions based on salary, increases if specific profits or sales goals are achieved, or benefits related to the value of the employer's stock.

- Termination of employment will typically cause loss or forfeiture of benefits, particularly for terminations followed by undesirable conduct, such as competing with the employer.

- The plan often will not provide immediate vesting of benefits, but vesting will occur over a period of time in order to retain employees.

- It is generally not in the employer's interest to fund the plan in advance or set aside funds for the plan prior to the commencement of benefit payments.

### Employee Objectives

An employee's personal financial planning objective is primarily to obtain additional forms of compensation for which income tax is deferred as long as possible, preferably until the money is actually received. Usually it is only highly compensated employees who wish to (or can afford to) defer compensation to a substantial extent, since only they have enough discretionary income to support substantial saving. From the employee's point of view, the tax deferral, and therefore the compounding of dollars that otherwise would be paid currently in taxes, is a major benefit of the plan. In addition, it is possible that plan benefits may be paid when the employee is in a lower marginal tax bracket. (However, due to frequent changes in the tax laws, this factor is difficult to predict.)

An employee who has enough bargaining power to influence the design of a nonqualified deferred compensation plan will favor the following types of provisions:

- Benefit certainty is usually more important than incentive provisions; employees rarely seek contingent features unless the company is definitely growing and the employee wants a benefit based on company growth.

- Employees will want a benefit that is immediately 100% vested without forfeiture provisions, for cause or otherwise.

- Employees like to have funds available for various purposes during employment to the extent possible under the tax law ( see "Withdrawals During Employment" below).

- Concern for benefit security is significant, and employees will want to explore some of the financing (informal funding) arrangements described later, such as corporate-owned life insurance (COLI), rabbi trusts, or surety bonds.

### Types of Benefit and Contribution Formulas

The benefit formula is the basic starting point in designing or explaining a nonqualified deferred compensation plan. Executives covered under the plan want to know first what benefits the plan provides, rather than methods of financing those benefits, such as corporate-owned life insurance (COLI) arrangements. Benefit formula design is almost wide open for nonqualified deferred compensation plans; great flexibility is possible and formulas can be designed for the specific needs of specific employees. Some common benefit formula approaches include:

- *Salary Continuation Formula.* Salary continuation generally refers to a type of nonelective nonqualified deferred compensation plan that provides a specified deferred amount payable in the future. A salary continuation plan provides benefits in addition to other benefits provided under other plans and requires no reduction in the covered employee's salary. *For example*: The contract might provide: "At retirement, disability, or death, the XYZ Corporation will pay you or your designated beneficiary $50,000 a year for 10 years starting at age 65."

  A salary continuation formula generally uses a defined benefit type of formula to calculate the benefit amount, but the formula is not subject to the limitations applicable to qualified defined benefit plans, such as the limitation on benefits, or the amount of salary used in the formula. A nonqualified salary continuation plan for a selected group of executives with similar formulas for the entire group is sometimes referred to as a "SERP" (for "supplemental executive retirement plan").

- *Salary Reduction Formula.* A salary reduction formula involves an elective deferral of a specified amount of the compensation that the employee would have otherwise received. The employer contribution under this type of plan can be in the form of a "bonus," without actual reduction of salary. The plan is somewhat similar to a defined contribution type of qualified plan, although the qualified plan restrictions do not apply.

  The amount deferred each year under a salary reduction formula is generally credited to the employee's "account" under the plan. When benefits are due, the amount accumulated in this account determines the amount of payments. Payment is generally in the form of a lump sum, but the account balance can also be paid in an equivalent stream of periodic payments.

  The salary reduction formula generally provides a method by which earnings on the account are credited. These earnings credits can be based upon a specified interest rate, or an external standard, such as Moody's Bond Index, the federal rate or other indexed rate, or the rate of earnings on specified assets.[2]

  In a salary reduction arrangement, the employer has no obligation to actually set assets aside. The participant's account can be purely an accounting concept existing only on paper. In that case, when payment becomes due, the employer pays it from its current assets. This points out the fact that all nonqualified deferred compensation plans are essentially based only on the employer's contractual obligation to pay benefits. However, employees may seek greater security, as discussed below under "Financing Approaches."

- *Excess benefit plan.* Under ERISA section 4(b)(5), an excess benefit plan that is unfunded is not subject to Title I of ERISA (which contains the reporting and disclosure, participation, vesting, funding, and fiduciary responsibility provisions).[3]

  Excess benefit plans are those designed to provide benefits only for executives whose annual projected qualified plan benefits are limited under the dollar limits of Code section 415 (see Chapter 25). An excess benefit plan makes up the difference between the percentage of pay that top executives are allowed under Section 415 and that which rank and file employees are allowed. In other words, highly compensated employees receive the difference between the amounts payable under their qualified plan and the amount they would have received if there were no benefit limitations under Code section 415.

  For some time, it was believed that an excess benefit plan could not restore benefits lost under the Code section 401(a)(17) limitation on compensation ($200,000 in 2003, as indexed),[4] which would limit the usefulness of this type of plan.[5]

  Even if the excess benefit formula is not specifically based upon the Section 401(a)(17) compensation limitation, many nonqualified plan benefit formulas are related to qualified plan formulas and are designed to "make the executive whole"—that is, to provide an amount that makes up the difference between the benefit that the executive would have received under the employer's qualified plans without the limitations of either Section 415 or Section 401(a)(17) and the amount actually received.

- *Stock appreciation rights (SARs) and phantom stock formulas.* The benefit formula in the plan can be determined on the basis of the value of a specified number of shares of employer stock, or contributions to a salary-reduction formula can be stated in terms of shares of employer stock rather than cash.

Generally, no actual shares are set aside, nor are shares of stock necessarily actually distributed. The value of employer stock simply is the measure by which the benefits are valued. Obviously, this type of formula provides a substantial incentive for the executive, and, from the employer viewpoint, matches the size of benefits with company success.

No firm distinction between these two types of benefit formulas has been established among benefits practitioners. However, a phantom stock benefit generally refers to a plan formula based upon an amount of shares of stock, established for an employee when the plan is adopted, with a provision that the employee receives the actual shares or equivalent cash at the date of payment. An SAR (stock appreciation right) formula provides that the employee's future benefits are to be determined by a formula based on the appreciation value of the company's stock over the period between adoption of the plan and the date of payment.

*Form of Benefits.* Nonqualified deferred compensation plans usually provide payments at retirement in a lump sum or a series of annual payments. Life annuities or joint and survivor annuities for the participant and spouse can also be provided. Since the elaborate restrictions on qualified plan payouts do not apply, considerable design flexibility is available.

Payout options must avoid the triggering of the constructive receipt doctrine—that is, the taxation of benefits before they are actually received by the employee. Constructive receipt problems are discussed further in "Tax Implications," below.

## Withdrawals During Employment

Employees recognize that any kind of deferred compensation plan holds money that they could have received earlier in cash. Thus, certainty of receipt is a very important consideration. Similarly, employees like plan provisions that permit them to make use of the deferred funds when they need them. However, if a deferred compensation plan simply allowed the participant to withdraw from the plan at any time without restriction, the plan would fail to defer income taxes under the doctrine of constructive receipt, as discussed below.

Withdrawals must be subject to a restriction or limitation that prevents them from being currently available within the constructive receipt doctrine. Some withdrawal provisions that are commonly used include:

- *Penalty or "haircut" provisions.* This type of provision allows withdrawal for a wide range of reasons stated in the plan, or even upon the mere request of the participant, but there is a penalty for withdrawing before termination of employment, death, disability, or retirement. Typical penalties are based on a percentage of the withdrawal (for example, if the participant requests $10,000, he receives $10,000 less a stated percentage penalty, such as 6%).

- *Suspension of participation provision.* Another typical withdrawal provision suspends the employee's participation in the plan for a period (such as six months) after withdrawing money from the plan.

- *Hardship withdrawal provision.* Another way to avoid constructive receipt is to condition withdrawals upon events that are not within the employee's control. In effect, death and disability provisions are examples of this approach. Withdrawals may also be conditioned on other specific hardships, such as financial emergencies, health matters, purchase of a house, educational costs for family members, and the like. The specific hardship withdrawal rules for Section 401(k) plans need not be followed in a nonqualified plan. The withdrawal provision can be quite broad, as long as it provides a significant limitation or restriction on the employee's ability to gain access to the plan funds. It is very helpful if the plan gives the final decision concerning the withdrawal to a person or committee that is not controlled by the employee.[6]

There are no firm guidelines in the law on what penalties are sufficient; plan designers may wish to ask for an IRS ruling on questionable proposed provisions.

## Termination of Employment

If the plan emphasizes employer objectives, termination provisions will be designed to maximize incentive features and noncompetition and similar provisions. At the extreme, an employer-instituted plan may even provide a complete forfeiture of nonqualified benefits if the employee terminates employment before retirement.

Most employer-instituted plans will at least have a vesting schedule under which benefits do not become vested until a specified number of years of service has been attained. Graduated vesting can also be used. As discussed below, if the plan is unfunded, the ERISA vesting provisions generally do not apply and any type of vesting schedule generally can be used.

If an executive's termination of employment results from disability, special benefits may be provided, particularly if the employee has some bargaining power in designing the plan. An employee will generally want benefits paid immediately upon disability. For this purpose, the employee will also want to use a definition of disability that is somewhat less restrictive than the "total and permanent" disability required for social security disability benefits. A typical disability provision based on employee objectives would provide for disability payments if the employee is no longer able to continue working in his specific profession or executive position. Disability determinations can be shifted to a third party such as an insurer, or a physician chosen by the employer and employee, in order to minimize possible disputes.

## Funded versus Unfunded Plans

In the employee benefit area, the term *funded plan* has a very specialized meaning. In the tax sense, a plan is formally funded if the employer has set aside money or property to pay plan benefits through some means that restricts access to the fund by the employer's creditors— for example, setting assets aside in an irrevocable trust for the exclusive benefit of employees covered under the plan.[7] For ERISA purposes, the Department of Labor (the DOL) has not specifically endorsed this clear-cut definition of funding, but for plans that benefit a select group of management or highly compensated employees, if the plan is unfunded for tax purposes, it probably will be regarded as unfunded for ERISA purposes.[8]

Assets used to informally fund or "finance" the employer's obligation under a nonqualified plan can, and almost always should, be set aside, but if this fund is accessible by the employer's creditors, providing no explicit security to the employee ahead of other employer creditors, the plan is deemed to be unfunded for tax purposes. As indicated above, although the issue is not completely clear, such an arrangement is probably also an unfunded one for ERISA purposes.[9]

Most nonqualified deferred compensation plans are unfunded because of significant tax and ERISA considerations:

- In a funded plan, amounts in the fund are taxable to the employee at the time the employee's rights to the fund become "substantially vested."[10] As discussed in Chapter 49, under the rules of Code section 83, substantial vesting can occur before funds are actually received by the employee.

- Funded plans are generally subject to the ERISA vesting and fiduciary requirements, which create design inflexibility.[11] Under the ERISA vesting rules, the plan must have a vesting schedule that is at least as fast as either the 5-year schedule (no vesting up to five years of service, 100% vesting after five years) or the 3-year to 7-year schedule:

| Years of Service | Vested Percentage |
|---|---|
| 3 | 20% |
| 4 | 40% |
| 5 | 60% |
| 6 | 80% |
| 7 or more | 100% |

The vesting and fiduciary rules for funded nonqualified plans are the same as those for qualified plans, as discussed in Chapter 25.[12]

## Financing Approaches

Since almost all nonqualified deferred compensation plans are unfunded in the formal sense, employees initiating deferred compensation arrangements are likely to seek ways to increase benefit security. The following approaches are commonly used:

- *Reserve account maintained by employer.* The employer maintains an actual account, invested in securities of various types. There is no trust. Funds are fully accessible to the employer and its creditors. The plan is considered unfunded for tax and ERISA purposes.

- *Employer reserve account with employee investment direction.* With this variation, the employee obtains greater security by having the right to "direct" (select) investments in the account. This right must be limited to a choice of broad types of investment (equity, bonds, family of mutual funds, etc.); the ability to choose specific investments may lead to constructive receipt by the employee.[13] Also, the investment direction by the participant must be advisory only and not binding.[14]

- *Corporate-owned life insurance.* Life insurance policies on the employee's life, owned by and payable to the employer corporation, can provide financing for the employer's obligation under nonqualified deferred compensation plans. With life insurance financing, the plan can provide a substantial death benefit, even in the early years of the plan. This is of significant value to younger employees.

- *Rabbi trust.* A rabbi trust is a trust set up to hold property used for financing a deferred compensation plan, where the funds set aside are subject to the employer's creditors. The IRS has ruled that trusts designed this way do not constitute formal funding in the tax sense. The DOL has a working premise that rabbi trusts meeting with the approval of the IRS will not cause excess benefit plans or top-hat plans to be funded for ERISA purposes.[15] These trusts are referred to as "rabbi trusts" because an early IRS letter ruling involved an arrangement between a rabbi and the employing congregation. The design of rabbi trusts is discussed in the "Questions and Answers," below.

- *Third-party guarantees.* In these arrangements, there is a guarantee from a third party to pay the employee if the employer defaults. The guarantor may be an insurance company or other entity. On occasion, third-party guarantees have received favorable tax treatment.[16] But the law in this area is not entirely clear. Employer involvement raises the possibility that the guarantee will cause the plan to be deemed formally funded for tax purposes.[17] However, it appears that if the employee, independently of the employer, obtains a third-party guarantee, the IRS will not necessarily view the plan as formally funded.[18]

## TAX IMPLICATIONS

### Constructive Receipt

Under the constructive receipt doctrine (Code section 451), an amount is treated as received for income tax purposes, even if it is not actually received, if it is "credited to the employee's account, set aside, or otherwise made available."

Constructive receipt does not occur if the employee's control over the receipt is subject to a "substantial limitation or restriction." A requirement of a passage of time until money can be received by the employee is usually considered a substantial limitation or restriction.[19] In a typical deferred compensation plan, for example, if the plan provides that an amount is not payable for five years or not payable until the employee terminates employment or retires, it will not be constructively received before that time.

The view of the IRS is that an agreement to defer compensation generally must be made before the compensation is earned. In order to defer compensation *after* services have already been performed, the IRS view is that the plan must have a substantial risk of forfeiture of the benefits.[20]

Plan distribution provisions must also be designed to avoid constructive receipt. For example, if the plan provides for distribution in 10 equal annual installments, and if the employee can elect, at any time, to accelerate payments, then, under the constructive receipt doctrine, the employee would have to include in income each year the amount that the employee could have elected to receive. As another example, if the plan provides for a payout in 10 annual installments with an election at any time to spread payments out further, the constructive receipt doctrine may require taxation under the original 10 payment schedule, regardless of any election to further defer payments, unless the plan imposes a substantial risk of forfeiture.[21] A typical forfeiture provision found in nonqualified plan distribution provisions of this type is a requirement that the employee be available for consulting and refrain from competing with the employer. As discussed in Chapter 49, the question of whether this constitutes a substantial risk of forfeiture depends on the specific facts and circumstances of the situation.

### Economic Benefit

A compensation arrangement that provides a current "economic benefit" to an employee can result in current taxation, even though the employee has no current right to receive cash or property. For example, suppose that an employee is covered under a funded nonqualified deferred compensation plan that has an irrevocable trust for the benefit of the employee. Under the economic benefit doctrine, the employee will be taxed as soon as the employee is vested in contributions made to the fund, even though the employee does not, at that time, have a right to withdraw cash.[22] This factor makes funded plans extremely unattractive.

**Figure 15.1**
**(pg. 1)**

## NONQUALIFIED DEFERRED COMPENSATION

Design Worksheet

A.  EMPLOYER AND EMPLOYEE DATA

Employer _____

Employer's address_____

_____

_____ Zip _____

Telephone No. (    ) _____

Employer I.D. No. _____

S corporation election? Yes _____ No _____

Date of S election _____

Accounting year _____

Company contact (name and title) _____

Telephone No. (    ) _____


Employee _____

Title _____

Employee address_____

_____ Zip _____

Telephone No. (    ) _____

Social Security No. _____

Percent ownership of employer _____

Effective date of deferred compensation arrangement _____


B.  PLAN FORMULA

**Formula type** (check)

_____  Salary reduction

_____  Salary continuation

_____  Other _____

**Figure 15.1**
**(pg. 2)**

**Salary reduction formula** (if applicable)

Reduction amount _____

Per (month, year, other) _____

Date of initial election _____

Annual election date thereafter _____

Other election date (specify) _____

Company contribution, if any _____

Conditions on company contribution _____

Company guarantee of interest on account balance (check one)

_____ fixed rate of _____ percent

_____ rate based on

_____ adjusted (how often)_____

**Salary continuation formula** (if applicable)

Benefits payable at (check)

_____ age 65

_____ other specified age _____

Benefit formula

_____ percent of compensation monthly

(times years of service)(up to _____ years)

Compensation means

_____ Annual compensation over highest _____ years

_____ Other (specify) _____

_____

Offset for other benefits

_____percent of social security benefits actually received

_____percent of qualified retirement plan benefits

Other (describe — e.g., workers compensation, disability)

_____

_____

**Benefit payable at termination of employment prior to retirement**

_____ No benefit

_____ Account balance

_____ Vested accrued benefit determined as follows _____

_____

_____

**Figure 15.1**
**(pg. 3)**

C.   VESTING

**Vesting Schedule**

_____      Immediate 100 percent vesting

_____      Graduated schedule (specify) _____

_____

**Forfeiture provisions**

_____      None

_____      Forfeiture for _____

_____

D.   DISABILITY BENEFIT

_____      Disability treated like other termination of employment

or

_____      Special disability provisions

           _____      Special benefit computation (specify)_____

           _____

           _____      Service continues to accrue for purposes of this plan

Definition of disability _____

_____

E.   BENEFIT PAYMENT

Options

_____      Lump sum (actuarially equivalent to _____)

_____      Periodic payment options (specify) _____

_____

Optional forms must be elected before _____

_____

After benefits commence, payment option (cannot be changed) (can be changed or modified) (annually)

(other _____) by election prior to _____

After benefits commence, future benefits are forfeited if _____

_____

**Figure 15.1**
**(pg. 4)**

F.    DEATH BENEFITS

_____    Benefits forfeited at death

_____    Death benefit payable to named beneficiary or estate if no named beneficiary

_____    Other_____

_____

**Amount of Benefit**

_____    Amount that would have been paid to employee at termination of employment

_____    Face amount of insurance contracts (describe contracts) _____

_____

_____    Other    _____

_____

_____

**Payment Form**

_____    Lump sum only

_____    Beneficiary has same options employee would have had if terminated employment on date of death.

Describe how beneficiary makes elections _____

_____

_____    Other    _____

_____

G.    FINANCING

_____    Formal funding (specify) _____

_____

_____    Informal financing

_____    Insurance contracts (specify) _____

_____

_____    Rabbi trust (describe) _____

_____

_____    Third party guarantees, surety bonds, etc.

(describe)_____

_____

_____

_____    No financing arrangement

The economic benefit doctrine does not generally affect unfunded plans, and, as discussed earlier, almost all nonqualified deferred compensation plans are unfunded. It is possible that some incidental benefits in the plan could create an economic benefit. This issue has sometimes been raised where the plan includes an insured death benefit. Currently, however, the IRS does not claim that there is an economic benefit resulting from the insured death benefit in a properly designed nonqualified plan.

## Income Taxation of Benefits and Contributions

Employees must pay ordinary income tax on benefits from unfunded nonqualified deferred compensation plans in the first year in which the benefit is actually or constructively received.

Death benefits from nonqualified plans that are payable to a beneficiary are taxable as income in respect of a decedent to the recipient.[23]

## Social Security (FICA) Taxes

Amounts deferred under nonqualified deferred compensation plans are not subject to social security taxes until the year in which the employee no longer has any substantial risk of forfeiting the amount, provided the amounts are reasonably ascertainable.[24] In other words, as soon as the covered executive cannot lose his interest in the plan, he will be subject to social security taxes. Conceivably, this could be earlier than the year of actual receipt.

For example, if the plan provides that benefits are payable at retirement, but the benefits become vested five years after they are earned, then the amounts deferred will enter into the social security tax base five years after they are earned. Note that this is neither the year in which they are earned nor the year they are paid, a circumstance that complicates tax compliance in this situation.

Although part of the social security taxable wage base — the OASDI part — has an annual upper limit ($87,000 for 2003; $89,400 for 2002), the Medicare hospital insurance portion is unlimited. The Medicare tax rate is 1.45% for the employer and the same rate for the employee. For higher paid executives, the inclusion of deferred compensation in the wage base during a year of active employment will not result in additional OASDI

taxes if the executive's current (nondeferred) compensation is more than the OASDI wage base, but additional Medicare taxes will be payable. This factor must be taken into account in designing nonqualified deferred compensation plans.

## Federal Estate Tax Treatment

The amount of any death benefit payable to a beneficiary under a nonqualified deferred compensation plan is generally included in the deceased employee's estate for federal estate tax purposes, at its then present value. In other words, the commuted value of payments made to the employee's beneficiary will be included in the employee's gross estate. But such payments will be considered "income in respect of a decedent" (Code section 691 income), and an income tax deduction will be allocated to the recipient of that income for the additional estate tax the inclusion generated. To the extent that payments are made to the employee's spouse in a qualifying manner, the unlimited marital deduction will eliminate any federal estate tax.

A plan can be designed so that the decedent did not have a right to receive the benefit prior to death. A plan designed to provide only death benefits is referred to as a death benefit only (DBO) plan. For employees potentially liable for substantial federal estate taxes, the DBO plan may be an appropriate design. DBO plans are covered in Chapter 32.

## Taxation of the Employer

For a nonqualified deferred compensation plan, the employer does not receive a tax deduction until its tax year that includes the year in which the compensation is includable in the employee's taxable income.[25] If the plan is unfunded, the year of inclusion is the year in which the compensation is actually or constructively received. For a formally funded plan, compensation is included in income in the year in which it becomes substantially vested, as discussed earlier.

Payments under a deferred compensation plan, like other forms of compensation, are not deductible unless the amounts meet the reasonableness test discussed in Chapter 30. The same issues can arise with respect to deferred compensation as with regular cash compensation or bonus arrangements.

The reasonableness issue is raised by the IRS in the year in which an employer attempts to take a deduction.

For nonqualified deferred compensation, this is generally the year in which the employee includes the amount in income—that is, a year that is later than the year in which the services were rendered. Compensation can be deemed reasonable on the basis of prior service;[26] however, it is possible that a combination of deferred compensation and current compensation received in a given year could raise reasonableness issues, particularly if the deferred amount is very large.

Note that publicly held corporations generally cannot deduct compensation in excess of $1 million per tax year to certain top-level executives (see Chapter 30).[27]

If assets are set aside in a reserve used to informally finance the employer's obligation under the plan, income on these assets is currently taxable to the employer. Consequently, the use of assets that provide a deferral of taxation can be advantageous. Life insurance policies are often used because their cash value build-up from year to year is not currently taxed. Death proceeds from the policy are also free of tax, except for a possible alternative minimum tax (AMT) liability (see Chapter 42 for discussion).

If assets used to finance the plan are held in a rabbi trust, the employer's tax consequences are much the same as if assets were held directly by the employer. For tax purposes, the rabbi trust is a "grantor trust." A grantor trust's income, deductions, and tax credits are attributed to the grantor (here, the employer) for tax purposes.

## ERISA REQUIREMENTS

Two types of nonqualified deferred compensation plans are eligible for at least partial exemptions from the ERISA requirements. The first exemption is for an unfunded excess benefit plan. This type of nonqualified deferred compensation plan, designed solely to supplement the qualified retirement benefits limited in amount by Code section 415, is not subject to any ERISA requirements.[28] As discussed above, this exemption is rarely available.

The most important ERISA exemption involves a type of plan often referred to as a "top-hat" plan. Under ERISA, if a nonqualified plan is unfunded and maintained by an employer primarily for the purpose of providing deferred compensation for a "select group of management or highly compensated employees," the plan is exempt from all provisions of ERISA, except for the reporting and disclosure requirements, and ERISA's

administrative and enforcement provisions. Top-hat plans can satisfy the reporting and disclosure requirements by providing plan documents, upon request, to the Department of Labor, and by filing a simple, one time statement about the arrangement with the Department of Labor.[29] Figure 15.2 is an example of this simple reporting statement.

The term "highly compensated," for this purpose, is not as clearly defined as it is for qualified and other plans (see Chapter 25). The Department of Labor is responsible for interpreting this provision of ERISA and it has not yet issued clear guidelines.[30] However, a plan that covers only a few highly paid executives will probably meet this ERISA exemption.

If a plan does not meet one of these ERISA exemptions, it must generally comply with most of the ERISA provisions applicable to qualified pension plans, including the vesting, fiduciary, minimum funding, and reporting and disclosure provisions.

As a result of these ERISA aspects, almost all nonqualified deferred compensation plans are limited to management or highly compensated employees and are formally unfunded, even though they may utilize some informal financing methods as discussed earlier.

Finally, the courts have sometimes held that a nonqualified deferred compensation plan was not subject to ERISA because it was not a "plan" within the meaning of ERISA. This ERISA exemption has been generally held to apply to plans covering one or only a few employees, where there was no "ongoing administrative scheme" to maintain the plan.[31] Unless the situation is nearly identical to reported court cases, this exemption is not very practical to rely upon, because it is based on particular facts found by courts in each case, and the result of future court proceedings cannot be easily predicted.

## WHERE CAN I FIND OUT MORE ABOUT IT?

1.  Graduate Course: Executive Compensation (GS 842), The American College, Bryn Mawr, PA.

2.  Leimberg et al., *The Tools and Techniques of Estate Planning*, 11th ed., Cincinnati, OH: The National Underwriter Co., 1998.

3.  Brody, Lawrence and Richey, Louis, *Comprehensive Deferred Compensation*, 3d ed., Cincinnati, OH: The National Underwriter Co., 1997.

**Figure 15.2**

### ALTERNATIVE REPORTING AND DISCLOSURE STATEMENT
### FOR UNFUNDED NONQUALIFIED DEFERRED COMPENSATION PLANS
### FOR CERTAIN SELECTED EMPLOYEES

To:  Top Hat Plan Exemption
Pension and Welfare Benefits Administration
Room N-5644
U.S. Department of Labor
200 Constitution Avenue, N.W.
Washington, D.C. 20210

In compliance with the requirements of the alternative method of reporting and disclosure under Part 1 of Title I of the Employee Retirement Income Security Act of 1974 for unfunded or insured pension plans for a select group of management or highly compensated employees, specified in Department of Labor Regulations, 29 C.F.R. Sec. 2520.104-23, the following information is provided by the undersigned employer.

Name and Address of Employer: _____

_____

_____

Employer Identification Number:_____

(Name of employer) maintains a plan (or plans) primarily for the purpose of providing deferred compensation for a select group of management or highly compensated employees.

Number of Plans and Participants in Each Plan:

_____ Plan covering _____ employees (or)

_____ Plans covering _____, _____, and

_____ employees; respectively

Dated _____, 20____

(Name of Employer)

By _____
    Plan Administrator

4. Brody, Lawrence, Floridis, Ronald and Richey, Louis, *Comprehensive Split Dollar*, 4th ed., Cincinnati, OH, The National Underwriter Co., 1997, supplemented by, The Brody Richey Split Dollar Report: Making Sense of Notice 2001-10, 2001.

## QUESTIONS AND ANSWERS

**Question** — How is life insurance used to finance an employer's obligation under a nonqualified deferred compensation plan?

*Answer* — Life insurance can be used in many ways, much like any other asset set aside to finance the plan. Life insurance has several advantages, such as its tax-free build-up of cash values and the availability of substantial death benefits, even in the early years of the plan.

Because of the particular advantages of life insurance, many deferred compensation plans are designed specifically to make use of life insurance financing.

---

*Example.* Suppose Crood Petroleum Corporation enters into a deferred compensation agreement with its executive, Frank Furness, under which Frank agrees to defer an anticipated $10,000 annual salary increase in return for the following specified benefits: (1) if Frank dies before retirement, $10,000 a year will be paid to his widow for a period equal to the number of years he was covered under the plan; and (2) if Frank remains employed by Crood until retirement at age 65, he will receive $20,000 per year for ten years, in addition to other company retirement benefits.

---

Frank's deferred $10,000 per year of compensation would have had an after-tax cost of $6,500 to the corporation if paid currently (assuming a 35% marginal corporate tax bracket). The corporation can use this $6,500 instead to finance Frank's benefits by purchasing a life insurance policy on Frank's life. If Frank is age 45, about $150,000 of cash value insurance (paid up at 65) can be purchased with this $6,500 annually. The corporation would be both the policyowner and the policy beneficiary and would pay the premiums, which would be nondeductible. (The tax implications of corporate-owned insurance are discussed in detail in Chapter 42.)

If Frank died at age 50, the corporation would receive approximately $150,000 of tax free policy proceeds (in addition to policy dividends and perhaps interest, but reduced by any corporate AMT liability). It would have paid $32,500 in premiums over the past five years. It is obligated to pay a total of $50,000 ($10,000 a year for five years) to Frank's widow, but since these payments are deductible, their after-tax cost is only $32,500 (65% of $50,000). This results in a net gain to the corporation of approximately $85,000 ($150,000 insurance proceeds less $32,500 of premiums and less $32,500 of after-tax cost of benefit payments). (This example does not take into account the time value of money, but to do so does not change the result significantly, since the corporation's loss of the use of five annual premium payments is balanced by being reimbursed in advance for the five years of benefit payments due Frank's widow.)

If Frank had retired before his death, policy cash values and the corporation's current cash flow could be used to finance Frank's annual benefit payments. However, a better solution in most cases is to keep the policy intact and use current corporate cash to make benefit payments. Then, when the employee dies, policy proceeds will reimburse the employer and often add to the company's surplus. This approach is often referred to as "cost recovery" nonqualified deferred compensation.

The employer should purchase enough insurance to offset any corporate AMT liability on the proceeds. Although the AMT should be no more than about 15% of policy proceeds, to be on the safe side it is suggested that the employer obtain about 17% or 18% more than the amount targeted to meet nonqualified deferred compensation needs.

**Question** — When should a benefit planner recommend using a rabbi trust?

*Answer* — Factors indicating that a rabbi trust might be advantageous include (1) a fear that the ownership or management of the business might change before deferred compensation benefits are paid; (2) a situation where new management might be hostile to the key employee in the future and fail to honor its contractual obligation to pay deferred compensation; and (3) situations where litigation to enforce payment of deferred compensation in the future would likely be too costly to be practical.

**Question** — What costs or risks are involved in the use of a rabbi trust-type of financing arrangement for deferred compensation?

*Answer* — Costs and risks include: (1) the legal and administrative costs of setting up the rabbi trust agreement in a manner that will meet IRS requirements; (2) the loss of the use of plan assets by the employer corporation (since they must be put in trust for the employee) except in bankruptcy or liquidation; (3) the rate of return on plan assets is limited by trust investments (assets could yield a higher return if invested in the employer's business); and (4) from the employee's standpoint, the employee is not protected against the employer's insolvency.

**Question** — What provisions should (or should not) be included in a "rabbi trust" agreement?

*Answer* — A rabbi trust can be valid without obtaining a specific IRS ruling. However, most clients will either want to obtain a ruling or, at a minimum, will want to use a form of rabbi trust that conforms with IRS' known ruling requirements.

Revenue Procedures 92-64 and 92-65, 1992-2 CB 422 and 428, contain the IRS' ruling position for rabbi trusts. The IRS will generally rule on a nonqualified deferred compensation arrangement using a rabbi trust *only* if the IRS' model rabbi trust (reproduced at the end of this chapter) is used. If a rabbi trust does not conform with the model, a ruling will be issued only in "rare and unusual circumstances."

The model trust generally conforms with IRS guidelines already well-known from its prior private letter rulings. Optional paragraphs are provided to allow some degree of customization. The model contains some relatively favorable provisions. For example, it allows the use of "springing" irrevocability—that is, a triggering event, like a change of ownership of the employer, can cause the trust to become irrevocable or can obligate the employer to make an irrevocable contribution sufficient to cover its obligations as of the time of the triggering event. Also, the model permits the rabbi trust to own employer stock. However, the model does not contain trigger provisions to allow acceleration of payments if the employer moves toward insolvency; the employee's rights must never be better than those of the employer's general, unsecured creditors. The model rabbi trust also has no

provision giving employees investment authority over rabbi trust assets.

While it is somewhat puzzling in light of the IRS' claim that it will not rule on plans using a rabbi trust other than the model trust, Revenue Procedure 92-64 allows the employer to add additional text to the model trust as long as that additional language is not inconsistent with the model language. How much latitude this provides to employers is not clear.

**Question** — Can a corporation provide a nonqualified deferred compensation plan to an executive who is a controlling shareholder (more than 50%) in the corporation?

*Answer* — In principle, a deferred compensation arrangement can be provided for a controlling shareholder under the rules discussed in this chapter. However, the IRS will not issue an advance private letter ruling on the tax effect of such a plan.[32] The IRS will carefully scrutinize such an arrangement because of the controlling shareholder's legal right to require corporate distributions at any time. Here are seven ways to increase the likelihood that the IRS will find that such an arrangement results in deferral of compensation and receives the tax treatment thereof:

(1) Research key cases on point. In particular, see *Casale v. Comm., Moline Properties, Inc. v. Comm.,* and Revenue Ruling 59-184,[33] which support the proposition that a corporation is a separate entity from its stockholders as long as the corporation is carrying on a valid business activity and is not a sham. See also *Carnahan v. Comm., Commerce Union Bank v. U.S., First Trust Company of St. Paul v. U.S.,* and Revenue Ruling 77-139,[34] which suggest that mere stock ownership by a plan participant is insufficient to invoke the doctrine of constructive receipt.

(2) Separate the financing of the employer's obligation from the plan itself. For example, if a life insurance policy is to be used, do not match the policy benefit to the promises made. When benefits under the financing vehicle are identical to and directly keyed into the benefits promised under the plan, the IRS will likely deny favorable tax treatment.[35] If the life insurance is maintained by the employer as key employee coverage and is kept totally separate from the agreement, there should be no constructive receipt (or economic benefit) problem.

(3) Include at least one highly compensated person other than a shareholder employee in the plan. The participation of a nonshareholder employee greatly enhances the argument that the plan is for corporate, rather than shareholder, purposes and will be of great help in justifying a corporate income tax deduction when benefits are to be paid.

(4) Create full documentation, in the corporate minutes and in the agreement itself, detailing the advantages to the corporation and the business purpose of the plan. Use wording that indicates that other successful competitive companies are providing similar supplemental compensation in their benefit programs. Incorporate wording from trade journals indicating that this type of plan is often used in the industry as a form of compensation helpful in recruiting, retaining, or retiring employees.

(5) A rabbi trust (discussed above) can be implemented to substantially limit even a controlling shareholder's ability to reach deferred amounts until the occurrence of specific events. The trust should have an independent trustee with the fiduciary responsibility, under state law, to deny access to anyone until the covered person satisfies the plan's triggering criteria (e.g., disability, death, or reaching the specified retirement age). Thus, the rabbi trust negates any "raw power" that a controlling shareholder may have.

(6) Establish an independent compensation review committee with the power to deny benefits to participants who do not meet plan criteria. The committee should actually meet and review the operation of the plan and police its provisions.

(7) Be sure the plan benefits do not fail the "HOG" test[36] by providing overgenerous benefit amounts that would not be provided to nonshareholder employees. Provide that contributions or benefits on behalf of shareholder employees cannot be proportionately greater than those provided to key employees who are not shareholders. In other words, base the plan benefit formula on a reasonable and uniform percentage of salary.

**Question** — How can an executive determine whether it is better to defer compensation and pay the taxes later or to receive the compensation currently and pay taxes at relatively low income tax rates?

*Answer* — Because of the uncertainty of future tax rates and investment return, there can never be a certain answer to this question. However, some simple computations can provide a "handle" on the question. Figure 15.3 shows the "break-even" point or the number of years of deferral required to make deferral pay, given a higher estimated rate of tax in future years.

As an example of the use of Figure 15.3, suppose an executive is currently in the 28% marginal income tax bracket. If the marginal tax rate is assumed to be 40% in future years, and investments can earn 9% before taxes, then it will take 4.14 years of deferral for deferred compensation to be better than current taxable compensation. Figure 15.3 indicates that deferred compensation is generally still a good idea for a relatively wide range of assumptions and reasonably short periods of deferral.

This computation does not take into account the effect of a corporate tax bracket that is higher than the individual employee's. This situation increases the value of a current tax deduction and accordingly decreases the overall tax value of deferral to the corporation and employee together. "Secular trust" plans, discussed in the following question, are responsive to this situation.

**Question** — What is a "secular trust?"

*Answer* — The secular trust (so named to contrast it with a rabbi trust) is an arrangement that meets two current employee objections to deferred compensation plans: the fear that tax savings will disappear because future tax rates will be very high, and the lack of security to the employee in relying on a formally unfunded plan.

A secular trust is an irrevocable trust for the exclusive benefit of the employee, with funds placed beyond the reach of the employer's creditors. Use of a secular trust is generally thought to result in taxation to the employee in the year in which assets are placed in the trust,[37] with a corresponding deduction to the employer in that year.[38] The amounts already taxed can be distributed tax free to the employee at retirement, even if tax rates have gone up considerably.[39]

The secular trust arrangement provides considerable security of benefits to the employee, as well as the ability to take advantage of currently low income tax rates. Before 1993, the top corporate tax

**Figure 15.3**

## YEARS UNTIL BREAK EVEN FOR DEFERRED COMPENSATION ASSUMING TAX RATES WILL INCREASE AND CURRENT RATE IS 28 PERCENT

| | | 28% | 28% | 28% | 28% | 28% |
|---|---|---|---|---|---|---|
| Current Tax Rate | | | | | | |
| Projected Tax Rate | | 35% | 40% | 45% | 50% | 55% |
| | | **Number of Years to Break Even*** | | | | |
| | 3% | 7.55 | 12.07 | 16.05 | 19.62 | 22.84 |
| | 4% | 5.69 | 9.09 | 12.10 | 14.78 | 17.21 |
| | 5% | 4.57 | 7.31 | 9.72 | 11.88 | 13.84 |
| | 6% | 3.83 | 6.12 | 8.14 | 9.95 | 11.59 |
| Before-tax | 7% | 3.30 | 5.27 | 7.01 | 8.57 | 9.98 |
| Return on Plan | 8% | 2.90 | 4.63 | 6.16 | 7.53 | 8.77 |
| Investments | 9% | 2.59 | 4.14 | 5.51 | 6.73 | 7.83 |
| | 10% | 2.34 | 3.74 | 4.98 | 6.08 | 7.08 |
| | 11% | 2.14 | 3.42 | 4.55 | 5.56 | 6.47 |
| | 12% | 1.97 | 3.15 | 4.19 | 5.12 | 5.96 |
| | 13% | 1.83 | 2.92 | 3.88 | 4.74 | 5.52 |

## YEARS UNTIL BREAK EVEN FOR DEFERRED COMPENSATION ASSUMING TAX RATES WILL INCREASE AND CURRENT RATE IS 33 PERCENT

| | | 33% | 33% | 33% | 33% | 33% |
|---|---|---|---|---|---|---|
| Current Tax Rate | | | | | | |
| Projected Tax Rate | | 35% | 40% | 45% | 50% | 55% |
| | | **Number of Years to Break Even** | | | | |
| | 3% | 1.99 | 6.51 | 10.49 | 14.06 | 17.28 |
| | 4% | 1.50 | 4.90 | 7.91 | 10.59 | 13.02 |
| | 5% | 1.21 | 3.94 | 6.36 | 8.52 | 10.47 |
| | 6% | 1.01 | 3.30 | 5.32 | 7.13 | 8.77 |
| Before-tax | 7% | 0.87 | 2.84 | 4.58 | 6.14 | 7.55 |
| Return on Plan | 8% | 0.76 | 2.50 | 4.03 | 5.40 | 6.64 |
| Investments | 9% | 0.68 | 2.23 | 3.60 | 4.82 | 5.93 |
| | 10% | 0.62 | 2.02 | 3.25 | 4.36 | 5.36 |
| | 11% | 0.56 | 1.84 | 2.97 | 3.98 | 4.89 |
| | 12% | 0.52 | 1.70 | 2.74 | 3.67 | 4.51 |
| | 13% | 0.48 | 1.57 | 2.54 | 3.40 | 4.18 |

$$*\text{number of years} = \frac{\text{natural log of (new tax rate/current tax rate)}}{\text{natural log of } (1 + \text{interest rate})}$$

Source: *Financial Services Professional's Guide to the State of the Art 1989*, The American College, Bryn Mawr, PA 19010, 1-800-841-8000, ext. 19. For further detailed analysis, see Doyle, "Creative Wealth Planning Techniques," *Financial Services Professional's Guide to the State of the Art*, Second Edition, 1991, The American College, Bryn Mawr, PA, 19010.

rate was higher than the top individual rate, and the acceleration of the employer's tax deduction provided more tax benefit than was lost by the employee in paying tax currently instead of deferring. However, this advantage may not apply under current tax rates.

Secular trust designers try to structure secular trusts as "grantor" trusts, in order to avoid possible double taxation. A grantor trust is generally ignored for tax purposes, with its income and tax reportable directly by the grantor. The IRS has previously ruled favorably on "employee-grantor" secular trusts, but employers are often more interested in the "employer-grantor" arrangement, because this allows employers to maintain more control of the trust assets, a major objective in the "golden handcuffs" type of plan.

Some letter rulings have reached strongly negative results on employer-funded secular trusts.[40] In a complex technical analysis applying Code sections 402(b) and 404(a)(5), the IRS held that an employer-funded secular trust cannot be taxed as an employer-grantor trust. Moreover, the rulings held that employer-funded secular trust earnings can be taxed twice, once to the trust and again to the employees.

At best, these rulings create confusion and uncertainty; a pessimistic view might be that without changes in the Internal Revenue Code, the employer-funded secular trust is not viable for executive compensation planning, particularly in view of the 1993 changes in corporate and individual tax rates.

## FOOTNOTES

1. With the passage of the Jobs and Growth Tax Reconciliation Act of 2003, the top marginal individual rate is now 35%, matching the top corporate rate.

2. Amounts representing "interest" credited on unfunded nonqualified deferred compensation cannot be currently deducted as interest under Section 163 by an accrual basis taxpayer. There has been great controversy over the proper timing of an accrual-basis employer's deduction for such amounts, but the current rule seems to be that the deduction must be delayed until such amounts are includable in employee income. *Albertson's, Inc. v. Comm.*, 42 F.3d 537 (9th Cir. 1994), *cert. denied*, 516 U.S. 807, 116 S. Ct. 51 (1995), vacating in part 12 F.3d 1529 (9th Cir. 1993), aff'g in part 95 TC 415 (1990) (divided court), en banc rehearing denied, 12 F.3d 1539 (9th Cir. 1994); Notice 94-38, 1994-1 CB 350; Let. Rul. 9201019; TAM 8619006.

3. ERISA Sections 4(b)(5), 201(7), 301(a)(9), 4021(b)(8).

4. The limit on compensation taken into account under qualified retirement plans has been increased to $200,000 for years beginning after December 31, 2001. In addition, the increment by which inflation adjustments will be made is lowered, from $10,000 to $5,000, which will result in more frequent increases in future years. IRC Sec. 401(a)(17), as amended by EGTRRA 2001.

5. One court has ruled that plans providing benefits in excess of the benefit limitations imposed by Section 415 satisfied the requirements of an excess benefit plan. When the plans were adopted, Section 415 was the only limit on qualified plan benefits. The plans were never amended to take into account the compensation limitation of Section 401(a)(17). This case suggests that a plan adopted to provide benefits in excess of the Section 415 limits can be an excess benefit plan, even if it also replaces benefits lost under Section 401(a)(17), as long as it was never amended for Section 401(a)(17). *Gamble v. Group Hospitalization*, 38 F.3d 126 (4th Cir. 1994).

6. See, e.g., Let. Rul. 9825007.

7. While money is not considered "property" subject to the rules of Section 83, a beneficial interest in money transferred or set aside from the claims of the employer's creditors, for example in a trust or escrow account, is Section 83 "property." Treas. Reg. §1.83-3(e).

8. See DOL Regs. §§2520.104-23(a)(1) and 2520.104-23(d)(2); DOL Adv. Ops. 94-31A, 92-13A, 91-16A, 90-14A, 89-22A; see also *Belsky v. First National Life Insurance Co.*, 818 F.2d 661 (8th Cir. 1987) (a plan is unfunded when benefits are paid from the employer's general assets); *Dependahl v. Falstaff Brewing Corp.*, 653 F.2d 1208 (8th Cir. 1981) (a plan is funded when there is property separate from the ordinary assets of the employer to which the employee can look for satisfaction of benefit obligations), aff'g in part 491 F. Supp. 1188 (E.D. Mo. 1980), cert. denied, 454 U.S. 968 (1981) and 454 U.S. 1084 (1981); *Miller v. Heller*, 915 F. Supp. 651 (S.D.N.Y. 1996) (a plan backed by insurance policies is unfunded despite employees' belief that the policies secured their deferred compensation because the language in each agreement clearly defeated their belief); *The Northwestern Mutual Life Ins. Co. v. Resolution Trust Corp.*, 848 F. Supp. 1515 (N.D. Ala. 1994) (insurance policies purchased in conjunction with a deferred compensation plan did not cause the plan to be funded); *Darden v. Nationwide Mutual Insurance Co.*, 717 F. Supp. 388 (E.D.N.C. 1989), aff'd, 922 F.2d 203 (4th Cir.), cert. denied, 502 U.S. 906 (1991) (a pension fund backed by annuities is unfunded when benefits are paid from employer's general assets); *Belka v. Rowe Furniture Corp.*, 571 F. Supp. 1249 (D. Md. 1983) (the distinction between funded and unfunded plans is whether there is property set apart from the employer's general funds for satisfaction of benefit obligations); DOL Adv. Op. 92-01A (refusing to find union arrangement to be an unfunded, dues-financed welfare benefit plan because there was no evidence the benefits were paid out of the union's general assets or that the assets of the arrangement were subject to the union's general creditors).

9. See DOL Adv. Ops. 94-31A, 92-13A, 91-16A, 90-14A, 89-22A.

10. Treas. Reg. §1.83-1(a). If a plan is formally funded through a trust, a special rule may instead tax highly compensated employees each year on their vested accrued benefit in the trust (minus amounts previously taxed). See IRC Section 402(b)(4).

11. ERISA Sections 201, 401(a).

12. For plan years beginning after December 31, 2001, new vesting rules apply to employer matching contributions of employees

with at least one hour of service after that effective date. The 5-year cliff vesting schedule is reduced to a 3-year cliff. Graduated vesting, which previously spanned 3-7 years of service is replaced with a 2-6 year graded vesting schedule (20% for each year of service, beginning with the second year, and 100% vesting after six years). IRC Section 411(a), as amended by EGTRRA 2001.

13. See Rev. Rul. 82-54, 1982-1 CB 11 and rulings cited therein; see also Let. Ruls. 9815039, 9805030.

14. Let. Ruls. 9008043, 8648011; see also Let. Ruls. 9504007, 9332038, 8834015, 8804057, 8607022.

15. E.g., DOL Adv. Op. 92-13A.

16. See *Berry v. U.S.*, 593 F. Supp. 80 (M.D. N.C. 1984) (shareholders of employer corporation guaranteed payment under plan), aff'd per curiam, 760 F.2d 85; *Robinson v. Comm.*, 44 TC 20 (1965) (while the issue was not raised by the IRS, payment of deferred prize fight proceeds was guaranteed by corporate fight promoter's parent corporation and one of its major shareholders), acq., 1970-2 CB xxi, 1976-2 CB 2 (correction); Let. Rul. 8906022 (parent guaranteed deferred compensation plan of subsidiary); Let. Rul. 8741078 (same); Let. Rul. 7902082 (shareholders guaranteed payment of corporate termination pay agreement to another shareholder-employee); Let. Rul. 7742098 (same); see also *Childs v. Comm.*, 103 TC 634 (1994) (a guarantee does not make a promise secured since the guarantee is itself a mere promise to pay); but see TAM 9336001 (the conclusion that victorious plaintiffs' promise to pay their attorney was funded and secured where they irrevocably ordered defendants' insurers to pay attorney out of plaintiffs' recovery and defendants' insurers paid attorney by buying annuities naming him annuitant was "strengthened" by the fact that a defendant and the defendants' insurers guaranteed to make the annuity payments should the annuity issuer default); compare Let. Rul. 9331006 (protecting benefits by giving employees certificates of participation secured by irrevocable standby letters of credit turned the promise into a secured promise subject to Section 83); Let. Rul. 9443006 (employer's purchase of irrevocable standby letter of credit beyond the reach of its general creditors to back its promise to pay accrued vacation benefits turned promise into a secured promise subject to Section 83).

17. See Let. Rul. 8406012 (current value of protection provided by employer-paid surety bond or other guarantee arrangement constitutes an economic benefit, the cost of which is taxable to the employee); compare Let. Rul. 9241006 (strongly hinting that at least employer-provided surety bonds might secure deferred compensation causing it to be immediately taxable to the extent benefits are substantially vested).

18. See Let. Ruls. 9344038 (employee-purchased indemnification insurance protecting deferred compensation does not accelerate taxation), and 8406012 (employee-purchased surety bond protecting deferred compensation does not accelerate taxation); but compare Let. Rul. 9241006 (suggesting that use of a surety bond to protect deferred compensation could accelerate taxation but not clearly distinguishing between employer-provided and employee-provided bonds).

19. Treas. Reg. §1.451-2(a).

20. Rev. Rul. 60-31, 1960-1 CB 174; Rev. Proc. 71-19, 1971-1 CB 698, as amplified by Rev. Proc. 92-65, 1992-2 CB 428; but see Let. Rul. 9506008 (plan allowing elections to defer bonus payments on or before May 31 of the compensation year with respect to which the deferral will be effective but not imposing forfeiture provisions did not cause constructive receipt).

21. See Rev. Rul. 67-449, 1967-2 CB 173; Rev. Proc. 71-19, 1971-1 CB 698, as amplified by Rev. Proc. 92-65, 1992-2 CB 428; TAM 8632003 (note, though, that the IRS did not analyze whether plan imposed substantial forfeiture provisions); but see *Childs v. Comm.*, 103 TC 634 (1994); *Martin v. Comm.*, 96 TC 814 (1991); *Veit v. Comm.*, 8 TCM 919 (1949).

22. *Sproull v. Comm.*, 16 TC 244 (1951), aff'd per curiam, 194 F.2d 541 (6th Cir. 1952); Rev. Rul. 72-25, 1972-1 CB 127; Rev. Rul. 68-99, 1968-1 CB 193; Rev. Rul. 60-31, 1960-1 CB 174. A special rule may tax highly compensated employees each year on their vested accrued benefit in the trust (minus amounts previously taxed). See IRC Section 402(b)(4).

23. If the decedent died on or before August 20, 1996, up to $5,000 can be excluded as an employee death benefit under Code section 101(b) if the employee did not have vested rights to the benefit immediately before death. (This employee death benefit exclusion has been repealed for decedents dying after August 20, 1996. SBJPA '96, Section 1402.)

24. IRC Section 3121(v)(2); Treas. Reg. §31.3121(v)(2)-1. See Notice 94-96, 1994-2 CB 564 for the IRS' enforcement position. Final regulations provide a twist to this special timing rule for certain amounts deferred that are not reasonably ascertainable at the later of (1) the time the services creating the right to the amount deferred are performed; or (2) when there is no substantial risk of forfeiting the right to the amount deferred. See Treas. Reg. §31.3121(v)(2)-1(e)(4)(i).

25. IRC Section 404(a)(5); Treas. Reg. §1.404(a)-12(b)(1). This rule seems to apply even to amounts credited as "interest" on unfunded deferred compensation by an accrual-basis employer. See footnote 2, above.

26. See, e.g., *Acme Construction Co., Inc. v. Comm.*, TC Memo 1995-6; *Comtech Systems, Inc. v. Comm.*, TC Memo 1995-4.

27. IRC Section 162(m).

28. ERISA Sections 4(b)(5), 4021(b)(8).

29. ERISA Sections 201(2), 301(a)(3), 401(a)(1), 503, 4021(b)(6); DOL Regs. §§2520.104-23, 2560.503-1(a), 2560.503-1(b).

30. The DOL's current position seems to be that the "select group of management or highly compensated employees" is limited to those employees who, by virtue of their position or compensation level, have the ability to affect or substantially influence the design and operation of their deferred compensation plan. E.g., DOL Adv. Op. 92-13A, footnote 1. However, in *Demery v. Extebank Deferred Compensation Plan*, 216 F. 3d 283 (2d Cir. 2000), the Second Circuit held that a plan met the top-hat requirement where it was made available to a group of middle-management employees comprising approximately 15% of the company's workforce, and those electing participation amounted to approximately 10% of the company's employees.

31. The leading case on this point is *Fort Halifax Packing Co. v. Coyne*, 48 U.S. 1 (Supreme Ct. 1987). However, in *Demery v. Extebank Deferred Compensation Plan*, 216 F. 3d 283 (2d Cir. 2000), the Second Circuit held that a plan met the top-hat requirement where it was made available to a group of middle-management employees comprising approximately 15% of the company's workforce, and those electing participation amounted to approximately 10% of the company's employees.

32. Rev. Proc. 99-3, Sec. 3.01(30), 1999-1 IRB 103, 108. This item has been on the IRS' annually revised list of "no ruling" items for many years. Active hostility to controlling shareholder-employee deferred compensation was expressed in a side discussion, or

"dictum," in Let. Rul. 8607029, a ruling otherwise favorable to the taxpayer. See also TAM 8828004.

33. *Casale v. Comm.*, 247 F.2d 440 (2nd Cir. 1957); *Moline Properties, Inc. v. Comm.*, 319 U.S. 436, 63 S.Ct. 1132 (1943); Rev. Rul. 59-184 1959-1 CB 65.

34. *Carnahan v. Comm.*, TC Memo 1994-163; *Commerce Union Bank v. U.S.*, 76-2 USTC ¶13,157 (M.D. Tenn. 1976); *First Trust Company of St. Paul v. U.S.*, 321 F. Supp. 1025 (D. Minn. 1970); Rev. Rul. 77-139, 1977-1 CB 278.

35. See *Casale v. Comm.*, above, footnote 28; *Goldsmith v. U. S.*, 78-1 USTC ¶9312 (Ct. Cl. Tr. Div. 1978), no appeal (adopted by full court), 586 F.2d 810 (Ct. Cl. 1978). But see Let. Ruls. 8103089 and 7940017.

36. See, e.g., *Willmark Service System, Inc. v. Comm.*, TC Memo 1965-294, aff'd, 368 F.2d 359 (2nd Cir. 1966).

37. The full picture of the taxation of employees participating in secular trusts is much more complex than this. For the rules applicable to participants in employer-funded secular trusts, see IRC Section 402(b); Treas. Regs. §§1.402(b)-1(a), 1.402(b)-1(b);

Let. Ruls. 9502030, 9417013, 9302017, 9212024, 9212019, 9207010, 9206009. For the rules applicable to employees participating in employee-funded secular trusts, see Let. Ruls. 9450004, 9437011, 9337016, 9328007, 9322011, 9316018, 9316008, 9235044, 9031031, 8843021, 8841023.

38. For more on the employer's deduction in the context of an employer-funded secular trust, see Treas. Reg. §1.404(a)-12(b)(1); Let. Ruls. 9502030, 9417013, 9302017, 9212024, 9212019, 9207010, 9206009. For more on the employer's deduction in the context of an employee-funded secular trust, see Let. Ruls. 9450004, 9437011, 9337016, 9328007, 9322011, 9316018, 9316008, 9235044, 9031031, 8843021, 8841023.

39. The IRS has pointed out that the taxation of distributions from employer-funded secular trusts to highly compensated employees participating in a plan that fails the minimum participation or the minimum coverage tests applicable to qualified plans is unclear. See Let. Ruls. 9502030, 9417013.

40. See Let. Ruls. 9417013, 9302017, 9212024, 9212019, 9207010, 9206009; see also Let. Rul. 9502030.

## IRS Model Rabbi Trust

### TRUST UNDER_____PLAN

*OPTIONAL*
*(a) This Agreement made this____day of_____, by and between_____(Company) and_____(Trustee);*

*OPTIONAL*
*(b) WHEREAS, Company has adopted the nonqualified deferred compensation Plan(s) as listed in Appendix_____.*

*OPTIONAL*
*(c) WHEREAS, Company has incurred or expects to incur liability under the terms of such Plan(s) with respect to the individuals participating in such Plan(s);*

(d) WHEREAS, Company wishes to establish a trust (hereinafter called "Trust") and to contribute to the Trust assets that shall be held therein, subject to the claims of Company's creditors in the event of Company's Insolvency, as herein defined, until paid to Plan participants and their beneficiaries in such manner and at such times as specified in the Plan(s);

(e) WHEREAS, it is the intention of the parties that this Trust shall constitute an unfunded arrangement and shall not affect the status of the Plan(s) as an unfunded plan maintained for the purpose of providing deferred compensation for a select group of management or highly compensated employees for purposes of Title I of the Employee Retirement Income Security Act of 1974;

(f) WHEREAS, it is the intention of Company to make contributions to the Trust to provide itself with a source of funds to assist it in the meeting of its liabilities under the Plan(s);

NOW, THEREFORE, the parties do hereby establish the Trust and agree that the Trust shall be comprised, held and disposed of as follows:

Section 1. *Establishment Of Trust*

(a) Company hereby deposits with Trustee in trust_____[insert amount deposited], which shall become the principal of the Trust to be held, administered and disposed of by Trustee as provided in this Trust Agreement.

*ALTERNATIVES—Select one provision.*

*(b) The Trust hereby established shall be revocable by Company.*

*(b) The Trust hereby established shall be irrevocable.*

*(b) The Trust hereby established is revocable by Company; it shall become irrevocable upon a Change of Control, as defined herein.*

*(b) The Trust shall become irrevocable_____[insert number] days following the issuance of a favorable private letter ruling regarding the Trust from the Internal Revenue Service.*

*(b) The Trust shall become irrevocable upon approval by the Board of Directors.*

(c) The Trust is intended to be a grantor trust, of which Company is the grantor, within the meaning of subpart E, part I, subchapter J, chapter 1, subtitle A of the Internal Revenue Code of 1986, as amended, and shall be construed accordingly.

(d) The principal of the Trust, and any earnings thereon shall be held separate and apart from other funds of Company and shall be used exclusively for the uses and purposes of Plan participants and general creditors as herein set forth. Plan participants and their beneficiaries shall have no preferred claim on, or any beneficial ownership interest in, any assets of the Trust. Any rights created under the Plan(s) and this Trust Agreement shall be mere unsecured contractual rights of Plan participants and their beneficiaries against Company. Any assets held by the Trust will be subject to the claims of Company's general creditors under federal and state law in the event Of Insolvency, as defined in Section 3(a) herein.

*ALTERNATIVES—Select one or more provisions, as appropriate.*

*(e) Company, in its sole discretion, may at any time, or from time to time, make additional deposits of cash or other property in trust with Trustee to augment the principal to be held, administered and disposed of by Trustee as provided in this Trust Agreement. Neither Trustee nor any Plan participant or beneficiary shall have any right to compel such additional deposits.*

*(e) Upon a Change of Control, Company shall, as soon as possible, but in no event longer than____[fill in blank] days following the Change of Control, as defined herein, make an irrevocable contribution to the Trust in an amount that is sufficient to pay each Plan participant or beneficiary the benefits to which Plan participants or their beneficiaries would be entitled pursuant to the terms of the Plan(s) as of the date on which the Change of Control occurred.*

*(e) Within____[fill in blank] days following the end of the Plan years, ending after the Trust has become irrevocable pursuant to Section l(b) hereof, Company shall be required to irrevocably deposit additional cash or other property to the Trust in an amount sufficient to pay each Plan participant or beneficiary the benefits payable pursuant to the terms of the Plan(s) as of the close of the Plan year(s).*

Section 2. *Payments to Plan Participants and Their Beneficiaries.*

(a) Company shall deliver to Trustee a schedule (the "Payment Schedule") that indicates the amounts payable in respect of each Plan participant (and his or her beneficiaries), that provides a formula or other instructions acceptable to Trustee for determining the amounts so payable, the form in which such amount is to be paid (as provided for or available under the Plan(s)), and the time of commencement for payment of such amounts. Except as otherwise provided herein, Trustee shall make payments to the Plan participants and their beneficiaries in accordance with such Payment Schedule. The Trustee shall make provision for the reporting and withholding of any federal, state or local taxes that may be required to be withheld with respect to the payment of benefits pursuant to the terms of the Plan(s) and shall pay amounts withheld to the appropriate taxing authorities or determine that such amounts have been reported, withheld and paid by Company.

(b) The entitlement of a Plan participant or his or her beneficiaries to benefits under the Plan(s) shall be determined by Company or such party as it shall designate under the Plan(s), and any claim for such benefits shall be considered and reviewed under the procedures set out in the Plan(s).

(c) Company may make payment of benefits directly to Plan participants or their beneficiaries as they become due under the terms of the Plan(s). Company shall notify Trustee of its decision to make payment of benefits directly prior to the time amounts are payable to participants or their beneficiaries. In addition, if the principal of the Trust, and any earnings thereon, are not sufficient to make payments of benefits in accordance with the terms of the Plan(s), Company shall make the balance of each such payment as it falls due. Trustee shall notify Company where principal and earnings are not sufficient.

Section 3. *Trustee Responsibility Regarding Payments to Trust Beneficiary When Company Is Insolvent.*

(a) Trustee shall cease payment of benefits to Plan participants and their beneficiaries if the Company is Insolvent. Company shall be considered "Insolvent" for purposes of this Trust Agreement if (i) Company is unable to pay its debts as they become due, or (ii) Company is subject to a pending proceeding as a debtor under the United States Bankruptcy Code.

*OPTIONAL*

*, or (iii) Company is determined to be insolvent by_____[insert names of applicable federal and/or state regulatory agency].*

(b) At all times during the continuance of this Trust, as provided in Section l(d) hereof, the principal and income of the Trust shall be subject to claims of general creditors of Company under federal and state law as set forth below.

(1) The Board of Directors and the Chief Executive Officer [or substitute the title of the highest ranking officer of the Company] of Company shall have the duty to inform Trustee in writing of Company's Insolvency. If a person claiming to be a creditor of Company alleges in writing to Trustee that Company has become Insolvent, Trustee shall determine whether Company is Insolvent and, pending such determination, Trustee shall discontinue payment of benefits to Plan participants or their beneficiaries.

(2) Unless Trustee has actual knowledge of Company's Insolvency, or has received notice from Company or a person claiming to be a creditor alleging that Company is Insolvent, Trustee shall have no duty to inquire whether Company is Insolvent. Trustee may in all events rely on such evidence concerning Company's solvency as may be furnished to Trustee and that provides Trustee with a reasonable basis for making a determination concerning Company's solvency.

(3) If at any time Trustee has determined that Company is Insolvent, Trustee shall discontinue payments to Plan participants or their beneficiaries and shall hold the assets of the Trust for the benefit of Company's general creditors. Nothing in this Trust Agreement shall in any way diminish any rights of Plan participants or their beneficiaries to pursue their rights as general creditors of Company with respect to benefits due under the Plan(s) or otherwise.

(4) Trustee shall resume the payment of benefits to Plan participants or their beneficiaries in accordance with Section 2 of this Trust Agreement only after Trustee has determined that Company is not Insolvent (or is no longer Insolvent).

(c) Provided that there are sufficient assets, if Trustee discontinues the payment of benefits from the Trust pursuant to Section 3(b) hereof and subsequently resumes such payments, the first payment following such discontinuance shall include the aggregate amount of all payments due to Plan participants or their beneficiaries under the terms of the Plan(s) for the period of such discontinuance, less the aggregate amount of any payments made to Plan participants or their beneficiaries by Company in lieu of the payments provided for hereunder during any such period of discontinuance.

Section 4. *Payments to Company.*

[The following need not be included if the first alternative under l(b) is selected.]

Except as provided in Section 3 hereof, after the Trust has become irrevocable, Company shall have no right or power to direct Trustee to return to Company or to divert to others any of the Trust assets before all payment of benefits have [*sic*] been made to Plan participants and their beneficiaries pursuant to the terms of the Plan(s).

Section 5. *Investment Authority.*

*ALTERNATIVES—Select one provision, as appropriate[.]*

*(a) In no event may Trustee invest in securities (including stock or rights to acquire stock) or obligations issued by Company, other than a de minimis amount held in common investment vehicles in which Trustee invests. All rights associated with assets of the Trust shall be exercised by Trustee or the person designated by Trustee, and shall in no event be exercisable by or rest with Plan participants.*

*(a) Trustee may invest in securities (including stock or rights to acquire stock) or obligations issued by Company. All rights associated with assets of the Trust shall be exercised by Trustee or the person designated by Trustee, and shall in no event be exercisable by or rest with Plan participants.*

*OPTIONAL*

*,except that voting rights with respect to Trust assets will be exercised by Company.*

*OPTIONAL*

*,except that dividend rights with respect to Trust assets will rest with Company.*

*OPTIONAL*

*Company shall have the right, at anytime, and from time to time in its sole discretion, to substitute assets of equal fair market value for any asset held by the Trust.*

[If the second Alternative 5(a) is selected, the trust must provide either (1) that the trust is revocable under Alternative l(b), or (2) the following provision must by included in the Trust]:

*"Company shall have the right at anytime, and from time to time in its sole discretion, to substitute assets of equal fair market value for any asset held by the Trust. This right is exercisable by Company in a nonfiduciary capacity without the approval or consent of any person in a fiduciary capacity."*

Section 6. *Disposition of Income.*

ALTERNATIVES—*Select one provision.*

*(a) During the term of this Trust, all income received by the Trust, net of expenses and taxes, shall be accumulated and reinvested.*

*(a) During the term of this Trust, all, or_____[insert amount] part of the income received by the Trust, net of expenses and taxes, shall be returned to Company.*

Section 7. *Accounting by Trustee.*

*OPTIONAL*

*Trustee shall keep accurate and detailed records of all investments, receipts, disbursements, and all other transactions required to be made, including such specific records as shall be agreed upon in writing between Company and Trustee. Within____[insert number] days following the close of each calendar year and within____[insert number] days after the removal or resignation of Trustee, Trustee shall deliver to Company a written account of its administration of the Trust during such year or during the period from the close of the last preceding year to the date of such removal or resignation, setting forth all investments, receipts, disbursements and other transactions effected by it, including a description of all securities and investments purchased and sold with the cost or net proceeds of such purchases or sales (accrued interest paid or receivable being shown separately), and showing all cash, securities and other property held in the Trust at the end of such year or as of the date of such removal or resignation, as the case may be.*

Section 8. *Responsibility of Trustee.*

*OPTIONAL*

*(a) Trustee shall act with the care, skill, prudence and diligence under the circumstances then prevailing that a prudent person acting in like capacity and familiar with such matters would use in the conduct of an enterprise of a like character and with like aims, provided, however, that Trustee shall incur no liability to any person for any action taken pursuant to a direction, request or approval given by Company which is contemplated by, and in conformity with, the terms of the Plan(s) or this Trust and is given in writing by Company. In the event of a dispute between Company and a party, Trustee may apply to a court of competent jurisdiction to resolve the dispute.*

*OPTIONAL*

*(b) If Trustee undertakes or defends any litigation arising in connection with this Trust, Company agrees to indemnify Trustee against Trustee's costs, expenses and liabilities (including, without limitation, attorneys' fees and expenses) relating thereto and to be primarily liable for such payments. If Company does not pay such costs, expenses and liabilities in a reasonably timely manner, Trustee may obtain payment from the Trust.*

*OPTIONAL*

*(c) Trustee may consult with legal counsel (who may also be counsel for Company generally) with respect to any of its duties or obligations hereunder.*

*OPTIONAL*

*(d) Trustee may hire agents, accountants, actuaries, investment advisors, financial consultants or other professionals to assist it in performing any of its duties or obligations hereunder.*

(e) Trustee shall have, without exclusion, all powers conferred on Trustees by applicable law, unless expressly provided otherwise herein, provided, however, that if an insurance policy is held as an asset of the Trust, Trustee shall have no power to name a beneficiary of the policy other than the Trust, to assign the policy (as distinct from conversion of the policy to a different form) other than to a successor Trustee, or to loan to any person the proceeds of any borrowing against such policy.

*OPTIONAL*

*(f) However, notwithstanding the provisions of Section 8(e) above, Trustee may loan to Company the proceeds of any borrowing against an insurance policy held as an asset of the Trust.*

(g) Notwithstanding any powers granted to Trustee pursuant to this Trust Agreement or to applicable law, Trustee shall not have any power that could give this Trust the objective of carrying on a business and dividing the gains therefrom, within the meaning of section 301.7701-2 of the Procedure and Administrative Regulations promulgated pursuant to the Internal Revenue Code.

Section 9. *Compensation and Expenses of Trustee.*

*OPTIONAL*

*Company shall pay all administrative and Trustee's fees and expenses. If not so paid, the fees and expenses shall be paid from the Trust.*

Section 10. *Resignation and Removal of Trustee.*

(a) Trustee may resign at any time by written notice to Company, which shall be effective_____[insert number] days after receipt of such notice unless Company and Trustee agree otherwise.

*OPTIONAL*

*(b) Trustee may be removed by Company on_____[insert number] days notice or upon shorter notice accepted by Trustee.*

*OPTIONAL*

*(c) Upon a Change of Control, as defined herein, Trustee may not be removed by Company for_____[insert number] year(s).*

*OPTIONAL*

*(d) If Trustee resigns within_____[insert number] year(s) after a Change of Control, as defined herein, Company shall apply to a court of competent jurisdiction for the appointment of a successor Trustee or for instructions.*

*OPTIONAL*

*(e) If Trustee resigns or is removed within____[insert number] year(s) or a Change of Control, as defined herein, Trustee shall select a successor Trustee in accordance with the provisions of Section 11(b) hereof prior to the effective date of Trustee's resignation or removal.*

(f) Upon resignation or removal of Trustee and appointment of a successor Trustee, all assets shall subsequently be transferred to the successor Trustee. The transfer shall be completed within____[insert number] days after receipt of notice of resignation, removal or transfer, unless Company extends the time limit.

(g) If Trustee resigns or is removed, a successor shall be appointed, in accordance with Section 11 hereof, by the effective date of resignation or removal under paragraph(s) (a) [or (b)] of this section. If no such appointment has been made, Trustee may apply to a court of competent jurisdiction for appointment of a successor or for instructions. All expenses of Trustee in connection with the proceeding shall be allowed as administrative expenses of the Trust.

Section 11. *Appointment of Successor.*

*OPTIONAL*

*(a) If Trustee resigns or is removed in accordance with Section 10(a) [or (b)] hereof, Company may appoint any third party, such as a bank trust department or other party that may be granted corporate trustee powers under state law, as a successor to replace Trustee upon resignation or removal. The appointment shall be effective when accepted in writing by the new Trustee, who shall have all of the rights and powers of the former Trustee, including ownership rights in the Trust assets. The former Trustee shall execute any instrument necessary or reasonably requested by Company or the successor Trustee to evidence the transfer.*

*OPTIONAL*

*(b) If Trustee resigns or is removed pursuant to the provisions of Section 10(e) hereof and selects a successor Trustee, Trustee may appoint any third party such as a bank trust department or other party that may be granted corporate trustee powers under state law. The appointment of a successor Trustee shall be effective when accepted in writing by the new Trustee. The new Trustee shall have all the rights and powers of the former Trustee, including ownership rights in Trust assets. The former Trustee shall execute any instrument necessary or reasonably requested by the successor Trustee to evidence the transfer.*

*OPTIONAL*

(c) The successor Trustee need not examine the records and acts of any prior Trustee and may retain or dispose of existing Trust assets, subject to Sections 7 and 8 hereof. The successor Trustee shall not be responsible for and Company shall indemnify and defend the successor Trustee from any claim or liability resulting from any action or inaction of any prior Trustee or from any other past event, or any condition existing at the time it becomes successor Trustee.

Section 12. *Amendment or Termination.*

(a) This Trust Agreement may be amended by a written instrument executed by Trustee and Company. [Unless the first alternative under 1(b) is selected, the following sentence must be included.] Notwithstanding the foregoing, no such amendment shall conflict with the terms of the Plan(s) or shall make the Trust revocable after it has become irrevocable in accordance with Section 1(b) hereof.

(b) The Trust shall not terminate until the date on which Plan participants and their beneficiaries are no longer entitled to benefits pursuant to the terms of the Plan(s) [unless the second alternative under 1(b) is selected, the following must be included:], "unless sooner revoked in accordance with Section 1(b) hereof." [*Sic*] Upon termination of the Trust any assets remaining in the Trust shall be returned to Company.

*OPTIONAL*
*(c) Upon written approval of participants or beneficiaries entitled to payment of benefits pursuant to the terms of the Plan(s), Company may terminate this Trust prior to the time all benefit payments under the Plan(s) have been made. All assets in the Trust at termination shall be returned to Company.*

*OPTIONAL*
*(d) Section(s)_____[insert number(s)] of this Trust Agreement may not be amended by Company for_____[insert number] year(s) following a Change of Control, as defined herein.*

Section 13. *Miscellaneous.*

(a) Any provision of this Trust Agreement prohibited by law shall be ineffective to the extent of any such prohibition, without invalidating the remaining provisions hereof.

(b) Benefits payable to Plan participants and their beneficiaries under this Trust Agreement may not be anticipated, assigned (either at law or in equity), alienated, pledged, encumbered or subjected to attachment, garnishment, levy, execution or other legal or equitable process.

(c) This Trust Agreement shall be governed by and construed in accordance with the laws of_____.

*OPTIONAL*
*(d) For purposes of this Trust, Change of Control shall mean: [insert objective definition such as: "the purchase or other acquisition by any person, entity or group of persons, within the meaning of section 13(d) or 14(d) of the Securities Exchange Act of 1934 ("Act"), or any comparable successor provisions, of beneficial ownership within the meaning of Rule 13d-3 promulgated under the Act) of 30 percent or more of either the outstanding shares of common stock or the combined voting power of Company's then outstanding voting securities entitled to vote generally, or the approval by the stockholders of Company of a reorganization, merger, or consolidation, in each case, with respect to which persons who were stockholders of Company immediately prior to such reorganization, merger or consolidation do not, immediately thereafter, own more than 50 percent of the combined voting power entitled to vote generally in the election of directors of the reorganized, merged or consolidated Company's then outstanding securities, or a liquidation or dissolution of Company or of the sale of all or substantially all of Company's assets"].*

Section 14. *Effective Date.*

The effective date of this Trust Agreement shall be_____, 20[___].

# Chapter 16

# PROFIT SHARING PLAN

## WHAT IS IT?

A profit sharing plan is a qualified, defined contribution plan featuring a flexible employer contribution provision. The major characteristics are:

- The employer's contribution to the plan each year can be either a purely discretionary amount (or nothing at all, if the employer wishes) or can be based on some type of formula, usually relating to the employer's annual profits.

- Each participant has an individual account in the plan. The employer's contribution is allocated to the individual participant accounts on the basis of a nondiscriminatory formula. The formula usually allocates employer contributions in proportion to each employee's compensation for the year. (Age-weighted formulas can also be used—see Chapter 22.)

- Plan benefits consist of the amount accumulated in each participant's account at retirement or termination of employment. This is the total of (a) employer contributions, (b) forfeitures from other employees' accounts (discussed below), and (c) the interest, capital gains, and other investment return realized over the years on plan assets.

- The plan usually distributes the employee's account balance in a lump sum at termination of employment, although other forms of payout may be available or, in the case of certain plans, may be required.

## WHEN IS IT INDICATED?

1. When an employer's profits, or financial ability to contribute to the plan, varies from year to year. A profit sharing plan is particularly useful as an alternative to a qualified pension plan where the employer anticipates that there may be years in which no contribution can be made.

2. When the employer wants to adopt a qualified plan with an incentive feature by which employee accounts increase with the employer's profits.

3. When the employee group has the following characteristics:

   - many employees are relatively young and have substantial time to accumulate retirement savings

   - employees can, and are willing to, accept a degree of investment risk in their accounts in return for the potential benefits of good investment results.

4. When the employer wants to supplement an existing defined benefit plan. The advantages of a profit sharing plan tend to provide exactly what is missing in a defined benefit plan—and vice versa—so that the two together provide an ideal balanced tax-deferred savings and retirement program.

## ADVANTAGES

1. A profit sharing plan provides the maximum contribution flexibility from the employer's viewpoint.

2. Contributions can be made even if there are no current or accumulated profits.[1] Even a nonprofit organization can have a qualified profit sharing plan.

3. As with all qualified plans, a profit sharing plan provides a tax-deferred retirement savings medium for employees.

4. The plan is relatively simple and inexpensive to design, administer, and explain to employees.

5. Individual participant accounts allow participants to benefit from good investment results in the plan fund.

## DISADVANTAGES

1. Retirement benefits may be inadequate for employees who enter the plan at older ages. This is dis-

cussed, with some illustrations, in Chapter 14 relating to money purchase plans. The problem of adequate benefits is even worse in a profit sharing plan than in a money purchase plan because a profit sharing plan does not involve any required minimum annual contribution by the employer. Thus, ultimate retirement benefits in a profit sharing plan are quite speculative. Some planners argue that a profit sharing plan should be considered primarily as a supplemental form of incentive-based deferred compensation and not as a retirement plan. Note that this disadvantage can be reduced by using an age-weighted formula, as discussed in Chapter 22.

2. Because of the limits applicable to profit sharing plans as well as other defined contribution plans, the relative amount of plan funding available for highly compensated employees-typically business owners or key employees—represents a smaller percentage of their compensation than can be contributed for lower-paid employees. Annual additions to a participant's account are limited to the lesser of (a) 100% of compensation or (b) $40,000 (in 2003, as indexed). Compensation taken into account for plan purposes is limited to $200,000 (in 2003, as indexed). So for an employee earning $40,000 annually, up to 100% of compensation ($40,000) can be contributed to his or her plan account (although contributions are rarely this high), whereas for an employee earning $300,000 annually, only $40,000 can be contributed—that is, less than 14% of compensation. The relative disadvantage of the allocation to highly compensated employees can be alleviated in part by using an integrated formula (described later in this chapter), or through the use of an age-weighted or cross-tested formula (Chapter 22).

3. Employees bear investment risk under the plan. While bearing investment risk is a potential disadvantage to employees, from the employer's viewpoint it is an advantage compared with a defined benefit plan. The employer's risk and costs tend to be lower for a profit sharing plan.

4. From the employee's standpoint, profit sharing plans are disadvantageous because there is no predictable level of employer funding under the plan. However, employees have a right to expect that employer contributions will be "substantial and recurring," as discussed below.

## DESIGN FEATURES

### Employer Contribution Arrangements

Employer contributions to a profit sharing plan can be based on either (a) a discretionary provision or (b) a formula provision.

Under a *discretionary* provision, the employer can determine each year the amount to be contributed. A contribution can be made to a profit sharing plan even if there are no current or accumulated profits. If the employer desires to make a contribution, any amount up to the maximum deductible limit can be contributed.

An employer can omit a contribution under a discretionary provision, but IRS regulations require "recurring and substantial" contributions.[2] There are no clear guidelines from the IRS as to how often contributions can be omitted. If too many years go by without contributions, the IRS will likely claim that the plan has been terminated. When a qualified plan is terminated, all nonvested amounts in participants' accounts become 100% vested. This is usually an undesirable result from the employer's viewpoint.

Under a *formula* provision, a specified amount must be contributed to the plan whenever the employer has profits. For example, a formula might provide that the employer will contribute 10% of all company profits in excess of $100,000 (but not to exceed the deduction limit discussed below under "Tax Implications"). The IRS does not dictate how to define profits for this purpose, so the employer can specify any appropriate formula. The most common approach is to define profits as determined on a before-tax basis under generally accepted accounting principles. As mentioned earlier, even a nonprofit corporation can adopt a profit sharing plan with purely discretionary contributions or contributions based on some appropriately defined surplus account.

Once a formula approach has been adopted, the employer is legally obligated to contribute the amount determined under the formula. However, formulas can be drafted that allow an omitted contribution if certain adverse financial contingencies occur. A suitable "fail-safe" provision of this type will avoid the necessity of amending the plan in the future if financial difficulties arise.

## Allocation to Participant Accounts

All profit sharing plans, regardless of how the total amount of employer contributions is determined, must have a formula under which the employer's contribution is allocated to employee accounts. This allocation formula must not discriminate in favor of highly compensated employees.

Most formulas make allocation to participants on the basis of their compensation as compared with the compensation of all participants.

---

*Example*: Participant Fred earns $50,000 this year. Total payroll for all plan participants this year is $500,000. For this year, the employer contributes $100,000 to the plan and the amount allocated to Fred's account is determined as follows:

$$\text{Total employer contribution} \quad \times \quad \frac{\text{Fred's Compensation}}{\text{Compensation of All Participants}}$$

$$\$100,000 \quad \times \quad \frac{\$50,000}{\$500,000} \quad = \quad \$10,000$$

The allocation to Fred's account equals 1/10 of $100,000, or $10,000.

---

The plan must define the term "compensation" in a nondiscriminatory way.[3] For example, if compensation is defined to include bonuses and exclude overtime pay, and only highly compensated employees receive bonuses and only lower paid employees receive overtime pay, the formula would likely be found discriminatory.

There is a limit on the amount of each employee's compensation that can be taken into account in the allocation formula, as well as for the 25% deduction limit discussed below under "Tax Implications." For 2003, the compensation limit is $200,000.[4]

Some profit sharing allocation formulas also take into account the years of service of each employee. Such a formula can satisfy the nondiscrimination requirements by meeting the requirements for one of the safe harbors provided in the regulations or by utilizing cross testing (see Chapter 22).[5]

The allocation formula can be "integrated" with Social Security. This helps the employer avoid duplicating Social Security benefits that are already provided to the employee. It also reduces the employer's cost for the plan. Treasury regulations specify the limits for this "permitted disparity," as it is technically described.

An integrated formula defines a level of compensation known as the "integration level." The plan then provides a higher rate of allocation of the employer contribution for compensation above that integration level than the rate for compensation below that integration level.

---

*Example*: For the year 2003, a profit sharing plan has two participants with compensation as shown below. For 2003, the employer contributes $15,000 to the plan. The plan's integration level is $20,000. Under the plan's allocation formula, each participant's account is to receive the maximum permitted percent allocation for compensation above $20,000. (As discussed in the "Questions and Answers," below, integration levels below the taxable wage base—$87,000 in 2003—require a reduction of the 5.7% factor. In this case, since the integration level is between 20% and 80% of the taxable wage base, the factor is 4.3%, as shown in column III.) The remaining amount of the employer contribution is allocated in proportion to total compensation. Plan allocations would then be as follows:

| Employee | I<br>2003<br>Compensation | II<br>Compensation<br>above<br>$20,000 | III<br>4.3%<br>of<br>Excess | IV<br>Allocation<br>of<br>Remainder | V<br><br>Total<br>Allocation |
|---|---|---|---|---|---|
| Al | $100,000 | $80,000 | $3,440 | $10,052 | $13,492 |
| Betty | 15,000 | 0 | 0 | 1,508 | 1,508 |
| | | | | | $15,000 |

The amount in column IV is determined as follows: (a) subtract the excess allocations (total of column III) from the $15,000 employer contribution ($15,000 - $3,440 = $11,560); (b) for each participant, this difference ($11,560) is then multiplied by a fraction; the numerator is the participant's total compensation and the denominator is the total payroll of $115,000. This allocation satisfies the permitted disparity regulations. (It should be noted these contribution levels could subject this plan to the top heavy requirements explained in Chapter 25.)

---

Regulations specify the degree of disparity permitted in a plan—the integration levels and the percentages allowed. Considerations involved in choosing the optimal integration level within the limits of these rules are discussed in the "Questions and Answers," below.

## Vesting

Generally, any vesting (nonforfeiture) provision permitted by the Code can be used in a profit sharing plan; however, special vesting requirements must be met with respect to matching contributions. Vesting is sometimes more generous in a profit sharing plan since it is designed as an employee incentive.

Many employers use the graded "3- to 7-year" vesting provision. This provides 20% vesting after three years of service. Vesting increases by 20% for each subsequent year of service and reaches 100% after seven years of service. Graded vesting with respect to matching contributions must begin with at least 20% after two years of service, reaching 100% after six years.[6] (See Chapter 25.)

If an employee leaves before becoming fully vested in his or her account balance, the nonvested amount, referred to as a "forfeiture," is left behind in the plan. In profit sharing plans, forfeitures are usually added to remaining participants' account balances. Adding forfeitures to participants' account balances tends to favor key employees, since they are more likely to participate in the plan over a long time period. For this reason, forfeitures must be allocated in a nondiscriminatory manner.[7] This usually requires forfeiture allocation in proportion to participants' compensation rather than in proportion to their existing account balances. In profit sharing plans, the formula for allocating forfeitures is usually the same as the formula for allocating employer contributions to participants' accounts.

## Distributions

Benefits from a profit sharing plan are usually payable at termination of employment or at the plan's stated normal retirement age. Profit sharing plans usually provide payment in the form of either a lump sum or a series of installment payments. The minimum installment payment must meet the minimum distribution rules discussed in Chapter 26. Some profit sharing plans also offer annuity options with a life contingency, but this is relatively uncommon. (Note, however, that certain plans are subject to the joint and survivor annuity requirements discussed in Chapter 26.)

Profit sharing plans typically allow "in service distributions"—that is, benefits payable before termination of employment. Many plans allow such distributions only in the event of "hardship" as specified in the plan. Typical hardship situations might include medical emergencies, home repair, or educational expenses. Employers traditionally administer such hardship provisions fairly liberally for the benefit of employees. The strict hardship definition applicable to Section 401(k) plans (see the "Questions and Answers" in Chapter 19) does not apply to other types of profit sharing plans.

The amount that a participant can withdraw before retirement or termination of employment cannot exceed the participant's vested account balance. In addition, the IRS has generally required that employer contributions not be withdrawn from the plan before termination of employment unless they have been in the plan for at least a 2-year period.[8] In some cases, the 2-year period can be waived if the participant has a minimum specified number of years of service, such as five.[9] In order to control and limit withdrawals to prevent depletion of plan funds, many plans impose a "plan penalty" for withdrawals, such as suspending an employee from the plan for a period of six months after a withdrawal. No plan penalty, however, can take away any of the participant's vested benefits.

In addition to any plan penalties that may apply, there is a 10% early distribution penalty for many distributions to participants before age 59½. This penalty is explained further in Chapter 26.

Because of the impact of the 10% early distribution penalty, it is very much in plan participants' interests to have a loan provision in a profit sharing plan. Loan provisions allow participants access to plan funds for emergencies and other financial needs without incurring the tax penalty of an early withdrawal. Plan loans are explained further in Chapter 26.

Profit sharing plan funds are generally invested in a pooled account managed (through a trustee or insurance company) by the employer or a fund manager designated by the employer. Either a trust fund or group or individual insurance contract can be used. Chapter 13 explains how life insurance can be used in the plan.

In a profit sharing plan, it is common to use "participant investment direction" or "earmarking" of participants' accounts. Earmarked accounts can be invested at the participant's direction. Usually, the plan limits the number of possible investments to reduce administrative costs. If the participant-directed account provision meets certain requirements set forth in Department of Labor (DOL) regulations,[10] the plan trustee is generally relieved of fiduciary responsibility for any losses resulting from an investment chosen by the participant. Typically, the plan will offer the participant a choice of investments from a family of mutual funds. Under the DOL regulations, at least three diversified choices must be permitted.[11]

## TAX IMPLICATIONS

1.  Employer contributions to the plan are deductible when made, so long as the plan remains "qualified." A plan is qualified if it meets the eligibility, vesting, funding, and other requirements explained in Chapter 25. In addition, the plan must designate that it is a profit sharing plan.[12]

    The maximum deductible employer contribution to the plan cannot exceed 25% of the payroll of all employees covered under the plan.[13] Any excess over these limits is not only nondeductible, but is also generally subject to a 10% penalty.[14] (However, contributions to one or more defined contribution plans that are nondeductible when contributed solely because of the combined plan deduction limit may be subject to an exception from the 10% penalty.[15]) Only the first $200,000 (in 2003, as indexed) of each employee's compensation can be taken into account for purposes of this limit.[16]

    If an employer maintains a defined benefit plan covering some of the same employees, the total deductible contribution for both plans is limited to 25% of compensation of the covered employees (or, if greater, the amount necessary to meet the minimum funding standard for the defined benefit plan, in which case the contribution to the profit sharing plan is not deductible).[17]

2.  Assuming the plan remains qualified, taxation of the employee is deferred. That is, (1) employer contributions, (2) forfeitures added to the participant's account, (3) investment earnings on the account and (4) capital gains realized in the account, are all nontaxable to a plan participant until withdrawn.[18]

3.  Code section 415 limits annual additions to each participant's account in a defined contribution plan to the *lesser of* (a) 100% of the participant's compen-

sation or (b) $40,000.[19] Annual additions include (1) employer contributions to the participant's account; (2) forfeitures from other participants' accounts; and (3) employee contributions to the account.[20]

4.  Distributions from a plan must follow the rules for qualified plan distributions. These distribution rules are explained in Chapter 26.

5.  Lump sum distributions may be eligible for the 10-year averaging (for certain employees born before 1936) tax computations available for qualified plans. Not all distributions are eligible for these special tax calculations; Chapter 26 covers the applicable rules and includes the appropriate IRS forms for making the calculation.

6.  Certain employers adopting a plan may be eligible for a business tax credit of up to $500 for "qualified startup costs." See Chapter 27 for details.

7.  A plan may permit employees to make voluntary contributions to a "deemed IRA" established under the plan. Amounts so contributed reduce the limit for other traditional or Roth IRA contributions. See Chapter 13 for details.

8.  The plan is subject to the ERISA reporting and disclosure rules outlined in Appendix A.

## ALTERNATIVES

1.  Money purchase pension plans are defined contribution plans similar to profit sharing plans except that the employer is *required* to make a contribution to a money purchase plan each year. (See Chapter 14.) Both types of plans allow a contribution (and deduction) of up to 25% of each participant's compensation.

2.  Cross-tested, age-weighted and target plans are defined contribution alternatives that have some similarities to defined benefit plans. With these plans, the employer contribution percentage can be based on age at plan entry—higher for older entrants. One of these plans may be favorable where the employer wants to provide adequate benefits for older (often key) employees. (See Chapter 22.)

3.  Defined benefit plans provide more security of retirement benefits and proportionately greater con-

tributions for older plan entrants, but are more complex to design and administer. (See Chapter 9.)

4. Nonqualified deferred compensation plans can be provided exclusively for selected executives. But the employer's tax deduction when a nonqualified plan is used is generally deferred until benefit payments are made. This can be as much as 20 or 30 years after the employer's contribution is made. (See Chapter 15.)

5. Individual retirement saving is an alternative or a supplement to an employer plan. But there is little or no tax deduction and tax deferral available except for the limited traditional and Roth IRA provisions (see Chapter 17 and Chapter 24).

See also the discussion in Chapter 2, "Designing the Right Pension Plan."

## HOW TO INSTALL A PLAN

Installation of a profit sharing plan follows the qualified plan installation procedure described in Chapter 27.

## WHERE CAN I FIND OUT MORE ABOUT IT?

1. Graduate Course: Advanced Pension and Retirement Planning I (GS 814), The American College, Bryn Mawr, PA.

## QUESTIONS AND ANSWERS

**Question** — Can a self-employed person adopt a profit sharing plan?

*Answer* — A self-employed person (sole proprietor or partner in a partnership) can adopt a profit sharing plan covering not only his or her regular employees, if any, but also covering the self-employed person(s). Such a plan is one type of "Keogh" or "HR 10" plan discussed in Chapter 12. Generally the self-employed person is treated the same as regular employees in a profit sharing plan, but there are some special rules that apply.

**Question** — Can employees make contributions to a profit sharing plan?

*Answer* — Employees can contribute to the plan on an after-tax basis. For employees to contribute on a

before-tax (salary reduction) basis, the plan must meet the additional requirements of Section 401(k); these are explained in Chapter 19. Furthermore, if the plan allows employee after-tax contributions, the additional nondiscrimination requirements under Code section 401(m) must be met. These are explained in Chapter 18.

**Question** — How can an employer decide when a profit sharing plan should be integrated with Social Security, and what are the factors involved in choosing the integration level?

*Answer* — A "stand alone" profit sharing plan—where the employer has no qualified defined benefit or other plan—is often integrated with Social Security because (1) employer costs are reduced and (2) the employer contribution in an integrated plan is disproportionately allocated to higher paid employees.

If an employer has two or more qualified plans covering even one employee in common, the regulations do not allow both plans to be fully integrated; the degree of integration in one or all plans must be cut back under complex guidelines. Planners generally find that if an employer has both a defined benefit plan and a profit sharing plan covering a common group of employees, it is most favorable to the employer and key employees to maximize the integration in the defined benefit plan and not to integrate the profit sharing plan at all.

Similarly, where an executive or owner of a small, closely-held business wants to obtain the full annual deductible contribution with the minimum cost for regular employees, a combination of an integrated money purchase plan and nonintegrated profit sharing plan often provides good results.

The regulations governing permitted disparity (i.e., integration) for defined contribution plans essentially provide as follows:

A defined contribution plan is integrated by providing a higher rate of contributions for compensation *above* a specified earnings level (excess contribution percentage) than for compensation below a specified earnings level (base contribution percentage).[21]

The maximum difference (i.e., the permitted disparity) between the excess contribution percentage and the base contribution percentage depends on the earnings level (integration level) chosen. If the integration level is the taxable wage base (TWB) used for Social Security purposes ($87,000 in 2003), the excess contribution percentage above the integration level cannot exceed the *lesser* of: (a) double the base percentage or (b) the base percentage plus 5.7%.[22] For example, if the employer contributes 5% for the first $87,000 of compensation, a contribution of up to 10% contribution can be made for compensation above that level. If, however, the base contribution percentage is 6% of the first $87,000, only an 11.7% contribution (not a 12% contribution) can be made for compensation above that level.

The regulations do not permit a defined contribution plan to use an integration level greater than the TWB plan;[23] however, an integration level *below* the TWB can be used. If an integration level below the TWB is chosen, then the permitted disparity is reduced as follows, depending on the amount of the integration level:[24]

- The maximum excess contribution percentage used in a plan where the integration level is 80% or more of the TWB ($69,600 to $86,999 in 2003) is the lesser of (a) double the base percentage or (b) the base percentage plus 5.4%.

- The maximum excess contribution percentage used in a plan where the integration level is 20% or more, but less than 80% of the TWB ($17,400 to $69,599 in 2003) is the lesser of (a) double the base percentage or (b) the base percentage plus 4.3%.

**Question** — What "integration level" should an employer choose?

*Answer* — Most small business owners will want to set the integration level at a point that will maximize contributions for owners and key employees. This can be accomplished by carefully looking at the employee census and assessing where a proper cutoff level would be.

Under prior law, the "optimum" integration level for a small business was just above the compensation level of the highest paid nonowner employee. This level gave *only* the owners the benefit of the extra percentage—the permitted disparity—under the integration rules.

Under the permitted disparity regulations, choosing an optimum integration level is *much more com-*

*plicated.* Because of the stepwise nature of the reduction in permitted disparity (see above), a reduction in the integration level sometimes increases the owner's benefit from the permitted disparity and in some cases it does not.

In deciding on a reduced integration level, in most cases it will not pay to reduce the integration level if the reduction reduces the owner's benefit level, so certain integration levels are unfavorable.

While in some cases the difference between the optimum integration level and simply using the TWB of $87,000 (in 2003) may be relatively small, can a financial planner afford not to point it out to a client before somebody else does?

**Question** — Can a participant in a qualified profit sharing plan use his profit sharing account to purchase insurance on the life of his spouse (or the joint lives of himself and his spouse)?

*Answer* — Yes. IRS rulings have permitted a participant in a profit sharing account to direct the plan trustee to purchase life insurance on the life of a person in whom he has an insurable interest.[25] Note that the plan must (a) include a "directed investment" (earmarking) provision and (b) permit the purchase of such life insurance. A plan that does not have these two provisions cannot be used for this purpose until it is amended to include the provisions.

The amount of the insurance that can be purchased on the participant's life is governed by the "incidental" limits discussed in Chapter 13. Note that for a profit sharing plan, these rules allow all amounts that have been in the plan for at least two years to be used for insurance. Therefore, profit sharing plans offer an opportunity to provide substantial amounts of insurance using tax-sheltered plan funds.

When an individual and his or her spouse have potentially large estates subject to federal estate tax, the tax becomes payable primarily at the death of the second, not the first to die. The advantage of a survivorship policy on an individual and spouse is that it provides substantial liquid funds when they are actually needed, and at an annual premium cost substantially lower than that for first-death insurance. If an individual in this situation has a substantial profit sharing account, that account provides a source of funds to pay premiums for this insurance.

As with insurance for the participant alone under a qualified plan, survivorship insurance results in current, annual taxable income to the participant. This income is not measurable under the P.S. 58 or Table 2001 rates, but rather using a lower annual cost reflecting the second-death feature.[26]

If the participant spouse dies first under this arrangement, the policy should be continued outside the plan. The participant (while living) should direct that at his death the policy (which is part of his profit sharing account balance) should be transferred to an irrevocable life insurance trust for the benefit of his family. If the nonparticipant spouse is the first to die, the participant should consider purchasing the policy from the plan, then contributing it to a life insurance trust.

Any purchase of a life insurance contract from the plan by the participant (or other party in interest, such as a relative) will be a "prohibited transaction" subject to penalties unless it meets the requirements set forth by the Department of Labor in Prohibited Transaction Exemption (PTE) 92-6. PTE 92-6 requires the following:

- the sale must be to a participant, a relative of the participant who is a beneficiary under the contract, an employer, or certain other employee benefit plans,

- the plan, but for the sale, would surrender the contract,

- if the purchaser is not the insurance-participant, the insured-participant must be given an opportunity to purchase the contract first, and

- the purchase price must put the plan in the same cash position as if it had retained the contract, surrendered it, and distributed the participant's vested interest in the plan.

The Department of Labor has clarified and confirmed that the sale of a second-to-die policy covering the participant and his spouse is covered under PTE 92-6.[27]

It should be noted that there are no other Treasury or IRS rulings (official or otherwise) which specifically sanction the use of survivorship policies in profit sharing plans.

## FOOTNOTES

1. IRC Section 401(a)(27)(A).

2. Treas. Reg. §1.401-1(b)(2).

3. IRC Section 414(s). See Treas. Reg. §1.414(s)-1.

4. IRC Section 401(a)(17).

5. Alternative methods for satisfying nondiscrimination requirements include satisfying a general nondiscrimination test, restructuring or cross-testing (testing defined contribution plans on the basis of benefits). See Treas. Reg. §1.401(a)(4)-2.

6. IRC Section 411(a)(12).

7. Treas. Reg. §1.401(a)(4)-1(b)(2)(ii).

8. Treas. Reg. §1.401-1(b)(1)(ii); Rev. Rul. 73-553, 1973-2 CB 130; Rev. Rul. 71-295, 1971-1 CB 184; Rev. Rul. 80-155, 1980-1 CB 84.

9. Rev. Rul. 68-24, 1968-1 CB 150.

10. See DOL Reg. §2550.404c-1.

11. DOL Reg. §2550.404c-1(b)(3).

12. IRC Section 401(a)(27)(B).

13. IRC Section 404(a)(3).

14. IRC Section 4972.

15. The exception generally applies to the extent that such contributions do not exceed the greater of (1) 6% of compensation (within the meaning of IRC Section 404(a) and as adjusted under Section 404(a)(12)) paid or accrued during the taxable year for which the contributions were made, to beneficiaries under the plans; or (2) the sum of employer matching contributions plus elective deferrals. See IRC Section 4972(c)(6)(B).

16. IRC Section 401(a)(17).

17. IRC Section 404(a)(7).

18. IRC Section 402(a).

19. IRC Section 415(c).

20. IRC Section 415(c)(2).

21. IRC Section 401(l)(2). See also, Treas. Regs. §§1.401(l)-1, -2, -4.

22. IRC Section 401(l)(2)(A).

23. IRC Section 401(l)(5)(A)(ii).

24. Treas. Reg. §1.401(l)-2(d).

25. Let Ruls. 8445095, 8108110 (co-shareholder).

26. Where the spouse or dependent coverage is available only through the purchase of a rider to the policy on the life of the participant, the cost of the insurance currently includable in the participant's income may not be measured by the actual cost of the rider, but must be measured using the P.S. 58 (or Table 2001) rate. See Let. Rul. 9023044.

27. DOL Adv. Op. 98-07A, September 24, 1998.

# Chapter 17

# ROTH IRAs

## WHAT IS IT?

A Roth IRA is a form of IRA under which contributions may be made up to a specified limit (see below) on a nondeductible basis, but withdrawals are tax free within certain limitations. Many provisions relating to Roth IRAs are best understood by comparison with traditional IRAs, so Chapter 24 on traditional IRAs should be reviewed as well.

Roth IRAs, like traditional IRAs, are primarily plans of individual savings. They are an alternative form of a tax-favored individual retirement plan. While they are not employee benefits, their features should be understood by benefit planners since they fit into an employee's plan of retirement savings and therefore they influence the form of employer retirement plans to some degree.

## WHEN IS IT INDICATED?

1. Like traditional IRAs, Roth IRAs are indicated when:

   • It is desirable to defer taxes on investment income.

   • Long-term accumulation, especially for retirement purposes, is an important objective.

   • A supplement or alternative to a qualified pension or profit sharing plan is needed.

2. The Roth IRA is indicated as an alternative to a traditional IRA when the particular tax benefits available under the Roth IRA are a better match to the individual's planning needs than the tax benefits from a traditional IRA. (See "Questions and Answers," below.)

## ADVANTAGES

1. Eligible individuals may contribute up to a specified limit (see below) to an IRA annually.

2. Withdrawals from a Roth IRA after (1) a five-year wait and (2) upon death or disability, for first-time home-buying expenses, or after age 59½ are tax-free in their entirety. That is, the initial investment as well as all investment income, capital gains, or other gains are entirely tax-free at the time of withdrawal.

3. Unlike traditional IRAs, Roth IRA contribution eligibility is not restricted by active participation in an employer's retirement plan.

4. Unlike traditional IRAs, Roth IRA contributions can be made after age 70½.

5. Roth IRAs are not subject to minimum distribution rules until the death of the Roth IRA owner. (For traditional IRAs, minimum distribution rules apply beginning at age 70½. Moreover, minimum distributions from traditional IRAs are generally taxable.)

## DISADVANTAGES

1. The Roth IRA contribution is limited each year for each individual, and this limit is reduced for single annual adjusted gross income (AGI) above $95,000 and eliminated entirely for single AGI of $110,000 or more. (The corresponding limits for joint-return filers are $150,000 and $160,000.)

2. Premature Roth IRA withdrawals in excess of contributions are taxed in full and are also subject to a 10% penalty on premature withdrawals similar to that applicable to traditional IRAs. (See the section on "Tax Implications," below.)

## TAX IMPLICATIONS

### Contribution Rules

1. *Contribution Limits.* The maximum Roth IRA contribution for an individual is the lesser of:

   (a) the dollar limit in the table below or (b) 100% of the individual's earned income, less contributions to traditional deductible or nondeductible IRAs (not including rollovers to such IRAs). As an example, for 2003, if an individual contributes $2,500 to a traditional deductible IRA, then no more than an additional $500 can be contributed to a Roth IRA.[1] "Earned income" means income from employment or self-employment; investment income cannot be counted. Earned income is computed the same for both traditional and Roth IRAs—for example, taxable alimony payments are included for both types of IRAs.

Generally, the annual dollar limit is as follows[2]:

| Taxable year beginning in | Dollar limit |
| --- | --- |
| 2002 through 2004 | $3,000 |
| 2005 through 2007 | $4,000 |
| 2008 | $5,000 |

After 2008, the dollar limit is scheduled to be adjusted for cost-of-living increases.[3]

For individuals who have attained age 50 before the close of the tax year, an additional dollar amount is allowable[4]—the resulting *total* amount is as follows:

| Year | Total dollar limit |
| --- | --- |
| 2002 through 2004 | $3,500 |
| 2005 | $4,500 |
| 2006 and 2007 | $5,000 |
| 2008 | $6,000 |

2. *AGI phaseout.* The contribution limit described in the preceding paragraph is phased out for taxpayers with higher adjusted gross incomes. The phaseout AGI limits are[5]:

| | |
| --- | --- |
| Unmarried individuals: | $95,000-110,000 |
| Married joint return filers: | $150,000-160,000 |
| Married separate filers: | $0—10,000 |

The adjusted gross income used for these limits is "modified" AGI, which excludes taxable income from a conversion of a traditional to a Roth IRA (see below).[6]

The reduction in the dollar limit in the phaseout AGI region is proportional to the amount by which the AGI exceeds the lower limit. For example, suppose that a single taxpayer's AGI is $102,500. The taxpayer is halfway into the $15,000 phaseout region, so his annual contribution limit for 2003 is reduced by half of the maximum amount (½ of $3,000, or $1,500). His annual contribution limit is therefore $3,000 less $1,500, or $1,500.

There is a $200 "floor" under the contribution limit; that is, the taxpayer can always contribute at least $200 until the AGI limit has been completely phased out. For example, if the taxpayer in the preceding example earned $109,900, he could still contribute up to $200 to a Roth IRA in that year.[7]

3. *Time Limits.* As with a traditional IRA, eligible persons may establish a Roth IRA account any time prior to the due date of their tax return, without extensions, even if taxpayers actually receive an extension of the filing date.[8] For most individuals or married couples the contribution cutoff date is April 15th. However, since earnings on a Roth IRA account accumulate tax-free, taxpayers may want to make contributions as early as possible in the tax year.

There is no restriction on contributions to a Roth IRA after the taxpayer reaches age 70½, unlike with a traditional IRA.[9]

4. *Nonrefundable Credit.* A limited nonrefundable tax credit is available to certain lower income taxpayers who make contributions to a Roth IRA. (see "Questions and Answers," below).

5. *Employer-sponsored Roth IRAs.* Employers can sponsor Roth IRAs for employees, as a limited alternative to an employer-sponsored qualified retirement plan. Employers who have a qualified plan can also sponsor a "deemed IRA" as part of the qualified plan to provide an alternative form of retirement savings for employees. See Chapter 24.

6. *Qualified Roth Contribution Programs.* After 2005, employers may amend their Section 401(k) or Section 403(b) plan to provide that participants' elective deferrals may be contributed to a "qualified Roth contribution program," which would be a separate account under the Section 401(k) or Section 403(b) plan. Contributions and distributions would be treated generally like Roth IRA amounts.[10]

## Distribution Rules

1. Account holders with more than one Roth IRA must treat them as a single account when calculating the tax consequences of distributions from any of them.[11]

Distributions from a Roth IRA are tax-free if the distribution meets both of the following requirements[12]:

(1) The distribution must be made after the 5-year period beginning with the first taxable year that the individual made a Roth IRA contribution, and

(2) The distribution must be

- made on or after the individual attains age 59½,

- made to a beneficiary or the individual's estate after the individual's death,

- attributable to the individual's being disabled ("total and permanent" social security definition of disability), or

- made for a first-time home purchase.

The 5-year holding period is defined as beginning with the first taxable year for which the account holder has a Roth IRA contribution of any kind. Subsequent rollovers into a Roth IRA will not require the running of a "new" 5-year holding period.

The "first-time homebuyer" exception is somewhat misleadingly titled. It is available for purchasing a principal residence of the individual, spouse, child, grandchild, or ancestor of the individual or spouse. Basically, it can be used at any time if the individual and spouse did not own a principal residence within the preceding 2 years. The exception can be used more than once. However (and this final rule severely limits the usefulness of this exception) there is a $10,000 lifetime limitation on the use of the first-time homebuyer exception for Roth IRAs.[13]

2. If a Roth IRA distribution is not tax-free under the rules described above, the distribution is subject to federal income tax, except that the total of the original nondeductible contributions are distributed first. Only after all contributions have been distributed will the earnings be deemed to have been withdrawn. In addition, there is a 10% penalty imposed on the taxable amount of any distribution, unless the distribution meets one of the exceptions to the 10% penalty for traditional IRAs (see Chapter 24).[14]

3. There are no minimum distribution requirements at age 70½ as there are for traditional IRAs, and the Roth IRA owner can therefore accumulate the fund until death if this is appropriate.

4. However, at the owner's death, the Roth IRA must be distributed within 5 years of the owner's death unless the owner has designated a beneficiary. If there is a designated beneficiary, the Roth IRA amount can be distributed over the life or life expectancy of the designated beneficiary as long as distributions begin within one year of the decedent's death.[15] If the beneficiary is the owner's spouse the surviving spouse can elect to treat the Roth IRA as his or her own. Distributions to beneficiaries after the owner's death are tax-free to the recipients, but they lose their character as Roth IRAs when distributed—that is, further investment returns on the amounts distributed are currently taxable.

## Rollovers

1. A Roth IRA can be rolled over to another Roth IRA tax-free.[16] As with traditional IRA rollovers, the transaction must be completed within 60 days, and only one rollover is permitted within a 12-month period.

2. There is no Code provision for rolling over a Roth IRA to a traditional IRA. A withdrawal can be made from a Roth IRA and contributed to a traditional IRA (deductible or nondeductible) within the annual limit for the year of the contribution. There is also no provision for rolling over a Roth IRA to a qualified plan or tax-deferred annuity (Section 403(b)) plan.

3. A traditional IRA (or any part of a traditional IRA) can be rolled over to a Roth IRA (generally this is referred to as a conversion of the traditional IRA to a Roth IRA). However, no conversion is permitted in a year in which the IRA owner's AGI exceeds $100,000.[17] AGI is determined on a joint-return basis if the IRA owner is married; conversions are not permitted for married individuals who file separately. According to the IRS, the fact that the owner's individual AGI is less than $100,000 is not material if the joint AGI exceeds $100,000. For tax years beginning in 2005, the definition of adjusted gross income has been modified to exclude minimum required distributions to IRA owners aged 70½ or older, solely for purposes of determining eligibility to convert a traditional IRA to a Roth IRA.[18]

The chief disadvantage of conversion is that the entire amount of the traditional IRA that is converted to a Roth IRA is generally taxable to the owner as ordinary income in the year of the conversion. This income is not included in AGI in determining whether the $100,000 limit has been met. Thus conversion accelerates all the taxes on the traditional IRA that could otherwise be deferred within the limits of the minimum distribution rules. To avoid bunching of income into high tax brackets, the conversion can be broken into a series of annual partial conversions.

See "Questions and Answers," below for criteria for determining whether a Roth IRA conversion is a good idea.

## WHERE CAN I FIND OUT MORE ABOUT IT?

1.  Most banks, savings and loans, insurance companies, and brokerage firms actively market IRAs, and can provide brochures describing their IRA plans. These firms will indicate the type of investments available as well as any charges that may be applied to such accounts.

2.  IRS Publication 590, *Individual Retirement Arrangements (IRAs)*, is available without charge from the IRS or the U.S. Government Printing Office. This publication covers traditional IRAs and Roth IRAs.

## QUESTIONS AND ANSWERS

**Question** — If a taxpayer is eligible for the maximum annual contribution to either a traditional or a Roth IRA, which should be chosen?

*Answer* — The analysis is somewhat complex, but from a strictly accounting viewpoint based on simple assumptions, the Roth IRA tends to provide slightly more money at retirement. However, individual circumstances may dictate otherwise. Figure 17.1 shows a comparison of various features of Roth and traditional IRAs.

The accounting analysis can be found in Auster and Chang, "Roth IRAs or Deductible IRAs: The Contribution and Conversion Decision," *Journal of Pension Planning and Compliance*, Vol. 24, Number 1.

To summarize the difference between the two, first note that if a taxpayer has $2,000 to invest on a before-tax basis, Roth IRAs and traditional IRAs are actuarially equivalent, assuming no change in tax rates.

---

*Example:* If a taxpayer invests $2,000 a year in a Roth IRA, this is a net investment of $1,440 (at a 28% tax rate). After 30 years at 10%, this grows to **$236,871**, free of taxes. If the taxpayer invests the full $2,000 each year in a traditional IRA, at 10% this grows in 30 years to $328,988; after paying 28% taxes the net amount is **$236,871**, the exact same amount as the Roth alternative.

---

This analysis is incomplete, however, because it fails to recognize that most taxpayers will invest the full $2,000 in the Roth IRA, not $1,440; they will find the tax money somewhere else. Likewise, the analysis thus far does not include contributing the tax savings from the traditional IRA to a side fund.

---

*Example:* In the article cited above, a comparison is made between (a) a $2,000 investment in a Roth IRA and (b) a $2,000 investment in a traditional IRA plus the results of investing the tax savings from the IRA deduction. For the same investment rates and tax rates, the Roth IRA always produces at least slightly better results. If you add in the fact that traditional IRAs must make minimum distributions beginning at age 70½ and Roth IRAs can be accumulated until death, the Roth IRA looks even better.

---

If you assume that tax rates increase at retirement, the benefits of Roth IRAs versus traditional IRAs increase further. An assumption that tax rates decrease at retirement improves the traditional IRA performance, but not generally by a great deal. Most advisors would hesitate to recommend a course of financial action based on a prediction of income tax rates far in the future (in the last 40 years the maximum federal income tax rate has varied from 28% to 91% with no predictable relation to politics or the economy) so these tax-rate arguments are mostly academic.

The increase in contributions and deduction limits after 2001 does not change the conclusions discussed here.

**Figure 17.1**

| COMPARISON OF TRADITIONAL AND ROTH IRA | | |
|---|---|---|
| | **TRADITIONAL IRA** | **ROTH IRA** |
| Contributions must be made out of earned income, not investment income | Yes | Yes |
| Annual dollar limit | Yes (before-tax). [total for sum of Roth and traditional IRA contributions] | Yes (after-tax). [total for sum of Roth and traditional IRA contributions] |
| Restrictions based on AGI | No, unless active participant in tax-favored employer plan | Yes, contribution limit phased out between $95,000 and $110,000 (single); $150,000 and $160,000 (joint) |
| Restrictions on deduction or contribution if active participant in tax-favored employer plan | Yes, deduction limited based on AGI | No |
| Tax-free buildup during accumulation period | Yes | Yes |
| Withdrawals tax-free | No | Yes, after waiting period |
| 10% penalty on early withdrawals | Yes | Yes |
| Required minimum distributions | Yes, beginning at earlier of age 70½ or death | Yes, beginning at death |
| Can rollover to (another) regular IRA | Yes (once annually) | No |
| Can rollover to (another) Roth IRA | Yes, if joint AGI $100,000 or less; must pay tax | Yes |
| Can rollover to qualified plan, TDA or Section 457 governmental plan | Yes | No |

**Question** — Is it advisable to convert a traditional IRA to a Roth IRA, assuming that the $100,000 AGI test has been met?

*Answer* — The strict accounting analysis of this issue is the same as for the $2,000 annual deduction, as discussed in the Auster and Chang article cited above. The Roth IRA conversion produces better results on this basis (especially if taxes are not paid out of the amount converted) and is therefore a good idea on paper. The longer the converted assets remain in the Roth IRA before withdrawal, the greater the advantage. Considering how long taxes can be deferred on traditional IRAs (see Appendix J) this is a surprising but irrefutable result. The big stumbling point is that the conversion requires all the federal income taxes on the converted amount to be paid up front. In the future tax rates could be drastically reduced or the income tax even eliminated; nobody can predict this.

**Question** — If I decide to convert my traditional IRA to a Roth IRA, can I move the money back to a traditional IRA within the same year (or before the tax return due date) if that is advantageous (for example if the value of the assets decline, making the tax bite too severe to proceed with the conversion, or AGI increases above $100,000)?

*Answer* — If the transfer from traditional IRA to Roth IRA was made in a direct trustee-to-trustee transfer, the amount can be "recharacterized" as a traditional IRA under a procedure in the Regulations.[19]

**Question** — Who is eligible to claim a nonrefundable credit for contributions to a Roth IRA?

*Answer* — Certain lower-income taxpayers may claim a temporary, nonrefundable credit for "qualified retirement savings contributions" in taxable years beginning after 2001 and before 2007.[20] "Qualified retirement savings contributions" include contributions to Roth or traditional IRAs, as well as elective deferrals to certain plans. (However, the total is reduced by certain distributions received by the taxpayer or his spouse during the prior two taxable years and the current taxable year for which the credit is claimed, including the period up to the due date (plus extensions) for filing the federal income tax return for the current taxable year.)

The credit is allowed against the sum of the regular tax and the alternative minimum tax (minus certain other credits) and is allowed in addition to any other deduction or exclusion that would otherwise apply. In addition, to be eligible, the taxpayer must be at least 18 as of the end of the tax year and must not be claimed as a dependent by someone else or be a full-time student.

The amount of the credit is limited to an "applicable percentage" of IRA contributions and elective deferrals up to $2,000. The "applicable percentages" are as follows:

### ADJUSTED GROSS INCOME

| Joint return | | Head of a household | | All other cases | | Applicable percentage |
| Over | Not over | Over | Not over | Over | Not over | |
| --- | --- | --- | --- | --- | --- | --- |
| 0 | $30,000 | 0 | $22,500 | 0 | $15,000 | 50% |
| 30,000 | 32,500 | 22,500 | 24,375 | 15,000 | 16,250 | 20% |
| 32,500 | 50,000 | 24,375 | 37,500 | 16,250 | 25,000 | 10% |
| 50,000 | | 37,500 | | 25,000 | | 0% |

*Example:* Ben and Fran have adjusted gross income of $31,000 for 2002. They each contribute $2,000 to a Roth IRA. Neither has received any distributions in the current or two preceding taxable years. Ben and Fran will be able to claim a credit of $400 (20% x $2,000) on their joint return (for a total of $800) for 2002.

## FOOTNOTES

1. IRC Section 408A(c)(2).

2. IRC Sections 408A(c)(2), 219(b)(5), as amended by The Economic Growth and Tax Relief Reconciliation Act of 2001 (EGTRRA 2001). Note that all provisions of EGTRRA 2001 are scheduled to sunset, or expire, after December 31, 2010.

3. IRC Section 219(b)(5)(C), as added by EGTRRA 2001.

4. IRC Section 219(b)(5)(B), as added by EGTRRA 2001.

5. IRC Section 408A(c)(3); Treas. Reg. §1.408A-3, Q&A 3.

6. IRC Section 408A(c)(3)(C)(i); Treas. Regs. §§1.408A-3, Q&A 5, Q&A 6.

7. IRC Section 408A(c)(3)(A), flush left language; Treas. Reg. §1.408A-3, Q&A-3.

8. See IRC Section 219(f)(3). Except for rules added by IRC Section 408A, Roth IRAs are subject to the same rules as traditional IRAs. IRC Section 408A(a).

9. IRC Section 408A(c)(4).

10. IRC Section 402A, as added by EGTRRA 2001.

11. IRC Section 408A(d)(4)(A), referencing IRC Section 408(d)(2).

12. IRC Section 408A(d)(2).

13. IRC Sections 408A(d)(5), 72(t)(8).

14. Treas. Reg. §1.408A-6, Q&A 5.

15. IRC Section 408A(c)(5).

16. IRC Section 408A(c)(3)(B).

17. IRC Section 408A(c)(3)(B)(i).

18. IRC Section 408A(c)(3)(C)(i).

19. Treas. Reg. §1.408A-5.

20. IRC Section 25B, as added by EGTRRA 2001.

# Chapter 18

# SAVINGS/MATCH PLAN

## WHAT IS IT?

A savings plan (or "thrift plan") is a qualified defined contribution plan that is similar to a profit sharing plan, with features that provide for and encourage after-tax employee contributions to the plan.

A typical savings plan provides for after-tax employee contributions with matching employer contributions. Each employee elects to contribute a certain percentage of his or her compensation, and these employee contributions are matched—either dollar for dollar or under some other formula—by employer contributions to the plan. Employee contributions are not deductible—the employee pays tax on the money before contributing it to the plan.

"Pure" savings plans, featuring only after-tax employee contributions are rare. However, a savings plan with after-tax employee contributions (often matched by the employer) is often part of a Section 401(k) plan or profit-sharing plan.

## WHEN IS IT INDICATED?

1. As an add-on feature to a Section 401(k) plan to allow employees to increase contributions beyond the annual limit on salary reductions under Section 401(k) plans. However, after-tax contributions are subject to their own complex limitations as discussed under "Tax Implications," below.

2. When the employee group has the following characteristics:

   • Many employees are relatively young and have substantial time to accumulate retirement savings.

   • Many employees are willing to accept a degree of investment risk in their plan accounts in return for the potential benefits of good investment results.

   • There is a wide variation among employees in the need or desire for retirement savings.

3. When the employer wants to supplement the company's defined benefit pension plan with a plan that features individual participant accounts and the opportunity for participants to save on a tax-deferred basis. The use of a combination of plans provides a balanced retirement program. The defined benefit plan appeals to older employees with a desire for secure retirement benefits, while the savings plan (or other defined contribution plan such as a profit sharing or Section 401(k) plan) generally appeals to younger employees who prefer to see their savings build up year-by-year rather than anticipating a projected benefit when they retire.

## ADVANTAGES

1. As with all qualified plans, a savings plan provides a tax-deferred retirement savings medium for employees. The tax on the employee contributions themselves are not deferred (since they are made on an after-tax basis); however, income taxes on subsequent investment earnings are deferred until distributions are made to employees from the plan.

2. The plan allows employees to control the amount of their savings. Employees have the option of taking all their compensation in cash and not contributing to the plan. (However, if they do so, they generally lose any employer matching contributions under the plan.)

3. Lump-sum distributions from the plan may be eligible for a special 10-year averaging tax computation (available to certain employees born before 1936).

4. Individual participant accounts allow participants to benefit from good results in the plan fund.

## DISADVANTAGES

1. The plan cannot be counted on by employees to provide an adequate benefit. First, benefits will not

be significant unless employees make substantial contributions to the plan on a regular basis. Furthermore, employees who enter the plan at older ages may not be able to make sufficient contributions to the plan, even if they wish to do so, because of (a) the limits on annual contributions discussed under "Tax Implications," below, and (b) the limited number of years remaining for plan contributions prior to retirement.

2. Employees bear investment risk under the plan. Bearing the investment risk is a potential disadvantage to employees, but from the employer's perspective the shift of risk is a positive feature. Employer costs are lower for a defined contribution plan such as a savings plan, as compared with a defined benefit plan.

3. Since employee accounts and matching amounts must be individually accounted for in the plan, the administrative costs for a savings plan are greater than those for a money purchase or a profit sharing plan without employee contributions.

4. The annual addition to each employee's account in a savings plan is limited to the *lesser of* (a) 100% of compensation or (b) $40,000 (in 2003 as indexed).[1] This may limit the relative tax advantage available to highly compensated employees under a savings plan or any other defined contribution plan.

## DESIGN FEATURES

Typical savings plans provide after-tax employee contributions with employer matching contributions. Participation in the plan is voluntary; each employee elects to contribute a chosen percentage of compensation up to a maximum percentage specified in the plan. The employee receives no tax deduction for this contribution and the contribution is fully subject to income tax as if it were in the employee's hands.

The employer makes a matching contribution to the savings plan. The employer match can be dollar-for-dollar, or the employer may put in some percentage of the employee contribution. A typical plan might permit an employee to contribute annually any whole percentage of compensation from 1% to 6%, with the employer contributing at the rate of half the chosen employee percentage. In this example then, if the employee elected to contribute 4% of compensation, the employer would be obligated to contribute an additional 2%.

Employer matching contributions are subject to the same vesting requirements as are applied to top-heavy plans; that is, 100% cliff vesting after three years, or graded vesting starting with 20% after two years, increasing by 20% each year until 100% is reached after six years.[2] This represents faster vesting than the normal 3-to-7-year rule.

In general, higher paid employees are in a position to contribute considerably more to this type of plan than lower paid employees. To prevent discrimination in savings plans, Section 401(m) imposes tests that effectively limit contributions by highly compensated employees (discussed under "Tax Implications," below). One of the principal administrative burdens in a savings plan is a need to monitor employee contribution levels to be sure the Section 401(m) nondiscrimination tests are met.

Apart from the employee contribution features, savings plans have features similar to profit sharing plans. Emphasis is usually put on the "savings account-like" features of the plan. Usually there are generous provisions for employee withdrawal of funds and for plan loans. Savings plans often feature participant-investment direction or earmarking. Earmarking is usually provided by allowing employees a choice among several specified pooled investment funds (such as mutual funds). However, it is possible, although administratively burdensome, to allow participants to direct virtually any type of investment for their account. If certain Department of Labor regulations are satisfied, the plan trustee and the employer are relieved of fiduciary liability for unsatisfactory investment results from investments chosen by the participant under a participant-directed investment provision.[3] The regulations include the requirement that at least three different diversified investment alternatives be made available to the employee. Life insurance can be used in the plan, as discussed in Chapter 13.

Although savings plans with only after-tax employee contributions and employer matching contributions were very popular in the past, the after-tax employee contribution approach is used more often as an add-on to a Section 401(k) plan. Employers often adopt a plan that combines all the features of a regular profit sharing plan, a savings plan, and Section 401(k) salary reductions. These combined plans can have one or more of the following features:

- employee after-tax contributions

- employer matching of employee after-tax contributions

- employee (before-tax) salary reductions (Section 401(k) amounts)

- employer matching of Section 401(k) amounts

- employer contributions based on a formula

- discretionary employer contributions

These are discussed further in Chapter 19.

## TAX IMPLICATIONS

1. Employer contributions to the plan are deductible when made so long as the plan remains "qualified" and separate accounts are maintained for all participants in the plan.[4] A plan is qualified if it meets eligibility, vesting, funding and other requirements discussed in Chapter 25. Employer matching contributions are subject to an accelerated vesting schedule (see Chapter 25).

2. Employee contributions to the plan, whether or not matched, are not tax deductible. (Before-tax employee salary reductions must meet the requirements of Section 401(k) discussed in Chapter 19.)

3. Assuming a plan remains qualified, taxation of the employee is deferred with respect to (a) employer contributions to the plan and (b) investment earnings on both employer and employee contributions. These amounts are nontaxable to plan participants until a distribution is made from the plan.[5] Recovery of the nontaxable amount differs depending on whether the after-tax contributions were made before 1987 or after 1986. See Chapter 26, Section IV, "Nontaxable and Taxable Amounts."

4. In order to be deemed nondiscriminatory (i.e., to prevent the plan from discriminating in favor of highly compensated employees), the plan must meet an *actual contribution percentage* (ACP) test under Code section 401(m). This test is applied to employee contributions, as well as to matching contributions; however, *employee* contributions must be tested under the first alternative (alternative (a)), while *matching* contributions can meet the ACP test in any of the following three alternative ways:

   (a) The ACP test is satisfied for a plan year if, for highly compensated employees, the average ratio (expressed as a percentage) *of* employee contributions (both matched and non-matched) plus employer matching contributions *to compensation for the plan year* does not exceed the greater of:

   (i) 125 percent of the contribution percentage (i.e., ratio) for all other eligible employees *for the preceding plan year*, or

   (ii) the lesser of (a) 200 percent of the contribution percentage for all other eligible employees, or (b) such percentage plus two percentage points *for the preceding plan year*.

   For example, if employee contributions and employer matching contributions for nonhighly compensated employees equaled 6% of compensation in 2003, those for highly compensated employees could be up to 8% (6% plus 2%) in 2003. Under the Code and regulations, the employer may take into account certain 401(k) salary reduction contributions and certain employer plan contributions in meeting this test.[6]

   (b) Alternatively, the ACP test can be satisfied with respect to matching contributions by meeting the requirements for a SIMPLE 401(k) plan (see Chapter 19).

   (c) Under a simplified safe harbor test, the plan satisfies the nondiscrimination test with respect to matching contributions if it satisfies (i) a contribution requirement, (ii) a notice requirement and (iii) a matching contribution limitation. This test generally parallels the requirements for a safe harbor 401(k) plan (described in Chapter 19) as follows:

   The *contribution requirement* for the safe harbor test states that the employer must make either matching contributions (equal to 100% of elective contributions but not exceeding 3% of compensation, *plus* 50% of elective contributions that exceed 3% but do not exceed 5% of compensation; however, in no event can the rate for highly compensated employees exceed the rate for nonhighly compensated employees) OR nonelective contributions (on behalf of all employees, equal to at least 3% of compensation).

   Under the *notice requirement*, each employee eligible to participate must, before the plan year begins, be given written notice that (i) the plan may be amended during the plan year to provide a nonelective contribution of at least

3%, and (ii) if it is, a supplemental notice will be given to eligible employees 30 days prior to the last day of the plan year informing them of the amendment. If the plan is amended, the supplemental notice must then be provided to each eligible employee at least 30 days prior to the end of the plan year (i.e., by December 1 for a calendar year).[7]

The *matching contribution limitation* is met if (i) no employer match can be made for employee deferrals in excess of 6% of compensation, (ii) the rate of match does not increase as the employee deferral rate increases, and (iii) matching contribution rates for highly compensated employees are not greater than those for nonhighly compensated employees.[8]

Under alternative (a), the employer must conduct annual testing to monitor the level of contributions made by nonhighly compensated employees, and then make sure that highly compensated employees do not exceed this level the following year, in order for the plan to remain qualified. Alternatives (b) and (c) are design-based so that annual testing of matching contributions is not necessary, but both include a funding requirement.

The definition of highly compensated employee for purposes of these tests is the same as that applicable to all benefit plans (and is discussed in detail in Chapter 25).

5. Certain employers adopting a new plan may be eligible for a business tax credit of up to $500 for "qualified startup costs." See Chapter 27 for details.

6. A plan may permit employees to make voluntary contributions to a "deemed IRA" established under the plan. Amounts so contributed reduce the limit for other traditional or Roth IRA contributions. See Chapter 24 for details.

7. Distributions from the plan must follow the rules for qualified plan distributions. Certain premature distributions are subject to penalties. The distribution rules are discussed in Chapter 26.

8. Certain employees born before 1936 may be eligible for a 10-year averaging tax calculation on lump-sum distributions. Not all distributions are eligible for these special tax calculations. The rules are discussed in detail in Chapter 26.

9. The plan is subject to the ERISA reporting and disclosure rules outlined in Appendix A.

## HOW TO INSTALL A PLAN

Installation of a savings plan follows the qualified plan installation procedures described in Chapter 27.

## WHERE CAN I FIND OUT MORE ABOUT IT?

1. *Tax Facts 1*, Cincinnati, OH: The National Underwriter Company, (revised annually).

## FOOTNOTES

1. IRC Section 415(c). Note that all provisions of EGTRRA 2001 are scheduled to sunset, or expire, after December 31, 2010.
2. IRC Section 411(a)(12).
3. DOL Reg. §2550.404c-1.
4. IRC Section 404(a)(3).
5. IRC Section 402(a).
6. IRC Section 401(m)(3); Treas. Reg. §1.401(m)-1(b)(5).
7. Notice 2000-3, 2000-1 CB 413.
8. IRC Sections 401(m)(11)(a)(i), 401(k)(12)(C).

# Chapter 19

# SECTION 401(k) PLAN

## WHAT IS IT?

A Section 401(k) plan (also known as a "cash or deferred arrangement" or CODA) is a qualified profit sharing or stock bonus plan under which plan participants have an option to put money in the plan or receive the same amount as taxable cash compensation. Contributions are permitted of up to $12,000 annually for years beginning in 2003 plus "catch-up contributions" (see below).[1] Amounts contributed to the plan under these options are not taxable to the participants until withdrawn. Aside from features related to the cash or deferred option, a traditional Section 401(k) plan is much like a regular qualified profit sharing plan described in Chapter 16. SIMPLE 401(k) plans and safe harbor 401(k) plans (see the Questions and Answers at the end of this chapter) vary from the traditional arrangements in that each has a funding requirement; however, such plans are exempt from the special ADP nondiscrimination testing that applies to traditional 401(k) plans.

## WHEN IS IT INDICATED?

1. When an employer wants to provide a qualified retirement plan for employees but can afford only minimal extra expense beyond existing salary and benefit costs. Traditional 401(k) plans can be funded entirely from employee salary reductions, except for installation and administration costs. In most plans, however, additional direct employer contributions to the plan will enhance its effectiveness.

2. When an employer is willing to meet a minimal funding requirement for nonhighly compensated employees and wants to maximize the contributions available to highly compensated employees without annual ADP testing. A SIMPLE 401(k) plan or a safe harbor plan (see the Questions and Answers at the end of this chapter) can offer many of the advantages of a traditional plan, without the nondiscrimination testing.

3. When the employee group has one or more of the following characteristics:

- Many would like some choice as to the level of savings—that is, a choice between various levels of current cash compensation and tax deferred savings. A younger, more mobile work force often prefers this option.

- Many employees are relatively young and have substantial time to accumulate retirement savings.

- Many employees are willing to accept a degree of investment risk in their plan accounts in return for the potential benefits of good investment results.

4. When an employer wants an attractive, "savings-type" supplement to its existing defined benefit or other qualified retirement plan. Such a supplement can make the employer's retirement benefit program attractive to both younger and older employees by providing both security of retirement benefits and the opportunity to increase savings and investment on a tax-deferred basis.

5. When the organization is a private taxpaying or tax-exempt organization. Governmental employers may not adopt Section 401(k) plans.

## ADVANTAGES

1. As with all qualified plans, a Section 401(k) plan provides a tax-deferred retirement savings medium for employees.

2. A Section 401(k) plan allows employees a degree of choice in the amount they wish to save under the plan. The amounts—both as dollar amounts and as percentages of payroll—that can be contributed to 401(k) plans by employees and employers are scheduled for substantial increases (see "Design Features" below).

3. The employer's deduction for plan contributions is 25% of the total payroll of employees covered under the plan. Furthermore, "total payroll" for purposes

of the 25% limit includes elective deferral amounts. However, the deduction limit does not apply to elective deferral amounts. In other words, an employer may contribute and deduct up to 25% in addition to elective deferrals.[2] A higher deduction limit applies to SIMPLE 401(k) plans.

4. Traditional Section 401(k) plans can be funded entirely through salary reductions by employees. As a result, an employer can adopt the plan with no additional cost for employee compensation; the only extra cost is plan installation and administration. The plan may actually result in some savings as a result of lower state or local (but not federal) payroll taxes.

5. Plan distributions may be eligible for a special 10-year averaging tax computation (available to certain employees born before 1936) on lump-sum distributions that may reduce tax rates on the benefit.

6. In-service withdrawals by employees for certain "hardships" are permitted; these are not available in qualified pension plans.

## DISADVANTAGES

1. As with all defined contribution plans (except target plans), account balances at retirement age may not provide adequate retirement savings for employees who entered the plan at later ages.

2. The annual employee salary reduction under the plan is limited to $12,000 in 2003. (However, employees over age 50 as of the end of the plan year may supplement this amount with "catch-up" contributions of up to $2,000 in 2003, as explained below.) In addition, employers may make matching or nonelective contributions to provide additional tax-deferred savings. For details and scheduled increases of these limits, see "Design Features," below.

3. Because of the "actual deferral percentage" (ADP) nondiscrimination test described below, a Section 401(k) plan can be relatively costly and complex to administer. Safe harbor 401(k) plans and SIMPLE 401(k) plans are not subject to this test; however, both require that certain funding requirements be met. (See "Questions and Answers" below for the requirements of each of these plans.)

4. Employees bear investment risk under the plan. (However, they can also potentially benefit from good investment results.)

## DESIGN FEATURES

### Salary Reductions

Section 401(k) plans are generally built around salary reduction contributions elected by employees. A possible alternative is for the employer to provide an annual "bonus" to employees that the employees can either receive in cash or contribute to the plan. "Negative election" provisions are also permitted; these are plan provisions whereby the employer automatically contributes a specified portion of each employee's salary to the 401(k) plan unless the employee specifically requests to receive the amount in cash.[3]

Salary reductions must be elected by employees *before* compensation is earned—that is, before they render the services for which compensation is paid. Salary reductions elected after compensation is earned are ineffective as a result of the tax doctrine of "constructive receipt."

The usual practice is to provide plan participants with a salary reduction election form that they must complete before the end of each calendar year. The election specifies how much will be contributed to the plan from each paycheck received for the forthcoming year. Usually the plan will permit the employee to reduce or entirely withdraw the election for pay not yet earned, if circumstances dictate. The plan must restrict each participant's salary reductions to no more than the annual limits set forth in the Code (see below).

The participant is always 100% vested in any salary reductions contributed to the plan and any plan earnings on those salary reductions. Even if a participant leaves employment after a short time, his portion of his plan account attributable to salary reductions cannot be forfeited. Usually plan account balances are distributed in a lump sum when a participant terminates employment.

Salary reductions, as well as any other plan contribution which the employee has the option to receive in cash (referred to as "elective deferrals"), are subject to an annual limit. The limit is a "per employee" rather than a "per plan" limit. The employee must add together each year all elective deferrals from (1) Section 401(k) plans, (2) salary reduction SEPs (available if established before 1997-see Chapter 21), (3) SIMPLE IRAs (see Chapter 20), and (4) Section 403(b) tax deferred annuity plans (see Chapter 23). (Note that deferrals from a 457 plan need not be aggregated, see Chapter 11). The total must not exceed the following limits:[4]

| Year | Amount |
|------|--------|
| 2003 | $ 12,000 |
| 2004 | 13,000 |
| 2005 | 14,000 |
| 2006 and thereafter | 15,000 |

In addition to the foregoing salary reductions, employees who have reached age 50 during the plan year can make "catch-up" contributions. For traditional and safe harbor 401(k) plans (but not SIMPLE 401(k) plans), the elective deferral limit is increased by the following "catch-up" amounts:[5]

| Year | Amount |
|------|--------|
| 2003 | $ 2,000 |
| 2004 | 3,000 |
| 2005 | 4,000 |
| 2006 and thereafter | 5,000 |

SIMPLE 401(k) plans are subject to a lower annual elective deferral limit; the following limits apply:[6]

| Year | Amount |
|------|--------|
| 2002 | $ 7,000 |
| 2003 | 8,000 |
| 2004 | 9,000 |
| 2005 and thereafter | 10,000 |

The corresponding age-50-or-over catch-up limit for SIMPLE 401(k) plans is[7]

| Year | Amount |
|------|--------|
| 2002 | $ 500 |
| 2003 | 1,000 |
| 2004 | 1,500 |
| 2005 | 2,000 |
| 2006 and thereafter | 2,500 |

Finally, a plan may permit employees to make voluntary contributions to a "deemed IRA" established under the plan. Amounts so contributed reduce the limit for other traditional or Roth IRA contributions. See Chapter 13 for details. Contributions under this provision may also (as with elective deferrals and with other IRA contributions) count toward the nonrefundable "saver's credit" for lower-income taxpayers, explained in the Questions and Answers below.

## Employer Contributions

Many Section 401(k) plans provide matching or nonelective employer contributions in order to encourage employee participation and make the plan more valuable to employees. In fact, in the case of safe harbor 401(k) plans and SIMPLE 401(k) plans, the Code requires that the terms of the plan provide for certain matching or nonelective contributions. (See "Questions and Answers" below, for details.) Section 401(k) plans typically use one or more of the following types of employer contributions:

- Formula matching contributions. The employer matches employee salary reductions, either dollar for dollar or under another formula. For example, the plan might provide that the employer contributes an amount equal to 50% of the amount the employee elects as a salary reduction. So, if an employee elected a salary reduction of $6,000, the employer would put an additional $3,000 into the employee's plan account.

- Discretionary matching contributions. Under this approach, the employer has discretion to make a contribution to the plan each year; the employer contribution is allocated to each participant's plan account in proportion to the amount elected by the participant as a salary reduction during that year. For example, at the end of a year the employer might decide to make a discretionary matching contribution of 40% of each participant's salary reduction for the year. Thus, if a participant had salary reductions of $5,000 for that year, the employer would contribute another $2,000 to that participant's account.

- Pure discretionary or "profit sharing" contributions. The employer makes a discretionary nonelective contribution to the plan that is allocated simply on the basis of each employee's compensation, without regard to the amount of salary reductions elected by that employee. For example, at the end of a year the employer might decide to contribute another $100,000 to the plan. This contribution would be allocated to plan participants' accounts in the same manner as a discretionary profit sharing contribution, as described in Chapter 16.

- Formula contributions. For example, the plan might provide that the employer will contribute 3% of compensation to the plan for employees whose annual compensation is less than $50,000.

So, for an employee who earned $30,000, the employer would contribute 3%, or $900, to that employee's plan account.

Chapter 18, Savings/Match Plan, covers design and advantages of employer matching arrangements as well as the use of employee after-tax contributions, whether in a stand-alone plan or as part of a Section 401(k) arrangement. Matching contributions may be subject to a test for nondiscrimination under Code Section 401(m). This "ACP" test is explained in Chapter 18.

## Plan Distributions

Distributions from Section 401(k) plans are subject to the qualified plan distribution rules detailed in Chapter 26. Most plans provide for distributions in a lump sum at termination of employment, which typically are rolled over to IRAs.

Section 401(k) plans can allow participants to make in-service withdrawals (withdrawals before termination of employment); however, there are a variety of restrictions that reduce the availability of such distributions to employees. These restrictions apply whether the plan is a traditional, safe harbor, or SIMPLE 401(k) plan.

First, there is a special rule that Section 401(k) account funds attributable to elective deferrals cannot be distributed prior to occurrence of one of the following:

- retirement

- death

- disability

- severance from employment with the employer

- attainment of age 59½ by the participant

- plan termination (if the employer has no other defined contribution plan other than an ESOP)

- hardship.[8]

"Hardship" is defined more restrictively than many participants may think, as discussed in the "Questions and Answers," below.

Note also that many pre-retirement distributions will not only be taxable, but will also be subject to the 10% early withdrawal penalty tax discussed in Chapter 26. To summarize, a 10% penalty tax applies to the taxable amount (amount subject to regular income tax) of any qualified plan distribution, except for distributions:

- after age 59½

- on the employee's death

- upon the employee's disability

- that are part of a joint or life annuity payout following separation from service

- that are paid after separation from service after attaining age 55, or

- that do not exceed the amount of medical expenses deductible as an itemized deduction for the year.[9]

From this list, it is evident that many "hardship" distributions from a Section 401(k) plan, though permitted by the terms of the plan, will be subject to the 10% penalty tax.

Many Section 401(k) plans have provisions for plan loans to participants. A plan loan provision may be extremely valuable to employees because it allows them access to their plan funds without the "hardship" restriction or the 10% penalty tax. Plan loans are discussed in detail in Chapter 26.

## TAX IMPLICATIONS

1.  Employee elective deferrals (i.e., salary reductions) up to the annual limit ($12,000 in 2003, plus any permitted catch-up contributions) are not subject to income tax to the employee in the year of deferral.[10] However, elective deferrals are subject to Social Security tax (both employer and employee).[11] In other words, even though salary has been deferred for income tax purposes, it is treated as received for Social Security purposes.

2.  The sum of all types of employer contributions to a traditional or safe harbor 401(k) plan are deductible by the employer for federal income tax purposes up to a limit of 25% of the total payroll of all employees covered under the plan. The employer deduction limit for SIMPLE 401(k) plan contributions is the greater of 25% of payroll or the amount of contributions required under the Code for such plans.[12]

Employee elective deferrals (salary reductions) do not have to be counted toward the 25% limit for any type of 401(k) plan. In other words, the employer may deduct as much as 25%, in addition to the employees' elective deferral amounts.

---

*Example:* Anxious Corp. has a traditional 401(k) plan, and its payroll for 2003 for employees covered under the plan is $400,000. In addition, employee elective deferrals in 2003 total $60,000. For 2003, Anxious Corp. can deduct up to a total of $115,000 for the 401(k) plan (25% of [$400,000 plus $60,000]). Furthermore, the $60,000 of elective deferrals can, but does not have to be, counted as part of this $115,000. (The $60,000 representing elective deferrals is subject to Social Security tax and FUTA—see below).

---

3. Elective deferrals, but not nonelective employer contributions, are subject to Social Security (FICA) and federal unemployment (FUTA) payroll taxes. The impact of state payroll taxes depends on the particular state's law. Both elective deferrals and nonelective employer contributions may be exempt from state payroll taxes in some states.

4. Elective deferrals in a traditional 401(k) plan must meet a special test for nondiscrimination—the "actual deferral percentage" or ADP test. (No ADP testing is necessary in the case of a SIMPLE 401(k) plan or a safe harbor plan; see the questions and answers at the end of this chapter for details.) To meet this requirement, the plan must satisfy, in actual operation, one of two alternative ADP tests as follows:[13]

> *Test 1* — The ADP for eligible highly compensated employees for the plan year is not more than the ADP of all other eligible employees *for the preceding plan year* multiplied by 1.25.

> *Test 2* — The ADP for eligible highly compensated employees for the plan year does not exceed the ADP for other eligible employees *for the preceding plan year* by more than 2% *and* the ADP for eligible highly compensated employees for the plan year is not more than the ADP of all other eligible employees *for the preceding plan* year multiplied by two.

This ADP testing method is referred to as "prior year testing." As an alternative, the ADP for

nonhighly compensated employees for the *current plan year* may be used under either test, but certain restrictions apply to a plan that uses current year testing and later wishes to change to prior year testing. No special restrictions apply to employers wishing to change from prior year testing back to current year testing.[14]

---

*Example:* If the ADP for nonhighly compensated employees in 2003 was 3%, the ADP for highly compensated employees in 2004 could be as high as 5% (3% plus 2%), using prior year testing. This meets the second test. The plan document must state whether the plan uses current year testing or prior year testing.

---

"Highly compensated employee" is defined (for this and all qualified plan purposes; see Chapter 25) as an employee who:[15]

- was during the current or preceding plan year, a more than 5% owner of the employer, or

- received compensation *for the preceding year* from the employer over $90,000 (in 2003 as indexed) *and* (if the employer elects the use of a "top-paid group" provision) was in the "top-paid group" for the preceding year.

5. Whether the 401(k) plan is a traditional, SIMPLE or safe harbor plan, it is subject to the limits of Code section 415. This means that annual additions to each participant's account are limited to the *lesser of* (a) 100% of compensation or (b) $40,000.[16] Annual additions include the total of (1) nonelective employer contributions to the participant's account, (2) salary reductions or other elective deferrals contributed to the account, (3) forfeitures from other participants' accounts, and (4) after-tax employee contributions to the account.[17]

6. Distributions from the plan to employees are subject to income tax when received. Lump sum distributions may be eligible for the special 10-year averaging (for certain employees born before 1936) tax computation available for qualified plans. Not all distributions are eligible for this calculation. Details on the taxation of distributions are discussed in Chapter 26.

7. A limited nonrefundable tax credit, known as the "saver's credit," is available to certain lower income

taxpayers who make salary deferrals (see Questions and Answers below).

8. Certain employers adopting a new plan may be eligible for a business tax credit of up to $500 for "qualified startup costs." See Chapter 27 for details.

## HOW TO INSTALL A PLAN

Installation of a Section 401(k) plan follows the qualified plan installation procedures described in Chapter 27.

In addition, elective deferral or salary reduction forms must be completed by plan participants *before* the plan's effective date so that salary reduction elections will be immediately effective. The plan may provide for a *negative election*, under which a fixed percentage of each employee's salary is contributed unless he elects *not* to participate, so long as each eligible employee is afforded the opportunity to receive the amount as cash or as a contribution.[18]

The establishment of a safe harbor plan or a SIMPLE 401(k) plan, requires that participants be provided with notice of the availability (or potential availability) of the plan prior to the commencement of the plan year.[19]

The success of a traditional Section 401(k) plan in meeting the employer's objectives and passing the ADP test depends on effective communication with employees. Effective employer-employee communication is always important in employee benefit plans, but it is particularly essential for a traditional 401(k) plan because of the active role of employees in the plan.

In those situations where the deferral rates by nonhighly compensated employees severely limit the ability of highly compensated employees to benefit from a traditional 401(k) plan, employers willing to meet certain funding requirements can remove the plan from ADP testing by adopting a safe harbor plan or a SIMPLE 401(k) plan (see "Questions and Answers" below). In both cases, the benefits available to highly compensated employees are unaffected by the participation levels of nonhighly compensated employees.

## WHERE CAN I FIND OUT MORE ABOUT IT?

1. Graduate Course: Advanced Pension and Retirement Planning I (GS 814), The American College, Bryn Mawr, PA.

2. IRS Publication 560, Retirement Plans for Small Business. This publication is available free from the IRS and is revised annually.

3. *Tax Facts 1*, The National Underwriter Company, updated annually.

## QUESTIONS AND ANSWERS

**Question** — What kinds of organizations can adopt Section 401(k) plans?

*Answer* — In general, any private for-profit business can adopt a Section 401(k) plan (whether traditional, SIMPLE, or safe harbor) for its employees; however, the availability of SIMPLE 401(k) plans is limited to employers with 100 or fewer employees.[20] The plan of an unincorporated business can cover partners or a sole proprietor as well as regular employees.

Private (nongovernmental) nonprofit organizations may also adopt 401(k) plans. Certain types of private nonprofits—specifically 501(c)(3) organizations—also have the option of adopting a Section 403(b) tax deferred annuity plan. For a summary of a 501(c)(3) organization's criteria for choosing between 401(k) and 403(b) plans, see the Questions and Answers for Chapter 23.

Governmental (federal, state, or local) organizations are generally not eligible to maintain a Section 401(k) plan.[21] Both nonprofit and governmental organizations can adopt Section 457 plans (see Chapter 11), which provide some features similar to a Section 401(k) plan.

**Question** — Can a Section 401(k) plan participant make deductible contributions to a traditional IRA as well as salary reductions under a Section 401(k) plan?

*Answer* — Yes, but only within the reduced deductible IRA limits allowed for active qualified plan participants—see Chapter 17.

**Question** — What is a "hardship" for purposes of a Section 401(k) plan withdrawal?

*Answer* — Regulations require that a hardship distribution meet two conditions: (a) the distribution must be necessary in light of immediate and heavy financial needs of the employee, and (b) funds must not be reasonably available from other resources of the employee.

As guidance in interpreting the first requirement, the regulations[22] list the following as meeting the "immediate and heavy" requirement:

- Medical expenses incurred by the participant or the participant's spouse or dependents.

- Purchase of a principal residence for the participant (mortgage payments do not typically constitute a hardship).

- Payment of tuition, educational fees, and room and board for the next 12 months of post-secondary education for a participant or his spouse, children, or dependents.

- Payments of amounts necessary to prevent the eviction of the participant from his principal residence or from foreclosure on the mortgage.

The second issue—the existence of other resources—is determined on the basis of individual facts and circumstances. To simplify plan administration, there is a "safe harbor" test for this—the requirement will be deemed met if the following circumstances exist:

(1) The distribution does not exceed the amount of the immediate and heavy financial need,

(2) the employee has obtained all distributions other than hardship distributions and all nontaxable loans available under all plans maintained by the employer, and

(3) the plan provides that the employee's elective deferral contributions and nondeductible contributions will be suspended for 12 months after the distribution and that the maximum contribution in the year following the suspension will be reduced by the amount contributed in the prior year.

**Question** — What are the requirements for a SIMPLE 401(k) plan?

*Answer* — The principal SIMPLE 401(k) plan requirements are:[23]

- the employer must have 100 or fewer employees (only employees with at least $5,000 in compensation for the preceding year are counted) on any day in the year

- employees who earned at least $5,000 from the employer in any two preceding years, and are reasonably expected to earn at least $5,000 in the current year, can make salary reduction contributions of up to $8,000 (in 2003, as indexed) annually

- the employer is required to make a contribution to the employee's 401(k) account an amount equal to either

    (a) a dollar for dollar matching contribution up to 3% of the employee's compensation, or

    (b) a nonelective contribution of 2% of compensation for all eligible employees earning at least $5,000 (whether or not they elect salary reductions).[24]

- employees must be 100% vested in all contributions (whether they are salary deferral, matching, or nonelective contributions) at all times.[25] No deferred vesting schedules are available;

- the limitations on distributions that apply to traditional 401(k) plans apply to SIMPLE 401(k) plans.

A SIMPLE 401(k) is deemed to meet the nondiscrimination requirement of Section 401(a)(4) (thus, it is not subject to ADP testing), and it is exempt from the top-heavy rules. However, it is otherwise subject to the reporting, disclosure, fiduciary responsibility, and other requirements for traditional 401(k) plans (e.g., the Section 415 limits, the compensation limit, and the prohibition on state and local governments operating a 401(k) plan).

**Question** — What are the requirements for a safe harbor 401(k) plan?[26]

*Answer* — A safe harbor plan satisfies the ADP test under an alternative safe harbor provided the employer meets a notice requirement and satisfies one of the following contribution requirements:

(a) the employer makes a matching contribution of 100% of the employee contribution up to 3% of compensation, *plus* 50% of deferrals from 3% to 5%, OR

(b) the employer makes a nonelective (nonmatching) contribution for all eligible nonhighly compensated employees equal to at least 3% of compensation.[27]

- The vesting requirements and withdrawal restrictions that apply to employer contributions in a traditional 401(k) plan are met with respect to all employer contributions (including matching contributions) required under the safe harbor provisions.[28]

- The rate of matching contributions for highly compensated employees may not at any time exceed the rate of matching contributions for nonhighly compensated employees.

- An alternative matching plan design that produces the same result as the contributions described above may, nevertheless, meet the safe harbor requirements if:[29]

  (i) the rate of the employer's contribution does not increase as an employee's rate of contribution increases, and

  (ii) the aggregate amount of matching contributions under the alternative formula is at least equal to the aggregate amount of matching contributions that would be made if matching contributions were made on the basis of the percentages described above.

- Safe harbor plans are subject to the same elective deferral limits (see "Design Features" above) as traditional 401(k) plans. A safe harbor plan is deemed to meet the nondiscrimination requirement of Section 401(a)(4) (thus, it is not subject to ADP testing), and it is generally exempt from the top-heavy rules.[30] However, it is otherwise subject to the reporting, disclosure, fiduciary responsibility, and other requirements for traditional 401(k) plans (e.g., the Section 415 limits, the compensation limit, and the prohibition on state and local governments operating a 401(k) plan).

**Question** — What is a Roth 401(k) plan?

Answer — The Economic Growth and Tax Relief Reconciliation Act of 2001 (EGTRRA 2001) included a provision that will permit 401(k) plans (as well as 403(b) plans, to offer a "qualified Roth contribution program," which will basically be a Roth account for elective deferrals. The provision takes effect in 2006 (at which time the limit on elective deferrals is scheduled to reach $15,000, and the after-50 "catch-up" amount will have reached $5,000).

Essentially, participants of plans establishing such a program will be able to designate all, or a portion, of their elective deferrals as Roth contributions. The Roth contributions would be included in the participant's gross income in the year made, and then be held in a separate account with separate record keeping. Earnings allocable to the Roth contributions will remain in the separate account.

A "qualified distribution" from a Roth account will not be includable in the participant's gross income, and rollovers will be available only to another Roth account or Roth IRA. The requirements for a "qualified distribution" are nearly identical to those for a Roth IRA (see Chapter 17), except that no exception is permitted for first-time home purchases. In other words, a qualified distribution is any distribution made after the 5-year "nonexclusion period" and after the participant has (a) reached age 59½, (b) died or (c) become disabled. (Distributions of excess deferrals are not included in this definition.)

The nonexclusion period is the 5-taxable year period beginning with the earlier of (1) the first year a contribution is made to the Roth account, or (2) if a rollover has been made to the Roth account from another Roth account under another employer plan, the first year a contribution was made to the earlier Roth account.

Aside from being currently included in gross income, amounts designated as Roth contributions under this provision will be treated in all other respects as elective deferrals. They will, together with other elective deferrals, be subject to the otherwise-applicable elective deferral limit (see "Design Features," above); thus, a single total limit will continue to apply to all elective deferrals.[31]

**Question** — What types of investments are appropriate for Section 401(k) plans?

*Answer* — Generally, investments traditionally used in qualified profit sharing plans are also used in Section 401(k) plans. Employee accounts in the plan fund are usually pooled for investment purposes. Investment tends toward bonds, money market, and liquid, cash-type media. Smaller plans often use a "family" of mutual funds for plan investments. The level of equity investment (common stocks) in Section 401(k) plans is usually lower than in defined benefit plans.

Many plans use a "directed investment" or "earmarking" provision that allows participants some degree of choice in the investment of their plan accounts. Directed investment provisions increase administrative costs of the plan. But they are attractive to employees and, if the directed investment provision meets certain standards set forth in Labor Department regulations,[32] the employer is relieved of fiduciary responsibility for unsatisfactory results from any investment directed by the participant.

Life insurance is sometimes provided in Section 401(k) plans in much the same way as it is used in a regular profit sharing plan. The use of life insurance in a qualified plan is discussed in Chapter 13.

**Question** — Is it better for a 401(k) plan participant to contribute to the 401(k) plan or to use the same amount to pay off a home mortgage?

*Answer* — With the widespread availability of 401(k) plans, many people must routinely make investment decisions that once only relatively affluent people were faced with. One involves the advisability of paying off existing debt as an alternative to investment. This can be a complex issue. In the case of mortgage interest, if the taxpayer does not itemize deductions, or if the expected return from the 401(k) plan is significantly less than the mortgage interest rate, a mortgage paydown may be better than increasing the 401(k) contribution in some circumstances.[33]

**Question** — How can an employer provide retirement benefits to replace 401(k) benefits lost by an executive as a result of the $200,000 (in 2003, as indexed) compensation "cap?"

*Answer* — In applying the ADP test, described under "Tax Implications" above, under Code section 401(a)(17) only the first $200,000 (in 2003) of each participant's salary can be taken into account. This has the effect of imputing a higher ADP percentage for executives than is actually the case. For example, if an executive earns $300,000 and defers $6,000 under the 401(k) plan, although this represents a 2% (6,000/300,000) deferral, for ADP purposes in 2003 it would be treated as a 3% (6,000/200,000) deferral. If this results in excess deferrals under the ADP test, generally the excess deferrals must be returned to highly compensated employees.

Executives in this situation might like a plan under which excess deferrals "pour over" into a nonqualified deferred compensation plan. IRS rulings originally were unfavorable to this approach, on the ground that the election to defer compensa-

tion was made too late (i.e., after compensation was earned), but more recent rulings have allowed this approach.[34] Here is an example of how IRS rulings suggest it could be done:

- Executive Nat enters into a salary reduction agreement no later than December 31, 2002 providing for a salary reduction of, say, $20,000 for 2003 to be credited to Nat's account in the Company's nonqualified deferred compensation (NQDC) plan. At this time, Nat also can elect to make an irrevocable "pourover 401(k) election" for 2003 (see below). The company can also agree to provide matching contributions.

- At the end of 2003, and not later than January 31, 2004, the plan administrator performs the ADP test and calculates Nat's elective deferral limit at $8,000.

- Pursuant to the 401(k) plan and the NQDC plan, this $8,000 (more specifically, the lesser of $8,000 or the total 2003 salary reduction, $20,000 in this case) will be paid in cash to Nat not later than March 15, 2004 (and be taxable for 2004) unless Nat has made the pourover 401(k) election for 2003. If Nat has done so, the $8,000 will be contributed directly by the employer to the 401(k) plan. No earnings on amounts held in the NQDC plan will be contributed to the 401(k) plan (relevant only where the "lesser salary reduction" rule applies). [Apparently the principal balance of Nat's account in the NQDC plan will be reduced accordingly, providing for a net 2003 deferral of $8,000 in the 401(k) plan and $12,000 in the NQDC.]

- Any employer matching contributions for Nat required under the 401(k) plan will be taken from employer matching contributions already made under the NQDC plan, and NQDC employer matches will be reduced accordingly.

**Question** — Who is eligible to claim the nonrefundable "saver's credit" for salary reduction contributions to a 401(k) plan?

*Answer* — Certain lower-income taxpayers may claim a temporary, nonrefundable credit for "qualified retirement savings contributions" in taxable years beginning after 2001 and before 2007.[35] "Qualified retirement savings contributions" include elective deferrals to 401(k) plans as well as other elective deferrals and contributions to Roth or traditional

IRAs. (However, the total is reduced by certain distributions received by the taxpayer or his spouse during the prior two taxable years and the current taxable year for which the credit is claimed, including the period up to the due date (plus extensions) for filing the federal income tax return for the current taxable year.)

The credit is allowed against the sum of the regular tax and the alternative minimum tax (minus certain other credits) and is allowed in addition to any other deduction or exclusion that would otherwise apply. In addition, to be eligible, the taxpayer must be at least 18 as of the end of the tax year and must not be claimed as a dependent by someone else or be a full-time student.

The amount of the credit is limited to an "applicable percentage" of IRA contributions and elective deferrals up to $2,000. The "applicable percentages" are as follows:

### ADJUSTED GROSS INCOME

| Joint return Over | Not over | Head of a household Over | Not over | All other cases Over | Not over | Applicable percentage |
|---|---|---|---|---|---|---|
| 0 | $30,000 | 0 | $22,500 | 0 | $15,000 | 50% |
| 30,000 | 32,500 | 22,500 | 24,375 | 15,000 | 16,250 | 20% |
| 32,500 | 50,000 | 24,375 | 37,500 | 16,250 | 25,000 | 10% |
| 50,000 | | 37,500 | | 25,000 | | 0% |

*Example:* Mickey and Minnie work for the same employer and together have adjusted gross income of $31,000 for 2003. Their employer sponsors a 401(k) plan and they each elected to make a salary reduction contribution of $2,000 to the plan. Neither has received any distributions in the current or two preceding taxable years. Mickey and Minnie will be able to exclude their salary reduction contributions as well as each being eligible to claim a credit of $400 (20% x $2,000) on their federal income tax return ($800 if married filing jointly) for 2003.

## FOOTNOTES

1. IRC Sections 402(g)(1)(B), 414(v)(2)(B). Note that all provisions of EGTRRA 2001 are scheduled to sunset, or expire, after December 31, 2010.
2. IRC Sections 404(a)(3)(A), 404(n). For further explanation of these changes, see Chapter 25, at "Deduction Limits."
3. Rev. Rul. 2000-35, 2000-2 CB 138.
4. IRC Section 402(g).
5. IRC Section 414(v)(2)(B)(i). Note that the limit will be lower if the amount of a participant's compensation, (after reduction for other elective deferrals) is less than the catch-up amounts.
6. IRC Sections 401(k)(11), 408(p)(2)(A)(ii).
7. IRC Section 414(v)(2)(B)(ii). Note that the limit will be lower if the amount of a participant's compensation, (after reduction for other elective deferrals) is less than the catch-up amounts.
8. IRC Section 401(k)(2)(B).
9. IRC Section 72(t).
10. IRC Section 402(g).
11. IRC Section 3121(v)(1).
12. IRC Section 404(a)(3).
13. IRC Section 401(k)(3)(A).
14. IRC Section 401(k)(3)(A), Notice 98-1, 1998-1 CB 327.
15. IRC Section 414(q).
16. IRC Section 415(c)(3).
17. IRC Section 415(c)(2).
18. See footnote 3, above.
19. A 60-day notice period is mandated by the Code for participants in SIMPLE 401(k) plans. IRC Section 401(k)(11)(B)(iii)(II). For safe harbor plans, eligible employees must be notified before the start of the plan year that the plan may be amended, and that if it is, a supplemental notice will be provided to each employee at least 30 days before the end of the plan year. Notice 2000-3, 2000-1 CB 413.
20. IRC Sections 401(k)(11)(D)(i), 408(p)(2)(C)(i). Only employees who earned at least $5,000 of compensation from the employer in the preceding year are counted. In the event that an eligible employer who establishes and maintains a SIMPLE 401(k) plan for one or more years subsequently becomes ineligible (i.e., exceeds the 100-employee limit), it will continue to be treated as eligible for the two years following the last year of eligibility. Special rules apply in the event of a merger or acquisition. See IRC Section 408(p)(2)(C)(i)(II).
21. IRC Section 401(k)(4)(B). Certain employers' pre-1987 plans were "grandfathered." See TRA '86, Section 1116(f)(2)(B); TAMRA '88, Section 1101(k)(8).
22. Treas. Reg. §1.401(k)-1(d)(2).
23. See IRC Section 401(k)(11).
24. If this election is made, notice must be provided to employees at least 60 days before the beginning of the plan year. See IRC Section 401(k)(11)(B)(ii).
25. IRC Section 401(k)(11)(A)(iii).
26. IRC Section 401(k)(12).
27. IRC Sections 401(k)(12)(B)(i), 401(k)(12)(C).
28. IRC Section 401(k)(12)(e)(i).
29. IRC Section 401(k)(12)(B)(iii).
30. IRC Section 416(g)(3)(H).
31. IRC Section 402A.
32. See DOL Reg. §2550.404c-1.
33. See Auster and Sennetti, "Should Participants in a 401(k) Contribute to the Plan or Pay Off Their Mortgages?," *Journal of Pension Planning & Compliance*, Spring 1994, for a discussion of the many factors involved in making this decision.
34. See e.g., Let. Ruls. 199924067, 9807010, 9530038.
35. IRC Section 25B.

# Chapter 20

# SIMPLE IRAs

## WHAT ARE THEY?

SIMPLE (Savings Incentive Match Plans for Employees) IRAs are employer-sponsored plans under which plan contributions are made to a participating employee's IRA.[1] Tax-deferred contribution levels are significantly higher than the $3,000/$6,000 (in 2003) limit for traditional and Roth IRAs (see Chapter 17). SIMPLE IRAs feature employee salary reduction contributions (elective deferrals) coupled with employer matching or nonelective contributions.

The term "SIMPLE plan," as used in the Internal Revenue Code refers to a SIMPLE IRA plan. Section 401(k) plans are permitted to satisfy the nondiscrimination in amount requirement (ADP test) by adopting provisions that are similar to the SIMPLE IRA requirements, but they are subject to additional requirements. See Chapter 19 for details on SIMPLE 401(k) plans.

SIMPLE IRAs are easy to adopt and to administer while providing employees with tax-deferred retirement savings benefits much like those of a qualified plan. However, qualified plans potentially can provide higher contribution levels. An employee's salary reductions under a SIMPLE IRA can be no greater than $8,000 annually (in 2003), plus catch-up amounts, if available (see below).[2]

## WHEN IS IT INDICATED?

1. When the employer is looking for an alternative to a qualified profit sharing plan that is easier and less expensive to install and administer. For very small employers, a SIMPLE IRA is one of the simplest types of tax-deferred employee retirement plans available. For larger employers, the cost of installing and administering a regular qualified plan can be spread over enough employees that the advantages of these plans are less significant.

2. When an employer has 100 or fewer employees and wants an easy-to-administer plan funded through employee salary reductions.

3. Where an individual has a relatively small amount of self-employment income and the SIMPLE IRA contribution limit is higher than that available for any other form of tax-favored plan, such as a Keogh plan or a SEP.

## ADVANTAGES

1. A SIMPLE IRA can be adopted by completing an IRS form (Forms 5304-SIMPLE or 5305-SIMPLE, reproduced at the end of this chapter) rather than by the complex procedure required for qualified plans (described in Chapter 27). However, if the employer adopts a master or prototype qualified plan, the installation costs and complexity may not actually be much greater than that for a SIMPLE IRA, even though the documentation is more voluminous.

2. Benefits of a SIMPLE IRA are totally portable by employees since funding is held entirely in an IRA for each employee and employees are always 100% vested in their benefits. Employees own and control their accounts, even after they terminate employment with the original employer.

3. Individual IRA accounts allow participants to benefit from good investment results (as well as run the risk of bad results).

4. A SIMPLE IRA can be funded in part through salary reductions by employees, if the conditions described in "Tax Implications," below, are met.

## DISADVANTAGES

1. Employees cannot rely upon a SIMPLE IRA to provide an adequate retirement benefit. First, benefits are not significant unless the employee makes significant regular salary reduction contributions. Such regular contributions are not a requirement of the plan. Furthermore, employees who enter the plan at older ages have only a limited number of years remaining prior to retirement to build up their SIMPLE IRA balances.

2. Annual contributions generally are restricted to lesser amounts than would be available in a qualified plan. SIMPLE IRA salary reduction contributions are limited by the maximum $8,000 (in 2003) salary reduction permitted for each participant (plus the employer's matching contribution). This contrasts with the $12,000 (in 2003) annual salary reduction permitted for traditional 401(k) plans or for 403(b) plans. The "catch-up" contribution limits are also lower for SIMPLE IRAs (and SIMPLE 401(k) plans) than for traditional 401(k) plans and 403(b) plans.

3. Distributions from SIMPLE IRAs are not eligible for the 10-year averaging provisions available for certain qualified plan distributions.

4. If an employer adopts a SIMPLE IRA plan, it cannot also maintain a qualified plan, SEP, 403(a) annuity, 403(b) tax-sheltered annuity, or a governmental plan (other than a Section 457 plan) for that year. However, certain collectively bargained plans will not affect an employer's eligibility to establish a SIMPLE IRA; see item two under "Tax Implications" below.

## TAX IMPLICATIONS

1. The employer may deduct contributions (both employee salary reduction amounts and employer matching contributions) to a SIMPLE IRA if certain Code requirements are met. The principal requirements are:[3]

   • the employer must have 100 or fewer employees (only employees with at least $5,000 in compensation for the preceding year are counted) on any day in the year

   • contributions may be made to an IRA established for each employee

   • employees who earned at least $5,000 from the employer in any two preceding years, and are reasonably expected to earn at least $5,000 in the current year, can contribute (through salary reductions) up to the following limit:

   | Year | Amount |
   |------|--------|
   | 2003 | $8,000 |
   | 2004 | 9,000 |
   | 2005 and thereafter | 10,000 |

   • participants who have reached the age of 50 during the plan year may be permitted to make "catch-up" contributions in addition to the limits

listed above. The limits for catch-up contributions are as follows:

| Year | Amount |
|------|--------|
| 2003 | 1,000 |
| 2004 | 1,500 |
| 2005 | 2,000 |
| 2006 and thereafter | 2,500 |

   • the employer is required to make a contribution equal to either

   (a) a dollar for dollar matching contribution up to 3% of the employee's compensation (the employer can elect a lower percentage, not less than 1%, in no more than two out of the five years ending with the current year),[4] or

   (b) 2% of compensation for all eligible employees earning at least $5,000 (whether or not they elect salary reductions).[5]

2. If the employer maintains a SIMPLE IRA, it may not maintain a qualified plan, SEP, 403(a) annuity, 403(b) tax sheltered annuity, or a governmental plan (other than a Section 457 plan) for that year. However, an employer who has only a collectively bargained qualified plan (but not any other qualified plan) may adopt a SIMPLE IRA plan for the non-collectively bargained employees, provided none of the SIMPLE IRA participants are participants in the collectively bargained plan.[6]

3. Each participating employee maintains an IRA for the SIMPLE IRA plan contributions. Employer contributions are made directly to the employee's IRA, as are any employee salary reduction contributions. Employer contributions and employee salary reductions, with the limits discussed above, are not included in the employee's taxable income.[7]

4. Direct employer contributions are not subject to Social Security (FICA) or federal unemployment (FUTA) taxes. However, employee salary reduction contributions are subject to FICA and FUTA.[8] The impact of state payroll taxes depends on the particular state's laws. Both salary reductions and employer contributions may be exempt from state payroll taxes in some states.

5. Distributions to employees are generally treated as distributions from a traditional IRA.[9] All the restrictions on traditional IRA distributions apply and the distributions are taxed the same; however, the 10% penalty on premature distributions is increased to

25% during the first two years of participation.[10] Furthermore, while a rollover may be made at any time from one SIMPLE IRA to another SIMPLE IRA, a rollover from a SIMPLE IRA to a traditional IRA during the first two years of participation is permitted only in the case of distributions to which the 25% early distribution penalty does not apply.[11] The taxation of traditional IRA distributions is discussed in Chapter 17. In particular, note that the 10-year averaging provisions are not available for SIMPLE IRA distributions.

6.  A limited nonrefundable tax credit (known as the "saver's credit") is available to certain lower income taxpayers who make salary deferrals to a SIMPLE IRA (see Questions and Answers, below).

7.  Certain employers adopting a new plan may be eligible for a business tax credit of up to $500 for "qualified startup costs." See Chapter 27 for details.

## HOW TO INSTALL A PLAN

Installation of a SIMPLE IRA plan can be very easy. The employer merely completes Form 5304-SIMPLE or Form 5305-SIMPLE. Copies of these forms and instructions are reproduced at the end of this chapter. Form 5304-SIMPLE does not provide for a "designated financial institution" for participant investments, while Form 5305-SIMPLE does, which some plan sponsors and participants may find restrictive. Salary reduction elections must be made by employees during a 60-day period prior to January 1 of the year for which the elections are made. The form does not have to be sent to the IRS or any other government agency.

## ERISA REQUIREMENTS

The reporting and disclosure requirements for SIMPLE IRA plans are simplified, particularly if the employer uses Form 5304-SIMPLE or 5305-SIMPLE. The annual report forms (5500 series) are not required for SIMPLE IRA plans.

## WHERE CAN I FIND OUT MORE ABOUT IT?

1.  IRS Publication 334, *Tax Guide for Small Business,* and Publication 535, *Business Expense Deductions,* available free from the IRS; revised annually.

## QUESTIONS AND ANSWERS

**Question** — Can an unincorporated business adopt a SIMPLE IRA covering partners or a sole proprietor?

*Answer* — Yes. Partners and proprietors can be covered under the SIMPLE IRA plan of an unincorporated employer, as well as regular employees.

For a person with a limited amount of self-employment income, such as a moonlighting business, the SIMPLE IRA may allow the maximum retirement plan contribution. Alternatives such as Keogh plans and SEPs have various limitations based on percentages of compensation or earned income. The limit for a SIMPLE IRA is not a percentage limit, but a dollar limit of $8,000 (for 2003) on salary reductions, with matching or nonelective contributions required by the employer. (SIMPLE IRAs are not subject to the limits of Section 415 of the Code, nor to the deduction limits of Section 404(a); see Chapter 25.)

**Question** — Can an employee who is over age 70½ participate in a SIMPLE IRA plan?

*Answer* — An individual cannot make deductible contributions to his or her own IRA after attaining age 70½. However, employers can make contributions to SIMPLE IRAs (including both matching contributions and salary reductions) for employees who are over age 70½. In fact, the age discrimination law, if applicable, would generally require such contributions to be made.

**Question** — Can an employee participating in a SIMPLE IRA also make deductible contributions to his or her own traditional IRA?

*Answer* — For purposes of any potential deduction for contributions to a traditional IRA, a SIMPLE IRA participant is treated the same as a participant in a regular qualified plan. That is, if the individual is an "active participant" in the SIMPLE IRA plan, traditional IRA contributions can be made, but the deduction limit of $3,000/$6,000 (in 2003) is reduced if adjusted gross income (AGI) exceeds certain limits. If the individual is not an active participant in the plan, the full IRA deduction may be available. These rules are discussed in detail in Chapter 17.

An employee covered under a SIMPLE IRA would be considered an active participant in any year in which salary reductions or employer contributions were allocated to his or her account. However, in a year in which no allocation was made to the individual's account, the individual would have any otherwise-available IRA deduction (up to the $3,000/$6,000 limit in 2003).[12] The higher SIMPLE IRA limit is not available for individual IRA contributions, only for employer contributions or salary reductions under a SIMPLE IRA plan.

**Question** — Who is eligible to claim the nonrefundable "saver's credit" for salary contributions to a SIMPLE IRA?

*Answer* — Certain lower-income taxpayers may claim a temporary, nonrefundable credit for "qualified retirement savings contributions" in taxable years beginning after 2001 and before 2007.[13] This is known as the "saver's credit." "Qualified retirement savings contributions" include elective deferrals to SIMPLE IRAs, as well as other elective deferrals and contributions to Roth or traditional IRAs. (However, the total is reduced by certain distributions received by the taxpayer or his spouse during the prior two taxable years and the current taxable year for which the credit is claimed, including the period up to the due date (plus extensions) for filing the federal income tax return for the current taxable year.)

The credit is allowed against the sum of the regular tax and the alternative minimum tax (minus certain other credits) and is allowed in addition to any other deduction or exclusion that would otherwise apply. In addition, to be eligible, the taxpayer must be at least 18 as of the end of the tax year and must not be claimed as a dependent by someone else or be a full-time student.

The amount of the credit is limited to an "applicable percentage" of IRA contributions and elective deferrals up to $2,000. The "applicable percentages" are as follows:

### ADJUSTED GROSS INCOME

| Joint return Over | Not over | Head of a household Over | Not over | All other cases Over | Not over | Applicable percentage |
|---|---|---|---|---|---|---|
| 0 | $30,000 | 0 | $22,500 | 0 | $15,000 | 50% |
| 30,000 | 32,500 | 22,500 | 24,375 | 15,000 | 16,250 | 20% |
| 32,500 | 50,000 | 24,375 | 37,500 | 16,250 | 25,000 | 10% |
| 50,000 | | 37,500 | | 25,000 | | 0% |

*Example:* Max and Erma work for the same employer and together have adjusted gross income of $31,000 for 2003. Their employer sponsors a SIMPLE IRA and they each elected to make a salary reduction contribution of $2,000 to the plan. Neither has received any distributions in the current or two preceding taxable years. Max and Erma will be able to exclude their salary reduction contributions as well as each being eligible to claim a credit of $400 (20% x $2,000) on their federal income tax return ($800 if married filing jointly) for 2003.

## FOOTNOTES

1. The provisions for SIMPLE IRAs are set forth in IRC Section 408(p). See Chapter 19 and IRC Section 401(k)(11) for the rules governing SIMPLE 401(k) plans.

2. IRC Section 408(p)(2)(A)(ii). Note that all provisions of EGTRRA 2001 are scheduled to sunset, or expire, after December 31, 2010.

3. See IRC Section 408(p).

4. IRC Section 408(p)(2)(A)(iii). The compensation limit under IRC Section 401(a)(17) is not applicable for purposes of the matching contribution; thus, for example, a 3% match could reach the maximum limit in 2003 of $7,000 if an employee has compensation of about $233,300 in a year. See also Notice 97-6, 1997-1 CB 353.

5. IRC Section 408(p)(2)(B). "Compensation" for purposes of the 2% nonelective contribution *is* subject to the limits of Code section 401(a)(17) ($200,000 for years beginning in 2003). Consequently, the maximum that could be contributed in nonelective contributions for an employee in 2003 would be $4,000 (i.e., 2% of $200,000). See IRC Section 408(p)(2)(B)(ii).

6. IRC Section 408(p)(2)(D).

7. See IRC Sections 402(k), 402(h)(1), 402(e)(3); Notice 97-6, 1997-1 CB 353.

8. IRC Sections 3121(a), 3306(a), 3401(a)(12); Notice 97-6, 1997-1 CB 353.

9. IRC Sections 402(k), 402(h)(3); General Explanation of Tax Legislation Enacted in the 104th Congress (JCT-12-96), p. 141 (the 1996 Blue Book).

10. IRC Section 72(t)(6).

11. IRC Section 408(d)(3)(G). During the two-year period that the 25% penalty is imposed, such a transfer would be treated as a distribution from the SIMPLE IRA and a contribution to the regular IRA that does not qualify as a rollover contribution. Notice 97-6, 1997-1 CB 353.

12. Notice 87-16, 1987-1 CB 446, I.

13. IRC Section 25B.

Form **5304-SIMPLE**
(Rev. March 2002)

Department of the Treasury
Internal Revenue Service

### Savings Incentive Match Plan for Employees of Small Employers (SIMPLE)—Not for Use With a Designated Financial Institution

OMB No. 1545-1502

**Do not** file with the Internal Revenue Service

_____ establishes the following SIMPLE
Name of Employer

IRA plan under section 408(p) of the Internal Revenue Code and pursuant to the instructions contained in this form.

## Article I—Employee Eligibility Requirements _(complete applicable box(es) and blanks—see instructions)_

**1** **General Eligibility Requirements.** The Employer agrees to permit salary reduction contributions to be made in each calendar year to the SIMPLE IRA established by each employee who meets the following requirements (select either 1a or 1b):

**a** ☐ **Full Eligibility.** All employees are eligible.

**b** ☐ **Limited Eligibility.** Eligibility is limited to employees who are described in both (i) and (ii) below:

    **(i)** **Current compensation.** Employees who are reasonably expected to receive at least $ _____ in compensation (not to exceed $5,000) for the calendar year.

    **(ii)** **Prior compensation.** Employees who have received at least $ _____ in compensation (not to exceed $5,000) during any _____ calendar year(s) (insert 0, 1, or 2) preceding the calendar year.

**2** **Excludable Employees.**

    ☐ The Employer elects to exclude employees covered under a collective bargaining agreement for which retirement benefits were the subject of good faith bargaining. **Note:** _This box is deemed checked if the Employer maintains a qualified plan covering only such employees._

## Article II—Salary Reduction Agreements _(complete the box and blank, if applicable—see instructions)_

**1** **Salary Reduction Election.** An eligible employee may make an election to have his or her compensation for each pay period reduced. The total amount of the reduction in the employee's compensation for a calendar year cannot exceed the applicable amount for that year.

**2** **Timing of Salary Reduction Elections**

**a** For a calendar year, an eligible employee may make or modify a salary reduction election during the 60-day period immediately preceding January 1 of that year. However, for the year in which the employee becomes eligible to make salary reduction contributions, the period during which the employee may make or modify the election is a 60-day period that includes either the date the employee becomes eligible or the day before.

**b** In addition to the election periods in 2a, eligible employees may make salary reduction elections or modify prior elections _____ _____. If the Employer chooses this option, insert a period or periods (e.g. semi-annually, quarterly, monthly, or daily) that will apply uniformly to all eligible employees.

**c** No salary reduction election may apply to compensation that an employee received, or had a right to immediately receive, before execution of the salary reduction election.

**d** An employee may terminate a salary reduction election at any time during the calendar year. ☐ If this box is checked, an employee who terminates a salary reduction election not in accordance with 2b may not resume salary reduction contributions during the calendar year.

## Article III—Contributions _(complete the blank, if applicable—see instructions)_

**1** **Salary Reduction Contributions.** The amount by which the employee agrees to reduce his or her compensation will be contributed by the Employer to the employee's SIMPLE IRA.

**2a** **Matching Contributions**

    **(i)** For each calendar year, the Employer will contribute a matching contribution to each eligible employee's SIMPLE IRA equal to the employee's salary reduction contributions up to a limit of 3% of the employee's compensation for the calendar year.

    **(ii)** The Employer may reduce the 3% limit for the calendar year in (i) only if:

        **(1)** The limit is not reduced below 1%; **(2)** The limit is not reduced for more than 2 calendar years during the 5-year period ending with the calendar year the reduction is effective; and **(3)** Each employee is notified of the reduced limit within a reasonable period of time before the employees' 60-day election period for the calendar year (described in Article II, item 2a).

**b** **Nonelective Contributions**

    **(i)** For any calendar year, instead of making matching contributions, the Employer may make nonelective contributions equal to 2% of compensation for the calendar year to the SIMPLE IRA of each eligible employee who has at least $ _____ (not more than $5,000) in compensation for the calendar year. No more than $200,000* in compensation can be taken into account in determining the nonelective contribution for each eligible employee.

    **(ii)** For any calendar year, the Employer may make 2% nonelective contributions instead of matching contributions only if:

        **(1)** Each eligible employee is notified that a 2% nonelective contribution will be made instead of a matching contribution; and

        **(2)** This notification is provided within a reasonable period of time before the employees' 60-day election period for the calendar year (described in Article II, item 2a).

**3** **Time and Manner of Contributions**

**a** The Employer will make the salary reduction contributions (described in 1 above) for each eligible employee to the SIMPLE IRA established at the financial institution selected by that employee no later than 30 days after the end of the month in which the money is withheld from the employee's pay. See instructions.

**b** The Employer will make the matching or nonelective contributions (described in 2a and 2b above) for each eligible employee to the SIMPLE IRA established at the financial institution selected by that employee no later than the due date for filing the Employer's tax return, including extensions, for the taxable year that includes the last day of the calendar year for which the contributions are made.

\* For 2003 and later years, this amount is subject to annual cost-of-living adjustments. The IRS announces the increase, if any, in a news release, in the Internal Revenue Bulletin, and on the IRS's internet web site at **www.irs.gov.**

**For Paperwork Reduction Act Notice, see page 6.**    Cat. No. 23377W    Form **5304-SIMPLE** (Rev. 3-2002)

## Article IV—Other Requirements and Provisions

**1** **Contributions in General.** The Employer will make no contributions to the SIMPLE IRAs other than salary reduction contributions (described in Article III, item 1) and matching or nonelective contributions (described in Article III, items 2a and 2b).

**2** **Vesting Requirements.** All contributions made under this SIMPLE IRA plan are fully vested and nonforfeitable.

**3** **No Withdrawal Restrictions.** The Employer may not require the employee to retain any portion of the contributions in his or her SIMPLE IRA or otherwise impose any withdrawal restrictions.

**4** **Selection of IRA Trustee.** The employer must permit each eligible employee to select the financial institution that will serve as the trustee, custodian, or issuer of the SIMPLE IRA to which the employer will make all contributions on behalf of that employee.

**5** **Amendments To This SIMPLE IRA Plan.** This SIMPLE IRA plan may not be amended except to modify the entries inserted in the blanks or boxes provided in Articles I, II, III, VI, and VII.

**6** **Effects Of Withdrawals and Rollovers**

**a** An amount withdrawn from the SIMPLE IRA is generally includible in gross income. However, a SIMPLE IRA balance may be rolled over or transferred on a tax-free basis to another IRA designed solely to hold funds under a SIMPLE IRA plan. In addition, an individual may roll over or transfer his or her SIMPLE IRA balance to any IRA after a 2-year period has expired since the individual first participated in any SIMPLE IRA plan of the Employer. Any rollover or transfer must comply with the requirements under section 408.

**b** If an individual withdraws an amount from a SIMPLE IRA during the 2-year period beginning when the individual first participated in any SIMPLE IRA plan of the Employer and the amount is subject to the additional tax on early distributions under section 72(t), this additional tax is increased from 10% to 25%.

## Article V—Definitions

**1** **Compensation**

**a** **General Definition of Compensation.** Compensation means the sum of the wages, tips, and other compensation from the Employer subject to federal income tax withholding (as described in section 6051(a)(3)) and the employee's salary reduction contributions made under this plan, and, if applicable, elective deferrals under a section 401(k) plan, a SARSEP, or a section 403(b) annuity contract and compensation deferred under a section 457 plan required to be reported by the Employer on Form W-2 (as described in section 6051(a)(8)).

**b** **Compensation for Self-Employed Individuals.** For self-employed individuals, compensation means the net earnings from self-employment determined under section 1402(a), without regard to section 1402(c)(6), prior to subtracting any contributions made pursuant to this plan on behalf of the individual.

**2** **Employee.** Employee means a common-law employee of the Employer. The term employee also includes a self-employed individual and a leased employee described in section 414(n) but does not include a nonresident alien who received no earned income from the Employer that constitutes income from sources within the United States.

**3** **Eligible Employee.** An eligible employee means an employee who satisfies the conditions in Article I, item 1 and is not excluded under Article I, item 2.

**4** **SIMPLE IRA.** A SIMPLE IRA is an individual retirement account described in section 408(a), or an individual retirement annuity described in section 408(b), to which the only contributions that can be made are contributions under a SIMPLE IRA plan and rollovers or transfers from another SIMPLE IRA.

## Article VI—Procedures for Withdrawal (*The employer will provide each employee with the procedures for withdrawals of contributions received by the financial institution selected by that employee, and that financial institutionís name and address (by attaching that information or inserting it in the space below) unless: **(1)** that financial institutionís procedures are unavailable, or **(2)** that financial institution provides the procedures directly to the employee. See **Employee Notification** on page 5.)*

## Article VII—Effective Date

This SIMPLE IRA plan is effective _____ . See instructions.

\*     \*     \*     \*     \*

_____

Name of Employer

_____

Address of Employer

By: _____ Signature _____        Date _____

Name and title _____

Form **5304-SIMPLE** (Rev. 3-2002)

## Model Notification to Eligible Employees

### I. Opportunity to Participate in the SIMPLE IRA Plan

You are eligible to make salary reduction contributions to the _____ SIMPLE IRA plan. This notice and the attached summary description provide you with information that you should consider before you decide whether to start, continue, or change your salary reduction agreement.

### II. Employer Contribution Election

For the _____ calendar year, the employer elects to contribute to your SIMPLE IRA *(employer must select either (1), (2), or (3)):*

☐ **(1)** A matching contribution equal to your salary reduction contributions up to a limit of 3% of your compensation for the year;

☐ **(2)** A matching contribution equal to your salary reduction contributions up to a limit of _____% *(employer must insert a number from 1 to 3 and is subject to certain restrictions)* of your compensation for the year; or

☐ **(3)** A nonelective contribution equal to 2% of your compensation for the year (limited to $200,000*) if you are an employee who makes at least $ _____ *(employer must insert an amount that is $5,000 or less)* in compensation for the year.

### III. Administrative Procedures

To start or change your salary reduction contributions, you must complete the salary reduction agreement and return it to _____ *(employer should designate a place or individual)* by _____ *(employer should insert a date that is not less than 60 days after notice is given).*

### IV. Employee Selection of Financial Institution

You must select the financial institution that will serve as the trustee, custodian, or issuer of your SIMPLE IRA and notify your employer of your selection.

## Model Salary Reduction Agreement

### I. Salary Reduction Election

Subject to the requirements of the SIMPLE IRA plan of _____ *(name of employer)* I authorize _____ % or $ _____ (which equals _____ % of my current rate of pay) to be withheld from my pay for each pay period and contributed to my SIMPLE IRA as a salary reduction contribution.

### II. Maximum Salary Reduction

I understand that the total amount of my salary reduction contributions in any calendar year cannot exceed the applicable amount for that year. See instructions.

### III. Date Salary Reduction Begins

I understand that my salary reduction contributions will start as soon as permitted under the SIMPLE IRA plan and as soon as administratively feasible or, if later, _____. *(Fill in the date you want the salary reduction contributions to begin. The date must be after you sign this agreement.)*

### IV. Employee Selection of Financial Institution

I select the following financial institution to serve as the trustee, custodian, or issuer of my SIMPLE IRA.

_____
Name of financial institution

_____
Address of financial institution

_____
SIMPLE IRA account name and number

I understand that I must establish a SIMPLE IRA to receive any contributions made on my behalf under this SIMPLE IRA plan. If the information regarding my SIMPLE IRA is incomplete when I first submit my salary reduction agreement, I realize that it must be completed by the date contributions must be made under the SIMPLE IRA plan. If I fail to update my agreement to provide this information by that date, I understand that my employer may select a financial institution for my SIMPLE IRA.

### V. Duration of Election

This salary reduction agreement replaces any earlier agreement and will remain in effect as long as I remain an eligible employee under the SIMPLE IRA plan or until I provide my employer with a request to end my salary reduction contributions or provide a new salary reduction agreement as permitted under this SIMPLE IRA plan.

Signature of employee _____   Date _____

\* *For 2003 and later years, this amount is subject to cost-of-living adjustments. The IRS announces the increase, if any, in a news release, in the Internal Revenue Bulletin, and on the IRS Web Site at www.irs.gov.*

Form **5304-SIMPLE** (Rev. 3-2002)

# General Instructions

*Section references are to the Internal Revenue Code unless otherwise noted.*

## Purpose of Form

Form 5304-SIMPLE is a model Savings Incentive Match Plan for Employees of Small Employers (SIMPLE) plan document that an employer may use to establish a SIMPLE IRA plan described in section 408(p), under which each eligible employee is permitted to select the financial institution for his or her SIMPLE IRA.

These instructions are designed to assist in the establishment and administration of the SIMPLE IRA plan. They are **not** intended to supersede any provision in the SIMPLE IRA plan.

**Do not** file Form 5304-SIMPLE with the IRS. Instead, keep it with your records.

For more information, see **Pub. 560,** Retirement Plans for Small Business (SEP, SIMPLE, and Qualified Plans), and **Pub. 590,** Individual Retirement Arrangements (IRAs).

## Which Employers May Establish and Maintain a SIMPLE IRA Plan?

To establish and maintain a SIMPLE IRA plan, you must meet **both** of the following requirements:

**1.** Last calendar year, you had no more than 100 employees (including self-employed individuals) who earned $5,000 or more in compensation from you during the year. If you have a SIMPLE IRA plan but later exceed this 100-employee limit, you will be treated as meeting the limit for the 2 years following the calendar year in which you last satisfied the limit.

**2.** You do not maintain during any part of the calendar year another qualified plan with respect to which contributions are made, or benefits are accrued, for service in the calendar year. For this purpose, a qualified plan (defined in section 219(g)(5)) includes a qualified pension plan, a profit-sharing plan, a stock bonus plan, a qualified annuity plan, a tax-sheltered annuity plan, and a simplified employee pension (SEP) plan. A qualified plan that only covers employees covered under a collective bargaining agreement for which retirement benefits were the subject of good faith bargaining is disregarded if these employees are excluded from participating in the SIMPLE IRA plan.

If the failure to continue to satisfy the 100-employee limit or the one-plan rule described in **1** and **2** above is due to an acquisition or similar transaction involving your business, special rules apply. Consult your tax advisor to find out if you can still maintain the plan after the transaction.

Certain related employers (trades or businesses under common control) must be treated as a single employer for purposes of the SIMPLE IRA requirements. These are: **(1)** a controlled group of corporations under section 414(b); **(2)** a partnership or sole proprietorship under common control under section 414(c); or **(3)** an affiliated service group under section 414(m). In addition, if you have leased employees required to be treated as your own employees under the rules of section 414(n), then you must count all such leased employees for the requirements listed above.

## What is a SIMPLE IRA Plan?

A SIMPLE IRA plan is a written arrangement that provides you and your employees with an easy way to make contributions to provide retirement income for your employees. Under a SIMPLE IRA plan, employees may choose whether to make salary reduction contributions to the SIMPLE IRA plan rather than receiving these amounts as part of their regular compensation. In addition, you will contribute matching or nonelective contributions on behalf of eligible employees (see **Employee Eligibility Requirements** below and **Contributions** on page 5). All contributions under this plan will be deposited into a SIMPLE individual retirement account or annuity established for each eligible employee with the financial institution selected by him or her.

## When To Use Form 5304-SIMPLE

A SIMPLE IRA plan may be established by using this Model Form or any other document that satisfies the statutory requirements.

**Do not** use Form 5304-SIMPLE if:

**1.** You want to require that all SIMPLE IRA plan contributions initially go to a financial institution designated by you. That is, you do not want to permit each of your eligible employees to choose a financial institution that will initially receive contributions. Instead, use **Form 5305-SIMPLE,** Savings Incentive Match Plan for Employees of Small Employers (SIMPLE)—for Use With a Designated Financial Institution.

**2.** You want employees who are nonresident aliens receiving no earned income from you that constitutes income from sources within the United States to be eligible under this plan; or

**3.** You want to establish a SIMPLE 401(k) plan.

## Completing Form 5304-SIMPLE

Pages 1 and 2 of Form 5304-SIMPLE contain the operative provisions of your SIMPLE IRA plan. This SIMPLE IRA plan is considered adopted when you have completed all applicable boxes and blanks and it has been executed by you.

The SIMPLE IRA plan is a legal document with important tax consequences for you and your employees. You may want to consult with your attorney or tax advisor before adopting this plan.

## Employee Eligibility Requirements (Article I)

Each year for which this SIMPLE IRA plan is effective, you must permit salary reduction contributions to be made by all of your employees who are reasonably expected to receive at least $5,000 in compensation from you during the year, and who received at least $5,000 in compensation from you in any 2 preceding years. However, you can expand the group of employees who are eligible to participate in the SIMPLE IRA plan by completing the options provided in Article I, items 1a and 1b. To choose full eligibility, check the box in Article I, item 1a. Alternatively, to choose limited eligibility, check the box in Article I, item 1b, and then insert "$5,000" or a lower compensation amount (including zero) and "2" or a lower number of years of service in the blanks in (i) and (ii) of Article I, item 1b.

In addition, you can exclude from participation those employees covered under a collective bargaining agreement for which retirement benefits were the subject of good faith bargaining. You may do this by checking the box in Article I, item 2. Under certain circumstances, these employees must be excluded. See **Which Employers May Establish and Maintain a SIMPLE IRA Plan?** above.

## Salary Reduction Agreements (Article II)

As indicated in Article II, item 1, a salary reduction agreement permits an eligible employee to make a salary reduction election to have his or her compensation for each pay period reduced by a percentage (expressed as a percentage or dollar amount). The total amount of the reduction in the employee's compensation cannot exceed the applicable amount for any calendar year. The applicable amount is $7,000 for 2002. That amount will increase to $8,000 for 2003, $9,000 for 2004, and $10,000 for 2005 and later years. In the case of an eligible employee who will be 50 or older before the end of the calendar year, the above limitation is increased to $7,500 for 2002, $9,000 for 2003, $10,500 for 2004, $12,000 for 2005, and $12,500 for 2006 and later years.

### Timing of Salary Reduction Elections

For any calendar year, an eligible employee may make or modify a salary reduction election during the 60-day period immediately preceding January 1 of that year. However, for the year in which the employee becomes eligible to make salary reduction contributions, the period during which the employee may make or modify the election is a 60-day period that includes either the date the employee becomes eligible or the day before.

You can extend the 60-day election periods to provide additional opportunities for eligible employees to make or modify salary reduction elections using the blank in Article II, item 2b. For example, you can provide that eligible employees may make new salary reduction elections or modify prior elections for any calendar quarter during the 30 days before that quarter.

You may use the **Model Salary Reduction Agreement** on page 3 to enable eligible employees to make or modify salary reduction elections.

Employees must be permitted to terminate their salary reduction elections at any time. They may resume salary reduction contributions for the year if permitted under Article II, item 2b. However, by checking the box in Article II, item 2d, you may prohibit an employee who terminates a salary reduction election outside the normal election cycle from resuming salary reduction contributions during the remainder of the calendar year.

## Contributions (Article III)

Only contributions described below may be made to this SIMPLE IRA plan. No additional contributions may be made.

### Salary Reduction Contributions

As indicated in Article III, item 1, salary reduction contributions consist of the amount by which the employee agrees to reduce his or her compensation. You must contribute the salary reduction contributions to the financial institution selected by each eligible employee.

### Matching Contributions

In general, you must contribute a matching contribution to each eligible employee's SIMPLE IRA equal to the employee's salary reduction contributions. This matching contribution cannot exceed 3% of the employee's compensation. See **Definition of Compensation,** below.

You may reduce this 3% limit to a lower percentage, but not lower than 1%. You cannot lower the 3% limit for more than 2 calendar years out of the 5-year period ending with the calendar year the reduction is effective.

**Note:** *If any year in the 5-year period described above is a year before you first established any SIMPLE IRA plan, you will be treated as making a 3% matching contribution for that year for purposes of determining when you may reduce the employer matching contribution.*

To elect this option, you must notify the employees of the reduced limit within a reasonable period of time before the applicable 60-day election periods for the year. See **Timing of Salary Reduction Elections** above.

### Nonelective Contributions

Instead of making a matching contribution, you may, for any year, make a nonelective contribution equal to 2% of compensation for each eligible employee who has at least $5,000 in compensation for the year. Nonelective contributions may not be based on more than $200,000* of compensation.

To elect to make nonelective contributions, you must notify employees within a reasonable period of time before the applicable 60-day election periods for such year. See **Timing of Salary Reduction Elections** above.

**Note:** *Insert "$5,000" in Article III, item 2b(i) to impose the $5,000 compensation requirement. You may expand the group of employees who are eligible for nonelective contributions by inserting a compensation amount lower than $5,000.*

## Effective Date (Article VII)

Insert in Article VII, the date you want the provisions of the SIMPLE IRA plan to become effective. You must insert January 1 of the applicable year unless this is the first year for which you are adopting any SIMPLE IRA plan. If this is the first year for which you are adopting a SIMPLE IRA plan, you may insert any date between January 1 and October 1, inclusive of the applicable year.

## Additional Information

### Timing of Salary Reduction Contributions

The employer must make the salary reduction contributions to the financial institution selected by each eligible employee for his or her SIMPLE IRA no later than the 30th day of the month following the month in which the amounts would otherwise have been payable to the employee in cash.

The Department of Labor has indicated that most SIMPLE IRA plans are also subject to Title I of the Employee Retirement Income Security Act of 1974 (ERISA). Under Department of Labor regulations at 29 CFR 2510.3-102, salary reduction contributions must be made to each participant's SIMPLE IRA as of the earliest date on which those contributions can reasonably be segregated from the employer's general assets, but in no event later than the 30-day deadline described above.

### Definition of Compensation

"Compensation" means the amount described in section 6051(a)(3) (wages, tips, and other compensation from the employer subject to federal income tax withholding under section 3401(a)). Usually, this is the amount shown in box 1 of **Form W-2,** Wage and Tax Statement. For further information, see **Pub. 15,** Circular E, Employer's Tax Guide. Compensation also includes the salary reduction contributions made under this plan, and, if applicable, compensation deferred under a section 457 plan. In determining an employee's compensation for prior years, the employee's elective deferrals under a section 401(k) plan, a SARSEP, or a section 403(b) annuity contract are also included in the employee's compensation.

For self-employed individuals, compensation means the net earnings from self-employment determined under section 1402(a), without regard to section 1402(c)(6), prior to subtracting any contributions made pursuant to this SIMPLE IRA plan on behalf of the individual.

### Employee Notification

You must notify each eligible employee prior to the employee's 60-day election period described above that he or she can make or change salary reduction elections and select the financial institution that will serve as the trustee, custodian, or issuer of the employee's SIMPLE IRA. In this notification, you must indicate whether you will provide:

**1.** A matching contribution equal to your employees' salary reduction contributions up to a limit of 3% of their compensation;

**2.** A matching contribution equal to your employees' salary reduction contributions subject to a percentage limit that is between 1 and 3% of their compensation; or

**3.** A nonelective contribution equal to 2% of your employees' compensation.

You can use the **Model Notification to Eligible Employees** on page 3 to satisfy these employee notification requirements for this SIMPLE IRA plan. A **Summary Description** must also be provided to eligible employees at this time. This summary description requirement may be satisfied by providing a completed copy of pages 1 and 2 of Form 5304-SIMPLE (including the information described in Article VI—Procedures for Withdrawal).

If you fail to provide the employee notification (including the summary description) described above, you will be liable for a penalty of $50 per day until the notification is provided. If you can show that the failure was due to reasonable cause, the penalty will not be imposed.

If the financial institution's name, address, or withdrawal procedures are not available at the time the employee must be given the summary description, you must provide the summary description without this information. In that case, you will have reasonable cause for not including this information in the summary description, but only if you ensure that it is provided to the employee as soon as administratively feasible.

## Reporting Requirements

You are not required to file any annual information returns for your SIMPLE IRA plan, such as Forms 5500 or 5500-EZ. However, you must report to the IRS which eligible employees are active participants in the SIMPLE IRA plan and the amount of your employees' salary reduction contributions to the SIMPLE IRA plan on Form W-2. These contributions are subject to social security, medicare, railroad retirement, and federal unemployment tax.

## Deducting Contributions

Contributions to this SIMPLE IRA plan are deductible in your tax year containing the end of the calendar year for which the contributions are made.

Contributions will be treated as made for a particular tax year if they are made for that year and are made by the due date (including extensions) of your income tax return for that year.

## Summary Description

Each year the SIMPLE IRA plan is in effect, the financial institution for the SIMPLE IRA of each eligible employee must provide the employer the information described in section 408(l)(2)(B). This requirement may be satisfied by providing the employer a current copy of Form 5304-SIMPLE (including instructions) together with the financial institution's procedures for withdrawals from SIMPLE IRAs established at that financial institution, including the financial institution's name and address. The summary description must be received by the employer in sufficient time to comply with the **Employee Notification** requirements above.

There is a penalty of $50 per day imposed on the financial institution for each failure to provide the summary description described above. However, if the failure was due to reasonable cause, the penalty will not be imposed.

---

**Paperwork Reduction Act Notice.** You are not required to provide the information requested on a form that is subject to the Paperwork Reduction Act unless the form displays a valid OMB control number. Books or records relating to a form or its instructions must be retained as long as their contents may become material in the administration of any Internal Revenue law. Generally, tax returns and return information are confidential, as required by section 6103.

The time needed to complete this form will vary depending on individual circumstances. The estimated average time is:

**Recordkeeping** . . . 3 hr., 38 min.

**Learning about the law or the form** . . . 2 hr., 26 min.

**Preparing the form** . . . . 47 min.

If you have comments concerning the accuracy of these time estimates or suggestions for making this form simpler, we would be happy to hear from you. You can write to the Tax Forms Committee, Western Area Distribution Center, Rancho Cordova, CA 95743-0001. **Do not** send this form to this address. Instead, keep it with your records.

Form **5305-SIMPLE**
(Rev. March 2002)

Department of the Treasury
Internal Revenue Service

### Savings Incentive Match Plan for Employees of Small Employers (SIMPLE)— for Use With a Designated Financial Institution

OMB No. 1545-1502

**Do not** file with the Internal Revenue Service

_____ establishes the following SIMPLE
Name of Employer

IRA plan under section 408(p) of the Internal Revenue Code and pursuant to the instructions contained in this form.

### Article I—Employee Eligibility Requirement *(complete applicable box(es) and blanks—see instructions)*

**1  General Eligibility Requirements.** The Employer agrees to permit salary reduction contributions to be made in each calendar year to the SIMPLE individual retirement account or annuity established at the designated financial institution (SIMPLE IRA) for each employee who meets the following requirements (select either 1a or 1b):

**a** ☐ **Full Eligibility.** All employees are eligible.

**b** ☐ **Limited Eligibility.** Eligibility is limited to employees who are described in both (i) and (ii) below:

    **(i)  Current compensation.** Employees who are reasonably expected to receive at least $ _____ in compensation (not to exceed $5,000) for the calendar year.

    **(ii)  Prior compensation.** Employees who have received at least $ _____ in compensation (not to exceed $5,000) during any _____ calendar year(s) (insert 0, 1, or 2) preceding the calendar year.

**2  Excludable Employees**

☐ The Employer elects to exclude employees covered under a collective bargaining agreement for which retirement benefits were the subject of good faith bargaining. **Note:** *This box is deemed checked if the Employer maintains a qualified plan covering only such employees.*

### Article II—Salary Reduction Agreements *(complete the box and blank, if applicable—see instructions)*

**1  Salary Reduction Election.** An eligible employee may make an election to have his or her compensation for each pay period reduced. The total amount of the reduction in the employee's compensation for a calendar year cannot exceed the applicable amount for that year. See instructions.

**2  Timing of Salary Reduction Elections**

**a** For a calendar year, an eligible employee may make or modify a salary reduction election during the 60-day period immediately preceding January 1 of that year. However, for the year in which the employee becomes eligible to make salary reduction contributions, the period during which the employee may make or modify the election is a 60-day period that includes either the date the employee becomes eligible or the day before.

**b** In addition to the election periods in 2a, eligible employees may make salary reduction elections or modify prior elections _____
_____ . If the Employer chooses this option, insert a period or periods (e.g. semi-annually, quarterly, monthly, or daily) that will apply uniformly to all eligible employees.

**c** No salary reduction election may apply to compensation that an employee received, or had a right to immediately receive, before execution of the salary reduction election.

**d** An employee may terminate a salary reduction election at any time during the calendar year. ☐ If this box is checked, an employee who terminates a salary reduction election not in accordance with 2b may not resume salary reduction contributions during the calendar year.

### Article III—Contributions *(complete the blank, if applicable—see instructions)*

**1  Salary Reduction Contributions.** The amount by which the employee agrees to reduce his or her compensation will be contributed by the Employer to the employee's SIMPLE IRA.

**2 a  Matching Contributions**

    **(i)** For each calendar year, the Employer will contribute a matching contribution to each eligible employee's SIMPLE IRA equal to the employee's salary reduction contributions up to a limit of 3% of the employee's compensation for the calendar year.

    **(ii)** The Employer may reduce the 3% limit for the calendar year in (i) only if:

        **(1)** The limit is not reduced below 1%; **(2)** The limit is not reduced for more than 2 calendar years during the 5-year period ending with the calendar year the reduction is effective; and **(3)** Each employee is notified of the reduced limit within a reasonable period of time before the employees' 60-day election period for the calendar year (described in Article II, item 2a).

**b  Nonelective Contributions**

    **(i)** For any calendar year, instead of making matching contributions, the Employer may make nonelective contributions equal to 2% of compensation for the calendar year to the SIMPLE IRA of each eligible employee who has at least $ _____ (not more than $5,000) in compensation for the calendar year. No more than $200,000* in compensation can be taken into account in determining the nonelective contribution for each eligible employee.

    **(ii)** For any calendar year, the Employer may make 2% nonelective contributions instead of matching contributions only if:

        **(1)** Each eligible employee is notified that a 2% nonelective contribution will be made instead of a matching contribution; and

        **(2)** This notification is provided within a reasonable period of time before the employees' 60-day election period for the calendar year (described in Article II, item 2a).

**3  Time and Manner of Contributions**

**a** The Employer will make the salary reduction contributions (described in 1 above) to the designated financial institution for the IRAs established under this SIMPLE IRA plan no later than 30 days after the end of the month in which the money is withheld from the employee's pay. See instructions.

**b** The Employer will make the matching or nonelective contributions (described in 2a and 2b above) to the designated financial institution for the IRAs established under this SIMPLE IRA plan no later than the due date for filing the Employer's tax return, including extensions, for the taxable year that includes the last day of the calendar year for which the contributions are made.

*\* For 2003 and later years, this amount is subject to annual cost-of-living adjustments. The IRS announces the increase, if any, in a news release, in the Internal Revenue Bulletin, and on the IRS's internet web site at www.irs.gov.*

**For Paperwork Reduction Act Notice, see page 6.**         Cat. No. 23063F         Form **5305-SIMPLE** (Rev. 3-2002)

## Article IV—Other Requirements and Provisions

**1  Contributions in General.** The Employer will make no contributions to the SIMPLE IRAs other than salary reduction contributions (described in Article III, item 1) and matching or nonelective contributions (described in Article III, items 2a and 2b).

**2  Vesting Requirements.** All contributions made under this SIMPLE IRA plan are fully vested and nonforfeitable.

**3  No Withdrawal Restrictions.** The Employer may not require the employee to retain any portion of the contributions in his or her SIMPLE IRA or otherwise impose any withdrawal restrictions.

**4  No Cost Or Penalty For Transfers.** The Employer will not impose any cost or penalty on a participant for the transfer of the participant's SIMPLE IRA balance to another IRA.

**5  Amendments To This SIMPLE IRA Plan.** This SIMPLE IRA plan may not be amended except to modify the entries inserted in the blanks or boxes provided in Articles I, II, III, VI, and VII.

**6  Effects Of Withdrawals and Rollovers**

**a** An amount withdrawn from the SIMPLE IRA is generally includible in gross income. However, a SIMPLE IRA balance may be rolled over or transferred on a tax-free basis to another IRA designed solely to hold funds under a SIMPLE IRA plan. In addition, an individual may roll over or transfer his or her SIMPLE IRA balance to any IRA after a 2-year period has expired since the individual first participated in any SIMPLE IRA plan of the Employer. Any rollover or transfer must comply with the requirements of section 408.

**b** If an individual withdraws an amount from a SIMPLE IRA during the 2-year period beginning when the individual first participated in any SIMPLE IRA plan of the Employer and the amount is subject to the additional tax on early distributions under section 72(t), this additional tax is increased from 10% to 25%.

## Article V—Definitions

**1  Compensation**

**a  General Definition of Compensation.** Compensation means the sum of wages, tips, and other compensation from the Employer subject to federal income tax withholding (as described in section 6051(a)(3)) and the employee's salary reduction contributions made under this plan, and, if applicable, elective deferrals under a section 401(k) plan, a SARSEP, or a section 403(b) annuity contract and compensation deferred under a section 457 plan required to be reported by the Employer on Form W-2 (as described in section 6058(a)(8)).

**b  Compensation for Self-Employed Individuals.** For self-employed individuals, compensation means the net earnings from self-employment determined under section 1402(a), without regard to section 1402(c)(6), prior to subtracting any contributions made pursuant to this plan on behalf of the individual.

**2  Employee.** Employee means a common-law employee of the Employer. The term employee also includes a self-employed individual and a leased employee described in section 414(n) but does not include a nonresident alien who received no earned income from the Employer that constitutes income from sources within the United States.

**3  Eligible Employee.** An eligible employee means an employee who satisfies the conditions in Article I, item 1 and is not excluded under Article I, item 2.

**4  Designated Financial Institution.** A designated financial institution is a trustee, custodian, or insurance company (that issues annuity contracts) for the SIMPLE IRA plan that receives all contributions made pursuant to the SIMPLE IRA plan and deposits those contributions to the SIMPLE IRA of each eligible employee.

## Article VI—Procedures for Withdrawal *(The designated financial institution will provide the instructions (to be attached or inserted in the space below) on the procedures for withdrawals of contributions by employees.)*

## Article VII—Effective Date

This SIMPLE IRA plan is effective _____ . See instructions.

\*          \*          \*          \*          \*

Name of Employer _____        By: Signature _____        Date _____

Address of Employer _____        Name and title _____

The undersigned agrees to serve as designated financial institution, receiving all contributions made pursuant to this SIMPLE IRA plan and depositing those contributions to the SIMPLE IRA of each eligible employee as soon as practicable. Upon the request of any participant, the undersigned also agrees to transfer the participant's balance in a SIMPLE IRA established under this SIMPLE IRA plan to another IRA without cost or penalty to the participant.

Name of designated financial institution _____        By: Signature _____        Date _____

Address _____        Name and title _____

Form **5305-SIMPLE** (Rev. 3-2002)

Form 5305-SIMPLE (Rev. 3-2002)

## Model Notification to Eligible Employees

### I. Opportunity to Participate in the SIMPLE IRA Plan

You are eligible to make salary reduction contributions to the _____
SIMPLE IRA plan. This notice and the attached summary description provide you with information that you should consider before you decide whether to start, continue, or change your salary reduction agreement.

### II. Employer Contribution Election

For the _____ calendar year, the employer elects to contribute to your SIMPLE IRA *(employer must select either (1), (2), or (3)):*

☐ **(1)** A matching contribution equal to your salary reduction contributions up to a limit of 3% of your compensation for the year;

☐ **(2)** A matching contribution equal to your salary reduction contributions up to a limit of _____% *(employer must insert a number from 1 to 3 and is subject to certain restrictions)* of your compensation for the year; or

☐ **(3)** A nonelective contribution equal to 2% of your compensation for the year (limited to $200,000*) if you are an employee who makes at least $ _____ *(employer must insert an amount that is $5,000 or less)* in compensation for the year.

### III. Administrative Procedures

To start or change your salary reduction contributions, you must complete the salary reduction agreement and return it to _____ *(employer should designate a place or individual)* by _____ *(employer should insert a date that is not less than 60 days after notice is given).*

## Model Salary Reduction Agreement

### I. Salary Reduction Election

Subject to the requirements of the SIMPLE IRA plan of _____ *(name of employer)* I authorize _____ % or
$ _____ (which equals _____ % of my current rate of pay)
to be withheld from my pay for each pay period and contributed to my SIMPLE IRA as a salary reduction contribution.

### II. Maximum Salary Reduction

I understand that the total amount of my salary reduction contributions in any calendar year cannot exceed the applicable amount for that year. See instructions.

### III. Date Salary Reduction Begins

I understand that my salary reduction contributions will start as soon as permitted under the SIMPLE IRA plan and as soon as administratively feasible or, if later, _____. *(Fill in the date you want the salary reduction contributions to begin. The date must be after you sign this agreement.)*

### IV. Duration of Election

This salary reduction agreement replaces any earlier agreement and will remain in effect as long as I remain an eligible employee under the SIMPLE IRA plan or until I provide my employer with a request to end my salary reduction contributions or provide a new salary reduction agreement as permitted under this SIMPLE IRA plan.

Signature of employee _____ Date _____

* For 2003 and later years, this amount is subject to cost-of-living adjustments. The IRS announces the increase, if any, in a news release, in the Internal Revenue Bulletin, and on the IRS Web Site at **www.irs.gov.**

Form **5305-SIMPLE** (Rev. 3-2002)

# General Instructions

*Section references are to the Internal Revenue Code unless otherwise noted.*

## Purpose of Form

Form 5305-SIMPLE is a model Savings Incentive Match Plan for Employees of Small Employers (SIMPLE) plan document that an employer may use in combination with SIMPLE IRAs to establish a SIMPLE IRA plan described in section 408(p).

These instructions are designed to assist in the establishment and administration of the SIMPLE IRA plan. They are **not** intended to supersede any provision in the SIMPLE IRA plan.

**Do not** file Form 5305-SIMPLE with the IRS. Instead, keep it with your records.

For more information, see **Pub. 560,** Retirement Plans for Small Business (SEP, SIMPLE, and Qualified Plans), and **Pub. 590,** Individual Retirement Arrangements (IRAs).

# Instructions for the Employer

## Which Employers May Establish and Maintain a SIMPLE IRA Plan?

To establish and maintain a SIMPLE IRA plan, you must meet **both** of the following requirements:

**1.** Last calendar year, you had no more than 100 employees (including self-employed individuals) who earned $5,000 or more in compensation from you during the year. If you have a SIMPLE IRA plan but later exceed this 100-employee limit, you will be treated as meeting the limit for the 2 years following the calendar year in which you last satisfied the limit.

**2.** You do not maintain during any part of the calendar year another qualified plan with respect to which contributions are made, or benefits are accrued, for service in the calendar year. For this purpose, a qualified plan (defined in section 219(g)(5)) includes a qualified pension plan, a profit-sharing plan, a stock bonus plan, a qualified annuity plan, a tax-sheltered annuity plan, and a simplified employee pension (SEP) plan. A qualified plan that only covers employees covered under a collective bargaining agreement for which retirement benefits were the subject of good faith bargaining is disregarded if these employees are excluded from participating in the SIMPLE IRA plan.

If the failure to continue to satisfy the 100-employee limit or the one-plan rule described in **1** or **2** above, is due to an acquisition or similar transaction involving your business, special rules apply. Consult your tax advisor to find out if you can still maintain the plan after the transaction.

Certain related employers (trades or businesses under common control) must be treated as a single employer for purposes of the SIMPLE requirements. These are: **(1)** a controlled group of corporations under section 414(b); **(2)** a partnership or sole proprietorship under common control under section 414(c); or **(3)** an affiliated service group under section 414(m). In addition, if you have leased employees required to be treated as your own employees under the rules of section 414(n), then you must count all such leased employees for the requirements listed above.

## What is a SIMPLE IRA Plan?

A SIMPLE IRA plan is a written arrangement that provides you and your employees with an easy way to make contributions to provide retirement income for your employees. Under a SIMPLE IRA plan, employees may choose whether to make salary reduction contributions to the SIMPLE IRA plan rather than receiving these amounts as part of their regular compensation. In addition, you will contribute matching or nonelective contributions on behalf of eligible employees (see **Employee Eligibility Requirements** below and **Contributions** on page 5). All contributions under this plan will be deposited into a SIMPLE individual retirement account or annuity established for each eligible employee with the designated financial institution named in Article VII.

## When To Use Form 5305-SIMPLE

A SIMPLE IRA plan may be established by using this Model Form or any other document that satisfies the statutory requirements.

**Do not** use Form 5305-SIMPLE if:

**1.** You want to permit each of your eligible employees to choose a financial institution that will initially receive contributions. Instead, use **Form 5304-SIMPLE,** Savings Incentive Match Plan for Employees of Small Employers (SIMPLE)—Not for Use With a Designated Financial Institution.

**2.** You want employees who are nonresident aliens receiving no earned income from you that constitutes income from sources within the United States to be eligible under this plan; or

**3.** You want to establish a SIMPLE 401(k) plan.

## Completing Form 5305-SIMPLE

Pages 1 and 2 of Form 5305-SIMPLE contain the operative provisions of your SIMPLE IRA plan. This SIMPLE IRA plan is considered adopted when you have completed all appropriate boxes and blanks and it has been executed by you and the designated financial institution.

The SIMPLE IRA plan is a legal document with important tax consequences for you and your employees. You may want to consult with your attorney or tax advisor before adopting this plan.

## Employee Eligibility Requirements (Article I)

Each year for which this SIMPLE IRA plan is effective, you must permit salary reduction contributions to be made by all of your employees who are reasonably expected to receive at least $5,000 in compensation from you during the year, and who received at least $5,000 in compensation from you in any 2 preceding years. However, you can expand the group of employees who are eligible to participate in the SIMPLE IRA plan by completing the options provided in Article I, items 1a and 1b. To choose full eligibility, check the box in Article I, item 1a. Alternatively, to choose limited eligibility, check the box in Article I, item 1b, and then insert "$5,000" or a lower compensation amount (including zero) and "2" or a lower number of years of service in the blanks in (i) and (ii) of Article I, item 1b.

In addition, you can exclude from participation those employees covered under a collective bargaining agreement for which retirement benefits were the subject of good faith bargaining. You may do this by checking the box in Article I, item 2. Under certain circumstances, these employees must be excluded. See **Which Employers May Establish and Maintain a SIMPLE IRA Plan?** above.

## Salary Reduction Agreements (Article II)

As indicated in Article II, item 1, a salary reduction agreement permits an eligible employee to make an election to have his or her compensation for each pay period reduced by a percentage (expressed as a percentage or dollar amount). The total amount of the reduction in the employee's compensation cannot exceed the applicable amount for any calendar year. The applicable amount is $7,000 for 2002. That amount will increase to

$8,000 for 2003, $9,000 for 2004, and $10,000 for 2005 and later years. In the case of an eligible employee who will be 50 or older before the end of the calendar year, the above limitation is increased to $7,500 for 2002, $9,000 for 2003, $10,500 for 2004, $12,000 for 2005, and $12,500 for 2006 and later years.

### Timing of Salary Reduction Elections

For a calendar year, an eligible employee may make or modify a salary reduction election during the 60-day period immediately preceding January 1 of that year. However, for the year in which the employee becomes eligible to make salary reduction contributions, the period during which the employee may make or modify the election is a 60-day period that includes either the date the employee becomes eligible or the day before.

You can extend the 60-day election periods to provide additional opportunities for eligible employees to make or modify salary reduction elections using the blank in Article II, item 2b. For example, you can provide that eligible employees may make new salary reduction elections or modify prior elections for any calendar quarter during the 30 days before that quarter.

You may use the **Model Salary Reduction Agreement** on page 3 to enable eligible employees to make or modify salary reduction elections.

Employees must be permitted to terminate their salary reduction elections at any time. They may resume salary reduction contributions for the year if permitted under Article II, item 2b. However, by checking the box in Article II, item 2d, you may prohibit an employee who terminates a salary reduction election outside the normal election cycle from resuming salary reduction contributions during the remainder of the calendar year.

## Contributions (Article III)

Only contributions described below may be made to this SIMPLE IRA plan. No additional contributions may be made.

### Salary Reduction Contributions

As indicated in Article III, item 1, salary reduction contributions consist of the amount by which the employee agrees to reduce his or her compensation. You must contribute the salary reduction contributions to the designated financial institution for the employee's SIMPLE IRA.

### Matching Contributions

In general, you must contribute a matching contribution to each eligible employee's SIMPLE IRA equal to the employee's salary reduction contributions. This matching contribution cannot exceed 3% of the employee's compensation. See **Definition of Compensation** below.

You may reduce this 3% limit to a lower percentage, but not lower than 1%. You cannot lower the 3% limit for more than 2 calendar years out of the 5-year period ending with the calendar year the reduction is effective.

**Note:** *If any year in the 5-year period described above is a year before you first established any SIMPLE IRA plan, you will be treated as making a 3% matching contribution for that year for purposes of determining when you may reduce the employer matching contribution.*

To elect this option, you must notify the employees of the reduced limit within a reasonable period of time before the applicable 60-day election periods for the year. See **Timing of Salary Reduction Elections** above.

### Nonelective Contributions

Instead of making a matching contribution, you may, for any year, make a nonelective contribution equal to 2% of compensation for each eligible employee who has at least $5,000 in compensation for the year. Nonelective contributions may not be based on more than $200,000* of compensation.

To elect to make nonelective contributions, you must notify employees within a reasonable period of time before the applicable 60-day election periods for such year. See **Timing of Salary Reduction Elections** above.

**Note:** *Insert "$5,000" in Article III, item 2b(i) to impose the $5,000 compensation requirement. You may expand the group of employees who are eligible for nonelective contributions by inserting a compensation amount lower than $5,000.*

## Effective Date (Article VII)

Insert in Article VII, the date you want the provisions of the SIMPLE IRA plan to become effective. You must insert January 1 of the applicable year unless this is the first year for which you are adopting any SIMPLE IRA plan. If this is the first year for which you are adopting a SIMPLE IRA plan, you may insert any date between January 1 and October 1, inclusive of the applicable year.

## Additional Information

### Timing of Salary Reduction Contributions

The employer must make the salary reduction contributions to the designated financial institution for the SIMPLE IRAs of all eligible employees no later than the 30th day of the month following the month in which the amounts would otherwise have been payable to the employee in cash.

The Department of Labor has indicated that most SIMPLE IRA plans are also subject to Title I of the Employee Retirement Income Security Act of 1974 (ERISA). Under Department of Labor regulations, at 29 CFR 2510.3-102, salary reduction contributions must be made to the SIMPLE IRA at the designated financial institution as of the earliest date on which those contributions can reasonably be segregated from the employer's general assets, but in no event later than the 30-day deadline described above.

### Definition of Compensation

"Compensation" means the amount described in section 6051(a)(3) (wages, tips, and other compensation from the employer subject to federal income tax withholding under section 3401(a)). Usually, this is the amount shown in box 1 of **Form W-2,** Wage and Tax Statement. For further information, see **Pub. 15,** Circular E, Employer's Tax Guide. Compensation also includes the salary reduction contributions made under this plan, and, if applicable, compensation deferred under a section 457 plan. In determining an employee's compensation for prior years, the employee's elective deferrals under a section 401(k) plan, a SARSEP, or a section 403(b) annuity contract are also included in the employee's compensation.

For self-employed individuals, compensation means the net earnings from self-employment determined under section 1402(a), without regard to section 1402(c)(6), prior to subtracting any contributions made pursuant to this SIMPLE IRA plan on behalf of the individual.

### Employee Notification

You must notify eligible employees prior to the employees' 60-day election period described above that they can make or change salary reduction elections. In this notification, you must indicate whether you will provide:

**1.** A matching contribution equal to your employees' salary reduction contributions up to a limit of 3% of their compensation;

**2.** A matching contribution equal to your employees' salary reduction contributions subject to a percentage limit that is between 1 and 3% of their compensation; or

**3.** A nonelective contribution equal to 2% of your employees' compensation.

You can use the **Model Notification to Eligible Employees** on page 3 to satisfy these employee notification requirements for this SIMPLE IRA plan. A **Summary Description** must also be provided to eligible employees at this time. This summary description requirement may be satisfied by providing a completed copy of pages 1 and 2 of Form 5305-SIMPLE (including the Article VI Procedures for Withdrawals and transfers from the SIMPLE IRAs established under this SIMPLE IRA plan).

If you fail to provide the employee notification (including the summary description) described above, you will be liable for a penalty of $50 per day until the notification is provided. If you can show that the failure was due to reasonable cause, the penalty will not be imposed.

## Reporting Requirements

You are not required to file any annual information returns for your SIMPLE IRA plan, such as Forms 5500 or 5500-EZ. However, you must report to the IRS which eligible employees are active participants in the SIMPLE IRA plan and the amount of your employees' salary reduction contributions to the SIMPLE IRA plan on Form W-2. These contributions are subject to social security, Medicare, railroad retirement, and federal unemployment tax.

## Deducting Contributions

Contributions to this SIMPLE IRA plan are deductible in your tax year containing the end of the calendar year for which the contributions are made.

Contributions will be treated as made for a particular tax year if they are made for that year and are made by the due date (including extensions) of your income tax return for that year.

## Choosing the Designated Financial Institution

As indicated in Article V, item 4, a designated financial institution is a trustee, custodian, or insurance company (that issues annuity contracts) for the SIMPLE IRA plan that would receive all contributions made pursuant to the SIMPLE IRA plan and deposit the contributions to the SIMPLE IRA of each eligible employee.

Only certain financial institutions, such as banks, savings & loan associations, insured credit unions, insurance companies (that issue annuity contracts), or IRS-approved nonbank trustees may serve as a designated financial institution under a SIMPLE IRA plan.

You are not required to choose a designated financial institution for your SIMPLE IRA plan. However, if you do not want to choose a designated financial institution, you cannot use this form (see **When to Use Form 5305-SIMPLE** on page 4).

## Instructions for the Designated Financial Institution

### Completing Form 5305-SIMPLE

By completing Article VII, you have agreed to be the designated financial institution for this SIMPLE IRA plan. You agree to maintain IRAs on behalf of all individuals receiving contributions under the plan and to receive all contributions made pursuant to this plan and to deposit those contributions to the SIMPLE IRAs of each eligible employee as soon as practicable. You also agree that upon the request of a participant, you will transfer the participant's balance in a SIMPLE IRA to another IRA without cost or penalty to the participant.

## Summary Description

Each year the SIMPLE IRA plan is in effect, you must provide the employer the information described in section 408(l)(2)(B). This requirement may be satisfied by providing the employer a current copy of Form 5305-SIMPLE (including instructions) together with your procedures for withdrawals and transfers from the SIMPLE IRAs established under this SIMPLE IRA plan. The summary description must be received by the employer in sufficient time to comply with the **Employee Notification** requirements on page 5.

If you fail to provide the summary description described above, you will be liable for a penalty of $50 per day until the notification is provided. If you can show that the failure was due to reasonable cause, the penalty will not be imposed.

**Paperwork Reduction Act Notice.** You are not required to provide the information requested on a form that is subject to the Paperwork Reduction Act unless the form displays a valid OMB control number. Books or records relating to a form or its instructions must be retained as long as their contents may become material in the administration of any Internal Revenue law. Generally, tax returns and return information are confidential, as required by section 6103.

The time needed to complete this form will vary depending on individual circumstances. The estimated average time is:

**Recordkeeping** . . . 3 hr., 38 min.

**Learning about the law or the form** . . . 2 hr., 26 min.

**Preparing the form**. . . . 47 min.

If you have comments concerning the accuracy of these time estimates or suggestions for making this form simpler, we would be happy to hear from you. You can write to the Tax Forms Committee, Western Area Distribution Center, Rancho Cordova, CA 95743-0001. **Do not** send this form to this address. Instead, keep it for your records.

# Chapter 21

# SIMPLIFIED EMPLOYEE PENSIONS (SEPs)

## WHAT ARE THEY?

SEPS (simplified employee pensions) are employer-sponsored plans under which plan contributions are made to the participating employee's IRA. Tax-deferred contribution levels are generally significantly higher than the maximum contribution limit for traditional IRAs (Chapter 24). A SEP provides for employer contributions only, except for salary reduction SEPs (SAR-SEPs), which had to be adopted before 1997.

SEPs are easy to adopt and generally simple to administer while providing employees with the tax-deferred retirement savings benefits of a qualified plan. However, qualified plans potentially can provide higher contribution levels. Annual SEP contributions are effectively limited to the lesser of 25% of compensation or $40,000 (in 2003).[1]

## WHEN IS IT INDICATED?

1.  When the employer is looking for an alternative to a qualified profit sharing plan that is easier and less expensive to install and administer. For very small employers, a SEP is one of the simplest types of tax-deferred employee retirement plans available. For larger employers (more than about 10 employees) the cost of installing and administering a qualified plan can be spread over enough employees that the advantages of a SEP are less significant.

2.  When an employer wants to install a tax-deferred plan and it is too late to adopt a qualified plan for the year in question. (Qualified plans must be adopted before the end of the year in which they are to be effective. SEPs can be adopted as late as the tax return filing date for the year in which they are to be effective.)

3.  When an employer who adopted a SAR-SEP prior to 1997 wants to continue to operate a simplified plan funded through employee salary reductions (before-tax contributions). While such plans may not be adopted after 1996, plans in existence before 1997 may continue to operate and add new partici-

pants. (See #4 under "Tax Implications," below for more details.) Employers wishing to adopt a simplified plan that is funded through employee salary reductions should consider a SIMPLE IRA plan (see Chapter 20).

## ADVANTAGES

1.  A SEP can be adopted by completing IRS Form 5305-SEP, reproduced at the end of this chapter, rather than by the complex procedure required for qualified plans (described in Chapter 27). However, if the employer adopts a master or prototype qualified plan, the installation costs and complexity may not actually be much greater than that for a SEP, even though the documentation is more voluminous.

2.  Benefits of a SEP are totally portable by employees since funding consists entirely of IRAs for each employee and employees are always 100 percent vested in their benefits. Employees own and control their SEP/IRA accounts, even after they terminate employment with the original employer.

3.  A SEP provides as much or more flexibility in the timing of contributions as a qualified profit sharing plan. The employer is free at its discretion to make no contribution to the plan in any given year.

4.  Individual IRA accounts allow participants to benefit from good investment results (however, they also assume the risk of bad investment results).

5.  A SAR-SEP that was adopted before 1997 can be funded through salary reductions by employees, if the conditions described in item #4 under "Tax Implications," below, are met.

## DISADVANTAGES

1.  Employees cannot rely upon a SEP to provide an adequate retirement benefit. First, benefits are not significant unless the employer makes sub-

stantial, regular contributions to the SEP. Such regular contributions are not a requirement for a SEP. Furthermore, employees who enter the plan at older ages have only a limited number of years remaining prior to retirement to build up their SEP accounts.

2. Annual contributions may be restricted to lesser amounts than would be available in a qualified plan. Although SEPs are subject to the same Section 415 limit as a defined contribution plan (i.e., the lesser of (a) 100% of compensation or (b) $40,000 (in 2003 as indexed), the deduction and exclusion amounts may be lower than they would be for a qualified plan, as explained below.

3. Distributions from SEPs are not eligible for special averaging available for certain qualified plan distributions (see Chapter 26).

## TAX IMPLICATIONS

1. An employer may deduct contributions to a SEP, up to 25% of the total payroll of all employees covered under the plan, if the contributions are made under a written formula that meets various requirements of the Internal Revenue Code.[2]

2. The major SEP coverage requirements are[3]:

   - A SEP must cover all employees who are at least 21 years of age and who have worked for the employer during 3 out of the preceding 5 calendar years. Part-time employment counts in determining years of service.

   - Contributions need not be made on behalf of employees whose compensation for the calendar year was less than $450 (as indexed for 2003).

   - The plan can exclude employees who are members of collective bargaining units if retirement benefits have been the subject of good-faith bargaining; nonresident aliens can also be excluded.

3. The employer need not contribute any particular amount to a SEP or make any contribution at all. The "recurring and substantial contributions" requirement applicable to qualified profit sharing plans (as discussed in Chapter 16) has no effect on SEPs, so SEP contributions are more flexible than those to a qualified plan. An employer can freely omit any year's contribution to a SEP without any concern about adverse tax consequences.

4. The employer contribution, if made, must be allocated to plan participants under a written formula that does not discriminate in favor of highly compensated employees. The definition of "highly compensated" is that used for most employee benefit purposes, as discussed in Chapter 25. SEP formulas usually provide allocations as a uniform percentage of total compensation of each employee. In the allocation formula, only the first $200,000 (as indexed for 2003) of each employee's compensation can be taken into account. SEP allocation formulas can be integrated with Social Security under the integration rules applicable to qualified defined contribution plans; these are discussed in Chapter 25.

5. *Salary Reduction SEPs (SAR-SEPs):* While new SAR-SEPs may not be adopted after 1996, an employer who has 25 or fewer eligible employees and who adopted a salary reduction SEP (i.e., one funded through employee salary reductions) prior to 1997 may continue to operate the plan and may add new participants (up to the 25-employee limit). Under a salary reduction plan, employees have an election to receive cash or have amounts contributed to the SEP. The arrangement works similarly to a Section 401(k) salary reduction arrangement described in Chapter 19. The rules changed by JCWAA 2002 with respect to the exclusion for SEPs also apply to SAR-SEPs, but the picture is a little more complex for SAR-SEPs. The definition of "compensation" for purposes of the SEP provisions does not include elective deferrals. As a result, the "25% of compensation" limit will produce a smaller total than in the case, for example, of a 401(k) plan, where "compensation" may include elective deferrals.[4]

   Salary reductions are subject to an annual limit. The employee must add together each year all elective deferrals to (1) salary reduction SEPS, (2) Section 401(k) plans (see Chapter 19), (3) SIMPLE IRAs (see Chapter 20), and (4) Section 403(b) tax deferred annuity plans (see Chapter 23). All elective deferrals from all employer plans that cover the employee must be aggregated. The total must not exceed the following limits[5]:

| Year | Amount |
|------|--------|
| 2003 | 12,000 |
| 2004 | 13,000 |
| 2005 | 14,000 |
| 2006 and thereafter | 15,000 |

In addition to the foregoing salary reductions, employees who have reached age 50 during the plan year are generally eligible to make "catch-up" contributions. For salary reduction SEPs, the elective deferral limit is increased by the following amounts[6]:

| Year | Amount |
|------|--------|
| 2003 | 2,000 |
| 2004 | 3,000 |
| 2005 | 4,000 |
| 2006 and thereafter | 5,000 |

Note that the above limits are higher than those applicable to SIMPLE IRAs and SIMPLE 401(k) plans (see Chapter 19 and Chapter 20), so employers with grandfathered salary reduction SEPs may wish to continue them.

An employer cannot use a salary reduction SEP unless 50 percent or more of the employees eligible to participate elect to make SEP contributions. In addition, rules similar to the "actual deferral percentage" (ADP) test apply to a salary reduction SEP.[7] Under the ADP rules for SAR-SEPs, the deferral percentage for each highly compensated eligible employee who participates must be no more than 1.25 times the ADP of nonhighly compensated eligible employees. For example, if nonhighly compensated employees elect salary reductions averaging 6 percent of compensation, no highly compensated employee can elect more than a 7.5 percent salary reduction.

Salary reductions, but not direct employer contributions, are subject to Social Security (FICA) and federal unemployment (FUTA) taxes.[8] The impact of state payroll taxes depends on the particular state's law. Both salary reductions and employer contributions may be exempt from state payroll taxes in some states.

6. If an employer maintains both a SEP and a qualified plan, employer contributions to the SEP reduce the amount that can be deducted for contributions to the qualified plan.

7. In a SEP plan, each participating employee maintains a traditional IRA. Employer contributions are made directly to the employee's IRA. Employer contributions, within the limits discussed above, are not included in the employee's taxable income.

8. Direct employer contributions to a SEP are not subject to Social Security (FICA) or federal unem-

ployment (FUTA) taxes. The impact of state payroll taxes depends on the particular state's laws. Both salary reductions and employer contributions may be exempt from state payroll taxes in some states.

9. Certain employers adopting a plan may be eligible for a business tax credit of up to $500 for "qualified startup costs." See Chapter 27 for details.

10. A limited nonrefundable tax credit, known as the "saver's credit," is available to certain lower income taxpayers who make salary deferrals to a salary reduction SEP. (see "Questions and Answers," below).

11. Distributions to employees from the plan are treated as distributions from an IRA. All the restrictions on traditional IRA distributions apply and the distributions are taxed in the same manner. The taxation of distributions from traditional IRAs is discussed in Chapter 24.

## HOW TO INSTALL A PLAN

Installation of a SEP can be very easy. The employer merely completes Form 5305-SEP. A copy of the form and instructions is reproduced at the end of this chapter. To adopt a SEP, the employer completes the form and signs it prior to the tax filing date for the year in which the SEP is to take effect.[9] The form does not have to be sent to the IRS or any other government agency.

A SEP adopted by filling out Form 5305-SEP is somewhat inflexible since it must follow the provisions set out on the IRS model form. Some of the provisions in this form are more stringent than are actually required by the SEP rules; in particular:

1. The plan set out on Form 5305-SEP is not integrated with Social Security.

2. By its terms, Form 5305-SEP cannot be used if the employer (a) currently maintains a qualified plan, or (b) maintained a qualified defined benefit plan at any time in the past covering one or more of the employees to be covered under the SEP.

If the employer wants to adopt a SEP plan that avoids the limitations of the IRS model form, the plan must be custom designed. Costs for custom designing and installing a SEP are comparable to those for a qualified profit sharing plan.

## ERISA REQUIREMENTS

The reporting and disclosure requirements for SEPs are simplified if the employer uses Form 5305-SEP. The annual report form (5500 series) need not be filed if these forms are used. In other cases, reporting and disclosure requirements are similar to those for a qualified profit sharing plan.

## WHERE CAN I FIND OUT MORE ABOUT IT?

1. IRS Publication 334, Tax Guide for Small Business, and Publication 535, Business Expense Deductions, available free from the IRS; revised annually.

## QUESTIONS AND ANSWERS

**Question** — How does the "last minute" adoption feature of a SEP operate?

*Answer* — Suppose an employer reviews financial results shortly after the close of the employer's tax year—say it's a calendar year—and decides that the company should have had a qualified plan for the year just ended. It is not possible to adopt a qualified plan after the close of the taxable year, as discussed in Chapter 27. However, a SEP can be adopted at any time up to the tax return filing date for the year, including extensions. For example, if an incorporated employer uses the calendar year, the tax return filing date for the year 2003 is March 15, 2004, with extensions possible to September 15, 2004. Therefore a SEP could be adopted for 2003 as late as September 15, 2004.

**Question** — Can an unincorporated business adopt a SEP covering partners or a sole proprietor?

*Answer* — Yes. Partners and proprietors can be covered under the SEP of an unincorporated employer, as well as regular employees. As discussed in Chapter 12 (relating to HR 10 plans), for a partner or proprietor, "earned income" is used in place of compensation in computing SEP contributions.

**Question** — Can an employer make contributions to a SEP for employees who are over age 70½?

*Answer* — An individual cannot make contributions to his or her own traditional IRA after attaining age 70½. However, employers can make contributions to SEPs for employees who are over age 70½. In fact, the age

discrimination law, if applicable, would generally require such contributions to be made.

**Question** — Can an employee participating in a SEP also make deductible contributions to his or her own traditional IRA?

*Answer* — For individual IRA purposes, a SEP participant is treated the same as a participant in a regular qualified plan. That is, if the individual is an "active participant" in the plan, individual IRA contributions can be made and deducted, but the deduction is reduced or eliminated if adjusted gross income exceeds certain limits (see Chapter 24 for details). The full IRA deduction may be available to an individual who is not an active participant in a plan.

An employee covered under a SEP would be considered an active participant in any year in which salary reductions or employer contributions were allocated to his or her account. However, in a year in which no allocation was made to the individual's account, the individual would have a full individual IRA deduction available (within the limits explained in Chapter 24).[10] The higher SEP limit is not available for individual IRA contributions.

**Question** — Who is eligible to claim a nonrefundable credit for salary contributions to a salary reduction SEP?

*Answer* — Certain lower-income taxpayers may claim a temporary, nonrefundable credit for "qualified retirement savings contributions" in taxable years beginning after 2001 and before 2007.[11] This is known as the "saver's credit." "Qualified retirement savings contributions" include elective deferrals to salary reduction SEPs, as well as other elective deferrals and contributions to Roth or traditional IRAs. (However, the total is reduced by certain distributions received by the taxpayer or his spouse during the prior two taxable years and the current taxable year for which the credit is claimed, including the period up to the due date (plus extensions) for filing the federal income tax return for the current taxable year.)

The credit is allowed against the sum of the regular tax and the alternative minimum tax (minus certain other credits) and is allowed in addition to any other deduction or exclusion that would otherwise apply. In addition, to be eligible, the taxpayer must be at least 18 as of the end of the tax year and must not be claimed as a dependent by someone else or be a full-time student.

The amount of the credit is limited to an "applicable percentage" of IRA contributions and elective deferrals up to $2,000. The "applicable percentages" are as follows:

### ADJUSTED GROSS INCOME

| Joint return | | Head of a household | | All other cases | | Applicable |
|---|---|---|---|---|---|---|
| Over | Not over | Over | Not over | Over | Not over | percentage |
| 0 | $30,000 | 0 | $22,500 | 0 | $15,000 | 50% |
| 30,000 | 32,500 | 22,500 | 24,375 | 15,000 | 16,250 | 20% |
| 32,500 | 50,000 | 24,375 | 37,500 | 16,250 | 25,000 | 10% |
| 50,000 | | 37,500 | | 25,000 | | 0% |

---

*Example:* Max and Erma have adjusted gross income of $31,000 for 2003. Their employers sponsor salary reduction SEPs and they each elected to make a salary reduction contribution of $2,000 to the plan. Neither has received any distributions in the current or two preceding taxable years. Max and Erma will be able to exclude their salary reduction contributions as well as each being eligible to claim a credit of $400 (20% x $2,000) on their federal income tax return ($800 if married filing jointly) for 2003.

---

## FOOTNOTES

1. This is the result of the combination of the IRC Section 415(c) limit (i.e., the lesser of $40,000 or 100% of compensation) and the IRC Section 402(h)(2) exclusion for contributions (which is 25% of compensation). Note that all provisions of EGTRRA 2001 are scheduled to sunset, or expire, after December 31, 2010.

2. IRC Section 404(h)(1)(C).

3. The rules described in this chapter for SEPS are contained in IRC Section 408(k) unless otherwise indicated in the footnotes. The IRC formerly contained provisions for SEPs funded through salary reductions (SAR-SEPs). No new SAR-SEPs may be adopted after 1996; however, SAR-SEPs existing on December 31, 1996 may continue in effect and add new participants.

4. IRC Secs. 402(h)(2)(A), 404(a)(12), 404(n).

5. IRC Section 402(g).

6. IRC Section 414(v). Note that the limit will be lower if the amount of a participant's compensation, (after reduction for other elective deferrals) is less than the catch-up amounts.

7. IRC Sec. 408(k)(6).

8. IRC Sections 3121(a)(5)(C), 3306(b)(5)(C).

9. Prop. Treas. Reg. §1.408-7(b).

10. Notice 87-16, 1987-1 CB 446, I.

11. IRC Section 25B.

Form **5305A-SEP**
(Rev. March 2002)

Department of the Treasury
Internal Revenue Service

**Salary Reduction Simplified Employee Pension—
Individual Retirement Accounts
Contribution Agreement**

(Under section 408(k) of the Internal Revenue Code)

OMB No. 1545-1012

**Do not** file
with the Internal
Revenue Service

_____ amends its salary reduction SEP by adopting the following Model Salary
Name of employer
Reduction SEP under Internal Revenue Code section 408(k) and the instructions
to this form.

**Note:** *An employer may not establish a salary reduction SEP after 1996.*

### Article I—Eligibility Requirements (check applicable boxes—see instructions)

Provided the requirements of Article III are met, the employer agrees to permit elective deferrals to be made in each calendar year to the individual retirement accounts or individual retirement annuities (IRAs), established by or for all employees who are at least _____ years old (not to exceed 21 years) and have performed services for the employer in at least _____ years (not to exceed 3 years) of the immediately preceding 5 years. This simplified employee pension (SEP) ☐ includes ☐ **does not** include employees covered under a collective bargaining agreement, ☐ includes ☐ **does not** include certain nonresident aliens, and ☐ includes ☐ **does not** include employees whose total compensation during the year is less than $450*.

### Article II—Elective Deferrals (see instructions)

**A. Salary Reduction Amount.** An eligible employee may elect to have his or her compensation reduced by a specified percentage or amount per pay period, as designated in writing to the employer.

**B. Timing of Elective Deferrals.** No deferral election may be based on compensation an eligible employee received, or had a right to receive, before execution of the deferral election.

### Article III—SEP Requirements (see instructions)

The employer agrees that each employee's elective deferrals to the SEP will be:

**A.** Based only on the first $200,000* of compensation.

**B.** Limited annually to the smaller of: **(1)** 25% of compensation; **or (2)** the section 402(g) limit for the tax year.

**C.** Limited further, under section 415, if the employer makes nonelective contributions to this or another SEP.

**D.** Paid to the employee's IRA trustee, custodian, or insurance company (for an annuity contract) or, if necessary, an IRA established for an employee by the employer.

**E.** Made only if at least 50% of the employer's employees eligible to participate elect to have amounts contributed to the SEP. If the 50% requirement is not satisfied as of the end of any calendar year, then all of the elective deferrals made by the employees for that calendar year will be considered "disallowed deferrals" (IRA contributions that are not SEP-IRA contributions).

**F.** Made only if the employer had 25 or fewer employees eligible to participate at all times during the prior calendar year.

**G.** Adjusted only if deferrals to this SEP for any calendar year do not meet the "deferral percentage limitation" described on page 3.

### Article IV—Excess SEP Contributions (see instructions)

Elective deferrals by a "highly compensated employee" must satisfy the deferral percentage limitation under section 408(k)(6)(A)(iii). Amounts in excess of this limitation will be deemed excess SEP contributions for the affected highly compensated employee or employees.

### Article V—Notice Requirements (see instructions)

**A.** The employer will notify each highly compensated employee, by March 15 following the end of the calendar year to which any excess SEP contributions relate, of the excess SEP contributions to the highly compensated employee's SEP-IRA for the applicable year. The notification will specify the amount of the excess SEP contributions, whether they must be withdrawn, the calendar year in which any excess contributions are includible in income, and must provide an explanation of applicable penalties if the excess contributions that must be withdrawn are not withdrawn on time.

**B.** The employer will notify each employee who makes an elective deferral to a SEP that, until March 15 after the year of the deferral, any transfer or distribution from that employee's SEP-IRA of SEP contributions (or income on these contributions) attributable to elective deferrals made that year will be includible in income for purposes of sections 72(t) and 408(d)(1).

**C.** The employer will notify each employee by March 15 of each year of any disallowed deferrals to the employee's SEP-IRA for the preceding calendar year. Such notification will specify the amount of the disallowed deferrals and the calendar year in which those deferrals are includible in income and must provide an explanation of applicable penalties if the disallowed deferrals are not withdrawn on time.

### Article VI—Top-Heavy Requirements (see instructions)

**A.** Unless paragraph B is checked, the employer will satisfy the top-heavy requirements of section 416 by making a minimum contribution each year to the SEP-IRA of each employee eligible to participate in this SEP (other than a key employee as defined in section 416(i)). This contribution, in combination with other nonelective contributions, if any, is equal to the smaller of 3% of each eligible nonkey employee's compensation or a percentage of such compensation equal to the percentage of compensation at which elective (not including catch-up elective deferral contributions) and nonelective contributions are made under this SEP (and any other SEP maintained by the employer) for the year for the key employee for whom such percentage is the highest for the year.

* *For 2003 and later years, this amount is subject to annual cost-of-living adjustments. The IRS announces the increase, if any, in a news release, in the Internal Revenue Bulletin, and on the IRS Web Site at* **www.irs.gov.**

**For Paperwork Reduction Act Notice, see page 7.**        Cat. No. 64362R        Form **5305A-SEP** (Rev. 3-2002)

# Simplified Employee Pensions (SEPs)

within which the calendar year ends. Contributions made for a particular tax year must be made by the due date of your income tax return (including extensions) for that tax year.

**Completing the agreement.** This agreement is considered adopted when:

- IRAs have been established for all your eligible employees;
- You have completed all blanks on the agreement form without modification; and
- You have given all your eligible employees the following information:

1. A copy of Form 5305-SEP.

2. A statement that traditional IRAs other than the traditional IRAs into which employer SEP contributions will be made may provide different rates of return and different terms concerning, among other things, transfers and withdrawals of funds from the IRAs.

3. A statement that, in addition to the information provided to an employee at the time the employee becomes eligible to participate, the administrator of the SEP must furnish each participant within 30 days of the effective date of any amendment to the SEP, a copy of the amendment and a written explanation of its effects.

4. A statement that the administrator will give written notification to each participant of any employer contributions made under the SEP to that participant's IRA by the later of January 31 of the year following the year for which a contribution is made or 30 days after the contribution is made.

Employers who have established a SEP using Form 5305-SEP and have furnished each eligible employee with a copy of the completed Form 5305-SEP and provided the other documents and disclosures described in **Instructions to the Employer** and **Information for the Employee,** are not required to file the annual information returns, Forms 5500 or 5500-EZ for the SEP. However, under Title I of the Employee Retirement Income Security Act of 1974 (ERISA), this relief from the annual reporting requirements may not be available to an employer who selects, recommends, or influences its employees to choose IRAs into which contributions will be made under the SEP, if those IRAs are subject to provisions that impose any limits on a participant's ability to withdraw funds (other than restrictions imposed by the Code that apply to all IRAs). For additional information on Title I requirements, see the Department of Labor regulation at 29 CFR 2520.104-48.

## Information for the Employee

The information below explains what a SEP is, how contributions are made, and how to treat your employer's contributions for tax purposes. For more information, see Pub. 590.

**Simplified employee pension.** A SEP is a written arrangement (a plan) that allows an employer to make contributions toward your retirement. Contributions are made to a traditional individual retirement account/annuity (traditional IRA). Contributions must be made to either a Model traditional IRA executed on an IRS form or a master or prototype traditional IRA for which the IRS has issued a favorable opinion letter.

An employer is not required to make SEP contributions. If a contribution is made, however, it must be allocated to all eligible employees according to the SEP agreement. The Model SEP (Form 5305-SEP) specifies that the contribution for each eligible employee will be the same percentage of compensation (excluding compensation greater than $200,000*) for all employees.

Your employer will provide you with a copy of the agreement containing participation rules and a description of how employer contributions may be made to your IRA. Your employer must also provide you with a copy of the completed Form 5305-SEP and a yearly statement showing any contributions to your IRA.

All amounts contributed to your IRA by your employer belong to you even after you stop working for that employer.

**Contribution limits.** Your employer will determine the amount to be contributed to your IRA each year. However, the amount for any year is limited to the smaller of $40,000* or 25% of your compensation for that year. Compensation does not include any amount that is contributed by your employer to your IRA under the SEP. Your employer is not required to make contributions every year or to maintain a particular level of contributions.

**Tax treatment of contributions.** Employer contributions to your SEP-IRA are excluded from your income unless there are contributions in excess of the applicable limit. Employer contributions within these limits will not be included on your Form W-2.

**Employee contributions.** You may make regular IRA contributions to an IRA. However, the amount you can deduct may be reduced or eliminated because, as a participant in a SEP, you are covered by an employer retirement plan.

**SEP participation.** If your employer does not require you to participate in a SEP as a condition of employment, and you elect not to participate, all other employees of your employer may be prohibited from participating. If one or more eligible employees do not participate and the employer tries to establish a SEP for the remaining employees, it could cause adverse tax consequences for the participating employees.

An employer may not adopt this IRS Model SEP if the employer maintains another qualified retirement plan. This does not prevent your employer from adopting this IRS Model SEP and also maintaining an IRS Model Salary Reduction SEP or other SEP. However, if you work for several employers, you may be covered by a SEP of one employer and a different SEP or pension or profit-sharing plan of another employer.

**SEP-IRA amounts—rollover or transfer to another IRA.** You can withdraw or receive funds from your SEP-IRA if, within 60 days of receipt, you place those funds in the same or another IRA. This is called a "rollover" and can be done without penalty only once in any 1-year period. However, there are no restrictions on the number of times you may make "transfers" if you arrange to have these funds transferred between the trustees or the custodians so that you never have possession of the funds.

**Withdrawals.** You may withdraw your employer's contribution at any time, but any amount withdrawn is includible in your income unless rolled over. Also, if withdrawals

occur before you reach age 59½, you may be subject to a tax on early withdrawal.

**Excess SEP contributions.** Contributions exceeding the yearly limitations may be withdrawn without penalty by the due date (plus extensions) for filing your tax return (normally April 15), but are includible in your gross income. Excess contributions left in your SEP-IRA after that time may have adverse tax consequences. Withdrawals of those contributions may be taxed as premature withdrawals.

**Financial institution requirements.** The financial institution where your IRA is maintained must provide you with a disclosure statement that contains the following information in plain, nontechnical language:

1. The law that relates to your IRA.

2. The tax consequences of various options concerning your IRA.

3. Participation eligibility rules, and rules on the deductibility of retirement savings.

4. Situations and procedures for revoking your IRA, including the name, address, and telephone number of the person designated to receive notice of revocation. This information must be clearly displayed at the beginning of the disclosure statement.

5. A discussion of the penalties that may be assessed because of prohibited activities concerning your IRA.

6. Financial disclosure that provides the following information:

a. Projects value growth rates of your IRA under various contribution and retirement schedules, or describes the method of determining annual earnings and charges that may be assessed.

b. Describes whether, and for when, the growth projections are guaranteed, or a statement of the earnings rate and the terms on which the projections are based.

c. States the sales commission for each year expressed as a percentage of $1,000.

In addition, the financial institution must provide you with a financial statement each year. You may want to keep these statements to evaluate your IRA's investment performance.

**Paperwork Reduction Act Notice.** You are not required to provide the information requested on a form that is subject to the Paperwork Reduction Act unless the form displays a valid OMB control number. Books or records relating to a form or its instructions must be retained as long as their contents may become material in the administration of any Internal Revenue law. Generally, tax returns and return information are confidential, as required by section 6103.

The time needed to complete this form will vary depending on individual circumstances. The estimated average time is:

**Recordkeeping** . . . . 1 hr., 40 min.

**Learning about the law or the form** . . . . 1 hr., 35 min.

**Preparing the form** . . . . 1 hr., 41 min.

If you have comments concerning the accuracy of these time estimates or suggestions for making this form simpler, we would be happy to hear from you. You can write to the Tax Forms Committee, Western Area Distribution Center, Rancho Cordova, CA 95743-0001. **Do not** send this form to this address. Instead, keep it with your records.

| Form **5305A-SEP** | **Salary Reduction Simplified Employee Pension—** | OMB No. 1545-1012 |
|---|---|---|
| (Rev. March 2002) | **Individual Retirement Accounts** | |
| | **Contribution Agreement** | **Do not** file with the Internal Revenue Service |
| Department of the Treasury Internal Revenue Service | (Under section 408(k) of the Internal Revenue Code) | |

_____ amends its salary reduction SEP by adopting the following Model Salary
Name of employer
Reduction SEP under Internal Revenue Code section 408(k) and the instructions to this form.

**Note:** _An employer may not establish a salary reduction SEP after 1996._

## Article I—Eligibility Requirements (check applicable boxes—see instructions)

Provided the requirements of Article III are met, the employer agrees to permit elective deferrals to be made in each calendar year to the individual retirement accounts or individual retirement annuities (IRAs), established by or for all employees who are at least _____ years old (not to exceed 21 years) and have performed services for the employer in at least _____ years (not to exceed 3 years) of the immediately preceding 5 years. This simplified employee pension (SEP) ☐ includes ☐ **does not** include employees covered under a collective bargaining agreement, ☐ includes ☐ **does not** include certain nonresident aliens, and ☐ includes ☐ **does not** include employees whose total compensation during the year is less than $450*.

## Article II—Elective Deferrals (see instructions)

**A. Salary Reduction Amount.** An eligible employee may elect to have his or her compensation reduced by a specified percentage or amount per pay period, as designated in writing to the employer.

**B. Timing of Elective Deferrals.** No deferral election may be based on compensation an eligible employee received, or had a right to receive, before execution of the deferral election.

## Article III—SEP Requirements (see instructions)

The employer agrees that each employee's elective deferrals to the SEP will be:

**A.** Based only on the first $200,000* of compensation.

**B.** Limited annually to the smaller of: **(1)** 25% of compensation; or **(2)** the section 402(g) limit for the tax year.

**C.** Limited further, under section 415, if the employer makes nonelective contributions to this or another SEP.

**D.** Paid to the employee's IRA trustee, custodian, or insurance company (for an annuity contract) or, if necessary, an IRA established for an employee by the employer.

**E.** Made only if at least 50% of the employer's employees eligible to participate elect to have amounts contributed to the SEP. If the 50% requirement is not satisfied as of the end of any calendar year, then all of the elective deferrals made by the employees for that calendar year will be considered "disallowed deferrals" (IRA contributions that are not SEP-IRA contributions).

**F.** Made only if the employer had 25 or fewer employees eligible to participate at all times during the prior calendar year.

**G.** Adjusted only if deferrals to this SEP for any calendar year do not meet the "deferral percentage limitation" described on page 3.

## Article IV—Excess SEP Contributions (see instructions)

Elective deferrals by a "highly compensated employee" must satisfy the deferral percentage limitation under section 408(k)(6)(A)(iii). Amounts in excess of this limitation will be deemed excess SEP contributions for the affected highly compensated employee or employees.

## Article V—Notice Requirements (see instructions)

**A.** The employer will notify each highly compensated employee, by March 15 following the end of the calendar year to which any excess SEP contributions relate, of the excess SEP contributions to the highly compensated employee's SEP-IRA for the applicable year. The notification will specify the amount of the excess SEP contributions, whether they must be withdrawn, the calendar year in which any excess contributions are includible in income, and must provide an explanation of applicable penalties if the excess contributions that must be withdrawn are not withdrawn on time.

**B.** The employer will notify each employee who makes an elective deferral to a SEP that, until March 15 after the year of the deferral, any transfer or distribution from that employee's SEP-IRA of SEP contributions (or income on these contributions) attributable to elective deferrals made that year will be includible in income for purposes of sections 72(t) and 408(d)(1).

**C.** The employer will notify each employee by March 15 of each year of any disallowed deferrals to the employee's SEP-IRA for the preceding calendar year. Such notification will specify the amount of the disallowed deferrals and the calendar year in which those deferrals are includible in income and must provide an explanation of applicable penalties if the disallowed deferrals are not withdrawn on time.

## Article VI—Top-Heavy Requirements (see instructions)

**A.** Unless paragraph B is checked, the employer will satisfy the top-heavy requirements of section 416 by making a minimum contribution each year to the SEP-IRA of each employee eligible to participate in this SEP (other than a key employee as defined in section 416(i)). This contribution, in combination with other nonelective contributions, if any, is equal to the smaller of 3% of each eligible nonkey employee's compensation or a percentage of such compensation equal to the percentage of compensation at which elective (not including catch-up elective deferral contributions) and nonelective contributions are made under this SEP (and any other SEP maintained by the employer) for the year for the key employee for whom such percentage is the highest for the year.

* _For 2003 and later years, this amount is subject to annual cost-of-living adjustments. The IRS announces the increase, if any, in a news release, in the Internal Revenue Bulletin, and on the IRS Web Site at **www.irs.gov.**_

**For Paperwork Reduction Act Notice, see page 7.**   Cat. No. 64362R   Form **5305A-SEP** (Rev. 3-2002)

Form 5305A-SEP (Rev. 3-2002)                                                                                    Page **2**

## Article VI—Top-Heavy Requirements *(continued)*

**B.** ☐ The top-heavy requirements of section 416 will be satisfied through contributions to nonkey employees' SEP-IRAs under this employer's other SEP.

**C.** To satisfy the minimum contribution requirement under section 416, all nonelective SEP contributions will be taken into account but elective deferrals will not be taken into account.

## Article VII—Effective Date (see instructions)

This SEP will be effective upon adoption and establishment of IRAs for all eligible employees.

---

Employer's signature                                    Date          Name and title

---

## Instructions

*Section references are to the Internal Revenue Code unless otherwise noted.*

### Purpose of Form

Form 5305A-SEP is a model salary reduction simplified employee pension (SEP) used by an employer to permit employees to make elective deferrals to a SEP described in section 408(k).

**Do not** file Form 5305A-SEP with the IRS. Instead, keep it with your records.

**Note:** *SEPs permitting elective deferrals cannot be established after 1996. If you established a SEP before 1997 that permitted elective deferrals, under current law you may continue to maintain such SEP for years after 1996.*

### Instructions for the Employer

#### What Is A SEP?

A SEP is a written arrangement (a plan) that provides you with an easy way to make contributions towards your employees' retirement income. Under a salary reduction SEP, employees may choose whether or not to make elective deferrals to the SEP or to receive the amounts in cash. If elective deferrals are made, you contribute the amounts deferred by your employees directly into a traditional individual retirement arrangement (traditional IRA) set up by or for each employee with a bank, insurance company, or other qualified financial institution. The traditional IRA, established by or for an employee, must be one for which the IRS has issued a favorable opinion letter or a model traditional IRA published by the Service as **Form 5305,** Traditional Individual Retirement Trust Account, or **Form 5305-A,** Traditional Individual Retirement Custodial Account. It cannot be a SIMPLE IRA (an IRA designed to accept contributions made under a SIMPLE IRA Plan described in section 408(p)) or a Roth IRA. Adopting Form 5305A-SEP does not establish an employer IRA described in section 408(c).

The information provided below is intended to help you understand and administer the elective deferral rules of your SEP.

#### When To Use Form 5305A-SEP

Use this form only if you intend to permit elective deferrals to a SEP. If you want to establish a SEP to which nonelective employer contributions may be made, use **Form 5305-SEP,** Simplified Employee Pension—Individual Retirement Accounts Contribution Agreement, or a nonmodel SEP instead of, or in addition to, this form.

**Do not** use Form 5305A-SEP if you:

**1.** Have any leased employees as defined in section 414(n)(2).

**2.** Currently maintain any other qualified retirement plan. This does not prevent you from also maintaining a Model SEP (Form 5305-SEP) or other SEP to which either elective or nonelective contributions are made.

**3.** Have more than 25 employees eligible to participate in the SEP at any time during the prior calendar year. If you are a member of one of the groups described in paragraph 2 under **Excess SEP Contributionsó Deferral Percentage Limitation** on page 3, you may use this SEP only if in the prior year there were never more than 25 employees eligible to participate in this SEP, in total, of all the members of such groups, trades, or businesses. In addition, all eligible employees of all the members of such groups, trades, or businesses must be eligible to make elective deferrals to this SEP.

**4.** Are a state or local government or a tax-exempt organization.

#### Completing the Agreement

This SEP agreement is considered adopted when:

**1.** You have completed all blanks on the form.

**2.** You have given all eligible employees the following information:

**a.** A copy of Form 5305A-SEP. Any individual who in the future becomes eligible to participate in this SEP must be given Form 5305A-SEP, upon becoming an eligible employee.

**b.** A statement that traditional IRAs other than the traditional IRAs into which employer SEP contributions will be made may provide different rates of return and different terms concerning, among other things, transfers and withdrawals of funds from the IRAs.

**c.** A statement that, in addition to the information provided to an employee at the time the employee becomes eligible to participate, the administrator of the SEP must furnish each participant within 30 days of the effective date of any amendment to the SEP, a copy of the amendment and a written explanation of its effects.

**d.** A statement that the administrator will give written notification to each participant of any employer contributions made under the SEP to that participant's IRA by the later of January 31 of the year following the year for which a contribution is made or 30 days after the contribution is made.

Employers who have established a salary reduction SEP using Form 5305A-SEP and have provided each participant a copy of the completed Form 5305A-SEP and the other documents and disclosures described in **Instructions for the Employer** and **Instructions for the Employee,** are not required to file the annual information returns, Forms 5500 or 5500-EZ, for the SEP. However, under Title I of the Employee Retirement Income Security Act of 1974 (ERISA), this relief from the annual reporting requirements may not be available to an employer who selects, recommends, or influences its employees to choose IRAs into which contributions will be made under the SEP, if those IRAs are subject to provisions that impose any limits on a participant's ability to withdraw funds (other than restrictions imposed by the Code that apply to all IRAs). For additional information on Title I requirements, see the Department of Labor regulations at 29 CFR 2520.104-49.

#### Forms and Publications You May Use

An employer may need to use any of the following forms or publications:

• **Form W-2,** Wage and Tax Statement.

• **Form 5330,** Return of Excise Taxes Related to Employee Benefit Plans. Employers who are liable for the 10% tax on excess contributions use this form to pay the excise tax.

• **Pub. 560,** Retirement Plans for Small Business (SEP, SIMPLE, and Qualified Plans).

• **Pub. 590,** Individual Retirement Arrangements (IRAs).

#### Deducting Contributions

You may deduct, subject to any applicable limits, contributions made to a SEP. This SEP is maintained on a calendar year basis, and contributions to the SEP are deductible for your tax year with or within which the particular calendar year ends. See section 404(h). Contributions made for a particular tax year and contributed by the due date of your income tax return, including extensions, are deemed made in that tax year and the contributions are deductible if they would otherwise be deductible had they actually been contributed by the end of that tax year. See Rev. Rul. 90-105, 1990-2 C.B. 69. However, the deductibility of your contributions may be limited if the contributions are excess contributions. See **Excess SEP Contributions—Deferral Percentage Limitation** on page 3 and the **Deferral Percentage Limitation Worksheet** on page 8.

# Simplified Employee Pensions (SEPs)

## Effective Date

Insert the date the provisions of this agreement are effective.

## Eligible Employees

All eligible employees must be allowed to participate in the SEP. An eligible employee is any employee who: **(1)** is at least 21 years old, and **(2)** has performed "service" for you in at least 3 of the immediately preceding 5 years.

You can establish less restrictive eligibility requirements, but not more restrictive ones.

Service means any work performed for you for any period of time, however short. If you are a member of an affiliated service group, a controlled group of corporations, or trades or businesses under common control, service includes any work performed for any period of time for any other member of such group, trades, or businesses.

## Excludable Employees

The following employees do not have to be covered by the SEP: **(1)** employees covered by a collective bargaining agreement whose retirement benefits were bargained for in good faith by you and their union, **(2)** nonresident alien employees who did not earn U.S. source income from you, and **(3)** employees who received less than $450* in compensation during the year.

## Elective Deferrals

You may permit your employees to make elective deferrals through salary reduction that, at the employee's option, may be contributed to the SEP or received by the employee in cash during the year.

Notwithstanding any limit in Article IIIB(1) or IIIC, an eligible employee who is 50 or older before the end of the calendar year can defer an additional amount of compensation during the year up to the catch-up elective deferral contribution limit (see **Section 402(g) Limit** below).

You must inform your employees how they may make, change, or terminate elective deferrals. You must also provide a form on which they may make their deferral elections. You may use the **Model Salary Reduction SEP Deferral Form** (elective form) on page 5, or a form that explains the information contained in this form in a way that is written to be understood by the average plan participant.

## SEP Requirements

• Elective deferrals may not be based on more than $200,000* of compensation. Compensation, for purposes other than the $450* rule (see **Excludable Employees** above), is defined as wages under section 3401(a) for income tax withholding at the source but without regard to any rules that limit the remuneration included in wages based on the nature or location of the employment or the services performed (such as the exception for agricultural labor in section 3401(a)(2)). Compensation also includes earned income under section 401(c)(2). Compensation does not include any employer SEP contributions, including elective deferrals. Compensation, for purposes of the $450* rule, is the same, except it includes deferrals made to this SEP and any amount not includible in gross income under section 125 or section 132(f)(4).

• The maximum an employee may elect to defer under this SEP for a year is the smaller of 25% of the employee's compensation or the limitation under section 402(g), as explained below.

**Note:** *The deferral limit is 25% of compensation (minus any employer SEP contributions, including elective deferrals). Compute this amount using the following formula: Compensation (before subtracting employer SEP contributions) X 20%.*

• If you make nonelective contributions to this SEP for a calendar year, or maintain any other SEP to which contributions are made for that calendar year, then contributions to all such SEPs may not exceed the smaller of $40,000* or 25% of compensation for any employee.

• Catch-up elective deferral contributions (see **Section 402(g) Limit** below) are not subject to the 25% limit.

## Section 402(g) Limit

Section 402(g) limits the maximum amount of compensation an employee may elect to defer under a SEP (and certain other arrangements) during the calendar year. This limit is $11,000 for 2002, $12,000 for 2003, $13,000 for 2004, $14,000 for 2005, and $15,000 for 2006 and later years. In the case of an eligible employee who is 50 or older before the end of the calendar year, an additional amount of compensation ("catch-up elective deferral contributions") may be deferred during the year. The limit on catch-up elective deferral contributions is $1,000 for 2002, $2,000 for 2003, $3,000 for 2004, $4,000 for 2005, and $5,000 for 2006 and later years.

## Excess Elective Deferrals

Amounts deferred for a year in excess of the section 402(g) limit are considered "excess elective deferrals" and are subject to the rules described below.

The limit applies to the **total** elective deferrals the employee makes for the calendar year, from all employers, under the following arrangements:

• Salary reduction SEPs under section 408(k)(6);

• Cash or deferred arrangements under section 401(k);

• Salary reduction arrangements under section 403(b); and

• SIMPLE IRA Plans under section 408(p).

Thus, an employee may have excess elective deferrals even if the amount deferred under this SEP alone does not exceed the section 402(g) limit.

If an employee who elects to defer compensation under this SEP and any other SEP or arrangement has made excess elective deferrals for a calendar year, the employee must withdraw those deferrals by April 15 following the calendar year to which the deferrals relate. Deferrals not withdrawn by April 15 will be subject to the IRA contribution limits of sections 219 and 408 and may be considered excess contributions to the employee's IRA. For the employee, these excess elective deferrals are subject to a 6% tax on excess contributions under section 4973. Income on excess elective deferrals is includible in the employee's income in the year it is withdrawn from the IRA. The income must be withdrawn by April 15, following the calendar year for which the deferrals were made. If the income is withdrawn after that date and the recipient is not 59½ years of age, it may be subject to the 10% tax on early distributions under section 72(t).

## Excess SEP Contributions—Deferral Percentage Limitation

The amount each of your "highly compensated employees" may contribute to an salary reduction SEP is also limited by the "deferral percentage limitation." This is based on the amount of money deferred, on average, by your nonhighly compensated employees. Deferrals made by a highly compensated employee that exceed this deferral percentage limitation for a calendar year are considered "excess SEP contributions" and must be removed from the employee's SEP-IRA, as discussed below, unless the following exception applies. Excess SEP contributions of a highly compensated employee who is 50 or older before the end of the calendar year do not have to be removed from the employee's SEP-IRA to the extent the amount of the excess SEP contributions is less than the catch-up elective deferral contribution limit (see **Section 402(g) Limit** above) reduced by any catch-up elective deferral contributions already made for the year.

The deferral percentage limitation for your highly compensated employees is computed by first averaging the "deferral percentages" (defined below) for the eligible nonhighly compensated employees for the year and then multiplying this result by 1.25.

Only elective deferrals are included in this computation. Nonelective SEP contributions may not be included. The determination of the deferral percentage for any employee is made under section 408(k)(6).

For purposes of this computation, the calculation of the number and identity of highly compensated employees, and their deferral percentages, is made on the basis of the entire "affiliated employer" (defined below).

A worksheet is provided on page 8 to assist in figuring the deferral percentage. You may want to photocopy it for yearly use.

The following definitions apply for purposes of computing the deferral percentage limitation under this SEP:

**1. Deferral percentage** is the ratio (expressed as a percentage to 2 decimal places) of an employee's elective deferrals for a calendar year to the employee's compensation for that year. For this purpose, an employee's elective deferrals does not include any catch-up elective deferral contributions that exceed the limit in Article IIIB(1) or IIIC or the section 402(g) limit applicable to employees under 50. No more than $200,000* of compensation per individual is taken into account. The deferral percentage of an employee who is eligible to make an elective deferral, but who does not make a deferral during the year, is zero. If a highly compensated employee also makes elective deferrals under another salary reduction SEP

# Simplified Employee Pensions (SEPs)

maintained by the employer, then the deferral percentage of that highly compensated employee includes elective deferrals made under the other SEP.

**2. Affiliated employer** includes **(a)** any corporation that is a member of a controlled group of corporations, described in section 414(b) that includes the employer, **(b)** any trade or business that is under common control, defined in section 414(c) with the employer, **(c)** any organization that is a member of an affiliated service group, defined in section 414(m) that includes the employer, and **(d)** any other entity required to be aggregated with the employer under regulations under section 414(o).

**3. A highly compensated employee** is an individual described in section 414(q) who:

**a.** Was a 5% owner defined in section 416(i)(1)(B)(i) during the current or preceding year; or

**b.** For the preceding year had compensation in excess of $85,000* and was in the top-paid group (the top 20% of employees, by compensation).

## Excess SEP Contributions— Notification

You must notify each affected employee, if any, by March 15 of the amount of any excess SEP contributions made to that employee's SEP-IRA for the preceding calendar year and what amount must be withdrawn. If needed, use the model form on page 5 of these instructions. Excess SEP contributions that must be withdrawn are includible in the employee's gross income in the preceding calendar year. However, if these excess SEP contributions (not including allocable income) total less than $100, then the excess contributions that must be withdrawn are includible in the employee's gross income in the calendar year of notification. Income allocable to these excess SEP contributions is includible in gross income in the year of withdrawal from the IRA.

If you do not notify any of your employees by March 15 of an excess SEP contribution that must be withdrawn, you must pay a 10% tax on such excess SEP contribution for the preceding calendar year. The tax is reported in Part XII of Form 5330. If you do not notify your employees by December 31 of the calendar year following the calendar year in which the excess SEP contributions arose, the SEP no longer will be treated as meeting the rules of section 408(k)(6). In this case, any contribution to an employee's IRA will be subject to the IRA contribution limits of sections 219 and 408 and thus may be considered an excess contribution to the employee's IRA.

Your notification to each affected employee of the excess SEP contributions must specifically state in a manner written

to be understood by the average employee:

- The amount of the excess SEP contributions attributable to that employee's elective deferrals;
- The amount of these excess SEP contributions that must be withdrawn;
- The calendar year in which the excess SEP contributions that must be withdrawn are includible in gross income; and
- Information stating that the employee must withdraw the excess SEP contributions that must be withdrawn (and allocable income) from the SEP-IRA by April 15 following the calendar year of notification by the employer. Excess contributions not withdrawn by April 15 following the year of notification will be subject to the IRA contribution limits of sections 219 and 408 for the preceding calendar year and may be considered excess contributions to the employee's IRA. For the employee, the excess contributions may be subject to the 6% tax on excess contributions under section 4973. If income allocable to an excess SEP contribution is not withdrawn by April 15 following the calendar year of notification by the employer, the employee may be subject to the 10% tax on early distributions under section 72(t) when withdrawn.

For information on reporting excess SEP contributions that must be withdrawn, see Notice 87-77, 1987-2 C.B. 385, Notice 88-33, 1988-1 C.B. 513, Notice 89-32, 1989-1 C.B. 671, and Rev. Proc. 91-44, 1991-2 C.B. 733.

To avoid the complications caused by excess SEP contributions, you may want to monitor elective deferrals on a continuing basis throughout the calendar year to insure that the deferrals comply with the limits as they are paid into each employee's SEP-IRA.

## Disallowed Deferrals

If you determine at the end of any calendar year that more than half of your eligible employees have chosen **not** to make elective deferrals for that year, then **all** elective deferrals made by your employees for that year will be considered **disallowed deferrals,** i.e., IRA contributions that are not SEP-IRA contributions.

You must notify each affected employee by March 15 that the employee's deferrals for the previous calendar year are no longer considered SEP-IRA contributions. Such disallowed deferrals are includible in the employee's gross income in that preceding calendar year. Income allocable to the disallowed deferrals is includible in the employee's gross income in the year of withdrawal from the IRA.

Your notification to each affected employee of the disallowed deferrals must clearly state:

- The amount of the disallowed deferrals;
- The calendar year in which the disallowed deferrals and earnings are includible in gross income; and
- That the employee must withdraw the disallowed deferrals (and allocable income) from the IRA by April 15 following the calendar year of notification by the employer. Those disallowed deferrals not withdrawn by April 15 following the year of notification will be subject to the IRA contribution limits of sections 219 and 408 and thus may be considered an excess contribution to the employee's IRA. For the employee, these disallowed deferrals may be subject to the 6% tax on excess contributions under section 4973. If income allocable to a disallowed deferral is not withdrawn by April 15 following the calendar year of notification by the employer, the employee may be subject to the 10% tax on early distributions under section 72(t) when withdrawn.

Disallowed deferrals should be reported the same way excess SEP contributions are reported.

## Restrictions on Withdrawals

Your highly compensated employees may not withdraw or transfer from their SEP-IRAs any SEP contributions (or income on these contributions) attributable to elective deferrals made for a particular calendar year until March 15 of the following year. Before that date, however, you may notify your employees when the deferral percentage limitation test has been completed for a particular calendar year and that this withdrawal restriction no longer applies. In general, any transfer or distribution made before March 15 of the following year (or notification, if sooner) will be includible in the employee's gross income and the employee may also be subject to a 10% tax on early withdrawal. This restriction does not apply to an employee's excess elective deferrals.

## Top-Heavy Requirements

Elective deferrals may not be used to satisfy the minimum contribution requirement under section 416. In any year in which a **key employee** makes an elective deferral, this SEP is deemed top-heavy for purposes of section 416, and you are required to make a minimum top-heavy contribution under either this SEP or another SEP for each nonkey employee eligible to participate in this SEP.

A key employee under section 416(i)(1) is any employee who, at any time during the preceding year was:

- An officer of the employer with compensation greater than $130,000*;
- A 5% owner of the employer, as defined in section 416(i)(1)(B)(i); or
- A 1% owner of the employer with compensation greater than $150,000.

## Model Salary Reduction SEP Deferral Form

### I. Salary reduction deferral

Subject to the requirements of the Model Salary Reduction SEP of _____ , I authorize the

(name of employer)

following amount or percentage to be withheld from each of my paychecks and contributed to my SEP-IRA:

**(a)** _____ % (not to exceed 25%) of my salary; or **(b)** $ _____ .

This salary reduction authorization shall remain in effect until I provide written modification or termination of its terms to my employer.

### II. Amount of deferral

I understand that the total amount I defer in any calendar year may not exceed the smaller of:

**(a)** 25% of my compensation (determined without including any SEP-IRA contributions); or **(b)** the section 402(g) limit for the year.

### III. Commencement of deferral

The deferral election specified in **I** above shall not become effective before _____. Specify a

(Month, day, year)

date no earlier than the first day of the first pay period beginning after this authorization.

### IV. Distributions from SEP-IRAs

I understand that I should not withdraw or transfer any amounts from my SEP-IRA that are attributable to elective deferrals and income on elective deferrals for a particular calendar year (except for excess elective deferrals) until March 15 of the subsequent year or, if sooner, when my employer notifies me that the deferral percentage limitation test for that plan year has been completed. Any such amounts that I withdraw or transfer before this time will be includible in income for purposes of sections 72(t) and 408(d)(1).

Signature of employee ▶ _____          Date ▶ _____

## Notification of Excess SEP Contributions

To: _____

(name of employee)

   Our calculations indicate that the elective deferrals you made to your SEP-IRA for calendar year_____ exceed the maximum permissible limits under section 408(k)(6), and that $ _____ must be withdrawn from your SEP-IRA.

   These excess SEP contributions are includible in your gross income for the _____ (insert the year identified above, or if less than $100, the following year) calendar year.

   These excess SEP contributions must be distributed from your SEP-IRA by April 15, 20 _____ (insert year after the calendar year in which this notice is given) in order to avoid possible penalties. Income allocable to the excess amounts must be withdrawn at the same time and is includible in income in the year of withdrawal. Excess SEP contributions remaining in your SEP-IRA account after that time are subject to a 6% excise tax, and the income on these excess SEP contributions may be subject to a 10% penalty when finally withdrawn.

   You made total excess contributions for the year of $ _____ . This amount may be different from the amount you have to withdraw if you have unused catch-up elective deferral contributions under this SEP for the year.

Signature of employer ▶ _____          Date ▶ _____

Form **5305A-SEP** (Rev. 3-2002)

# Simplified Employee Pensions (SEPs)

## Instructions for the Employee

The following instructions explain what a simplified employee pension (SEP) is, how contributions to a SEP are made, and how to treat these contributions for tax purposes. For more information, see the SEP agreement on pages 1 and 2 and the **Instructions for the Employer** beginning on page 2.

### What Is A SEP?

A SEP is a written arrangement (a plan) that allows an employer to make contributions toward your retirement without becoming involved in more complex retirement plans. A SEP may include a **salary reduction arrangement**, like the one provided on this form. Under this arrangement, you can elect to have your employer contribute part of your pay to your own traditional individual retirement account or annuity (traditional IRA), set up by you or on your behalf with a bank, insurance company, or other qualified financial institution. The part contributed is tax deferred. Only the remaining part of your pay is currently taxable. This type of SEP is available only to an employer with 25 or fewer eligible employees.

The traditional IRA must be one for which the IRS has issued a favorable opinion letter or a model traditional IRA published by the IRS as **Form 5305,** Traditional Individual Retirement Trust Account, or **Form 5305-A,** Traditional Individual Retirement Custodial Account. It cannot be a SIMPLE IRA (an IRA designed to accept contributions made under a SIMPLE IRA Plan described in section 408(p)) or a Roth IRA.

Your employer must provide you with a copy of the SEP agreement containing eligibility requirements and a description of the basis upon which contributions may be made.

All amounts contributed to your IRA belong to you, even after you quit working for your employer.

### Forms and Publications You May Use

An employee may use either of the two forms and the publication listed below.

- **Form 5329,** Additional Taxes on Qualified Plans (including IRAs) and Other Tax-Favored Accounts. Use Form 5329 to pay tax on excess contributions and/or tax on early distributions.
- **Form 8606,** Nondeductible IRAs and Coverdell ESAs. Use Form 8606 to report nondeductible IRA contributions.
- **Pub. 590,** Individual Retirement Arrangements (IRAs).

### Elective Deferrals

#### Annual Limitation

The maximum amount that you may defer to a SEP for a calendar year is limited to the smaller of 25% of compensation or the **section 402(g) limit.** The 25% limit is reduced if your employer makes **nonelective contributions** on your behalf to this or another SEP for the year. In that case, the total contributions on your behalf to all such SEPs may not exceed the smaller of $40,000* or 25% of compensation.

### Section 402(g) Limit

Section 402(g) limits the maximum amount of compensation you can defer in each calendar year to all salary reduction SEPs, SIMPLE IRA plans under section 408(p), section 403(b) salary reduction arrangements, and cash or deferred arrangements under section 401(k), regardless of the number of employers you may have worked for during the year. This limit is $11,000 for 2002, $12,000 for 2003, $13,000 for 2004, $14,000 for 2005, and $15,000 for 2006 and later years. If you are 50 or older before the end of the calendar year, you can defer an additional amount of compensation ("catch-up elective deferral contributions") during the year. The limit on catch-up elective deferral contributions is $1,000 for 2002, $2,000 for 2003, $3,000 for 2004, $4,000 for 2005, and $5,000 for 2006 and later years.

For a **highly compensated employee,** there may be a further limit on the amount you can defer. Figured by your employer and known as the **deferral percentage limitation,** it limits the percentage of pay that a highly compensated employee can elect to defer to a SEP-IRA. Your employer will notify any highly compensated employee who has exceeded the limitation.

### Tax Treatment

Elective deferrals that do not exceed the limits discussed above are excluded from your gross income in the year of the deferral. They are not included as taxable wages on **Form W-2,** Wage and Tax Statement. However, elective deferrals are treated as wages for social security, Medicare, and unemployment (FUTA) tax purposes.

### Excess Amounts

There are three situations which will result in excess amounts in a salary reduction SEP-IRA.

**1.** Making **excess elective deferrals** (i.e., amounts in excess of the **section 402(g) limit**). You must determine whether you have exceeded the limit in the calendar year.

**2.** Highly compensated employees who make **excess SEP contributions** (i.e., amounts in excess of the deferral percentage limitation referred to above). The employer must determine if an employee has made excess SEP contributions.

**3.** Having **disallowed deferrals** (i.e., more than half of your employer's eligible employees choose not to make elective deferrals for a year). All elective deferrals made by employees for that year are considered disallowed deferrals, as discussed below. Your employer must also determine if there are disallowed deferrals.

### Excess Elective Deferrals

Excess elective deferrals are includible in your gross income in the calendar year of deferral. Income earned on the excess elective deferrals is includible in the year of withdrawal from the IRA. You should withdraw excess elective deferrals and any allocable income by April 15 following the year to which the deferrals relate. These amounts **may not** be transferred or rolled over tax-free to another IRA.

If you do not withdraw excess elective deferrals and any allocable income by April 15, the excess elective deferrals will be subject to the IRA contribution limits of sections 219 and 408 and will be considered excess contributions to your IRA. Such excess deferrals are subject to a 6% excise tax for each year they remain in the SEP-IRA. The excise tax is reported in Part III of Form 5329.

Income earned on excess elective deferrals is includible in your gross income in the year you withdraw it from your IRA. The income should be withdrawn by April 15 following the calendar year in which the deferrals were made. If the income is withdrawn after that date and you are not 59½ years of age, it may be subject to the 10% tax on early distributions. Report the tax in Part I of Form 5329. Also see Pub. 590 for a discussion of exceptions to the age 59½ rule.

### Excess SEP Contributions

If you are a **highly compensated employee,** you may have excess SEP contributions for a calendar year that may have to be withdrawn from your SEP-IRA. If you have excess SEP contributions that do not have to be withdrawn (because you had unused catch-up elective deferral contributions), the following rules on including the contributions in income, withdrawing the contributions, and penalties if you don't withdraw them do not apply to these excess SEP contributions. Your employer must notify you of any excess contributions, whether or not they must be withdrawn. This notification should show the amount of the excess SEP contributions, the amount that must be withdrawn, the calendar year to include any excess contributions in income, and the penalties that may be assessed if the contributions that must be withdrawn are not withdrawn from your IRA within the applicable time period.

Your employer must notify you of the excess SEP contributions by March 15 following the calendar year for which you made the excess SEP contributions. Generally, you include the excess SEP contributions in income for the calendar year in which you made the original deferrals. This may require you to file an amended individual income tax return. However, any excess SEP contribution less than $100 (not including allocable income) must be included in income in the calendar year of notification. Income earned on these excess contributions must be included in your gross income when you withdraw it from your IRA.

You must withdraw these excess SEP contributions (and allocable income) from your IRA. You may withdraw these amounts without penalty, until April 15 following the calendar year in which you were notified by your employer of the excess SEP contributions. Otherwise, the excess SEP contributions are subject to the IRA contribution limits of sections 219 and 408 and will be considered an excess contribution to your IRA. Thus, the excess SEP contributions are subject to a 6% excise tax reportable in Part III of Form 5329 for each year the contributions remain in your IRA.

If you do not withdraw the income earned on the excess SEP contributions by April 15 following the calendar year of notification by your employer, the income may be subject to a 10% tax on early distributions if you are not 59½ years of age when you withdraw it. Report the tax in Part I of Form 5329. Also see Pub. 590.

If you have both **excess elective deferrals** and **excess SEP contributions,** the amount of excess elective deferrals that you withdraw by April 15 will reduce any excess SEP contributions that must be withdrawn for the corresponding calendar year.

### Disallowed Deferrals

You are not required to make elective deferrals to a SEP-IRA. However, if more than 50% of your employer's eligible employees choose not to make elective deferrals in a calendar year, then no employee may participate for that calendar year. If you make elective deferrals during a year in which this happens, then your deferrals for that year will be "disallowed," and the deferrals will be treated as ordinary IRA contributions (which may be excess IRA contributions) rather than SEP-IRA contributions.

Disallowed deferrals and any income the deferrals have earned may be withdrawn, without penalty until April 15 following the calendar year in which you are notified of the disallowed deferrals. Amounts left in the IRA after that date will be subject to the same penalties discussed in **Excess SEP Contributions** above.

### Income Allocable To Excess Amounts

The rules for determining and allocating income to excess elective deferrals, excess SEP contributions, and disallowed deferrals are the same as those governing regular IRA contributions. The trustee or custodian of your SEP-IRA will inform you of the income allocable to these amounts.

### Additional Top-Heavy Contributions

If you are not a **key employee,** your employer must make an additional contribution to your SEP-IRA for a year in which the SEP is considered "top heavy." (Your employer can tell you if you are a key employee. Also, see **Top-Heavy Requirements** on page 4 for the definition of a key employee.) This additional contribution will not exceed 3% of your compensation. It may be less if your employer has already made a contribution to your SEP-IRA, and for certain other reasons.

### IRA Contribution for SEP Participants

In addition to any SEP amounts, you may make regular IRA contributions to an IRA. However, the amount of your contribution that you may deduct on your income tax return is subject to various income limits. See Form 8606. Also, you may want to see Pub. 590.

### SEP-IRA Amounts—Rollover or Transfer To Another IRA

If you are a highly compensated employee, you may not withdraw or transfer from your SEP-IRA any SEP contributions (or income

on these contributions) attributable to elective deferrals made during the year until March 15 of the following year or, if sooner, at the time your employer notifies you that the deferral percentage limitation test (discussed under **Annual Limitation** on page 6) has been completed for that year. In general, any transfer or distribution made before this time is includible in your gross income and may also be subject to a 10% tax on early distribution. Report this tax in Part I of Form 5329. You may, however, remove excess elective deferrals from your SEP-IRA before this time but you may not roll over or transfer these deferrals to another IRA.

If the restrictions above do not apply, you may withdraw funds from your SEP-IRA and no more than 60 days later place those funds in the same or another IRA, but not in a SIMPLE IRA. This is called a "rollover" and can be done without penalty only once in any 1-year period. However, there are no restrictions on the number of times that you may make "transfers" if you arrange to have these funds transferred between the trustees or the custodians so that you never have possession of the funds.

You may not, however, roll over or transfer excess elective deferrals, excess SEP contributions, or disallowed deferrals from your SEP-IRA to another IRA. These amounts may be reduced only by a distribution to you.

### Employer To Provide Information on SEP-IRAs and Form 5305A-SEP

Your employer must give you a copy of the following information:

**1.** A copy of a completed Form 5305A-SEP, the **Model Salary Reduction SEP Deferral Form** (used to defer amounts to the SEP), and, if applicable, a copy of the **Notice of Excess SEP Contributions.** Your employer should also provide you with a statement of any contributions made during the calendar year to your SEP-IRA. Highly compensated employees must also be notified at the time the deferral percentage limitation test is completed.

**2.** A statement that traditional IRAs other than SEP-IRAs receiving contributions under this SEP may have different rates of return and different terms (e.g., transfers and withdrawals from the IRAs).

**3.** A statement that the administrator of an amended SEP must furnish to each participant within 30 days of the amendment, a copy of the amendment and an explanation of its effects.

**4.** A statement that the administrator must notify each participant in writing of any employer contributions to the SEP-IRA. The notification must be made by the later of January 31 following the year of the contribution or 30 days after the contribution is made.

### Financial Institution Requirements

The financial institution where your IRA is maintained must provide you with a **disclosure statement** that contains the following information in plain, nontechnical language:

**1.** The law that relates to your IRA.

**2.** The tax consequences of various options concerning your IRA.

**3.** Participation eligibility rules, and rules on the deductibility of retirement savings.

**4.** Situations and procedures for revoking your IRA, including the name, address, and telephone number of the person designated to receive notice of revocation. (This information must be clearly displayed at the beginning of the disclosure statement.)

**5.** A discussion of the penalties that may be assessed because of prohibited activities concerning the IRA.

**6.** Financial disclosure that provides the following information.

**a.** Projects value growth rates of the IRA under various contribution and retirement schedules, or describes the method of computing and allocating annual earnings and charges that may be assessed.

**b.** Describes whether, and for what period, the growth projections are guaranteed, or a statement of earnings rate and the terms on which these projections are based.

**c.** States the sales commission to be charged in each year expressed as a percentage of $1,000.

In addition, the financial institution must provide you with a financial statement each year. You may want to keep these statements to evaluate your IRA's investment performance and to report IRA distributions for tax purposes.

**Paperwork Reduction Act Notice.** You are not required to provide the information requested on a form that is subject to the Paperwork Reduction Act unless the form displays a valid OMB control number. Books or records relating to a form or its instructions must be retained as long as their contents may become material in the administration of any Internal Revenue law. Generally, tax returns and return information are confidential, as required by section 6103.

The time needed to complete this form will vary depending on individual circumstances. The estimated average time is:

**Recordkeeping** . . . . 4 hr., 29 min.
**Learning about the law or the form** . . . . 5 hr., 1 min.
**Preparing the form** . . . . 58 min.

If you have comments concerning the accuracy of these time estimates or suggestions for making this form simpler, we would be happy to hear from you. You can write to the Tax Forms Committee, Western Area Distribution Center, Rancho Cordova, CA 95743-0001. **Do not** send this form to this address. Instead, keep it for your records.

Form 5305A-SEP (Rev. 3-2002)

## Deferral Percentage Limitation Worksheet (see instructions on page 3)

| (a) Employee Name | (b) Status H = HCE* O = Other | (c) Compensation (see below) | (d) Deferrals (see below) | (e) Ratio (d) ÷ (c) | (f) Permitted ratio (for HCE* only, see below) | (g) Permitted amount (for HCE* only) (c) X (f) | (h) Excess (for HCE* only) (d) minus (g) |
|---|---|---|---|---|---|---|---|
| 1 | | | | | | | |
| 2 | | | | | | | |
| 3 | | | | | | | |
| 4 | | | | | | | |
| 5 | | | | | | | |
| 6 | | | | | | | |
| 7 | | | | | | | |
| 8 | | | | | | | |
| 9 | | | | | | | |
| 10 | | | | | | | |
| 11 | | | | | | | |
| 12 | | | | | | | |
| 13 | | | | | | | |
| 14 | | | | | | | |
| 15 | | | | | | | |
| 16 | | | | | | | |
| 17 | | | | | | | |
| 18 | | | | | | | |
| 19 | | | | | | | |
| 20 | | | | | | | |
| 21 | | | | | | | |
| 22 | | | | | | | |
| 23 | | | | | | | |
| 24 | | | | | | | |
| 25 | | | | | | | |

\* **Highly compensated employee.** See the definition on page 4.
**Column (c). Compensation.** Enter compensation from this employer and any related employers.
**Column (d). Deferrals.** Enter all SEP elective deferrals other than catch-up elective deferral contributions. See **Deferral percentage** on page 3.
**Column (f). Permitted ratio.**
**Column (h). Excess.** Amounts in this column may have to be withdrawn by the HCE. See instructions on page 3.

**A**  Enter the total of the ratios in column (e) for the employees marked as "O" in column (b) _____

**B**  Divide line A by the number of employees marked as "O" in column (b) _____

**C**  Permitted ratio. Multiply line B by 1.25 and enter the permitted ratio here _____

# Chapter 22

# CROSS–TESTED/AGE–WEIGHTED PLAN

## WHAT IS IT?

In general, the use of an age-weighted contribution allocation for a defined contribution plan allows higher contribution levels (as a percentage of compensation) for older plan entrants. That is, the formula for annual employer contributions or allocations to participant accounts is based not only on the participant's compensation but also on the participant's *age* on entering the plan.

Age-weighting permits adequate account balances to build up in the relatively short time available to older entrants before retirement. In addition, with an age-weighted formula, the employer's plan contributions tend to be weighted toward owners and key employees since in many businesses these employees will be older than rank-and-file employees when the plan is adopted.

The most common type of plan using age-weighting is the *cross-tested plan*, which is usually a *new comparability plan*; other marketing designations are sometimes used. A cross-tested plan does not use a fixed age-weighted formula as such. Instead, the plan is designed to provide maximized benefits to highly compensated employees, and benefits for other employees are designed to provide whatever is required by nondiscrimination regulations under IRC Section 401(a)(4). For example, a plan covering 13 employees plan might provide for a $40,000 annual contribution for each of the three highly compensated employees, and for the remaining 10 employees the plan would provide a flat percentage of compensation that meets certain tests under the nondiscrimination regulations. A minimum of 5% of compensation for the nonhighly compensated employees is generally required, as discussed below.

Plans can also be designed using fixed formulas based on each participant's age and compensation. An *age-weighted profit sharing plan* is a profit sharing plan in which the allocation formula contains an actuarial age-weighting factor (i.e., providing a higher allocation for older plan entrants). A target plan is a pension plan with an age-weighted contribution formula. A target plan, unlike an age-weighted profit sharing plan, requires annual employer contributions to meet the Code's minimum funding standards.

## WHEN IS IT INDICATED?

1. When business owners and key employees are generally older than rank-and-file employees and the objective is to provide the maximum contribution for the owners and key employees in a defined contribution plan ($40,000 annually as indexed for 2003), while minimizing costs for covering remaining employees.

2. When the features of a regular defined contribution plan would be attractive to the employer, except that there are older employees whose retirement benefits would be inadequate because of the relatively few years remaining for participation in the plan. The age-weighted formula allows proportionately greater employer contributions for these older employees (greater percentages of their compensation).

3. When the employer is looking for an alternative that provides adequate retirement benefits to older employees but has the lower cost and simplicity of a defined contribution plan.

4. When an employer wants to terminate an existing defined benefit plan in order to avoid the increasing cost and regulatory burdens associated with these plans. If an age-weighted plan is substituted for the defined benefit plan, in many cases the new plan will provide approximately the same benefits to most employees, and it will be relatively easy to obtain IRS approval for the defined benefit plan termination.

5. When a closely held business or professional corporation has key employees who are approximately age 50 or older and who generally want to contribute less than the annual additions dollar limit of $40,000 (as indexed for 2003). The age-weighted plan is generally the ideal qualified plan to adopt in this situation, because its benefit level is just as high

as would be available in a defined benefit plan (given the $40,000 (in 2003) annual restriction), but is much simpler and less expensive to install and administer.

## ADVANTAGES

1. Retirement benefits can be maximized for employees who enter the plan at older ages. The following comparison of a target plan with a money purchase plan illustrates this. The illustration shows how the annual contribution and retirement benefit vary for three employees, each earning $30,000 annually:

| | Annual Contribution | | Accumulation at 65 (5½% return) | |
|---|---|---|---|---|
| Employee age at entry | Money Purchase (14%) | Target | Money Purchase | Target |
| 30 | $4,200 | $1,655 | $444,214 | $175,000 |
| 40 | 4,200 | 3,243 | 226,657 | 175,000 |
| 50 | 4,200 | 7,402 | 99,292 | 175,000 |

2. From the viewpoint of a business owner, particularly in a small, closely held business, the feature illustrated in the paragraph above also means that in an age-weighted plan, more of the total employer contributions in the age-weighted plan will likely be allocated to owners and key employees, as compared with a money purchase or other defined contribution plan. This will be the case if the owners and key employees are older than the average of all employees when the plan is adopted.

3. As with all qualified plans, an age-weighted plan provides a tax-deferred retirement savings medium for employees.

4. The age-weighted plan is relatively simple and inexpensive to design, administer, and explain to employees, compared with a defined benefit plan. Plans with fixed age-weighted formulas are similar in this regard than a cross-tested plan.

5. Plan benefits may be eligible for a special 10-year averaging tax computation (available to certain employees born before 1936) on lump-sum distributions.

6. Individual accounts for participants allow participants to benefit from good investment results in the plan fund.

## DISADVANTAGES

1. As with any defined contribution plan, the annual addition to each employee's account is limited to the lesser of (a) 100% of compensation, or (b) $40,000 (as indexed for 2003).[1] While this increased limit dramatically increased the funding opportunities for younger and lower paid employees, it still limits the relative amount of funding for highly compensated employees. For older employees, a defined benefit plan may allow a much higher level of employer contributions to the plan, as discussed further under "Design Features," below.

2. Employees bear investment risk under the plan. While this is a disadvantage to employees, it also tends to reduce employer costs compared to a defined benefit plan. This is because the employer bears the investment risk in a defined benefit plan.

3. A target pension plan is subject to the Code's minimum funding requirements. Employers are obligated to make minimum contributions each year under the plan's contribution formula or be subject to minimum funding penalties. While an age-weighted or cross-tested profit sharing plan is not subject to the minimum funding requirements, contributions must be recurring and substantial as discussed in Chapter 16.

4. If the age-weighted plan is a profit sharing plan, the ultimate benefits to participants are particularly uncertain since the employer is not necessarily committed to any specific funding level and may even omit funding in some years.

5. In the case of a target pension plan or a cross-tested plan, actuarial services maybe needed on an annual basis.

## CROSS–TESTED PLAN DESIGN

A cross-tested plan is designed to meet the nondiscrimination requirements of the regulations under Code Section 401(a)(4). Highly-compensated employees are assumed to receive a large annual allocation, generally the maximum amount permitted under the Section 415 annual additions limit (the lesser of $40,000, as indexed for 2003, or 100% of compensation). Then, the remaining employees are provided with an allocation that meets the requirements of the cross-testing regulations.

In general, the underlying approach of the cross-testing regulations is to test the plan's ultimate benefits for nondiscrimination, even though the plan is a defined contribution plan rather than a defined benefit plan (hence the term "cross-testing"). This is done by projecting the year's contribution for each employee to that employee's retirement age (at an assumed rate of interest) and analyzing the benefit provided by the projected amount, as a percentage of the employee's compensation. If these projected benefits, as a percentage of compensation, do not discriminate in favor of highly compensated employees, then the plan is considered nondiscriminatory.

In order to use cross-testing, the regulations have a "gateway" requirement. For most small-business plans, this gateway generally requires a minimum allocation of 5% of compensation for nonhighly compensated employees.[2] Note that this is higher than the 3%-of-compensation minimum required under the top-heavy rules (see Chapter 25).

While the cross-testing rules are complex, a simple example showing their application will illustrate the characteristics and advantages of the cross-tested plan.

---

*Example:* Dr. Ace, a solo medical practitioner, has an incorporated medical practice of which he and four others are employees. Dr. Ace is highly compensated and the others are nonhighly compensated within the meaning of the qualified plan rules (see Chapter 25). A cross-tested plan is proposed with the following characteristics[3]:

| Participant | Age | Compensation | Plan contribution | % of compensation |
|---|---|---|---|---|
| Dr. Ace | 53 | 200,000 | 40,000 | 20 |
| A | 55 | 50,000 | 2,500 | 5 |
| B | 30 | 30,000 | 1,500 | 5 |
| C | 25 | 30,000 | 1,500 | 5 |
| D | 25 | 30,000 | 1,500 | 5 |

---

The proposed plan provides a contribution of 5% of pay to meet the gateway required for the use of cross-testing. The next step is to project the contribution to each participant's age 65, at an assumed rate of 8½% interest (a rate between 7½% and 8½% must be used;[4] choosing the maximum of 8½% provides the best result for the highly compensated employees). For example, for Dr. Ace, his $40,000 contribution accumulates to $83,354 at age 65 at an 8½% rate. The accumulated contribution is then expressed as a life annuity and the annuity as a percentage of compensation is determined.[5] For example, for Dr. Ace, the $83,354 accumulation

equates to an $8,937 annuity which is 4.47% of his compensation of $200,000.

| Participant | Compensation | Plan Contribution | Plan Cont. proj. to Age 65 | Projected benefit | Projected Benefit as % of Compensation |
|---|---|---|---|---|---|
| Dr. Ace | 200,000 | 40,000 | 83,354 | 8,937 | 4.47 |
| A | 50,000 | 2,500 | 4,425 | 474 | .95 |
| B | 30,000 | 1,500 | 20,410 | 2,188 | 7.29 |
| C | 30,000 | 1,500 | 30,690 | 3,291 | 10.97 |
| D | 30,000 | 1,500 | 30,690 | 3,291 | 10.97 |

The final step is to test the projected benefit under the coverage tests of Section 410(b). These benefits must satisfy either the ratio percentage test of the average benefit test of that section (see Chapter 25 for general discussion of Section 410). The ratio percentage test is applied to a hypothetical "plan" consisting of the highly compensated participant (Dr. Ace) and all nonhighly compensated participants whose projected benefits are equal to or greater than those of Dr. Ace. In this case, this consists of Dr. Ace and participants B, C, and D. Under the ratio percentage test, at least 70% of the nonhighly compensated employees must be covered. The ratio percentage test is met since the percentage of nonhighly compensated participants who are covered is 75% (3 out of 4), Therefore, this plan meets the requirements of the cross-testing regulations.

If there is more than one highly compensated employee in the plan, the test may be more complicated. In that case, the plan must be broken into "rate groups" consisting of each highly compensated participant and all the employees who have projected benefits equal to or greater than the highly compensated participant. The IRC Section 410 coverage tests are then applied to the rate groups.

## Disadvantages of Cross-Tested Plans

Disadvantages of cross-tested plans include:

- Design of the plan is somewhat unstable since hiring of new employees may make the plan suddenly impractical, depending on the age distribution of employees under the new employee census.

- If there are too many rank-and-file employees who are relatively older (ages comparable to that of the highly compensated participants) the cost of the cross-tested plan for the rank and file employees may be higher than that of other alternatives, such as a profit sharing plan integrated with Social Security.

- Similarly, if many highly compensated employees are relatively young, the plan provides fewer advantages as well.

- An analysis of the plan to determine whether it meets the cross-testing requirements must be done at least as often as new employees join the plan, and this can be costly. Software is available, however, for employers to do this "in-house" at relatively low cost.

- Having a plan like this in effect inhibits the hiring of new employees who are relatively old, and this could put the employer in danger of violating age discrimination laws as well as depriving it of the services of valuable and experienced employees with critical skills.

## FIXED-FORMULA AGE-WEIGHTED PLANS

### Age-Weighted Profit Sharing Plan

An age-weighted profit sharing plan with a fixed age-weighted (actuarial) formula for allocating employer contributions will automatically pass the cross-testing requirements since all participants will (by design) have the same projected benefit as a percentage of compensation. Use of a formula thus reduces the complexity of the plan and the costs of compliance, since periodic cross-testing is not required.

*Disadvantages of fixed-formula profit sharing plans.* Although it is not immediately obvious from the nature of the plan, a fixed-formula plan is more difficult to communicate to employees and more difficult for them to understand than a cross-tested plan. The complicated mechanics of cross-testing are not a factor in explaining a cross-tested plan; employees simply understand that their annual allocation is 5% of compensation, generally applicable to all but the business owners. A fixed-formula plan has a different percentage of compensation for each age represented in the plan, and employees often have difficulty understanding why this is the case. For example in the illustration used above for cross-testing, if the employee group in question had a fixed formula plan, the percentage of compensation allocated each year to plan accounts would be much greater for employee A, aged 55, than for employees C and D, aged 25. Employees tend to question the fairness of this, particularly younger employees who consider themselves valuable, and who in fact might be making a greater relative contribution to the business than the older employees.

### Age-Weighted Pension (Target Benefit) Plan

A pension plan with a fixed age-weighted formula is similar to a profit sharing plan with a fixed formula except that as a pension plan, it is subject to the Code's minimum funding requirements. This means that an annual contribution equal to the amount required under the plan formula *must* be made or penalties are imposed. By comparison, a profit sharing plan is not subject to any annual funding requirement and annual contributions by the employer can be discretionary in amount. Profit sharing contributions can even be omitted in certain years, if permitted by the plan document, as long as they meet the IRS requirement of "substantial and recurring" contributions that applies to all profit sharing plans.

An age-weighted pension plan is generally referred to as a "target" plan since its design (with its requirement of mandatory annual employer funding) implies a funding target at each employee's retirement. However, as a defined contribution plan there is no guarantee of benefits or account balances, and the investment risk remains with the employee as with all defined contribution plans.

The disadvantages of target plans are the employee communication problem described in connection with fixed-formula profit sharing plans, and also the inflexibility from the employer's standpoint resulting from the requirement of fixed annual funding.

## TAX IMPLICATIONS

1. Employer contributions to an age-weighted plan are deductible when made, so long as the plan remains "qualified." A plan must meet the eligibility, vesting, funding and other requirements discussed in Chapter 25 to be qualified.

2. Assuming the plan remains qualified, taxation of the employee on plan contributions is deferred. Both employer contributions and earnings on plan assets are nontaxable to plan participants until withdrawn.[6]

3. Annual additions to each participant's account are limited to the lesser of (a) 100% of the participant's compensation or (b) $40,000 (in 2003, as indexed).[7] Annual additions include (1) employer contributions to participants' accounts; (2) forfeitures from other participants' accounts; and (3) employee contributions to the account.[8]

4. Distributions from the plan must follow the rules for qualified plan distributions. Certain premature distributions are subject to penalties. The distribution rules are discussed in Chapter 26.

5. Lump sum distributions made after age 59½ may be eligible for the special 10-year averaging (for certain employees born before 1936) tax computation available for qualified plans. Chapter 26 covers these rules and includes IRS forms.

6. A target pension plan, but not a profit sharing plan, is subject to the minimum funding rules of IRC Section 412. This requires minimum annual contributions,[9] subject to a penalty imposed on the employer if less than the minimum amount is contributed. For a target plan, the minimum funding requirement is generally the amount required under the plan's contribution formula. The minimum funding requirement, therefore, will be satisfied so long as the employer contributes to each participant's account the percentage of compensation required by the plan. Chapter 25 discusses the minimum funding rules further.

7. Certain employers adopting a plan may be eligible for a business tax credit of up to $500 for "qualified startup costs." See Chapter 27 for details.

8. A plan may permit employees to make voluntary contributions to a "deemed IRA" established under the plan. Amounts so contributed reduce the limit for other traditional or Roth IRA contributions. See Chapter 13 for details.

9. The plan is subject to the ERISA reporting and disclosure rules outlined in Appendix A.

## ALTERNATIVES

1. Defined benefit plans provide more benefit security because of the employer and government guarantee of benefit levels. Defined benefit plans also allow greater tax deductible employer contributions for older plan entrants who are highly compensated, because the annual additions limit does not apply. However, defined benefit plans are more complex and costly to design and administer.

2. Money purchase plans offer an alternative similar to target plans, but without the age-related contribution feature.

3. Nonqualified deferred compensation plans can be provided exclusively for selected executives. But with those plans the employer's tax deduction is generally deferred until benefit payments are made. This can be as much as 20 or 30 years after the employer's contribution is made.

4. Individual retirement savings is available as an alternative or supplement to an employer plan, but the amounts that may be subject to deduction or deferral are limited. See Chapters 24 and 17.

## HOW TO INSTALL THE PLAN

Installation of an age-weighted plan follows the qualified plan installation procedure described in Chapter 27.

## WHERE CAN I FIND OUT MORE ABOUT IT?

1. Graduate Course: Advanced Pension and Retirement Planning I (GS 814), The American College, Bryn Mawr, PA.

## QUESTIONS AND ANSWERS

**Question** — Can a self-employed person adopt a cross-tested or other age-weighted plan?

*Answer* — Yes. The plan can cover not only regular employees of the business, but also the self-employed person(s) who own the business—the sole proprietor or partners. Plans covering self-employed persons are known as "Keogh" or "HR 10" plans. These plans are basically the same as regular qualified plans, but some of the special rules that apply are covered in Chapter 12 of this book.

Any contribution or allocation formula applied to self-employed individuals must be based on their "earned income" as contrasted with the "compensation" base for regular employees. The definition of earned income is covered in Chapter 12.

**Question** — How is an age-weighted formula applied where shareholder-employees of an S corporation are covered?

*Answer* — For an S corporation, the plan contribution or allocation formula cannot provide an employer contribution for all of the shareholder-employee's income from the corporation. The formula must be based only on the shareholder's compensation for services rendered to the corporation. Any portion of the shareholder's income that represents dividends from the S corporation must be excluded from the plan formula.

## FOOTNOTES

1.   IRC Section 415(c)(3).
2.   Treas. Reg. §1.401(a)(4)-8(b)(1)(iv).
3.   This example is based on an example used by Bruce Temkin, MSPA, EA, at an ALI-ABA Course, "Representing the Professional and Closely Held Business," Scottsdale, AZ, Feb. 13-15, 2003.
4.   See definition of "standard interest rate," Treas. Reg. §1.401(a)(4)-12.
5.   A standard interest rate and mortality table, with no mortality prior to retirement, is used. Treas. Reg. §1.401(a)(4)-8(b)(2)(ii). Standard interest rate and mortality tables are defined in Treas. Reg. §1.401(a)(4)-12. The interest rate is not less than 7.5% and not greater than 8.5%. A list of permissible mortality tables is provided in the regulation.
6.   IRC Section 402(a).
7.   IRC Section 415(c).
8.   IRC Section 415(c)(2).
9.   Estimated quarterly required contributions of Section 412(m) apply only to certain underfunded defined benefit pension plans, not defined contribution pension plans. See IRC Section 412(m).

# Chapter 23

# TAX DEFERRED ANNUITY

## WHAT IS IT?

A tax deferred annuity plan (also called a "TDA" plan or Section 403(b) plan) is a tax deferred employee retirement plan that can be adopted only by certain tax-exempt organizations and certain public school systems.[1] Employees have accounts in a TDA plan to which employers contribute (or employees contribute through salary reductions).

The benefits of a TDA plan to employees are similar to those of a qualified profit sharing plan, particularly the Section 401(k) type of plan (see Chapter 19): (1) the TDA contribution is, within limits, not currently taxable to employees; (2) plan account balances accumulate tax free; and (3) tax on plan contributions and account earnings is deferred until the employee actually withdraws amounts from the plan.

## WHEN IS IT INDICATED?

1.  When (and only when) the employer organization is eligible under the TDA provisions of the Code. An organization must be one of the following in order to adopt a TDA plan:

    (a) A tax-exempt employer described in section 501(c)(3) of the Code. This means that:

        (1) The employer must be "organized and operated exclusively for religious, charitable, scientific, testing for public safety, literary, or educational purposes, or to foster national or international amateur sport competition...or for the prevention of cruelty to children or animals."

        (2) The organization must benefit the public, rather than a private shareholder or individual.

        (3) The organization further must refrain from political campaigning or propaganda intended to influence legislation.

    In other words, most familiar non-profit institutions such as churches, hospitals, private schools and colleges, and charitable institutions are eligible to adopt a TDA.

    (b) An educational organization with (1) a regular faculty and curriculum and (2) a regularly enrolled student body in attendance, that is operated by a state or municipal agency. In other words, most public schools and colleges may adopt a TDA plan. A TDA plan can also be adopted for certain employees outside of the schools who perform services involving the operation or direction of the public school education program.

2.  Assuming the employer organization is eligible, the positive indications for a TDA plan are:

    (a) When the employer wants to provide a tax deferred retirement plan for employees but can afford only minimal extra expense beyond existing salary and benefit costs. A TDA plan can be funded entirely from employee salary reductions (except for installation and administration costs, which must be paid for by the employer). In most plans, however, some additional employer contribution to the plan can enhance its effectiveness.

    (b) When the employee group has one or more of the following characteristics:

        •   Many would like some choice as to the level of savings—that is, a choice between various levels of current cash compensation and tax deferred savings. A younger, more mobile work force often prefers this option.

        •   Many employees are relatively young and have substantial time to accumulate retirement savings.

        •   Many employees are willing to accept a degree of investment risk in their plan accounts in return for the potential benefits of good investment results.

    (c) When an employer wants an attractive, "savings-type" supplement to its existing defined benefit or other qualified plan. Such a supplement can make the employer's retirement benefit program attractive to both younger and older employees by providing both security of retirement benefits and the opportunity to increase savings and investment on a tax deferred basis.

Non-governmental, tax-exempt employers are also permitted to offer Section 401(k) plans (see Chapter 19).[2] See the "Questions and Answers," below, for considerations to take into account when choosing between a Section 401(k) plan and a TDA. Also, tax-exempt employers and governmental entities are permitted to maintain SIMPLE IRA plans (see Chapter 20).[3]

## ADVANTAGES

1. As with qualified plans, a TDA plan provides a tax-deferred retirement savings medium for employees.

2. A salary reduction-type TDA plan allows employees a degree of choice in the amount they wish to save under the plan.

3. TDA plans can be funded entirely through salary reductions by employees. As a result, an employer can adopt the plan with no additional cost for employee compensation; the only extra cost is plan installation and administration. The plan may actually result in some savings as a result of lower state or local (but not federal) payroll taxes.

4. In-service withdrawals by employees are permitted; these are not available in qualified pension plans, although they are available in profit sharing plans.

## DISADVANTAGES

1. As with qualified defined contribution plans, account balances at retirement age may not provide adequate retirement savings for employees who enter the plan at later ages.

2. For each employee the annual salary reduction under the plan is subject to the elective deferral limit (see below). However, this amount can be supplemented by employer contributions to provide additional tax deferred savings.

3. Because of the nondiscrimination tests described below, a TDA plan can be relatively costly and complex to administer.

4. Employees bear investment risk under the plan. However, TDA funds are in large part invested in low risk annuity contracts. Only the mutual fund (custodial account—see below) type of TDA investment (and possibly some variable annuity contracts) involves significant investment risk, and employees usually are given a choice of mutual fund investments so they can control the degree of risk.

## DESIGN FEATURES

### Salary Reductions

Like Section 401(k) plans, TDA plans are generally built around salary reduction contributions elected by employees. A possible alternative is for the employer to provide an annual "bonus" to employees that the employees can either receive in cash or contribute to the plan. "Negative election" provisions should also be permitted; these are plan provisions whereby the employer automatically contributes a specified portion of each employee's salary to the plan, unless the employee specifically requests to receive the amount in cash. Negative elections have been approved for 401(k) plans and should be acceptable for TDAs as well.[4]

Salary reductions must be elected by employees *before* compensation is earned — that is, before they render the services for which compensation is paid. Salary reductions elected after compensation is earned are ineffective as a result of the tax doctrine of "constructive receipt."[5]

The usual practice is to provide plan participants with a salary reduction election form that they must complete before the end of each calendar year. The election specifies how much will be contributed to the plan from each paycheck received for the forthcoming year. Usually the plan will permit the employee to reduce or entirely withdraw the election for pay not yet earned, if circumstances dictate. The plan must restrict each participant's salary reductions to no more than the annual limits set forth in the Code (see below). In general, the procedural rules for salary reductions are the same as those for 401(k) plans.[6]

Salary reductions, as well as any other plan contribution that the employee has the option to receive in cash (referred to as "elective deferrals"), are subject to an annual limit. The limit is a "per employee" rather than a "per plan" limit. The employee must add together each year all elective deferrals from (1) Section 401(k) plans, (2) salary reduction SEPs (available if established before 1997 — see Chapter 21), (3) SIMPLE IRAs (see Chapter 20), and (4) Section 403(b) TDA plans. (Note that deferrals from a 457 plan need not be aggregated, which creates a "double dip" opportunity--see Chapter 11). The total must not exceed the following limits:[7]

| Year | Amount |
|------|--------|
| 2003 | $12,000 |
| 2004 | 13,000 |
| 2005 | 14,000 |
| 2006 | 15,000 |
| as indexed in $500 increments | |

In addition to the foregoing salary reductions, employees who have reached age 50 during the plan year[8] can make "catch-up" contributions. All participants must have the same right to make this election. Under this catch-up, the elective deferral limit is increased by the following amounts:[9]

| Year | Amount |
|------|--------|
| 2003 | $ 2,000 |
| 2004 | 3,000 |
| 2005 | 4,000 |
| 2006 or thereafter | 5,000 |

## The TDA Salary Reduction Catch–Up

TDA plans have an additional catch-up feature that is unique to TDAs. If a covered employee has completed 15 years of service for the employer, and the employer is (1) an educational organization, (2) a hospital, (3) a home health care agency, (4) a health and welfare service agency, or (5) a church, synagogue or related organization, the elective deferral limit (see above) is increased by an additional sum equal to the least of

- $3,000

- $15,000, reduced by any amounts excluded from gross income for prior taxable years by reason of the catch-up provision, or

- $5,000 times the employee's years of service with the employer, less all prior salary reductions with that employer.[10]

Notwithstanding these all of these limits, the amount contributed by salary reduction cannot exceed 100% of the employee's compensation, except that the age-50 catch-up is not limited by Section 415 limits (see below).[11]

## Employer Contributions

Many TDA plans provide for employer contributions, in addition to or instead of salary reduction contributions, in order to encourage employee participation and make the plan more valuable to employees. TDA plans most often use a "formula matching contribution." Under this approach, the employer matches employee salary reductions, either dollar for dollar or under another formula. For example, the plan might provide that the employer contributes an amount equal to 50% of the amount the employee elects as a salary reduction. So if an employee elects a salary reduction of $6,000, the employer puts an additional $3,000 into the employee's plan account. Other employer contribution approaches can be used similar to those used in Section 401(k) plans, as discussed in Chapter 19.

The level of employer match can be increased for employees with longer service. However, whenever there are employer contributions, complex nondiscrimination requirements must be met — see below. These impose additional administrative costs for the employer.

## Section 415 Limits

A TDA plan is subject to the same limits under Code Section 415 as a qualified defined contribution plan. (See Chapter 25). That is, the annual addition to each participant's account cannot exceed the lesser of (a) 100% of compensation or (b) $40,000 (2003 indexed figure). "Annual additions" refers to the total of employer contributions, employee contributions, and forfeitures from other participants' accounts (forfeitures are unlikely in 403(b) plans because of the 100% vesting requirement discussed below). The 100% limit is applied to the participant's gross compensation, unreduced by any salary reduction contributions to the 403(b) or to a Section 401(k), 457, SIMPLE, or FSA (flexible spending account) plan.

The following are some examples that apply these limits:

*Example 1:* Employee Bob, age 45, earns $80,000 in 2003. He is covered under a TDA plan funded exclusively through employee salary reduction. The maximum amount he may contribute to the TDA plan for 2003 is $12,000.

*Example 2:* Employee Barb, age 33, earns $90,000 in 2003. She is covered under a TDA plan that provides for salary reductions and employer discretionary contributions. Barb elects a salary reduction of $12,000 for 2003. The employer can contribute up to a total of $28,000 for Barb (a total of $40,000 for 2003).

*Example 3:* Employee Bill, age 40, earns $10,000 in 2003. His TDA plan provides for salary reductions and discretionary employer contributions. Bill elects a salary reduction of $5,000 for 2003. The employer can contribute up to an additional $5,000, for a total of $10,000 contributed to the plan (100% of compensation, unreduced by Bill's salary reduction election). Bill pays taxes currently only on the $5,000 of cash compensation that he receives in 2003.

## Nondiscrimination Requirements

*Salary reduction nondiscrimination requirement.* All plans must allow all employees to make salary reduction contributions to the plan if any employee is permitted to do so. The employer can require a minimum salary reduction of up to $200 as a condition for participation. Coverage is not required for employees who participate in a Section 401(k) or Section 457 plan, another TDA plan, nor for certain other employees.[12]

*Nondiscrimination requirements for employer contributions—all employers.* For all employers, only the first $200,000 (2003 figure) of each participant's compensation can be taken into account in any plan contribution formula (not applicable to a salary reduction formula).[13]

*Nondiscrimination requirements for employer contributions—private nonprofits.* Additional nondiscrimination requirements apply to plans of private nonprofit organizations (i.e., these do not apply to government or church plans). Employer contributions and any other contributions *except for* salary reduction contributions (elective deferrals) in plans of private nonprofit organizations must comply with the following nondiscrimination requirements that are generally applicable to qualified plans:[14]

- Contributions or benefits must not discriminate in favor of highly compensated employees.[15]

- The plan must meet the nondiscrimination rules for employer contributions and matching contributions.[16]

- The plan's coverage must meet certain percentage tests.[17]

- Integration with Social Security is governed by Code section 401(a)(5) (although Social Security integration is rarely used in 403(b) plans).

These requirements as applied to 403(b) plans have not been fully worked out by the IRS as they have been for regular qualified plans. In particular, there is no procedure for obtaining advance determination letters for 403(b) plans. The current status of these rules is discussed further in "Questions and Answers," below.

## Vesting

The participant is always 100% vested in all amounts contributed to the TDA plan by salary reduction and in any plan earnings on those amounts. Even if a participant leaves employment after a short time, his or her plan account attributable to such contributions cannot be forfeited. However, participants need not be immediately vested in employer contributions. Note though that plans with employer contributions are generally subject to ERISA and that ERISA imposes minimum vesting standards. In addition, in years beginning after 2001, employer matching contributions are subject to the same vesting requirements as are applied to top-heavy plans; that is, 100% cliff vesting after three years, or graded vesting starting with 20% after two years, increasing by 20% each year until 100% is reached after six years.[18]

## Plan Investments

Generally, all plan funds in TDA plans must be invested in either (1) annuity contracts purchased by the employer from an insurance company, or (2) mutual fund (regulated investment company) shares held in custodial accounts.[19] Many plans provide both types of investments and allow participants full discretion to divide their accounts between the two investment media.

Annuities used in TDA plans can be either group or individual contracts, level or flexible premium annuities, or fixed dollar or variable annuities. Face amount certificates providing a fixed maturity value and a schedule of redemptions are also permitted. Annuity contracts can give participants a degree of choice as to investment strategy. For example, the participant can be given a choice of investment mix between equity funds and fixed investment funds.

"Incidental life insurance" protection under annuity contracts is also permitted. The amount of life insurance is limited by the "incidental" tests discussed in Chapter 13 (i.e., the limits are the same as those for qualified plans). As with qualified plans, the value of the life insurance protection is taxed annually to the employee using the interim rates set forth in Table 2001 (see Chapter 13), and these insurance costs may be recovered tax-free on a subsequent plan distribution.

## Plan Distributions

Distributions from TDA plans are subject to the qualified plan distribution rules detailed in Chapter 26. Many plans provide for distributions in a lump sum at termination of employment. However, a plan subject to ERISA must either provide for a qualified joint and survivor annuity as its automatic benefit or provide that if the participant dies, 100% of his nonforfeitable benefit will be paid to his surviving spouse unless the spouse is deceased or has consented to another beneficiary.[20]

TDA plans often allow participants to make in-service withdrawals (i.e., withdrawals before termination of employment). The Code restricts the types of withdrawals permitted; the plan itself can be even more restrictive or can prohibit in-service withdrawals entirely. Because of poor legislative craftsmanship, the Code restrictions are unduly complex and not entirely clear. The table in Figure 23.1 appears to be the best possible interpretation of current law.[21] The headings "employer contributions" and "salary reductions" refer to the portions of the employee's account attributable to employer contributions or salary reductions respectively. The term "pre-1989 assets" refers to assets held as of the close of the last plan year beginning before January 1, 1989; the term "post-1988 assets" refers to assets contributed after the close of the last plan year beginning before January 1, 1989. In order to make it easier for employees to determine what amounts they can withdraw, plan administrators should provide account information in this form, although currently few do so. Notwithstanding the restrictions summarized in Figure 23.1, distributions may also be made to former spouses under the rules for qualified domestic relations orders (QDROs).

**Figure 23.1**

| ALLOWABLE DISTRIBUTIONS FROM 403(b) PLANS | | | | |
|---|---|---|---|---|
| | Insurance Contract Plans | | 403(b)(7) (Mutual Fund) Plans | |
| Events | Employer contributions | Salary reductions | Employer contributions | Salary reductions |
| At or after age 59½, death, severance from employment, disability | All amounts | All amounts | All amounts | All amounts |
| Hardship | All amounts | All amounts attributable to pre-1989 assets; for post-1988 assets, principal only (no income) | Amounts attributable to pre-1989 assets only[22] | All amounts attributable to pre-1989 assets; for post 1988 assets, principal only (no income) |
| Other | All amounts | Amounts attributable to pre-1989 assets only | No distributions permitted[23] | No distributions permitted[24] |

All withdrawals are subject to income tax. In addition, many in-service distributions will be subject to the 10% early withdrawal penalty tax discussed in Chapter 26, even if the distribution is permitted under the terms of the TDA plan. To summarize, a 10% penalty tax applies to the taxable amount (i.e., amount subject to regular income tax) of any qualified plan or TDA distribution, except for distributions:

- on or after age 59½

- on or after the employee's death

- attributable to the employee's disability

- that are part of substantially equal periodic payments (made at least annually) following separation from service and for the life or life expectancy of the employee or the joint lives or joint life expectancies of the employee and his beneficiary

- that are paid after separation from service after age 55

- that do not exceed the amount of medical expenses deductible as an itemized deduction for the year.[25]

Many TDA plans have provisions for plan loans to participants. A plan loan provision is extremely valuable to employees because it allows them access to their plan funds without the 10% penalty tax. Plan loans are discussed in detail in Chapter 26.[26]

## TAX IMPLICATIONS

1. Employees are not taxed currently on either salary reductions or employer contributions under a TDA plan, so long as these in total do not exceed the limits discussed above.

2. Salary reductions, but not employer contributions, are generally subject to Social Security (FICA) and federal unemployment (FUTA) payroll taxes.[27] The impact of state payroll taxes depends on the particular state's law. Both elective deferrals and employer contributions may be exempt from state payroll taxes in some states.

3. A limited nonrefundable tax credit is available to certain lower income taxpayers who make salary deferrals to a TDA (see "Questions and Answers," below).

4. Beginning after 2002, a plan may permit employees to make voluntary contributions to a "deemed IRA" established under the plan. Amounts so contributed reduce the limit for other traditional or Roth IRA contributions. See Chapter 13 for details. Contributions under this provision may also (as with elective deferrals and other IRA contributions) count toward the nonrefundable credit for lower-income taxpayers, explained in the "Questions and Answers," below.

5. Plan participants may exclude from income amounts directly transferred (i.e., from trustee to trustee) from a TDA plan to a governmental defined benefit plan if the transferred funds are used to purchase permissible service credits or to repay contributions or earnings that were previously refunded because of a forfeiture of service credit.[28]

6. Distributions from the plan must follow the rules for qualified plan distributions. Certain premature distributions are subject to penalties. The distribution rules are discussed in Chapter 26.

7. Distributions from the plan to employees are subject to income tax when received. Single sum distributions are *not* eligible for the special 10-year averaging computations applicable to qualified plan distributions.

## ERISA REQUIREMENTS

In general, ERISA applies to a TDA plan to the same extent it applies to a qualified plan. In addition, a plan subject to ERISA must observe its other requirements, including fiduciary requirements and plan requirements protecting spousal benefits. However, TDAs of certain employers may be subject to the ERISA exemption applicable to governmental and church plans. In addition, an ERISA exemption under Labor Department regulations applies to plans that are (1) funded purely through voluntary salary reductions by employees, and (2) not considered "established or maintained by the employer."[29] This exemption permits only minimal employer involvement with the plan.

## HOW TO INSTALL A PLAN

Installation of a TDA plan is not subject to the qualified plan rules. Furthermore, some employers having TDA plans are not subject to any provisions of ERISA (e.g., church or governmental organizations). Government approval of a TDA plan is not necessary and is not now generally sought by plan installers (although the IRS reportedly is considering a determination letter program for TDAs similar to that for qualified plans). However, a written plan document similar to a qualified plan document is required if ERISA applies to the plan, and should be adopted as a matter of good policy even where not required by law.

In addition, salary reduction forms must be completed by plan participants before the plan's effective date so that salary reduction elections will be immediately effective.

The success of a TDA plan in meeting the employer's objectives and the nondiscrimination tests depends on effective communication with employees. Effective employer-employee communication is always important in employee benefit plans. But it is particularly essential for a TDA plan because of the active role of employees in the plan.

## WHERE CAN I FIND OUT MORE ABOUT IT?

1. Graduate Course: Retirement Savings Plans for Employees (GS 814), The American College, Bryn Mawr, PA.

2. *Advanced Sales Reference Service*, Section 61, The National Underwriter Co.

3. IRS final audit guidelines for tax deferred annuities, reprinted in *IRM Handbook 7.7.1, Employee Plans Examination Guidelines Handbook*, Chapter 13, Section 403 Plans. This document can be viewed, printed, or downloaded from the IRS web site: http://www.irs.ustreas.gov/bus_info/ep/GUIDE.pdf.

## QUESTIONS AND ANSWERS

**Question** — How can a planner determine if an employer organization meets the technical eligibility requirements in the Code?

*Answer* — Most organizations that are tax-exempt under Section 501(c)(3) have obtained a government ruling letter to that effect. Also, organizations that have been ruled tax-exempt are listed in a government publication available at libraries, and on the IRS web site (http://www.irs.ustreas.gov/bus_info/eo/eosearch.html). Planners should ask

the prospective TDA client for a copy of the ruling letter, if any, and keep it in their files. If there is no ruling letter, or if the organization is not a Section 501(c)(3) organization, the planner should at a minimum obtain an attorney's or accountant's written opinion that the organization meets the TDA criteria. In questionable cases, an IRS ruling should be sought.

**Question** — Can TDA plans cover "independent contractors" — for example, anesthesiologists or radiologists associated with, but not formally employed by, hospitals?

*Answer* — No. TDA plan participants must be employees of the plan sponsor. The best way for a planner to verify this is to ask the sponsor how these individuals are treated by the sponsor for employment tax purposes—Social Security (FICA) and federal unemployment (FUTA). Employees and independent contractors are treated differently under these taxes (the employer pays no employment taxes for independent contractors) and the treatment of these individuals in the TDA plan should be consistent.

**Question** — Can a TDA plan participant make deductible IRA contributions as well as salary reductions under the TDA plan?

*Answer* — Yes. However, in a year in which an individual makes salary reduction contributions to a TDA plan or the employer contributes to his TDA account, the individual is considered an "active participant" under the IRA rules. IRA contributions are deductible only within the reduced deductible IRA limits allowed for active plan participants — see Chapter 17. There is a phaseout of IRA deductibility based on adjusted gross income. After-tax contributions to a Roth IRA may be made, subject to certain income limitations. See Chapter 24.

**Question** — Can a TDA participant transfer funds from one annuity contract or mutual fund investment to another without adverse tax effect?

*Answer* — Yes; such a transfer is not a taxable event. The transfer can be structured as a "direct rollover" or "rollover" as described in Chapter 26. However, for TDAs it is also possible to make a direct transfer. As approved by the IRS in Rev. Rul. 90-24,[30] the plan participant simply directs the insurance company or mutual fund now holding the participant's account to transfer part or all of it directly to the new insurance company contract or mutual fund designated by the participant. No distribution to the participant should be made.

There is no income tax or early distribution penalty on a direct transfer. However, some annuity contracts may have a penalty provision for withdrawals that will reduce the net amount available for withdrawal.

**Question** — What nondiscrimination rules currently apply to TDA plans providing employer contributions?

*Answer* — The nondiscrimination rules that apply where there are employer contributions are very complicated and require expert administrative guidance for the employer in these cases. There are two main sets of rules: the general guidelines and the 401(m) tests.[31]

*General guidelines.* The IRS has not issued final guidance on the application of these rules to TDAs. IRS Notice 89-23[32] provides "safe harbors" that employers can use until final rules are established.[33] In applying the safe harbors, an employer can aggregate its TDA and qualified plans. If any one of the following three safe harbors is met, the aggregated arrangement is deemed to comply with the nondiscrimination rules:

1. The *maximum disparity* safe harbor is satisfied if (a) the highest percentage of compensation contributed on behalf of any highly compensated employee (HCE) who is earning benefits under the aggregated arrangement does not exceed 180% of the lowest percentage of compensation contributed on behalf of any nonhighly compensated employee (NHCE) who is earning benefits, (b) at least 50% of the NHCEs are earning benefits under the aggregated arrangement, and (c) the percentage of employees earning benefits under the aggregated arrangement who are NHCEs is at least 70%.

2. The *lesser disparity* safe harbor is satisfied if (a) the highest percentage of compensation contributed on behalf of any HCE who is earning benefits under the aggregated arrangement does not exceed 140% of the lowest percentage of compensation contributed on behalf of any NHCE who is earning benefits, (b) at least 30% of the NHCEs are earning benefits under the aggregated arrangement, and (c) the percentage of employees

earning benefits under the aggregated plans who are NHCEs is at least 50%.

3. The *no disparity* safe harbor is satisfied if (a) the highest percentage of compensation contributed on behalf of any HCE who is earning benefits under a plan or plans in the aggregated arrangement does not exceed the percentage of compensation contributed on behalf of any NHCE who is earning benefits and (b) either of the following tests is satisfied: (i) at least 20% of the NHCEs must be earning benefits under the aggregated arrangement and the percentage of participants in the aggregated arrangement who are NHCEs must be at least 70%; or (ii) at least 80% of the NHCEs must be earning benefits under the aggregated arrangement and the percentage of participants in the aggregated arrangement who are NHCEs must be at least 30%.

In applying these tests, employees who have not met the plan's minimum age and service requirements may be excluded. If a plan fails to meet these safe harbors, it is still possible to comply with the general nondiscrimination rules as discussed in the regulations. A plan will be deemed to be in compliance if the employer operates the plan in accordance with a reasonable, good faith interpretation of the rules. The IRS is currently working on more extensive nondiscrimination rules for TDA plans. When these are completed, the IRS may begin issuing determination letters for TDA plans similar to the determination letters they now issue for qualified plans.

*401(m) tests.* If the plan provides employer matching contributions or employee after-tax contributions, it must meet the nondiscrimination tests of Code section 401(m). Under these tests, the ratio of employer matching contributions and employee after-tax contributions (as a percentage of each eligible employee's compensation) is computed. The average of these ratios for highly compensated employees *for the plan year* cannot exceed the average of these ratios for all other eligible employees *for the preceding plan year* by more than the greater of:

- 125%, or

- the lesser of (a) 200%, or (b) the percentage of all other eligible employees *for the preceding plan year* plus 2 percentage points.[34]

For example, if the average of employee after-tax contributions and employer matching contributions to compensation for nonhighly compensated employees is 6% of compensation, the average for highly compensated employees can be up to 8% (6% plus 2%).

Administratively, the employer must monitor the level of contributions made by nonhighly compensated employees, and then make sure that highly compensated employees do not exceed this level by too much for the plan to remain qualified.

To meet this test, the employer may take into account Section 401(k) contributions to a plan maintained by the employer, or employer contributions to which the Section 401(k) vesting and withdrawal restrictions apply.[35]

*Definition of highly compensated employee.* "Highly compensated employee" is defined as it is for qualified plan purposes (see Chapter 25). In summary, a highly compensated employee is an employee who

- was during the current or preceding plan year a more than 5% owner of the employer, or

- received compensation for the preceding year from the employer over $80,000 (as indexed, $90,000 in 2003) *and* (if the employer elects the use of a "top-paid group" provision) was in the "top-paid group" for the preceding year.[36]

**Question** — Since a 501(c)(3) organization can sponsor both Section 401(k) plans and TDA plans, what are the considerations in choosing between the two?

*Answer* — Most practitioners believe that TDA plans are generally more favorable in this situation. The advantages of the TDAs include:

- no ADP testing (although employer contributions are subject to Section 401(m) tests)

- no ERISA applicability for salary-reduction-only plans

- entire plan not disqualified for exceeding salary reduction limit for one employee[37]

- increased limit on salary reduction contributions for employees who have completed 15 years of service with certain employers

- top-heavy plan rules generally do not apply (although employer matching contributions are subject to the faster top-heavy vesting requirements).

By contrast, Section 401(k) plans have only a few advantages over TDA plans including:

- a somewhat broader investment flexibility—not limited like TDA plans to annuity contracts and mutual funds

- availability of special 10-year averaging for participants born before 1936, a steadily diminishing advantage.

Because of potential complexities in actual situations, however, this choice should always be carefully studied for the individual case at issue.

**Question** — Who is eligible to claim a nonrefundable credit for salary contributions to a TDA?

*Answer* — Certain lower-income taxpayers may claim a temporary, nonrefundable credit for "qualified retirement savings contributions" in taxable years beginning after 2001 and before 2007.[38] "Qualified retirement savings contributions" include elective deferrals to TDAs, as well as other elective deferrals and contributions to Roth or traditional IRAs. (However, the total is reduced by certain distributions received by the taxpayer or his spouse during the prior two taxable years and the current taxable year for which the credit is claimed, including the period up to the due date (plus extensions) for filing the federal income tax return for the current taxable year.)

The credit is allowed against the sum of the regular tax and the alternative minimum tax (minus certain other credits) and is allowed in addition to any other deduction or exclusion that would otherwise apply. In addition, to be eligible, the taxpayer must be at least 18 as of the end of the tax year and must not be claimed as a dependent by someone else or be a full-time student.

The amount of the credit is limited to an "applicable percentage" of IRA contributions and elective deferrals up to $2,000. The "applicable percentages" are as follows:

## ADJUSTED GROSS INCOME

| Joint return | | Head of a household | | All other cases | | Applicable |
|---|---|---|---|---|---|---|
| Over | Not over | Over | Not over | Over | Not over | percentage |
| 0 | $30,000 | 0 | $22,500 | 0 | $15,000 | 50% |
| 30,000 | 32,500 | 22,500 | 24,375 | 15,000 | 16,250 | 20% |
| 32,500 | 50,000 | 24,375 | 37,500 | 16,250 | 25,000 | 10% |
| 50,000 | | 37,500 | | 25,000 | | 0% |

*Example:* Joe and Jenny together have adjusted gross income of $31,000 for 2003. Their employer sponsors a TDA plan and they each elected to make a salary reduction contribution of $2,000 to the plan. Neither has received any distributions in the current or two preceding taxable years. Joe and Jenny will be able to exclude their salary reduction contributions as well as each being eligible to claim a credit of $400 (20% x $2,000) on their federal income tax return ($800 if married filing jointly) for 2003.

**Question** — What is a Roth 403(b) plan?

*Answer* — A new provision included in the Economic Growth and Tax Relief Reconciliation Act of 2001 (EGTRRA 2001) will permit 403(b) plans (as well as 401(k) plans) to offer a "qualified Roth contribution program," which will basically be a Roth account for elective deferrals. The provision does not take effect until 2006 (at which time the limit on elective deferrals is scheduled to reach $15,000, and the after-50 "catch-up" amount will have reached $5,000).

Essentially, participants of plans establishing such a program will be able to designate all, or a portion, or their elective deferrals as Roth contributions. The Roth contributions would be included in the participant's gross income in the year made, and then be held in a separate account with separate record keeping. Earnings allocable to the Roth contributions will remain in the separate account.

A "qualified distribution" from a Roth account will not be includable in the participant's gross income, and rollovers will be available only to another Roth account or Roth IRA. The requirements for a "qualified distribution" are nearly identical to those for a Roth IRA (see Chapter 17), except that no exception is permitted for first-time home purchases. In other words, a qualified distribution is any distribution made after the 5-year "nonexclusion period"

and after the participant has (a) reached age 59½, (b) died or (c) become disabled. (Distributions of excess deferrals are not included in this definition.)

The nonexclusion period is the 5-taxable year period beginning with the earlier of (1) the first year a contribution is made to the Roth account, or (2) if a rollover has been made to the Roth account from another Roth account under another employer plan, the first year a contribution was made to the earlier Roth account.

Aside from being currently included in gross income, amounts designated as Roth contributions under this provision will be treated in all other respects as elective deferrals. They will, together with other elective deferrals, be subject to the otherwise-applicable elective deferral limit; thus, a single total limit will continue to apply to all elective deferrals.[39]

**Question** — How were excludable 403(b) plan contributions determined before 2002?

*Answer* — Prior to 2002, the determination of the amount of 403(b) salary reductions and employer contributions that a plan participant could make on a before-tax basis was very complicated. In addition to the provisions of post-2001 law, there was an "exclusion allowance" that had to be determined and also a complex catch-up provision applicable to the Section 415 limits. Generally, current law permits higher annual contributions.

## ENDNOTES

1. Unless other references are provided, the rules in this chapter are found in IRC Section 403(b).
2. IRC Sec. 401(k)(4)(B).
3. IRC Sec. 408(p); see also Notice 97-6, 1997-1 CB 353.
4. Rev. Rul 2000-35, 2000-2 CB 138.
5. See Chapter 15, "Nonqualified Deferred Compensation," for discussion.
6. SBJPA '96, Sec. 1450(a).
7. IRC Sec. 402(g).
8. A participant who is projected to attain age 50 before the end of a calendar year is deemed to be age 50 as of January 1 of such year. The necessary rules for coordinating with non-calendar plan years are in proposed regulations. Prop. Treas. Reg. §§1.414(v)-1(a)(4)(B), 1.414(v)-1(b)(2).
9. IRC Sec. 414(v)(2)(B)(ii).
10. IRC Sec. 402(g)(7).
11. IRC Sec. 414(v)(3)(a)(1).

12. IRC Sec. 403(b)(12)(A)(ii).

13. IRC Sec. 403(b)(12)(A)(ii).

14. IRC Sec. 403(b)(12)(A)(i).

15. IRC Sec. 401(a)(4).

16. IRC Sec. 401(m).

17. IRC Sec. 410(b).

18. IRC Sec. 411(a)(12).

19. Churches and certain related organizations can make TDA plan contributions to retirement income accounts; it seems that such retirement income accounts need not limit their investments to annuities and mutual fund custodial accounts. See IRC Section 403(b)(9); Conf. Rep. No. 760, 97th Cong., 2nd Sess. 637-638 (TEFRA '82), reprinted in 1982-2 CB 681; Secs. 13.3 and 13.3.3 of the final audit guidelines for TDA plans, reprinted in *IRM Handbook 7.7.1, Employee Plans Examination Guidelines Handbook*, Chapter 13, Section 403 Plans (this document can be viewed or printed from the IRS web site: http://www.irs.ustreas.gov/bus_info/ep/GUIDE.pdf); ERISA Section 203(a)(2).

20. ERISA Sec. 205.

21. See IRC Sec. 403(b)(11); IRC Sec. 403(b)(7)(A)(ii), as amended by TRA '86, Sec. 1123(c)(1)-(2); TRA '86, Sec. 1123(e)(2), as amended by TAMRA '88, Sec. 1011A(c)(11)(B).

22. IRC Section 403(b)(7) can be interpreted to indicate that earnings on employer contributions (both pre-1989 assets and post-1988 assets) can be distributed at any time.

23. *Ibid*.

24. The rules can be interpreted to indicate that earnings on pre-1989 salary reduction assets can be distributed at any time.

25. IRC Sec. 72(t).

26. Note that if the plan is not subject to ERISA (i.e., governmental plans, church plans and certain employee-contribution-only plans—see "ERISA Requirements" in the text), loans are subject to Code section 72(p), but not to ERISA regulations (DOL Reg. §2550.408b-1).

27. IRC Secs. 3121(a)(5) [FICA], 3306(b)(5) [FUTA].

28. IRC Sec. 403(b)(13).

29. DOL Reg. §2510.3-2(f).

30. 1990-1 CB 97.

31. TDA plans maintained by churches and qualified church-controlled organizations are not subject to the nondiscrimination rules. IRC Secs. 403(b)(1)(D), 403(b)(12)(B); see IRC Secs. 3121(w)(3)(A) and 3121(w)(3)(B) for the applicable definitions of "church" and "qualified church-controlled organizations." IRC Sec, 403(b)(1)(D). Except for the IRC Section 401(a)(17) limit on compensation, plans maintained by governmental employers are not subject to the nondiscrimination rules. IRC Sec. 403(b)(12)(C).

32. 1989-1 CB 654.

33. Subsequent notices have extended the use of the safe harbors and the "good faith" compliance standard until specific guidance is issued under Section 403(b). Notice 90-73, 1990-2 CB 353; Notice 92-36, 1992-2 CB 364; and Notice 96-64, 1996-2 CB 229.

34. IRC Sec. 401(m)(2)(A). In addition, alternative methods of satisfying these tests may be available (see Chapter 18).

35. IRC Sec. 401(m); Treas. Reg. §1.401(m)-1(b)(5).

36. IRC Sec. 414(q)(1).

37. IRC Sec. 403(b)(1)(E).

38. IRC Sec. 25B.

39. IRC Sec. 402A.

# Chapter 24

# TRADITIONAL IRAs

## WHAT IS IT?

A traditional IRA (which stands for either individual retirement account or individual retirement annuity) is a type of retirement savings arrangement under which IRA contributions, up to certain limits, and investment earnings are tax-deferred. That is, interest earned and gains received inside the traditional IRA are free of federal income tax until withdrawn from the IRA.

Traditional IRAs are primarily plans of individual savings, rather than employee benefits. However, their features should be understood since they fit into an employee's plan of retirement savings and therefore they influence the form of employer retirement plans to some degree.

Employers can sponsor traditional IRAs for employees, as a limited alternative to an employer-sponsored qualified retirement plan. Employers who have a qualified plan can also sponsor a "deemed IRA" as part of the qualified plan to provide an alternative form of retirement savings for employees. Employer-sponsored IRAs and deemed IRAs are discussed in the "Questions and Answers" at the end of this chapter. An arrangement similar to the employer-sponsored IRA which allows greater annual employer contributions is the SEP (simplified employee pension) discussed in Chapter 21. SIMPLE IRA plans involve employee salary reduction contributions and employer matching or nonelective contributions that are contributed to an IRA. SIMPLE plans are discussed in Chapter 20.

See also the chapter on the Roth IRA. The Roth IRA provides benefits comparable to those from a traditional IRA. Detailed comparisons between the two are covered in Chapter 17. Education IRAs are discussed in the "Questions and Answers," below.

## WHEN IS IT INDICATED?

1. When there is a need to shelter current compensation or earned income from taxation.

2. When it is desirable to defer taxes on investment income.

3. When long-term accumulation, especially for retirement purposes, is an important objective.

4. When a supplement or alternative to a qualified pension or profit sharing plan is needed.

## ADVANTAGES

1. Eligible individuals may contribute up to the maximum annual contribution amount (see below) to a traditional IRA (and up to the maximum annual contribution amount for a spouse if a traditional spousal IRA is available) and possibly deduct this amount from their current taxable income.

2. Investment income earned on the assets held in a traditional IRA is not taxed until it is withdrawn from the account. This deferral applies no matter what the nature of the investment income. It may be in the form of interest, dividends, rents, capital gain, or any other form of income. Such income will generally be taxed only when it is withdrawn from the account and received as ordinary income.

## DISADVANTAGES

1. The traditional IRA deduction is limited to the maximum contribution amount each year (and up to the maximum contribution amount for a spouse if a traditional spousal IRA is available), with even more stringent limits, or a complete unavailability of the deduction, if the individual or spouse is an active participant in a tax-favored employer retirement plan, as discussed below.

2. Traditional IRA withdrawals are subject to the 10% penalty on premature withdrawals applicable to all tax-favored retirement plans.

3. Traditional IRA withdrawals are not eligible for the special averaging tax computation that applies to certain lump sum distributions from qualified plans. This is discussed in Chapter 26.

4. Traditional IRAs cannot be established once an individual reaches age 70½ (except in the case of rollover-IRAs) and withdrawals from the account are required by April 1 of the year after the year in which the individual reaches age 70½. For additional information on required distributions, see Chapter 26.

## TAX IMPLICATIONS

### Contribution Rules

1. *Deduction Limits.* The maximum annual deductible IRA contribution for an individual is the lesser of (a) the maximum annual contribution amount or (b) 100% of the individual's earned income—that is, income from employment or self-employment; investment income cannot be counted.[1] A provision for traditional spousal IRAs permits additional contributions up to an additional maximum annual contribution amount for the spouse in some cases. The provision works like this: if individual Pat's spouse Chris is not working or receives lesser includable compensation for the year than Pat, the couple may contribute up to $3,000 in 2001 to an IRA for Chris, for a total contribution for the couple of up to $6,000. More technically, assuming the "active participant" restrictions of item 2 below do not apply, the maximum allowable deductible contribution for Chris is the lesser of (1) $3,000 or (2) 100% of Chris's includable compensation, plus 100% of Pat's includable compensation minus the amount of the deduction taken by Pat for IRA contributions for the year. In order to contribute to a traditional spousal IRA, the couple must file a joint return.[2]

If both spouses have earned income, each can have a traditional IRA. The deduction limit for each spouse with earned income is the maximum annual contribution amount/100% limit. However, traditional IRA contribution limits are combined with Roth IRAs. The maximum annual contribution amount is reduced for each dollar contributed by the same taxpayer to a Roth IRA.

Generally, the maximum annual contribution amount is as follow:

| Taxable year beginning in | Dollar limit |
|---|---|
| 2002 through 2004 | $3,000 |
| 2005 through 2007 | $4,000 |
| 2008 | $5,000 |

After 2008, the maximum annual contribution amount is scheduled to be adjusted for cost-of-living increases.[3]

For individuals who have attained age 50 before the close of the tax year, an additional contribution amount is allowable[4]—the resulting *total* maximum contribution amount is as follows:

| Year | Total dollar limit |
|---|---|
| 2002 through 2004 | $3,500 |
| 2005 | $4,500 |
| 2006 and 2007 | $5,000 |
| 2008 | $6,000 |

2. *Active Participant Restrictions.* Current law imposes income limitations on the deductibility of traditional IRA contributions for those persons who are "active participants" in an employer retirement plan that is tax-favored—including a qualified retirement plan, simplified employee pension (SEP), Section 403(b) tax deferred annuity plan, or SIMPLE IRA.[5]

If an otherwise eligible person actively participates in the employer plan, the available traditional IRA deduction is reduced below the maximum annual contribution amount if the AGI of the taxpayer is within the phaseout ranges indicated below, with the deduction eliminated entirely if the AGI is above the upper limit of the phaseout range.

#### IRA Active Participant AGI phaseout ranges

| Year | Single | Married filing jointly | Married filing separately |
|---|---|---|---|
| 2002 | $ 34,000-44,000 | $ 54,000-64,000 | $ 0-10,000 |
| 2003 | 40,000-50,000 | 60,000-70,000 | 0-10,000 |
| 2004 | 45,000-55,000 | 65,000-75,000 | 0-10,000 |
| 2005 | 50,000-60,000 | 70,000-80,000 | 0-10,000 |
| 2006 | 50,000-60,000 | 75,000-85,000 | 0-10,000 |
| 2007 and later | 50,000-60,000 | 80,000-100,00 | 0-10,000 |

The reduction in the maximum annual contribution amount in the phaseout AGI region is proportional to the amount by which the AGI exceeds the lower limit. For example, suppose that in 2003 a single taxpayer's AGI is $42,000 and he is an active participant under age 50. The taxpayer is $2,000 into the phaseout region of $10,000, so his annual traditional IRA deduction is reduced by $2,000/$10,000 or 20%. This is a reduction of $600 (20% of $3,000), so the maximum IRA deduction is $2,400 ($3,000 less $600).

There is a $200 "floor" under the reduction formula. That is, as long as the taxpayer is below the AGI cutoff level, at least $200 can be contributed and deducted. For example, if the taxpayer in the preceding example had an AGI of $49,900, he could contribute and deduct up to $200.

An individual is not subject to the "active participant" restrictions just because his or her spouse is an active participant in a tax-favored retirement plan. However, this provision phases out for joint adjusted gross incomes from $150,000 to $160,000.

For example, suppose Chris and Pat are married and file jointly. Both are working and Chris, but not Pat, actively participates in an employer-sponsored qualified plan. Chris and Pat each earn $75,000 in 2003. Pat may contribute and deduct up to $3,000 to an IRA. Chris may not make any deductible contributions to an IRA. However, if Chris and Pat each earned $85,000 or more in 2003, neither one could make a deductible IRA contribution since this "no spousal attribution of active participation" rule would be fully phased out at their joint AGI level of $160,000. If joint AGI was between $150,000 and $160,000, Pat's deduction limit would be reduced ratably below $3,000.

3. *Nondeductible IRAs.* An individual or married couple can also make *nondeductible* traditional IRA contributions, within limits.[6] The limit is the same regardless of income level; it is the *excess of* the maximum annual contribution amount *over* the amount deductible. If the individual or couple make no deductible contributions, they can therefore contribute up to the maximum annual contribution limit in the case of an individual, and up to an additional maximum annual contribution amount in accordance with the spousal IRA rules set out above, on a nondeductible basis. Nondeductible contributions will be free of tax when they are distributed, but income earned on such contributions will be taxed. If nondeductible contributions are made to a traditional IRA, amounts withdrawn will be treated as partly tax free and partly taxable. Because nondeductible IRA contributions impose additional accounting problems, and provide generally no better result than simply investing in tax-free or tax-deferred non-IRA investments, most advisers do not recommend them.

For a discussion of nondeductible Roth IRAs, see Chapter 17.

4. *Time Limits.* Eligible persons may establish an IRA account and claim the appropriate tax deduction any time prior to the due date of their tax return, *without* extensions, even if the taxpayer actually receives an extension of the filing date.[7] For most individuals or married couples the contribution cutoff date is April 15th. However, since earnings on an IRA account accumulate tax-free, taxpayers may want to make contributions as early as possible in the tax year. The advantage of making an IRA contribution at the beginning of the year can be seen in the following table which assumes $2,000 annual contributions and a rate of return of eight percent.

| Years Of Growth | Beginning Of Year January 1 | End Of Year December 31 | Advantage Of Early Contributions |
|---|---|---|---|
| 5 | $ 12,572 | $ 11,733 | $ 939 |
| 10 | 31,291 | 28,973 | 2,318 |
| 15 | 58,649 | 54,304 | 4,344 |
| 20 | 98,846 | 91,524 | 7,322 |
| 25 | 157,909 | 146,212 | 11,697 |
| 30 | 244,692 | 226,566 | 18,125 |
| 35 | 372,204 | 344,634 | 27,571 |
| 40 | 559,562 | 518,113 | 41,449 |
| 45 | 834,852 | 773,011 | 61,841 |

The advantage of early contributions continues with the increased contribution limits after 2001; of course, the accumulations would be even greater the larger the contributions to the traditional IRA.

5. *Nonrefundable Credit.* A limited nonrefundable tax credit is available to certain lower income taxpayers who make contributions to a traditional IRA (see "Questions and Answers," below).

## Distribution and Rollover Rules

1. The government penalizes certain early withdrawals from IRAs. The premature distribution penalty is 10% of the taxable amount withdrawn from the IRA.[8] Therefore, IRA contributions should be made from funds that can be left in the account until one of the "non-penalty" events listed below occurs.

For IRAs, the premature distribution penalty (discussed further in Chapter 26) does *not* apply to:

- distributions made on or after attainment of age 59½,

- distributions made to the IRA participant's beneficiary or estate on or after the participant's death,

- distributions attributable to the participant's disability,

- distributions that are part of a series of substantially equal periodic payments made at least annually over the life or life expectancy of the participant, or the participant and a designated beneficiary,

- distributions for medical care, within the 7.5% of itemized deduction "floor" for such expenses,

- distributions to unemployed individuals for health insurance premiums under certain conditions,

- distributions for higher education costs (tuition, fees, books, supplies and equipment) for the taxpayer, spouse, child or grandchild, and

- distributions to pay acquisition costs of a first home for the participant, spouse, child, grandchild or ancestor of the participant or spouse, up to a $10,000 lifetime maximum.

The exception for *periodic payments* provides some flexibility and can be very favorable in some cases. For example, suppose Ira Participant decides at age 52 to take some money out of his IRA. Ira can do so without penalty, as long as the amount taken out annually is substantially what the annual payment would be under a life annuity (or joint life annuity) purchased with his IRA account balance. No actual annuity purchase is required.[9] Then, when Ira reaches age 59½, he can withdraw all the rest of the money in his IRA account. Ira doesn't have to continue the annuity payments since he is now relying on a different penalty exception, the exception for payments after age 59½.

However, if the series of payments is changed before the participant reaches age 59½ or, if after age 59½, within five years of the date of the first payment, the tax that would have been imposed, but for the periodic exception, is imposed with interest in the year the change occurs. In the example above, if Ira Participant had begun receiving payments un-

der the periodic payment exception when he was 57, he would have to continue the annuity payments for at least five years to avoid the penalty.[10]

2. Distributions must begin by April 1 of the year after the year in which age 70½ is reached.[11] The minimum distribution requirements are discussed in Chapter 26.

3. An IRA can be used to receive a "rollover" of certain distributions of benefits from employer-sponsored retirement plans. The distribution must be directly transferred or rolled over to the rollover IRA within 60 days after it is received.[12] IRA rollovers are usually straightforward, but there are some complicated rules in special situations. These are discussed further in Chapter 26.

4. When an IRA owner dies, a somewhat complex pattern of tax rules applies. Planners need to understand the tax treatment of this common situation in order to prevent unnecessary tax penalties for their clients. These rules are generally designed to prevent IRA distributions from being "stretched out" unduly to increase tax deferral. See Appendix J for a detailed discussion.

## WHERE CAN I FIND OUT MORE ABOUT IT?

1. Most banks, savings and loans, insurance companies, and brokerage firms actively market IRAs, and can provide brochures describing their IRA plans. These firms will indicate the types of investments available as well as any charges that may be applied to such accounts.

2. IRS Publication 590, *Individual Retirement Arrangements (IRAs)*, is available without charge from the IRS or the U.S. Government Printing Office.

## QUESTIONS AND ANSWERS

**Question** — If neither an individual nor his or her spouse is an active participant in a tax-favored retirement plan, are there any limitations on the deductibility of IRA contributions?

*Answer* — No. If neither the individual nor the spouse is an active participant in a qualified retirement plan, simplified employee pension (SEP), Section 403(b) annuity plan, or SIMPLE IRA, they may contribute up to the maximum annual contribution deduction limit, as set out above, and deduct the full amount of the contribution regardless of the level of AGI.

---

*Example:* Minnie (age 35) and Bill (age 40), a married couple, each earn $75,000 annually. Neither is an active participant in any qualified plan, SEP, Section 403(b) plan, or SIMPLE IRA. For 2003, Minnie and Bill can each contribute and deduct up to $3,000 to their own IRA plan (a total of $6,000 for both).

*Example:* Mabel earns $75,000 annually. Her husband, Alf, has no earned income (although he has investment income over $100,000 annually). Neither spouse is over 49 or an active participant in a tax-favored plan. For 2003, Mabel can contribute and deduct up to $3,000 to an IRA for herself and up to $3,000 to an IRA for her spouse (for a total of $6,000) provided they file a joint return.

---

**Question** — What does it mean to be an "active participant" in a qualified plan, SEP, TDA, or SIMPLE IRA plan?

*Answer* — A person is an active participant in an employer's retirement plan for a given year if the participant actually receives an employer contribution or accrues a benefit under an employer's defined benefit plan for any part of that year. A person is an active participant in a defined contribution-type plan if any contribution or forfeiture is allocated to his account during the year.

For example, in a qualified profit sharing plan it is possible for an employer to omit making a plan contribution in a given year. For such a year, an employee is *not* considered an active plan participant even though covered under the plan, so long as there was no contribution made (or forfeiture allocated) to the employee's account under the plan.

Note, however, that an employee is considered an active participant if a contribution is made for him by the employer but the employee is not vested in the amount in his account. If the employee stays long enough to become vested, he will acquire full rights to that amount, so he is considered an active participant for the year in which the contribution was made.

**Question** — If only one spouse is an active participant, can the other spouse receive a full IRA deduction?

*Answer* — A non-active participant spouse filing a joint return may receive a full IRA deduction if joint income is less than $150,000. The non-participant spouse may receive a partial deduction if joint income is between $150,000 and $160,000.

**Question** — Is there any minimum contribution required each year?

*Answer* — No, there is no required minimum contribution to an IRA. An individual can put aside relatively small amounts each year and still see them grow into a considerable sum for retirement. Also, a contribution does not have to be made every year. It is possible to skip a year or any number of years without jeopardizing the tax-deferred status of the account. However, failure to make contributions reduces the value of the account for tax-shelter purposes and limits the amount of earnings that will build up on a tax-free basis.

**Question** — Who can claim a nonrefundable credit for a contribution to an IRA?

*Answer* — Certain lower-income taxpayers may claim a temporary, nonrefundable credit for "qualified retirement savings contributions" in taxable years beginning after 2001 and before 2007.[13] "Qualified retirement savings contributions" include elective deferrals to SIMPLE IRAs, as well as other elective deferrals and contributions to Roth or traditional IRAs. (However, the total is reduced by certain distributions received by the taxpayer or his spouse during the prior two taxable years and the current taxable year for which the credit is claimed, including the period up to the due date (plus extensions) for filing the federal income tax return for the current taxable year.)

The credit is allowed against the sum of the regular tax and the alternative minimum tax (minus certain other credits) and is allowed in addition to any other deduction or exclusion that would otherwise apply. In addition, to be eligible, the taxpayer must be at least 18 as of the end of the tax year and must not be claimed as a dependent by someone else or be a full-time student.

The amount of the credit is limited to an "applicable percentage" of IRA contributions and elective deferrals up to $2,000. The "applicable percentages" are as follows:

## ADJUSTED GROSS INCOME

| Joint return | | Head of a household | | All other cases | | Applicable |
|---|---|---|---|---|---|---|
| Over | Not over | Over | Not over | Over | Not over | percentage |
| 0 | $30,000 | 0 | $22,500 | 0 | $15,000 | 50% |
| 30,000 | 32,500 | 22,500 | 24,375 | 15,000 | 16,250 | 20% |
| 32,500 | 50,000 | 24,375 | 37,500 | 16,250 | 25,000 | 10% |
| 50,000 | | 37,500 | | 25,000 | | 0% |

---

*Example:* Joe and Jennifer have an adjusted gross income of $31,000 for 2003 and they each contributed at least $2,000 to a traditional IRA. Neither participates in an employer-provided retirement plan and neither have received any distributions. Not only could Joe and Jennifer each deduct their $2,000 contributions, they each can also claim a credit of $400 (20% x $2,000) on their federal income tax return for 2002.

---

**Question** — What kind of income is eligible to be contributed to an IRA account?

*Answer* — The income must be produced from personal services which would include wages, salaries, professional fees, sales commissions, tips, and bonuses.

Unearned income such as dividends, interest, or rent cannot be used in determining the amount of the IRA contribution.

**Question** — Do married couples with two incomes contribute to one or two regular IRAs?

*Answer* — Two. Each should establish a separate IRA account. Contributions are based on each separate income and each contribution is a separate tax deduction. This is true even though a couple may live in a community property state.

**Question** — How are IRA benefits paid?

*Answer* — An IRA account belongs to the participant and the participant is free to take the money out at any time, in any amount, or leave it in indefinitely. However, the tax penalty provisions described in "Distribution and Rollover Rules" above impose significant penalties that effectively require money to be left in until age 59½(with some exceptions to the 10% early withdrawal penalty) and also require distributions to begin after age 70½ on a joint-life annuity basis or faster.

If IRA assets are a significant part of the participant's savings, planning for distributions to minimize taxes can be extremely important. The rules (unfortunately very complex) for distributions are discussed in Chapter 26.

**Question** — Must a participant's spouse consent to an IRA distribution?

*Answer* — Generally, no. The federal consent requirements enacted under the Retirement Equity Act of 1984 apply to qualified plans but not to IRAs. Spousal consent may be required when a qualified plan distribution is rolled over to an IRA, but distributions thereafter can be made without spousal consent. This underscores the importance of making careful long-range retirement and estate plans for both spouses when a significant qualified plan distribution is rolled over to an IRA. Notwithstanding the absence of federal consent requirements, however, a spouse's property rights in an IRA account are a matter of state law, and may differ depending on whether the state is a common law or community property jurisdiction.

**Question** — Can an IRA owner borrow from his IRA?

*Answer* — Loans from IRAs to the IRA owner or a related party are prohibited transactions subject to penalty. However, an IRA owner can use the 60-day IRA rollover provision to, in effect, make a 60-day interest free loan from an IRA.[14] The owner simply takes the money out, uses it during the 60-day period, and then deposits it in the same or another IRA on or before the 60th day after withdrawal.[15] This type of transaction may be helpful as part of a "swing loan" when selling one residence and buying another, or for similar financial needs.

**Question** — When are taxes paid on IRA plans?

*Answer* — Generally, the entire amount of an IRA distribution including principal and earnings is ordinary income in the year of receipt. However, if nondeductible contributions have been made to the account, they are recovered tax-free. If money is withdrawn periodically in installments or an annuity, only the amount received each year is taxable. If nondeductible contributions have been made, a portion of each payment is received tax-free.

**Question** — What happens if too much is contributed to an IRA account in any one year?

*Answer* — If more than the maximum allowable amount is contributed in any year, a 6% excise tax will be imposed on the excess contribution. However, the 6% tax can be avoided by withdrawing the excess contribution and earnings prior to the filing date for the federal income tax return (normally April 15). If the excess contribution plus earnings is not withdrawn by the tax return filing date, the 6% excise tax will be imposed in each succeeding year until the excess is eliminated.[16]

**Question** — How can an employer sponsor IRAs for employees?

*Answer* — (1) *Employer-sponsored IRA.* An employer (or a labor union) can sponsor IRAs for its employees as an alternative to a pension plan. There is no requirement of nondiscrimination in coverage. The IRAs can be made available to any employee or a discriminatory group of employees. Contributions to the IRA can be made either as additional compensation from the employer or as a salary reduction elected by the employee. If the employer contributes extra compensation, it is taxable to the employee, but the employee may be eligible for the IRA deduction. The maximum annual contribution limit for an employer-sponsored IRA is the same as for traditional individual IRAs. Employers may establish payroll deduction IRA plans for employees under Department of Labor guidelines without the arrangement becoming subject to the employee benefit provisions and restrictions of ERISA.[17]

(2) *Deemed IRA.* After 2002, an employer that has a qualified plan, Section 403(b) tax sheltered annuity, or eligible Section 457 governmental plan may allow employees to make voluntary contributions to an account or annuity set up under the plan that meets the rules for traditional IRAs.[18] Such deemed IRAs will not be subject to the IRC rules governing the employer plan but will be subject to the exclusive benefit and fiduciary rules of ERISA (to the extent they apply to the employer plan).

(3) *SEP.* An arrangement similar to the employer-sponsored IRA is the SEP (simplified employee pension) discussed in Chapter 21. SEPs allow greater annual employer contributions; however, SEPs require nondiscriminatory coverage of employees. See Chapter 21.

(4) *SIMPLE IRAs.* This arrangement involves employee salary reduction contributions and employer matching or nonelective contributions that are contributed to an IRA. See Chapter 20.

**Question** — Are IRA contributions locked into any one particular investment?

*Answer* — No. First, the IRA participant may select more than one organization that sponsors IRA programs, as long as the total of all investments made each year is within the maximum annual contribution limit. For example, part of the contribution could be placed in a savings account and the remainder in a mutual fund plan. Second, at any time the IRA participant may request an IRA sponsor to transfer IRA assets directly from one sponsoring organization to another; not all IRA sponsors will agree to do this, however. Alternatively, assets may be taken out of an IRA and reinvested with another IRA sponsor within 60 days without any tax consequences. However, the IRA participant is allowed to make this type of transaction from an IRA—a "rollover"—only once every 12 months.[19]

**Question** — In what types of assets may IRA funds be invested?

*Answer* — IRA funds can be invested in any type of asset, with three specific limitations:

(1) An IRA cannot be invested in a "collectible" as defined in Code section 408(m). A collectible is any work of art, rug, antique, metal or gem, stamp, coin, alcoholic beverage, or any other item designated as a collectible by the IRS. The IRA can, however, invest in certain state or federally-issued coins.[20]

(2) IRAs cannot be invested in life insurance contracts.[21]

(3) Since IRAs cannot make loans to an IRA participant,[22] the participant's note is in effect another type of property the IRA cannot invest in. That is, an IRA owner cannot lend IRA funds to himself or to a related person or business. IRAs can, however, make loans to individuals or companies that are not "disqualified persons" under the prohibited transaction rules,' if the underlying IRA documents permit. For example, Letter Ruling 8723082 states that an IRA owner could make loans from the IRA to an unrelated company that was in the business of owning and managing shopping centers.

**Question** — How are IRAs treated for state tax law purposes?

*Answer* — State tax laws vary, and not every state accords IRAs the same favorable tax treatment as does federal law. Three issues can arise:

1.  Is the IRA contribution deductible for state (or local) income tax purposes?

2.  Are IRA withdrawals taxable under state income tax law?

3.  If an IRA owner takes a deduction for an IRA contribution in State A and then moves to State B, does the owner owe income tax to State A when making an IRA withdrawal? Some states apparently took the position that taxes were due in that situation. However, Title 4 United States Code Section 114, enacted by Congress in 1996, prohibits a state from imposing taxes on certain retirement income (including IRA withdrawals) of individuals who are not residents or legally domiciled in that state.

**Question** — If a participant's spouse is the beneficiary of the participant's IRA, is the amount eligible for the marital deduction for federal estate tax purposes?

*Answer* — In general, amounts transferred to a spouse at death are eligible for the marital deduction. There is no problem with this if the spouse receives the IRA directly. However, if a trust for the spouse's benefit receives the IRA assets, the trust must qualify as a "QTIP" (qualified terminable interest property) trust in order to be eligible for the marital deduction.

In Revenue Ruling 2000-2,[23] the IRS indicated the requirements that must be met for an IRA-beneficiary trust to qualify as a QTIP trust. Generally, income must be distributable currently to the spousal beneficiary.

**Question** — What is an Education IRA?

*Answer* — An Education IRA is a trust or custodial account that is created for the express purpose of funding the "qualified education" expenses of the designated beneficiary.[24]

The designated beneficiary of an Education IRA must be a life-in-being at the time it is established.[25] Contributions cannot exceed the annual cumulative limit of $2,000 (in 2003; $500 for prior years), must be made in cash and are not tax deductible. In addition, contributions must be made on or before the date on which the beneficiary attains age 18.

The contribution limit is phased out for single contributors with AGI between $95,000 and $110,000. That is no contribution is available for 2003 for a single taxpayer with AGI above $110,000. The phase-out for joint filers is between $190,000 and $220,000.[26]

Distributions from an Education IRA that are made for the payment of "qualified higher education expenses" are penalty free and tax free. "Qualified higher education expenses" are defined as tuition, fees, books, supplies, and equipment required for the enrollment or attendance at an eligible higher education institution.[27] An "eligible higher education institution" is any college, university, vocational school or other postsecondary educational institution described in section 481 of the Higher Education Act of 1965.[28] After 2001, distributions can also be used for elementary and secondary public, private or religious school expenses.[29]

## FOOTNOTES

1.  IRC Sections 219(a), 219(b), as amended by The Economic Growth and Tax Relief Reconciliation Act of 2001 (EGTRRA 2001). Note that all provisions of EGTRRA 2001 are scheduled to sunset, or expire, after December 31, 2010.

2.  IRC Section 219(c).

3.  IRC Section 219(b)(5)(C), as added by EGTRRA 2001.

4.  IRC Section 219(b)(5)(B), as added by EGTRRA 2001.

5.  IRC Section 219(g).

6.  IRC Section 408(o).

7.  IRC Section 219(f)(3).

8.  IRC Section 72(t).

9.  Rules for calculating the annual annuity payment are provided by the IRS in IRS Notice 89-25, 1989-1 CB 662, Question 12. Three methods of calculating payments are listed with approval: (1) use of the minimum distribution rules of Section 401(a)(9); (2) amortizing the account balance over single or joint life expectancies of owner and beneficiary; (3) using an annuity factor using a "reasonable" interest rate and mortality table; eight percent and the UP-1984 table are used in the IRS' example. See also IRS Publication 590.

10.  IRC Section 72(t)(4).

11.  IRC Sections 408(a)(6), 408(b)(3), 401(a)(9).

12.  IRC Section 408(d)(3)(A)(ii).

13.  IRC Section 25B, as added by EGTRRA 2001.

14.  Let. Rul. 9010008.

15.  Note, however, that there may be tax consequences with more than one rollover. In *Martin v. Comm.*, TC Memo 1992-331, a taxpayer made "rollovers" *from* two separate IRAs within one 12-month period. The Tax Court characterized the second transac-

tion as a distribution taxable under Code section 408(d)(1), noting only that Section 408(d)(3)(B) states that the rollover exemption can only be used once during any one year period.

16. IRC Sections 4973, 408(d)(4).

17. IB 99-1, 64 Fed. Reg. 32999 (6-18-99).

18. IRC Section 408(q), as added by EGTRRA 2001.

19. Prop. Reg. §1.408-4(b). But see footnote 15.

20. IRC Section 408(m)(3).

21. IRC Section 408(a)(3).

22. It is a prohibited transaction under IRC Section 4975(c)(1)(B).

23. Rev. Rul. 2000-2, 2000-3 IRB 305.

24. IRC Sections 530(b), as amended by EGTRRA 2001, 530(g).

25. IRC Section 530(b)(1), as amended by EGTRRA 2001.

26. IRC Section 530(c)(1), as amended by EGTRRA 2001.

27. IRC Section 530(b)(2)(A)(i), as amended by EGTRRA 2001.

28. IRC Sec. 529(e)(5).

29. IRC Section 530(b)(4), as added by EGTRRA 2001.

# Chapter 25

# QUALIFIED PLANS: GENERAL RULES FOR QUALIFICATION

The design of qualified pension and profit sharing plans is a very complex subject, and the complete details are beyond the scope of this book. However, because of the great importance of these plans in an employer's benefit program and for individual financial and retirement planning, every planner should have a basic understanding of how these plans are structured, what they can do, and the rules for "qualifying" these plans.

In order to obtain the tax advantages of qualified plans, complex Internal Revenue Code and regulatory requirements must be met (but special rules apply to governmental plans[1]). The following will summarize these requirements as briefly as possible. These rules have many exceptions and qualifications that will not be covered in detail.

## ELIGIBILITY AND COVERAGE

A qualified plan must cover a broad group of employees, not just key employees and business owners. Two types of rules must be satisfied: the "age and service" ("waiting period") requirements, and the "overall coverage" and "participation" requirements.

Minimum waiting period and age requirements are often used in plans to avoid burdening the plan with employees who terminate after short periods of service. However, the plan cannot require more than one year of service for eligibility, and any employee who has attained the age of 21 must be allowed to enter the plan upon meeting the plan's waiting period requirement. As an alternative, the plan waiting period can be up to two years if the plan provides immediate 100% vesting upon entry. No plan can impose a maximum age for entry. For eligibility purposes, a year of service means a 12-month period during which the employee has at least 1,000 hours of service.[2]

In addition to the rules restricting age- and service-related eligibility provisions, qualified plan coverage is further regulated through two alternative overall coverage tests. A qualified plan must satisfy one of the two following tests:[3]

1. *Ratio percentage test*. The plan must cover a percentage of nonhighly compensated employees that is at least 70% of the percentage of highly compensated employees covered.

2. *Average benefit test*. The plan must benefit a nondiscriminatory classification of employees, and the average benefit, as a percentage of compensation, for all nonhighly compensated employees of the employer must be at least 70% of that for highly compensated employees (see below).

"Highly compensated" is a concept defined in detail in Code section 414(q) (see below).

In addition, for a *defined benefit* plan to be qualified, it must cover, on each day of the plan year, the lesser of (1) 50 employees of the employer or (2) the greater of (a) 40% or more of all employees of the employer, or (b) two employees (or, if there is only one employee, that employee). This test is commonly known as the 50/40 test.[4]

The average benefit test is a two-pronged test—it requires (1) a *nondiscriminatory classification* and (2) the *70% average benefit* requirement.[5]

The nondiscriminatory classification test is expanded upon in some detail in the regulations under Section 410(b). First, the regulations provide a "safe harbor" table (Figure 25.1) under which certain plans are deemed to meet the nondiscriminatory classification requirement automatically. The safe harbor test is best explained through an example using the table.

---

*Example:* Suppose Average Co. has 700 salaried office employees, including 100 highly compensated employees, and 9,300 production employees, of whom 300 are highly compensated. Average Co. would like to maintain a qualified plan just for the office employees. The office plan will not meet the ratio percentage test since its ratio percentage is 25% [(600/9,600)/(100/400)]. Does it meet the average benefit test under the regulations? Its nonhighly compensated concentration percentage is 9,600/10,000 or 96%. From the table, the "safe harbor"

Figure 25.1

| Nonhighly compensated employee concentration percentage | Safe harbor percentage | Unsafe habor percentage | Nonhighly compensated employee concentration percentage | Safe harbor percentage | Unsafe harbor percentage |
|---|---|---|---|---|---|
| 0-60 | 50.00 | 40.00 | 80 | 35.00 | 25.00 |
| 61 | 49.25 | 39.25 | 81 | 34.25 | 24.25 |
| 62 | 48.50 | 38.50 | 82 | 33.50 | 23.50 |
| 63 | 47.75 | 37.75 | 83 | 32.75 | 22.75 |
| 64 | 47.00 | 37.00 | 84 | 32.00 | 22.00 |
| 65 | 46.25 | 36.25 | 85 | 31.25 | 21.25 |
| 66 | 45.50 | 35.50 | 86 | 30.50 | 20.50 |
| 67 | 44.75 | 34.75 | 87 | 29.75 | 20.00 |
| 68 | 44.00 | 34.00 | 88 | 29.00 | 20.00 |
| 69 | 43.25 | 33.25 | 89 | 28.25 | 20.00 |
| 70 | 42.50 | 32.50 | 90 | 27.50 | 20.00 |
| 71 | 41.75 | 31.75 | 91 | 26.75 | 20.00 |
| 72 | 41.00 | 31.00 | 92 | 26.00 | 20.00 |
| 73 | 40.25 | 30.25 | 93 | 25.25 | 20.00 |
| 74 | 39.50 | 29.50 | 94 | 24.50 | 20.00 |
| 75 | 38.75 | 28.75 | 95 | 23.75 | 20.00 |
| 76 | 38.00 | 28.00 | 96 | 23.00 | 20.00 |
| 77 | 37.25 | 27.25 | 97 | 22.25 | 20.00 |
| 78 | 36.50 | 26.50 | 98 | 21.50 | 20.00 |
| 79 | 35.75 | 25.75 | 99 | 20.75 | 20.00 |

ratio percentage is 23%. Since the plan has an actual ratio percentage of 25%, it is deemed to meet the nondiscriminatory classification test without actually looking at the classification itself. (Of course, the plan also has to meet the average benefit percentage portion of the average benefit test.)

---

If a plan's ratio percentage falls between the safe and "unsafe harbor" percentages in the table, the IRS will examine the facts and circumstances of the classification to determine whether it is, in fact, discriminatory. If the ratio percentage is *below* the unsafe harbor percentage, the plan is considered automatically discriminatory.[6]

In applying the above coverage tests, certain employees are not counted, which means that they can effectively be excluded from the plan. In particular, employees included in a collective bargaining unit can be excluded if there was good faith bargaining on retirement benefits.[7]

When the coverage rules are applied, all related employers must be treated as a single employer. Thus, an employer generally cannot break up its business into a number of corporations or other separate units to avoid covering rank-and-file employees. Appendix B discusses these complex rules in further detail.

However, if the employer actually has bona fide "separate lines of business," it is possible to apply the coverage test and the 50/40 test (as necessary) separately to employees in each line of business. This allows plans to be provided only to one line of business, or several different plans tailored to different lines of business.[8]

## Highly Compensated— Definition for Employee Benefit Purposes

An employee is a *highly compensated employee* with respect to a plan year if he—

(1) was a 5% owner (as defined for top-heavy purposes) at any time during either the current year or the preceding year, or

(2) received compensation for the preceding year in excess of $80,000 ($90,000 in 2003, as indexed) from the employer, *and* if the employer elects the application of this clause for the preceding year, was in the "top-paid group" for that year.[9]

The "top-paid group" of employees for a year is the group of employees in the top 20%, ranked on the basis of compensation paid for the year. For the purpose of determining the top-paid group, the following employees may be excluded: (1) employees with less than six months of service, (2) employees who normally work less than 17½ hours per week, (3) employees who normally work during not more than six months in any year, (4) employees under the age of 21, (5) except as provided by regulations, employees covered by a collective bargaining agreement, and (6) nonresident aliens with no U.S. earned income. At the employer's election, a shorter period of service, smaller number of hours or months, or lower age than those specified in (1) through (4) may be used.[10]

Former employees are treated as highly compensated employees if (1) they were highly compensated employees when they separated from service, or (2) they were highly compensated employees at any time after attaining age 55.[11]

The controlled group, common control, affiliated service group, and employee leasing provisions of Section 414 (see Appendix B) are to be applied before applying the highly compensated employee rules.

## NONDISCRIMINATION IN BENEFITS AND CONTRIBUTIONS

Qualified plans must be nondiscriminatory with respect to highly compensated employees either in terms of benefits or in terms of employer contributions to the plan.[12] Some nondiscriminatory formulas will, however, provide a higher benefit for highly compensated employees; for example, contributions or benefits can be based on compensation or years of service.

Detailed regulations govern the application of the nondiscrimination requirements for contributions and benefits under Code section 401(a)(4). A defined contribution plan will generally be tested under the "contributions" test,[13] although the plan accounts can be converted to benefits and tested under the "benefits" test.[14] However, ESOPs (see Chapter 10), Section 401(k) plans (see Chapter 19), and plans with after-tax employee contributions and/or employer matching contributions (see Chapter 18) may not be tested on a benefits basis.[15] Section 401(k) plans and plans with after-tax employee contributions/and or employer matching contributions must continue to meet the special nondiscrimination tests for those plans, as discussed in the chapters referenced.

Under the final regulations, a defined benefit plan will be nondiscriminatory if it meets a *general* test or a uniformity requirement and one of three "safe harbors."[16] These nondiscrimination rules for defined benefit plans compare the rate at which benefits accrue for highly compensated employees to the rate at which benefits accrue for other employees. The implications of these rules for defined benefit plans are discussed in the "Questions and Answers" in Chapter 9.

## Integration with Social Security

Qualified plan benefit or contribution formulas can be "integrated" with Social Security.[17] In an integrated plan, greater contributions or benefits generally are provided for higher paid employees whose compensation is greater than an amount based on the Social Security taxable wage base. The difference in contributions or benefits permitted under these rules is referred to as "permitted disparity."

Since most employees will receive Social Security benefits when they retire, a calculation of an employee's retirement needs must take these into account. Since Social Security benefits are effectively paid out of employer compensation costs, an employer is permitted by law to take Social Security benefits into account by integrating a qualified plan's benefit formula with Social Security benefits. However, the rules for doing so are quite complex. The details will not be discussed here, but the financial planner should be familiar with the basic integration rules which follow.

Social Security integration benefits employers from a cost point of view since it effectively reduces the cost of the qualified plan. Also, since Social Security provides a higher retirement income, relatively speaking, for lower paid employees, Social Security integration of qualified plans permits such plans to provide relatively greater benefits for highly compensated employees, which is often an employer objective.

### Defined Benefit Plans

There are two methods for integrating defined benefit formulas with Social Security: the "excess" method and the "offset" method.

Under the excess method of integration with Social Security, the plan defines a level of compensation called the integration level. The plan then provides a higher rate of benefits for compensation above the integration level. A plan's integration level is an amount of compensation specified under the plan by a dollar amount or formula. Benefits under the plan expressed as a percentage of compensation are lower for compensation below the integration level than they are for compensation above the integration level.[18]

---

*Example:* Plan A's integrated formula provides an annual benefit of 30% of final average annual compensation plus 25% of compensation above the plan's integration level. Labelle, born in 1938, is a participant in plan A. He retires in 2004. Labelle's final average compensation is $50,000. The integration level (rounded covered compensation—see below) is $45,000. Labelle's annual retirement benefit is determined as follows:

— 30% of final average compensation of $50,000, or $15,000, plus

— 25% of $5,000 ($50,000 - $45,000) or $1250.

The total benefit is $16,250 ($15,000 plus $1250).

---

The Code and regulations provide various rules specifying what maximum integration level a plan can use, and how large the percentage spread above and below the integration level can be. As a general rule, a plan's integration level cannot exceed an amount known as "covered compensation," which is specified by the IRS in a table. Covered compensation is the average of the contribution and benefit base under the Social Security Act for each year during the 35-year period ending with the year in which an employee attains Social Security retirement age.[19] Therefore, the covered compensation amount for each employee depends upon the year in which the employee retires (see Figure 25.2). Under the regulations, a plan may determine an employee's covered compensation by use of a different IRS table that is developed by rounding the actual amounts of covered compensation for different years of birth (see Figure 25.2).[20]

The Code and Treasury regulations also restrict the percentage spread between the benefit as a percentage of compensation above and below the integration level. The "base benefit percentage" is the percentage of compensation that the plan provides for compensation below the integration level, and the "excess benefit percentage" is the percentage of compensation above the integration level.

The excess benefit percentage cannot exceed the base benefit percentage by more than ¾ of one percentage point for any year of service, or participant's years of service up to 35.[21]

For example, if a defined benefit plan provides a benefit of 1% of compensation below the integration level for each year of service, then it can provide not more than 1.75% of compensation above the integration level for each year of service. Or, for a participant with 35 years of service, if the plan provides a benefit of 30% of final average compensation below the integration level, it cannot provide more than 56.25% of compensation above the integration level. (The spread of 26.25% is ¾ of one percentage point multiplied by 35 years of service.) The difference between the base and excess benefit percentages—the *maximum excess allowance*—can be no greater than the base percentage. Thus if a plan provides 10% of final average compensation below the integration level, it can provide no more than 20% of compensation above the integration level.[22]

Under the offset method of integration, the plan formula is reduced by a fixed amount or a formula amount that is designed to represent the existence of Social Security benefits.[23] There is no integration level in an offset plan. The Code and regulations provide limits on the extent of an offset for Social Security. In particular, the rules provide that no more than half of the benefit provided under the formula without the offset may be taken away by an offset. For example, if a plan formula provides 50% of final average compensation with an offset, even the lowest paid employee must receive at least 25% of final average compensation from the plan.

## Defined Contribution Plans

Defined contribution plans can be integrated only under the excess method. Generally, if the integration level is equal to the Social Security taxable wage base in effect at the beginning of the plan year ($87,000 for plan years beginning in 2003), the difference in the allocation percentages above and below the integration level can be no more than the lesser of:

(1) the percentage contribution below the integration level or

Figure 25.2

| 2003 COVERED COMPENSATION TABLE | | | | | |
|---|---|---|---|---|---|
| Calendar Year of Birth | Calendar Year of Social Security Retirement | 2003 Covered Compensation | Calendar Year of Birth | Calendar Year of Social Security Retirement | 2003 Covered Compensation |
| 1907 | 1972 | $ 4,488 | 1939 | 2005 | $46,236 |
| 1908 | 1973 | 4,704 | 1940 | 2006 | 48,492 |
| 1909 | 1974 | 5,004 | 1941 | 2007 | 50,724 |
| 1910 | 1975 | 5,316 | 1942 | 2008 | 52,908 |
| 1911 | 1976 | 5,664 | 1943 | 2009 | 55,008 |
| 1912 | 1977 | 6,060 | 1944 | 2010 | 57,096 |
| 1913 | 1978 | 6,480 | 1945 | 2011 | 59,148 |
| 1914 | 1979 | 7,044 | 1946 | 2012 | 61,152 |
| 1915 | 1980 | 7,692 | 1947 | 2013 | 63,132 |
| 1916 | 1981 | 8,460 | 1948 | 2014 | 64,968 |
| 1917 | 1982 | 9,300 | 1949 | 2015 | 66,720 |
| 1918 | 1983 | 10,236 | 1950 | 2016 | 68,352 |
| 1919 | 1984 | 11,232 | 1951 | 2017 | 69,912 |
| 1920 | 1985 | 12,276 | 1952 | 2018 | 71,376 |
| 1921 | 1986 | 13,368 | 1953 | 2019 | 72,780 |
| 1922 | 1987 | 14,520 | 1954 | 2020 | 74,136 |
| 1923 | 1988 | 15,708 | 1955 | 2022 | 76,656 |
| 1924 | 1989 | 16,968 | 1956 | 2023 | 77,856 |
| 1925 | 1990 | 18,312 | 1957 | 2024 | 78,972 |
| 1926 | 1991 | 19,728 | 1958 | 2025 | 79,992 |
| 1927 | 1992 | 21,192 | 1959 | 2026 | 80,952 |
| 1928 | 1993 | 22,716 | 1960 | 2027 | 81,852 |
| 1929 | 1994 | 24,312 | 1961 | 2028 | 82,692 |
| 1930 | 1995 | 25,920 | 1962 | 2029 | 83,448 |
| 1931 | 1996 | 27,576 | 1963 | 2030 | 84,180 |
| 1932 | 1997 | 29,304 | 1964 | 2031 | 84,876 |
| 1933 | 1998 | 31,128 | 1965 | 2032 | 85,500 |
| 1934 | 1999 | 33,060 | 1966 | 2033 | 86,028 |
| 1935 | 2000 | 35,100 | 1967 | 2034 | 86,436 |
| 1936 | 2001 | 37,212 | 1968 | 2035 | 86,748 |
| 1937 | 2002 | 39,444 | 1969 | 2036 | 86,940 |
| 1938 | 2004 | 43,968 | 1970 or later | 2037 | 87,000 |

| 2003 Rounded Covered Compensation Table | |
|---|---|
| Year of Birth | Covered Compensation |
| 1937 | $39,000 |
| 1938-1939 | 45,000 |
| 1940 | 48,000 |
| 1941 | 51,000 |
| 1942-1943 | 54,000 |
| 1944 | 57,000 |
| 1945-1946 | 60,000 |
| 1947 | 63,000 |
| 1948-1949 | 66,000 |
| 1950-1951 | 69,000 |
| 1952-1953 | 72,000 |
| 1954 | 75,000 |
| 1955-1957 | 78,000 |
| 1958-1960 | 81,000 |
| 1961-1964 | 84,000 |
| 1965 and later | 87,000 |

(2) the greater of (a) 5.7% or (b) the old age portion of the Social Security tax rate.[24]

Thus, for a plan year beginning in 2003, if an integrated plan has an integration level of $87,000 and the plan allocates employer contributions plus forfeitures at the rate of 15.7% of compensation above the integration level, then it would have to provide at least a 10% allocation for compensation below the integration level (making the difference 5.7%).

Further rules, and considerations in choosing an "optimum" integration level for a defined contribution plan, are discussed in the "Questions and Answers" in Chapter 16.

## VESTING

If a qualified plan provides for employee contributions, the portion of the benefit or account balance attributable to employee contributions must at all times be 100% vested (nonforfeitable).[25] The portion attributable to employer contributions must be vested under a specified vesting schedule that is at least as favorable as one of two alternative minimum standards[26]:

1. *5-year vesting.* A plan's vesting schedule satisfies this minimum requirement if an employee with at least five years of service is 100% vested. No vesting at all is required before five years of service.

2. *3- to 7-year vesting.* The plan must provide vesting that is at least as fast as the following schedule:

| Years of Service | Vested Percentage |
|---|---|
| 3 | 20 |
| 4 | 40 |
| 5 | 60 |
| 6 | 80 |
| 7 or more | 100 |

Employer matching contributions (i.e., contributions made by an employer on account of an employee contribution or elective deferral, or forfeiture allocated on the basis of employee contributions, matching contributions, or elective deferrals) must vest under a faster vesting schedule that is at least as favorable as one of the following two standards:[27]

1. *3-year vesting.* A plan's vesting schedule satisfies this minimum requirement if an employee with at least three years of service is 100% vested. No

vesting at all is required before three years of service.

2. *2- to 6-year vesting.* The plan must provide vesting that is at least as fast as the following schedule:

| Years of Service | Vested Percentage |
|---|---|
| 2 | 20 |
| 3 | 40 |
| 4 | 60 |
| 5 | 80 |
| 6 or more | 100 |

This faster vesting schedule is also applicable to top-heavy plans (discussed below).

## FUNDING REQUIREMENTS

Employer and employee contributions to a qualified plan must be deposited into an irrevocable trust fund or insurance contract that is for the "exclusive benefit" of plan participants and their beneficiaries.[28] The *minimum funding standard* provides a mathematical calculation of the minimum amount that must be contributed to a qualified pension plan.[29] Pension plans, both defined benefit and defined contribution, must meet these annual minimum funding standards or be subject to a penalty. Profit sharing plans are not subject to the minimum funding standards as such, but contributions must be "recurring and substantial" or the IRS can deem the plan to be terminated. Substantial and recurring is not clearly defined in the law so that there is always some risk in repeatedly omitting contributions.[30]

The minimum funding standards applicable to defined benefit plans depend on the method by which an annual cost for these plans is determined. The annual cost is based on an *actuarial cost method*.

### Actuarial Cost Methods

An actuarial cost method determines the employer's annual cost for a defined benefit plan. Actuaries use a number of different actuarial cost methods, which can be relatively complex mathematically. However, these methods are based on simple principles that should be understood by financial planners even though the computational complexities are left to the actuary. An actuarial cost method develops a series of annual deposits to the plan fund that will grow to the point where as each employee retires the fund is sufficient to fully fund the employee's retirement benefit.

There are two basic ways of spreading these costs over future working careers of employees. Under the *projected benefit* or level funding method, the total cost is divided into equal deposits for each employee's benefit spread over the period remaining until the employee's retirement. With the *accrued benefit* method the annual deposit is based on the benefit accrued each year. The accrued benefit method produces a generally rising series of deposits for a given employee, because as retirement approaches there is less time to fund each additional piece of accrued benefit. The overall plan cost does not necessarily rise, however, with the accrued benefit method, because employees may enter and leave the plan from time to time.

If a defined benefit plan provides past service benefits, the cost of these can be made part of the annual cost using a projected benefit or accrued benefit method. Alternatively, the past service benefit can be funded separately by developing what is known as an *unfunded past service liability* or a *supplemental liability*. The supplemental liability is paid off through deposits to the plan fund over a fixed period of years, up to 30, regardless of actual retirement dates for employees. The use of a supplemental liability can provide additional funding flexibility in many cases.

Projected benefit actuarial cost methods can be either individual or aggregate. With the individual methods, a separate cost is determined for each employee, with the total employer deposit being the sum of all the separate pieces. With the aggregate method, the cost is developed for the employer's payroll as a whole and is expressed as a percentage of payroll.

Because there are so many different approaches in determining the annual cost using an actuarial cost method, there is no one single annual cost applicable to a given defined benefit plan for a given group of employees. Different actuarial methods should be developed giving a variety of annual cost approaches as part of the design stage for a defined benefit plan.

## Actuarial Assumptions

Actuarial cost methods depend on making assumptions about various cost factors, since actual results

cannot be known in advance. The annual cost developed under an actuarial cost method depends significantly on these assumptions, and there is some flexibility in choosing assumptions. Under the Code, each assumption must be reasonable, within guidelines in the Code and regulations.[31] Actuarial assumptions include:

- investment return on the plan fund

- salary scale—an assumption about increases in future salaries; this is particularly significant if the plan uses a final average type of formula

- mortality—the extent to which some benefit will not be paid because of the death of employees before retirement

- annuity purchase rate—this determines the funds needed at retirement to provide annuities in the amount designated by the plan formula

- the annuity purchase rate, in turn, depends on assumptions about future investment return and post-retirement mortality

- turnover—the extent to which employees will terminate employment before retirement and thereby receive limited or no benefit.

## Deduction Limits

An employer's maximum annual deduction for contributions to a defined benefit plan is limited to the amount determined actuarially under standards set forth in Section 404(a) of the Code, or the amount required to meet the minimum funding standards, if greater.[32]

The maximum amount an employer can deduct for contributions to a defined contribution plan became subject to three favorable changes in years beginning after 2001, under EGTRRA 2001 amendments:

1. The deduction limit increased to 25% of *compensation* for profit sharing and stock bonus plans. In years beginning before 2002, profit sharing and stock bonus plans were subject to a deduction limit of 15% of compensation.[33]

2. The definition of *compensation* for purposes of the preceding paragraph includes elective deferrals to a qualified plan, 403(b) plan, 457 plan, SEP,

SIMPLE, or Section 125 FSA plan.[34] This means that the payroll upon which the 25% is based is higher than it was before 2002, resulting in a higher deduction limit for employer contributions to the plan.

3. For purposes of calculating the total amount that the employer has contributed to a plan, elective deferrals do not have to be counted.[35] The following example illustrates the effect of these changes:

---

*Example:* ABC Corporation sponsors a 401(k) plan to which ABC's employees made elective deferrals totalling $10,000 in 2001. ABC's total payroll for all employees covered under the plan in 2001 was $100,000. In 2001, ABC Corporation used a safe harbor definition of "compensation" based on Box 1 of Form W-2, meaning that the deduction limit was applied to the net income-taxable payroll of $90,000. Since the deduction limit was 15% in 2001, ABC's total deduction was limited to $13,500 (15% of $90,000). In addition to the elective deferrals of $10,000 (which count toward this limit), ABC can contribute and deduct only another $3,500 as an employer contributions.

---

In 2003, ABC's payroll still totals $100,000 and its employees still make elective deferrals totalling $10,000, but the deduction limit is 25% of compensation. Furthermore, the 25% limit is based on gross compensation ($100,000), so that ABC's deduction limit is $25,000. Finally, elective deferrals do not count toward the $25,000 limit, so ABC may contribute and deduct as much as $25,000 to its employees' accounts in addition to the $10,000 of elective deferrals.

For a combination of defined benefit and defined contribution plans, the deduction limit is the greater of (1) 25% of the compensation of all participants or (2) the amount required to meet the minimum standard for the defined benefit plan.[36]

There is a penalty of 10% on nondeductible contributions by the employer—that is, contributions in excess of these limits.[37]

## Timing of Contributions

Under the minimum funding rules, defined benefit plan contributions must be paid within 8½ months after the end of the plan year, and defined contribution pension plan contributions must be paid within 2½ months (subject to a 6-month extension) after the end of the plan year.[38] Penalties apply if the minimum funding requirements are not met. Profit sharing plans are not subject to the minimum funding rules.

If a defined benefit plan fails to meet certain funding requirements for a plan year, a quarterly payment requirement must be met in the following plan year. For a calendar year taxpayer, contributions are due April 15, July 15, October 15 and January 15 of the following year; corresponding dates apply to fiscal year taxpayers. A failure to make timely payments subjects the taxpayer to interest on the missed installment.[39]

Each quarterly payment must be 25% of the lesser of (a) 90% of the annual minimum funding amount or (b) 100% of the preceding year's minimum funding amount.[40]

## Fiduciary Rules

There are strict limits on the extent to which an employer can exercise control over the plan fund.[41] The plan trustee can be a corporation or an individual, even a company president or shareholder, but plan trustees are subject to stringent federal fiduciary rules requiring them to manage the fund solely in the interest of plan participants and beneficiaries. Loans to employees are permitted within limits (see Chapter 26), but generally the employer is penalized for borrowing from the plan.

## LIMITATIONS ON BENEFITS AND CONTRIBUTIONS

To prevent a qualified plan from being used primarily as a tax shelter for highly compensated employees, there is a limitation on plan benefits or employer contributions.

## Defined Benefit Limits

Under a defined benefit plan, the highest annual benefit payable under the plan must not exceed the lesser of:

- 100% of the participant's compensation averaged over the three years of highest compensation, or

- $160,000 (in 2003, as indexed).[42]

The $160,000 limit is adjusted in $5,000 increments under a cost-of-living indexing formula.[43]

The $160,000 limit (in 2003, as indexed) is also adjusted actuarially for retirement ages earlier than age 62 or later than age 65.

## Defined Contribution Limits

For a defined contribution plan, the "annual additions" (employer contributions, employee salary reductions, employee contributions, and plan forfeitures reallocated from other participants' accounts) to each participant's account is limited. This annual additions limit cannot exceed the lesser of:

- 100% of the participant's annual compensation, or

- $40,000[44] (in 2003, as indexed)

The $40,000 limit is subject to indexing in increments of $1,000.[45]

## Compensation Limit

A further limitation on plan benefits or contributions is that only the first $200,000 of each employee's annual compensation (in 2003, as indexed) can be taken into account in the plan's benefit or contribution formula.[46] The $200,000 limit is scheduled to be indexed for inflation in increments of $5,000.[47] Thus, for example, if an employee earns $300,000 annually in 2003, and the employer has a 10% money purchase plan, the maximum contribution for that employee would be $20,000 (10% of $200,000).

## TOP–HEAVY REQUIREMENTS

A *top-heavy* plan is one that provides more than 60% of its aggregate accrued benefits or account balances to *key employees*, as defined below. These plans must meet certain additional qualification rules.[48] SIMPLE IRA plans (see Chapter 20), as well as SIMPLE 401(k) plans that allow contributions only under Section 401(k)(11) (see Chapter 19), are exempt from the top-heavy requirements,[49] as are safe harbor 401(k) plans.[50]

If a plan is top-heavy for a given year, it must provide more rapid vesting than generally required.[51] The plan can either provide 100% vesting after three years of service, or 6-year graded vesting as follows:

| Years of Service | Vested Percentage |
|---|---|
| 2 | 20 |
| 3 | 40 |
| 4 | 60 |
| 5 | 80 |
| 6 or more | 100 |

In addition, a top-heavy plan must provide minimum benefits or contributions for non-key employees.[52]

For defined benefit plans the benefit for each non-key employee during a top-heavy year must be at least 2% of compensation multiplied by the employee's years of service, up to 20%. The average compensation used for this formula is based on the highest five years of compensation.

For a defined contribution plan, employer contributions during a top-heavy year must be at least 3% of compensation.

A *key employee* for purposes of the top-heavy rules is an employee who, at any time during the plan year is:

- an officer of the employer having annual compensation greater than $130,000 (in 2003, as indexed)

- a more-than-5% owner of the employer, or

- a more-than-1% owner of the employer having annual compensation from the employer of more than $150,000.[53]

For these purposes, no more than 50 employees (or, if lesser, the greater of three or 10% of the employees) will be treated as officers.

## FOOTNOTES

1. Nondiscrimination testing by governmental plans was virtually eliminated by TRA '97. See IRC Sections 401(a)(5), 401(a)(26), 410(c)(2), 401(k)(3) and 403(b)(12).

2. IRC Section 410(a).

3. IRC Section 410(b); Treas. Reg. §1.410(b)-2.

4. IRC Section 401(a)(26). More lenient rules apply to governmental plans. See Notice 2001-9, 2001-1 CB 375.

5. See Treas. Reg. §1.410(b)-2(b)(3).

6. Treas. Reg. §1.410(b)-4.

7.  IRC Section 410(b)(3).

8.  IRC Section 410(b)(5). The requirement that a separate line of business have at least 50 employees does not apply in determining whether a plan satisfies the 50/40 test on a separate line of business basis. IRC Section 401(a)(26)(G).

9.  IRC Section 414(q)(1).

10. IRC Section 414(q)(5).

11. IRC Section 414(q)(6).

12. IRC Section 401(a)(4).

13. Treas. Reg. §1.401(a)(4)-2.

14. Treas. Reg. §1.401(a)(4)-8; see Chapter 22.

15. Treas. Reg. §1.401(a)(4)-2(b)(3).

16. Treas. Reg. §1.401(a)(4)-3.

17. IRC Section 401(l).

18. IRC Section 401(l)(3)(A).

19. Treas. Reg. §1.401(l)-1(c)(7).

20. Treas. Reg. §1.401(l)-1(c)(7)(ii)(A).

21. IRC Section 401(l)(4)(A).

22. IRC Section 401(l)(4)(A), flush language.

23. IRC Section 401(l)(3)(B).

24. IRC Section 401(l)(2). The IRS will publish the percentage rate of the portion attributable to old age insurance when it exceeds 5.7%.

25. IRC Section 411(a)(1).

26. IRC Section 411(a)(2).

27. IRC Section 411(a)(12). Note that all provisions of EGTRRA 2001 are scheduled to sunset, or expire, after December 31, 2010.

28. IRC Section 401(a)(2).

29. IRC Section 412. For penalties for noncompliance, see IRC Section 4971.

30. See Chapter 16.

31. IRC Section 412(c)(3).

32. IRC Section 404(a)(1). There is a "full funding limitation" within the minimum funding standards that limits this deduction. See IRC Section 412(c)(7). The computation of this has been liberalized for years beginning in 2005 and thereafter.

33. See IRC Section 404(a)(3).

34. IRC Section 404(A)(12).

35. See IRC Section 404(n).

36. IRC Section 404(a)(7).

37. IRC Section 4972.

38. IRC Section 404(a)(1).

39. IRC Section 412(m).

40. IRC Section 412(m)(4).

41. ERISA, Part 4 (section 401, et seq.). The "prohibited transaction" rules are reiterated in IRC Section 4975.

42. IRC Section 415(b).

43. IRC Section 415(d)(4)(A).

44. IRC Section 415(c).

45. IRC Section 415(d)(4)(B).

46. IRC Section 401(a)(17)(A).

47. IRC Section 401(a)(17)(B).

48. IRC Section 416(a).

49. IRC Sections 416(g)(4)(G), 401(k)(11)(D)(ii).

50. IRC Section 416(g)(4)(H). This rule applies to a plan that consists solely of contributions meeting the requirements of IRC Section 401(k)(12) and safe harbor matching contributions meeting the requirements of IRC Section 401(m)(11).

51. IRC Section 416(b).

52. IRC Section 416(c).

53. IRC Section 416(i).

## Chapter 26

# QUALIFIED PLANS: DISTRIBUTIONS AND LOANS

### CONTENTS OF THIS CHAPTER

## I. PLANNING RETIREMENT DISTRIBUTIONS

Distributions from qualified pension, profit sharing, employer stock plans, and Section 403(b) tax deferred annuity plans are subject to numerous special rules and distinctive federal income tax treatment. Advance consideration of all the potential implications of plan distributions is an important part of overall plan design.

Furthermore, in advising clients who are plan participants, a clear understanding of the qualified plan rules is important. A qualified plan or Section 403(b) tax deferred annuity plan can allow employees to accumulate substantial retirement benefits. Even a middle-level employee may have an account balance of hundreds of thousands of dollars available at retirement or termination of employment. Careful planning is important in order to make the right choices of payment options and tax treatment for a plan distribution, to obtain the right result in financial planning for retirement, and also to avoid adverse tax results or even a tax disaster.

The retirement plan distribution rules are astonishingly complicated. They are a maze full of tax traps that have developed in the law over many years, with Congress and the IRS adding new twists and turns almost every year. This chapter is only a basic outline of these rules, but even this basic outline is quite complex.

One way to thread the maze and give some structure to the subject is to look at the issue from the standpoint of advice to a plan participant who is about to retire. What questions need to be asked and what decisions must be made? Typically, the process might proceed by asking and answering these questions—

1.  What kinds of distributions does the plan itself allow? The retiree's advisor should review plan documents, particularly the summary plan description (SPD), to determine what options are available. Sections II and III of this chapter discuss these issues.

2.  Should the distribution be made in a lump sum or in a periodic payout? Section V of this chapter discusses the basic tax tradeoffs. Can or should the distribution be rolled over? (Section IX.)

3.  If periodic payments are chosen, what kind of payment schedule is best?

    —Note the requirement of spousal consent for a payment option that "cuts out" the spouse. (Section II.)

    —Are the minimum distribution requirements satisfied? (Section VIII.)

—Is the payment subject to a 10% early distribution penalty? (Section VIII.)

—How will the payments be taxed? (Section IV, A and B.)

4. If a lump sum payment is chosen—

—Is it eligible for 10-year averaging? (Section IV.)

—If eligible for 10-year averaging, is the election of 10-year averaging beneficial? (Section IV.)

—How much tax is payable? (Section IV.)

5. What are the potential future estate tax consequences of the form of distribution chosen? (Sections IV G and VIII.)

## II. PLAN PROVISIONS— REQUIRED SPOUSAL BENEFITS

All qualified pension plans must provide two forms of survivorship benefits for spouses: (1) the *"qualified pre-retirement survivor annuity"* and (2) the *"qualified joint and survivor annuity."* Stock bonus plans, profit sharing plans, and ESOPs generally need not provide these survivorship benefits for the spouse if the participant's nonforfeitable account balance is payable as a death benefit to that spouse.[1]

### Qualified Pre–retirement Survivor Annuity

Once a participant in a plan requiring these spousal benefits is vested, the nonparticipant spouse acquires the right to a pre-retirement survivor annuity, payable to the spouse in the event of the participant's death before retirement. This right is an actual property right created by federal law.

In a defined benefit plan, the survivor annuity payable under this provision of law is the amount that would have been paid under a qualified joint and survivor annuity if the participant had either (1) retired on the day before his or her death (in the case of the participant dying after attaining the earliest retirement age under the plan); or (2) separated from service on the earlier of the actual time of separation or death and survived to the plan's earliest retirement age, then retired with an immediate joint and survivor annuity (in the case of the participant dying before attaining such age).[2] The calculation of joint and survivor annuity amounts is discussed below.

If the plan is a defined contribution plan, the qualified pre-retirement survivor annuity is an annuity for the life of the surviving spouse that is the actuarial equivalent of at least 50% of the participant's vested account balance, determined as of the date of death.[3]

The pre-retirement survivor annuity is an automatic benefit. If no other election is made, a pre-retirement survivor annuity is provided. If the plan permits, a participant can elect to receive some other form of retirement survivorship benefit, including no pre-retirement survivorship benefit at all, or survivorship benefits payable to a beneficiary other than the spouse. However, the spouse must understand the rights given up and must consent, in writing, to the participant's choice of another form of benefit.[4]

The right to make an election of a benefit other than the pre-retirement survivor annuity must be communicated to all vested participants who have attained age 32.[5] The participant can elect to receive some benefit other than the pre-retirement survivor annuity at any time after age 35.[6] The participant can also change this election at any time before retirement.

Consideration of "electing out" of the pre-retirement survivorship benefit becomes more important as a participant nears retirement age. Electing out of the pre-retirement survivorship benefit will generally increase the participant's benefit after retirement, unless the plan specifically subsidizes the retirement benefit. Thus, a participant may want to elect out of the benefit to increase the size of the monthly check received during the post-retirement period. Alternatively, the participant may wish to provide a pre-retirement survivorship benefit for a beneficiary other than the surviving spouse.

Such elections must be considered very carefully, particularly by the nonparticipant spouse. Generally a nonparticipant spouse would (and should) not agree to waive this benefit unless the couple's overall retirement planning provides some compensating benefit to the spouse. The existence and amount of any such compensating benefit to the spouse should be documented in connection with the spouse's benefit waiver.

The consent of the nonparticipant spouse to waiver of the pre-retirement survivorship benefit in favor of an optional benefit form selected by the participant must

(1) be in writing; (2) acknowledge the effect of the waiver; and (3) be witnessed, either by a plan representative or a notary public.[7] For this reason, full disclosure—in writing—to the nonparticipant spouse must be made, and the spouse should be advised to consult an independent legal (and possibly financial) advisor in connection with the waiver. For large benefits, this advice to the spouse is an extremely important consideration.

## Qualified Joint and Survivor Annuity

A qualified joint and survivor annuity is a post-retirement death benefit for the plan participant's spouse. If the plan is subject to these requirements, it must automatically provide, as a retirement benefit, an annuity for the life of the participant with a survivor annuity for the life of the participant's spouse. The survivor annuity must not be less than 50% nor greater than 100% of the annuity payable during the joint lives of the participant and spouse.[8] For example, if $1,000 per month is payable during the joint lives, the annuity to the surviving spouse can be any specified amount from $500 per month to $1,000 per month. The spouse's annuity must be continued even if the spouse remarries.[9]

As with the pre-retirement survivor annuity, a participant may elect to receive another form of benefit if the plan permits. However, as with a qualified pre-retirement survivor annuity, the spouse must consent in writing to the election.[10] An election to waive the joint and survivor form must be made during the 90-day period ending on the "annuity starting date"—the date on which benefit payments should have begun to the participant, not necessarily the actual date of payment.[11] The waiver can be revoked—that is, the participant can change the election during the 90-day period. Administrators of affected plans must provide participants with a notice of the election period and an explanation of the consequences of the election within a reasonable period before the annuity starting date.[12]

Since the joint and survivor annuity must be the actuarial equivalent of other forms of benefit, the participant may wish to increase the monthly pension by waiving the joint and survivor annuity and receiving a straight life annuity or some other form of benefit. Just as in the case of the pre-retirement survivorship benefit, discussed above, the nonparticipant spouse's consent to waiver of the joint and survivor annuity in favor of an optional benefit form selected by the participant must (1) be in writing; (2) acknowledge the effect of the

waiver; and (3) be witnessed, either by a plan representative or a notary public.[13] It is extremely important that spouses are made aware of what they are giving up if they consent to some other benefit form.

## III. PLAN PROVISIONS— OTHER BENEFIT OPTIONS

A qualified plan can offer a wide range of distribution options. Participants benefit from having the widest possible range of options, because this increases their flexibility in personal retirement planning. However, a wide range of options increases administrative costs. Also, the IRS makes it difficult to withdraw a benefit option once it has been established.[14] Consequently, most employers provide only a relatively limited "menu" of benefit forms for participants to choose from.

In addition, a qualified plan generally must provide for "direct rollovers" of certain distributions.[15] Failure to elect a "direct rollover" will subject the distribution to mandatory 20% withholding. Plan administrators must provide a written explanation to the distributee of his right to elect a "direct rollover" and the withholding consequences of not making the election.[16] See "Tax Treatment of Rollovers," under Section IX.

## Defined Benefit Plan Distribution Provisions

Defined benefit plans must provide a married participant with a *joint and survivor annuity* as the automatic form of benefit, as described earlier. For an unmarried participant, the plan's automatic form of benefit is usually a *life annuity*—typically monthly payments to the participant for life, with no further payments after the participant's death.

Many plans allow participants to elect to receive some other form of benefit from a list of options in the plan. However, to elect any option that eliminates the benefit for a married participant's spouse, the spouse must consent on a notarized written form to waive the spousal right to the joint and survivor annuity. As discussed earlier, this is not just a legal formality; in consenting to another form of benefit, the spouse gives up important and often sizable property rights in the participant's qualified plan benefit that are guaranteed under federal law.

Typically, plans offer, as an option to the joint or single life annuity, a *period-certain* annuity. A period-certain annuity provides payments for a specified period of time—usually 10 to 20 years—even if the participant, or the participant and spouse, both die before the end of that period. Thus, the period-certain annuity makes it certain that periodic (usually monthly) benefits will continue for the participant's heirs even if the participant and spouse die early. Because of this guarantee feature, the annual or monthly payments under a period-certain option are less than they would be under an option where payments end at death (see table below).

### MONTHLY PAYMENTS — VARIOUS ANNUITY FORMS

Assumptions: plan participant aged 65, spouse aged 62, lump sum equivalent at age 65 of $200,000

| Form of annuity | Monthly benefit |
| --- | --- |
| Life | $1,818 |
| Life — 10 years certain | 1,710 |
| Life — 20 years certain | 1,560 |
| Joint and survivor — 50% | 1,696 |
| Joint and survivor — 66⅔% | 1,626 |
| Joint and survivor — 100% | 1,504 |

As the above comparison indicates, a period-certain option should be chosen if the participant wants to make sure that his heirs are provided for in case both he and his spouse die shortly after retirement. The reduction in monthly income is relatively small, since it is based on the average life expectancy of all annuitants and assumes that the average annuitant (male or female) lives about 20 years after attaining age 65. Thus, the participant and spouse should consider a period-certain option if they are both in poor health, or if they want to make sure that children (or other heirs) with large financial needs are provided for in the event of their deaths. On the other hand, if the participant wants the largest possible monthly income from the plan, a life annuity should be chosen.

Defined benefit plans may allow a participant to choose a joint annuity with a beneficiary other than a spouse—for example, an annuity for the life of a participant with payments continuing after the parent-participant's death to a son or daughter. Proposed tax regulations limit the amount of annuity payable to a much younger beneficiary in order to ensure that the participant personally receives (and therefore is taxed on) at least a minimum portion of the total value of the plan benefit and that plan payments are not unduly deferred beyond the participant's death. (See the minimum distribution rules discussed below in Section VIII.) Thus, a much younger beneficiary (except for a spouse) generally would not be allowed to receive a 100% survivor annuity benefit.

## Defined Contribution Plan Distribution Provisions

Defined contribution plans include such plans as profit sharing, 401(k), and money purchase plans. Section 403(b) tax-deferred annuity plans also have distribution provisions similar to defined contribution plans. Some defined contribution plans provide annuity benefits like those in defined benefit plans. In fact, money purchase plans, target benefit plans and Section 403(b) tax deferred annuity plans subject to ERISA must meet the pre-retirement and joint and survivor annuity rules discussed above. Other defined contribution plans do not have to meet these rules if (1) there is no annuity option; and (2) the plan participant's account balance is payable to the participant's spouse in the event of the participant's death.[17] Avoiding the required joint and survivor provisions simplifies plan administration and therefore reduces the plan's cost.

Annuity benefits are computed by converting the participant's account balance in the defined contribution plan into an equivalent annuity. In some plans, the participant can elect to have his account balance used to purchase an annuity from an insurance company. The same considerations in choosing annuity options as have already been discussed would then apply. If the plan offers annuity options, the required joint and survivor provisions apply, as discussed earlier.

Defined contribution plans often provide a lump sum benefit at retirement or termination of employment. Defined contribution plans often also allow the option of taking out non-annuity distributions over the retirement years. That is, the participant simply takes out money as it is needed, subject to the minimum distribution requirements discussed later. Such distribution provisions provide much flexibility in planning.

## IV. TAX IMPACT

For many plan participants, retirement income adequacy is more important than minimizing taxes to the last dollar. Nevertheless, taxes on both the federal and state levels must never be ignored, since they reduce the participant's "bottom line": financial security. The greater the tax on the distribution, the less financial security the participant has.

A qualified plan distribution may be subject to federal, state, and local taxes, in whole or in part. This section will focus only on the federal tax treatment. The federal tax treatment is generally the most significant, because federal tax rates are usually higher than state and local rates. Also, many state and local income tax laws provide a full or partial exemption or specially favorable tax treatment for distributions from qualified retirement plans.

## Nontaxable and Taxable Amounts

Qualified plans often contain after-tax employee money—that is, contributions that have already been taxed. These amounts can be received by the employee free of federal income taxes, although the order in which they are recovered for tax purposes depends on the kind of distribution.

The first step in determining the tax on any distribution, then, is to determine the participant's cost basis in the plan benefit.

The participant's cost basis can include[18]:

- the total after-tax contributions made by the employee to a contributory plan;

- the total cost of life insurance protection actually reported as taxable income on federal income tax returns by the participant, if the plan distribution is received under the same contract that provides the life insurance protection (If the plan trustee cashes in the life insurance contract before distribution, this cost basis amount is not available. For a person who is now or was self-employed, the cost of life insurance protection is not includable in basis.);[19]

- any employer contributions previously taxed to the employee—for example, where a nonqualified plan later becomes qualified;

- certain employer contributions attributable to foreign services performed before 1963; and

- the amount of any plan loans included in income as a taxable distribution (see VI, below).

*In-service (Partial) Distributions.* If a participant takes out a partial plan distribution before termination of employment (as is provided for in many savings or thrift plans), the distribution is deemed to include both nontaxable and taxable amounts; the nontaxable amount will be in proportion to the ratio of total after-tax contributions (i.e., the employee's cost basis) to the plan account balance (similar to the computation of the annu-

ity exclusion ratio discussed below).[20] Expressed as a formula it looks like this:

$$\text{nontaxable amount} = \text{distribution} \ \times \ \frac{\text{employee's cost basis}}{\text{total account balance}}$$

However, there is a "grandfather" rule for pre-1987 after-tax contributions to the plan. If certain previously existing plans include contributions made before 1987, it is possible to withdraw after-tax money first. That is, if a distribution from the plan is made (at any time, even after 1987) that is *less* than the total amount of pre-1987 after-tax contributions, the entire distribution is received tax free. Once a participant's pre-1987 amount (if any) has been used up, the regular rule applies.[21]

A taxable in-service distribution may also be subject to the early distribution penalty, discussed later. In addition, in-service distributions generally will be subject to mandatory withholding at 20%, unless the distribution is transferred to an eligible retirement plan by means of a "direct rollover" (see "Retirement Plan Rollovers," below).[22]

*Total Distributions.* If the participant begins annuity payments based on the entire account balance, the nontaxable amount will be proportionate to the ratio of total after-tax contributions (i.e., the employee's cost basis) in the plan to the total annuity payments expected to be received (see below). If the participant withdraws his or her entire account balance, the distribution may be eligible for the lump sum distribution treatment discussed below. Total distributions may also be subject to the early distribution penalty, discussed below. In addition, certain distributions may be subject to mandatory withholding at 20%, unless such distributions are rolled over by means of a "direct rollover" (see "Retirement Plan Rollovers," below).

## Taxation of Annuity Payments

An employee who has no cost basis (described above) for his interest in the plan must include as ordinary income the full amount of each annuity payment (i.e., periodic plan distributions made over more than one taxable year of the employee in a systematic liquidation of the participant's benefit).

If the employee has a cost basis, one of two tables is used to determine the excludable portion of each monthly payment.[23] If the annuity is payable over one life, the table set forth following the paragraph below is used.

| Age on annuity starting date | Number of anticipated payments |
|---|---|
| Not more than 55 | 360 |
| More than 55-60 | 310 |
| More than 60-65 | 260 |
| More than 65-70 | 210 |
| More than 70 | 160 |

If the annuity is payable over two or more lives, the excludable portion of each monthly payment is determined by dividing the employee's investment in the contract by the number of anticipated payments, based on the combined ages of the recipients, as follows:

| Combined age of annuitants | Number of payments |
|---|---|
| Not more than 110 | 410 |
| More than 110 but not more than 120 | 360 |
| More than 120 but not more than 130 | 310 |
| More than 130 but not more than 140 | 260 |
| More than 140 | 210 |

These tables do not apply if the annuitant is age 75 or over, unless there are fewer than five years of guaranteed payments under the annuity.[24] If a lump sum is paid to the taxpayer in connection with the commencement of the annuity payments, it will be taxable as an amount not received as an annuity under Section 72(e), and treated as received before the annuity starting date. Such a taxpayer's investment in the contract will be determined as if the lump sum payment has been received.[25]

After the cost basis is fully recovered, payments received subsequently are taxable in full.[26] If the participant dies before the cost basis is fully recovered, an income tax deduction for the unrecovered basis is allowed on the participant's final income tax return.[27]

If the annuity starting date was before November 19, 1996, different rules were applicable.[28]

## Lump Sum Distributions

A lump sum distribution may be desirable for retirement planning purposes, but the participant may not want a lump sum if it is taxed in a high tax bracket. However, certain lump sum distributions from qualified plans (distributions from IRAs, SEPs, or Section 403(b) tax deferred annuity plans are not technically "lump sum distributions") may be eligible for a special, favorable tax calculation.

Lump sum distributions may be subject to the early distribution penalty (see Section VIII). In addition, lump sum distributions generally will be subject to mandatory withholding at 20%.[29]

## "Grandfather" Rules

The tax break for lump sum distributions was "10-year averaging" from 1974 through 1986. For an individual who attained age 50 before January 1, 1986, the 10-year averaging provision is "grandfathered." Such an individual may elect to use 10-year averaging using the 1986 tax rates (taking into account the prior law zero bracket amount).[30]

A further grandfather rule retained the capital gain rate of 20% for the capital gain portion of distributions (the portion attributable to pre-1974 accumulations, if any) to participants who attained age 50 before January 1, 1986 and elected capital gain treatment. However, under the lower capital gain rates that were restored in 1997 and the additional long-term capital gain rate reductions by JGTRRA 2003, such treatment is no longer beneficial.

## When to Elect 10–year Averaging

*Ten-year Averaging.* A plan participant is eligible to elect the 10-year averaging provision if he or she attained age 50 before January 1, 1986 (i.e., was born before January 1, 1936).

It should also be noted that for a participant who attained age 50 before January 1, 1986, not only the 10-year averaging calculation, but also the other favorable lump sum rules of earlier law were grandfathered. Thus, 10-year averaging could be elected for a distribution on separation from service prior to age 59½, if the participant attained age 50 before January 1, 1986.

## Taxation of Death Benefits

In general, the same income tax treatment applies to death benefits paid to beneficiaries as to lifetime benefits payable to participants. The special lump sum provision can be used by the beneficiary. If the employee had attained age 50 before January 1, 1986, the beneficiary may elect 10-year averaging, even if the participant was not 59½ or older at his or her death.[31] For an annuity distribution, the beneficiary uses the same annuity rules described earlier.

There are also some additional income tax benefits available.

ayable under a life insurance
...ied plan, the pure insurance
...it is excludable from income
...nce amount is the difference
...amount and its cash value at

...ployee, aged 64, dies in
...t. Her beneficiary receives
...nefit of $100,000 from the
...s the proceeds of a cash
...ntract; the contract's cash
...h was $60,000. Ellen re-
...00 of Table 2001 insurance
...on her income tax returns
...he taxable amount of the
...n to the beneficiary is
...wing items:

...nce amount of $40,000
...n value of $60,000),

...of $10,000.

...t of this benefit is there-

...nerally used in determining
...e protection after 2000.[33] For
...es were used to calculate the
...lowever, the IRS revoked this
...ts P.S. 58 rates as the proper
...protection generally for tax
...ber 31, 2002.

...the treatment of death ben-
...n IRA. A spouse can roll over
the death benefit received from a participant to the
spouse's IRA, or, after 2002, to another eligible retirement plan.[35] However, a nonspouse beneficiary is not
allowed to roll over the benefit (see below regarding the
treatment of amounts received under a QDRO).

## Federal Estate Tax

The entire value of a qualified plan death benefit is
subject to inclusion in the decedent's gross estate for
federal estate tax purposes. However, only high-income
plan participants will actually be subject to estate tax.
First, there is a substantial minimum tax credit applicable to the estate tax. This essentially eliminates estate
taxes for gross estates of less than $1,000,000 for 2002

and 2003; $1,500,000 for 2004 and 2005; $2,000,000 for
2006, 2007, and 2008; and $3,500,000 for 2009. In 2010, the
estate tax is repealed for a year. Finally, in 2011, the
exemption equivalent of the unified credit reverts to
$1,000,000 (as it was scheduled to increase before the
law change).[36] In addition, the unlimited marital deduction for federal estate tax purposes defers federal estate
tax on property transferred at death to a spouse in a
qualifying manner until the death of the second spouse.[37]

In some cases, however, avoiding federal estate tax
can be significant. For example, the estate may be relatively large and the participant may be single, or, for
whatever reason, unwilling to pay the death benefit to
the spouse. Therefore, the marital deduction would not
be available. Also, even when the death benefit is payable to a spouse, federal estate tax is merely delayed and
is not really avoided; a spouse is often about the same
age as the decedent, and thus within a few years much
of the property transferred to the spouse is potentially
subject to federal estate tax at the surviving spouse's
death.

Some authorities believe it is possible to design a
qualified plan so that death benefits can be excluded
from the participant's estate. Here is the rationale: the
federal estate tax law provides that all of a decedent's
property is includable in the estate unless there is a
specific exclusionary provision. Qualified plan death
benefits are not subject to any specific exclusion, so they
are generally includable. There is, however, a specific
provision in the estate tax law for life insurance—Section 2042. Life insurance proceeds are includable in a
decedent's estate only if the decedent had "incidents of
ownership" (some valuable property right) in the insurance policies (or if proceeds are payable to the decedent's
estate).

An incident of ownership includes the right to designate the beneficiary, as well as similar rights under the
policy. Some planners have attempted to design qualified plan death benefits using life insurance policies in
which the decedent has no incidents of ownership.
Some methods for doing this include the use of separate
trusts or subtrusts under the plan for holding insurance
policies, together with irrevocable beneficiary designations.

At this point, the law is not entirely clear on whether
these provisions will, in fact, avoid incidents of ownership. A conservative view is that they will not. However,
if the amount is large enough so that the participant is
willing to incur the costs of drafting the subtrust ar-

rangement and the potential court costs if the arrangement is challenged by the IRS, there may be little to lose in the use of this technique, since estate inclusion is certain without it.

## V. LUMP SUM VS. DEFERRED PAYMENTS— THE TRADEOFFS

Often plan participants have a choice between a single lump sum plan distribution and a series of deferred payments. This requires a choice between competing advantages.

Advantages of a lump sum distribution include:

- 10-year averaging for eligible distributions to an individual born before 1936; and

- freedom to invest plan proceeds at the participant's—not the plan administrator's—discretion.

The contrasting advantages of a deferred payout are:

- deferral of taxes until money is actually distributed;

- continued tax shelter of income on the plan account while money remains in the plan; and

- security of retirement income.

There is not one single favored alternative, but rather competing advantages. In a given situation, a lump sum distribution may save more taxes or provide a higher potential for investment returns, and in others, the deferred payment may be a better tax choice. And taxes are not the only factor to consider.

A full analysis for an individual may be complex, considering all the factors involved. A complete analysis should certainly be done where very large sums are involved. In other cases, it may be adequate to make a good estimate of the result.

The factors involved in determining which alternative to choose include:

- the age of the participant (or the participant and beneficiary, if a survivorship annuity is involved); this affects the expected number of years of payout;

- the health of the participant (and beneficiary), which also affects the expected number of payout years;

- the expected return on investment;

- the current and future expected tax rates for the participant; this involves estimating not only what the rates will be, but also what tax bracket the participant will be in (i.e., the amount of total taxable income the participant will have);

- the nontax aspects—the amounts of income needed, and when it will be needed; and

- the total amount of the benefit; if the amount is large, the relative benefit of averaging is reduced, since most of the distribution is taxed in higher brackets, even under the averaging calculation.

In a sense, it is impossible to make an exact determination of this issue. For example, the planner cannot predict what future tax rates will be or the amount of investment earnings that would actually be received in the future. However, by making reasonable assumptions in a given case, some conclusions can usually be drawn.

## VI. LOANS

Because of the 10% penalty tax on "early" distributions from qualified plans (see below), a plan provision allowing loans to employees may be attractive. This allows employees access to plan funds without extra tax cost. However, a loan provision increases administrative costs for the plan and may deplete plan funds available for pooled investments.

For participants to borrow from a plan, the plan must specifically permit such loans. Any type of qualified plan (or Section 403(b) tax deferred annuity plan) may permit loans. Loan provisions are most common in defined contribution plans, particularly profit sharing plans. There are considerable administrative difficulties connected with loans from defined benefit plans because of the actuarial approach to plan funding. Loans from IRAs and SEPs are not permitted.

Loans to participants are generally prohibited transactions, subject to penalties unless such loans (1) are exempted from the prohibited transaction rules by an administrative exemption; or (2) meet the requirements set out in Code section 4975(d)(1). The requirements of that section are met if:

(1) loans made by the plan are available to all participants and beneficiaries on a reasonably equivalent basis;

(2) loans are not made available to highly compensated employees in an amount greater than the amounts made available to other employees;

(3) loans are made in accordance with specific provisions regarding such loans set forth in the plan;

(4) the loans bear reasonable rates of interest; and

(5) the loans are adequately secured.[38]

For years beginning after 2001, plan loans may be made from a qualified plan to a sole proprietor, a more-than-10% partner in an unincorporated business, and an S corporation employee who is a more-than-5% shareholder in the corporation.[39] For years prior to 2002, such loans were prohibited transactions, subject to penalties.[40]

A loan from a qualified plan (or a Section 403(b) tax deferred annuity) will be treated as a taxable distribution if it does not meet the requirements of Code section 72(p). Section 72(p) provides that aggregate loans from qualified plans to any individual plan participant cannot exceed the *lesser* of:

- $50,000, reduced by the excess of the highest outstanding loan balance during the preceding one-year period over the outstanding balance on the date when the loan is made; or

- one-half the present value of the participant's vested account balance (or accrued benefit, in the case of a defined benefit plan).

A loan of up to $10,000 can be made, even if this is more than one-half of the participant's vested benefit.[41] For example, a participant having a vested account balance of $17,000 could borrow up to $10,000.

Loans must be repayable, by their terms, within five years, except for loans used to acquire a principal residence of the participant.

Interest on a plan loan, in most cases, will be consumer interest, which is generally not deductible by the employee, unless the loan is secured by a home mortgage. Interest deductions are specifically prohibited in two situations: (1) if the loan is to a key employee, as defined in the Code's rules for top-heavy plans (Section 416); or (2) if the loan is secured by a Section 401(k) or Section 403(b) tax deferred annuity plan account based on salary reductions.[42]

## VII. QUALIFIED DOMESTIC RELATIONS ORDERS (QDROs)

In general, a qualified plan benefit cannot be assigned or "alienated" by a participant, voluntarily or involuntarily.[43] The idea behind this rule is to protect the participant's retirement fund from attachment by creditors. However, after a series of conflicting state court cases, an exception to this rule was added for the claims of spouses and dependents in domestic relations situations.

This exception permits an assignment of a qualified plan benefit under a *qualified domestic relations order* (QDRO), as defined in Code section 414(p). A QDRO is a decree, order, or property settlement under state law relating to child support, alimony, or marital property rights, which assigns part or all of a participant's plan benefits to a spouse, former spouse, child, or other dependent of the participant. Consequently, a participant's plan benefits are now generally part of the negotiable assets in domestic disputes. The pension law does not indicate how such benefits are to be divided; this is still a matter of state domestic relations law and the negotiation between the parties. The QDRO provisions of the Code simply provide a means by which state court domestic relations orders can be enforced against plan trustees.

To protect plan administrators and trustees from conflicting claims, a QDRO cannot assign a benefit that the plan does not provide. Also, a QDRO cannot assign a benefit that is already assigned under a previous order.[44]

If, under the plan, a participant has no right to an immediate cash payment from the plan, a QDRO cannot require the trustees to make such a cash payment. If an immediate cash settlement is desired, the parties will generally agree to allow the participant to keep the entire plan benefit and pay compensating cash to the nonparticipant spouse. (Such compensating cash payments are not, however, treated as qualified plan distributions to the nonparticipant spouse.) If compensating cash payments are not possible, QDROs have been used to segregate plan assets into a subtrust for the benefit of the spouse making the claim, with cash distributions made at the earliest time that the plan provisions would permit distributions to the participant.

An alternate payee who is the spouse or former spouse of the participant and who receives a distribution by reason of a QDRO may roll over the distribution in the same manner as if he or she were the participant.

## VIII. PENALTY TAXES

In addition to the complicated regular tax rules, distributions must be planned so that recipients avoid— or at least are not surprised by— tax penalties for withdrawals made too early or too late. These are summarized as follows.

### Early Distribution Penalty

This is, in effect, a penalty for making distributions "too soon." Early distributions from qualified plans, Section 403(b) tax deferred annuity plans, IRAs, and SEPs are subject to a penalty of 10% of the taxable portion of the distribution.[45] In the case of SIMPLE IRAs, the penalty is increased to 25% during the first two years of participation.

The penalty does *not* apply to distributions:

- made on or after attainment of age 59½.

- made to the plan participant's beneficiary or estate on or after the participant's death.

- attributable to the participant's disability.

- that are part of a series of substantially equal periodic payments made at least annually over the life or life expectancy of the participant, or the participant and a designated beneficiary (separation from the employer's service is required, except for IRAs).

- made upon separation from service after attainment of age 55 (not applicable to IRAs).

- made to a former spouse, child, or other dependent of the participant under a qualified domestic relations order (not applicable to IRAs).

- to the extent of medical expenses deductible for the year under Code section 213, whether or not actually deducted.

- to pay health insurance costs while unemployed (IRAs only).

- for higher education costs (tuition, fees, books, supplies, and equipment) for the taxpayer, spouse, child, or grandchild (IRAs only).

- to pay acquisition costs of a first home of the participant, spouse, child, grandchild, or ancestor of the participant or spouse, up to a $10,000 lifetime maximum (IRAs only).

In the case of the periodic payment exception, if the series of payments is changed before the participant reaches age 59½ or, if after age 59½, within five years of the date of the first payment, the tax is generally recaptured. In other words, the penalty that would have been imposed, but for the perio dic exception, is imposed, with interest, in the year the change occurs.[46] Detailed guidance on the calculation of such payments and an exception for a "one time election" to lower the payments were set forth in IRS guidance in 2002.[47]

### Minimum Distribution Requirements and Penalty

Minimum distributions from qualified plans, Section 403(b) tax deferred annuity plans, IRAs, SEPs, SIMPLE IRAs and Section 457 governmental deferred compensation plans must begin not later than April 1 of the calendar year following the later of: (1) the calendar year in which the employee attains age 70½; or (2) the employee retires.[48] The second (retirement year) alternative is not available for a more-than-5% owner of the business sponsoring the qualified plan,[49] or for an IRA owner.

If the annual distribution is less than the minimum amount required, there is a penalty of 50% of the amount not distributed that should have been.[50] But a participant can always take out more than the required minimum. The required minimum distribution rules are designed to determine the rate at which income taxes must be paid on the retirement accumulation; the minimum distribution amounts do not have to be spent by the participant, but can be reinvested in a nonqualified investment medium.

The rules for determining and paying required minimum distributions were greatly simplified by regulations finalized in April, 2002.[51] Under these provisions, the required minimum distribution each year is generally determined by dividing the account balance (determined as of the last valuation date in the preceding year) by the appropriate number in the lifetime required minimum distribution table set forth in the final regulations (see Figure 26.1).[52]

---

*Example*: Kermudgen reaches age 73 in 2003. His qualified account balance as of the end of 2002 was $400,000. Kermudgen's required distribution for 2002 is $16,194.28, ($400,000 divided by 24.7, the lifetime distribution factor for a 73-year old).

---

The lifetime minimum distribution factors in Figure 26.1 are generally used regardless of who is named as beneficiary, but note the following:

- A more favorable minimum distribution (lower required annual amount) is available for a participant whose beneficiary is a spouse more than 10 years younger than the participant. In this case, a minimum distribution can be determined using the actual joint life expectancy of the participant and the spouse.[53]

- At the participant's death, the minimum distribution to the participant's designated beneficiary is generally based on the beneficiary's remaining life expectancy. Under the current minimum distribution rules, there is likely to be a amounts remaining at the owner's death, so the minimum distribution rules for survivors are significant in retirement and estate planning. This is discussed further in Appendix J of this book.

- The designated beneficiary for purposes of after-death distributions is determined as of September 30 of the year following the year of the participant's death.

## IX. RETIREMENT PLAN ROLLOVERS

Tax-free "rollovers" of distributions to and from qualified plans, Section 403(b) tax deferred annuity plans, traditional IRAs, SEPs, and eligible Section

**Figure 26.1**

| UNIFORM LIFETIME TABLE | | | | | |
|---|---|---|---|---|---|
| Age of Employee | Distribution Period | Age of Employee | Distribution Period | Age of Employee | Distribution Period |
| 70 | 27.4 | 86 | 14.1 | 101 | 5.9 |
| 71 | 26.5 | 87 | 13.4 | 102 | 5.5 |
| 72 | 25.6 | 88 | 12.7 | 103 | 5.2 |
| 73 | 24.7 | 89 | 12.0 | 104 | 4.9 |
| 74 | 23.8 | 90 | 11.4 | 105 | 4.5 |
| 75 | 22.9 | 91 | 10.8 | 106 | 4.2 |
| 76 | 22.0 | 92 | 10.2 | 107 | 3.9 |
| 77 | 21.2 | 93 | 9.6 | 108 | 3.7 |
| 78 | 20.3 | 94 | 9.1 | 109 | 3.4 |
| 79 | 19.5 | 95 | 8.6 | 110 | 3.1 |
| 80 | 18.7 | 96 | 8.1 | 111 | 2.9 |
| 81 | 17.9 | 97 | 7.6 | 112 | 2.6 |
| 82 | 17.1 | 98 | 7.1 | 113 | 2.4 |
| 83 | 16.3 | 99 | 6.7 | 114 | 2.1 |
| 84 | 15.5 | 100 | 6.3 | 115 | 1.9 |
| 85 | 14.8 | | | | |

457 governmental plans are specifically allowed by the Internal Revenue Code.[54] Thus, rollovers between different types of plans are permitted—for example, from a qualified plan to a Section 403(b) tax deferred annuity. A rollover of a distribution from a SIMPLE IRA during the first two years of participation may be made only to another SIMPLE IRA, except in the case of distributions to which the premature distribution penalty does not apply (see above).[55] The most commonly-used form of rollover is a rollover to an IRA from an employer plan at the employee's termination of employment.

If a rollover is made within 60 days of receipt of the distribution and follows statutory rules, the tax on the distribution is deferred; in other words, the receipt is not a taxable event to the participant. However, "eligible rollover distributions" from qualified plans, Section 403(b) tax deferred annuity plans, and eligible Section 457 governmental plans are subject to mandatory withholding at 20%, unless the rollover is effected by means of a "direct rollover" (see "Tax Treatment of Rollovers," below.)

## When Are Rollovers Used?

1. When a retirement plan participant receives a plan distribution and wants to defer taxes (and avoid any early distribution penalties) on part or all of the distribution.

2. When a qualified retirement plan, Section 403(b) tax deferred annuity plan or eligible Section 457 governmental plan is terminated by the employer, and an individual participant will receive a large termination distribution from the plan, has no current need for the income, and wishes to defer taxes on it.

3. When a participant in a qualified plan, Section 403(b) tax deferred annuity plan, eligible Section 457 governmental plan, or IRA would like to continue to defer taxes on the money in the plan, but wants to change the form of the investment or gain greater control over it.

## Tax Treatment of Rollovers

1. Any distribution from an "eligible retirement plan"—that is, a qualified plan, Section 403(b) tax deferred annuity plan, eligible Section 457 governmental plan, SEP, or IRA is eligible for rollover, except the following:

- a required minimum distribution (generally beginning at age 70½),

- a distribution that is one of a series of substantially equal periodic payments payable (a) for a period of ten years or more, or (b) for the life or life expectancy of the employee or the employee and a designated beneficiary, or

- a "hardship" distribution.[56]

2. Eligible rollover distributions received from an eligible retirement plan must be either transferred to another eligible retirement plan by means of a "direct rollover," pursuant to the employee's election, or transferred by the participant to the other plan not later than the 60th day after the distribution from the plan. A "direct rollover" is defined as an eligible rollover distribution that is paid directly to another eligible retirement plan for the benefit of the distributee. It can be accomplished by any reasonable means of direct payment, including the use of a wire transfer or a check that is negotiable only by the trustee of the new plan or rollover IRA.[57] If the "direct rollover" method is not chosen in the case of a distribution from a qualified plan, Section 403(b) plan, or eligible Section 457 governmental plan, the distribution is subject to mandatory withholding at 20%.[58]

Failure to roll over the distribution within 60 days subjects it to income taxes (although the employee may be eligible to elect 10-year averaging to cushion the blow, if the distribution qualifies for special averaging). The Secretary of the Treasury has the authority to waive the 60-day rule where it would be against equity or good conscience to enforce it, including cases of disaster, casualty, or other events beyond the participant's control.[59]

3. Distributions *from* a rollover IRA are not eligible for 10-year averaging tax treatment.

4. Distributions from a rollover IRA are subject to the same rules and limitations as all traditional IRA distributions, discussed in Chapter 24. To summarize, distributions must: (a) begin no later than April 1 of the year after the participant attains age 70½, and (b) be made in minimum amounts, based on a life or joint life payout. Distributions are taxable as ordinary income, without 10-year averaging. Distributions prior to age 59½ are also subject to the 10% early withdrawal penalty, subject to the exceptions discussed earlier in this chapter.

5.  Loans from a rollover IRA, like loans from any other IRA, are not permitted.

6.  If a participant dies before withdrawing all of the rollover IRA account, the death benefit is includable in the deceased participant's estate for federal estate tax purposes. If payable to the participant's surviving spouse in a qualifying manner, the marital deduction will defer estate taxes.

7.  If the participant wishes to preserve any available capital gains and special averaging treatment for a qualified plan distribution, a "conduit IRA" must still be used to hold qualified plan funds for transfer from one qualified plan to another when an employee changes employers. The initial transfer from the qualified plan to the IRA is tax-free if the amount is transferred within 60 days. (Although the distribution will be subject to 20% mandatory withholding unless transferred by means of a "direct rollover"—see (2) above.) If the IRA contains no assets other than those attributable to the distribution from the qualified plan, then the amount in the IRA may subsequently be transferred, tax free, to another qualified plan, if that plan allows such transfers and the special tax treatment is preserved. Thus, an existing IRA should not be used for conduit rollovers; a new IRA should be established.[60]

## Alternatives to Rollovers

In cases where a rollover IRA is an alternative to leaving the money in the existing qualified plan, it may be better—or no worse—to leave the money in the plan if the participant is satisfied with the qualified plan's investment performance and the payout options available under that plan meet the participant's needs.

Results similar to a rollover IRA can be achieved if the qualified plan distributes an annuity contract to a participant in lieu of a cash distribution. The annuity contract does not have to meet the requirements of an IRA, but the tax implications and distribution restrictions are generally similar.

## WHERE CAN I FIND OUT MORE ABOUT RETIREMENT PLAN DISTRIBUTIONS?

1.  *Tax Facts 1*, National Underwriter Co., Cincinnati, OH; revised annually.

2.  IRS Publications 575, *Pension and Annuity Income*, and 590, *Individual Retirement Arrangements*, available from local IRS offices.

## FOOTNOTES

1.  IRC Section 401(a)(11).
2.  IRC Section 417(c)(1).
3.  IRC Section 417(c)(2).
4.  IRC Section 417(a).
5.  IRC Section 417(a)(3)(B).
6.  IRC Section 417(a)(6)(B).
7.  IRC Section 417(a)(2)(A).
8.  IRC Section 417(b).
9.  Treas. Reg. §1.401(a)-11(b)(2). See also Treas. Reg. §1.401(a)-11(g).
10. IRC Section 417(a)(2).
11. IRC Section 417(a)(6)(A).
12. IRC Section 417(a)(3)(A).
13. IRC Section 417(a)(2)(A).
14. IRC Section 411(d)(6)(B)(ii); Treas. Reg. §1.411(d)(4), Q&A 1, Q&A 2. This "anti-cutback" rule was eased somewhat for plan years beginning after 2001. IRC Section 411(d)(6). However, all provisions of EGTRRA 2001 are scheduled to sunset, or expire, after December 31, 2010.
15. IRC Section 401(a)(31).
16. IRC Section 402(f). The notice must include an explanation of the tax consequences and any restrictions on distributions from the eligible plan receiving the distribution that are different from those applicable to the distributing plan. IRC Section 402(f)(1)(E).
17. IRC Section 401(a)(11)(B)(iii).
18. IRC Section 72(f); Regs. §§1.72-8, 1.72-16(b)(4), 1.402(a)-1(a)(6), 1.403(a)-2; Rev. Rul. 72-149, 1972-1 CB 218.
19. The IRS has stated that it will accept "Table 2001" rates generally for determining the value of life insurance protection after 2001. See Notice 2002-8, 2002-4 IRB 398. For details, see Chapter 13. Table 2001 rates replaced P.S. 58 rates as the proper measure of life insurance protection.
20. IRC Section 72(e)(8).
21. IRC Section 72(e)(8)(D).
22. IRC Section 3405(c)(1).
23. IRC Section 72(d)(1). This provision is effective for annuity starting dates (i.e., the first date for which an amount is payable) after 1997.
24. IRC Section 72(d)(1)(E). It would appear that for an annuitant who is 75 or older and whose contract provides for 5 or more years of guaranteed payments, the rules for annuities with a starting date after July 1, 1986 and before November 19, 1996 would be applied.
25. IRC Section 72(d)(1)(D).
26. IRC Section 72(b)(2).
27. IRC Section 72(b)(3).
28. See IRC Sections 402(a), 72, 403(a); Treas. Reg. §1.72-4(a).
29. IRC Sections 3405(b), 3405(c).

30. Tax Reform Act of 1986, Section 1122(h).

31. Tax Reform Act of 1986, Section 1122(h)(5).

32. Treas. Reg. §1.72-16(c)(4).

33. Notice 2002-8, 2002-4 IRB 398.

34. Rev. Rul. 55-747, 1955-2 CB 228.

35. IRC Section 402(c)(9). For distributions received before 2002, spousal rollovers could be made only to IRAs.

36. IRC Section 2010(c).

37. IRC Sections 2001(c), 2010(a), 2505(a), 6018(a).

38. IRC Section 4975(d)(1). Loans from Section 403(b) tax deferred annuity plans are subject to the prohibited transactions rules and penalties if the plan is subject to ERISA. ERISA Sections 408(b), 502(i); Labor Reg. §2550.408b-1.

39. IRC Section 4975(f)(6)(iii). A similar provision was added to ERISA.

40. IRC Section 4975(f)(6), prior to amendment by EGTRRA 2001.

41. IRC Section 72(p)(2). However, additional security may be required in order to insure that such a loan meets the "adequate security" requirement. See Labor Reg. §2550.408b-1(f)(2).

42. IRC Section 72(p)(3).

43. IRC Section 401(a)(13).

44. IRC Section 414(p)(3).

45. IRC Section 72(t).

46. IRC Section 72(t)(4).

47. Rev. Rul. 2002-62, 2002-42 IRB 710, modifying Notice 89-25, 1989-1 CB 662, A-12.

48. A minimum distribution is required for the year in which the participant attains age 70½ or retires, even if the actual distribution is deferred until April 1 of the following year. However, all other minimum distributions must be made during the year to which they apply. So, for example, an individual who attains age 70½ in 2002 and defers the initial minimum distribution to April 1, 2003 must receive two minimum distributions during 2003: the deferred 2002 distribution, and the 2003 distribution.

49. As defined in the top-heavy rules; see IRC Sections 401(a)(9), 403(b)(10), 408(a)(6), 408(b)(3), and 457(d)(2).

50. IRC Section 4974.

51. See TD 8987, 67 Fed. Reg. 18988 (4-17-02).

52. See Treas. Reg. §1.401(a)(9)-9, A-2. The rules described here are effective for distributions for calendar years beginning after 2002. Treas. Reg. §1.401(a)(9)-1, A-2. Distributions for 2002 could be made under the 2001 proposed regulations, the 2002 final regulations or earlier 1987 proposed regulations. The 1987 proposed regulations, in effect for years before 2001, were considerably more complicated.

53. See Treas. Reg. §1.401(a)(9)-5, A-4. This joint life expectancy is determined from the Joint and Last Survivor Life Expectancy Table set forth in the final regulations at Treas. Reg. §1.401(a)(9)-9, A-3.

54. IRC Section 402(c)(8)(B).

55. IRC Section 408(d)(3)(G)

56. IRC Section 402(c)(4)(C). Prior to 2002 only hardship distributions from Section 401(k) plans and Section 403(b) plans were prohibited from receiving rollover treatment. EGTRRA 2001 broadened this limitation to include hardship distributions from any eligible retirement plan.

57. Treas. Reg. §1.401(a)(31)-1, A-3.

58. IRC Section 3405(c)(1).

59. IRC Sections 402(c)(3), 408(d)(3)(I). Prior to amendments by EGTRRA 2001, there was no legislative basis for waiving the 60-day rule for pre-2002 distributions, even where the delays were the result of erroneous advice or the inaction of third parties.

60. IRC Section 408(d)(3).

☐ VOID   ☐ CORRECTED

| PAYER'S name, street address, city, state, and ZIP code | **1** Gross distribution<br><br>$ | OMB No. 1545-0119<br><br>20**03**<br><br>Form **1099-R** | **Distributions From Pensions, Annuities, Retirement or Profit-Sharing Plans, IRAs, Insurance Contracts, etc.** |
|---|---|---|---|
| | **2a** Taxable amount<br><br>$ | | |
| | **2b** Taxable amount not determined ☐ | Total distribution ☐ | **Copy A**<br>**For**<br>**Internal Revenue Service Center** |
| PAYER'S Federal identification number | RECIPIENT'S identification number | **3** Capital gain (included in box 2a)<br><br>$ | **4** Federal income tax withheld<br><br>$ | **File with Form 1096.** |
| RECIPIENT'S name | **5** Employee contributions or insurance premiums<br><br>$ | **6** Net unrealized appreciation in employer's securities<br><br>$ | For Privacy Act and Paperwork Reduction Act Notice, see the **2003 General Instructions for Forms 1099, 1098, 5498, and W-2G.** |
| Street address (including apt. no.) | **7** Distribution code(s) | IRA/ SEP/ SIMPLE ☐ | **8** Other<br>$          % | |
| City, state, and ZIP code | **9a** Your percentage of total distribution        % | **9b** Total employee contributions<br>$ | |
| Account number (optional) | **10** State tax withheld<br>$<br>$ | **11** State/Payer's state no. | **12** State distribution<br>$<br>$ |
| | **13** Local tax withheld<br>$<br>$ | **14** Name of locality<br>$ | **15** Local distribution<br>$<br>$ |

Form **1099-R**                    Cat. No. 14436Q          Department of the Treasury - Internal Revenue Service

**Do Not Cut or Separate Forms on This Page — Do Not Cut or Separate Forms on This Page**

☐ VOID   ☐ CORRECTED

| PAYER'S name, street address, city, state, and ZIP code | **1** Gross distribution<br><br>$ | OMB No. 1545-0119<br><br>20**03**<br><br>Form **1099-R** | **Distributions From Pensions, Annuities, Retirement or Profit-Sharing Plans, IRAs, Insurance Contracts, etc.** |
|---|---|---|---|
| | **2a** Taxable amount<br><br>$ | | |
| | **2b** Taxable amount not determined ☐ | Total distribution ☐ | **Copy 1**<br>**For**<br>**State, City, or Local Tax Department** |
| PAYER'S Federal identification number | RECIPIENT'S identification number | **3** Capital gain (included in box 2a)<br><br>$ | **4** Federal income tax withheld<br><br>$ | |
| RECIPIENT'S name | **5** Employee contributions or insurance premiums<br><br>$ | **6** Net unrealized appreciation in employer's securities<br><br>$ | |
| Street address (including apt. no.) | **7** Distribution code(s) | IRA/ SEP/ SIMPLE ☐ | **8** Other<br>$          % | |
| City, state, and ZIP code | **9a** Your percentage of total distribution        % | **9b** Total employee contributions<br>$ | |
| Account number (optional) | **10** State tax withheld<br>$<br>$ | **11** State/Payer's state no. | **12** State distribution<br>$<br>$ |
| | **13** Local tax withheld<br>$<br>$ | **14** Name of locality<br>$ | **15** Local distribution<br>$<br>$ |

Form **1099-R**                              Department of the Treasury - Internal Revenue Service

☐ CORRECTED (if checked)

| PAYER'S name, street address, city, state, and ZIP code | **1** Gross distribution $ | OMB No. 1545-0119 20**03** Form **1099-R** | **Distributions From Pensions, Annuities, Retirement or Profit-Sharing Plans, IRAs, Insurance Contracts, etc.** |
|---|---|---|---|
| | **2a** Taxable amount $ | | |

| | | **2b** Taxable amount not determined ☐ | Total distribution ☐ | **Copy B** **Report this income on your Federal tax return. If this form shows Federal income tax withheld in box 4, attach this copy to your return.** |
|---|---|---|---|---|
| PAYER'S Federal identification number | RECIPIENT'S identification number | **3** Capital gain (included in box 2a) $ | **4 Federal income tax withheld** $ | |
| RECIPIENT'S name | | **5** Employee contributions or insurance premiums $ | **6** Net unrealized appreciation in employer's securities $ | |
| Street address (including apt. no.) | | **7** Distribution code(s) | IRA/ SEP/ SIMPLE ☐ | **8** Other $ % | This information is being furnished to the Internal Revenue Service. |
| City, state, and ZIP code | | **9a** Your percentage of total distribution % | **9b** Total employee contributions $ | |
| Account number (optional) | | **10** State tax withheld $ _____ $ | **11** State/Payer's state no. | **12** State distribution $ _____ $ |
| | | **13** Local tax withheld $ _____ $ | **14** Name of locality $ | **15** Local distribution $ |

Form **1099-R**        Department of the Treasury - Internal Revenue Service

## Instructions for Recipient

Generally, distributions from pensions, annuities, profit-sharing and retirement plans (including section 457 state and local government plans), IRAs, insurance contracts, etc., are reported to recipients on Form 1099-R.

**Qualified plans.** If your annuity starting date is after 1997, you must use the simplified method to figure your taxable amount if your payer did not show the taxable amount in box 2a. See **Pub. 575,** Pension and Annuity Income.

**IRAs.** For distributions from a traditional individual retirement arrangement (IRA), simplified employee pension (SEP), or savings incentive match plan for employees (SIMPLE), generally the payer is not required to compute the taxable amount. Therefore, the amounts in boxes 1 and 2a will be the same most of the time. See the Form 1040 or 1040A instructions to determine the taxable amount. If you are at least age 70½, you must take minimum distributions from your IRA (other than a Roth IRA). If you do not, you may be subject to a 50% excise tax on the amount that should have been distributed. See **Pub. 590,** Individual Retirement Arrangements (IRAs), and **Pub. 560,** Retirement Plans for Small Business (SEP, SIMPLE, and Qualified Plans), for more information on IRAs.

**Roth IRAs.** For distributions from a Roth IRA, generally the payer is not required to compute the taxable amount. You must compute any taxable amount on **Form 8606,** Nondeductible IRAs. An amount shown in box 2a may be taxable earnings on an excess contribution.

**Loans treated as distributions.** If you borrow money from a qualified plan, tax-sheltered annuity, or government plan, you may have to treat the loan as a distribution and include all or part of the amount borrowed in your income. There are exceptions to this rule. If your loan is taxable, Code L will be shown in box 7. See Pub. 575.

**Box 1.** Shows the total amount you received this year. The amount may have been a direct rollover, a transfer or conversion to a Roth IRA, a recharacterized IRA contribution; or you may have received it as periodic payments, as nonperiodic payments, or as a total distribution. Report the amount on Form 1040 or 1040A on the line for "IRA distributions" or "Pensions and annuities" (or the line for "Taxable amount"), and on Form 8606, whichever applies. However, if this is a lump-sum distribution, report it on **Form 4972,** Tax on

Lump-Sum Distribution. If you have not reached minimum retirement age, report your disability payments on the line for "Wages, salaries, tips, etc." Also report on that line corrective distributions of excess deferrals, excess contributions, or excess aggregate contributions.

If a life insurance, annuity, or endowment contract was transferred tax free to another trustee or contract issuer, an amount will be shown in this box and Code 6 will be shown in box 7. You need not report this on your tax return.

**Box 2a.** This part of the distribution is generally taxable. If there is no entry in this box, the payer may not have all the facts needed to figure the taxable amount. In that case, the first box in box 2b should be checked. You may want to get one of the following publications from the IRS to help you figure the taxable amount: **Pub. 560, Pub. 571,** Tax-Sheltered Annuity Plans (403(b) Plans) for Employees of Public Schools and Certain Tax-Exempt Organizations, **Pub. 575, Pub. 590, Pub. 721,** Tax Guide to U.S. Civil Service Retirement Benefits, or **Pub. 939,** General Rule for Pensions and Annuities. For an IRA distribution, see **IRAs** and **Roth IRAs** above. For a direct rollover, zero should be shown, and you must enter zero (-0-) on the "Taxable amount" line of your tax return.

If this is a total distribution from a qualified plan (other than an IRA or tax-sheltered annuity) and you were born before January 2, 1936 (or you are the beneficiary of someone born before January 2, 1936), you may be eligible for the 10-year tax option. See the **Instructions for Form 4972** for more information.

**Box 2b.** If the first box is checked, the payer was unable to determine the taxable amount, and box 2a should be blank. However, if this is a traditional IRA, SEP, or SIMPLE distribution, then see **IRAs** above. If the second box is checked, the distribution was a total distribution that closed out your account.

**Box 3.** If you received a lump-sum distribution from a qualified plan and were born before January 2, 1936 (or you are the beneficiary of someone born before January 2, 1936), you may be able to elect to treat this amount as a capital gain on Form 4972 (not on Schedule D (Form 1040)). See the Instructions for Form 4972. For a charitable gift annuity, report as a long-term capital gain on Schedule D (Form 1040).

*(Continued on the back of Copy C.)*

☐ CORRECTED (if checked)

| PAYER'S name, street address, city, state, and ZIP code | **1** Gross distribution $ | OMB No. 1545-0119 **20**03 Form **1099-R** | **Distributions From Pensions, Annuities, Retirement or Profit-Sharing Plans, IRAs, Insurance Contracts, etc.** |
|---|---|---|---|
| | **2a** Taxable amount $ | | |
| | **2b** Taxable amount not determined ☐   Total distribution ☐ | | **Copy C For Recipient's Records** |
| PAYER'S Federal identification number / RECIPIENT'S identification number | **3** Capital gain (included in box 2a) $ | **4** Federal income tax withheld $ | |
| RECIPIENT'S name | **5** Employee contributions or insurance premiums $ | **6** Net unrealized appreciation in employer's securities $ | This information is being furnished to the Internal Revenue Service. |
| Street address (including apt. no.) | **7** Distribution code(s)  IRA/SEP/SIMPLE ☐ | **8** Other $ % | |
| City, state, and ZIP code | **9a** Your percentage of total distribution % | **9b** Total employee contributions $ | |
| Account number (optional) | **10** State tax withheld $ $ | **11** State/Payer's state no. $ | **12** State distribution $ |
| | **13** Local tax withheld $ $ | **14** Name of locality | **15** Local distribution $ $ |

Form **1099-R**   (keep for your records)   Department of the Treasury - Internal Revenue Service

## Instructions for Recipient (Continued)

**Box 4.** This is the amount of Federal income tax withheld. **Include this on your income tax return as tax withheld, and if box 4 shows an amount (other than zero), attach Copy B to your return.** Generally, if you will receive payments next year that are not eligible rollover distributions, you can change your withholding or elect not to have income tax withheld by giving the payer **Form W-4P**, Withholding Certificate for Pension or Annuity Payments.

**Box 5.** Generally, this shows the employee's investment in the contract (after-tax contributions), if any, recovered tax free this year; the part of premiums paid on commercial annuities or insurance contracts recovered tax free; or the nontaxable part of a charitable gift annuity. This box does not show any IRA contributions.

**Box 6.** If you received a lump-sum distribution from a qualified plan that includes securities of the employer's company, the net unrealized appreciation (NUA) (any increase in value of such securities while in the trust) is taxed only when you sell the securities unless you choose to include it in your gross income this year. See Pub. 575 and the Instructions for Form 4972. If you did not receive a lump-sum distribution, the amount shown is the NUA attributable to employee contributions, which is not taxed until you sell the securities.

**Box 7.** The following codes identify the distribution you received. **1–** Early distribution, no known exception (in most cases, under age 59½). See **Form 5329**, Additional Taxes on Qualified Plans (Including IRAs) and Other Tax-Favored Accounts. For a rollover to a traditional IRA of the entire taxable part of the distribution, do not file Form 5329. See the Form 1040/1040A instructions. **2–** Early distribution, exception applies (under age 59½)*. **3–** Disability*. **4–** Death*. **5–** Prohibited transaction. **6–** Section 1035 exchange (a tax-free exchange of life insurance, annuity, or endowment contracts). **7–** Normal distribution. **8–** Excess contributions plus earnings/excess deferrals (and/or earnings) taxable in 2003. **9–** Cost of current life insurance protection (premiums paid by a trustee or custodian for current insurance protection, taxable to you currently). **A–** May be eligible for 10-year tax option. See Form 4972. **D–** Excess contributions plus earnings/excess deferrals taxable in 2001. **E–** Excess annual additions under section 415 and certain excess amounts under section 403(b) plans. Report on Form 1040/1040A on the line for taxable pension or annuity income*. **F–** Charitable gift

annuity. **G–** Direct rollover to a qualified plan, a tax-sheltered annuity, a governmental 457(b) plan, or an IRA. May also include a transfer from a conduit IRA to a qualified plan*. **J–** Early distribution from a Roth IRA, no known exception (in most cases, under age 59½). Report on Forms 1040 and 8606 and see Form 5329. **L–** Loans treated as distributions. **N–** Recharacterized IRA contribution made for 2003 and recharacterized in 2003. Report on 2003 Form 1040/1040A and Form 8606, if applicable. **P–** Excess contributions plus earnings/excess deferrals taxable in 2002. **Q–** Roth IRA qualified distribution. You are age 59½ or over and meet the 5-year holding period for a Roth IRA. See the Form 1040/1040A instructions*. **R–** Recharacterized IRA contribution made for 2002 and recharacterized in 2003. Report on 2002 Form 1040/1040A and Form 8606, if applicable. **S–** Early distribution from a SIMPLE IRA in first 2 years, no known exception (under age 59½). May be subject to an additional 25% tax. See Form 5329. **T–** Roth IRA distribution, exception applies. You are either age 59½ or over or an exception (code 3 or 4) applies. See the Form 1040/1040A instructions.

If the IRA/SEP/SIMPLE box is checked, you have received a traditional IRA, SEP, or SIMPLE distribution.

**Box 8.** If you received an annuity contract as part of a distribution, the value of the contract is shown. It is not taxable when you receive it and should not be included in boxes 1 and 2a. When you receive periodic payments from the annuity contract, they are taxable at that time. If the distribution is made to more than one person, the percentage of the annuity contract distributed to you is also shown. You will need this information if you use the 10-year tax option (Form 4972).

**Box 9a.** If a total distribution was made to more than one person, the percentage you received is shown.

**Box 9b.** For a life annuity from a qualified plan or from a tax-sheltered annuity (with after-tax contributions), an amount may be shown for the employee's total investment in the contract. It is used to compute the taxable part of the distribution. See Pub. 575.

**Boxes 10–15.** If state or local income tax was withheld from the distribution, these boxes may be completed. Boxes 12 and 15 may show the part of the distribution subject to state and/or local tax.

*You are not required to file Form 5329.

☐ CORRECTED (if checked)

| PAYER'S name, street address, city, state, and ZIP code | 1 Gross distribution $ | OMB No. 1545-0119 **20**03 Form **1099-R** | **Distributions From Pensions, Annuities, Retirement or Profit-Sharing Plans, IRAs, Insurance Contracts, etc.** |
|---|---|---|---|
| | 2a Taxable amount $ | | |
| | 2b Taxable amount not determined ☐ | Total distribution ☐ | |
| PAYER'S Federal identification number / RECIPIENT'S identification number | 3 Capital gain (included in box 2a) $ | 4 Federal income tax withheld $ | **Copy 2** File this copy with your state, city, or local income tax return, when required. |
| RECIPIENT'S name | 5 Employee contributions or insurance premiums $ | 6 Net unrealized appreciation in employer's securities $ | |
| Street address (including apt. no.) | 7 Distribution code(s) / IRA/ SEP/ SIMPLE ☐ | 8 Other $ % | |
| City, state, and ZIP code | 9a Your percentage of total distribution % | 9b Total employee contributions $ | |
| Account number (optional) | 10 State tax withheld $ $ | 11 State/Payer's state no. $ | 12 State distribution $ |
| | 13 Local tax withheld $ $ | 14 Name of locality | 15 Local distribution $ $ |

Form **1099-R**     Department of the Treasury - Internal Revenue Service

☐ VOID   ☐ CORRECTED

| PAYER'S name, street address, city, state, and ZIP code | 1 Gross distribution $ | OMB No. 1545-0119 **20**03 Form **1099-R** | **Distributions From Pensions, Annuities, Retirement or Profit-Sharing Plans, IRAs, Insurance Contracts, etc.** |
|---|---|---|---|
| | 2a Taxable amount $ | | |
| | 2b Taxable amount not determined ☐ | Total distribution ☐ | |
| PAYER'S Federal identification number / RECIPIENT'S identification number | 3 Capital gain (included in box 2a) $ | 4 Federal income tax withheld $ | **Copy D** **For Payer** |
| RECIPIENT'S name | 5 Employee contributions or insurance premiums $ | 6 Net unrealized appreciation in employer's securities $ | For Privacy Act and Paperwork Reduction Act Notice, see the **2003 General Instructions for Forms 1099, 1098, 5498, and W-2G.** |
| Street address (including apt. no.) | 7 Distribution code(s) / IRA/ SEP/ SIMPLE ☐ | 8 Other $ % | |
| City, state, and ZIP code | 9a Your percentage of total distribution % | 9b Total employee contributions $ | |
| Account number (optional) | 10 State tax withheld $ $ | 11 State/Payer's state no. $ | 12 State distribution $ |
| | 13 Local tax withheld $ $ | 14 Name of locality | 15 Local distribution $ $ |

Form **1099-R**     Department of the Treasury - Internal Revenue Service

# Chapter 27

# INSTALLING A QUALIFIED RETIREMENT PLAN

This chapter covers the complicated and distinctive steps involved in installing a qualified retirement plan. Qualified plans include the following plans covered in this book:

Installing a plan involves various steps, some of which must comply with a fairly strict legal timetable. To help focus this discussion, an installation checklist for a typical qualified plan is set out in Figure 27.1 for reference.

## Plan Adoption

An employer must legally "adopt" a qualified plan during the employer's taxable year in which it is to be effective.[1] (By contrast, a simplified employee pension (SEP) can be adopted as late as the tax filing date for the year—see Chapters 20 and 21.) The plan sponsor should adopt (and document the adoption of) the plan before the end of the year in which the plan is to become effective. The plan can be made effective to the beginning of the year of adoption. An adoption that is made later and reflected in "backdated" documents is not legally effective for purposes of the tax treatment of a qualified plan.

The reason for this requirement is basically one of tax accounting. An employer cannot obtain a deduction for an expense accrued during a year unless it meets the "all events" test for accrual. That is, all events that make the accrual a legally binding obligation of the employer must have occurred by the end of the tax year. Thus, a qualified plan must have been legally adopted by the end of a particular tax year if the employer wishes to take a tax deduction for contributions to the plan for that year.

A corporation adopts a plan by a formal action of the corporation's board of directors. An unincorporated business should adopt a written resolution in a form similar to a corporate resolution. The plan does not have to be in final form in order to be legally adopted; the corporate resolution can simply set out the principal terms of the plan such as coverage, benefit formula, vesting, etc.

If the plan will use a trust for funding, a trust must be established before the end of the year of adoption and must be valid under the law of the state in which it is established. A nominal plan contribution may be required for that purpose. If the plan is to be funded through an insurance contract, the insurer must accept the application for the contract before the end of the year, but the contract need not be formally adopted in final form at that time.

## Credit for Startup Costs

Certain small employers are eligible for a business tax credit of up to $500 for startup costs or employee education expenses incurred in connection with the adoption of a retirement plan. The credit is nonrefundable, and may be taken only during the plan's first three years, or for the year preceding the year the plan becomes effective and the first two years of the plan. To be eligible, the employer must have no more than 100 employees with compensation in excess of $5,000 for the previous year, and the plan must cover at least one nonhighly compensated employee. Amounts eligible for the credit include 50% of the qualified startup costs paid or incurred during the year. No credit is allowed for the portion of expenses that are used to determine the amount of the credit.[2]

## Advance Determination Letter

Because of the complexity of the qualification provisions, and the tax cost of having a plan considered "disqualified" by the IRS, most plan sponsors apply to the IRS for a ruling that the plan provisions meet Code requirements for favorable tax treatment as a qualified

**Figure 27.1**

## PLAN INSTALLATION CHECKLIST AND TIMETABLE

**ASSUMPTIONS:**
1. Employer uses calendar year for tax reporting.
2. Plan is to be effective January 1, 2003.

**BEFORE DECEMBER 31, 2003**
1. Corporate board must pass a resolution adopting the plan. Plan document does not have to be in final form.
2. Trust agreement must be signed and trust established under state law; or application for group pension contract must be made and accepted by insurance company.
3. Plan must be "communicated to employees." This can be done orally at employee meetings or through a written communication. The summary plan description (SPD) can be used for this purpose simply by distributing it earlier than its regular due date (see below).

**BEFORE EMPLOYER'S TAX FILING DATE**
(March 15, 2004, with extensions to September 15, 2004 if applied for)
1. Plan should be drafted in final form and signed by plan sponsor and trustee.
2. Employer must make the 2003 contribution to the plan by this date in order for it to be deductible on the 2003 tax return.
3. Application for IRS determination letter should be filed before this date in order to extend the retroactive amendment period. However, there is no specific deadline for filing the application for determination.

**WITHIN 120 DAYS AFTER PLAN IS ADOPTED**
(i.e., Board of Directors' resolution)
1. Furnish SPD to participants (see Appendix A of this book).

**BEFORE FILING APPLICATION FOR DETERMINATION WITH IRS**
1. Provide "Notice to Interested Parties" to employees as required by IRS regulations. This is a prescribed formal notice to employees of their rights in connection with the determination letter process. The notice must be provided 10 to 24 days before filing if the notice is mailed, and 7 to 20 days before filing if the notice is posted.

**ON OR BEFORE JULY 31, 2004**
(and each July 31 thereafter)
1. File Annual Report (Form 5500 series) — (see Appendix A).

**ON OR BEFORE SEPTEMBER 30, 2004**
(and each September 30 thereafter)
1. Furnish Summary Annual Report to participants (see Appendix A).

plan. This letter is generally referred to as a "determination letter."

Technically, a plan does not have to receive a favorable determination letter in order to be qualified. If the plan provisions in letter and in operation meet Code requirements, the plan is qualified and entitled to the appropriate tax benefits. However, without a determination letter, the issue of plan qualification for a given year does not arise until the IRS audits the employer's tax returns for that year. By that time, it is generally too late for the employer to amend the plan to correct any disqualifying provisions. So if the plan has a disqualifying provision or lacks an essential provision, the

employer's tax deduction for the year being audited is lost. (In addition, the plan fund will lose its tax-exempt status and employees will become taxable on their vested benefits—a true all-around tax disaster.) A determination letter helps to avoid this problem since auditing agents generally will not raise the issue of plan qualification if the employer has a current determination letter—that is, one that shows the plan complies with current law.

Plans generally must be amended periodically to conform to changes in the law. Each time there is a significant amendment to the plan a new determination letter should be obtained.

It is always possible for the IRS to raise the issue that a plan is discriminatory *in operation*—as opposed to merely having discriminatory provisions on paper. A determination letter cannot prevent this. For those plans in which discrimination or other failures have occurred, a combination of voluntary correction programs offers corrective measures ranging from self-correction of insignificant operational errors to correction of document or other errors found during a plan audit. The purpose of these programs, known collectively as the Employee Plans Compliance Resolution System (EPCRS), is to prevent plan disqualification.[3]

The Code contains a "retroactive amendment" procedure that allows plan sponsors to amend a plan retroactively to eliminate certain disqualifying provisions.[4] Retroactive plan amendments may be made up to the employer's tax filing date for the year in question, including extensions. For example, if a corporate employer uses a calendar tax year, the tax filing date for the year 2003 is March 15, 2004, with possible extensions to September 15, 2004. A plan effective January 1, 2003 can be retroactively amended as late as September 15, 2004 under this provision.

An additional advantage of the determination letter procedure is that it can extend the time for retroactive amendments. If the determination letter request is filed before the tax filing date, retroactive amendments can be made as long as the determination letter request is still pending.

Determination letter requests are made on IRS forms. Copies of Form 5300, used for custom designed plans, and Form 5307, used for master or prototype plans (see below), are reproduced at the end of this chapter. A "short form," Form 6406, is available for determination letter requests involving plan amendments only (not a new plan).

Specific IRS requirements for documentation of determination letter requests change frequently. Practitioners should consult the annually revised IRS Revenue Procedure on this subject. The 2003 version is Revenue Procedure 2003-6, 2003-1 IRB 191.

The IRS once provided determination letters as a free service, but a fee schedule was instituted in 1988. For 2003, the fee ranges from $100 to $1,250, depending on the type of plan and the nature of the advice sought. Form 8717 (reproduced at the end of this chapter) is filed along with the fee and the form from the appropriate member of the 5300 family. A limited exemption from the fee applies for employers with 100 or fewer employees, during the first

five years of the plan.[5] Also, a limited tax credit for small employers is available (see above) to help defray the costs of implementing a retirement plan.[6]

## Master and Prototype Plans

Custom design of a qualified plan can be costly because the plan document must be very lengthy to reflect all of the complex requirements of current law. The benefits profession has developed methods to reduce the cost of plan drafting; these are particularly important to smaller employers, since the cost of installation must be spread over relatively few employees.

One of the most common methods of reducing drafting costs is to use a "master" or "prototype" plan offered by a financial institution as an inducement to use that institution's investment products to fund the plan. Insurance companies, banks, mutual funds, and various service providers frequently offer master or prototype plans. These plans are standardized plans of various types—for example prototype profit sharing or prototype money purchase—that use standardized language approved by the IRS. The plan sponsor has some degree of choice in basic provisions of the plan such as the vesting schedule, the contribution or benefit formula, etc.

A master plan is distinguished from a prototype in that a master plan usually refers to a plan under which various employers use a single financial institution for funding, while a prototype plan generally does not commit the plan sponsor to use any particular funding institution or medium.

The use of master or prototype plans greatly simplifies plan installation in many cases. The fee for adopting a master or prototype plan is usually much less than the cost of drafting a custom designed plan. The determination letter procedure is also simplified, because the "boilerplate" provisions of the plan have already been approved by the IRS. All the IRS has to do is determine whether the basic vesting schedule, contribution or benefit formula, etc., as applied to the employer in question, is nondiscriminatory.

The cost of drafting a custom designed plan has also been addressed by pension professionals. There are "document preparation services" that will generate documents from their central word processors based on a checklist of plan provisions submitted by the plan installer. Usually, the use of a document preparation service will speed IRS approval of a plan, because the

IRS becomes familiar with the standard language used by various document preparers.

## FOOTNOTES

1.  Treas. Reg. §1.401-1(a)(2). See also, *Engineered Timber Sales, Inc. v. Comm.*, 74 TC 808 (1980).

2.  IRC Section 45E. Note that all provisions of EGTRRA 2001 are scheduled to sunset, or expire, after December 31, 2010.

3.  See Rev. Proc. 2002-29, 2002-29 IRB 133. The self-correction portion of this initiative requires that the plan have a favorable determination letter.

4.  IRC Section 401(b).

5.  P.L. 107-16 (EGTRRA 2001), Sec. 620.

6.  See IRC Section 45E.

| Form **5300** | **Application for** | OMB No. 1545-0197 |
|---|---|---|
| (Rev. September 2001) | **Determination for Employee Benefit Plan** | **For IRS Use Only** |
| Department of the Treasury Internal Revenue Service | (including collectively bargained plans formerly filed on Form 5303) (Under sections 401(a) and 501(a) of the Internal Revenue Code) | |

Review the **Procedural Requirements Checklist** on page 5 before submitting this application.

**1a** Name of plan sponsor (employer if single-employer plan)

**1b** Employer identification number

Number, street, and room or suite no. (If a P.O. box, see instructions.)

**1c** Employer's tax year ends—Enter (MM)

City　　　　　State　　　　　ZIP code

**1d** Telephone number ( )

**2a** Person to contact if more information is needed. (See instructions.) (If **Form 2848**, Power of Attorney and Declaration of Representative, or other written designation is attached, check box and do not complete the rest of this line.) . . . . . . . . . . . . . . . . . . ▶ ☐

**1e** Fax number ( )

Name

Number, street, and room or suite no. (If a P.O. box, see instructions.)

**2b** Telephone number ( )

City　　　　　State　　　　　ZIP code

**2c** Fax number ( )

**3a** Determination requested for (enter applicable number(s) in the box and fill in required information). (See instructions.)

☐ Enter 1 for Initial Qualification—Date plan signed ▶ ......../....../..........

☐ Enter 2 for a request after initial qualification—Is complete plan attached? (See instructions.) ▶ Yes ☐ No ☐
Date amendment signed ▶ .........../....../........... Date amendment effective ▶ .........../....../.........

☐ Enter 3 for Affiliated Service Group status (section 414(m))—Date effective ▶ .........../....../.........

☐ Enter 4 for Leased Employee status

☐ Enter 5 for Partial termination—Date effective ▶ .........../....../.........

☐ Enter 6 for Termination of collectively bargained multiemployer or multiple-employer plan covered by PBGC insurance—Date of Termination ▶ .........../....../.........

**b** Has the plan received a determination letter? . . . . . . . . . . . . . Yes ☐ No ☐
Date of letter ▶ .........../....../.........
If "Yes" submit a copy of the latest letter and subsequent amendments.
Number of amendments ▶ ............................
If "No," submit all prior plan(s) and/or adoption agreement(s). (See instructions.)

**c** Have interested parties been given the required notification of this application? (See instructions). Yes ☐ No ☐

**d** Does the plan have a cash or deferred arrangement (section 401(k))? . . . . . . . . Yes ☐ No ☐

**e** Does the plan have matching contributions (section 401(m))? . . . . . . . . . Yes ☐ No ☐

**f** Does the plan have after-tax employee voluntary contributions (section 401(m))? . . . . . Yes ☐ No ☐

**g** Does this plan benefit noncollectively bargained employees or are more than 2% of the employees who are covered under a collective bargaining agreement for professional employees? . . . . Yes ☐ No ☐
See Regulations section 1.410(b)-9.

**h** Does the plan provide for disparity in contributions or benefits that is intended to meet the permitted disparity requirements of section 401(l)? . . . . . . . . . . . . . . . Yes ☐ No ☐

**4a** Name of plan (Plan name may not exceed 66 characters, including spaces.):

......................................................

............... **b** Enter 3-digit plan number ....../....../...... **d** Enter plan's **original** effective date (MMDDYYYY)

......./....... **c** Enter date plan year ends (MMDD) ............... **e** Enter number of participants (See instructions.)

Under penalties of perjury, I declare that I have examined this application, including accompanying statements and schedules, and to the best of my knowledge and belief, it is true, correct, and complete.

**Print Name** ▶　　　　　　　　　**Title** ▶

**Signature** ▶　　　　　　　　　　　　　　　**Date** ▶

**For Paperwork Reduction Act Notice, see separate instructions.**　　Cat. No. 11740X　　Form **5300** (Rev. 9-2001)

**5** Indicate type of plan by entering the number from the list below.

| | |
|---|---|

1—profit-sharing and/or 401(k)    4—defined benefit but not cash balance    7—non-leveraged ESOP

2—money purchase    5—cash balance    8—stock bonus

3—target benefit    6—leveraged ESOP    9—safe harbor 401(k)

| | Yes | No |
|---|---|---|

**6a** Is the employer a member of an affiliated service group? . . . . . . . . . . . . . .

**b** Is the employer a member of a controlled group of corporations or a group of trades or businesses under common control? . . . . . . . . . . . . . . . . . . . . . . . . . . . . .

If **a** and/or **b** above is "Yes," complete required statement (see instructions).

**7a** Is this a governmental plan? . . . . . . . . . . . . . . . . . .

If "Yes," is the plan a state level plan? . . . . . . . . . . . . .

**b** Is this a nonelecting church plan? . . . . . . . . . . . . . . . .

**c** Is this a collectively bargained plan? (See Regulations section 1.410(b)-9.) . . . . . . . . .

**d** Is this a section 412(i) plan? . . . . . . . . . . . . . . . . . .

**e** Is this a multiple-employer plan? Enter number of participating employers ................... . . . . . .

**f** Is this a multiemployer plan as described in section 414(f)? . . . . . . . . . . . . .

**8a** Do you maintain any other qualified plan(s) under section 401(a)? . . . . . . . . . . . . .

If "Yes," attach required statement (see instructions).

If "No," skip to line 8d.

**b** Do you maintain another plan of the same type (i.e., both this plan and the other plan are defined contribution plans or both are defined benefit plans) that covers non-key employees who are also covered under this plan?

If yes, when the plan is top-heavy, do the non-key employees covered under both plans receive the required top-heavy minimum contribution or benefit under:

(1)  This plan? . . . . . . . . . . . . . . . . . . . . .

(2)  The other plan? . . . . . . . . . . . . . . . . . . .

**c** If this is a defined contribution plan, do you maintain a defined benefit plan (or if this is a defined benefit plan, do you maintain a defined contribution plan) that covers non-key employees who are also covered under this plan? . . . . . . . . . . . . . . . . . . . . . . . . . . . . .

If yes, when the plan is top-heavy, do non-key employees covered under both plans receive:

(1)  the top-heavy minimum benefit under the defined benefit plan? . . . . . . . . . . .

(2)  at least a 5% minimum contribution under the defined contribution plan? . . . . . . . . .

(3)  the minimum benefit offset by benefits provided by the defined contribution plan? . . . . . . . .

(4)  benefits under both plans that, using a comparability analysis, are at least equal to the minimum benefit? (See instructions.) . . . . . . . . . . . . . . . . . . . .

**d** Does the plan prevent the possibility that the section 415 limitations will be exceeded for any employee who is (or was) a participant in this plan and any other plan of the employer? . . . . . . . . . . . . .

**General Eligibility Requirements** (Complete all lines.)

**9a** Check all that apply:

(1) ☐ All employees

(2) ☐ Hourly rate employees

(3) ☐ Salaried employees

(4) ☐ Other (Specify) --------------------------------------

**b** Minimum years of service required to participate ......................... If no minimum, check ▶ ☐

**c** Minimum age required to participate (Specify)                    If no minimum, check ▶ ☐

**Vesting** (Check one box to indicate the regular (non-top heavy) vesting provisions of the plan.)

**10a** ☐ Full and immediate

**b** ☐ Full vesting after 2 years of service

**c** ☐ Full vesting after 3 years of service

**d** ☐ Full vesting after 5 years of service

**e** ☐ 2 to 6 year graded vesting

**f** ☐ 3 to 7 year graded vesting

**g** ☐ Other

Form **5300** (Rev. 9-2001)

**Benefits and Requirements for Benefits**

**11a** For defined benefit plans—Method for determining accrued benefit ▶ ------------------------------------------------

  (1) Benefit formula at normal retirement age is -----------------------------------------------------------

  -----------------------------------------------------------------------------------------------------------

  (2) Benefit formula at early retirement age is -----------------------------------------------------------

  -----------------------------------------------------------------------------------------------------------

  (3) Normal form of retirement benefit is -----------------------------------------------------------------

  -----------------------------------------------------------------------------------------------------------

  **b** For defined contribution plans—Employer contributions:

  (1) Profit-sharing or stock bonus plan contributions are determined under:
  ☐ A definite formula    ☐ A discretionary formula    ☐ Both

  (2) Matching contributions are determined under:
  ☐ A definite formula    ☐ A discretionary formula    ☐ Both

  (3) Money purchase plan—Enter rate of contribution ---------------------------------------------------

  -----------------------------------------------------------------------------------------------------------

  (4) Target benefit plan—state target benefit formula -------------------------------------------------

  -----------------------------------------------------------------------------------------------------------

  -----------------------------------------------------------------------------------------------------------

**Miscellaneous**

|  | N/A | Yes | No |
|---|---|---|---|

**12a** Does any amendment to the plan reduce or eliminate any section 411(d)(6) protected benefit, including an amendment adopted after September 6, 2000, to eliminate a joint and survivor annuity form of benefit? (See instructions.) . . . . . . . . . . . . . . . . . .

  **b** Are trust earnings and losses allocated on the basis of account balances in a defined contribution plan? If "No," attach a statement explaining how they are allocated.

  **c** Is this plan or trust currently under examination or is any issue related to this plan or trust currently pending before:
  - The Internal Revenue Service . . . . . . . . . . . . . .
  - The Department of Labor . . . . . . . . . . . . . . .
  - The Pension Benefit Guaranty Corporation, or . . . . . . . . . . . . . .
  - Any court? . . . . . . . . . . . . . . .

  If "Yes," attach a statement explaining the issues involved, the contact person's name (IRS Agent, DOL Investigator, etc.) and their telephone number. Do not answer "Yes" if the plan has been submitted under the Voluntary Compliance Program of the Employee Plans Compliance Resolution System (EPCRS).

Form **5300** (Rev. 9-2001)

Form 5300 (Rev. 9-2001)    Page **4**

**Optional determination request regarding the ratio percentage test. A determination regarding the average benefit test may be requested by attaching Schedule Q (Form 5300).**

| | | Yes | No |
|---|---|---|---|
| **13** | Is this a request for a determination regarding the ratio percentage test of Regs. section 1.410(b)-2(b)(2) or a request for a determination regarding one of the special requirements of Regs. section 1.410(b)-2(b)(5), (6), or (7)? . . | | |

**If "Yes,"** complete only lines 13a through 13n for a ratio percentage test determination, or complete only line 13o for a determination regarding one of the special requirements.

**If "No,"** skip to line 14.

**a** Is this plan disaggregated into two or more separate plans that are not 401(k), 401(m), or profit sharing plans?
If "Yes," see the instructions and attach separate schedules for each disaggregated portion . . . . .

**b** Does the employer receive services from any leased employees as defined in section 414(n)? . . . . . .

**c** Coverage date (MMDDYYYY). See instructions for inserting date . . . . . . . . . . . .

**d** Total number of employees (include self-employed individuals) (employer-wide) . . . . . .

**e** Statutory and regulatory exclusions under this plan (do not count an employee more than once):

  (1) Number of employees excluded because of minimum age or years of service required . .

  (2) Number of employees excluded because of inclusion in a collective bargaining unit . . .

  (3) Number of employees excluded because they terminated employment with less than 501 hours of service and were not employed on last day of plan year . . . . . . . . . .

  (4) Number of employees excluded because employed by other qualified separate lines of business (QSLOBs) . . . . . . . . . . . . . . . . . . . . . . .

  (5) Number of employees excluded because they were nonresident aliens with no earned income from sources within the United States . . . . . . . . . . . . . .

**f** Total statutory and regulatory exclusions (add lines 13e(1) through 13e(5)) . . . . . . .

**g** Nonexcludable employees (subtract line 13f from line 13d) . . . . . . . . . . .

**h** Number of nonexcludable employees on line 13g who are highly compensated employees (HCEs) .

**i** Number of nonexcludable HCEs on line 13h benefiting under the plan . . . . . . . .

**j** Number of nonexcludable employees who are nonhighly compensated employees (NHCEs) (subtract line 13h from line 13g) . . . . . . . . . . . . . . . . . . .

**k** Number of nonexcludable NHCEs on line 13j benefiting under the plan . . . . . . . .

**l** Ratio percentage (See instructions.) . . . . . . . . . . . . . . . . .

**m** Enter the ratio percentage for the following, if applicable:

  (1) Section 401(k) part of the plan . . . . . . . . . . . . . . . .

  (2) Section 401(m) part of the plan . . . . . . . . . . . . . . . .

| | | Yes | No |
|---|---|---|---|
| **n** | Are the results on line 13l or 13m based on the aggregated coverage of more than one plan? . . . . . | | |

If "Yes," attach a statement showing the names, plan numbers, EINs, and benefit/allocation formulas of the other plans.
**All aggregated plans should be filed concurrently.**

**o** If the plan satisfied coverage using one of the special requirements of Regulations section 1.410(b)-2(b)(5), (6), or (7), enter the letter from the list below that identifies the special requirement:

☐ A—1.410(b)-2(b)(5)—No NHCEs employed
   B—1.410(b)-2(b)(6)—No HCEs benefit
   C—1.410(b)-2(b)(7)—Collectively bargained only

**Optional determination request regarding the nondiscrimination design-based safe harbors of section 401(a)(4).**

**Section 401(k) and/or section 401(m) plans that do not contain a provision for discretionary contributions should not complete this line.**

| | | Yes | No |
|---|---|---|---|
| **14** | Is this a request for a determination regarding a design-based safe harbor under section 401(a)(4)? . . . | | |

If "Yes," complete the following:
Design-based nondiscrimination safe harbors:

**a** Does the plan provide for disparity in contributions or benefits that is intended to meet the permitted disparity requirements of section 401(l)? . . . . . . . . . . . . . . . . .
If "Yes," answer line 14b. Otherwise, skip to line 14c.

**b** Do the provisions of the plan ensure that the overall permitted disparity limits will not be exceeded? . . .

**c** Enter the letter ("A" – "G") from the list below that identifies the safe harbor intended to be satisfied ▶
A—1.401(a)(4)-2(b)(2) defined contribution (DC) plan with uniform allocation formula
B—1.401(a)(4)-3(b)(3) unit credit defined benefit (DB) plan          E—1.401(a)(4)-3(b)(5) insurance account
C—1.401(a)(4)-3(b)(4)(i)(C)(1) unit credit DB fractional rule plan    F—1.401(a)(4)-8(b)(3) target benefit plan
D—1.401(a)(4)-3(b)(4)(i)(C)(2) flat benefit DB plan                   G—1.401(a)(4)-8(c)(3)(iii)(b) cash balance plan

**d** List the plan section(s) that satisfy the safe harbor (including, if applicable, the permitted disparity requirements) here:

Form **5300** (Rev. 9-2001)

## Procedural Requirements Checklist
**********Form 5300**********

**Use this list to ensure that your submitted package is complete. Failure to supply the appropriate information may result in a delay in the processing of the application.**

☐ **1** Is **Form 8717,** User Fee for Employee Plan Determination Letter Request, attached to your submission?

☐ **2** Is the appropriate user fee for your submission attached to Form 8717?

☐ **3** If appropriate, is **Form 2848,** Power of Attorney and Declaration of Representative, or a privately designated authorization attached? (For more information, see the **Disclosure Request by Taxpayer** in the instructions.)

☐ **4** Is a copy of your plan's latest determination letter, if any, attached?

☐ **5** Is the Employer Identification Number (EIN) of the **plan sponsor/employer** (NOT the trust's EIN) entered on line 1b?

☐ **6** Does line 4d list the plan's original effective date?

☐ **7** Is the application signed and dated?

☐ **8** Have interested parties been given the required notification of this application?
(See the instructions for line 3c.)

☐ **9** If you are requesting a determination as an **Affiliated Service Group,** have you included the information requested in the instructions?
**NOTE:** You can request a ruling from the IRS as to whether or not you are an **Affiliated Service Group** by listing your request on line 3 of Form 5300.

☐ **10** If you answered "Yes" to line(s) 6a and/or line 6b, have you included the information requested in the instructions?

☐ **11** **For Multiple Employer Plans:** Have you included the required information as specified in the instructions under **Specific Plans—Additional Requirements?**

☐ **12** **For Partial Termination Requests:** If requesting a determination for the plan and one or more employers maintaining the plan, have you included the required information as specified in the instructions under **Types of Determination Letters, Partial Termination?**

☐ **13** If you answered "Yes" to line 8a, have you included the requested information?

☐ **14** If you are requesting additional determinations, is page 4 completed and/or Schedule Q attached?

☐ **15** If filing a Schedule Q, are all appropriate demonstrations attached?
(See Instructions for Schedule Q)

| | | | |
|---|---|---|---|
| ☐ Demo 1 | ☐ Demo 5 | ☐ Demo 8 | ☐ Demo 11 |
| ☐ Demo 3 | ☐ Demo 6 | ☐ Demo 9 | |
| ☐ Demo 4 | ☐ Demo 7 | ☐ Demo 10 | |

☐ **16** Have you included a copy of the plan, trust, and all amendments since your last determination letter?

☐ **17** **For Employee Stock Ownership Plans (ESOP):** Have you attached **Form 5309,** Application for Determination of Employee Stock Ownership Plan, to your submission?

☐ **18** **For PBGC Terminations:** Have you included the required information as specified in the instructions under **Types of Determination Letters?**

Form **5300** (Rev. 9-2001)

**SCHEDULE Q**
**(Form 5300)**
(Rev. August 2001)
Department of the Treasury
Internal Revenue Service

## Elective Determination Requests

**File as an attachment to Form 5300, 5307, or 5310 to request specific determinations.**

**See the instructions before completing this schedule.**

OMB No. 1545-0197

Name of plan sponsor (employer, if single-employer plan) as shown on Form 5300, 5307, or 5310

Employer identification number

Name of plan

| | | Yes | No |
|---|---|---|---|
| **1** | Is this a request for a determination on whether a plan that uses the qualified separate lines of business rules of section 414(r) satisfies the gateway test of section 410(b)(5)(B) or satisfies the special requirements for employer-wide plans? . . . . . . . . . . . . . . . . . . . . .  If "Yes," see instructions and attach **Demo 1.** | | |
| **2** | Sections 401(a)(26) and 410(b). See instructions. | | |
| **3** | Is this a request for a determination that specified benefits, rights, or features meet the nondiscriminatory current availability requirement? . . . . . . . . . . . . . . . . . . . . .  If "Yes," see instructions and attach **Demo 3.** | | |
| **4** | Is this a request for a determination regarding the plan being restructured, mandatorily disaggregated, or permissively aggregated? (See instructions.) . . . . . . . . . . . . . . . . .  If "Yes", see the instructions and attach **Demo 4.** | | |
| **5** | If Form 5300 line 13 or Form 5307 line 11 is answered "No," is this a request for a determination regarding Regulations section 1.410(b)-2(b)(5) average benefit test? If "Yes," see instructions and attach **Demo 5** . . | | |
| **6** | If Form 5300 line 14 or Form 5307 line 12 is answered "No," is this a request for a determination regarding a nondesign-based safe harbor or a general test under 401(a)(4)? . . . . . . . . . . . . . . .  If "Yes," see instructions and attach **Demo 6.** Also, enter the letter (A, B, or C) corresponding to the type of determination requested . . . . . . . . . . . . . . . . . . . . . . . . ▶ **Type** A = General test, involving "safety valve" rule in Regulations section 1.401(a)(4)-3(c)(3) (defined benefit plans only) B = General test, **not** involving "safety valve" rule C = Nondesign-based safe harbor | | |
| **7** | (i) Is this a request for a determination regarding a plan provision that provides for pre-participation or imputed service? . . . . . . . . . . . . . . . . . . . . . . . . . . . . .  (ii) Is this a request for a determination regarding a plan amendment (or, for an initial determination, a plan provision) providing a period of past service in excess of the safe harbor? . . . . . . . . . . .  If (i) or (ii) is "Yes," see instructions and attach **Demo 7.** | | |
| **8** | Is this a request for a determination regarding a floor offset arrangement intended to satisfy the safe harbor in Regulations section 1.401(a)(4)-8(d)?. . . . . . . . . . . . . . . . . . . .  If "Yes," see instructions and attach **Demo 8.** | | |
| **9** | Is this a request for a determination that a definition of compensation is nondiscriminatory? (See instructions.)  If "Yes," see instructions and attach **Demo 9.** | | |
| **10** | Is this a request for a determination for a defined benefit plan with employee contributions not allocated to separate accounts? . . . . . . . . . . . . . . . . . . . . . . . . . . .  If "Yes," complete lines 11 and 12. | | |
| **11** | Enter the letter (A, B, C, D, or E) corresponding to the method used to determine the employer-provided benefit:. . . . . . . . . . . . . . . . . . . . . . . . . . . . . . . ▶ **Method** A = Composition-of-workforce method B = Minimum benefit method (also enter the plan factor, if applicable (.4 or .6)) C = Grandfather rule D = Government plan method E = Cessation of employee contributions method If "A," see instructions and attach **Demo 10.** If applicable, list the plan provisions and indicate the plan factor here: _____ | | |
| **12** | Enter the letter (A, B, or C) corresponding to the method used to show that the employee-provided benefit is nondiscriminatory in amount: . . . . . . . . . . . . . . . . . . . . ▶ **Method** A = Same rate of contributions B = Total benefits method C = Grandfather rule If "C," see instructions and attach **Demo 11.** | | |

**For Paperwork Reduction Act Notice, see the Instructions for Form 5300.**     Cat. No. 21811R     **Schedule Q (Form 5300) (Rev. 8-2001)**

| Form **5307**<br>(Rev. September 2001)<br>Department of the Treasury<br>Internal Revenue Service | **Application for Determination for Adopters of Master or Prototype or Volume Submitter Plans**<br>(Under sections 401(a) and 501(a) of the Internal Revenue Code) | OMB No. 1545-0200 |
|---|---|---|
| | | **For IRS Use Only** |

Review the **Procedural Requirements Checklist** on page 4 before submitting this application.

**1a** Name of plan sponsor (employer if single-employer plan)

**1b** Employer identification number

Number, street, and room or suite no. (If a P.O. box, see instructions.)

**1c** Employer's tax year ends—Enter (MM)

City                State        ZIP code

**1d** Telephone number

( )

**2a** Person to contact if more information is needed. (See instructions.) (If **Form 2848**, Power of Attorney and Declaration of Representative, or other written designation is attached, check box and do not complete the rest of this line.) . . . . . . . . . . . . . . . . . . . . . . . . ☐

**1e** Fax number

( )

Name

Number, street, and room or suite no. (If a P.O. box, see instructions.)

**2b** Telephone number

( )

City                State        ZIP code

**2c** Fax number

( )

**3a** Determination requested for (enter applicable number(s) in the box and fill in required information.) (See instructions.)

☐ Enter 1 for Initial Qualification—Date plan signed ▶ ......../......./........

☐ Enter 2 for a request after Initial Qualification
Date amendment signed ▶ ......../......./........
Date amendment effective ▶ ......../......./........

☐ Enter 3 for Standardized Plans (See instructions)

**b** Has the plan received a determination letter? . . . . . . . . . . . . . . . Yes ☐ No ☐
Date of letter ▶ ......../......./........
If "Yes" submit a copy of the latest letter and subsequent amendments.
Number of amendments ▶ ............
If "No," submit all prior plan(s) and/or adoption agreement(s). (See instructions.)

**c** Have interested parties been given the required notification of this application? (See instructions) . . Yes ☐ No ☐
**d** Does the plan have a cash or deferred arrangement (section 401(k))? . . . . . . . . . Yes ☐ No ☐
**e** Does the plan have matching contributions (section 401(m))? . . . . . . . . . . Yes ☐ No ☐
**f** Does the plan have after-tax employee voluntary contributions (section 401(m))? . . . . . . . Yes ☐ No ☐
**g** Does the plan provide for disparity in contributions or benefits that is intended to meet the permitted disparity requirements of section 401(l)? . . . . . . . . . . . . . . . . . . Yes ☐ No ☐

**4a** Name of plan (Plan name may not exceed 66 characters, including spaces.):

-----------------------------------------------------------------

............ **b** Enter 3-digit plan number    ....../....../...... **d** Enter plan's **original** effective date (MMDDYYYY)
....../...... **c** Enter date plan year ends (MMDD)    ............ **e** Enter number of participants (See instructions.)

**5** Indicate type of plan by entering the number from the list below.
☐ 1—profit-sharing and/or 401(k)
2—money purchase
3—target benefit
4—defined benefit but not cash balance

Under penalties of perjury, I declare that I have examined this application, including accompanying statements and schedules, and to the best of my knowledge and belief it is true, correct, and complete.

Print Name ▶                Title ▶

Signature ▶                            Date ▶

**For Paperwork Reduction Act Notice, see separate instructions.**        Cat. No. 11832Y        Form **5307** (Rev. 9-2001)

| | Yes | No |
|---|---|---|

**6a** Is the employer a member of an affiliated service group? . . . . . . . . .

**b** Is the employer a member of a controlled group of corporations or a group of trades or businesses under common control? . . . . . . . . . . . . . . . . . . .

If **a** and/or **b** above is "Yes," complete required statement (see instructions).

**7a** Is this a master or prototype plan? . . . . . . . . . . . . . . . . .
If "Yes," Date of Opinion Letter ▶ .........../...../........... Serial Number ▶ _____

**b** Is this an approved volume submitter plan? . . . . . . . . . . . . .
If "Yes," Date of Advisory Letter ▶ .........../...../........... Serial Number ▶ _____

**c** Are there modifications to the volume submitter plan or are there addenda to the adoption agreement? . .
If "Yes," attach a list of the modifications and see the instructions under **What to File** and **Who May Not File.**

**d** Are there any "Other" boxes selected in the adoption agreement? . . . . . . . . . . .

**8a** Is this a governmental plan? . . . . . . . . . . . . . . . . . .
If "Yes," is the plan a state level plan? . . . . . . . . . . . . . .

**b** Is this a nonelecting church plan? . . . . . . . . . . . . . . . .

**c** Is this a collectively bargained plan? (See Regulations section 1.410(b)-9) . . . . . . . . . .

**d** Is this a section 412(i) plan? . . . . . . . . . . . . . . . . . .

**9a** Do you maintain any other qualified plan(s) under section 401(a)? . . . . . . . . . . . .
If "Yes," attach required statement in the instructions for line 9a.
If "No," skip to line 9d.

**b** Do you maintain another plan of the same type (i.e., both this plan and the other plan are defined contribution plans or both are defined benefit plans) that covers non-key employees who are also covered under this plan?
If "Yes," when the plan is top-heavy, do the non-key employees covered under both plans receive the required top-heavy minimum contribution or benefit under:
(1) This plan? . . . . . . . . . . . . . . . . . . . . . . .
(2) The other plan? . . . . . . . . . . . . . . . . . . . . .

**c** If this is a defined contribution plan, do you maintain a defined benefit plan (or if this is a defined benefit plan, do you maintain a defined contribution plan) that covers non-key employees who are also covered under this plan? . . . . . . . . . . . . . . . . . . . . . . . . . .
If "Yes," when the plan is top-heavy, do non-key employees covered under both plans receive:
(1) the top-heavy minimum benefit under the defined benefit plan? . . . . . . . . .
(2) at least a 5% minimum contribution under the defined contribution plan? . . . . . . .
(3) the minimum benefit offset by benefits provided by the defined contribution plan? . . . . . . .
(4) benefits under both plans that, using a comparability analysis, are at least equal to the minimum benefit? (See instructions.) . . . . . . . . . . . . . . . . . . . . .

**d** Does the plan prevent the possibility that the section 415 limitations will be exceeded for any employee who is (or was) a participant in this plan and any other plan of the employer? . . . . . . . . . . . .

---

**Miscellaneous**

| | N/A | Yes | No |
|---|---|---|---|

**10a** Does any amendment to the plan reduce or eliminate any section 411(d)(6) protected benefit including an amendment adopted after September 6, 2000, to eliminate a joint and survivor annuity form of benefit? (See instructions.) . . . . . . . . . . . . . . . . . . . . . . . .

**b** Are trust earnings and losses allocated on the basis of account balances in a defined contribution plan? . . . . .
If "No," attach a statement explaining how they are allocated.

**c** Is this plan or trust currently under examination or is any issue related to this plan or trust currently pending before:

• The Internal Revenue Service, . . . . . . . . . . . . . . .
• The Department of Labor, . . . . . . . . . . . . . . . . .
• The Pension Benefit Guaranty Corporation, or . . . . . . . . . . . .
• Any court . . . . . . . . . . . . . . . . . . . . . .

If "Yes," attach a statement explaining the issues involved, the contact person's name (IRS Agent, DOL Investigator, etc.) and their telephone number. Do not answer "Yes" if the plan has been submitted under the Voluntary Compliance Program of the Employee Plans Compliance Resolution System (EPCRS).

**Optional determination request regarding the ratio percentage test. A determination regarding the average benefit test may be requested by attaching Schedule Q (Form 5300).**

|  |  | Yes | No |
|---|---|---|---|
| **11** | Is this a request for a determination regarding the ratio percentage test of Regs. section 1.410(b)-2(b)(2) or a request for a determination regarding one of the special requirements of Regs. section 1.410(b)-2(b)(5), (6), or (7)? | | |

**If "Yes,"** complete only lines 11a through 11n for a ratio percentage test determination, or complete only line 11o for a determination regarding one of the special requirements.

**If "No,"** skip to line 12.

**a** Is this plan disaggregated into two or more separate plans that are not 401(k), 401(m), or profit-sharing plans? If "Yes," see the instructions and attach separate schedules for each disaggregated portion . . . . . .

**b** Does the employer receive services from any leased employees as defined in section 414(n)? . . . . .

**c** Coverage date (MMDDYYYY). See instructions for inserting date . . . . . . .

**d** Total number of employees (include self-employed individuals) (employer-wide) . . . . . .

**e** Statutory and regulatory exclusions under this plan (do not count an employee more than once):

    (1) Number of employees excluded because of minimum age or years of service required . .

    (2) Number of employees excluded because of inclusion in a collective bargaining unit . . .

    (3) Number of employees excluded because they terminated employment with less than 501 hours of service and were not employed on last day of plan year . . . . . . . . .

    (4) Number of employees excluded because employed by other qualified separate lines of business (QSLOBs) . . . . . . . . . . . . . . . . . . . .

    (5) Number of employees excluded because they were nonresident aliens with no earned income from sources within the United States. . . . . . . . . . . .

**f** Total statutory and regulatory exclusions (add lines 11e(1) through 11e(5)) . . . . . .

**g** Nonexcludable employees (subtract line 11f from line 11d) . . . . . . . . . .

**h** Number of nonexcludable employees on line 11g who are highly compensated employees (HCEs) .

**i** Number of nonexcludable HCEs on line 11h benefiting under the plan . . . . . . . .

**j** Number of nonexcludable employees who are nonhighly compensated employees (NHCEs) (subtract line 11h from line 11g) . . . . . . . . . . . . . . . . .

**k** Number of nonexcludable NHCEs on line 11j benefiting under the plan . . . . . . .

**l** Ratio percentage (See instructions.) . . . . . . . . . . . . . . .

**m** Enter the ratio percentage for the following, if applicable:

    (1) Section 401(k) part of the plan . . . . . . . . . . . . . .

    (2) Section 401(m) part of the plan . . . . . . . . . . . . . .

|  |  | Yes | No |
|---|---|---|---|
| **n** | Are the results on line 11l or 11m based on the aggregated coverage of more than one plan? . . . . . | | |

If "Yes," attach a statement showing the names, plan numbers, EINs, and benefit/allocation formulas of the other plans. **All aggregated plans should be filed concurrently.**

**o** If the plan satisfied coverage using one of the special requirements of Regulations section 1.410(b)-2(b)(5), (6), or (7), enter the letter from the list below that identifies the special requirement:

      A—1.410(b)-2(b)(5)—No NHCEs employed
      B—1.410(b)-2(b)(6)—No HCEs benefit
      C—1.410(b)-2(b)(7)—Collectively bargained only

**Optional determination request regarding the nondiscrimination design-based safe harbors of section 401(a)(4).**

**Section 401(k) and/or section 401(m) plans that do not contain a provision for discretionary contributions should not complete this line.**

|  |  | Yes | No |
|---|---|---|---|
| **12** | Is this a request for a determination regarding a design-based safe harbor under section 401(a)(4)? . . . | | |

If "Yes," complete the following:

Design-based nondiscrimination safe harbors:

**a** Does the plan provide for disparity in contributions or benefits that is intended to meet the permitted disparity requirements of section 401(l)? . . . . . . . . . . . . . . .
If "Yes," answer line 12b. Otherwise, skip to line 12c.

**b** Do the provisions of the plan ensure that the overall permitted disparity limits will not be exceeded? . . . .

**c** Enter the letter ("A" – "G") from the list below that identifies the safe harbor intended to be satisfied ▶

    A—1.401(a)(4)-2(b)(2) defined contribution (DC) plan with uniform allocation formula
    B—1.401(a)(4)-3(b)(3) unit credit defined benefit (DB) plan      E—1.401(a)(4)-3(b)(5) insurance account
    C—1.401(a)(4)-3(b)(4)(i)(C)(1) unit credit DB fractional rule plan    F—1.401(a)(4)-8(b)(3) target benefit plan
    D—1.401(a)(4)-3(b)(4)(i)(C)(2) flat benefit DB plan      G—1.401(a)(4)-8(c)(3)(iii)(b) cash balance plan

**d** List the plan section(s) that satisfy the safe harbor (including, if applicable, the permitted disparity requirements) here:

Form **5307** (Rev. 9-2001)

## Procedural Requirements Checklist
**********Form 5307**********

**Use this list to ensure that your submitted package is complete. Failure to supply the appropriate information may result in a delay in the processing of the application.**

☐ 1 Is **Form 8717**, User Fee for Employee Plan Determination Letter Request, attached to your submission?

☐ 2 Is the appropriate user fee for your submission attached to Form 8717?

☐ 3 If appropriate, is **Form 2848**, Power of Attorney and Declaration of Representative, or a privately designated authorization attached? (For more information, see the **Disclosure Request by Taxpayer** in the instructions.)

☐ 4 Is a copy of your plan's latest determination letter, if any, attached?

☐ 5 Is the Employer Identification Number (EIN) of the **plan sponsor/employer** (NOT the trust's EIN) entered on line 1b?

☐ 6 Does line 4d list the plan's original effective date?

☐ 7 Is the application signed and dated?

☐ 8 Have interested parties been given the required notification of this application?
(See the instructions for line 3c.)

☐ 9 If your plan is a master or prototype, have you included a copy of the adoption agreement and opinion letter?

☐ 10 If your plan is a volume submitter, have you included:
   ☐ A copy of the plan document;
   ☐ The current advisory letter;
   ☐ A list of modifications from the approved plan;
   ☐ A copy of the trust instrument; and
   ☐ A copy of the plan amendments?
(See **What To File** in the instructions.)

☐ 11 If you answered "Yes" to line(s) 6a and/or 6b, have you included the information requested in the instructions for lines 6a and 6b?

☐ 12 If you answered "Yes" to line 9a, have you included the information specified in the instructions for line 9a?

☐ 13 If you are requesting additional determinations, is page 3 completed and/or the Schedule Q attached?

☐ 14 If filing a Schedule Q, are all appropriate demonstrations attached?
(See Instructions for Schedule Q)
   ☐ Demo 1   ☐ Demo 5   ☐ Demo 8   ☐ Demo 11
   ☐ Demo 3   ☐ Demo 6   ☐ Demo 9
   ☐ Demo 4   ☐ Demo 7   ☐ Demo 10

Form **5307** (Rev. 9-2001)

| Form **8717** | **User Fee for Employee Plan** | For IRS Use Only | OMB No. 1545–1772 |
|---|---|---|---|

Form **8717**
(Rev. February 2002)

Department of the Treasury
Internal Revenue Service

**User Fee for Employee Plan Determination Letter Request**

▶ Attach to determination letter application.

For IRS Use Only

OMB No. 1545–1772

Control number _____

Amount paid _____

User fee screener

**1** Name of plan sponsor (employer if single-employer plan)

**2** Sponsor's employer identification number

**3** Plan name

**4** Plan number

**Caution:** *If you qualify for the exemption from user fees for small business employers, complete only the certification below (see the instructions on page 2 for details). For all other applications, leave the certification blank and check the appropriate box in column A or B of line 5.*

### Certification

I certify that the application for a determination letter on the qualified status of _____ _____ (name of the plan) meets the conditions for exemption from user fees described in section 620 of the Economic Growth and Tax Relief Reconciliation Act of 2001.

Signature ▶ _____  Title ▶ _____  Date ▶ _____

| Form Submitted | Fee Schedule | |
|---|---|---|
| | **A** | **B** |
| **5a Form 5300:** | with Demo 5 and/or Demo 6:<br>☐ $1,250 | no Demo 5 and no Demo 6<br>☐ $700 |
| **b Form 5307:** | with Demo 5 and/or Demo 6:<br>☐ $1,000 | no Demo 5 and no Demo 6<br>☐ $125 |
| **c Form 5310:** | with Demo 5 and/or Demo 6:<br>☐ $375 | no Demo 5 and no Demo 6<br>☐ $225 |
| **d Form 6406:** | Not applicable | ☐ $125 |
| **e Multiple employer plans (Form 5300):** | with Demo 5 and/or Demo 6: | no Demo 5 and no Demo 6 |
| (1) 2 to 10 Forms 5300 submitted | ☐ (1) $1,250 | ☐ (1) $700 |
| (2) 11 to 99 Forms 5300 submitted | ☐ (2) $2,000 | ☐ (2) $1,400 |
| (3) 100 to 499 Forms 5300 submitted | ☐ (3) $3,500 | ☐ (3) $2,800 |
| (4) Over 499 Forms 5300 submitted | ☐ (4) $6,500 | ☐ (4) $5,600 |
| **f Multiple employer plans (Form 5310):** | with Demo 5 and/or Demo 6: | no Demo 5 and no Demo 6 |
| (1) 2 to 10 employers maintaining the plan | ☐ (1) $375 | ☐ (1) $225 |
| (2) 11 to 99 employers maintaining the plan | ☐ (2) $600 | ☐ (2) $450 |
| (3) 100 to 499 employers maintaining the plan | ☐ (3) $1,000 | ☐ (3) $900 |
| (4) Over 499 employers maintaining the plan | ☐ (4) $2,000 | ☐ (4) $1,800 |
| **g Volume submitter:** | | |
| (1) Specimen plan | | ☐ (1) $1,500 |
| (2) Lead specimen plan (see Rev. Proc. 2000-20) | | ☐ (2) $3,000 |
| (3) Specimen plan identical to lead specimen plan (see Rev. Proc. 2000-20) | | ☐ (3) $100 |
| **h Group trust** | | ☐ $750 |

Attach Check or Money Order Here

Cat. No. 64727O

Form **8717** (Rev. 2-2002)

## Instructions

*(Section references are to the Internal Revenue Code unless otherwise noted.)*

### A Change To Note

Small business employers may qualify for an exemption from user fees for determination letter requests made after December 31, 2001. See **Exemption from User Fees** below for details.

Generally, a user fee is required with each application for a determination letter. The user fees are shown on page 1. For more information, see Rev. Proc. 2002-8, 2002-1 I.R.B. 252, and Rev. Proc. 2000-20, 2000-6 I.R.B. 553.

### Exemption from User Fee

The exemption from the user fee (section 620 of the Economic Growth and Tax Relief Reconciliation Act of 2001) applies to all eligible employers (defined below) who request a determination letter within the first five plan years or, if later, the end of the remedial amendment period that begins within the first five plan years with respect to a plan. An application from an eligible employer for a plan that was first effective on or after December 9, 1989, will automatically meet this requirement, provided the application is made by the end of the plan's GUST (i.e., the Small Business Job Protection Act of 1996 and other laws) remedial amendment period. See Rev. Proc. 2001-55, 2001-49 I.R.B. 552, and Rev. Proc. 2000-20, 2000-6 I.R.B. 553, as modified by Notice 2001-42, 2001-30 I.R.B. 70, regarding the GUST remedial amendment period.

An **eligible employer** as defined in section 408(p)(2)(C)(i)(l) is an employer which had no more than 100 employees who received at least $5,000 of compensation from the employer for the preceding year. In addition, an eligible employer must have at least one employee who is not a highly compensated employee (as defined in section 414(q)) and is participating in the plan.

The determination of whether an employer is an eligible employer under this section is made as of the date of the request described above. If your application meets these requirements, complete **only** the Certification. Do **not** complete any part of line 5.

### Payment of User Fee

If you do not met the conditions for exemption discussed above, a user fee is due.

Check the appropriate box in column A of line 5 if **(a)** your plan uses the average benefit test to satisfy minimum coverage requirements and/or the general test to demonstrate nondiscrimination in the amount of contributions or benefits, and **(b)** you want to receive a determination letter that covers these issues (i.e., your application includes **Schedule Q (Form 5300)**, Elective Determination Requests and a demonstration labeled Demo 5 and/or Demo 6).

Check the appropriate box in column B of line 5 if you do not want to receive a determination letter that covers the average benefit test and/or the general test (i.e., the plan is not required to use these tests or you do not want these issues considered). A general test plan is a plan that is other than a design-based safe harbor or nondesign-based safe harbor plan.

Attach a check or money order payable to the **"United States Treasury"** for the full amount of the user fee to Form 8717, if applicable. If you do not include the full amount, your application will be returned. Attach Form 8717 to your determination letter application.

If you have multiple plans (e.g., a profit-sharing plan and a money purchase plan), submit a separate determination letter application and Form 8717 for each plan.

### Where To File

• Send the determination letter application and Form 8717 to:

Internal Revenue Service
P.O. Box 192
Covington, KY 41012-0192

If you are using a private delivery service, send the application and Form 8717 to:

Internal Revenue Service
201 West Rivercenter Blvd.
Covington, KY 41011
Attn: Extracting Stop 312

• Send a request for approval of a **volume submitter specimen plan** to the Volume Submitter Coordinator at:

Internal Revenue Service
P.O. Box 2508
Cincinnati, OH 45201
Attn: VSC
Room 5106

If you are using a private delivery service, send the request for approval of the **volume submitter specimen plan** to:

Internal Revenue Service
550 Main Street
Cincinnati, OH 45202
Attn: VSC
Room 5106

**Paperwork Reduction Act Notice.** We ask for the information on this form to carry out the Internal Revenue laws of the United States. If you want to have your plan approved by the IRS, you are required to give us the information. We need it to determine whether you meet the legal requirements for plan approval.

You are not required to provide the information requested on a form that is subject to the Paperwork Reduction Act unless the form displays a valid OMB control number. Books or records relating to a form or its instructions must be retained as long as their contents may become material in the administration of any Internal Revenue law. Generally, tax returns and return information are confidential, as required by section 6103.

The time needed to complete and file this form will vary depending on individual circumstances. The estimated average time is 5 minutes.

If you have comments concerning the accuracy of this time estimate or suggestions for making this form simpler, we would be happy to hear from you. You can write to the Tax Forms Committee, Western Area Distribution Center, Rancho Cordova, CA 95743-0001. Do **not** send this form to this address. Instead, see **Where To File** above.

# Chapter 28

# BONUS PLAN

## WHAT IS IT?

A bonus is an addition to regular salary or compensation that is provided, usually near year end, to enable employees to share in profits resulting from a successful year. This chapter discusses the tax and other planning considerations that apply.

## WHEN IS IT INDICATED?

1. Bonuses are often used in closely held companies to enable shareholder-employees to withdraw the maximum compensation income from the company each year.

2. Bonuses are used for executives of larger companies as an incentive-oriented form of compensation, based on the attainment of profit or other goals during the year.

3. Bonuses may be used to assist executives in funding cross-purchase buy-sell agreements or in contributing their share of the premium to a split dollar arrangement.

## ADVANTAGES

1. For executives of larger companies, bonuses represent an incentive-based form of compensation that is very effective because of the close connection between performance and receipt. Often, the executive uses the bonus to purchase a life insurance policy which provides death benefit protection and tax-deferred accumulation of cash value.

2. Bonuses allow flexibility in compensation to reflect company performance, both in closely held and larger corporations.

3. Bonus arrangements are flexible and simple to design, within the tax constraints discussed below.

## DISADVANTAGES

1. Bonuses generally do not offer an opportunity for the employee to defer taxation of compensation for more than one year.

2. Bonuses are limited by the requirement of "reasonableness" for the deductibility of compensation payments by the employer.

3. Bonuses are taxable to the employee as ordinary income.

## TAX IMPLICATIONS

Bonus payments are deductible under the same rules as other forms of cash compensation. These rules are discussed in detail in Chapter 30, but will be covered in summary here as they apply to bonuses.

A bonus, together with other compensation, cannot be deducted unless it constitutes (a) a reasonable allowance for (b) services actually rendered. Factors indicating reasonableness—the first part of the test—are listed in the general discussion in Chapter 30. Also discussed in Chapter 30 is the fact that no deduction is permitted for compensation in excess of $1,000,000 paid to certain top executives of publicly held corporations.

Bonuses can be very large if they are based on profits or earnings and the company has a very good year. For example, suppose a sales manager receives a $400,000 bonus in addition to his regular $100,000 base salary, under a sales-target bonus formula. Although $500,000 of compensation might, as a general rule, be considered unreasonably high for this type of sales manager, this arrangement might be sustained by the IRS for two reasons:

- Reasonableness of compensation is often tested in accordance with circumstances existing when the bonus agreement is entered into rather than when the bonus is actually paid.

- In testing the reasonableness of a bonus, both the IRS and the courts will usually take into account the element of risk involved to the employee. That is, an employee presumably had a choice between a relatively lower amount of guaranteed compensation and a higher amount of contingent compensation. So the two should be deemed equivalent for purposes of testing reasonableness. For instance, a sales manager who receives a $100,000 base salary and a bonus of 10% of the gross sales increase in 2004, producing a $400,000 bonus for 2004, probably could not at the beginning of 2004 have negotiated a contract for $500,000 of guaranteed compensation without bonus. The reasonableness of the bonus contract should be based on the reasonableness of the equivalent fixed salary agreement that the sales manager could have negotiated, not on the $500,000 total resulting from taking a chance and then having a good year.

This emphasizes the importance of planning ahead when using bonuses as an employee benefit technique. If reasonableness might become an issue, decide upon a bonus formula well in advance of the time the bonus is paid. (Preferably, in advance of the year in which the bonus will be earned). In other words, a formula for determining a bonus for year-end 2004 should be determined in writing before the beginning of 2004 to help support the reasonableness of the amount.

The timing of income to the employee and deductions to the corporation are governed by the rules discussed in detail in Chapter 30 with regard to cash compensation. Since bonuses are often payable after the end of the year in which they are earned, the "2½ month safe-harbor rule" is important for bonus planning. Under this rule, an accrual method corporation can deduct a compensation payment that is properly accrued before the end of a given year, so long as the payment is made no later than 2½ months after the end of the corporation's taxable year. For example, for a calendar year accrual method corporation, a bonus earned for services completed in 2004 can be deducted by the corporation for 2004, so long as it is paid on or before March 15, 2005. Note, however, that the 2½ month rule does not apply to payments to employees who own or control (50% or more) the corporation under Code section 267(b). For those employees, the corporation must pay the bonus during its taxable year in order to deduct it during that taxable year.

For regular employees who can make use of the 2½ month safe harbor technique, the ability to move taxable income into the employee's next taxable year is a significant advantage of the bonus form of compensation. For example, a bonus might be earned (and deducted by the corporation) in 2004, paid on March 15, 2005, and the employee could defer the payment of tax to April 15, 2006 (the employee's due date for the 2005 tax return.)

## ALTERNATIVES

1. As with cash compensation in general, as discussed in Chapter 30, taxation can be avoided or deferred by various types of noncash compensation plans that are discussed throughout this book, including qualified pension and profit sharing plans, nonqualified deferred compensation plans, and medical benefit plans.

2. Stock option, incentive stock option (ISO), or restricted stock plans are forms of deferred compensation with many of the same incentive features as a cash bonus plan. These are discussed in later chapters.

## HOW ARE THESE PLANS SET UP?

Bonus plans can be informal or even oral. There are no tax or other legal requirements for a written plan or for filing anything with the government. However, a written plan is often desirable, and in that case employer and employee might want to consult with an attorney experienced in handling employee compensation matters.

## WHERE CAN I FIND OUT MORE ABOUT THESE PLANS?

1. Graduate Course: Executive Compensation (GS 842), The American College, Bryn Mawr, PA.

2. FSP (formerly CLU/ChFC Courses): Income Taxation (HS 321) and Planning for Business Owners and Professionals (HS 331), The American College, Bryn Mawr, PA.

3. CFP Course: Retirement Planning and Employee Benefits (CFP V), College for Financial Planning, Denver, CO.

## QUESTIONS AND ANSWERS

**Question** — What are the advantages of a written bonus plan?

*Answer* — A written agreement has at least two advantages:

First, a written plan, particularly one drafted in advance of the year in which compensation is earned, helps to avoid disallowance of the corporation's deduction on the ground that the amount is unreasonable. Without a written plan, the IRS is likely to claim that a bonus is simply a discretionary payment that is excessive and therefore nondeductible. If this payment is made to a shareholder, the payment may be characterized as a dividend instead of deductible compensation. This means that the corporation will not receive a tax deduction, even though the entire distribution will probably be taxable as dividend income to the shareholder-recipient.

A second reason for a written agreement is that it defines the terms of the bonus and assures the employee of legal grounds to require the corporation to live up to the agreement. The terms of the agreement should be clearly defined for this reason.

**Question** — If a bonus is based on "profits," is there any specific definition of profits that must be used?

*Answer* — There is no tax or legal reason for any specific definition of profits in a bonus agreement. But it is important to use a clear definition in order to protect against later misunderstandings. Profits can be defined as the amount shown in financial statements, as taxable income for federal income tax purposes, or based upon some other method of defining profits. If the definition relies on company accounting methods or federal tax laws, the agreement should take possible changes in accounting method or the tax laws into account. Paying a bonus may, in itself, affect profits. So, the agreement must specify whether profits are determined before or after bonus payments. For a company with more than one division or subsidiary, an executive may want to tie the bonus to profits in one particular unit rather than the company as a whole.

# Chapter 29

# CAFETERIA PLAN

## WHAT IS IT?

A cafeteria plan is one under which employees may, within limits, choose the form of employee benefits from a "cafeteria" of benefit plans provided by their employer. Cafeteria plans must include a "cash option"—an option to receive cash in lieu of noncash benefits of equal value.[1]

## WHEN IS IT INDICATED?

1. When employee benefit needs vary within the employee group—for example, where the employee mix includes young, unmarried people with minimal life insurance and medical benefit needs as well as older employees with families who need maximum medical and life insurance benefits.

2. When employees want to choose the benefit package most suited to their needs.

3. When an employer seeks to maximize employee satisfaction with the benefit package, and thereby maximize the employer's benefit from its compensation expenditures.

4. When the employer is large enough to afford the expense of such a plan. Because of administrative costs and complexity, cafeteria plans, in general, tend to be used by larger employers. However, there is one type of cafeteria plan—the flexible spending account or FSA—that provides very specific tax benefits and is often used even by smaller employers including closely held businesses. FSAs feature benefit funding through salary reductions by employees. FSA plans are discussed in detail in Chapter 35.

## ADVANTAGES

1. Cafeteria plans help give employees an appreciation of the value of their benefit package.

2. The flexibility of a cafeteria benefit package helps meet varied employee needs.

3. Cafeteria plans can help control employer costs for the benefit package because provision of benefits that employees do not need is minimized.

## DISADVANTAGES

1. Cafeteria plans are more complex and expensive for the employer to design and administer than fixed, standardized benefit packages.

2. Benefit packages usually include some insured benefits—medical and life insurance benefits, for example—and not all insurers will provide these programs on a cafeteria plan basis.

3. Complex tax requirements apply to the plan under Section 125 of the Internal Revenue Code.

4. Highly compensated employees may lose the tax benefits of the plan if it is discriminatory. Key employees may lose tax benefits if more than 25% of aggregate benefits under the plan are provided to them.

## EXAMPLE OF CAFETERIA PLAN

1. All employees receive a "basic benefit package" consisting of:

   • Term life insurance equal to 1½ times salary;

   • Medical expense insurance for employee and dependents; and

   • Disability income insurance (long and short term).

2. Each employee receives an additional "credit" based on salary and years of service (3% of salary for zero to five years of service, 4½% for five to 10 years of service, and 6% for 10 or more years). Each year the employee can elect to apply this credit to one or more of a list of additional benefits specified by the employer. These benefits might include:

- Cash only;

- Additional term life insurance up to one times salary;

- Dental insurance for employee or dependents; and

- Up to two weeks additional vacation time.

## TAX IMPLICATIONS

1. A cafeteria plan must comply with the provisions of Code section 125. This code section provides an exception from the "constructive receipt" doctrine for cafeteria plans. Under that doctrine, an employee is taxed on money or property that he has a free election to receive, even if he chooses not to receive it. So, if the terms of Section 125 are not met in a cafeteria plan, an employee is taxed on the value of any taxable benefits available from the plan, even if the participant chooses nontaxable benefits, such as medical insurance.

2. Under Section 125 and its regulations, only certain benefits—"qualified benefits"—can be made available in a cafeteria plan.[2] Qualifying benefits include cash and most tax-free benefits provided under the Code, *except*:

   - medical savings account contributions under Section 106(b).

   - scholarships and fellowships under Section 117.

   - educational assistance provided under a plan governed by Section 127.

   - employee discounts (for example, those for department store employees), no-additional-cost services (for example, standby airline travel for airline employees), and other fringe benefits provided under Section 132.[3]

   - retirement benefits, such as qualified or nonqualified deferred compensation; however, a 401(k) arrangement can be included.[4]

   - long-term care insurance.[5]

3. There are nondiscrimination requirements for cafeteria plans:

*Participation.* The plan must be made available to a group of employees in a manner that does not discriminate in favor of "highly compensated" employees.[6] A highly compensated employee, for this purpose, is one who is an officer, a shareholder owning more than 5% of the employer, a highly compensated employee, or the spouse or dependent of any of these.[7] The following "safe-harbor" eligibility provision is permitted: the plan will not be considered discriminatory if it benefits a group of employees under a classification that does not discriminate in favor of highly compensated employees *and* it covers all employees with three years of service beginning no later than the first day of the plan year after the three years' service is attained.[8]

*Benefits.* The plan must not discriminate in favor of highly compensated employees as to contributions and benefits.[9] Also, qualified benefits provided to key employees (as defined in the top-heavy plan rules under Section 416(i) — see Chapter 25) under the plan must not exceed, in value, 25% of the aggregate value of plan benefits provided to all employees.[10]

If these nondiscrimination tests are not met by the plan, the result is that otherwise nontaxable benefits become taxable to highly compensated employees or key employees—but not to regular employees.

In addition, any type of benefit offered under the plan must meet its own nondiscrimination tests—for example, any group term life insurance offered under the plan would also have to meet the nondiscrimination requirements of Section 79. These requirements are discussed in the chapters of this book covering these plans.

In many cases, it is not difficult to meet the nondiscrimination tests. In other cases, the result of not meeting the tests—some taxation to highly compensated employees only—may not be objectionable in view of the overall advantages of the plan.

## ALTERNATIVES

1. The FSA, or flexible spending account, is a cafeteria plan funded through salary reductions. It is not just an alternative but a special type of cafeteria plan design that should be thoroughly investigated whenever cafeteria benefits are considered—see Chapter 35.

2. Fixed benefit programs without employee choice may be adequate where most employees have the same benefit needs or where the employer cannot administer a more complex program.

3. Cash compensation as an alternative to benefits gives up tax advantages in favor of maximum employee choice, and assumes that employees will have adequate income to provide benefits on their own.

## HOW ARE THESE PLANS SET UP?

1. First, the employer must decide on a plan design. This involves a survey of employee needs and employer costs, and a business decision as to the best alternative.

2. A written plan must be drafted and adopted by the employer. IRS or other governmental approval of the plan is generally not necessary, but an IRS ruling can be obtained if there is any doubt about some aspect of the tax treatment of the plan as designed.

3. Employee election (choice of benefit) forms must be designed and distributed to employees. Generally, employees must make benefit choices in advance of the year in which the benefits are earned.[11] For example, for benefits to be earned and used in 2005, employees should complete and file their election forms with the employer before the end of 2004.

4. Skillful communication with employees is the most important element in the success of a cafeteria plan; these plans are often complicated.

## HOW DO I FIND OUT MORE ABOUT THESE PLANS?

1. Beam, Burton T., Jr. and John J. McFadden, *Employee Benefits*, 6th ed. Chicago, IL: Dearborn Financial Publishing, Inc., 2001.

2. Graduate Course: Executive Compensation (GS 842), The American College, Bryn Mawr, PA.

## FOOTNOTES

1. IRC Section 125(d)(1).
2. IRC Section 125(d)(1)(B).
3. IRC Section 125(f).
4. IRC Section 125(d)(2).
5. IRC Section 125(f).
6. IRC Section 125(b)(1)(A).
7. IRC Section 125(e).
8. IRC Section 125(g)(3).
9. IRC Section 125(b)(1)(B).
10. IRC Section 125(b)(2).
11. Prop. Treas. Reg. §1.125-1, Q&A 15.

# Chapter 30

# CASH COMPENSATION PLANNING

## WHAT IS IT?

Although cash compensation—the employee's compensation paid currently (during the year in which it is earned)—is not generally thought of as an employee benefit, it is actually the core of any compensation and benefit package. Any proposed employee benefit has to be compared in effectiveness with equivalent cash compensation. In addition, many employee benefit plans such as pension and life insurance plans have benefit or contribution schedules that are based on the employee's cash compensation. Finally, from a tax point of view, cash compensation is not as simple as it might appear. Financial planners must understand the rules to avoid adverse tax results from inappropriate planning.

## WHEN IS IT INDICATED?

Opportunities for planning cash compensation primarily arise for employees, including shareholder-employees, of regular or "C" corporations (not "S" corporations). In an unincorporated business or an "S" corporation, all income and losses pass directly through to the owners' tax returns, so there are few compensation planning opportunities.

## ADVANTAGES

1.  Compared with noncash benefits or deferred payments, cash compensation provides certainty and, therefore, greater security to the employee.

2.  Cash compensation tends to set an employee's status in the company and community; the amount of annual salary must be carefully considered for this reason.

3.  Cash compensation is an important part of overall financial planning for shareholder-employees of closely held corporations.

4.  For employers, cash compensation is preferable to noncash benefits because it is easier to budget, with no unknown or uncontrollable costs.

5.  Cash compensation plans rarely involve design and administrative complexities, including ERISA aspects, that may apply to medical benefits, pensions, and other types of noncash or deferred compensation.

## DISADVANTAGES

1.  In general, cash compensation that is paid currently is currently taxable at ordinary income rates.

2.  Cash compensation must meet the reasonableness test for deductibility and other tax issues discussed below. In some cases, other forms of compensation can avoid or defer these problems.

## TAX IMPLICATIONS

### Reasonableness of Compensation

The Internal Revenue Code allows an employer who carries on a trade or business to deduct "a reasonable allowance for salaries or other compensation for personal services actually rendered."[1] This "reasonableness" test is the main tax issue in determining whether an employer's payments for compensating an employee are deductible. If the company's payment does not meet this reasonableness test, its deduction is disallowed.

In addition to the reasonableness requirement, there is an upper limitation on the amount of compensation paid to certain executives that may be deducted by a publicly-held corporation. Generally, no deduction is permitted for compensation in excess of $1,000,000 paid by a publicly-held corporation to the company's chief executive officer or any employee who is one of the four highest compensated officers of the company (other than the chief executive officer).[2] There are, however, exceptions to this rule for compensation payable on a commission basis, and other forms of performance-based compensation.

At a corporate income tax rate of 35%, the corporation's deduction saves 35 cents for every deductible dollar.

Stated in another manner, the out-of-pocket cost for reasonable (deductible) compensation is 65 cents of each dollar paid, as opposed to one dollar for nondeductible payments. Since state income tax deductibility usually follows the federal rules, the true difference between deductibility and nondeductibility can be even greater.

The IRS does not usually raise the reasonableness issue if salaries are not particularly high. However, as the amount paid and deducted increases, it becomes important for a company to "build a case" that compensation is reasonable. Steps to suggest to a client include:

- Determine compensation levels prior to the beginning of each fiscal year, before salary has been earned, instead of simply determining salaries from year-to-year on a purely discretionary basis. This avoids the impression that the amount of salary is based simply on the amount that shareholder-employees wish to withdraw from the corporation for a given year.

- Written employment contracts should be provided and signed before compensation is earned.

- The company's board of directors should document, in the minutes of directors' meetings, how the amount of salary was determined.

- Court cases and IRS publications mention many factors in determining what constitutes reasonable compensation. These factors, listed below, should be reviewed in documenting the amount of salary and other compensation.

### Factors in Determining Reasonable Compensation

Factors mentioned by the courts in "reasonableness of compensation" cases, and by the IRS in its publications, include the following:

- Comparison with compensation paid to executives in comparable positions for comparable employers.

- The employee's qualifications for the position.

- The nature and scope of the employee's duties.

- The size and complexity of the business enterprise.

- Comparison of the compensation paid with the company's gross and net income.

- The company's compensation policy for all employees.

- Economic conditions—including the condition of the industry and the local economy as well as the overall national economy.

- Comparison with dividend distributions to shareholders. Abnormally low dividends can create an inference that a so-called salary payment to a shareholder-employee is really a disguised dividend.

In recent cases, courts have increasingly stressed the "hypothetical independent investor" test. Under this test, the court compares rates of return on investment in the corporation that is under IRS challenge with the rates of return that an independent investor in the same type of business would demand. If the target corporation's rate of investment return is significantly lower, the implication is that corporate profits are being paid out in the form of compensation to employees, which in turn implies that the compensation amounts are unreasonable.

### Treatment of Disallowed Compensation

A deduction for compensation that is disallowed because it is unreasonable is treated in various ways depending on the circumstances. IRS regulations state that if a corporation makes excessive payments and such payments are made primarily to shareholders, these payments will be treated as dividends.[3] Dividend treatment is the most typical situation for disallowed compensation. Other types of treatment are possible, depending on the facts. For example, if an employee at some point had transferred property to the corporation, excessive compensation payments could be treated as payments for this property, which would be nondeductible capital expenditures to the corporation.

From the recipient's point of view, in the absence of any other evidence, any excessive payments for salaries or compensation will be taxable as ordinary income to the recipient. In other words, from the employee's point of view, the reasonableness issue may not have much tax effect.

However, if the employee is a shareholder in the corporation, the corporation's tax picture and the possible loss of a compensation deduction at the corporate level can be very important.

*Example:* Larry Sharp owns 100% of Sharp Corporation and is its sole employee. Sharp Corporation earns $400,000 in 2003. If the corporation pays all $400,000 to Larry as deductible compensation, the only tax burden on the $400,000 is the individual income tax that Larry pays. But if the IRS disallows $100,000 of the compensation deduction and treats it as a nondeductible dividend, then Larry still has $400,000 of taxable ordinary income, but the corporation also has $100,000 of taxable income. The corporation's tax on this—$22,250—is a direct reduction in Larry's wealth since he is a 100% shareholder.

Note however, that with the passage of the Jobs and Growth Tax Relief Reconciliation Act of 2003, the maximum income tax on certain dividends may be reduced to 15%, which may increase compensation planning opportunities for business owners.

## Reimbursement Agreements

Because of the uncertainty of the reasonable compensation issue, companies often enter into reimbursement agreements with employees under which the employee is required to pay back the excessive portion of the compensation to the corporation if the IRS disallows a deduction for compensation. The employee does not generally have to pay income tax on the amount repaid. These agreements can be useful, but they do not necessarily solve the reasonableness problem. In fact, they may be a "red flag" to the IRS examiner. The IRS sometimes asserts that such an agreement is evidence that the corporation intended to pay unreasonable compensation. Therefore, such an agreement can make the compensation even more likely to attract attention during a tax audit and more difficult to defend in litigation.

An agreement to reimburse is rarely in the direct financial interest of the employee, since the employee would usually be better off keeping the money rather than returning it. The employee's tax on any excessive portion is treated as a dividend, so the tax paid from the employee's perspective may be less than if the entire payment was compensation. Reimbursement agreements are primarily used by shareholder-employees where the corporation's tax status is of indirect financial

interest to the employee. In those cases, what hurts the corporation hurts the employee as a stockholder.

## Timing of Income and Deductions

The tax rules for the timing of a corporation's deduction for compensation are more complicated than one might expect, primarily because the IRS sees potential for abuse in compensation payment situations.

Under the usual tax accounting rules for accrual method taxpayers, an item is deductible for an accounting period if that item has been properly accrued, even if not actually paid. Accrual occurs, for tax purposes, in the taxable year when all events have happened that legally require the corporation to pay the amount—the so-called "all events" test. Usually, the all events test is satisfied as soon as the employee has performed all the services required under the terms of the employment contract. Because of the apparent potential for abuse of compensation arrangements, particularly for closely held businesses, there are specific rules for deducting compensation payments that override the usual accrual rules in some cases. These are summarized below.

If the company uses the cash method of accounting, deductions for compensation cannot be taken before the year in which the compensation is actually paid.

No employer, whether using the cash method or the accrual method, can take a deduction for compensation for services that are not rendered before the end of the taxable year for which the deduction is claimed. Any compensation paid in advance must be deducted pro rata over the period during which services are actually rendered.

## Timing of Corporate Deductions for Compensation Payments

The tax rules for timing of deductions distinguish between *current compensation* and *deferred compensation*. If the compensation qualifies as current compensation, then the employer can deduct it in the year in which it is properly accrued to the corporation under the tax accounting accrual rules. If the amount qualifies as deferred compensation, then the employer corporation cannot deduct it until the taxable year of the corporation in which, or with which, ends the taxable year of the employee in which the amount is includable in the employee's income.[4] For example, if an employer sets up a deferred compensation arrangement in 2004 for work performed in 2004 with compensation payable in 2006 and taxable to the employee in 2006, the corporation cannot deduct the compensation amount until 2006.

Whether an amount is considered current or deferred compensation depends on the type of employee:

- For a regular employee—an employee who is not a controlling shareholder or otherwise related to the employer corporation—the IRS takes the position that a plan is deferred compensation if the payment is made more than 2½ months after the end of the taxable year of the corporation.[5] In other words, there is a 2½ month *safe harbor rule*. For example, if a calendar year accrual-method corporation declares and accrues a bonus to an employee before the end of 2004, the employer is entitled to a 2004 deduction for the bonus as long as the bonus is paid before March 15, 2005. The employee would include this bonus in income for 2005. However, if the bonus was paid on April 1, 2005—beyond the 2½ month limit—then, the employee still includes the amount in income for 2005, but the employer's deduction is delayed until 2005.

- If the employee is related to the corporation (directly or indirectly owns more than 50% of the corporation), then the 2½ month safe harbor rule does not apply.[6] Deductions and income are matched in all cases. So, if a calendar year accrual-method corporation declares and accrues a bonus to its controlling shareholder before the end of 2004, but pays it on February 1, 2005, the corporation cannot deduct the bonus until 2005.

## ALTERNATIVES

1. Taxation can be avoided or deferred by various types of noncash compensation plans, which are discussed throughout this book. Some examples of plans that defer taxation, usually until cash is actually received by the employee, are:

    - nonqualified deferred compensation plans,

    - qualified pension, profit sharing, ESOP, 401(k) and similar plans, and

    - stock option and restricted stock plans.

Compensation options that are completely tax free (no taxation either currently or deferred) include such plans as:

- health and accident plans (provided that certain nondiscrimination and eligibility requirements are met),

- disability income plans of certain types,

- dependent care and educational assistance plans (subject to certain maximum limits on amounts that may be excluded from income by employees),

- group term life insurance up to $50,000 (unless the plan discriminates in favor of key employees), and

- the pure death benefit amount from any life insurance plan, even if the premium is currently taxable.

2. Where the employer may lose a deduction for cash compensation due to a reasonableness of compensation problem, part of the compensation might be provided in a form that is both tax-deferred to the employee and deduction-deferred to the employer. This is discussed further under nonqualified deferred compensation plans. The reasonableness of compensation issue does not arise until the year in which the employer takes the deduction, so deferring the deduction can be helpful.

## HOW IS THE PLAN SET UP?

Cash compensation planning is simple and is often not even thought of as a form of employee benefit planning. However, for a complex employment agreement involving cash and other forms of compensation, and in situations where reasonableness of compensation may be an issue, a tax accountant, tax attorney, or financial planner specializing in employee benefits and compensation planning can provide useful guidance.

## WHERE CAN I FIND OUT MORE ABOUT IT?

1. IRS Publication 334, *Tax Guide for Small Business*, has a simple explanation of the IRS position on the employer's tax treatment of employee pay and benefits. IRS Publication 17, *Your Federal Income Tax*, covers the tax treatment from the employee side.

Both these publications are available free from the IRS and are revised annually.

2.  Graduate Course: Executive Compensation (GS 842), The American College, Bryn Mawr, PA.

3.  FSP (formerly CLU/ChFC) Courses: Income Taxation (HS 321) and Planning for Business Owners and Professionals (HS 331), The American College, Bryn Mawr, PA.

4.  CFP Course: Retirement Planning and Employee Benefits (CFP V), College for Financial Planning, Denver, CO.

## QUESTIONS AND ANSWERS

**Question** — If an executive's compensation is based on profits or sales, will it be deemed unreasonable (and therefore nondeductible) if the employer has an unusually good year and the payment is therefore very high?

*Answer* — The reasonableness of salary is typically tested according to the circumstances existing at the time a profit-oriented compensation agreement is entered into rather than when it is actually paid. Thus, if the percentage or formula itself is not unreasonable at the time the agreement becomes binding on the parties, the actual amount may be deemed reasonable, however high. In addition, the issue of reasonableness can also take into account the element of risk involved to the employee. That is, suppose an employer agrees to pay an employee $100,000, plus 25% of profits for the upcoming year. The company has an extremely good year and the employee receives $600,000. While a $600,000 guaranteed salary might be deemed unreasonable, the fact that the executive took some risk in accepting a contingent type of compensation may bring the $600,000 amount within the limits of reasonableness.

**Question** — What is the significance of cash compensation planning for an employee of an S corporation?

*Answer* — An S corporation is a corporation that has made an election under federal tax law to be taxed essentially as a partnership. In an S corporation, all corporate income and losses are passed through to stockholders in proportion to their stock ownership. Corporate income is taxable to shareholders whether or not it is actually distributed as dividends. For S corporation shareholder-employees, there is no opportunity to defer taxation of their share of current income, except through a qualified retirement plan, which is discussed in other chapters of this book.

When S corporation shareholders are also employees of the corporation, as is often the case, it is important to distinguish between compensation for services to the shareholder-employees, as opposed to their share of corporate earnings passed through to them from the corporation. This distinction between compensation and dividend income has a significant effect on the various qualified and nonqualified employee benefit plans, discussed later in this book. For example, pension plans and group-term life insurance plans often base their benefits on the employee's compensation income, which does not include any element of income from the corporation that is characterized as a dividend.

## FOOTNOTES

1.  IRC Section 162(a)(1).
2.  IRC Section 162(m).
3.  Treas. Reg. §1.162-8.
4.  IRC Section 404(a)(5); Reg. §1.404(a)-12(b)(2).
5.  Temp. Treas. Reg. §1.404(b)-1T, Q 2.
6.  IRC Sections 267(a)(2), 267(b)(2).

# Chapter 31

# COMPANY CAR OR REIMBURSEMENT PLAN

## WHAT IS IT?

A car is often an essential business tool for an employee or someone who is self-employed. Employers often provide cars or reimburse expenses for business use of personally owned vehicles. Company cars or car expense reimbursement plans are not employee benefits as such, since their purpose is not actually to compensate the employee. However, an employer's policy regarding business use of cars is often viewed as part of the employer's fringe benefit package.

There are three possible types of arrangements between an employer and employee regarding business use of cars:

(1) *Company car.* The business can provide the car directly to the employee.

(2) *Reimbursement plan.* The business can reimburse the employee for costs incurred in using the employee's car for business.

(3) *No plan.* The employee or self-employed person can assume the costs of business use of the car and deduct them on his or her tax return. (The employee's salary or other compensation implicitly will reflect the fact that the employee assumes this burden.)

For an employee, the first scenario—the company car—generally provides the best tax result, since it can allow all business related car expenses to be excluded from taxable income in all cases. A reimbursement approach, or the unreimbursed use of the employee's car (scenarios two or three) may not allow full deductions since the employee must deduct car expenses as a "miscellaneous expense." These are subject to a 2% of gross income "floor," as discussed below under "Reporting."

For a self-employed person, all business related car expenses are deductible without a 2% floor.

The tax rules for car expense deductions are inordinately complicated, apparently because Congress

and the IRS believe that taxpayers often abuse these provisions. This chapter will summarize the rules for handling deductions and reimbursements for car use.

## COMPANY CARS

### When is it Indicated?

Because of the administrative complexity of company car plans, company cars are provided primarily where employees use them substantially for business or commuting. They are also provided as a fringe benefit for selected executives in high tax brackets.

### Advantages of Company Car Programs

1. The "company car" approach can maximize tax benefits for the employee by avoiding the 2% of adjusted gross income floor for miscellaneous itemized deductions.

2. Companies can maintain maximum control over the cars employees use in business (type of car, maintenance, etc.).

### Disadvantages

1. Companies must bear the capital investment costs of car ownership. With the termination of the investment credit and less favorable depreciation rules, such an investment has fewer tax benefits than in past years.

2. Companies must bear substantial administrative costs. In particular, if the car is used for personal purposes to a significant extent, the company must bear the burden of determining the value of personal use if the employee is to avoid the 2% floor limitation on miscellaneous itemized deductions (see the rules discussed below).

## Tax Treatment of Employer

In a company car plan, the employer is the owner of the car and is entitled to deductions for depreciation, as well as for any other expenses it actually pays.

*Employer reporting.* The employer must report the value of car availability to affected employees. There are basically three options for reporting:

1.  The employer can report the entire value of car availability on the employee's W-2 and the employee can claim a deduction for business use. In this case, the employee is subject to the 2% floor requirement for miscellaneous itemized deductions;

2.  The employer can determine the amount of personal or commuting use and report that only; or

3.  If the plan meets the requirements for a written plan as discussed below under "Employee Recordkeeping," the employer can report only commuting use for which the employer has not been reimbursed by the employee.

The employer must withhold Social Security (FICA) and FUTA on the amount reported, but the employer can elect not to withhold federal income tax on this amount.[1] If so, the employee may have to increase withholding or estimated tax payments to avoid an underpayment penalty.

The employer can elect a special accounting rule under which fringe benefits, such as company cars, provided during the last two months of a calendar year can be treated as provided during the following calendar year.[2] If the employer elects this treatment, the employee must follow it also.

*Valuation of car availability.* The taxable value of a car to an employee is the amount an unrelated third party would charge for its use in an arms-length transaction.[3] A comparable lease value can be used.

Alternatively, the employer can elect one of three special valuation rules; if the employer does so, the employee must use either the same rule that the employer elected or the general arms-length rule.[4] The three special rules are:

*   A lease value from the IRS' Annual Lease Value Table.[5]

*   A mileage rate of 36 cents per mile (in 2003) for all business use.[6] To use the mileage rate the car must be (1) used more than 50% in business; (2) used each weekday in an employer sponsored commuting pool; or (3) driven at least 10,000 miles during the year and used primarily by employees. Also, the standard mileage rate cannot be used to value the use of any "luxury car" subject to the depreciation limitations of Code Section 280F.[7]

*   A "commuting valuation rule" of $1.50 per one-way commute or $3.00 per round trip. To use this rule, the employer must have (and enforce) a written policy that the employee must commute in the vehicle and cannot use the vehicle for other than minimal personal use. This election is unavailable to "control employees" (directors and certain officers and owners — see below).[8]

## Tax Treatment of Employee

To the extent used for business, providing a car to an employee is a "working condition fringe" under Code section 132 and, thus, its value is not included in income. (See Chapter 36, Fringe Benefits.) If the car is used for commuting or for personal purposes, the amount included in the employee's income for the year is:

$$\frac{\text{personal/commuting miles}}{\text{total miles}} \times \text{value of car availability}$$

See the "Questions and Answers" section at the end of this chapter for a definition of "commuting."

The employee is entitled to a business deduction for any expenses the employee actually pays for business use of the automobile (such as gasoline, etc.). The employee is also entitled to a deduction to the extent of business use if the employer chooses to report 100% of the car's availability value on the employee's W-2. (In that case, the employee's deduction on Form 2106, line 27 is the business use percentage of the total amount reported on the W-2.)

However, if the employee claims a deduction in either situation, it must be reported on Schedule A as a miscellaneous deduction and is therefore subject to the 2% of adjusted gross income limitation for such deductions. In other words, the most advantageous company car plan will be one which minimizes or eliminates the need for the employee to claim any business expense deductions.

*Employee recordkeeping.* If the car is used partly for business and partly for personal use, the employee must keep records substantiating the business use. These are necessary either to allow the employer to determine the amount of business use, or to allow the employee to claim a business deduction if the employer reports 100% of the car's value on the employee's W-2 (see above).

However, if the car is used only for business and commuting, with minimal personal use, the employee does not have to keep records if:

1. the company has a written policy statement (meeting requirements set out in IRS Regulations) of no personal use except for commuting;

2. the employee is not a control employee (director, officer earning $50,000 or more, employee earning $100,000 or more, or 1% or more owner);

3. the employer reports the commuting value on the employee's W-2 to the extent the commuting value is not reimbursed to the employer; and

4. the employee is required, for "bona fide noncompensatory business reasons," to travel to or from work in the vehicle.[9]

## REIMBURSEMENT PLANS AND "NO PLANS"

The IRS recognizes three types of reimbursement plans:

1. An *accountable plan* is one that requires the employee (a) to adequately account to the employer for expenses and (b) return any excess reimbursement to the employer.

2. A *nonaccountable plan* is one that *either* (a) does not require the employee to adequately account to the employer, or (b) allows the employee to keep excess reimbursements.

3. *No plan*—that is, the employer does not reimburse directly at all, and the employee is responsible for paying expenses and is entitled to any deduction for them. However, the employer can indirectly reimburse the employee in this situation by increasing salary or paying a bonus.

The IRS table shown in Figure 31.1 summarizes the employer and employee reporting treatment under these three situations. The IRS table shown in Figure 31.2

summarizes when local transportation expenses are deductible.[10]

## REPORTING

Employer W-2 reporting requirements have been discussed above.

For an *employee* claiming a car expense deduction, Form 2106 must be filed. A simplified Form 2106-EZ may be used in certain situations using the standard mileage rate. Forms 2106 and 2106-EZ are reproduced at the end of this chapter. The deductible amount determined on Form 2106 is entered on the employee's Schedule A, Form 1040, as a miscellaneous deduction. Miscellaneous deductions, in total, are allowable only to the extent that they exceed 2% of the employee's adjusted gross income.

A *self-employed person* does not file Form 2106. Instead, car expenses are computed and entered as a deduction on Schedule C, "Income From Business or Profession." There is no 2% of adjusted gross income limitation on Schedule C deductions.

## WHERE CAN I GET ADDITIONAL INFORMATION?

The rules in this area are extremely complex. A summary of these rules is found in IRS Publication 463, *Travel, Entertainment, Gift, and Car Expenses*, and IRS Publication 535, *Business Expenses*. IRS regulations under Code sections 61, 132, and 274 also deal with car expenses.

## QUESTIONS AND ANSWERS

**Question** — Is interest on a car loan deductible as a business expense?

*Answer* — Interest on a car loan is not deductible by most taxpayers. However, if the taxpayer is self-employed, the interest is deductible as a Schedule C deduction, to the extent of business use of the car.

**Question** — What types of "getting to work" trips are business expenses as opposed to commuting?

*Answer* — The IRS has persistently attempted to crack down on alleged abuses in this area. Some current IRS positions:

**Figure 31.1**

| REPORTING TRAVEL, ENTERTAINMENT, GIFT AND CAR EXPENSES AND REIMBURSEMENTS | | |
|---|---|---|
| **Type of Reimbursement (or Other Expense Allowance) Arrangement** | **Employer Reports on Form W-2** | **Employee Reports on Form 2106[1]** |
| *Accountable Plan* | | |
| Actual expense reimbursement<br><br>Adequate accounting made and excess returned | No amount. | No amount. |
| Actual expense reimbursement<br><br>Adequate accounting and return of excess both required but excess not returned | Excess reported as wages in Box 1. | No amount. |
| Per diem or mileage allowance up to federal rate<br><br>Adequate accounting made and excess returned | No amount. | All expenses and reimbursements *only* if excess expenses are claimed. Otherwise form is not filed. |
| Per diem or mileage allowance up to the federal rate<br><br>Adequate accounting and return of excess both required but excess not returned | Excess reported as wages in Box 1. Amount up to the federal rate is reported only in Box 13—it is *not* reported in Box 1. | No amount. |
| Per diem or mileage allowance exceeds the federal rate<br><br>Adequate accounting up to the federal rate only and excess not returned | Excess reported as wages in Box 1. Amount up to the federal rate is reported only in Box 13—it is *not* reported in Box 1. | All expenses (and reimbursements reported on Form W-2, box 13) *only* if expenses in excess of the federal rate are claimed. Otherwise, form is not filed. |
| *Nonaccountable Plan* | | |
| Either adequate accounting or return of excess, or both, not required by plan | Entire amount is reported as wages in Box 1. | All expenses. |
| *No Reimbursement Plan* | Entire amount is reported wages in Box 1. | All expenses. |

[1] You may be able to use Form 2106-EZ. See *Completing Forms 2106 and 2106-EZ* in Chapter 6 of IRS Pub. 463.

- Using a car telephone for business calls, carrying tools or instruments, or having advertising signs on your car will not cause a commute to be considered a business trip.

- If you work at two different workplaces, the cost of getting from one place to the other is deductible as a business expense. The cost of traveling between an office at home and other work locations is a deductible business expense *if* the home office is the principal place of business. But a commute to and from home to a part-time job is not a deductible expense. See the IRS chart at Figure 31.2.

- You can deduct the round trip cost of travel from your home to a temporary work assignment (i.e., where work is initially expected to last for a year or less and actually does last for a year or less) if the temporary work is located outside the metropolitan area where you live.[11]

**Figure 31.2**

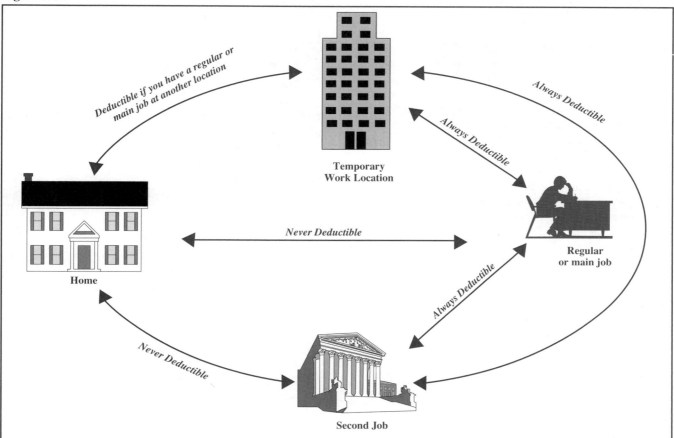

*Home*: The place where you reside. Transportation expenses between your home and your main or regular place of work are personal commuting expenses.

*Regular or main job:* Your principal place of business. If you have more than one job, you must determine which one is your regular or main job. Consider the time you spend at each, the activity you have at each, and the income you earn at each.

*Temporary work location*: A place where your work assignment is irregular or short-term, generally a matter of days or weeks. Unless you have a regular place of business, you can only deduct your transportation expenses to a temporary location <u>outside</u> your metropolitan area.

*Second job*: If you regularly work at two or more places in one day, whether or not for the same employer, you can deduct your transportation expenses of getting from one workplace to another. You cannot deduct your transportation costs between your home and a second job on a day off from your main job.

**Question** — How does the car expense deduction differ if the car is used 50% or less (as opposed to more than 50%) for business purposes?

*Answer* — The amount of the deduction allowed for depreciation is computed in a different, less favorable way if the car is used 50% or less for business.

If the car is used 50% or less for business, the taxpayer must compute depreciation on a straight-line basis over a five-year period. Neither accelerated depreciation nor the Section 179 election to expense[12] can be used.

**Question** — When can the "standard mileage rate" be used to compute car business expenses?

*Answer* — Generally, whenever a taxpayer wants to deduct car business expenses, there is a choice between determining the actual expenses and using the simpler standard mileage rate. The mileage rate for 2003 is 36 cents per mile for all business use.[13]

In order to use the standard mileage rate the taxpayer must choose the standard mileage rate method for the first year in which the car was placed in service in business. If actual expenses (using certain accelerated depreciation) are used in the first year, the mileage rate cannot be used in later years. But if the mileage rate is used in the first year the taxpayer can change to actual expenses in later years.

## FOOTNOTES

1. IRC Sections 3121(a)(20), 3402(s).
2. Ann. 85-113, 1985-31 IRB 31; see Treas. Reg. §1.61-21(c)(7).
3. Treas. Reg. §1.61-21(b)(4).
4. Treas. Reg. §1.61-21(b)(4).
5. Treas. Reg. §1.61-21(d)(2).
6. Rev. Proc. 2002-61, 2002-39 IRB 616.
7. Treas. Reg. §1.61-21(e)(1)(iii).
8. Treas. Reg. §1.61-21(f).
9. Treas. Regs. §§1.61-21(f), 1.132-5(f), 1.274-6T(a)(3), 1.274-6T(d).
10. These tables are found in IRS Pub. 463, *Travel, Entertainment, Gift, and Car Expenses*, revised annually.
11. Rev. Rul. 99-7, 1 CB 361.
12. Treas. Reg. §1.179-1(d).
13. Rev. Proc. 2002-61, 2002-39 IRB 616.

Form **2106**

Department of the Treasury
Internal Revenue Service  (99)

**Employee Business Expenses**

▶ See separate instructions.

▶ Attach to Form 1040.

OMB No. 1545-0139

20**02**

Attachment
Sequence No. **54**

| Your name | Occupation in which you incurred expenses | Social security number |
|---|---|---|

**Part I**  **Employee Business Expenses and Reimbursements**

**Step 1   Enter Your Expenses**

|  |  | Column A Other Than Meals and Entertainment | Column B Meals and Entertainment |
|---|---|---|---|
| 1 | Vehicle expense from line 22 or line 29. (Rural mail carriers: See instructions.) . . . . . . . . . . . . . . . . . . **1** |  | ///// |
| 2 | Parking fees, tolls, and transportation, including train, bus, etc., that **did not** involve overnight travel or commuting to and from work . . **2** |  | ///// |
| 3 | Travel expense while away from home overnight, including lodging, airplane, car rental, etc. **Do not** include meals and entertainment **3** |  | ///// |
| 4 | Business expenses not included on lines 1 through 3. **Do not** include meals and entertainment . . . . . . . . . . **4** |  | ///// |
| 5 | Meals and entertainment expenses (see instructions) . . . . **5** | ///// |  |
| 6 | **Total expenses.** In Column A, add lines 1 through 4 and enter the result. In Column B, enter the amount from line 5 . . . . . **6** |  | ///// |

**Note:** *If you were not reimbursed for any expenses in Step 1, skip line 7 and enter the amount from line 6 on line 8.*

**Step 2   Enter Reimbursements Received From Your Employer for Expenses Listed in Step 1**

| 7 | Enter reimbursements received from your employer that were **not** reported to you in box 1 of Form W-2. Include any reimbursements reported under code "L" in box 12 of your Form W-2 (see instructions) . . . . . . . . . . . . . . . . . . **7** |  | ///// |
|---|---|---|---|

**Step 3   Figure Expenses To Deduct on Schedule A (Form 1040)**

| 8 | Subtract line 7 from line 6. If zero or less, enter -0-. However, if line 7 is greater than line 6 in Column A, report the excess as income on Form 1040, line 7 . . . . . . . . . . . . . **8** | ///// | ///// |
|---|---|---|---|
|  | **Note:** *If **both columns** of line 8 are zero, you cannot deduct employee business expenses. Stop here and attach Form 2106 to your return.* |  |  |
| 9 | In Column A, enter the amount from line 8. In Column B, multiply line 8 by 50% (.50). (Employees subject to Department of Transportation (DOT) hours of service limits: Multiply meal expenses by 65% (.65) instead of 50%. For details, see instructions.) . . . . . . . . . . . . . . . . . **9** | ///// | ///// |
| 10 | Add the amounts on line 9 of both columns and enter the total here. **Also, enter the total on Schedule A (Form 1040), line 20.** (Fee-basis state or local government officials, qualified performing artists, and individuals with disabilities: See the instructions for special rules on where to enter the total.) . . . . . . . . . . . . . . . . . . . . . . ▶ **10** |  |  |

**For Paperwork Reduction Act Notice, see instructions.**          Cat. No. 11700N          Form **2106** (2002)

Form 2106 (2002)                                                                                           Page **2**

**Part II**   Vehicle Expenses

**Section A—General Information** (You must complete this section if you are claiming vehicle expenses.)

| | | | (a) Vehicle 1 | (b) Vehicle 2 |
|---|---|---|---|---|
| 11 | Enter the date the vehicle was placed in service | 11 | / / | / / |
| 12 | Total miles the vehicle was driven during 2002 | 12 | miles | miles |
| 13 | Business miles included on line 12 | 13 | miles | miles |
| 14 | Percent of business use. Divide line 13 by line 12 | 14 | % | % |
| 15 | Average daily roundtrip commuting distance | 15 | miles | miles |
| 16 | Commuting miles included on line 12 | 16 | miles | miles |
| 17 | Other miles. Add lines 13 and 16 and subtract the total from line 12 | 17 | miles | miles |
| 18 | Do you (or your spouse) have another vehicle available for personal use? | | ☐ Yes | ☐ No |
| 19 | Was your vehicle available for personal use during off-duty hours? | | ☐ Yes | ☐ No |
| 20 | Do you have evidence to support your deduction? | | ☐ Yes | ☐ No |
| 21 | If "Yes," is the evidence written? | | ☐ Yes | ☐ No |

**Section B—Standard Mileage Rate** (See the instructions for Part II to find out whether to complete this section or Section C.)

| | | | |
|---|---|---|---|
| 22 | Multiply line 13 by 36½¢ (.365) | 22 | |

**Section C—Actual Expenses**

| | | | (a) Vehicle 1 | | (b) Vehicle 2 | |
|---|---|---|---|---|---|---|
| 23 | Gasoline, oil, repairs, vehicle insurance, etc. | 23 | | | | |
| 24a | Vehicle rentals | 24a | | | | |
| b | Inclusion amount (see instructions) | 24b | | | | |
| c | Subtract line 24b from line 24a | 24c | | | | |
| 25 | Value of employer-provided vehicle (applies only if 100% of annual lease value was included on Form W-2—see instructions) | 25 | | | | |
| 26 | Add lines 23, 24c, and 25 | 26 | | | | |
| 27 | Multiply line 26 by the percentage on line 14 | 27 | | | | |
| 28 | Depreciation. Enter amount from line 38 below | 28 | | | | |
| 29 | Add lines 27 and 28. Enter total here and on line 1 | 29 | | | | |

**Section D—Depreciation of Vehicles** (Use this section only if you owned the vehicle and are completing Section C for the vehicle.)

| | | | (a) Vehicle 1 | | (b) Vehicle 2 | |
|---|---|---|---|---|---|---|
| 30 | Enter cost or other basis (see instructions) | 30 | | | | |
| 31 | Enter section 179 deduction and special allowance (see instructions) | 31 | | | | |
| 32 | Multiply line 30 by line 14 (see instructions if you claimed the section 179 deduction or special allowance) | 32 | | | | |
| 33 | Enter depreciation method and percentage (see instructions) | 33 | | | | |
| 34 | Multiply line 32 by the percentage on line 33 (see instructions) | 34 | | | | |
| 35 | Add lines 31 and 34 | 35 | | | | |
| 36 | Enter the limit from the table in the line 36 instructions | 36 | | | | |
| 37 | Multiply line 36 by the percentage on line 14 | 37 | | | | |
| 38 | Enter the **smaller** of line 35 or line 37. Also enter this amount on line 28 above | 38 | | | | |

♲                                                                                          Form **2106** (2002)

| | |
|---|---|
| Form **2106-EZ** | OMB No. 1545-1441 |

**Form 2106-EZ**

Department of the Treasury
Internal Revenue Service  (99)

### Unreimbursed Employee Business Expenses

▶ **Attach to Form 1040.**

20**02**

Attachment
Sequence No. **54A**

| Your name | Occupation in which you incurred expenses | Social security number |
|---|---|---|
| | | |

## You May Use This Form Only if All of the Following Apply.

- You are an employee deducting ordinary and necessary expenses attributable to your job. An ordinary expense is one that is common and accepted in your field of trade, business, or profession. A necessary expense is one that is helpful and appropriate for your business. An expense does not have to be required to be considered necessary.

- You **do not** get reimbursed by your employer for any expenses (amounts your employer included in box 1 of your Form W-2 are not considered reimbursements).

- If you are claiming vehicle expense, you are using the standard mileage rate for 2002.

**Caution:** *You can use the standard mileage rate for 2002* **only if: (a)** *you owned the vehicle and used the standard mileage rate for the first year you placed the vehicle in service* **or (b)** *you leased the vehicle and used the standard mileage rate for the portion of the lease period after 1997.*

| Part I | Figure Your Expenses | | |
|---|---|---|---|
| 1 | Vehicle expense using the standard mileage rate. Complete Part II and multipy line 8a by 36½¢ (.365) | **1** | |
| 2 | Parking fees, tolls, and transportation, including train, bus, etc., that **did not** involve overnight travel or commuting to and from work . . . . . . . . . . . | **2** | |
| 3 | Travel expense while away from home overnight, including lodging, airplane, car rental, etc. **Do not** include meals and entertainment . . . . . . . . . . . . | **3** | |
| 4 | Business expenses not included on lines 1 through 3. **Do not** include meals and entertainment | **4** | |
| 5 | Meals and entertainment expenses: $ _____ x 50% (.50) (Employees subject to Department of Transportation (DOT) hours of service limits: Multiply meal expenses by 65% (.65) instead of 50%. For details, see instructions.) . . . . . . . . | **5** | |
| 6 | **Total expenses.** Add lines 1 through 5. Enter here and **on line 20 of Schedule A (Form 1040).** (Fee-basis state or local government officials, qualified performing artists, and individuals with disabilities: See the instructions for special rules on where to enter this amount.) . . . . . | **6** | |

| Part II | Information on Your Vehicle. Complete this part **only** if you are claiming vehicle expense on line 1. |
|---|---|

**7** When did you place your vehicle in service for business use? (month, day, year) ▶ .......... / .......... / ..........

**8** Of the total number of miles you drove your vehicle during 2002, enter the number of miles you used your vehicle for:

**a** Business ........................  **b** Commuting ........................  **c** Other ........................

**9** Do you (or your spouse) have another vehicle available for personal use? . . . . . . . . . . .  ☐ Yes  ☐ No

**10** Was your vehicle available for personal use during off-duty hours? . . . . . . . . . . . .  ☐ Yes  ☐ No

**11a** Do you have evidence to support your deduction? . . . . . . . . . . . . . . .  ☐ Yes  ☐ No

**b** If "Yes," is the evidence written? . . . . . . . . . . . . . . . . . . .  ☐ Yes  ☐ No

## General Instructions

*Section references are to the Internal Revenue Code.*

### Changes To Note

**Standard mileage rate.** The standard mileage rate has been increased to 36½ cents for each mile of business use in 2002.

**Meal expenses.** The percentage of meal expenses that may be deducted by employees subject to Department of Transportation (DOT) hours of service limits has been increased to 65% for 2002.

### Purpose of Form

You may use Form 2106-EZ instead of Form 2106 to claim your unreimbursed employee business expenses if you meet all the requirements listed above Part I.

### Recordkeeping

You cannot deduct expenses for travel (including meals, unless you used the standard meal allowance), entertainment,

gifts, or use of a car or other listed property, unless you keep records to prove the time, place, business purpose, business relationship (for entertainment and gifts), and amounts of these expenses. Generally, you must also have receipts for all lodging expenses (regardless of the amount) and any other expense of $75 or more.

### Additional Information

For more details about employee business expenses, see:

**Pub. 463,** Travel, Entertainment, Gift, and Car Expenses

**Pub. 529,** Miscellaneous Deductions

**Pub. 587,** Business Use of Your Home (Including Use by Day-Care Providers)

**Pub. 946,** How To Depreciate Property

## Specific Instructions

### Part I—Figure Your Expenses

**Line 2.** See the line 8b instructions for the definition of commuting.

**Line 3.** Enter lodging and transportation expenses connected with overnight travel away from your tax home (defined below). You cannot deduct expenses for travel away from your tax home for any period of temporary employment of more than 1 year. **Do not** include expenses for meals and entertainment. For more details, including limits, see Pub. 463.

Generally, your **tax home** is your main place of business or post of duty regardless of where you maintain your family home. If you do not have a regular or main place of business because of the nature of your work, then your tax home is the place where you regularly live. If you do not fit in either of these categories, you are considered an itinerant and your tax home is wherever you work. As an itinerant, you are never away from home and cannot claim a travel expense deduction. For more details on your tax home, see Pub. 463.

**Line 4.** Enter other job-related expenses not listed on any other line of this form. Include expenses for business gifts, education (tuition and books), home office, trade publications,

For Paperwork Reduction Act Notice, see back of form.          Cat. No. 20604Q          Form **2106-EZ** (2002)

etc. For details, including limits, see Pub. 463 and Pub. 529. **Do not** include on line 4 any tuition and fees you deducted on Form 1040, line 26, or any educator expenses you deducted on Form 1040, line 23. If you are deducting home office expenses, see Pub. 587 for special instructions on how to report these expenses. If you are deducting depreciation or claiming a section 179 deduction on a cellular telephone or other similar telecommunications equipment, a home computer, etc., see **Form 4562,** Depreciation and Amortization, to figure the depreciation and section 179 deduction to enter on line 4.

 You may be able to take a credit for your educational expenses instead of a deduction. See **Form 8863,** Education Credits (Hope and Lifetime Learning Credits) for details.

Do not include expenses for meals and entertainment, taxes, or interest on line 4. Deductible taxes are entered on lines 5 through 9 of Schedule A (Form 1040). Employees **cannot** deduct car loan interest.

**Note:** If line 4 is your only entry, do not complete Form 2106-EZ unless you are claiming:

- Expenses for performing your job as a fee-basis state or local government official,
- Performing-arts-related business expenses as a qualified performing artist, or
- Impairment-related work expenses as an individual with a disability.

See the line 6 instructions for definitions. If you are not required to file Form 2106-EZ, enter your expenses directly on Schedule A (Form 1040), line 20.

**Line 5.** Generally, you may deduct only 50% of your business meal and entertainment expenses, including meals incurred while away from home on business. If you were an employee subject to the Department of Transportation (DOT) hours of service limits, that percentage is increased to 65% for business meals consumed during, or incident to, any period of duty for which those limits are in effect.

Employees subject to the DOT hours of service limits include certain air transportation employees, such as pilots, crew, dispatchers, mechanics, and control tower operators; interstate truck operators and interstate bus drivers; certain railroad employees, such as engineers, conductors, train crews, dispatchers, and control operations personnel; and certain merchant mariners.

Instead of actual cost, you may be able to claim the **standard meal allowance** for your daily meals and incidental expenses while away from your tax home overnight. Under this method, you deduct a specified amount, depending on where you travel, instead of keeping records of your actual meal expenses. However, you must still keep records to prove the time, place, and business purpose of your travel.

The standard meal allowance is the Federal M&IE rate. For travel in 2002, this rate is $30 a day for most small localities in the United States. Most major cities and many other localities in the United States are designated as high-cost areas and qualify for higher rates. You can find these rates on the Internet at **www.policyworks.gov/perdiem.** Click on "2002 Domestic Per Diem Rates" for the

period January 1, 2002 – September 30, 2002 and on "2003 Domestic Per Diem Rates" for the period October 1, 2002 – December 31, 2002. For locations outside the continental United States, the applicable rates are published monthly. You can find these rates on the Internet at **www.state.gov/m/a/als/prdm/2002.**

See Pub. 463 for details on how to figure your deduction using the standard meal allowance, including special rules for partial days of travel, transportation workers, and taxpayers related to their employer.

**Line 6.** If you were a **fee-basis state or local government official** (defined below), include the expenses you incurred for services performed in that job in the total on Form 1040, line 34. Write "FBO" and the amount in the space to the left of line 34. Your employee business expenses are deductible whether or not you itemize deductions. A fee-basis state or local government official is an official who is an employee of a state or political subdivision of a state and is compensated, in whole or in part, on a fee basis.

If you were a **qualified performing artist** (defined below), include your performing-arts-related expenses in the total on Form 1040, line 34. Write "QPA" and the amount in the space to the left of line 34. Your performing-arts-related business expenses are deductible whether or not you itemize deductions. The expenses are not subject to the 2% limit that applies to most other employee business expenses.

A qualified performing artist is an individual who:

**1.** Performed services in the performing arts as an employee for at least two employers during the tax year,

**2.** Received from at least two of those employers wages of $200 or more per employer,

**3.** Had allowable business expenses attributable to the performing arts of more than 10% of gross income from the performing arts, and

**4.** Had adjusted gross income of $16,000 or less before deducting expenses as a performing artist.

To be treated as a qualified performing artist, a married individual must also file a joint return, unless the individual and his or her spouse lived apart for all of 2002. On a joint return, requirements **1, 2,** and **3** must be figured separately for each spouse. However, requirement **4** applies to the combined adjusted gross income of both spouses.

If you were an **individual with a disability** and are claiming impairment-related work expenses (defined below), enter the part of the line 6 amount attributable to those expenses on Schedule A (Form 1040), line 27, instead of on Schedule A (Form 1040), line 20. Your impairment-related work expenses are not subject to the 2% limit that applies to most other employee business expenses. Impairment-related work expenses are the allowable expenses of an individual with physical or mental disabilities for attendant care at his or her place of employment. They also include other expenses in conneciton with the place of employment that enable the employee to work. See Pub. 463 for details.

## Part II—Information on Your Vehicle

If you claim vehicle expense, you must provide certain information on the use of your vehicle by completing Part II. Include an attachment listing the information requested in Part II for any additional vehicles you used for business during the year.

**Line 7.** Date placed in service is generally the date you first start using your vehicle. However, if you first start using your vehicle for personal use and later convert it to business use, the vehicle is treated as placed in service on the date you started using it for business.

**Line 8a.** Do not include commuting miles on this line; commuting miles are not considered business miles. See below for the definition of commuting.

**Line 8b.** If you do not know the total actual miles you used your vehicle for commuting during the year, figure the amount to enter on line 8b by multiplying the number of days during the year that you used your vehicle for commuting by the average daily roundtrip commuting distance in miles.

Generally, **commuting** is travel between your home and a work location. However, travel that meets **any** of the following conditions is not commuting.

**1.** You have at least one regular work location away from your home and the travel is to a temporary work location in the same trade or business, regardless of the distance. Generally, a temporary work location is one where your employment is expected to last 1 year or less. See Pub. 463 for details.

**2.** The travel is to a temporary work location outside the metropolitan area where you live and normally work.

**3.** Your home is your principal place of business under section 280A(c)(1)(A) (for purposes of deducting expenses for business use of your home) and the travel is to another work location in the same trade or business, regardless of whether that location is regular or temporary and regardless of distance.

---

**Paperwork Reduction Act Notice.** We ask for the information on this form to carry out the Internal Revenue laws of the United States. You are required to give us the information. We need it to ensure that you are complying with these laws and to allow us to figure and collect the right amount of tax.

You are not required to provide the information requested on a form that is subject to the Paperwork Reduction Act unless the form displays a valid OMB control number. Books or records relating to a form or its instructions must be retained as long as their contents may become material in the administration of any Internal Revenue law. Generally, tax returns and return information are confidential, as required by section 6103.

The time needed to complete and file this form will vary depending on individual circumstances. The estimated average time is: **Recordkeeping,** 40 min.; **Learning about the law or the form,** 12 min.; **Preparing the form,** 24 min.; **Copying, assembling, and sending the form to the IRS,** 20 min.

If you have comments concerning the accuracy of these time estimates or suggestions for making this form simpler, we would be happy to hear from you. See the Instructions for Form 1040.

# Chapter 32

# DEATH BENEFIT ONLY (DBO) PLAN

## WHAT IS IT?

A death benefit only plan, or DBO plan, (sometimes referred to as an "employer-paid death benefit" or a "survivor's income benefit plan") is a plan by which an employer defers employee compensation and pays it to the employee's designated beneficiary at the employee's death. No benefit is payable in any form to the employee during his or her lifetime.

## WHEN IS IT INDICATED?

1. The DBO type of plan is most valuable in the case of a highly compensated employee who: (1) expects to have a large estate; and (2) faces significant federal estate tax liability because the estate will be payable to a nonspouse beneficiary (i.e., will not be able to fully use the estate tax marital deduction). If the covered employee owns 50% or less of the corporation's stock and the plan is properly designed, the benefit from a DBO plan is not subject to federal estate tax. However, note that the estate tax is repealed for one year in 2010.

2. The plan can be used for selected employees as a supplement to qualified retirement plan benefits. Under current law, maximum qualified plan benefits to highly compensated employees may be significantly limited. A DBO plan can provide extra benefits not affected by such limitations.

3. The plan can be used to replace a split dollar plan (see Chapter 52) where the cost to the employee of the current insurance protection is increasing rapidly because of age—usually after age 60.

4. A DBO plan can be used for deferring compensation of younger employees with families and a need for insurance; the DBO plan can be converted to full nonqualified deferred compensation with lifetime benefits when the employee's value to the employer has increased to the point where this is indicated.

## ADVANTAGES

1. If the covered employee is not a controlling (more than 50%) shareholder, properly designed DBO benefits can be kept out of the deceased employee's estate for federal estate tax purposes.

2. The plan's death benefit provides valuable estate liquidity and a source of immediate and continuing cash to the beneficiary upon the employee's death.

3. The benefit is not taxable to the employee during lifetime.

4. The plan can be financed by the employer through the purchase of life insurance, which provides funds to pay the death benefit and avoids current tax on investment returns under the policy. (Some alternative minimum tax—AMT—on the death proceeds may be payable at the corporate level.)

## DISADVANTAGES

1. The entire benefit is income taxable to the beneficiary—as ordinary income. This applies even if the benefit is financed using life insurance.

2. Keeping the death benefit out of the gross estate requires very careful plan design and avoidance of technical tax traps, thus limiting flexibility in plan design.

3. The employer-corporation's tax deduction for the plan is deferred until the benefit is paid and the beneficiary includes the payments received in income. The employer must wait to take the deduction, even if it sets funds aside in advance (such as through the purchase of a life insurance contract).

## DESIGN FEATURES

The plan's benefit formula can take many forms:

1. The simplest formula is a fixed dollar amount— for example, $50,000 for each employee covered under the plan, or $10,000 per year for five years.

2. Benefits can be based on average compensation over a period of years—for example, the death benefit might be equal to a year's salary averaged over the five years prior to death.

3. Benefits are often related loosely to the death benefit under an insurance policy on the employee's life that is owned and purchased by the employer, in order to finance the plan. For example, suppose the employer and employee agree that the employee's salary will be reduced by $100 per month—or agree to extra employer payments of $100 per month—that will be used toward the premiums on an insurance policy. If the $1,200 per year will buy approximately a $50,000 life insurance policy for that employee, given his age and health, then the death benefit under the plan will be $50,000. Note, however, that most planners recommend against tying the benefit directly, dollar for dollar, to a life insurance policy. The plan should be designed to avoid any inference that it is simply the purchase of life insurance for the employee.[1]

## TAX IMPLICATIONS

1. The death benefit from the plan will not be included in the deceased employee's estate so long as: (1) the plan does not provide any benefits payable during the employee's lifetime; and (2) the employee does not have the right to change the beneficiary, once the plan is established.[2]

In determining whether the plan pays lifetime benefits, the IRS will look beyond the DBO plan itself. Another plan that provides benefits during lifetime can be taken into account for this purpose, even if the employee never actually lives to collect those benefits.[3] Thus, a DBO plan will not be excluded from an employee's estate, if the employer also maintains a nonqualified deferred compensation plan providing lifetime benefits. The two plans will be linked together for this purpose and the estate tax exclusion will be lost. However, a *qualified* pension or profit sharing plan is not taken into account for this purpose, so those plans can be provided in addition to DBOs.[4] After several court cases on the issue[5], the IRS also now agrees that an employer's long-term disability benefit plan will not "taint" a DBO, unless the disability plan requires that the employee be "retired on disability" to receive benefits.[6]

2. Benefits paid to the employee's beneficiary are taxable in full to the beneficiary as ordinary income.[7]

3. The benefit payments are deductible to the corporation when paid, so long as they constitute "reasonable compensation" for the services of the deceased employee in prior years. See Chapter 30 of this book for a detailed discussion of the "reasonableness" test. The reasonableness issue is most likely to be raised by the IRS if the decedent was a majority or controlling stockholder, particularly if the beneficiary is also a stockholder.

The IRS may also question whether the death benefit payment was "for services actually rendered" by the employee, as required for deductibility under Code section 162. This issue is most likely to be raised where: (1) the deceased employee was a majority shareholder; or (2) where there was no written agreement to pay the benefit prior to the employee's death. If the corporation's deduction is disallowed for this reason, the amount could be treated as a nondeductible dividend, or, in unusual cases, as a gift by the corporation, with deductibility limited to $25 under Code section 274(b).

## ERISA REQUIREMENTS

1. Whether a DBO plan is a pension plan or a welfare benefit plan for ERISA purposes is not clear.[8] In either case, if the plan is unfunded and limited to a "select group of management or highly compensated employees"—the "top hat" group—it should be exempt from most of the provisions of ERISA.[9] If such a DBO plan is considered a pension plan, it should be exempt from ERISA's participation, vesting, funding, and fiduciary responsibility requirements; the plan will be subject to ERISA's reporting and disclosure requirements and ERISA's administrative and enforcement provisions, but such a plan should be able to satisfy the reporting and disclosure requirements through a streamlined procedure including a simple notice to the Department of Labor (see Chapter 15, Nonqualified Deferred Compensation, at "ERISA REQUIREMENTS," for details and a sample notification form).[10] If such a DBO plan is considered a welfare benefit plan, it will be (like all welfare benefit plans) exempt from ERISA's participation, vesting, and funding requirements, and it will be relieved of ERISA's reporting and disclosure requirements, except for the requirement that it submit plan documents to the Secretary of

Labor upon request; the plan would appear to be subject to at least some of ERISA's fiduciary responsibility requirements and to ERISA's administrative and enforcement provisions.[11]

2.   If the plan covers a broader group of employees, the full scope of ERISA's requirements — including vesting, funding, and reporting and disclosure requirements — may apply.[12] The vesting and funding requirements are discussed in Chapter 25 of this book and the reporting and disclosure requirements are summarized in Appendix A.

## ALTERNATIVES

1.   Group-term life insurance.

2.   Life insurance in a qualified plan.

3.   Split dollar life insurance.

4.   Individually-owned life insurance (perhaps paid for through additional bonus compensation from the employer).

## HOW TO INSTALL A PLAN

Except for a "voluntary" plan (see "Questions and Answers," below), there should always be a written plan adopted under a corporate resolution by the board of directors, in advance of the time that payments are to be made under the plan. The plan document can be simple, but it should specify (a) the amount of the benefit, (b) what employee or group of employees is entitled to it, and (c) should indicate that the benefit is intended as compensation for services to be rendered by the employee. Nothing has to be filed with the government, except for the possible ERISA requirements listed earlier.

## WHERE CAN I FIND OUT MORE ABOUT IT?

1.   Leimberg, Stephan R., et al., *The Tools and Techniques of Estate Planning*, 12th ed. Cincinnati, OH: The National Underwriter Co., 2001.

2.   Richey, Louis R., and Brody, Lawrence, *Comprehensive Deferred Compensation*, 3d ed. Cincinnati, OH: The National Underwriter Co., 1997.

## QUESTIONS AND ANSWERS

**Question** — Should an employer finance its obligations under a death benefit plan in advance?

*Answer* — These plans, if provided to a select group of management or highly compensated employees, should not come within the funding requirements of ERISA. However, if they are formally funded, many ERISA requirements apply. This is discussed in detail in Chapter 15, Nonqualified Deferred Compensation. Therefore, "formal" funding (where the employee has rights to the fund ahead of corporate creditors) is undesirable.

Many plans are "informally funded"—a better term to use is "financed"—through the corporation's setting aside an asset or combination of assets that is designed to grow to the point where benefit payments can be made from it. The amount, however, must be available to corporate creditors. The IRS does not consider this type of arrangement to be a "fund" for tax purposes, and the Department of Labor (which administers ERISA) probably will not consider this type of arrangement to be a "fund" for ERISA purposes.[13]

One of the most common types of investment for this type of fund is life insurance, since the insurance guarantees that adequate amounts will be available, even if the employee dies at a relatively young age.

**Question** — How is life insurance used in a DBO plan?

*Answer* — As an example, suppose the plan provides a $100,000 death benefit to a key executive. If the employer corporation expects to be in a 34% tax bracket when the benefit is paid, it purchases a $66,000 policy on the employee's life. The corporation is owner and beneficiary of the policy and pays the premiums. The corporation's premium payments are nondeductible. If the employee dies, the corporation pays out $100,000 to the beneficiary and it deducts $100,000 as compensation, which saves $34,000 in taxes. The $66,000 in death proceeds from the policy is tax-free to the corporation, assuming no AMT tax. These proceeds reimburse the corporation for its out-of-pocket cost.

If the benefit is to be paid to the beneficiary over a period of years, rather than in a lump sum, the amount of life insurance needed by the corporation is further reduced. This is because investment earnings received by the corporation on the policy death proceeds are available to help fund the benefit payments.

**Question** — What mistakes in plan design or other circumstances would cause an employer death benefit to be included in the employee's estate?

*Answer* — The promise of the employer to pay a death benefit to a specified beneficiary, in return for the employee's promise to continue working for the employer, is considered a transfer by the employee of a property right.[14] If the agreement gives the employee the right to change the beneficiary, that retention of the power to designate who will enjoy the "transfer" has been held by the IRS to cause estate tax inclusion.[15]

If the beneficiary's right to receive the death benefit is conditioned on surviving the employee, and the employee retained a right to direct the disposition of the property (for example, where the death benefit is payable to the employee's spouse, but if the spouse does not survive the employee, the death benefit is payable to the employee's estate), that reversionary interest may cause inclusion.[16]

If the beneficiary is a revocable trust established by the employee, the right to alter, amend, or revoke the transfer by changing the terms of the trust would cause inclusion.[17]

Another problem relates to an employee who is also a controlling (more than 50% shareholder). The IRS argues that such an individual, by virtue of his or her voting control, has the right to alter, amend, revoke, or terminate the agreement. Therefore, the benefit should be includable in the estate of such an individual.[18]

If the employee already has postretirement benefits, such as a nonqualified deferred compensation agreement that pays a retirement benefit, the IRS could claim that the preretirement death benefit plan and the postretirement deferred compensation plan should be considered as a single plan. This would cause the present value of the death benefit to be treated, for estate tax purposes, as if it were a joint and survivor annuity; the present value of the death benefit would be includable in the deceased employee's estate.[19]

If the death benefit is payable to a trust over which the employee had a general power of ap-

pointment, the IRS might argue that the employee had a power of appointment over the death proceeds, which would result in inclusion for estate tax purposes.[20]

If the death benefit is funded with life insurance on the employee's life and the employee owned the policy or had veto rights over any change in the beneficiary, the IRS would probably attempt to include the policy proceeds because of the employee's incidents of ownership.[21]

**Question** — What is the advantage of a "voluntary" DBO plan?

*Answer* — A voluntary DBO is a payment not made under a contract or plan, but rather at the employer's discretion, after the employee's death. Such a payment probably will not be included in the employee's estate, because neither the employee nor the beneficiary possessed any right to compel the employer to pay the benefit and, therefore, there was no transfer to the employee.[22] However, if the employee owned more than 50% of the company's stock, the IRS is likely to argue for inclusion, for the reasons discussed above, even in this type of plan.

Even though there is no formal contract in this type of plan, it may be satisfactory, since the employee can reasonably expect the benefit to be paid in many cases. However, in other situations, this expectation may not be enough. The benefit will then provide the employee no peace of mind or financial security, and a written plan should be adopted.

## FOOTNOTES

1. See *Dependahl v. Falstaff Brewing Corp.*, 491 F.Supp. 1188 (E.D. Mo. 1980), aff'd in part, 653 F.2d 1208 (8th Cir. 1981), cert. denied, 454 U.S. 968 (1981) and 454 U.S. 1084 (1981); Department of Labor (DOL) Advisory Opinion 81-11A, regarding conditions under which life insurance is not considered a "plan asset"; see also *Belsky v. First National Life Insurance Co.*, 818 F.2d 661 (8th Cir. 1987); *Miller v. Heller*, 915 F. Supp. 651 (S.D.N.Y. 1996); *The Northwestern Mutual Life Ins. Co. v. Resolution Trust Corp.*, 848 F. Supp. 1515 (N.D. Ala. 1994); *Darden v. Nationwide Mutual Ins. Co.*, 717 F. Supp. 388 (E.D.N.C. 1989), aff'd, 922 F.2d 203 (4th Cir.), cert. denied, 502 U.S. 906 (1991); *Belka v. Rowe Furniture Corp.*, 571 F. Supp. 1249 (D. Md. 1983); DOL Advisory Opinions 94-31A, 92-22A, 92-02A.

2. See the question and answer above relating to "mistakes in plan design."

3. Treas. Reg. §20.2039-1(b).

4. *Est. of Fusz v. Comm.*, 46 TC 214 (1966), acq. 1967-2 CB 2; Rev. Rul. 76-380, 1976-2 CB 270.

5. *Est. of Wm. V. Schelberg v. Comm.*, 79-2 USTC ¶13,321 (2d Cir. 1979), rev'g 70 TC 690 (1978); *Est. of Glen J. Van Wye v. U.S.*, 82-2 USTC ¶13,485 (6th Cir. 1982).

6. The IRS has announced that it will follow the *Schelberg* decision in all circuits. See *Looney v. U.S.*, Docket No. 83-8709 (11th Cir., motion filed 1-26-84).

7. If the decedent died on or before August 20, 1996, up to $5,000 can be excluded as an employee death benefit under Code section 101(b) if the employee did not have vested rights to the benefit immediately before death. This employee death benefit exclusion has been repealed for decedents dying after August 20, 1996. SBJPA '96, Section 1402.

8. The definitions of "pension plan" and "welfare benefit plan" for ERISA purposes are sufficiently vague that a DBO plan could arguably be characterized as either (or perhaps both). See ERISA Sections 3(1), 3(2)(A); Labor Reg. §2510.3-1; see also *Dependahl*, above.

9. See ERISA Sections 201(1), 201(2), 301(a)(1), 301(a)(3), 401(a), 401(a)(1), 503, 4021(a), 4021(b)(6); Labor Regs. §§2520.104-23, 2520.104-24, 2560.503-1(a), 2560.503-1(b). If a DBO plan is considered *both* a pension plan and a welfare benefit plan, it might not be able to take advantage of the exemptions from ERISA's participation, vesting, funding, and fiduciary responsibility requirements available to an unfunded plan maintained primarily for the purpose of providing deferred compensation to the top hat group. The argument would be that because such a plan's benefits are equally pension and welfare benefits, such a plan does not *primarily* provide deferred compensation. See ERISA Sections 201(2), 301(a)(3), 401(a)(1). Under a similar argument, such a hybrid plan might also be ineligible for the streamlined reporting and disclosure procedure available to an unfunded pension plan *primarily* providing deferred compensation to the top hat group. See Labor Reg. §2520.104-23. The merit of such arguments is unclear, and they are subject to counter-arguments. For example, a potential response might point out that the top hat exemptions are not written in terms of a plan that is *primarily a pension plan*; they are written in terms of a *plan primarily providing deferred compensation*, and welfare benefits can be considered deferred compensation just as readily as can pension benefits — for they are a form of future compensation for current services. Thus, the response might conclude, a plan that is equally a pension plan and a welfare benefit plan could still provide deferred compensation primarily (or even solely!). The merits of this argument, too, are unclear.

10. ERISA Sections 201(2), 301(a)(3), 401(a)(1), 503; Labor Regs. §§2520.104-23, 2560.503-1(a), 2560.503-1(b). The streamlined procedure for satisfying the reporting and disclosure requirements is also available to pension plans providing benefits to the top hat group (1) exclusively through employer-paid insurance contracts or policies, or (2) through employer-paid insurance contracts or policies and from the employer's general assets. Labor Reg. §2520.104-23.

11. ERISA Sections 201(1), 301(a)(1); Labor Reg. §2520.104-24; See ERISA Sections 401(a), 503; Labor Reg. §2560.503-1(a). The almost complete exemption from the reporting and disclosure requirements also extends to welfare plans providing benefits to the top hat group (1) exclusively through employer-paid insurance contracts or policies, or (2) through employer-paid insurance contracts or policies and from the employer's general assets. Labor Reg. §2520.104-24. A creative argument might (1) point out that the exemptions from ERISA's participation, vesting, funding, and fiduciary responsibility requirements for an unfunded plan maintained primarily for the purpose of providing deferred compensation to the top hat group are written in terms of a *plan* rather than in terms of a *pension plan*, (2) claim that a DBO plan's promised death benefits are nothing but deferred compensation — that is, future compensation for current services — and (3) conclude that regardless of whether a DBO plan is characterized as a pension plan or a welfare benefit plan it should still be able to take advantage of the exemptions from ERISA's participation, vesting, funding, and fiduciary obligations for an unfunded *plan* maintained primarily for the purpose of providing *deferred compensation* to the top hat group. The merits of this argument are not clear.

12. Welfare benefit plans are not subject to ERISA's Title I participation, vesting, and funding requirements, nor to ERISA's Title IV plan termination insurance provisions. See ERISA Sections 201(1), 301(a)(1), 4021(a)(1).

13. See Chapter 15, Nonqualified Deferred Compensation, at "Funded versus Unfunded Plans," and the authorities cited in that discussion; see also Labor Reg. §2520.104-24; DOL Advisory Opinions 93-14A, 92-24A, 92-22A, 92-02A, 81-11A.

14. See, e.g., *Est. of Fried v. Comm.*, 445 F.2d 979 (2d Cir. 1971); *Est. of Bernard L. Porter v. Comm.*, 442 F.2d 915 (1st Cir. 1971).

15. IRC Section 2036; Rev. Rul. 76-304, 1976-2 CB 269.

16. IRC Section 2037; *Est. of Fried v. Comm.*, 54 TC 805 (1970), aff'd, 445 F.2d 979 (2nd Cir. 1971), cert. denied, 404 U.S. 1016 (1972); Rev. Rul. 78-15, 1978-1 CB 289.

17. IRC Section 2038.

18. *Est. of Levin v. Comm.*, 90 TC 723 (1988). The IRS' position in this case was a reversal of an earlier private ruling, TAM 8701003.

19. IRC Section 2039; *Est. of Fusz v. Comm.*, 46 TC 214 (1966).

20. IRC Section 2041.

21. IRC Section 2042.

22. *Edith L. Courtney v. U.S.*, 84-2 USTC ¶13580 (N.D. Ohio 1984).

# Chapter 33

# DEPENDENT CARE ASSISTANCE PLAN

## WHAT IS IT?

A dependent care assistance plan reimburses employees for day-care and other dependent care expenses or provides an actual day-care center or similar arrangement. If the program is properly structured, the day-care expenses are deductible to the employer under Code section 162 and non-taxable to the employee under Code section 129. (See below for a discussion of the employer-provided child care credit.) The dependent care plan can be funded using employee salary reductions under a flexible spending account (FSA) described in Chapter 35.

## WHEN IS IT INDICATED?

1. When the employer wants to attract and keep employees who need help in caring for small children or other dependents during working hours.

2. To provide an attractive tax benefit to all employees who have dependent care expenses.

## ADVANTAGES

1. The plan can be helpful in recruiting and keeping relatively low-paid employees who have dependent care needs.

2. The employer gets more benefit for each dollar spent on this form of compensation as opposed to cash compensation because benefits paid under a properly structured dependent care assistance program are tax-free to the employees.

3. The plan can be funded partially or entirely through FSA salary reductions.

## DISADVANTAGES

1. A fully-subsidized day-care or other dependent care program can be expensive while a partially-subsidized program may not be helpful in attracting and keeping employees.

2. A substantial day-care program may be seen by nonparticipating employees as discriminatory in favor of participating employees.

## DESIGN FEATURES

1. Dependent care can be provided in kind.[1] For example, the employer can provide a day-care and after-school center for employees' children right on the business premises or contract with a nearby center to provide day-care.

2. Alternatively, the benefit can be provided through full or partial reimbursement of qualifying employee expenses for dependent care. This is the approach usually taken when the plan is funded through employee salary reductions as part of an FSA plan.

## TAX IMPLICATIONS

1. The costs of the plan are deductible to the employer as employee compensation.

2. If the plan meets the requirements of Code section 129, the benefits are non-taxable to participating employees.

3. Section 129(d) imposes a variety of nondiscrimination rules summarized as follows:

   • Contributions or benefits must not discriminate in favor of highly compensated employees, as defined in Code section 414(q) (see Chapter 25).

   • The plan must cover a group that the IRS finds nondiscriminatory. The following may be excluded:

      —employees who have not completed 1 year of service, or attained age 21

—employees in a collective bargaining unit if there has been good faith bargaining on dependent care

- Benefits for all employees who own more than 5 percent of the employer, and their spouses and dependents, cannot be more than 25 percent of the total benefits each year.

- The average benefits provided to employees who are not highly compensated must be at least 55 percent of the average benefits provided to highly compensated employees. In applying this benefit test the employer can elect to exclude employees earning less than $25,000 (or a lower specified amount) if the plan is funded through salary reductions.

Failure to meet these rules makes plan benefits taxable, but only to "highly compensated" participants.[2]

4. Dependent care assistance eligible under Section 129 can be provided only to: (a) a child under 13 for whom the employee-taxpayer is entitled to take a dependency deduction on the income tax return; or (b) a taxpayer's dependent or spouse who is physically or mentally unable to care for himself.[3]

5. The amount of benefits excluded annually by the employee—the value of the services provided directly plus any employer reimbursements of expenses paid by the employee—cannot be more than the employee's earned income or, if the employee is married, the lesser of the employee's or spouse's earned income. Furthermore, the total amount excluded by the employee is limited to $5,000 annually, or $2,500 if the employee is married and files a separate return.[4]

6. Qualifying expenses must be for care alone, not for education above the kindergarten level. The following are items that qualify as care:[5]

- full preschool and kindergarten expenses (full tuition and fees for these programs);

- after-school programs for children under 13;

- summer camp for children under 13 (however, expenses for overnight summer camp do not qualify);

- cost of a housekeeper/sitter for children or other dependents cared for at home. (However, payments to a child under 19 or to a child that the employee is entitled to a personal exemption for do not qualify.)

7. A dependent care assistance plan must be in writing.[6]

8. In order to claim the exclusion for dependent care assistance benefits under Section 129 the taxpayer must report the correct name, address and taxpayer identification number of the care provider on his tax return.[7]

## ERISA AND OTHER REQUIREMENTS

The plan is considered a "welfare benefit plan" for ERISA purposes. This requires a written plan document, a summary plan description (SPD) explaining the plan that is provided to employees, a designated plan administrator, and a formal claims procedure. (Appendix A details these requirements more fully.) Further, Section 129 requires that the employer provide each employee with an annual statement of the expenses incurred in providing the prior year's benefits by January 31 of each year.[8]

## ALTERNATIVES

One alternative to dependent care assistance programs is the informal coverage of these expenses for selected employees through extra compensation or bonuses. However, this extra compensation is fully taxable to the employee.

## HOW TO INSTALL A PLAN

ERISA and the Code require a written plan and an SPD but no governmental approval. Some employers may want to obtain an IRS ruling stating that the plan complies with Section 129 if there are plan features, such as liberal benefits or limited employee eligibility, that raise compliance questions.

## WHERE CAN I FIND OUT MORE ABOUT IT?

1. IRS Publication 503, *Child and Dependent Care Expenses*, (annual IRS publication available at local IRS office).

2. IRS Publication 334, *Tax Guide for Small Business*, (annual IRS publication available at local IRS office).

3. Beam, Burton T., Jr. and John J. McFadden, *Employee Benefits*, 6th ed. Chicago, IL: Dearborn Financial Publishing, Inc., 2000.

## QUESTIONS AND ANSWERS

**Question** — Can an unincorporated business have a dependent care plan covering partners or proprietors as well as regular employees?

*Answer* — Yes. Section 129 allows self-employed individuals—partners or proprietors—to be treated as employees under the plan.[9] As with regular employees, dependent care benefits are excluded from the income of partners or proprietors who are covered by the plan.

**Question** — Can employees who receive tax-free benefits under a dependent care plan also use the dependent care tax credit of Code section 21?

*Answer* — Only if the employee receives benefits from the plan that are taxable to the employee or makes additional expenditures not paid for by the plan. Tax-free benefits from an employer dependent care plan are not eligible for the Section 21 tax credit. Additionally, the amount of expenses eligible for the dependent care credit must be offset dollar for dollar by the amount of expenses that the taxpayer excludes from income under the dependent care plan. For example, if a taxpayer has $2,400 of eligible dependent care expenses during the year and the employer's plan reimbursed him for $1,000 of the expenses only the remaining $1,400 would be eligible for the dependent care credit.[10]

**Question** — How can an employee decide between using the employer's dependent care assistance plan and using the dependent care tax credit (Section 21)?

*Answer* — Current law prohibits "double dipping" by taxpayers who pay child care expenses qualifying for the child care credit and who participate in a company sponsored dependent care assistance program.[11]

An employee's tax benefit from the child care credit is reduced to the extent he or she uses a company plan to cover expenses. Specifically, the maximum amount of qualifying expenses—$2,400 ($3,000 after 2002) for one child; $4,800 ($6,000 after 2002) for two or more children—a taxpayer may use for the child care credit is reduced dollar-for-dollar by amounts paid through a company plan. For example, if a company plan reimburses an employee with two children $4,000 for child care expenses in 2003, only $2,000 ($6,000 - $4,000) of additional child care expenses paid by the employee will qualify for the child care credit.

As a result, all employees who have child care expenses exceeding $4,800 ($6,000 after 2002) and who may participate in a company sponsored dependent care assistance program must choose between the company plan and the child care credit.

The choice depends on the employee's tax rate and whether or not amounts that would otherwise be allocated to child care under the company plan can be allocated to other benefits. For example, if the company dependent care assistance plan is part of a cafeteria plan or FSA salary-reduction plan where the employees can choose to allocate the amount that would otherwise go to child care expenses to fund other benefits such as medical expenses, health insurance premiums, or life insurance, the employees will generally be better off if they elect benefits other than child care reimbursements from their company plan. In this way they still get the full benefit of the company plan and may take the child care credit for the child care expenses they pay with after-tax dollars separately from the plan.

However, if the company plan does not allow the employees to use the amount that would otherwise go to child care expenses to fund other benefits, or for those employees who cannot fully use the other benefits that may be elected, the choice between the company plan and the child care credit depends on their tax rate (taxable income), filing status, and adjusted gross income (AGI).

The child care credit is equal to 35 percent of qualified expenses for persons with an AGI of $15,000 or less. The credit is reduced by one percentage point for each $2,000 of AGI above $15,000 with a floor of 20 percent for persons with AGI over $43,000.[12] Therefore, for each dollar of qualifying child care expenses the tax savings range from 35 cents to 20 cents for AGIs ranging from $15,000 to $43,000 and above.

In contrast, if child care expenses are reimbursed through a company salary-reduction plan, the tax savings will depend on the person's tax rate, which depends on taxable income and filing status. Employees whose taxable income falls in the 15 percent tax bracket will save only 15 cents on each qualifying dollar of child care expenses reimbursed through a company plan. Consequently, they should clearly opt out of the company plan and use the child care credit because they will save between 5 and 20 cents more on the dollar. However, if taxable income falls in a tax bracket above 25 percent, the employees will save at least 25 cents on each qualifying dollar of child care expenses reimbursed through the company plan. For these levels of taxable income the tax savings with the company plan will always equal or exceed the tax savings from the child care credit.

**Question** — What is the tax credit for employer-provided child care facilities?

*Answer* — Employers that provide child care for their employees may be able to claim a tax credit for the expenses associated with the expenses of providing the child care. The amount of the credit is 25 percent of certain child care expenditures and 10 percent of certain child care resource and referral expenditures. This credit may not exceed $150,000 for any tax year.[13]

There are recapture rules if the qualified child care facility ceases operation within 10 years of starting up or if there is a change in ownership in the child care facility. (However, special rules may apply if the purchaser agrees to assume the recapture liability.) If a taxpayer uses this credit with respect to property, the basis of the property is reduced by the amount of the credit. Also, no other deductions or credits may be taken for payments that result in this tax credit.

## FOOTNOTES

1. IRC Sections 129(a)(1), 129(e)(8).
2. IRC Section 129(d)(1).
3. IRC Sections 129(e)(1), 21(b).
4. IRC Sections 129(a)(2), 129(b)(1).
5. IRC Sections 129(e)(1), 21(b)(1), 21(b)(2), and 129(c); Treas. Reg. §1.44A-1(c)(3).
6. IRC Section 129(d)(1).
7. IRC Section 129(e)(9).
8. IRC Section 129(d)(7).
9. IRC Sections 129(e)(3), 129(e)(4).
10. IRC Sections 21(c), 129(e)(7).
11. IRC Section 21(c).
12. IRC Section 21(a), as amended by the Economic Growth and Tax Relief Reconciliation Act of 2001 (EGTRRA 2001). The percentage and dollar amount increases in effect after 2002 are scheduled to expire after December 31, 2010. EGTRRA 2001, Section 901.
13. IRC Section 45F, as added by EGTRRA 2001. It is scheduled to expire after December 31, 2010, unless extended by Congress.

# Chapter 34

# EDUCATIONAL ASSISTANCE PLAN

## WHAT IS IT?

An employer's educational assistance plan pays or reimburses employees for expenses incurred in educational programs aimed at improving job skills. Some broader plans provide assistance for education even if not job-related, or for education for children or dependents of employees.

## ADVANTAGES

1.  Employers benefit from improvement in employee skills through education that the employee might not be able to afford otherwise.

2.  Properly structured job-related educational benefits are not taxable income to employees.

## DISADVANTAGES

1.  A program that is too broad may simply train an employee for a job with another employer.

2.  Educational benefits beyond certain limits are taxable as compensation to the employee.

## TAX IMPLICATIONS

1.  An individual can deduct job-related educational expenses—including not only tuition but incidental expenses such as transportation, books, and supplies, if the education:

    (a) maintains or improves a skill required in the individual's employment, or

    (b) is expressly required by the individual's employer as a condition of keeping the individual's job.

    Job-related educational expenses are not deductible as a trade or business expense under Code section 162 if they do not meet these requirements. The IRS specifies that the costs for two types of education are not deductible: (a) education required to meet the minimum qualification requirements for an individual's present employment and (b) education that qualifies the individual for a new trade or business.[1]

    Some examples will illustrate this:

    *   Suppose an individual who has not completed a law degree begins working with a law firm on the understanding that the degree will be completed. Expenses for completing the law degree are nondeductible, because they are incurred simply to meet the minimum qualification requirements of the individual's current job.

    *   For a tax accountant in an accounting firm, law school expenses could be deductible if the accountant can prove to the IRS that the education will maintain or improve the accountant's skills as a tax expert.

    *   For an English teacher, expenses for law school probably would not be deductible since they would not maintain or improve skills in the teacher's existing job and would be seen as training to qualify in a new trade or business.

2.  Expenses for travel are not deductible as job-related educational expenses.[2]

3.  Employer reimbursements to employees for job-related educational expenses are deductible by the employer as compensation.[3]

4.  To the extent that the employer's deduction for reimbursements is matched by a corresponding deduction at the employee level, the educational assistance plan provides the employee with a form of tax-free income.

    Usually an employer's educational assistance plans are designed to reimburse only the deductible job-related expenses, both to provide the tax benefit and because the deductible job-related expenses will be the ones that the employer will be most interested in subsidizing. For example, it does not make sense for an employer to pay for education that qualifies an employee for a career with a different company.

5. There are several tax benefit provisions available to individuals incurring educational expenses, reimbursed or otherwise:

- An itemized deduction can be claimed for these amounts as employee business expenses. This deduction is available only if the employee itemizes deductions, and is subject to the 2%-of-adjusted-gross-income "floor" on total miscellaneous deductions under Code Section 67.

- Tuition and fees at an eligible post-secondary educational institution are deductible under Code Section 222 without any floor, and the deduction is available even if the taxpayer doesn't itemize deductions. However, the deduction is scheduled to expire after 2005 and is subject to an annual maximum based on adjusted gross income (AGI) as follows:

| Year | AGI $65,000 or less ($130,000 joint return) | AGI $65,000-80,000 ($130,000-160,000 joint) | Other |
|------|------|------|------|
| 2002 and 2003 | $3,000 | $3,000 | 0 |
| 2004 and 2005 | $4,000 | $2,000 | 0 |

- The taxpayer may be eligible for the Hope and Lifetime Learning tax ccredits. These are described in detail in IRS Publication 970.

6. Section 127 of the Code allows an employer to provide a broader range of educational reimbursements to employees on a tax-free basis. Such amounts are excludable from the employee's gross income.[4] While Congress has allowed Section 127 to expire several times in the past, it has been extended for expenses paid through 2010.[5]

Section 127 plans — "qualified educational assistance plans" — currently have the following characteristics:

- A broad range of educational benefits can be included in a Section 127 plan, including primary, secondary, undergraduate, and graduate programs as well as most other legitimate education programs.

- Under the plan, an employer can make payments up to a maximum of $5,250 annually for tuition, fees, books, supplies, and equipment for educational programs for an employee. Payments under the plan are deductible by the employer and excludable from the employee's gross income. The employer may pay these expenses directly, provide the education directly, or reimburse employees for expenditures they make.

- Courses taken by employees and covered under the plan need not be job related. However, course benefits may not involve sports, games, or hobbies unless they relate to the employer's business.

- Section 127 provides no tax benefits for tools or supplies retained by the employee after completion of the course or for meals, lodging, or transportation.

- A Section 127 plan must be in writing. However, it need not be funded in advance and does not have to be approved in advance by the IRS.

- A Section 127 plan must not discriminate in coverage in favor of highly compensated employees. In addition, there is a nondiscrimination rule for benefits: not more than five percent of the total amount paid or incurred annually by the employer for educational assistance under the plan may be provided for employees who are shareholders or owners of at least five percent of the business.

- Eligible employees must be notified of the program.

- A plan meets the requirements of Section 127(b) even if it provides benefits to former employees, which includes retired, disabled, or laid-off employees.[6]

7. Employer reimbursements of employee expenses for educating children or other dependents are taxable income to the employee and deductible as compensation by the employer. (Such expenses may be deductible by the employee if they meet the requirements for the new, "above the line" deduction for qualified higher education expenses explained under #2, above.) For a highly compen-

sated employee, such payments may create a question as to whether the overall compensation meets the reasonableness of compensation test for deductibility. This test is discussed in Chapter 30.

## ERISA REQUIREMENTS

An employer's educational assistance plan may be considered a "welfare benefit plan" for ERISA purposes, which means that the plan should be in writing, with a written claims procedure, and a Summary Plan Description (SPD) must be furnished to employees. If the plan is funded (most plans are not) additional requirements may apply. The ERISA rules are summarized in Appendix A.

## HOW TO INSTALL A PLAN

There should be a written plan, especially if the plan covers more than a few employees, but the document can be a simple one. An SPD should be drafted and distributed to meet ERISA requirements. No government approval is required, nor is it usually recommended. A request for an IRS ruling can be made if there are any tax questions.

## WHERE CAN I FIND OUT MORE ABOUT IT?

1. IRS Publications 17, *Your Federal Income Tax*, and 508, *Educational Expenses*, cover the deduction for educational expenses. They are revised annually and available from the IRS.

2. Beam, Burton T., Jr. and John J. McFadden, *Employee Benefits*, 6th ed. Chicago, IL: Dearborn Financial Publishing, Inc., 2000.

## QUESTIONS AND ANSWERS

**Question** — What is an "educational benefit trust" and how is it used?

*Answer* — An educational benefit trust is an arrangement under which an employer creates a trust fund to pay educational expenses for dependents of employees covered under the plan. Typically, this is used as an executive benefit, but it can also be provided to a larger group of employees or all employees.

Under current tax law, there is little, if any, tax advantage to this type of plan. The employer can deduct amounts paid into the trust fund for plan purposes. However, under Code section 419, the deduction is limited to the amount of benefits provided during the year. In other words, the employer cannot accelerate deductions by setting up the trust fund rather than paying benefits directly.

To the employee, benefits are taxable when they are paid to dependents for educational expenses. The amount paid to an employee's dependent is considered additional compensation income to the employee.

## FOOTNOTES

1. Reg. §1.162-5.
2. IRC Section 274(m)(2); but see Reg. §1.162-5(e).
3. Reg. §1.162-10.
4. IRC Section 127(a).
5. IRC Section 127(d), repealed by EGTRRA 2001.
6. Rev. Rul. 96-41, 1996-2 CB 8.

# Chapter 35

# FLEXIBLE SPENDING ACCOUNT

## WHAT IS IT?

A flexible spending account, or FSA, is a type of cafeteria plan—a plan under which employees can choose between cash and specified benefits—that is funded through salary reductions elected by employees each year.

## WHEN IS IT INDICATED?

1. When an employer wants to expand employee benefit choices without significant extra out-of-pocket costs (or possibly realize some actual dollar savings). Some situations where benefit choices are desirable:

    • Where many employees have employed spouses with duplicate medical coverage

    • Where employees contribute to health insurance costs

    • Where the employer's medical plans have large deductibles or coinsurance (co-pay) provisions

    • Where employees are nonunion (collective bargaining units prefer uniform benefit packages)

    • Where there is a need for benefits that are difficult to provide on a group basis, such as dependent care.

2. Where the costs of an employee benefit plan, such as health insurance, have increased and the employer must impose additional employee cost sharing in the form of (a) deductibles, or (b) coinsurance, the FSA approach minimizes employee outlay since the FSA converts after-tax employee expenditures to before-tax expenditures.

3. The FSA provides a tax benefit for employees (tax exclusion for various benefits) that is not available through any other plan.

4. Because of administrative costs, FSAs are usually impractical for businesses with only a few employ-

ees. Most FSAs involve employers with 25 or more employees, but the plan could be considered for as few as 10 employees.

5. FSA benefits cannot be provided to self-employed persons—partners or sole proprietors.

## ADVANTAGES

1. Since it is a type of cafeteria plan, the plan provides employees with some degree of choice as to whether to receive compensation in cash or benefits, and what form the benefits will take.

2. The FSA is funded through employee salary reductions, which means that no extra outlay by the employer is required, except for administrative costs.

3. The plan may result in a reduction in some employment taxes paid by the employer, since taxable payroll is reduced.

4. Salary reductions elected by employees to fund nontaxable benefits under the plan are not subject to federal income taxes.

5. The list of potential nontaxable benefits available from the plan is large and includes many benefits that employers might not otherwise provide to employees—for example, dependent care.

## DISADVANTAGES

1. An FSA must meet all of the complex nondiscrimination requirements for cafeteria plans (see Chapter 29). Monitoring compliance with these rules raises administrative costs. Also, particularly in some closely held corporations, there could be a loss of tax benefits to highly compensated employees if the nondiscrimination rules are not met.

2. FSAs require employees to evaluate their personal and family benefit situations and file a timely election form every year. They must estimate—at the

end of each year—the amount that will be required for covered expenses in the following year. This is sometimes both confusing and difficult, and some employees may not fully utilize the plan because of the perceived complexity or paperwork involved. Others may not want to risk the forfeiture required of any funds left in the account at the end of the year (see number 6 in the discussion below).

3. Administrative costs are greater than in a fixed benefit plan.

4. As discussed in the "Questions and Answers," below, IRS proposed regulations require an employer to be "at risk" regarding the total annual amount an employee elects to allocate to health benefits under his or her FSA.

## HOW IT WORKS—AND AN EXAMPLE

These are the basic features of an FSA plan:

1. The employer decides what benefits are to be provided in the FSA and adopts written plans to provide these benefits, if the plans are not already in place. (The design of these individual plans is generally covered in separate chapters of this book.) For example, the employer might decide that the FSA will allow employee salary reductions to be applied to:

   • medical expenses, such as deductibles and co-pays, not covered under the health insurance plan

   • expenses of dependent care (the employer must adopt a dependent care assistance plan)

2. The employer advises employees to review their benefit needs toward the end of each year and estimate their next year's expenses for items covered in the plan.

3. Before the end of the calendar year, employees file with the employer a written election to reduce salary by the amount they choose (the amount they estimate that they will spend on covered benefits) and allocate it among the benefits in the plan. A sample enrollment form is reproduced in Figure 35.1 at the end of this chapter. The chosen salary reduction goes into a "benefit account." The benefit account is a book account—it is not actually funded by the employer in most cases.

4. Each employee keeps a record of expenses in each benefit category and makes a claim on the plan for reimbursement. Claims are usually made on a quarterly basis for administrative convenience. (The employee does not have to make a written claim for expenses that would otherwise be a payroll deduction, such as the employee share of health insurance. Such claims are handled automatically by the plan.) A sample claim form appears in Figure 35.2 at the end of this chapter.

5. The employer issues checks to employees for reimbursement. These reimbursements are free of income tax.

6. At the end of the year, if anything is left in the employee's benefit account, it is forfeited. It cannot be carried over to the next year. This feature requires careful planning by the employee.

---

*Example:* Suppose employee Patella earns $40,000 per year and is covered under an FSA having the features noted in this discussion. On December 31, 2003, having reviewed his probable benefit needs for 2004, he files an FSA election with his employer to reduce his 2004 salary by $2,000. The $2,000 will go into his FSA benefit book account, and he elects to allocate it as follows:

   • $1,500 for medical expenses covered under the medical FSA but not the health insurance plan (Patella anticipates orthodontic expenses during 2004 for his daughter, Rubella)

   • $500 for expenses under the dependent care plan (Patella plans to send his daughter, age 11, to summer day camp costing about $500)

---

If Patella's expenses run as expected, the FSA will have turned $2,000 of nondeductible after-tax expenditures into before-tax payments, saving Patella the federal income tax on $2,000, and saving the employer the employment taxes on $2,000 of compensation paid.

If Patella's covered expenses are higher, he will simply lose the tax benefits that would have been available if he had made a larger salary reduction election.

However, if Patella's expenses are less than predicted, he will actually forfeit the amount remaining in his FSA benefit account at the end of the year. The amount forfeited in effect reverts to the employer, since it represents compensation that will not have to be paid.[1]

## DESIGN FEATURES

1.  An FSA is a cafeteria plan under Code section 125, and it must meet all the complex rules prohibiting discrimination in favor of highly compensated employees and prohibiting a concentration of benefits among the key employees. These rules are discussed in detail in Chapter 29, Cafeteria Plan.

    In general, these rules will be satisfied if all employees are allowed to participate and if benefits, as a percentage of compensation, are approximately equal for all employees. If the employer wants more selective coverage and benefits, compliance with the nondiscrimination rules must be carefully analyzed.

    The cost of noncompliance with the rules is not disqualification of the plan as a whole. Rather, the tax benefits for highly compensated employees only are lost.

2.  What benefits can be provided in the plan? These are the same as for cafeteria plans in general. Thus, employers can include the following types of benefits in an FSA arrangement:

    *   Medical reimbursement, including anything not covered in the health insurance plan—dental care, eyeglasses, hearing aids, etc. The potentially wide range of this option is discussed further in Chapter 47 of this book.

    *   Dependent Care Reimbursement (see Chapter 33).

    The Internal Revenue Code specifically prohibits some benefits from being provided under an FSA—

    — health insurance premiums (the FSA cannot be used to pay the employee's portion of the premium, but these can be paid on a pre-tax basis through a cafeteria plan, see Chapter 29)[2]

    — medical savings account contributions under Code section 106(b)

    — scholarships and fellowships under Code section 117

    — educational assistance provided under a plan governed by Code section 127

    — employee discounts (for example, those for department store employees), no-additional-cost services (for example, standby airline travel for airline employees) and other fringe benefits provided under Code section 132[3]

    —deferred compensation, other than under a Section 401(k) plan[4]

    —long-term care insurance[5]

3.  On the practical side, the critical design feature is *adequate employee communication*, so that employees use the plan, and the employer's efforts in instituting the plan pay off in employee appreciation.

## TAX IMPLICATIONS

1.  Employee salary reductions applied to nontaxable benefits are not subject to income tax. Highly compensated employees may be taxed on these benefits if the plan is discriminatory. Further, key employees may lose the tax benefits of an FSA if their benefits, as a percentage of compensation, is too large. See Chapter 29, Cafeteria Plan, for more details.

    Salary reductions, to be effective for tax purposes, must be made before the compensation is earned. IRS regulations require FSA elections to be made annually before the beginning of the calendar year for which the salary reduction is to be effective.[6]

2.  The employer gets a tax deduction for the amounts it pays to reimburse employees for covered expenditures.

3.  The employer's payroll subject to payroll taxes is reduced by the amount of any employee salary reductions under an FSA.[7] Payroll taxes include:

    (a) FICA (social security),

    (b) FUTA (federal unemployment tax),

    (c) state unemployment taxes, and

    (d) workers' compensation.

    State laws relating to unemployment taxes and workers' compensation may vary and should be checked.

## ERISA REQUIREMENTS

The ERISA requirements are those applicable to the various individual plans—health insurance, dependent care, etc.—that are part of the FSA arrangement. Generally, these plans are exempt from any requirement of advance funding and follow the rules applicable to welfare benefit plans under ERISA (see Appendix A). Written plans, a summary plan description, and a formal claims procedure are required under ERISA.

## HOW TO INSTALL A PLAN

Suppose an FSA plan is to be effective January 1, 2004. The essential step before this date is to obtain effective employee salary reduction elections. Thus, the plan must be designed, communicated to employees, and the salary reduction forms must be designed and furnished to employees before January 1, 2004. (See enrollment form in Figure 35.1 at the end of this chapter.)

Formal plan documents for the FSA and for each plan included in the FSA—medical reimbursement, dependent care, etc. — must be drafted and adopted by the employer. (All these can be incorporated in a single document, but separate documents are often convenient.) To be effective January 1, 2004, a corporation would have to formally adopt these documents, with a written resolution of the board of directors, before the end of the corporation's taxable year in which the effective date—January 1, 2004—falls. For example, a calendar-year corporation would have to formally adopt these plans no later than December 31, 2004.

## WHERE CAN I FIND OUT MORE ABOUT IT?

1. *Fundamentals of Employee Benefit Programs*, 5th ed. Washington, DC: Employee Benefit Research Institute, 1996.

2. Mamorsky, *Employee Benefits Handbook*, 3rd ed. Boston, Massachusetts: Warren, Gorham, & Lamont, 1992 (supplemented annually).

## QUESTIONS AND ANSWERS

**Question** — Is an employee "locked-in" for a full year to his or her FSA salary reduction amount and benefit allocation, or can it be changed during the year?

*Answer* — Changes are not generally allowed unless there are major life events that affect benefit needs.

The regulations list marriage, divorce, death of a spouse or child, birth of a child or addition of a dependent, and loss of a spouse's job as some of the permitted qualifying events.[8]

**Question** — Since FSA salary reductions eliminate Social Security taxes on the salary reduction, are Social Security benefits also affected?

*Answer* — If an FSA salary reduction reduces an employee's wages below the taxable wage base for the year ($87,000 for 2003), then Social Security benefit credit for that year will also be reduced. This probably will not reduce an employee's ultimate Social Security retirement benefit by very much, but it may deter FSA participation by lower-paid employees. It is advisable for employers to investigate exactly how much effect this will have and communicate it to employees to allay any unreasonable fears they may have. Also, for a relatively low cost, employers can provide an insurance or annuity benefit or qualified plan supplement to compensate employees for this loss.

**Question** — Are FSA salary reductions recognized for state or local income tax purposes?

*Answer* — If state or local income taxes are based on federal taxable income—as most are—then salary reductions are generally effective for state tax purposes. However, state and local laws vary.

**Question** — Is there a dollar limit on annual salary reductions in an FSA plan?

*Answer* — There is no dollar limit applicable to FSA salary reductions as such. However, the separate employee benefit plans that are part of an FSA program may have their own dollar limits. For example, there is a $5,000 annual limit for dependent care plans (see Chapter 33). Also, employers often limit salary reductions to a relatively small amount in order to meet the nondiscrimination rules of Section 125. If the plan permits large salary reductions, highly compensated employees are likely to use the plan disproportionately. Regulations require the plan to specify a maximum dollar limit or a maximum percentage of compensation.[9] For further discussion, see Baxendale and Coppage, "Choosing Between the Child Care Credit and Flexible Accounts," *Taxation for Accountants*, May, 1993. In addition, the employer may wish to limit the amount at risk. See discussion below.

**Question** — If an employee uses up his or her benefit account allocated to one form of benefit, can amounts allocated to another form of benefit be reallocated?

*Answer* — The IRS takes the position that there can be no such "crossover" of benefit allocations between medical FSAs and Dependent Care FSAs during the year.[10] This emphasizes the importance (and difficulty) of careful employee planning in making the annual salary reduction election and allocation of the benefit account.

**Question** — What are the implications of the IRS position that an employer must be "at risk" with respect to health benefits in an FSA?

*Answer* — Proposed regulations state that health care reimbursements under an FSA will not be tax free if the plan eliminates all "risk of loss" to an employer.[11] In effect, this forces the employer to be a health insurer with respect to the health care reimbursement aspect of the FSA.

---

*Example:* Suppose a law firm's FSA plan covers employee Ben DeLaws. Ben elects in December 2003 to reduce his 2004 salary by $100 per month (a total of $1,200 for 2004) and use the salary reduction amount for health benefits under the FSA plan. In February, 2004, Ben's daughter incurs orthodontia expenses of $1,000 which are covered under the plan. Can the plan reimburse Ben in March 2004 only the $200 that he has contributed so far, and reimburse the remaining $800 as Ben makes further salary reduction FSA contributions over the rest of 2004? The IRS says no; Ben is entitled to reimbursement of the entire $1,000 (at the subsequent claims period under the plan). If Ben quits his job and goes to work for another firm in June, 2004, he will never have contributed enough to the FSA to cover this reimbursement and his prior employer will have to cover the difference. This is what the IRS means by "risk of loss."

---

The IRS view is questionable and may be litigated eventually. Since this regulation is a proposed regulation, taxpayers who do not follow it are not subject to criminal or negligence penalties. However, if it is made permanent the IRS will undoubtedly enforce it retroactively. It appears advisable for employers to recognize the rights of employees to receive full current reimbursement of FSA claims even before their FSA accounts have accumulated

enough to pay the claim, but the employer may not have to pay the full amount in one installment unless the employee specifically requests immediate full payment.

**Question** — If an employer has an arrangement under which the amount elected as a salary reduction in an FSA is "reimbursed" to the employee to cover the employee's uninsured medical expenses, can this reimbursement be treated as a tax-free amount under Code Section 105(b) (payment to reimburse an employee's expenses for medical care)?

*Answer* — If the reimbursement is made only for actual uninsured medical expenses incurred during the year, as the expenses are incurred, Section 105(b) treatment could conceivably be applicable. However, in Rev. Rul 2002-80, 2002-49 IRB, the IRS concluded that purported reimbursements, whether in the form of direct reimbursements or purported "loans" were not subject to tax-free Section 105(b) treatment where the reimbursements were made regardless of whether the employee actually incurred uninsured medical expenses. The fact that the employer treated excess reimbursements (i.e. amounts in excess of actual uninsured medical expenses reported to the employer) as taxable income did not change this result.

## FOOTNOTES

1.  Prop. Treas. Reg. §1.125-1, Q&A 7.
2.  IRC Section 125(f).
3.  Prop. Treas. Reg. §1.125-2, A-7(b)(4). Similarly, group term life insurance on the employee's life up to $50,000, disability insurance premiums under an employer group arrangement, contributions to a Section 401(k) plan, and extra vacation days cannot be provided through an FSA but can be provided through a regular Section 125 Cafeteria Plan.
4.  IRC Section 125(d)(2).
5.  IRC Section 125(f).
6.  Prop. Treas. Reg. §1.125-1, Q&A 6, Q&A 15.
7.  IRC Sections 3121(a)(5)(G), 3306(b)(5)(G). Note that there is no exception for salary reductions under cafeteria plans as there is for 401(k) and 403(b) salary reductions.
8.  Prop. Treas. Reg. §1.125-2, Q&A 6. The Service has issued new proposed regulations and two sets of final regulations applicable to election changes for health and group term life insurance. The final regulations are effective March 23, 2000 (but applicable for cafeteria plan years beginning on or after January 1, 2001) and January 1, 2001. Treas. Reg. §1.125.4.
9.  Prop. Treas. Reg. §1.125-2, Q&A 3.
10. See Prop. Treas. Reg. §1.125-1, Q&A 17.
11. Prop. Treas. Reg. §1.125-2, Q&A 7.

**Figure 35.1**

---

**(Name of Employer)**
**FLEXIBLE SPENDING ACCOUNT (FSA)**
**ENROLLMENT - 2004**

---

Each employee must complete this form before December 31, 2003 and return it to the employer.

Name: _____    Social Security No. _____ \ _____ \ _____

(   )    NO, I do not wish to enroll in the FSA for 2004. I understand that I cannot enroll at any other time during the 2004 Plan Year.

(   )    YES, I elect to enroll in the FSA, effective January 1, 2004, and authorize the employer to reduce my pay by the following amount(s):

    *an allocation for anticipated health expenses ............................................................................. $_____
    *an allocation for dependent care expenses (not to exceed $5,000) ......................................... $_____

                    Total (Not to exceed $[0,000]) ................ $_____

I understand that the salary reduction I have elected for health expenses are recorded separately from the salary reduction for dependent care costs. If there is money recorded in one account at the end of the year, it is not transferable to meet expenses in the other category.

I understand that I cannot suspend, increase or decrease my salary reductions during the 2004 Plan Year unless I experience a major "life event" as described in federal regulations.

I understand that any money remaining in my Flexible Spending Account at the end of the 2004 Plan Year will be forfeited by me.

I have received a written explanation of the Flexible Spending Account. I understand that the employer cannot be responsible for any tax liabilities which may subsequently occur as a result of my FSA participation.

_____    _____
*Your signature*    *Date*

---

**Figure 35.2**

### (Name of Employer)
### FLEXIBLE SPENDING ACCOUNT (FSA)
### EMPLOYEE REIMBURSEMENT REQUEST

**INSTRUCTIONS:**
When to file a reimbursement request form:

This form is to be filed every time you request reimbursement under the FSA for *eligible health expenses* or for *dependent care expenses*. Please submit your *original* bills or cancelled checks with this form. Legible photocopies are acceptable.

**HEALTH EXPENSES**
I authorize reimbursement of the health expenses indicated below through my FSA. I certify that, to the best of my knowledge, the expenses I am submitting would qualify as tax deductible medical expenses. I further certify that these expenses are not reimbursable under any other plan, including a plan of another employer that covers me, my spouse or another member of my family.

| (1) | (2) | (3) | (4) |
|---|---|---|---|
| DESCRIPTION OF ELIGIBLE EXPENSES | DATE INCURRED | TOTAL AMOUNT OF BILL | AMOUNT PAID BY ANY OTHER PLAN |
| | | | |
| | | | |
| | | | |

| (5) | (6) |
|---|---|
| FSA Col. (3) - Col. (4) | EXPENSES FOR: NAME (If dependent, relationship and date of birth) |
| | |
| | |
| | |

**Figure 35.2 (continued)**

## DEPENDENT CARE EXPENSES

I authorize reimbursement of the expenses indicated below through my FSA. I certify that, to the best of my knowledge, the expenses I am submitting meet the requirements of employment-related dependent care expenses. If married, I further certify that these expenses, together with any other dependent day care expenses already reimbursed through FSA, do not exceed the lesser of my earned income or the earned income of my spouse. I also certify that my spouse was employed on the date these expenses were incurred.

| (1) | (2) | (3) | (4) |
|---|---|---|---|
| Name of Individual or Organizatin Providing Dependent Care Service | Provider Social Security or I.D. Number | Date Incurred | Total Amount of Bill |

| (5) | (6) |
|---|---|
| FSA Claim | Expenses for Care of: (Name, relationship, age) |

Employee Name: _____     Social Security No. _____

_____     _____
Employee Signature                                                    Date

Plan Administrator _____ Date _____

# Chapter 36

# "FRINGE" BENEFITS (SECTION 132)

## WHAT ARE THEY?

Fringe benefits are noncash compensation benefits to employees. Most miscellaneous fringe benefits not discussed in other chapters of this book are governed by Code section 132, which determines whether the benefits are taxable to employees. This chapter covers:

- employee discounts

- no-additional-cost services

- company cafeterias and meal plans

- qualified transportation

- qualified retirement planning services

- gyms and athletic facilities

- "working condition fringes"

- "de minimis fringes"

## EMPLOYEE DISCOUNTS

Employers in the retailing business often provide employees with discounts on merchandise sold in the employer's stores. For example, a department store may provide a 10% discount on clothing purchased by employees.

## Advantages

1. Discounts on merchandise are almost as valuable as cash to employees, but are very inexpensive for the employer because the employer can still make a profit on the items sold (or at least recover its cost) but does not have to bear the full cost of marketing and selling the items to the public.

2. In the retail fashion industry, discounts serve the retailer's interest in promoting its products by allowing sales employees to wear the retailer's fashion items (which they otherwise could not afford) on the job.

## Tax Implications

Employee discounts are not includable in the employee's taxable income if the following conditions are met.

1. For a "highly compensated" employee (see definition below), the discount is excludable from income only if the discount is available on substantially the same terms to each member of a classification of employees that does not discriminate in favor of highly compensated employees. For example, if a department store provided discounts only to its executives, most of whom fell under the "highly compensated" definition, the discounts would be taxable income, but only to those executives who were highly compensated.

2. The discount does not exceed the employer's "gross profit percentage" on the item. Gross profit percentage is the percentage of the ordinary retail price equal to

$$\frac{\text{sales price less cost for all such items}[1]}{\text{sales price for all such items}}$$

3. The items discounted must be property offered for sale to customers in the ordinary course of the line of business of the employer in which the employee is working.[2] However, real estate or investments are not available for employee discount programs, even if the employer is in the business of selling real estate or investment products.

Employee discounts can be offered not only to active employees but also to (1) retired and disabled employees, (2) a widow or widower of an employee of the business, or (3) a spouse or dependent child of an employee. Dependent child includes either an actual dependent for tax purposes or a child under age 25 both of whose parents are deceased.[3]

## NO-ADDITIONAL-COST SERVICES

Service businesses can provide discounted services to employees at low cost, but with considerable perceived value to the employees. Probably the best-known example of this type of fringe benefit is the free or discounted "standby" air travel available to some airline employees.

### Advantages

1. Free or discounted services to employees may be almost as valuable to them as cash, but they can be provided at almost no marginal cost to the employer if they primarily involve excess capacity that provides no revenue to the employer.

### Tax Implications

Services provided free or discounted to employees are not includable in the employee's taxable income if the following conditions are met:

1. For a highly compensated employee (see definition below), the value of the services used is excludable from income only if the services are available on substantially the same terms to each member of a classification of employees that does not discriminate in favor of highly compensated employees. For example, if an airline provided free standby air travel only to its executives, most of whom fell under the "highly compensated" definition, the value of any trips taken by highly compensated employees would be taxable income to them. Trips taken by nonhighly compensated employees would not be taxable.

2. Either of the following two conditions must be satisfied:

   - The employer must incur no substantial cost (including foregone revenues) in providing such service to the employee (determined without regard to any amount paid by the employee). For example, providing hotel employees free hotel accommodations on a standby basis—that is, where the rooms are not otherwise booked—would meet this condition, because there would be no foregone revenue, and no substantial additional cost to the employer. However, providing free hotel room reservations, thus "bumping" paying customers, would not meet this condition.[4]

   - Alternatively, if services are discounted to employees, the discount cannot be more than 20 percent of the price at which the services are offered by the employer to regular customers.[5]

3. The services must be those offered for sale to customers in the ordinary course of the line of business of the employer in which the employee is working.[6] For example, if a corporation operates both a hotel and an airline, employees of the hotel business can be provided with free standby hotel rooms in the employer's hotel, but not standby air transportation.

   Unrelated employers in the same line of business—for example, two unrelated airlines—can enter into reciprocal written agreements under which employees of both can obtain nontaxable services from either one of the employers.[7]

No-additional-cost services can be offered not only to active employees but also to (1) retired and disabled employees, (2) a widow or widower of an employee of the business, or (3) a spouse or dependent child of an employee. Dependent child includes either an actual dependent for tax purposes or a child under age 25 both of whose parents are deceased.[8] In addition, for air travel, the parent of an employee can be included in the plan.[9]

## COMPANY CAFETERIAS AND MEAL PLANS

Employers often provide cafeterias or dining rooms for employees for various business reasons: (1) time is saved by having employees eat on the premises rather than travel to outside restaurants; (2) nearby restaurants may be too expensive for many employees; (3) the work environment is enhanced by providing company dining facilities; (4) employees may even talk business at lunch and trade ideas or make business decisions.

Employers can almost always deduct the cost of these facilities as business expenses. The significant tax question is—are the meals taxable to employees? The rules are surprisingly complicated.

There are two types of cafeteria/dining room/meal plans provided by an employer for employees that do not result in extra taxable income to employees: (1) a Section 119 "on-premises" plan and (2) a Section 132(e)(2) "on or near" plan.[10]

Any *other* meals or meal plans, other than these two types, that are furnished to employees working at their regular workplace will constitute taxable income to the employee to the extent of the fair market value of the meal. However, meals and lodging furnished to employees who are working away from home are not taxable to the employees.[11]

*Section 119 on-premises plan.* If an employer furnishes meals for employees, or their spouses or dependents, the value of the meals is excluded from the employee's income if:

- the meals are for the "convenience of the employer"; and

- the meals are furnished on the business premises of the employer.[12]

The issue of whether the plan serves the convenience of the employer is a factual one, with guidelines set out in the regulations under Section 119.

If more than half of the employees are provided with meals that meet the above tests, all meals provided to employees on business premises are excluded from income.[13]

There is no requirement that the meals must be furnished for all employees or a broad or nondiscriminatory classification of employees.

The tax treatment of the plan is the same whether or not employees must pay for the meals, in full or in part. The amount the employee pays for individual meals is not tax-deductible by the employee. However, if the plan is structured so that the employee is *required* to pay a fixed periodic charge for the plan (not on a per-meal basis), then the fixed periodic charge is excluded from the employee's income for tax purposes.[14]

*Section 132(e) on-or-near plan.* If an employer operates an eating facility for employees, the value of meals is not taxable to employees if the following conditions are met:[15]

- the eating facility is located on or near the business premises of the employer;

- revenue derived from the facility normally equals or exceeds the "direct operating costs" of the facility. The direct operating costs are the costs of food and beverages and labor performed directly at the eating facility.[16]

- if the employee is "highly compensated" (see definition below) the meal is taxable unless ac-

cess to the eating facility is available on substantially the same terms to each member of a group of employees that is defined in a nondiscriminatory way.

In other words, an "executives only" dining room (including even a separate, posh dining room next to the employee mess[17]) can result in taxation of the meal's value to the executive, unless the plan meets the requirements of a Section 119 "on-premises" plan.[18]

## QUALIFIED TRANSPORTATION

A qualified transportation fringe is a plan that provides one or more of the following benefits for employees:[19]

- transportation in a "commuter highway vehicle";

- a transit pass for use on a transit system (public or private); or

- "qualified parking."

## Advantages

1.  The value of these benefits can be considerable in some cases. They are provided tax-free to employees while the cost is fully deductible to employers.

2.  Qualified transportation fringes, unlike other fringe benefits, can be provided to employees on a cash-option (salary reduction) basis.[20] For example, the employer can offer a group of employees the choice of receiving a monthly transit pass worth $50 or $50 more in cash that month. Those who choose the transit pass do not pay federal income taxes on its value; only those who choose the cash option must pay taxes on the $50 monthly benefit.

   By contrast, if an employer offered another fringe benefit on this basis, all employees would be taxable on the value of the benefit, whether they took cash or not. For example, if a department store offered employees a choice between $50 worth of monthly discounts on store merchandise or $50 monthly in cash, all employees covered by the plan would have $50 of taxable monthly income, whether or not they chose the cash option. Fringe benefits other than qualified transportation fringes must be offered as an employer-paid extra only, not under a cash option, or they lose their tax-free nature.

3.  There are no nondiscrimination requirements for qualified transportation fringes. For example, parking can be provided tax-free (up to the monthly limit described below) even if it is available only to selected executives. Planners of executive compensation programs, particularly for executives working in downtown office buildings, should make note of the compensation opportunity potentially available here.

## Benefits

*Commuter highway vehicle.* This benefit is available for transportation in vans seating at least six passengers and running on commuting trips when it is at least half-full. (This half-full provision is evidently designed to exclude chauffeured executive limos, etc.) The van can be operated by the employer or a contractor hired by the employer.[21] Tax-free benefits are limited to an aggregate per-employee monthly limit of $100 worth of transportation in commuter highway vehicles and transit passes.[22]

*Transit pass.* A transit pass applies to mass transit as normally understood, as well as costs for a van operated as a business by a third party (not the employer or a contractor hired by the employer) and having at least a six-passenger capacity.[23] As indicated, a $100 monthly aggregate limit applies for transit passes together with commuter highway vehicle benefits.

*Parking.* Although many employees probably do not think of parking as an employee benefit, particularly if they work in suburban locations, the value of parking to employees can be considerable.

Under the tax law, parking provided to employees is excludable from their taxable income up to $175 per month (as adjusted for inflation, $190 in 2003).[24] To qualify, the employer must provide the parking arrangement on or near the employer's place of business or near a location from which the employee can board some type of commuter vehicle.[25]

Although it is relatively easy to determine the value of a parking space in a commercial lot or garage, valuing spaces at suburban office or plant facilities may be a problem. The IRS has simplified this somewhat by taking the position that the value of the parking is zero if nobody but an employee would pay to park in the lot or garage.[26]

## QUALIFIED RETIREMENT PLANNING SERVICES

An employee and spouse may exclude from their income the value of certain retirement planning services provided by the employer maintaining their qualified retirement plan.[27] The exclusion will not be available to highly compensated employees, unless the services are also available, on substantially the same basis, to all employees that would normally be provided education and information regarding the employer's qualified plan.[28]

The services that may be excluded are not limited to information regarding the employer's qualified retirement plan. Thus, the services may include general advice regarding the employee's and the spouse's overall plan for retirement, of which the employer's qualified plan is only a part.[29] Services such as tax preparation, and accounting, legal, or brokerage services are excluded, without regard to whether they relate to retirement planning.

## GYMS AND ATHLETIC FACILITIES

An athletic facility available to employees is tax free to them if:

1.  it is located on the premises of the employer (but this can be somewhere other than the employer's *business* premises and can be either owned or leased[30]);

2.  it is operated by the employer; and

3.  substantially all of the facility's use is by employees, their spouses, and their dependent children.[31]

There are no nondiscrimination requirements for this provision. That is, an athletic facility that is provided only for selected executives is tax-free to the executives if it meets the three requirements listed above.[32]

## WORKING CONDITION FRINGES

Code section 132 contains a general provision that if an employer provides property or services to an employee, the value of these is not taxable to the employee if, had the employee paid for them himself, that payment would be allowable as an employee business expense deduction.[33] Such employer-provided property or services are referred to as "working condition fringes."

For example, if an employee is driven to an away-from-home work location in the company limousine, the value of that transportation is not taxable to the employee. This is because if the employee himself paid for travelling to a work location away from home, such costs would be deductible to him.

In the case of company cars and car expense reimbursement plans, the IRS has woven a vast web of regulation out of this seemingly simple provision, as discussed in Chapter 31.

## DE MINIMIS FRINGE

A final general rule in the fringe benefit area is a provision of Section 132 that property or services provided to the employee are not taxable to him if their value is so small as to make accounting for them "unreasonable or administratively impractical."[34] Such benefits are referred to as "de minimis fringes" after the legal term *de minimis* which means "among the small things (that can be ignored)."

Unfortunately, employers and employees still have to worry whether the IRS will agree that a "small" thing is small enough to be ignored. While the IRS is apparently not yet concerned about used pencils that employees take home from the office, there are many doubtful areas. Some current guidelines from the IRS regulations appear in Figure 36.1.[35]

## DEFINITION OF HIGHLY COMPENSATED

For purposes of the fringe benefit rules that include nondiscrimination provisions, the definition of highly compensated employee is the same one used for qualified pension and profit sharing plans.[36]

In summary, a highly compensated employee is any employee who, during the year or the preceding year:

1. was at any time an owner of *more* than 5 percent of the business; or

2. received compensation from the employer in excess of $80,000 (as indexed, $90,000 for 2003).[37]

**Figure 36.1**

| NOT TAXABLE | |
| --- | --- |
| Occasional money for meals or local transportation, not provided on a regular or routine basis | Occasional cocktail parties, group meals, picnics |
| Taxi fare for commute outside of normal work hours to or from unsafe area (employee must include only first $1.50 per trip in income but highly compensated must include full fare) | Traditional noncash birthday or holiday gifts with a "low" fair market value |
| | Occasional theater or sports tickets |
| Occasional typing of personal letters by company secretary | Coffee, doughnuts, or soft drinks |
| | Local telephone calls |
| Occasional personal use of copying machine (machine must be used 85 percent for business) | Flowers, gifts for illness, reward, family crisis |

| TAXABLE | |
| --- | --- |
| Season theater or sports tickets | Group-term life insurance on spouse or child |
| Commuting use of company car more than one day per month | Use of company apartment, lodge, etc. for weekend |
| Membership in private club | |

## FOOTNOTES

1. IRC Section 132(c)(2)(A). Regulations provide details for calculating this percentage.
2. IRC Section 132(c)(4).
3. IRC Section 132(h).
4. IRC Section 132(b).
5. IRC Section 132(c)(1)(B).
6. IRC Section 132(b)(1). For airlines, certain affiliated airlines are deemed to be in the same line of business. IRC Section 132(j)(5).
7. IRC Section 132(i).
8. IRC Section 132(h).
9. IRC Section 132(h)(3).
10. The two Code sections dealing with meals for employees, 119 and 132, were enacted at different times and are not coordinated. The only provision dealing with the overlap is Section 132(l), and it is not explicit and subject to differing interpretations. The interpretation adopted in this chapter is that meals are tax-free to employees if they meet *either* of these two Code provisions. For a discussion of the relationship of these provisions, see "Unraveling Recent Tax Law Changes for Free Meals to Employees at On-Premises Facilities," *Weekly Alert*, RIA, August 13, 1998.
11. See IRS Publication 463.
12. IRC Section 119(a).
13. IRC Section 119(b)(4).
14. IRC Section 119(b)(3).
15. IRC Section 132(e)(2).
16. Treas. Reg. §1.132-7(b).
17. Treas. Reg. §1.132-7(a)(1)(ii).
18. See footnote 10 as to whether Sections 119 and 132 are alternatives. A discriminatory executives-only dining facility could meet the requirements of Section 119, but it should be noted that the "convenience of the employer" test in the latter section must then be met; it has no counterpart in Section 132. "Convenience of the employer" appears to be a tough test to meet. See TAM 9143003.
19. IRC Section 132(f)(1).
20. IRC Section 132(f)(4).
21. IRC Sections 132(f)(5)(B), 132(f)(5)(D).
22. IRC Section 132(f)(2)(A).
23. IRC Section 132 (f)(5)(A).
24. IRC Sections 132(f)(2)(B), 132(f)(6).
25. IRC Section 132(f)(5)(C).
26. Notice 94-3, 1994-1 CB 327, Q-10.
27. IRC Section 132(a)(7), as added by the Economic Growth and Tax Relief Reconciliation Act of 2001 (EGTRRA 2001). Note that all provisions of EGTRRA 2001 are scheduled to sunset, or expire, after December 31, 2010.
28. IRC Section 132(m)(2), as added by EGTRRA 2001.
29. IRC Section 132(m)(1), as added by EGTRRA 2001.
30. Treas. Reg. §1.132-1(e)(2).
31. IRC Section 132(j)(4).
32. Treas. Reg. §1.132-1(e)(5).
33. IRC Section 132(d). The two-percent floor on itemized deductions is not considered. Reg. §1.132-5(a)(1)(vi).
34. IRC Section 132(e).
35. Treas. Reg. §1.132-6.
36. IRC Section 414(q).
37. Notice 2002-71, 2002-45 IRB 830.

# Chapter 37

# GOLDEN PARACHUTE PLAN

## WHAT IS IT?

A golden parachute plan is a compensation arrangement that provides special severance benefits to executives in the event that the corporation changes ownership and the covered executives are terminated.

An executive who accepts employment with a company that is a potential target for acquisition will often insist on a parachute-type compensation arrangement as a matter of self protection. Within limits, such agreements are an acceptable compensation practice.

Compensation arrangements of this type have a potential for abuse: inefficient managers could potentially grant themselves large parachute payments that would act merely as a financial obstacle to acquisition, or would unduly burden successor management. Therefore, Congress added provisions to the Internal Revenue Code that limit corporate deductions for these payments and impose a penalty on the recipient for payments beyond specified limits. These provisions do *not* generally apply, however, to closely held corporations (see below).

See also Chapter 50, Severance Pay Plan, for further general considerations in the design of severance pay arrangements.

## TAX IMPLICATIONS

1. An amount that is characterized as an "excess parachute payment" is subject to two tax sanctions:

   • no employer deduction is allowed[1] and

   • the person receiving the payment is subject to a penalty tax equal to 20% of the excess parachute payment.[2]

2. An excess parachute payment is: (1) the amount of any "parachute payment"; less (2) the portion of the "base amount" that is allocated to the payment. The formula to calculate the amount of a parachute payment considered to be excess is:

$$\text{Parachute payment} - \frac{\text{Present value of the parachute payment}}{\text{Present value of all parachute payments expected}} \times \text{Base amount}$$

*Definition of parachute payment.* A parachute payment is any compensatory payment made to an employee or independent contractor who is an officer, shareholder, or highly compensated individual (defined as one of the highest paid 1% of company employees, up to 250 employees[3]) that meets the following criteria[4]:

(a) the payment is contingent on a change (i) in the ownership or effective control of the corporation, or (ii) in the ownership of a substantial portion of the assets of the corporation, and

(b) the aggregate present value of the payments equals or exceeds three times the base amount.

Also included in the definition of a parachute payment is any payment made under an agreement that violates securities laws.[5]

If an agreement is made within one year of the ownership change, there is a presumption (which is rebuttable) that the payment is contingent on an ownership change.[6]

Any amount that the taxpayer can prove is "reasonable compensation" for personal services rendered before the takeover will not be treated as a parachute payment. Reasonable compensation is determined by reference to either the executive's historic compensation, or amounts paid by the employer or comparable employers to executives performing comparable services.[7]

Disallowance under this provision is coordinated with the Code provision generally disallowing deductions for compensation over $1,000,000; amounts disallowed under one provision are not allowed under the other.[8]

*Definition of base amount.* The base amount means the recipient individual's annualized includable (taxable) compensation for the "base period," which is the most recent five taxable years ending before the date on which the change of ownership or control occurs.[9]

---

*Example 1:* Roger Flabb, CEO of Wimpp Industries, Inc., has had annualized compensation of $700,000 annually for the past five years. His severance agreement provides a lump sum severance payment of $2,800,000 in the event he is fired after a corporate takeover. [Assume that $2,100,000, but not more than that, would be reasonable compensation as a severance payment.] Octopus, Inc. acquires Wimpp in 2004 and Roger is terminated and paid the $2,800,000 in 2004. Of that amount, $700,000 is an excess parachute payment (the excess of the total of $2,800,000 over three times the base amount, 3 x $700,000 = $2,100,000). Octopus (or whatever corporation pays the amount and is eligible to deduct compensation paid to Roger) is denied a deduction for the $700,000 excess parachute payment. The remaining $2,100,000 of the severance payment to Roger is deductible as a compensation payment. Roger must pay income tax on the entire $2,800,000 payment *plus* a 20% penalty tax on the excess parachute payment (20% of $700,000 or $140,000).

*Example 2:* Brenda Flabb, Vice President of Wimpp Industries, Inc., earned $20,000 each of the prior five years. She is entitled to two golden parachute payments, one of $200,000 at the time of her termination and a second payment of $400,000 at a future date. Assume that the present value of the second payment is $300,000. Applying the formula above, the portion of the base amount allocated to the first payment would be $40,000 ($200,000/$500,000 x $100,000) with $60,000 ($300,000/$500,000 x $100,000) al-

located to the second payment. Therefore, the amount of the first excess payment is $160,000 ($200,000 - $40,000) and the second excess payment is $340,000 ($400,000 - $60,000).

---

3. The parachute rules do not apply to corporations that have no stock that is readily tradable on an established securities market, provided that the payments are approved by a majority of shareholders who, immediately before the change in control, owned more than 75% of the voting power of all outstanding stock following disclosure to them of all material facts.[10] Further, the parachute rules do not apply to payments from small business corporations (S corporations) or generally to payments from qualified retirement plans, simplified employee pension plans and SIMPLE IRAs.[11]

## WHERE CAN I FIND OUT MORE ABOUT IT?

Hevener, Mary B. "Golden Parachutes: Proposed Regulations," *Tax Management Compensation Planning Journal* 17/8, August 4, 1989.

Feldman, "A Bird's-Eye View of Golden Parachutes," *Journal of Pension Planning and Compliance*, Spring, 1993.

## FOOTNOTES

1. IRC Section 280G(a).
2. IRC Section 4999.
3. IRC Section 280G(c).
4. IRC Section 280G(b)(2).
5. IRC Section 280G(b)(2)(B).
6. IRC Section 280G(b)(2)(C).
7. IRC Section 280G(b)(4); Prop. Reg. §1.280G-1, Q&A 40, 42(a).
8. IRC Section 162(m)(4)(f).
9. IRC Sections 280G(b)(3)(A), 280G(d)(2).
10. IRC Sections 280G(b)(5)(A)(ii), 280G(b)(5)(B); Prop. Reg. §1.280G-1, Q&A 6(a)(2), 7(a).
11. IRC Sections 280G(b)(5)(A)(i), 280G(b)(6).

# Chapter 38

# GROUP–TERM LIFE INSURANCE

## WHAT IS IT?

A group-term life insurance plan provides insurance for a group of employees under a group insurance contract held by the employer. If the plan qualifies under Code section 79, the cost of the first $50,000 of insurance is tax-free to employees.

## WHEN IS IT INDICATED?

Because virtually all employees have at least some basic need for life insurance, and as there are few other ways to obtain tax-free life insurance, most employers would find it difficult to find reasons not to provide a group-term plan, at least at levels up to the $50,000 tax-free limit.

At levels above $50,000, group-term plans may be a cost effective way to provide a life insurance benefit, both for employer and employee. However, group-term coverage may have costs and other disadvantages for coverage of amounts over $50,000; these disadvantages have led planners to investigate the "carve-out" concept discussed below.

## DESIGN FEATURES

### Nondiscrimination Requirements

Code section 79 prescribes rules to prevent discrimination in favor of "key employees" (key employee is defined under the top-heavy rules of Code section 416(i)—see Chapter 25). The nondiscrimination requirements do not apply to plans of churches, synagogues, or certain related organizations.

If these rules are not met, key employees lose the tax exclusion for the first $50,000 of coverage. Because coverage above $50,000 is included in taxable income, key employees must include the cost of the entire amount of coverage at the greater of Table I rates (see below) or the actual cost.

### Coverage Rules

The plan must:

- benefit at least 70 percent of all employees;

- benefit a group of which at least 85 percent are not key employees;

- benefit a nondiscriminatory classification of employees, as determined by the IRS; or

- in a cafeteria (Section 125) plan, meet the Section 125 nondiscrimination rules (see Chapter 29).[1]

### Benefit Rules

1. Benefits must not discriminate in favor of key employees.

2. All benefits available to key employees must be available to other plan participants.[2]

3. Life insurance coverage equal to the same percentage of compensation for all participants will not violate the benefit nondiscrimination rule. There is no dollar limit on the amount of compensation that can be taken into account for this purpose.[3]

### Who Can Be Excluded

In applying the percentage tests, the following may be excluded:

- employees who have not completed 3 years of service;

- part-time or seasonal employees; and

- employees not included in the plan who are part of a collective bargaining unit that has engaged in good faith bargaining on the issue of death benefits.

## Requirements of Section 79 Regulations

The regulations for Code section 79 require group-term insurance to have the following characteristics in order to obtain the $50,000 exclusion:[4]

1.  It must provide a *general death benefit*. Accident and health insurance, including double indemnity riders, or travel accident insurance are not considered part of the Section 79 plan. Also, life insurance as an incidental benefit in a qualified pension or profit sharing plan is not considered part of the Section 79 plan.

2.  It must be provided to a *group of employees* as compensation for services. The group can be all employees or a group defined in terms of employment-related factors—union membership, duties performed, etc.—or a group restricted solely on the basis of age or marital status. (Nondiscriminatory coverage requirements also apply, as discussed below.) The plan cannot cover company shareholders who are not employees, or a group consisting only of shareholder-employees.

3.  The insurance policy must be *carried directly or indirectly by the employer*. This requirement is met if the employer pays any part of the cost of the plan.

4.  Insurance amounts for employees must be determined under a *formula that precludes individual selection*. The formula must be based on factors such as age, years of service, compensation, or position in the company.

The plan can, however, provide a given level of coverage to persons in a position defined such that only a few (but at least more than one) highly compensated employees are in that category. (However, note the nondiscrimination rules discussed above.)

## Group Life Insurance Carve-out for Executives

### The Carve-out Concept

An executive covered under a company's group-term life insurance plan (Section 79 plan) may be able to obtain a better benefit if the executive is taken out of the group plan and given a separate individual policy provided by the employer. A group of selected executives can be similarly treated. Removing these executives does not affect the qualified status of the group-term plan for the remaining employees.[5]

### Advantages of Carve-Out Coverage Over Group-Term

1.  Executives can be provided with more insurance than would be available under a group-term plan. A group-term plan requires the same multiple of salary for all employees while the carve-out plan formula can be selective and discriminatory.

2.  The plan can provide cash growth which is a "portable" benefit for the executive. In a group-term plan, coverage after retirement can be provided only by an expensive policy conversion or purchasing new individual coverage.

3.  Cost to the employer can be favorable.

4.  Carving out the discriminatory benefits in a group-term plan can save an otherwise discriminatory plan.

### How To Structure the Carve-Out Coverage

All of the methods used to finance executive life insurance are generally available for carved-out benefits; that is —

*   bonus or "Section 162" plans

*   split dollar plans

*   death benefit only plans

For a comparison of carve-out with regular group-term coverage, see Figure 38.1 at the end of this chapter.

The IRS has taken a position that could create problems with the carve-out concept. In a Technical Advice Memorandum (TAM), the IRS concluded that the insurance for the carved-out group in question was itself a group-term plan subject to Section 79 rather than a split-dollar plan as the designers intended.[6] The Service concluded that the carve-out split-dollar plan had all four of the characteristics of Section 79 group-term insurance described under "Requirements of Section 79 Regulations" above. Accordingly, it was governed by Section 79 and taxation to employees was based on Table I (see below) rather than the P.S. 58 table or equivalent applicable to split-dollar plans (see Chapter 52).

It would appear that in order for carve-out programs to work as intended, the carve-out coverage will need to be actively designed to avoid Section 79 status. If the carve-out coverage involves a split-dollar plan, it may be possible to avoid Section 79 status if the plan provides more than a pure insurance benefit—that is, if the split dollar plan is an equity-type plan as described in Chapter 52. However, the full implications of the current IRS position on carve-outs as described in the TAM are not completely clear.

## TAX IMPLICATIONS

1. The cost of the first $50,000 of group-term insurance provided for each employee is tax-free to the employee. Key employees may lose this benefit if the plan does not meet the Section 79 nondiscrimination rules discussed above. The cost of any discriminatory coverage (including any coverage over $50,000) is included in the key employee's income at the greater of the Table I rates (see below) or the actual cost.[7]

2. For the cost of nondiscriminatory coverage above $50,000, the amount taxable to the employee is determined on a monthly basis.[8] The amount of coverage in excess of $50,000 is multiplied by the "Table I" rates (see below).[9] The annual taxable amount is the sum of the monthly amounts, less any premiums paid by the employee.

#### "TABLE I" RATES FOR GROUP TERM INSURANCE

| 5-year age bracket | Cost per $1,000 of insurance for 1-month period[9] |
|---|---|
| Under 25 | $ .05 |
| 25 to 29 | .06 |
| 30 to 34 | .08 |
| 35 to 39 | .09 |
| 40 to 44 | .10 |
| 45 to 49 | .15 |
| 50 to 54 | .23 |
| 55 to 59 | .43 |
| 60 to 64 | .66 |
| 65 to 69 | 1.27 |
| 70 and above | 2.06 |

NOTE
1. Age of the employee is attained age on the last day of the employee's taxable year.

For example, suppose an employee age 32 was covered under a group-term plan providing insurance of $100,000 for all twelve months of the year, and the employee paid $30 for this coverage for the year. The amount of coverage in excess of the $50,000 tax-free level is $50,000 ($100,000 - $50,000). Using Table I, 50 times $0.08 equals $4.00 of monthly cost, which multiplied by 12 (for 12 months) equals $48. The employee paid $30, and the difference between $48 and $30, $18, is taxable income for the year.

3. The death benefit from the insurance is tax-free to the beneficiary, just as if the insurance was personally-owned.

4. Premiums paid by the employer for group-term life insurance of employees are deductible business expenses.

5. The employer must pay employment taxes on the extra compensation that each employee includes in income as a result of plan coverage with insurance amounts over $50,000 or any coverage or benefits included by reason of the nondiscrimination rules.[11] Employment taxes include FICA (social security) and FUTA (federal unemployment tax). State unemployment and workers' compensation taxes may apply in some states—state laws vary and should be checked in each case.

## ERISA AND OTHER REQUIREMENTS

A group-term plan is a "welfare benefit plan" subject to the ERISA requirements discussed in Appendix A.

## ALTERNATIVES

1. Life insurance in a qualified plan

2. Split dollar life insurance

3. Death benefit only (employer death benefit)

4. Personally-owned insurance

## HOW TO INSTALL A PLAN

In addition to group insurance contracts, it is also advisable to adopt a written plan meeting the Section 79 requirements listed above.

## WHERE CAN I FIND OUT MORE ABOUT IT?

1. *Tax Facts 1*, Cincinnati, OH: The National Underwriter Co., (revised annually).

2. *Fundamentals of Employee Benefit Programs*, 5th ed. Washington, DC: Employee Benefit Research Institute, 1996.

3. Cady, Donald F., *Field Guide to Estate Planning, Business Planning, & Employee Benefits*, Cincinnati, OH: The National Underwriter Co., (revised annually).

## QUESTIONS AND ANSWERS

**Question** — Can group-term insurance be provided for self-employed persons or S corporation shareholders?

*Answer* — The exclusion from taxable income of the cost of the first $50,000 of group-term insurance under Code section 79 is not available to self-employed persons—partners or proprietors—or to shareholders of S corporations who own more than 2% of the corporation. (These more-than-2% shareholders are treated as partners for employee benefit purposes.)

However, self-employed persons and more-than-2% shareholders of S corporations can be included in the insured group for purposes of determining group coverage and premiums. The full cost of such insurance is taxable to the individual covered. (See Chapter 5.)

**Question** — How small a group can be covered under group-term insurance and are there any special rules for small groups?

*Answer* — Under the Section 79 regulations,[12] group insurance for fewer than 10 employees qualifies for the tax exclusion under Section 79 if

- it is provided for all full-time employees, and

- the amount of protection is computed either as a uniform percentage of compensation, or on the basis of coverage brackets established by the insurer under which no bracket exceeds 2½ times the next lower bracket and the lowest bracket is at least 10 percent of the highest bracket.

For example, a plan dividing employees into four classes with insurance amounts according to the following brackets would meet the test in the regulations:

| Class A: | $ 10,000 |
|---|---|
| Class B: | 25,000 |
| Class C: | 50,000 |
| Class D: | 100,000 |

Eligibility and amount of coverage may be based on evidence of insurability but this must be determined solely on the basis of a medical questionnaire completed by the employee and not by requiring a physical examination.

Meeting the under-10 employee regulations described in this answer is no guarantee that the plan will also be deemed nondiscriminatory. An under-10 employee plan must also meet the Section 79 nondiscrimination requirements.

**Question** — Can insurance providing a permanent benefit be used in a group-term life insurance plan?

*Answer* — Yes, under certain conditions. A policy is considered to provide a permanent benefit if it provides an economic value extending beyond one policy year. For example, a policy with a cash surrender value would be considered to provide a permanent benefit.

A policy with a permanent benefit may be treated as part of a group-term plan if

- the amount of death benefit considered part of the group-term plan is specified in writing, and

- the group-term portion of the death benefit each year complies with a formula in the regulations.

If permanent insurance is used in a group-term plan, the cost of the permanent benefit, less any amount contributed by the employee towards that permanent benefit, is included in the employee's taxable income for the year. The regulations contain a formula for computing the annual cost of permanent benefits.[13]

**Question** — Can "group universal life insurance programs" (sometimes referred to as "GULP") be used in a Section 79 group-term plan?

*Answer*—Group universal life programs are universal life insurance arrangements for a group of employees. These programs provide covered employees with (a) the advantages of universal life coverage—

variation in the timing and amount of premiums, and cash values with attractive rates of investment return—as well as (b) the advantages of group underwriting—convenience for employees, reduced costs, and coverage without evidence of insurability, within limits.

Group universal life contracts can be used as part of a plan of group-term insurance meeting the requirements of Section 79 and the regulations. However, application of this Code section to a GULP plan does not produce a good tax result due to the rules for taxing "permanent" insurance benefits contained in Section 79. Thus, most GULP plans are designed specifically to *avoid* the application of Section 79. This can be done by using an employee-pay-all arrangement and structuring coverage through a third party (such as a trustee) so that the policy is not deemed to be "carried directly or indirectly by the employer" as required under Section 79. Planning requires close adherence to technical requirements and must be done with the advice of an expert.

It is possible to provide Section 79 group-term insurance up to the tax-free level, and also provide the GULP benefit as a (non-Section 79) supplement to the Section 79 plan, if adequate coverage for group underwriting can be obtained.

**Question** — Do the Section 79 nondiscrimination rules require, in effect, that the plan must cover practically all employees of an employer and provide all of them with insurance equal to the same multiple of salary?

*Answer* — Do all employees of the company have to receive life coverage equal to the same percentage of compensation? Not necessarily. The company can set up two or more plans, having different benefit formulas, as long as *each* plan meets the coverage rules.

---

*Example:* Employer has 600 employees; 500 are nonunion hourly employees and 100 are salaried; of the 100 salaried, 10 are key employees. Plan 1 provides group insurance equal to 1 x compensation for all hourly employees. Plan 2 provides group insurance equal to 2 x compensation for all salaried employees. Both plans meet the coverage requirements (Plan 1: 100%

of participants are not key employees; Plan 2: 90% of participants are not key employees; both percentages are greater than 85%.)

---

**Question** — Should dependent coverage be included in a group-term plan?

*Answer* — A small amount of dependent coverage in a group-term plan is treated favorably for tax purposes. Dependent coverage is regarded as a "de minimis fringe" that is not included in income (see Chapter 36) if the face amount of employer-provided group-term life insurance payable on the death of a spouse or dependent of an employee does not exceed $2,000.[14] Additional dependent coverage can be provided by the employee on an after-tax basis, without affecting the nontaxability of the employer-paid $2,000 of insurance.

## FOOTNOTES

1. IRC Section 79(d)(3).
2. IRC Section 79(d)(2).
3. IRC Section 79(d)(5). Prior to its repeal by P. L. 101-140, Section 89 included a $200,000 limit on the amount of compensation that could be taken into account. P. L. 101-140 also includes a provision that even if Section 79 coverage is provided through a Section 501(c)(9) VEBA (see Chapter 54), the limit (in 2001, $170,000) applicable to VEBAs in general under Code section 505(b)(7) does not apply in determining whether the requirements of Section 79 are met. P. L. 101-140, Section 204(c).
4. Treas. Reg. §1.79-1.
5. In Letter Ruling 9701027, the IRS found that a plan could permit employees with coverage in excess of $50,000 to reduce the amount of their coverage without violating the "individual selection" rule of Section 79.
6. TAM 200002047. TAMs are applicable only to a specific taxpayer, but as indications of IRS positions they command considerable deference in planning.
7. IRC Section 79(d)(1).
8. Treas. Reg. §1.79-3.
9. Treas. Reg. §1.79-3(d)(2).
10. Treas. Reg. §§1.79-3(d)(2), 1.79-3(e). For purposes of determining whether a policy is "carried directly or indirectly" by the employer, the employer may use either the Table I rates effective July 1, 1999 or the prior rates until January 1, 2003.
11. IRC Section 3121(a)(2)(C); See Notice 88-82, 1988-2 CB 398 for current FICA reporting rules.
12. Treas. Reg. §1.79-1(c).
13. Treas. Reg. §§1.79-1(b), 1.79-1(d).
14. Notice 89-110, 1989-2 CB 447.

**Figure 38.1**

| | GROUP-TERM VS. CARVE-OUT | |
|---|---|---|
| | **Group-term** | **Carve-out** |
| Income tax to employee | 1. First $50,000 is income tax free. | 1. All coverage is taxable (except for DBO arrangement). |
| | 2. Coverage over $50,000 is taxed at Table I rates (cannot use insurer's lower term rate). | 2. Generally, coverage is taxed at lower of PS 58 (Table 2001 after 2001) rates or insurer's term rate. |
| Premium deductibility to corporation | Fully deductible | Varies; bonus-type plan is fully deductible, nondeductible if corporation is beneficiary |
| Cost to corporation | Rises if group ages; experience-rated (rises if group mortality or incidence of policy conversion at 65 increases). | Most plans involve level-premium insurance contracts with guaranteed premium. |
| Nondiscrimination coverage requirements | Section 79 coverage requirements apply; if not met, key employees lose the $50,000 exemption | None |
| Benefit nondiscrimination requirements | Section 79 requirements apply; generally benefits must be uniform percentage of compensation for all participants. | None; coverage can vary from executive to executive |
| Underwriting | Group, with guaranteed issue | Generally individual |
| Treatment at retirement | Coverage usually terminates or is reduced sharply because of increasing employer cost; also, higher Table I rates past age 64 increase cost to employee | Can be continued beyond retirement with no increased employer cost; employee cost is PS 58 (Table 2001 after 2001) or lower term cost |
| Use of cash value or permanent insurance | May result in unfavorable taxation to covered employee | Enhances planning flexibility |

# Chapter 39

# HEALTH INSURANCE

## WHAT IS IT?

Health insurance is the most widespread employee benefit, covering more than 75 million employees in the United States. It is widespread as an employee benefit not only because it meets a critical employee need, but also because it receives almost unique tax benefits: the entire cost is deductible to employers, but nothing is includable in employees' taxable income as a result of plan coverage or payment of plan benefits, if the plan meets the rules discussed below. Thus health insurance is a completely tax-free form of employee compensation.

There are two main types of health insurance plans:

- prepaid plans, in which health care providers are paid in advance of providing services; and

- postpaid plans, which pay health care providers for services rendered, or reimburse employees for payments to providers.

The principal form of prepaid plans is the Health Maintenance Organization, or HMO. HMOs are discussed separately in Chapter 40. This chapter will focus primarily on postpaid plans, which are the traditional form of health insurance.

## PLAN DESIGN

Health insurance plans provided by employers are usually complicated and may even be "customized" to some degree, particularly for larger employers. However, three fundamental types of plan design are usually identified—the "basic" plan, the "major medical" plan, and the "comprehensive" plan.

*Basic Plan.* A basic plan primarily provides health care services that are connected with hospitalization. The types of benefits provided in a basic plan are:

(1) Inpatient hospital charges, such as room and board, nursing care, supplies, and other hospital expenses.

(2) In-hospital visits by physicians. Home or office visits are not covered in a basic plan.

(3) Surgical fees, including surgeons' fees as well as anesthesiologists' and other surgical assistants' fees. These plans often cover fees for surgical procedures performed in a doctor's office or at an outpatient facility—not just those performed on patients admitted to a hospital.

*Major Medical Plan.* A major medical plan covers medical services excluded from basic plans. For this reason, it is sometimes referred to as a "supplemental major medical plan." Although the objective of the plan is to fill gaps in basic coverage, few plans cover all medical expenses. Routine doctors' office visits are usually excluded. Also, most plans do not cover dental, vision, and hearing care, although employers often provide these through separate plans.

*Comprehensive Plan.* The comprehensive type of plan combines the coverage of basic and major medical plans in a single plan. This is currently the dominant type of plan. Many employers have replaced basic and major medical plans with comprehensive plans.

## BENEFIT STRUCTURE

Many health plans do not pay the full cost of covered benefits. Major medical and comprehensive plans in particular, but also some basic plans, use "deductibles" and "coinsurance" to reduce plan costs by requiring employees to share benefit costs. The plan also usually has a per-individual maximum coverage limit on covered expenses.

*Deductibles.* A deductible is an amount of initial expense specified in the plan that is paid by the employee toward covered benefits. For example, if the plan has a $200 deductible, the participant pays the first $200 of covered expenses, and the plan covers the rest, up to a specified limit. Deductibles generally range from $100 to $500.

Deductibles are usually computed annually. For example, if the deductible is $500 and a covered individual incurs $400 of doctors' bills covered under the plan between January and November, the plan does not pay anything. However, if the same individual incurs an additional covered medical expense of $200 in December, the $500 deductible will have been satisfied and the plan will pay the $100 in excess of the deductible. Some plans have carryover provisions to avoid an unfair impact of the deductible. For example, with a three-month carryover provision, medical bills incurred during the last three months of the year can be used toward the next year's deductible. Thus, if an individual has a serious illness in December and incurs a $1,000 medical expense, subsequent bills in January and thereafter will not be subject to another deductible.

Most deductibles are *all-causes* deductibles—that is, the deductible is cumulative over the year or other period, even though the medical bills may reflect many different illnesses or medical conditions. However, some plans have *per-cause* deductibles. Under a per-cause deductible, the deductible amount must be satisfied for each separate illness or other medical condition.

Most employee plans use a *per-family* deductible as well as individual deductibles to minimize the payment burden for families. For example, the plan may have a $200 per individual deductible, but also a provision under which the plan pays for all covered expenses in full when total expenses for all family members exceed $500.

*Coinsurance.* Under a coinsurance provision, the plan participant is responsible for a specified percentage, usually 20%, of covered expenses. For example, if a plan has a $100 deductible, and a participant incurs expenses of $1,100 during the year, the plan pays $800 of these and the participant pays the rest (the $100 deductible plus 20% of the remaining $1,000 of expenses).

The participant's 20% share can become burdensome quickly in the event of a major illness, so good plan design requires an upper dollar limit on the participant's share. The participant's costs are usually limited to several thousand dollars on an annual basis.

*Maximum Coverage Limits.* To limit the plan's ultimate liability, there is usually an upper "lifetime limit" on the amount that the plan will pay for any one individual's medical expenses. This limit should be high enough so that only the rarest of medical events will cause it to be exceeded. Limits of $500,000 to $1 million are commonly used. If the limit is too low, the plan violates the basic principle of insurance, which is to share catastrophic losses that no one individual can bear. Also, extending

the upper limit substantially is usually not expensive because of the rarity of medical catastrophes. It is best to obtain coverage of $1 million, or unlimited coverage, whenever possible.

## PLAN FUNDING

Employers fund postpaid-type health plans in one or a combination of three ways:

(1) commercial insurance company contracts;

(2) Blue Cross/Blue Shield contracts; and

(3) "self-funding" or self insurance (without an insurance contract).

*Commercial Insurers.* A health insurance contract from a commercial insurance company usually provides reimbursement to employees for their expenses for covered medical procedures. Some insurers may pay health care providers directly, however. Reimbursement is usually limited to the "usual, customary, and reasonable" (UCR) charges for a given procedure in the employee's geographical area. Thus, an employee may not receive full reimbursement for a medical claim if the insurer's claims department considers the amount charged to be greater than the UCR amount.

Premiums for commercial health insurance contracts reflect six elements:

(1) expected benefit payments;

(2) administrative expenses;

(3) commissions;

(4) state premium taxes;

(5) risk charges; and

(6) return on the insurer's capital allocated to the contract (profit).

For groups of 50 employees or more, premiums are usually "experience rated." That is, the insurer keeps separate records for the employer group and adjusts charges to reflect above- or below-average benefit utilization by the group itself.

*Blue Cross/Blue Shield.* Blue Cross and Blue Shield plans were originally designed by organizations of hospitals and physicians in order to facilitate the payment of hospital and doctor bills. Blue Cross and Blue Shield plans generally provide direct payment in full to "participating" hospitals and doctors for medical benefits provided to covered employees. A participating hospital or doctor is one that agrees to pre-established rates and billing schedules with Blue Cross or Blue Shield. If an employee is admitted to a hospital or uses a doctor that is not participating, the Blue Cross or Blue Shield plan pays or reimburses on a UCR basis.

Blue Cross and Blue Shield plans can be obtained by individuals as well as by employers. A basic principle of the "Blues" is to offer coverage to any individual who requests it and to provide terminating employees under an employer plan with the ability to convert to an individual product.

Blue Cross (for hospital bills) and Blue Shield (for doctors' bills) are nonprofit organizations operating within a given geographical area. However, they must meet standards prescribed by their national associations. Federal tax law provides that these organizations are taxed on a basis similar to insurance companies.

*Self-Funding.* With self-funding (self insurance), the employer pays claims and other costs directly, either on a pay-as-you-go basis (that is, the employer pays claims out of current operating revenues as they are incurred by covered employees), or out of a reserve fund accumulated in advance. (However, as indicated below, the employer can accelerate its tax deductions for health and accident plans only to a limited extent, even if a fund is accumulated in advance.)

Self-funding can be combined with an insurance contract which provides "administrative services only" (an ASO contract). Also, the employer can obtain a "stop-loss" insurance contract, under which plan claims above a stated level are assumed by the insurer. This protects the employer against large unanticipated losses.

A self-funded plan should not be confused with a Health Reimbursement Arrangement (HRA). An HRA is a plan designed to supplement existing insured health plans and to provide special tax benefits. These plans are discussed in Chapter 47.

## Archer Medical Savings Accounts

Individuals employed by an employer having 50 or fewer employees and self-employed persons are eli-

gible for a pilot "medical savings account" program, originally effective for 1997 through 2002. The cut-off year for this pilot program has been extended from 2002 to 2003.[1] Similar to employer-sponsored IRAs, these plans (designated "Archer MSAs" in 2000) provide medical expense benefits. The employer's role is primarily to provide payroll deductions or direct contributions (subject to nondiscrimination requirements) and also possibly to provide a "high deductible" health insurance plan. A limit of 750,000 participants is provided under the law, on a first-come, first-served basis. IRS will announce when this cutoff is reached.[2]

In order to participate in an Archer MSA, the employee must be covered under a "high deductible" health insurance plan. For 2003, the deductible range for individual coverage is $1,700 to $2,500, with an out-of-pocket limitation of $3,350. For family coverage, these numbers for 2003 are $3,350, $5,050, and $6,150 respectively.[3]

An Archer MSA works like an IRA devoted to paying the employee's unreimbursed medical expenses and those of his spouse and dependents. Contributions by the employee are deductible from the employee's income for tax purposes and contributions by the employer to the Archer MSA are not includable in the employee's income. Contributions to an Archer MSA are subject to an annual limitation (an aggregate of monthly limitations), which is a percentage of the deductible of the required high deductible health plan. For an individual, it is 65% of that deductible and 75% for family coverage.

Unlike an IRA, however, distributions from the Archer MSA, when used to cover medical expenses that would be eligible for the Section 213 itemized medical expense deduction, are not taxable to the employee. Distributions from an Archer MSA used for other purposes are subject to income tax, plus an additional penalty tax of 15%, unless the distribution is made after age 65 or upon death or disability.

Generally, the effect of an Archer MSA is similar to that of a flexible spending account (FSA) devoted to medical expenses, except that there is no "risk of loss" provision in an Archer MSA. Archer MSA balances that are unused at the end of the year can be carried over and used for medical expenses in subsequent years.

If an employer contributes to an Archer MSA, there is a "comparability" rule designed to prevent discrimination in favor of highly compensated employees.

## ELIGIBILITY AND COVERAGE

Employer health insurance plans generally cover all employees. Employees are usually covered immediately upon being hired, or after a brief waiting period for coverage, such as three months. Some employers maintain separate plans for collective bargaining unit employees or other identifiable groups.

### Internal Revenue Code Eligibility and Coverage Requirements

The tax law provides certain requirements for group health plan coverage, subject to a penalty for noncompliance. Broadly, the requirements are:

- Exclusion of participants for preexisting conditions is limited to: (1) conditions for which medical advice or treatment was recommended or received within the six-month period ending on the enrollment date; and (2) the exclusion extends for no more than 12 months. Credit must be given against this period for previous coverage.[4]

- Participants may not be excluded (or required to pay an extra premium) on the basis of; (1) health status; (2) medical condition, physical and mental; (3) claims experience; (4) receipt of health care; (5) medical history; (6) genetic information; (7) evidence of insurability; or (8) disability.[5]

- The plan may not restrict benefits for any hospital length of stay in connection with childbirth for the mother or newborn child to less than 48 hours (96 hours for caesarean births).[6]

- Limits on benefits for mental illness must be no more restrictive than those for medical or surgical benefits. (This provision expires for services furnished after December 31, 2003.[7]

These provisions do not apply to governmental plans, or to plans that have fewer than two participants who are current employees. Other complex exclusions also apply.[8]

For noncompliance with these provisions, the penalty is generally $100 per day for each individual, up to a total of the lesser of: (1) 10% of the employer's payments under group health plans in the previous year; or (2) $500,000.[9] This is the same penalty amount that applies to COBRA violations (see below).

## COBRA Continuation of Coverage

Many employers have plans that continue health insurance coverage for employees and their dependents for a period of time after termination of employment. Some methods of funding continued coverage after retirement are discussed below.

Employer flexibility in this area is significantly limited since passage of the Consolidated Omnibus Budget Reconciliation Act of 1985 (COBRA).[10] The COBRA continuation coverage provisions apply for a given year if the employer had 20 or more employees on a typical business day in the preceding year. Final regulations provide that an employer is considered to have employed fewer than 20 employees during a calendar year if it had fewer than 20 employees on at least 50% of its typical business days during that year.[11] Only common law employees are taken into account for purposes of the small-employer exception. Self-employed individuals, independent contractors, and directors are not counted.[12] In the case of a multiemployer plan, a small-employer plan is a group health plan under which each of the employers contributing to the plan for a calendar year normally employed fewer than 20 employees during the preceding calendar year.[13] Government and church plans are exempt.

Under COBRA, the employer must offer continued health plan coverage for 18 months after termination of employment or reduction in hours of employment, other than for "gross misconduct."[14] If termination is due to disability, coverage must be continued for 29 months.

Also, under COBRA, the employer must generally provide the option to continue an employee's existing health plan coverage (including dependent coverage) for 36 months after the following "qualifying events":

(1) death of the employee;

(2) divorce or legal separation of the covered employee (coverage continues for the former spouse and dependents);

(3) the employee's entitlement to Medicare benefits;

(4) a bankruptcy proceeding under the United States Code, where the employee retired from the employer; and

(5) a child ceasing to be a dependent for plan purposes.

If an employee is on leave under the Family and Medical Leave Act of 1993 (FMLA) and does not return to work, the COBRA qualifying event generally is deemed to take place on the last day of the FMLA leave.[15]

Continuation coverage can be terminated before the 36, 29, or 18 month period if:

- the employer terminates its health plan for all employees;

- the employee or beneficiary fails to pay his or her share of the premium; or

- the employee or beneficiary becomes covered under any other plan providing medical care. However, if the new plan excludes a pre-existing condition, the employee must be allowed to continue coverage under the prior plan for the full COBRA period.

The employer can require the former employee or beneficiary to pay part of the cost of continuation coverage. However, this former employee or beneficiary's share cannot be more than 102% of the cost to the plan of coverage for similarly situated beneficiaries with respect to whom a qualifying event has not occurred (whether the cost is paid by the employer or employee). The premium for an employee disabled at the time of his termination or reduction in hours may be as much as 150% of the plan cost after the eighteenth month of continuation coverage.

Employees and beneficiaries must be notified of their right to continuing coverage when they become covered under the plan and when a qualifying event occurs. A sample notification form is reproduced in Figure 39.1. Similar information must be provided in the plan's Summary Plan Description (SPD).

The penalty for noncompliance with the benefit continuation requirements is, generally, a tax of $100 a day during the period that any failure with respect to a qualified beneficiary continues.

## Continuing Health Coverage For Retirees

Many employers want to continue company-paid health benefits for retirees, either for all employees or for a selected group. Rising costs as well as new developments in the tax and accounting treatment of such plans have required many of these plans to be redesigned.

The key issue is the method of funding or financing the plan. There is no one best way to design these plans, so the planner must weigh the advantages and disadvantages of each approach and fit it with the employer's unique situation. Currently, the alternatives are:

1. *Pay as you go.* With this alternative, there is no advance funding or financing; health insurance premiums are simply paid each year after the covered employee retires. This alternative is simple and offers the lowest initial cost. There are no nondiscrimination requirements if the plan is insured,[16] so the plan can be offered only to selected executives. However, costs of such plans can rise unpredictably and burden future cash flow of the company. Under FAS 106 (see Appendix E) a current accrual must nonetheless be made, so current earnings are reduced. Also, the employer's tax deduction for the payment is deferred to the year in which the premiums are actually paid.

2. *Earmarked corporate assets.* Under this approach, the plan is essentially a pay-as-you-go arrangement, but to provide a better indication of responsible financial management the corporation sets aside specified assets to offset the additional liability that the FASB rules would impose.

3. *Corporate-owned life insurance.* This is again a variation on the pay-as-you-go approach, but with a dedicated corporate asset reserve in the form of corporate-owned life insurance. The insurance is maintained on the life of each covered employee, with the corporation as owner and beneficiary. The tax-free cash buildup of the policy is used to pay the after-tax cost of health insurance premiums for retired employees. When the insured employee dies, the tax-free death benefit allows the company to recover part or all of its costs for the plan.

4. *Increase pension benefits.* Under this alternative, there is no formal health insurance continuation plan for retirees (except for the required COBRA coverage), but pension benefits are increased to provide employees with additional money to pay insurance premiums. This alternative allows a current deduction to the employer for the extra costs and tax-free accumulation of investment returns, but the pension nondiscrimination rules require that the increased benefits be provided to all employees covered under the pension plan. Also, the employee must pay taxes on the increased pension benefit, so the potentially tax-free nature of the health insurance benefit is lost. Also, there is no certainty or even

**Figure 39.1**

---

**ABC Corporation**
**Employees' Medical Benefit Plan**
**Continuation of Coverage**

### NOTICE OF RIGHT TO CONTINUE COVERAGE

Your coverage under the Employees' Medical Benefit Plan terminates as of [date of qualifying event]. If you [and your covered dependents] are not covered under any other group health care plan, you may continue [health care] coverage without interruption under the Plan for up to [18] [29] [36] months.

You have 60 days from [later of the date notice is received or date of qualifying event] to elect to continue coverage.

### COST OF CONTINUED COVERAGE

If you elect to continue coverage under the Plan, you must pay $ [amount equal to 102 percent or 150 percent (disability) of the total monthly cost of coverage for any similarly situated person covered by the Plan] on the first day of each month for which coverage is to be continued, in advance. Failure to pay this amount by the first of any month will result in loss of coverage.

### WHEN CONTINUED COVERAGE CEASES

The continued coverage will cease for any person when:

    (a) the cost of continued coverage is not paid on or before the date it is due; or
    (b) that person becomes eligible for Medicare; or
    (c) that person becomes covered under another health care plan; or
    (d) the Plan terminates for all employees.

### CONVERSION RIGHTS

Once continued coverage ceases for any person, that person may obtain a personal health care policy without evidence of insurability, as provided under the terms of the Plan. [Such a conversion right is not available for dental, vision care, or prescription drug coverages.]

### HOW TO ELECT CONTINUED COVERAGE

Complete the request for continued coverage below. Return it together with your check or money order payable to [ABC Corporation] for $ [one month's cost] to the address shown within 45 days after you elect continued coverage. You will be billed separately for any amount due for the period between [the date shown above] and the date your payment is made.

---

**Complete one form for each electing employee or beneficiary.**

I elect continuing coverage under the ABC Corporation Employees' Medical Benefit Plan.

---

Name                         Social Security No.               Date of Birth

---

Address

reasonable expectation that the increased benefits will, in fact, cover health insurance costs incurred many years after retirement.

5. *Incidental benefit in qualified plan.* Under this approach, continued health insurance coverage is provided as an incidental benefit under a qualified pension or profit sharing plan. The health insurance coverage is funded as part of the plan cost. Under Code section 401(h), the fund for health insurance must be kept in a separate account for each participant. Neither health insurance costs nor benefit payments are taxable income to the employee,[17] which means that the 401(h) alternative has the same tax benefit as direct health insurance coverage. See the Questions and Answers for some limitations applicable to "key employees." Incidental benefits in a qualified plan are limited to 25% of the aggregate contributions to the plan after establishment of the 401(h) account,[18] and many actuaries consider this limit inadequate for funding the full potential liability. Also see "Questions and Answers," below.

6. *VEBA or other trust fund.* Here assets are set aside to meet the future insurance liability in a separate trust fund. A VEBA is a tax-exempt arrangement that can be used for this purpose. (VEBAs are discussed in detail in Chapter 54.) The approach is similar to using a Section 401(h) account, but the limits on contributions are not subject to the 25% incidental benefit rule, but rather to the rules for prefunded welfare benefits under Sections 419 and 419A. Although a VEBA is generally tax exempt, the rules for "unrelated business taxable income" as applied to a VEBA in this situation would generally tax most of the VEBA's income.[19] VEBAs must meet nondiscrimination rules[20] similar to those for qualified plans, so the benefits cannot be provided just to a selected group of executives.

The chart in Figure 39.2 summarizes the advantages and disadvantages of these approaches to preretirement financing of retiree medical benefits.

## TAX IMPLICATIONS

1. The employer may deduct the cost of health insurance premiums in an insured plan or benefits paid in an uninsured plan as a general business expense. Plan administrative expenses are also deductible.

2. Deductions for prefunding medical benefits (that is, setting funds aside and deducting amounts for medical benefits to be paid in future years) are limited under rules set out in Code sections 419 and 419A. Generally, for a given year an employer can deduct expenditures for medical benefits up to a limit equal to the total of (a) the direct costs of the plan for the year—claims paid plus administrative costs, plus (b) contributions to an asset account up to 35% of the preceding year's direct costs.

3. The employee does not have taxable income (a) when the employer pays insurance premiums, (b) when benefits are paid, or (c) when the plan reimburses the employee for covered expenses (unless the employee is considered highly compensated and the plan is a discriminatory noninsured medical expense reimbursement plan).[21]

4. The employee is eligible for an itemized medical expense deduction under Code section 213 for (a) any portion of health insurance premiums paid by the employee, (b) unreimbursed out-of-pocket costs resulting from deductibles or coinsurance, and (c) any other medical expenses eligible for a Section 213 deduction. The Section 213 deduction is available only if the taxpayer itemizes deductions on the tax return. The deduction is limited to the amount by which the total of all eligible medical expenses exceeds 7.5% of the taxpayer's adjusted gross income.

## ERISA AND OTHER REQUIREMENTS

An employer's health and accident plan is a "welfare benefit plan" subject to the ERISA requirements discussed in Appendix A.[22]

## WHERE CAN I FIND OUT MORE ABOUT IT?

1. Beam, Burton T., Jr. and John J. McFadden, *Employee Benefits*, 6th ed. Chicago, IL: Dearborn Financial Publishing, Inc., 2000.

2. *Tax Facts 1*, Cincinnati, OH: *The National Underwriter Co.*, (revised annually).

3. Cady, Donald F., *Field Guide to Estate Planning, Business Planning, & Employee Benefits*, Cincinnati, OH: *The National Underwriter Co.*, (revised annually).

**Figure 39.2**

## FINANCING OF RETIREE MEDICAL BENEFITS

| | Advantages | Disadvantages |
|---|---|---|
| Pay-As-You-Go | • low initial cash flow<br>• simplicity<br>• no nondiscrimination requirements | • FASB standards require liability<br>• increasing cash flow requirements<br>• burdens future management/shareholders |
| Earmarked Corporate Assets | • demonstrates responsible financial management<br>• money managers can manage portfolio like pension fund<br>• no nondiscrimination requirements | • no tax deduction until benefits are paid<br>• investment income taxable<br>• rate of return could be inadequate |
| Corporate-Owned Life Insurance | • offset to balance sheet liability<br>• tax-free investment accumulation<br>• policy loan interest deductible (up to $50,000 loan on each key person)<br>• death benefits tax-free<br>• potentially high rate of return<br>• no nondiscrimination requirements | • high initial cash requirements<br>• no tax deduction until benefits are paid |
| Increased Pension Benefits | • no FASB balance sheet liability except for increased pension<br>• tax-free accumulation<br>• deductibility of contributions | • nondiscrimination requirements<br>• benefits taxable to employees<br>• Sec. 415 limits for higher paid |
| Incidental Qualified Plan Benefit (401(h)) | • deductibility of contributions<br>• tax-free accumulation | • nondiscrimination requirements<br>• contributions cannot exceed 25% of pension plan contributions<br>• reduces maximum pension<br>• tax deductions do not reflect future medical cost inflation |
| VEBA | • deductibility of contributions | • tax deductions do not reflect future medical cost inflation under Sections 419, 419A<br>• nondiscrimination requirements<br>• earnings in excess of current claims subject to UBIT (Unrelated Business Income Tax) |

## QUESTIONS AND ANSWERS

**Question** — How do employer health and accident benefits fit into a cafeteria plan?

*Answer* — Since employees have varying needs for health benefits (some may prefer lower deductibles, others may want broader coverage such as dental expense coverage, etc.), the plan can be made attractive to employees by offering a number of optional plans under a "cafeteria" arrangement.

The salary reduction type of cafeteria plan offers another attractive possibility in the health care area. Such A plan makes possible the conversion of after-tax employee expenditures in a health plan to nontaxable expenditures. Such expenditures include the employee share of health insurance, deductibles, coinsurance payments, and medical expenses not covered by the plan. These expenditures are technically deductible as itemized medical deductions under Code section 213, but because of the 7.5% of adjusted gross income floor, few employees will be able to deduct them. This approach in effect allows these items to be excluded from taxable income without any floor limit. FSA plans are discussed in detail in Chapter 35. Cafeteria plans are discussed further in Chapter 29.

**Question** — Can a self-employed person (sole proprietor or partner in an unincorporated business) or S corporation shareholder-employee be covered under his business's health insurance plan and obtain any tax advantage?

*Answer* — A self-employed person or S corporation shareholder-employee can be covered under a business's health insurance plan. This may provide a more economical means of obtaining health benefits than individual insurance, because of the group underwriting of an insured employer plan.

The cost of health insurance for a self-employed individual or a more than 2% shareholder-employee in an S corporation would ordinarily not be a deductible expense to the business because the self-employed individual is not considered an employee (and a more than 2% S corporation shareholder-employee is treated as a partner for fringe benefit purposes). However, a special provision, Code section 162(l), permits a special deduction in order to equalize the treatment of incorporated and unincorporated businesses in this regard. Under Section 162(l), a self-employed individual is entitled to a

business expense deduction equal to the amount paid for health insurance. The deduction cannot exceed the self-employed individual's earned income for the year from the trade or business with respect to which the plan is established. The deduction cannot be used to reduce self-employment income subject to self-employment tax. Rules are provided to prevent duplication of deductions for other medical insurance covering the taxpayer or itemized medical expense deductions.

**Question** — Do the COBRA requirements for continuing health benefits apply if the employer's plan is not health insurance?

*Answer* — The COBRA continuation requirements apply to any kind of group health care coverage, including HMOs and self-funded or noninsured plans. However, the covered employee has the right only to continue the kind of coverage that existed during employment. For example, the employer must offer continuing HMO coverage to an employee covered under an HMO, but the employer need not offer alternative health insurance, although the employer can do so if it wishes. Note, however, that an employee on COBRA continuation coverage be given the same right to switch coverage during an "open enrollment" period that is available to an active employee.

**Question** — Does COBRA's continuing coverage requirement preempt state law in states that require more generous continuing coverage in certain situations?

*Answer* — No; unlike ERISA, COBRA does not contain a preemption of state law. Therefore, planners must continue to be aware of state continuation requirements applicable to their clients.

**Question** — Is the 401(h) "incidental benefit" account an advantageous method of funding postretirement benefits for key employees?

*Answer* — Coverage of key employees in a Section 401(h) arrangement adds some extra complexities that have led some planners to recommend against covering key employees in 401(h)-type plans. First, there must be separate, individual 401(h) accounts for each key employee.[23] The total amount allocated to a key employee for pension plus incidental medical or other benefits is subject to the $40,000 (as indexed for 2003) annual additions dollar limitation under section 415 of the Code, which may limit the ability to prefund medical benefits for key employees in some cases.[24]

The definition of "key employee" in these rules is that used for purposes of the top-heavy rules, Code section 416(i). (See Chapter 25.)

**Question** — Can an employer use the excess assets in an "overfunded" pension plan to fund retiree medical benefits?

*Answer* — An employer with an overfunded pension plan can amend the plan to add postretirement health insurance as an additional incidental benefit. The amount allocated to all incidental benefits cannot exceed 25% of the aggregate plan contributions after establishment of the 401(h) account.[25] If a plan is at the "full funding limit," it is not allowed to make any further actual contributions for pension purposes, so (since 25% of zero is zero) no additional deductible contributions for medical benefits can be made.

Section 420, a temporary Code provision extended through the year 2005, allows an employer to make a transfer of excess pension assets to a Section 401(h) account without the employer having to pay either regular income tax or the pension reversion excise tax on the amount transferred. This provision, however, includes complex restrictions and regulatory requirements. Also, transferred assets may not be used for postretirement health benefits for key employees as defined in Code section 416(i).

It also appears unfeasible to withdraw excess funding from a qualified plan and transfer it to a VEBA to fund retiree benefits. The IRS apparently views this withdrawal as a "pension reversion" to the employer, which is fully income taxable to the employer and is also subject to the 20% pension reversion penalty tax under Code section 4980.

**Question** — How is health plan coverage for retirees reflected by the employer for accounting purposes?

*Answer* — The accounting profession's Financial Accounting Standards Board (FASB) has adopted a standard for accounting treatment of postretirement benefits other than pensions (FAS 106). This standard requires employers to reflect the promise of future benefits on an accrual basis—that is, as benefits are earned, rather than when they are ulti-

mately paid out. Accounting requirements for benefit plans are discussed further in Appendix E.

**Question** — May an employer drop retiree health insurance coverage after an employee has retired?

*Answer* — This is a complex issue involving both federal law (ERISA) and the interpretation of the retiree's employment contract which often results in litigation.

As a practical matter, the best way for an employer to maintain flexibility is to have a clear "reservation of rights" clause in its collective bargaining agreements, its plan documents, and other employment agreements, as well as its ERISA-required Summary Plan Descriptions (SPDs). This clause should clearly state that the employer reserves the right to change or withdraw the benefit at any time, both before and after the retirement of any covered employee. The procedure by which this change would be made should be specified and the company should strictly follow this procedure.[26] Although this may not prevent lawsuits by aggrieved employees, it will put the employer in the best possible position if these benefits must be revoked at some time in the future.

## FOOTNOTES

1. IRC Sections. 220(i)(2), 220(i)(3)(B), as amended by JCWAA 2002.
2. Archer Medical Savings Accounts are governed generally by Code sections 220 and 4980E.
3. IRC Section 220(c); Rev. Proc. 2001-59, 2001-52 IRB 623. The deductible and out-of-pocket expense amounts are adjusted for the cost of living. IRC Section 220(g).
4. IRC Section 9801.
5. IRC Section 9802.
6. IRC Section 9811.
7. IRC Section 9812.
8. IRC Section 9831.
9. IRC Section 4980D.
10. The COBRA rules are found IRC Section 4980B.
11. Treas. Reg. §54.4980B-2, A-5.
12. Treas. Reg. §54.4980B-2, A-5.
13. Treas. Reg. §54.4980B-2, A-5.
14. The definition of "gross misconduct" is not provided under COBRA, but has been developed through case law, often based on state law definitions.
15. Notice 94-103, 1994-2 CB 569.
16. IRC Section 105(h).

17. Treas. Reg. §1.72-15(h). See Let. Rul. 8747069.

18. IRC Section 401(h), last paragraph.

19. IRC Sections 512(a)(3)(E)(iii), 419A(c)(2).

20. IRC Section 505.

21. IRC Sections 105, 106.

22. Labor Reg. §2510.3-1.

23. IRC Sections 401(h)(6), 415(l); Treas. Reg. §1.401-14(c)(2).

24. IRC Sections 415(l)(1), 415(c)(1)(B), 415(c)(2), as amended by EGTRRA 2001.

25. IRC Section 401(h), last paragraph; Treas. Reg. §1.401-14(c)(1)(i).

26. *Curtis-Wright Corporation v. Schoonejongen*, 514 U.S. 73 (1995).

# Chapter 40

# HEALTH MAINTENANCE ORGANIZATION (HMO)

## WHAT IS IT?

A Health Maintenance Organization, or HMO, is an organization of physicians or other health care providers that provides a broad and nearly complete range of health care services on a prepaid basis. An HMO is an alternative to traditional health insurance.

## WHEN IS IT INDICATED?

1.  As an alternative to traditional health insurance, HMOs are attractive to younger employees and employees with many dependents, because the HMO typically covers all medical expenses without significant deductibles or co-pay provisions. Where such employees are predominant in an employer's work force, the employer may get the most perceived value for its benefit dollar by offering an HMO, or choice of HMOs, as its health benefit plan.

## ADVANTAGES

1.  HMOs typically cover more health care services than traditional health insurance, with fewer deductibles and lower co-payments.

2.  HMOs are said to emphasize preventive medicine, and thus control overall costs better than plans which pay only when employees are hospitalized or sick.

## DISADVANTAGES

1.  An HMO subscriber generally must receive care from a doctor or other service provider who is part of the HMO. Except for certain emergencies, the HMO will not pay for services of non-HMO providers.

2.  The cost advantage, if any, of HMOs may be due to the fact that they enroll younger and healthier participants than traditional health insurance plans, which emphasize coverage for major medical pro-

cedures. In time, therefore, it is argued that the cost advantage of HMOs will diminish.

## HMO BENEFIT STRUCTURE

Conventional health insurance reimburses employees for expenses or pays providers for health care as required by covered employees. By contrast, an HMO either employs the providers or contracts directly with providers (see the discussion below on types of HMOs). The providers agree to provide medical services to HMO subscribers when required, in return for an annual payment determined *in advance*. Each subscriber to the HMO (or employer who sponsors the plan) pays a fee based on the HMO's projected annual cost.

As a result of this arrangement, the HMO assumes the risk that services required will cost more than the annual payment. In other words, the HMO has an incentive to hold down the costs of health care to subscribers. In theory, these reduced costs will be passed along in the form of reduced costs to the HMO subscribers or to employers who pay for the plan.

HMO subscribers generally must use physicians and other health care providers who are part of the HMO contractual arrangement. Exceptions are usually allowed for emergency services out of the HMO's geographic area, and for medical specialties not available within the HMO, if referred by the primary HMO physician. In return for this reduction in freedom of choice, HMO plans provide for almost all health care services, including routine physician visits. Usually there are no deductibles. There may be a small co-payment fee for some services. For example, subscribers may be required to pay $10 for each visit to a doctor's office and $5 for each prescription.

A comparison of one employer's insured health plan with two alternative HMOs is included in Figure 40.1 at the end of this chapter to give some idea of the benefits provided under typical HMO plans and how they differ from insured plans.

## TYPES OF HMOs

HMOs are organized in one of three ways:

(1) the *staff model* HMO is an HMO organization which directly employs doctors and other health care providers who provide the HMO's services to subscribers.

(2) the *group practice* or medical group model involves contracts between the HMO and a medical group or groups that provide services to subscribers. The individual doctors and other providers are not directly employed by the HMO as an entity.

Both staff model and group practice HMOs are sometimes referred to as *closed panel* plans, because subscribers must use doctors and other providers who are employed by the HMO or under contract to the HMO.

(3) the *individual practice association* or IPA plan, under which the HMO is an association of individual doctors or medical groups that practice in their own offices. Most see non-HMO as well as HMO patients. These plans are often referred to as *open panel* plans, since HMO subscribers can choose any doctor who is part of the IPA. In some areas, many doctors participate in these plans, giving HMO subscribers a wide range of choice.

The structure of an HMO is relevant to an employer's benefit planning in that different types of HMOs may have varying attractiveness to employees. Many employees may be reluctant to give up their own doctors in order to sign up with an unfamiliar closed-panel type of HMO. On the other hand, the choice of doctors in a large IPA plan may be appealing. The IPA may even include some employees' own doctors already. So, an HMO affiliation may effectively change nothing from some employees' viewpoints except to drastically lower the cost of their doctor bills.

The appeal of HMOs in a given geographical area depends in large part on the local medical community's support of the HMO concept. If local doctors and hospitals, particularly the most prestigious ones, are in favor of HMOs, then many local health care providers will join HMOs. HMO subscribers will then have almost the same amount of choice as they would in a conventional insured plan.

## TAX IMPLICATIONS

The tax treatment of payments to HMOs and benefits received is the same as that for health insurance, described in Chapter 39. Eligibility and coverage requirements, including the COBRA provisions, are also the same as for health insurance.

## WHERE CAN I FIND OUT MORE ABOUT IT?

1. Beam, Burton T., Jr. and John J. McFadden, *Employee Benefits*, 6th ed. Chicago, IL: Dearborn Financial Publishing, Inc., 2000.

**Figure 40.1**

| | | | |
|---|---|---|---|
| **EMPLOYER, INC.**<br>**COMPARISON OF HEALTH CARE BENEFITS** | | | |
| | **Insured Plan** | **Health Maintenance Organization A** | **Health Maintenance Organization B** |
| **TYPE OF PLAN** | Health insurance plan covering full or partial cost of medical services after they are provided. | Prepaid Individual Practice Association — contracts with private physicians' offices located in the community. | Prepaid Group Practice Plan — a team of physicians and medical professionals practice together to provide members preventive, comprehensive care for a fixed, advanced payment. |
| **CHOICE OF PHYSICIAN** | Member may select any licensed physician or surgeon. | Member selects a physician from one of the 230 primary medical offices. All types of specialists are available by referral. | Member selects a personal physician from the medical group who coordinates and directs all health care needs including referrals to specialists. |
| **WHERE PRIMARY AND SPECIALTY CARE IS AVAILABLE** | Care provided in physician's office or outpatient facility. | Care provided in participating private physician's offices. | Care provided at five multi-specialty centers. |
| **CHOICE OF HOSPITALS** | Member may select any accredited hospital. Choice depends on where physician has admitting privileges. | Member goes to hospital where physician has admitting privileges. | Selection among participating hospitals (see brochure for locations). |
| **DEDUCTIBLE AND COINSURANCE** | Annual deductible; $200 individual, $500 family. 10% or 50% coinsurance on covered charges after satisfying deductible. Selected procedures/care covered in full, no deductible. No coinsurance on covered services after $4,000 individual/$10,000 family annual expense incurred. | No deductible. No coinsurance (except small co-payments for office visits, home visits, prescriptions and outpatient mental health and other deductibles as noted in the comparison). | No deductible. No coinsurance except small co-payments for outpatient mental health. |
| **MAXIMUM BENEFIT** | No lifetime maximum. | No overall maximum limit. | No overall maximum limit. |

**Figure 40.1 (continued)**

| | Insured Plan | Health Maintenance Organization A | Health Maintenance Organization B |
|---|---|---|---|
| **EMPLOYER, INC.** COMPARISON OF HEALTH CARE BENEFITS | | | |
| **PREVENTIVE CARE** | | | |
| Routine Physicians | Not covered. | Covered in full. | Covered in full. |
| Well Baby Care | Covered at 90%. | Covered in full. | Covered in full. |
| Pap Smears | Routine exams not covered. | Covered in full. | Covered in full; care provided by Gynecologist. |
| Immunizations | Not covered. | Covered in full. | Covered in full. |
| Eye Exam | Not covered. | Covered in full and $35 allowance for eyeglasses or contact lenses | Covered in full including written prescriptions for lenses. |
| Hearing Exam | Not covered. | Covered in full. | Covered in full. |
| Health Education | Available through some physicians' offices. | Weight watchers programs, YMCA physical fitness program, other programs offered periodically. | Periodic classes held on diet, prenatal care and physical fitness, smoking cessation, stress management, etc. Discount programs at many Nautilus clubs and health spas. |
| **PHYSICIAN CARE** | | | |
| Surgery | Outpatient—covered at 100% no deductible. (Charges for hospital, surgicenter or miscellaneous physician's expense connected to outpatient surgery covered at 90% after deductible.) Inpatient-covered at 90% after deductible. Specified elective procedures require second opinion to ensure unreduced benefits. | Covered in full. | Covered in full. |
| Inpatient Visits | Covered at 90% after satisfying deductible. | Covered in full. | Covered in full. |
| Office and Home | Covered at 90% after satisfying deductible. | Office visits covered with $2 co-pay at primary office. Physician home visits covered with $5 co-pay. No co-pay for specialist visits. | Office visits covered in full. Home visits covered in full. |
| X-rays and Lab | Pre-Admission status— covered at 100% with no deductible. Other instances covered at 90% after satisfying deductible when deemed medically necessary. | Covered in full. | Covered in full. |

**Figure 40.1 (continued)**

| | Insured Plan | Health Maintenance Organization A | Health Maintenance Organization B |
|---|---|---|---|
| **EMPLOYER, INC.**<br>**COMPARISON OF HEALTH CARE BENEFITS** | | | |
| **HOSPITAL SERVICES**<br>Room and Board | Covered at 90% for unlimited days after satisfying deductible. | Covered in full for unlimited days in semiprivate room. (Private room covered in full when medically necessary.) | Covered in full for unlimited days in semiprivate room. (Private room covered in full when medically necessary.) |
| Supplies, Tests, Medication, etc. | Covered at 90% after satisfying deductible. In hospital charges in connection with a scheduled surgical procedure incurred more than 24 hours prior are not covered. | Covered in full. | Covered in full. |
| Private Duty Nurse | Covered at 90% after satisfying deductible up to a maximum of $1,000 a year. | Covered in full when medically necessary. | Covered in full when medically necessary. |
| **EMERGENCY CARE** | Covered at 100% with no deductible if rendered in physician's office or an emergency care center within 48 hours of accidental injury. Hospital emergency room service covered at 90% after the deductible. | Covered with $15 co-pay at hospital and $5 co-pay at doctor's office. | Covered in full for around-the-clock emergency care by HMO-B physicians and in participating hospitals. Emergency care by non-HMO-B physicians or hospitals also covered when obtaining HMO-B care is not reasonable because of distance and urgency. |
| Ambulance Service | Covered at 90% for local transportation after satisfying deductible when medically necessary. | Covered in full when medically necessary. | Covered in full. |
| **MATERNITY CARE**<br>Hospital | Co-pays and deductibles apply. See Hospital Services. | Covered in full. | Covered in full. |
| Physician | Co-pay and deductibles apply. See Physician Care. | Covered in full. | Covered in full. |
| Waiting Period | No waiting period — limitation of pre-existing conditions apply. | No waiting period. | No waiting period. |

**Figure 40.1 (continued)**

| | Insured Plan | Health Maintenance Organization A | Health Maintenance Organization B |
|---|---|---|---|
| **EMPLOYER, INC.** COMPARISON OF HEALTH CARE BENEFITS | | | |
| **MENTAL HEALTH CARE** | | | |
| Hospital | Co-pays and deductibles apply. See Hospital Services | Covered in full for 35 days per year. | Covered in full for 45 days per 12 months. |
| Inpatient Physician | Co-pays and deductibles apply. See Physician Care. | Covered in full 35 days per year. | Covered in full for 45 days per 12 months. |
| Outpatient Physician | Covered at 50% up to $40 per visit and $1,000 per year. | Covered for 20 visits per year. First two visits covered in full. Next eight visits you pay $10 per visit. Next 10 visits, employee pays $25 per visit. Member charge never exceeds 50% of fee. | Covered for 30 visits per 12 months. First three visits covered in full. Next 27 visits employee pays $10 per visit. |
| Alcohol and Drug Addiction | Covered as other mental health services. | Covered in full for acute phase of alcohol or drug abuse. | No special limits. Covered as other medical and mental health services. Detoxification covered for acute phase only. |
| **DENTAL CARE** | | | |
| Hospital | Separate Dental option offered to all employees — Contact Personnel for details. | Covered for: hospital costs when confinement is necessary for dental care due to covered medical problem; treatment of accidental injury to natural teeth occurring while insured; impacted wisdom teeth, partially, or totally covered by bone. | Covered for: hospital costs when confinement is necessary for dental care; and treatment of accidental injury to natural teeth occurring while insured; and certain oral surgical procedures, e.g., impacted wisdom teeth partially or totally covered by bone. |
| Office visits | Separate Dental option offered to all employees. | Oral hygiene exams for children under 12, including cleaning and scaling of teeth, instruction and fluoride treatment. | Covered for: two checkups and one cleaning per year, 20% discount on other dental services including speciality areas and orthodontia at participating dental offices. |
| **OUTPATIENT MEDICATION** | | | |
| Prescription Drug | Covered at 90% after deductible. | Covered w/$2.50 co-pay. | Covered w/$2 co-pay. |
| Injections | Covered at 90% after deductible. | Covered in full. | Covered in full. |

**Figure 40.1 (continued)**

| | Insured Plan | Health Maintenance Organization A | Health Maintenance Organization B |
|---|---|---|---|
| **PRESCRIBED HOME HEALTH SERVICES** | Home Health Extension Services paid at 100% with no deductible if recommended by discharging hospital. | Covered in full except for travel. | Covered in full. |
| **ALLERGY CARE** | Covered at 90% after deductible. | Covered in full. | Covered in full. |
| **ELIGIBILITY** | Spouse; and unmarried dependent children to age 19 or age 23 if a full time student. | Spouse; and unmarried dependent children to age 19 or age 23 if a full time student. | Spouse; and unmarried dependent children to age 19 or age 23 if a full time student. |
| **MEDICARE** | Regular plan coverage continued, may be coordinated with Medicare. | Medicare plan available. | Medicare coordinated benefit available. |
| **CONVERSION** | Conversion to individual coverage available. | Conversion to Non-Group coverage available. RX is not available for conversion. | Conversion to Non-Group coverage available. |

Table heading: **EMPLOYER, INC. COMPARISON OF HEALTH CARE BENEFITS**

# Chapter 41

# INCENTIVE STOCK OPTION (ISO)

## WHAT IS IT?

An incentive stock option (ISO) plan is a tax-favored plan for compensating executives by granting options to buy company stock. Unlike regular stock options, ISOs generally do not result in taxable income to executives either at the time of the grant or the time of the exercise of the option. If the ISO meets the requirements of Internal Revenue Code section 422, the executive is taxed only when stock purchased under the ISO is sold. (Regular or "nonstatutory" stock options are discussed in Chapter 53. Also, see Appendix D for a comprehensive outline of stock option and similar plans used for compensating executives, particularly in large corporations.)

## WHEN IS IT INDICATED?

ISOs are primarily used by larger corporations to compensate executives. ISOs are generally not suitable for closely held corporations because (a) ISOs are valuable to executives only when stock can be sold, and there is usually no ready market for closely held stock, and (b) shareholders of closely held corporations often do not want unrelated outsiders to become shareholders of the company.

## ADVANTAGES

1. The ISO provides greater deferral of taxes to the executive than a nonstatutory stock option (see Chapter 53).

2. Income from the sale of the stock obtained through exercise of an ISO may be eligible for preferential capital gain treatment, enhancing the value of the tax deferral.

3. The ISO is a form of compensation with little or no out-of-pocket cost to the company. The real cost of stock options is that the company forgoes the opportunity to sell the same stock on the market and realize its proceeds for company purposes.

## DISADVANTAGES

1. The corporation granting an ISO does not ordinarily receive a tax deduction for it at any time.

2. The plan must meet complex technical requirements of Code section 422 and related provisions.

3. The exercise price of an ISO must be at least equal to the fair market value of the stock when the option is granted. There is no similar restriction on nonstatutory options.

4. As with all stock option plans, the executive gets no benefit unless he is able to come up with enough cash to exercise the option.

5. An executive may incur an alternative minimum tax (AMT) liability when an ISO option is exercised, thus increasing the executive's cash requirements in the year of exercise.

## TAX IMPLICATIONS

1. The executive is not subject to federal income tax on an ISO either at the time the option is granted or at the time he exercises the option (i.e., when he buys the stock). Tax consequences are deferred until the time of disposition of the stock.[1]

2. In order to obtain this tax treatment for incentive stock options, Section 422 prescribes the following rules:

   • the options must be granted under a written plan specifying the number of shares to be issued and the class of employees covered under the plan. There are no nondiscrimination rules; the plan can cover key executives only.

   • only the first $100,000 worth of ISO stock granted any one employee, which becomes exercisable for the first time during any one year, is entitled to the favorable ISO treatment; to the extent that the value of the stock exceeds $100,000, this amount is treated as a non-statutory (regular) stock option.

- no option, by its terms, may be exercisable more than ten years from the date of the grant.

- the person receiving the option must be employed by the company granting the option at all times between the grant of the option and three months before the date of exercise (twelve months in the case of permanent and total disability, and no limit in the event of death).

- stock acquired by an employee under the ISO must be held for at least two years after the grant of the option and one year from the date stock is transferred to the employee. (This requirement is waived upon the employee's death.)

- no options may be issued more than ten years from the date the ISO plan is adopted or approved, whichever occurs first.

- the option must not be transferable (except by will or descent and distribution) and must be exercisable only by the person receiving it.

- corporate stockholders must approve the ISO plan within twelve months of the time it is adopted by the company's board of directors.

- the exercise price of the option must be at least equal to the fair market value of the stock on the date the option is granted.

- ISOs may not be granted to any employee who owns, directly or indirectly, more than 10% of the corporation unless the term of the option is limited to not more than five years and the exercise price is at least 110% of the fair market value of the stock on the date of the grant.[2]

3. Although there is no regular income tax to the executive when an ISO is exercised, the alternative minimum tax (AMT) may have an impact. The excess of the stock's fair market value over the option price at the time of exercise is included in the individual's alternative minimum taxable income. (However, if the individual is subject to the alternative minimum tax, his basis in the stock for alternative minimum tax purposes will be increased by the amount included in income.)[3]

4. If the executive holds the stock for the periods specified above, (two years after grant and one year after exercise) the gain on any sale is taxed at preferential long-term capital gain rates.

5. If the stock is sold before the two year/one year holding periods specified above, the excess of the fair market value of the shares at the time of exercise over the exercise price is treated as compensation income to the executive in the year the stock is sold, depriving the executive of preferential capital gain treatment.[4]

---

*Example:* Executive Flo Through is covered under her company's ISO plan. Under the plan, Flo is granted an option in 2003 to purchase company stock for $100 per share. In January, 2005, Flo exercises this option and purchases 100 shares for a total of $10,000. The fair market value of the 100 shares in January, 2005, is $14,000. In October, 2005, Flo sells the 100 shares for $16,000. Flo's taxable gain is $6,000 ($16,000 amount realized less $10,000 cost). Of this amount, $4,000 (fair market value of $14,000 less $10,000 exercise price) is treated as compensation income for the year 2005. The remaining $2,000 is capital gain.

---

6. The corporation does not get a tax deduction for granting an ISO. Nor does it get a deduction when an executive exercises an option or sells stock acquired under an ISO plan.[5] However, the corporation *does* get a deduction for the compensation income element that an executive must recognize if stock is sold before the two year/one year holding period, as described in paragraph five above.

## WHERE CAN I FIND OUT MORE ABOUT IT?

1. Graduate Course: Executive Compensation (GS 842), The American College, Bryn Mawr, PA.

2. *Tax Facts On Investments (Tax Facts 2)*, The National Underwriter Co., Cincinnati, Ohio; revised annually.

## FOOTNOTES

1. IRC Section 421(a).

2. IRC Section 422(b)(6) provides that an incentive stock option can be granted to an individual only if such individual, at the time the option is granted, does not own stock possessing more than 10% of the total combined voting power of all classes of stock of the employer corporation or of its parent or subsidiary corporation.

3. IRC Section 56(b)(3).

4. IRC Section 421(b).

5. IRC Section 421(a)(2), 421(b).

# Chapter 42

# KEY EMPLOYEE LIFE INSURANCE

## WHAT IS IT?

Key employee life insurance, sometimes included within the broader description of corporate-owned life insurance or COLI, is insurance on a key employee's life owned by the employer, with the death benefit payable to the employer. Technically, key employee insurance is designed to compensate the employer for the loss of a key employee and is not an employee benefit for the key employee. However, in closely held corporations, key employee insurance can be used to indirectly benefit shareholder-employees by providing a source of liquid assets in the corporation. Key employee policies make assets available from policy cash values during the employee's lifetime and from the policy proceeds on the death of the employee. These assets can be used to finance the employer's obligation under one or more employee benefit plans.

## WHEN IS IT INDICATED?

1. When a corporation will incur an obligation to pay a specified beneficiary or class of beneficiaries at an employee's death under a death benefit only (DBO) plan—see Chapter 32.

2. When an employer has a nonqualified deferred compensation arrangement with one or more key executives or other employees and needs a way to finance its obligation upon the death of the employee. For example, such a plan might provide a benefit of $50,000 a year for 10 years if the employee lives to retirement or $50,000 a year for 10 years to a designated beneficiary if the employee dies either before or after retirement—see Chapter 15.

3. When a closely held corporation anticipates a need for liquid assets upon the death of a key employee to stabilize the corporation financially and enable it to continue contributing to employee benefit plans for surviving employees.

4. When a shareholder-employee expects the corporation to buy stock from his or her estate as part of an estate plan and the corporation needs additional liquid assets to carry out such a purchase.

## TAX IMPLICATIONS

### To the Employee

1. There is no income tax to a key employee or the key employee's estate when the corporation owns the policy, pays the premiums, and receives death proceeds from key employee life insurance.

2. Corporate-owned key employee life insurance may have some effect on the federal estate tax payable by the deceased key employee's estate.

- The value of corporate stock held by a decedent at death is included in the decedent's gross estate for federal estate tax purposes. If the corporation held life insurance on the decedent's life, the insurance proceeds increase the value of the corporation, and therefore can be included in the value of the stock held by the decedent. The general rule for key employee life insurance, where the corporation is the beneficiary, is that the insurance proceeds are taken into account in valuing the decedent's stock, but not necessarily included in the decedent's estate dollar for dollar.[1] However, in many situations the IRS attempts to increase the value of the stock as much as possible where the corporation held key employee life insurance.

- If the insured key employee was a majority shareholder (more than 50%), the tax law provides that policy proceeds, to the extent payable to or for the benefit of a party other than the corporation or its creditors, will be taxed in the insured key employee's estate as life insurance.[2] For this reason, policy proceeds of corporate-owned life insurance should generally be payable only to the corporation or its creditors.

### To the Corporation

1. Corporate-paid premiums on life insurance on the life of a key employee, where the corporation

is the owner and beneficiary of the life insurance contract, are not deductible for federal income tax purposes.[3]

2. The death proceeds of key employee life insurance are tax-free when paid to the corporation, except for the potential application of the alternative minimum tax (AMT) discussed below.[4]

3. If the corporation has accumulated earnings of more than $250,000 ($150,000 for certain service corporations) then the further accumulation of income to pay life insurance premiums for key employee insurance potentially exposes the corporation to the accumulated earnings tax. There are, however, many exceptions to the application of this tax. The purchase of life insurance to cover the potential loss of a bona fide key employee should not result in a significant risk of accumulated earnings tax exposure in most cases.

4. Key employee life insurance involves some potential corporate exposure to the corporate alternative minimum tax (AMT). The purpose of the AMT is to require corporations to pay a minimum level of income tax on actual economic income, even if taxable income has been reduced by significant amounts of tax-exempt or tax-preferred income. The AMT is a tax computed on a base of reported income plus certain "tax preferences." Generally, a corporation must pay the larger of its regular tax or the AMT.[5] Certain "small" corporations are exempt from AMT (generally, average gross receipts of $7,500,000 or less).[6]

The AMT is imposed on a base of "adjusted minimum taxable income" or AMTI. The AMTI includes regular income plus tax preferences. In addition, there is included in the AMTI an amount equal to 75% of the excess of corporate "adjusted current earnings" over the AMTI (computed without regard to the adjustment for current earnings), with various adjustments.[7]

Adjusted current earnings includes amounts that are income for accounting purposes and treated as "earnings and profits" under tax law (Code section 312) but are not included in taxable income. IRS regulations indicate that both death proceeds (in excess of the taxpayer's basis) and the annual increases in cash value are part of adjusted current earnings.[8]

The corporate AMT is equal to 20% of AMTI reduced by a $40,000 exemption which is phased

out at the rate of 25% of AMTI exceeding $150,000 (in other words, the exemption disappears for AMTI that is equal to or greater than $310,000 ($310,000 exceeds $150,000 by $160,000 and 25% of $160,000 is $40,000)).

A simple example will illustrate the impact of AMT on corporate-owned life insurance:

---

*Example.* Professional Services, Inc. (PSI) has regular taxable income of $200,000. Also, PSI receives $300,000 of net death proceeds from corporate-owned term life insurance. PSI's regular income tax on $200,000 is $61,250. The AMT is computed as follows:

| | | |
|---|---|---|
| Taxable income | | $200,000 |
| AMTI without adjustment for current earnings | | 200,000 |
| Current earnings | $500,000 | |
| Less AMTI w/o adjustment | -200,000 | |
| | $300,000 | |
| 75% of 300,000 | | $225,000 |
| AMTI | | 425,000 |
| Exemption amount | | 0 |
| AMTI less exemption | | 425,000 |
| AMT (20% of AMTI less exemption) | | 85,000 |
| Less regular tax | | -61,250 |
| Additional tax | | 23,750 |

This example shows an additional tax of $23,750, which is 7.9% of the insurance proceeds of $300,000. In general, the maximum tax that can be imposed on death proceeds is 20% of 75% of the death proceeds, or 15%.

---

Although the AMT is unfavorable to corporate-owned life insurance, its maximum impact is not extreme. Furthermore, the best way to avoid the impact of the AMT is to purchase additional life insurance, to insure that the corporation receives the full amount expected, after AMT.

## ALTERNATIVES

Personally-owned insurance can provide estate liquidity and funds to meet the needs of beneficiaries. Corporate funds can be used indirectly by paying extra compensation to the employee as discussed in Chapter 28. This extra compensation is deductible so long as it meets the reasonableness test discussed in Chapter 30. In a situation where the corporation's marginal income tax bracket is higher than the employee's, personally-owned insurance may provide a better tax result.

## WHERE CAN I FIND OUT MORE ABOUT IT?

1. Leimberg, Stephan R., et al., *The Tools and Techniques of Estate Planning*, 12th ed. Cincinnati, OH: The National Underwriter Co., 2001.

2. CLU/ChFC Course: Planning for Business Owners and Professionals (HS 331), The American College, Bryn Mawr, PA.

3. Graduate Courses: Advanced Estate Planning (GS 815 and 816), The American College, Bryn Mawr, PA.

## FOOTNOTES

1. Treas. Reg. §20.2031-2(f).
2. Treas. Reg. §20.2042-1(c)(6).
3. IRC Section 264(a)(1).
4. IRC Section 101(a)(1).
5. IRC Sections 55, 56.
6. IRC Section 55(e).
7. IRC Section 56(g).
8. Treas. Reg. §1.56(g)-1(c)(5).

# Chapter 43

# LEGAL SERVICES PLAN

## WHAT IS IT?

A legal services plan (sometimes referred to as a "prepaid legal services plan") is an employer-funded plan that makes legal services available to employees when needed. The expenses of the plan are deductible to the employer. Benefits are generally taxable as compensation to the employees.

## WHEN IS IT INDICATED?

In theory, any group of employees can benefit from the advantages of these plans. However, in practice they are used primarily by larger employers for employees in collective bargaining units. Such plans are usually funded through multiemployer trusteeships sponsored by labor unions. Group insurance for funding these plans is also available but is not yet widely used.

## ADVANTAGES

1. Many employees, particularly middle and lower income employees, are not well-served by the traditional fee-for-service system of delivering legal services and, as a result, often do without a lawyer when they really need one. For example, many middle income people do not have adequate legal advice in tax and domestic matters. A legal services plan provides these services without additional employee expenditure.

2. Legal expenses such as the cost of a criminal trial can be the kind of catastrophic expense that is best provided through an insurance-type or group benefit program such as a legal services plan.

## DISADVANTAGES

1. Since most employees rarely need a lawyer, or rarely perceive the need for one, a legal services plan may not be fully appreciated by employees compared with other forms of employee compensation.

2. Funding and administering a legal services plan is difficult in light of the limited availability of group legal insurance or multiemployer arrangements.

3. Some employers fear that a legal services plan will make it more likely that employees will sue the employer in the event of a dispute. However, legal services for actions by employees against the employer can be (and usually are) excluded from the plan.

4. Either employer expenditures for the plan or the value of legal services provided will be taxable income to covered employees.

## DESIGN FEATURES

1. Generally, any group of employees can be covered.

2. Benefits are usually provided on either a *scheduled* or a *comprehensive* basis.

   With a scheduled plan only those benefits listed in the plan are provided. Most plans provide at least the following benefits:

   - legal consultations and advice on any matter;

   - preparation of wills, deeds, powers-of-attorney and other routine legal documents;

   - personal bankruptcy;

   - adoption proceedings;

   - defense of civil and criminal matters;

   - juvenile proceedings; and

   - divorce, separation, child custody, and other domestic matters.

   A plan that provides comprehensive benefits pays for all legal services, with specified exclusions. The most common exclusions include:

- audits by the IRS;

- actions against the employer, the plan, or a labor union sponsoring the plan;

- contingent fee cases or class action suits; and

- actions arising out of the employee's separate business transactions.

3. Some plans provide benefits on an indemnity basis, that is, by reimbursing the employee for covered expenditures. In that case, benefits are usually limited to a flat amount for a given legal service or a maximum hourly rate. There may also be a maximum annual benefit such as $1,000.

Prepayment-type plans are more common than indemnity plans. In a prepayment plan there is no direct expenditure by employees. In a *closed-panel* prepayment plan, the most common type, employees must obtain covered services from specified groups of lawyers who are either employed by or under contract with the plan (similar to an HMO— see Chapter 40). In an *open-panel* prepayment plan employees can choose their own lawyer or choose a lawyer from an approved list. The lawyer must agree in advance to a fee schedule set by the legal services plan. A plan can combine both the closed panel and open panel approaches, allowing occasional use of top legal specialists for serious matters, while routine matters are handled by the closed panel.

## TAX IMPLICATIONS

1. Costs of a legal services plan are deductible to the employer,[1] with certain limitations:

   (a) as with all deductions for employee compensation, the overall compensation of each employee must meet the "reasonableness" test discussed in Chapter 30;

   (b) if the plan is funded in advance, the amount of deductible advance funding is limited to approximately the benefits provided during the taxable year plus administrative expenses.[2]

2. Employees are taxed as follows[3]:

   (a) if the plan is prefunded by the employer—for example, if the employer pays a group legal insurance premium to an insurance company— the employee is taxed on his or her share of the premium at the time the employer pays it, if the employee is fully vested in the benefit (legally entitled at that time to receive benefits under the plan). The benefits should then be received tax-free.

   (b) if the employer pays for benefits out of current revenues as employees receive benefits, the employee is taxed on the value of benefits as they are received.

## WHERE CAN I FIND OUT MORE ABOUT IT?

1. Beam, Burton T., Jr. and John J. McFadden, *Employee Benefits*, 6th ed. Chicago IL: Dearborn Financial Publishing, Inc., 2000.

## FOOTNOTES

1. IRC Section 162(a)(1).

2. See generally IRC Section 419.

3. The rules discussed here are the general rules for inclusion under Code sections 61 and 83. There is no longer a specific Code provision allowing for certain tax-free legal services benefit; Code section 120 expired for taxable years beginning after June 30, 1992.

# Chapter 44

# LOANS TO EXECUTIVES

Many employers make loans available to executives, usually restricted to loans for specified purposes. Typically such loans are interest-free or made at a favorable interest rate. Under guidance issued by the IRS, certain Split dollar plans may be treated as loans (see Chapter 52).

## WHEN IS IT INDICATED?

Employers rarely act as an unrestricted "bank" for executives. However, loan programs can be extremely attractive as a compensation supplement to help executives meet cash needs in special situations. Loans are typically offered for the following:

- Mortgage or "bridge" loan to help in the purchase of a home, where the employee is moving from one of the employer's business locations to another.

- College or private school tuition for members of the executive's family.

- Purchase of stock of the employer through a company stock purchase plan or otherwise.

- Meeting extraordinary medical needs, tax bills, or other personal or family emergencies such as divorce settlement costs.

- Purchase of life insurance.

- Purchase of a car, vacation home, or other expensive item.

## ADVANTAGES

1. Although the tax rules discussed under "TAX IMPLICATIONS," below, provide no tax advantage to executive loans, such loans still provide a valuable benefit by (a) making cash available where regular bank loans might be difficult to obtain and (b) providing loans at a favorable rate of interest.

2. Certain types of loans are generally exempt from the complex tax rules for "below-market" loans:

- mortgage and bridge loans made in connection with an employment-connected relocation,

- "de minimis" loans aggregating less than $10,000 (see below), and

- low interest loans without "significant tax effect" on the lender or borrower.

3. The cost of a loan program to the employer is only the administrative cost plus the loss of interest on the loan, if any, compared to what the employer could have obtained by another type of investment or investment in the business itself.

4. There are no nondiscrimination rules for executive loan programs. Loans can be provided to selected groups of executives or even a single executive. The terms, amounts, and conditions of executive loans can be varied from one executive to another as the employer wishes.

## DISADVANTAGES

1. The tax rules for "below-market" loans are complicated and confusing, which increases the administrative cost of the loan program for both employer and employee.

2. The tax treatment of term loans (as opposed to demand loans) is unfavorable—the employee must include a substantial portion of the loan in income immediately in some cases.

3. The employer must bear the cost of administering the loan (for example, determining whether the loan should be granted, monitoring the payback, and advising the executive as to the tax consequences), and also must bear the risk of default (either losing the money altogether or the costs of foreclosure on a house or other asset used as collateral).

## TAX IMPLICATIONS

1. The following tax rules apply if a loan is

   (a) a "below-market"[1] loan,

   (b) "compensation-related,"[2] and

   (c) a "demand" loan—a loan payable in full at any time upon demand of the lender. A "demand" loan also includes any loan (1) where the interest arrangements are conditioned on the future services of the employee, and (2) of which the interest benefits are not transferable by the employee.[3]

Most executive loan programs involve loans that meet these definitions. Term loans—those payable at a specified time in the future—are discussed in the "Questions and Answers" at the end of this chapter.

For federal income tax purposes, interest on a loan meeting conditions (a), (b), and (c) is treated as three transactions combined—the actual transaction plus two "deemed" transactions:

   (1) Interest *actually* paid by the executive borrower is taxable income to the company (lender) and that interest payment may be deductible by the borrower, subject to the usual limitations on interest deductions. For example, if the loan qualifies as a home mortgage loan, the interest is fully deductible, but if it is a personal loan not secured by a home mortgage, it is generally nondeductible.

   (2) The employer is treated as if it paid additional compensation to the employee in the amount of the difference between the actual rate of interest and the "applicable federal rate" (see below).[4] This additional compensation income is deductible by the employer (within the usual "reasonable compensation" limits) and is taxable to the executive.

   The applicable federal rate (AFR) is published monthly by the IRS as a Revenue Ruling (which appears monthly in the Internal Revenue Bulletin). For demand loans, the AFR is the short-term semiannual rate. For a term loan, the AFR is the short-term, mid-term, or long-term rate in effect as of the day the loan was made, also compounded semiannually. Each of these figures can be found in Table 1 of each month's Revenue Ruling establishing the AFR. If the loan is of a fixed principal amount that remains outstanding for the entire calendar year, the "blended annual rate" (published in July of each year) is the AFR.[5]

   (3) The executive is treated as if he paid the amount in (2), above, to the employer. This amount is additional taxable income to the employer. The amount is deductible by the executive borrower, again under the usual limitations on interest deductibility.

---

*Example:* Executive Flint borrows $100,000 from her employer. Assume that interest at the applicable federal rate for Year 1 would be $6,000, but actual interest under the loan agreement is only $2,000. This loan results in additional taxable compensation income to Flint for year 1 of $4,000 ($6,000 less $2,000). If interest is deductible (for example, if the loan qualifies as a home mortgage loan), Flint can deduct $6,000 (the actual $2,000 paid plus the deemed $4,000) as an interest payment. Flint's employer can deduct $4,000 as compensation paid to Flint for year 1, regardless of whether Flint can deduct any of the interest.

---

Are these loans advantageous to the employee in light of these rules? Yes, because with a low interest loan it still costs the employee less to borrow money even if it results in additional taxable income. For example, suppose that in the example above executive Flint had not been able to deduct any interest on the loan. Then, in this "worst-case" scenario, Flint would have had additional taxable income of $4,000; at a marginal rate of 30%, this would result in an additional tax of $1,200. The total cost of borrowing for year 1, therefore, would be the actual interest paid ($2,000) plus the additional tax ($1,200), or a total of $3,200. By comparison, a loan at the applicable federal rate (which presumably is close to the actual market rate) would have cost Flint $6,000 in year 1.

2. *Exceptions.*

*Mortgage and bridge loans.* The rules described above do not apply to certain mortgage and bridge loans used to help an employee purchase a house in connection with the employee's transfer to a new principal place of work. In other words, such loans are treated for tax purposes by the employer and employee just as they are actually negotiated, without any "deemed" transactions.

The following requirements must be met in order to qualify for the mortgage loan exception[6]:

(a) the loan is compensation-related and is a demand or a term loan, as defined earlier;

(b) the new principal residence is acquired in connection with the transfer of the employee to a new principal place of work (which meets the distance and time requirements for a moving expense deduction under Code section 217—see Chapter 48);

(c) the executive certifies to the employer that he or she reasonably expects to be entitled to and will itemize deductions while the loan is outstanding;

(d) under the loan agreement, loan proceeds may be used only to buy the executive's new principal residence; and

(e) the loan is secured by a mortgage on the new principal residence of the employee.

A bridge loan must satisfy the requirements above, as well as the following additional requirements[7]:

(a) the loan must be payable in full in 15 days after the old principal residence is sold;

(b) the aggregate principal of all bridge loans must not exceed the employer's reasonable estimate of the equity of the executive and his spouse in the old residence; and

(c) the old residence must not be converted to business or investment use.

*De minimis loans.* The below-market rules do not apply to a compensation-related loan for any day on which aggregate loans outstanding between the company and the executive do not exceed $10,000, provided that tax avoidance is not one of the principal purposes of the interest arrangements.[8] A husband and wife are treated as one borrower for this purpose.[9]

*No tax effect.* A loan is exempt from the below-market rules if the taxpayer can show that the interest arrangements will have no significant effect on any federal tax liability of the lender or borrower.[10] In making this determination the IRS will consider

- whether items of income and deduction generated by the loan offset each other;

- the amount of such items;

- the cost to the taxpayer of complying with the below-market loan rules; and

- any non-tax reasons for structuring the transaction as a below-market loan.[11]

## ERISA AND OTHER REGULATORY IMPLICATIONS

An executive loan program does not appear to fall within the definition of either a "welfare benefit plan" or a "pension plan" for ERISA purposes. Therefore, ERISA requirements should not apply and a Form 5500 need not be filed.

Federal "Truth in Lending" requirements may conceivably apply.[12]

Employers should investigate the Truth in Lending requirements if they extend more than 25 loans (or more than 5 loans secured by dwellings) in a calendar year. The Truth in Lending requirements primarily involve additional paperwork, but failure to meet them could result in penalties.

As part of the wave of corporate governance regulation arising out of the Enron collapse and similar events in 2001 and 2002, Congress enacted the Sarbanes-Oxley Act, which contains a range of corporate accountability provisions. Included in the Act is a provision that prohibits any publicly traded corporation from making a personal loan to any director or executive officer. The law does not apply to loans to employees who are not directors or officers, nor does it apply to loans of corporations that are not publicly traded.

## ALTERNATIVES

Because of the administrative cost and complexity of loan programs, employers may wish to investigate alternatives that would provide substantially the same benefits to executives. These could include:

- loans by the employer at full market rates, but "bonus" the interest cost to the executive as additional compensation.

- guarantees by the employer of regular bank loans taken out by executives. This works best where the bank is one with which the employer has an established business relationship.

## QUESTIONS AND ANSWERS

**Question** — How is a term loan to an executive treated for tax purposes?

*Answer* — A term loan is defined in the below-market loan rules as any loan that is not a demand loan.[13] Generally, a term loan is one with a fixed payment date such as five years—that is, a loan that does not by its terms have to be paid back until a specified date in the future.

A term loan is deemed to be below-market if the amount loaned is more than the present value of all payments due under the loan.[14] The present value is determined with a discount rate based on the applicable federal rate (AFR).

If a below-market compensation-related loan is made, the executive (borrower) is treated as if he immediately received an amount equal to the excess of (a) the amount of the loan, over (b) the present value of all payments required to be made under the loan.[15]

For example, suppose employer Rocks, Inc. lends executive Rubble $40,000, interest-free, payable in 5 years. Assume that based on the AFR for the first year of the loan, the present value of the loan is $22,000. Rubble is treated as having received additional compensation income of $18,000 ($40,000 less $22,000) in the first year of the loan. Rocks, Inc. can deduct this $18,000 as additional compensation paid (subject to the reasonable compensation rules). Over the five-year period of the loan, Rubble is also treated as paying interest to Rocks, Inc. at the applicable federal rate on the deemed "unpaid amount" of $22,000, and Rocks, Inc. must include this interest in income.

The $10,000 de minimis rule for term loans is similar to the one for demand loans; however, once a term loan has exceeded $10,000, it continues to be subject to the below-market loan rules, even if the balance later falls below $10,000.[16]

## FOOTNOTES

1. IRC Section 7872(e)(1) defines below-market loans; a demand loan is a below-market loan if interest is payable on it at a rate less than the "applicable federal rate" in effect for the loan period.

2. IRC Section 7872(c)(1)(B) provides that a below-market loan is compensation-related if it is directly or indirectly between (1) an employer and an employee, or (2) an independent contractor and the person for whom the independent contractor provides services.

3. IRC Section 7872(f)(5). The IRS is given authority to issue regulations treating any loan with an indefinite maturity as a demand loan.

4. The actual calculation is complicated; the rules are given in detail in the proposed treasury regulations under Code section 7872.

5. Rev. Rul. 86-17, 1986-1 CB 377.

6. Temp. Treas. Reg. §1.7872-5T(c)(1)(i).

7. Temp. Treas. Reg. §1.7872-5T(c)(1)(ii).

8. IRC Section 7872(c)(3).

9. IRC Section 7872(f)(7).

10. Temp. Treas. Reg. §1.7872-5T(b)(14).

11. Temp. Treas. Reg. §1.7872-5T(c)(3).

12. See Title I of the Consumer Protection Act, as amended, 15 U.S.C. 1601 *et seq.*

13. IRC Section 7872(f)(6).

14. IRC Section 7872(e)(1)(B).

15. IRC Section 7872(b)(1).

16. IRC Section 7872(f)(10).

# Chapter 45

# LONG–TERM CARE PLAN

## WHAT IS IT?

A long-term care plan is an employer-provided benefit similar to health insurance. Benefits generally cover "nursing home" or home health expenses for chronically ill beneficiaries; these are items not traditionally included in a health care plan. Tax benefits are similar to those for employer-provided health insurance — premium costs are deductible to the employer, and premiums and benefits are nontaxable to the employee or beneficiary within certain limits.

## WHEN IS IT INDICATED?

1. When an employer wishes to provide an additional tax-favored benefit to employees that might be too expensive for the employees to consider without the employer's involvement.

2. When the employee group is relatively old (the "aging baby boomer" group) and conscious of significant need for help with potential long-term care expenses and appreciative of employer assistance in providing this.

## PLAN DESIGN

Tax benefits for long-term care are relatively new, having been introduced in the Health Insurance Portability and Accountability Act of 1996. It is still not entirely clear what form the majority of employer plans will ultimately take, or whether these plans will be widely accepted. However, certain aspects of these plans can be noted:

- Long-term care insurance is expensive and most employer-sponsored plans probably will require substantial payments by employees; many might require employees to pay the full cost. This limits potential tax benefits because, unlike the employer's tax deduction for premium payments that is generally allowable in full, the employee's tax deductions are limited by the "floor" for medical expense deductions (see below).

- The employee's share of premiums, if any, cannot be paid from a cafeteria or flexible spending account type of plan.[1] This eliminates one of the most potentially promising methods of covering employee payments under such plans.

- Long-term care, in general, is treated as health insurance both as an employee benefit and for purposes of individual policies. Because of limitations on the ability of employers to provide this benefit on a cost-effective basis, individual policies may become more common than employer plans.

- For purposes of the tax benefits under these plans, the definition of long-term care insurance is strictly limited (see below) and plans generally will tend to be tailored to comply with this definition in order to receive tax benefits.

- The COBRA continuation coverage requirements (described in Chapter 39) do not apply to long-term care plans.[2] Further, certain provisions relating to preexisting conditions and other portability issues do not apply to long-term care plans if the plan is offered separately.[3]

- Subject to the portability requirements and general civil rights and similar nondiscrimination requirements applicable to all types of employee compensation, an employer can make a long-term care plan available to any employee or any group of employees.

- The plan apparently can cover spouses and dependents on the same basis as a health insurance plan.

## TAX IMPLICATIONS

1. If a plan meets the Code's definition of a "qualified long-term care insurance contract"[4] it is treated for tax purposes the same as an accident and health insurance contract. A qualified long-term care insurance contract is any insurance contract if:

- the only insurance protection provided under the contract is coverage of "qualified long-term care services";

- the contract does not pay or reimburse expenses that are reimbursable under Medicare;

- the contract is guaranteed renewable;

- the contract has no cash surrender value or other monetary value;

- refunds of premiums are used to reduce future premiums or increase future benefits; and

- certain consumer protection requirements are met.

Qualified long-term care services means specified services provided to a chronically ill individual as defined in Code section 7702B. For purposes of determining how much of the benefit payments may be excluded from income there is a per diem limitation that is indexed for inflation ($220 per day in 2003).

2. Treatment as a qualified long-term care insurance contract carries with it the same tax treatment as an accident and health contract. In the case of an employer plan:

- the employer's premium payments are tax-deductible under Code section 162(a);

- the employer's payment of the premium does not result in taxable income to the covered employee[5]; and

- benefits under the plan are not taxable to the employee or beneficiary subject to certain limitations.[6]

3. If the employee pays part or all of the cost of the plan, premiums that do not exceed certain dollar limits are treated as medical expenses available for an itemized deduction under Code section 213 for medical expenses subject to the "floor" of 7.5 per-

cent of adjusted gross income. In 2003, the dollar limits are:

| Individual with attained age before close of taxable year of | Limitation on premiums |
|---|---|
| 40 or less | $ 250 |
| 41 through 50 | 470 |
| 51 through 60 | 940 |
| 61 through 70 | 2,510 |
| Over 70 | 3,130 |

Similarly, unreimbursed expenses for qualified long-term care services for the taxpayer or his spouse or dependents are eligible for the Section 213 itemized deduction, again subject to the 7.5 percent floor.

4. A self-employed person may deduct 100% of premiums for a qualified long-term care insurance contract. However, the deductible premiums are first limited to those eligible for the Section 213 itemized deduction described above.[7]

## ERISA AND OTHER REQUIREMENTS

An employer's long-term care plan is a "welfare benefit plan" subject to the ERISA requirements discussed in Appendix A.

## FOOTNOTES

1. IRC Section 125(f).
2. IRC Section 4980B(g)(2) provides that the health care continuation rules (COBRA) do not apply to coverage under a "...plan substantially all of the coverage under which is for qualified long-term care services...." There is no such specific exclusion under Code section 4980D relating to preexisting conditions and other portability requirements.
3. IRC Sections 9831, 9832(c).
4. IRC Section 7702B(b).
5. IRC Section 106(a).
6. IRC Section 105. See IRC Section 7702B(d).
7. IRC Section 162(l).

# Chapter 46

# LONG TERM DISABILITY INSURANCE

## WHAT IS IT?

Long term disability insurance is an employer-sponsored program to provide disability income to employees who are disabled (unable to work) beyond a period specified in the plan, usually six months. Such plans are designed to supplement the Social Security disability coverage available to almost all employees. Disability income under an employer plan usually continues for the duration of the disability, or until death. The plan is usually funded through an insurance contract, particularly for smaller employers.

## WHEN IS IT INDICATED?

1. When employees have a need for income to provide for themselves and their families in the event of long term disability.

   Unfortunately, disability is a common event. It is more likely that an employee will become disabled before age 65 than that he or she will die before 65. Social Security disability benefits are available only for severe disabilities. Social Security benefit levels are not adequate for highly paid employees to maintain their standard of living. Disability income plans are very common as employee benefits because of the great perceived need for them. They would be even more common, or more generous, if it were not for their high cost to employers. The question employers face is not so much whether there is a need for these programs, but rather how they can be financed.

2. When an employer wants to provide a special benefit for executives, if the company has no regular long term disability program for all employees, or if the regular program provides limited benefits. Under current law, employers can provide disability plans on a discriminatory basis—that is, special plans can be provided for selected executives only. The employer is free to choose (1) who will be covered; (2) the amounts of coverage provided (amounts can vary from employee to employee); and (3) the terms and conditions of coverage.

## DESIGN FEATURES

### Eligibility

Since long term disability plans provided by employers are not subject to nondiscrimination rules, the employer has great flexibility in deciding who is covered under the plan. Many plans cover only full-time salaried employees, or only a select group of executive employees. This reduces plan costs, not only because fewer employees are covered, but also because experience in many firms indicates that disability claims are more frequent among non-salaried employees. Some plans simply use the approach of covering only employees above a specified salary level. Exclusions like these in an employer plan are not necessarily grossly inequitable to lower paid employees, because Social Security disability benefit levels—income replacement ratios—are relatively satisfactory for lower paid employees.

Most long term disability plans require a waiting period of three months to a year before an eligible employee becomes covered.

### Definition of Disability

The plan's definition of disability is very important in establishing its cost to the employer. The definition can be strict or liberal, or somewhere in between. Three common definitions will illustrate the range of options:

- the "Social Security" or "total and permanent" definition—disability is defined as a condition under which the individual "is unable to engage in any substantial gainful activity by reason of any medically determinable physical or mental impairment which can be expected to result in death or which has lasted or can be expected to last for a continuous period of not less than 12 months." This is the strictest (i.e., least favorable to the employee) definition that is commonly used.

- the "qualified for" definition—disability is defined as "the total and continuous inability of the employee to engage in any and every gainful occupation for which he or she is qualified or shall reasonably become qualified by reason of training, education, or experience." This definition is more liberal than the Social Security definition since it does not require the disabled employee to be incapable of any gainful employment, only employment for which the employee is qualified. This definition, or some variation of it, is commonly used in employer long term disability plans.

- the "regular occupation" or "own occupation" definition—disability is defined as the "total and continuous inability of the employee to perform any and every duty of his or her regular occupation." Although this definition is often used in short term disability plans (see Chapter 51), it is generally too liberal for an employer's long term plan. However, if the plan is designed purely as an extra benefit for a selected group of executives, a liberal definition might be used. Most individual disability policies also use a liberal definition, since individuals, for themselves, tend to define disability in terms of inability to do their current job.

As these definitions indicate, most long term disability plans require total disability in order to receive benefits. However, some plans provide payments for partial disabilities, particularly if the partial disability is preceded by a total disability. This may encourage rehabilitation and return to gainful employment, which is desirable for both employer and employee.

Disability plans usually contain specific exclusions under which benefits will not be paid even if the definition of disability is otherwise met. Common exclusions are (1) disabilities during periods when the employee is not under a physician's care; (2) disabilities caused by an intentionally self-inflicted injury; and (3) disabilities beginning before the employee became eligible for plan coverage.

## Benefit Formulas

Long term plans generally do not provide 100% of pre-disability income. The principal reason for this, from the employer's viewpoint, is to avoid disincentives to return to work. Insurers generally do not underwrite plans providing too high a replacement ratio. Disability income amounts of 50% to 70% of pre-disability income are typical.

Benefits are usually "integrated" with disability benefits from other plans. For example, a plan's benefit formula might provide that the disability benefit from the employer is 70% of the employee's pre-disability compensation, less disability benefits from specified other sources. This provides the employee with the desired 70% disability income level, but the employer only pays whatever additional amount is required after other sources are taken into account. Typical sources of disability benefits, other than the disability plan itself, include (1) Social Security; (2) workers' compensation; (3) qualified or nonqualified retirement plans; (4) other insurance; or (5) earnings from other employment.

Integration with other plans can use either a full (dollar for dollar) offset of the disability benefit by the other income sources, or an integration formula of some kind can be used, under which benefits from the employer plan are reduced by something less than a dollar for each dollar of other disability benefits. There are no federal tax law restrictions on integration similar to those applicable to qualified retirement plans. This means that the employer is free to design any kind of integration formula that meets its cost limits and other objectives for the plan.

## TAX IMPLICATIONS

1. Employer contributions to disability income plans, either insurance premium payments or direct benefit payments under an uninsured plan, are deductible as employee compensation. Like all compensation deductions, they are subject to the "reasonableness" requirement described in Chapter 30.

2. In some plans, employees pay part of the cost of the plan, usually through payroll deductions. These payments are not deductible by the employee.

3. Employer payments of premiums under an insured disability plan do not result in taxable income to the employee.[1]

4. Benefit payments under an employer plan are fully taxable to the employee (subject to the credit described below) if the plan was fully paid for by the employer. If the employer paid part of the cost, only a corresponding part of the benefit is taxable, again subject to the credit. For example, if the employer paid 75% of the disability insurance premiums and the employee paid the remaining 25%, only 75% of the disability benefit received by the employee is taxable.[2]

IRS regulations specify the time over which the employer and employee percentages are to be measured for this purpose. For group disability insurance, generally, payments over the three year period prior to the disability are taken into account in determining the percentages paid by employer and employee.[3]

5.  If an employee receiving benefits meets the "total and permanent" disability definition described earlier, a limited tax credit reduces the tax impact of disability payments for lower-income recipients.[4]

Generally, the disability credit is calculated by taking the maximum amount subject to the credit (see below) and subtracting one half of the amount by which the taxpayer's adjusted gross income exceeds the AGI limits (see below). The credit is equal to 15% of this amount. Thus, the maximum annual tax credit is $1,125 for a joint return, as indicated below. The chart below shows the maximum amounts eligible for the credit, the maximum credit that may be obtained, and the limitations to adjusted gross income (AGI):

### MAXIMUM AMOUNT SUBJECT TO CREDIT

| | |
|---|---|
| Single Person | $5,000 |
| Joint Return (where one spouse is a qualified individual) | $5,000 |
| Joint Return (where both spouses are qualified individuals)' | $7,500 |
| Married Filing Separately | $3,750 |

### MAXIMUM CREDIT

| | |
|---|---|
| Single Person | $750 |
| Joint Return (where one spouse is a qualified individual) | $750 |
| Joint Return (where both spouses are qualified individuals) | $1,125 |
| Married Filing Separately | $562.50 |

### ADJUSTED GROSS INCOME LIMITS

| | |
|---|---|
| Single Person | $7,500 |
| Married Filing Jointly | $10,000 |
| Married Filing Separately | $5,000 |

For example, if a disabled employee has adjusted gross income (from all sources, including taxable disability income) of $14,000, and is married, filing jointly, the amount on which his disability tax credit is calculated would be $5,000 (the maximum amount for a joint return where only one spouse receives disability income payments) less $2,000 (one half of the amount by which the taxpayer's AGI exceeds $10,000). In short, this is $5,000 - $2,000, or $3,000.

The taxpayer's credit is equal to 15% of $3,000, or $450. Accordingly, the employee's income tax bill for the year is reduced by $450. Note that to receive this credit, the employee must meet the Social Security total and permanent definition of disability. An employee might receive benefits under some employer plans without meeting this strict definition of disability, as discussed above.

This tax credit is even further reduced by 15% of any tax-free income received by the employee from a pension, annuity, or disability benefit, including Social Security. Since most disability plans are integrated with Social Security benefits, this further reduction makes the credit even less valuable.

In view of all the reductions applicable to this credit, and the extremely low AGI limits on full availability, the credit has become a minor factor in the design of disability benefits.

6.  Disability insurance premiums paid by the employer under the plan are not considered wages subject to employment taxes (FICA—Social Security—and FUTA—federal unemployment).[5] Generally, disability insurance premiums are not subject to state employment taxes either, but individual state laws should be consulted.

7.  Disability benefits are subject to federal income tax withholding if paid directly by the employer. If paid by a third party, such as an insurance company, withholding is required only if the employee requests it.[6]

8.  Disability benefits attributable to employer contributions are subject to Social Security taxes for a limited period (six months generally) at the beginning of a disability. Thereafter, they are not considered wages subject to Social Security tax.[7]

## ERISA REQUIREMENTS

A disability income plan is considered a welfare benefit plan under ERISA (see Appendix A). Such plans require a written summary plan description (SPD), the naming of a plan administrator, and a formal written claims procedure by which employees can make benefit claims and appeal denials. The plan is not subject to the eligibility, vesting, or funding requirements of ERISA. The plan administrator must provide plan participants with a summary plan description (SPD).

### WHERE CAN I FIND OUT MORE ABOUT IT?

1. Beam, Burton T., Jr. and John J. McFadden, *Employee Benefits,* 6th ed. Chicago, IL: Dearborn Financial Publishing, Inc., 2000.

2. *Tax Facts 1,* Cincinnati, OH: The National Underwriter Company. Revised annually.

### QUESTIONS AND ANSWERS

**Question** — What are the alternatives to the classic employer-paid long term disability plan?

*Answer* — When an employer considers providing a disability income to an executive or group of executives, the advantages and disadvantages of an employer-paid plan versus individual disability insurance must be weighed.

The employer plan results in no current taxable income to the employee, and thus provides deferral of taxes. Disability benefits are, however, fully taxable, except for a credit which benefits only low-income employees. This raises some planning issues. The amount of disability benefit for a particular employee may be, and in fact usually is, much more than what the employer paid for it. Thus, the total tax bill to the employee is usually larger if the employee does in fact become disabled. Also, if tax rates increase, each dollar of taxable disability income may be subject to more tax in the future than the value of a dollar's worth of current tax exclusion (ignoring the time value of money).

These factors may make individual disability income policies, or a group policy paid for totally by the employee, more attractive to some executives than an employer-paid long term disability plan. An employee-paid policy results in no current tax deduction, but benefits are free of tax. The cost of the policy to the executive can be minimized or eliminated if the employer pays additional compensation or an annual bonus in the amount of the employee's cost for the coverage, plus the income tax on the bonus itself—a so-called "double bonus" plan.

**Question** — Is there any type of disability plan that provides *both* employer payment of deductible premiums and non-taxation of benefits to the employee?

*Answer* — Under code section 105(c), disability benefits are tax-free if the amount of benefit is (1) based on

permanent loss of use of a member or function of the body; and (2) is computed by reference to the nature of the injury and not to the period the employee is absent from work. This Code provision is intended primarily to cover plans such as accidental death and dismemberment (AD&D) plans that pay a lump sum for loss of a leg, eye, etc. However, some planners have made use of this exclusion as a substitute for traditional disability insurance. This is done by designing a plan that pays a stated amount for a heart attack, for arthritis, or for other specified conditions, with benefits based on a schedule in the plan and not specifically on the employee's compensation. These benefits can be paid by the employer directly, or in some cases can be paid out of a qualified pension or profit sharing plan.

Another approach—one with less validity—that is sometimes used in order to get the best of both worlds is to design a plan under which the decision as to whether the employer or the employee pays premiums is postponed to the last possible time each year. This permits an employee to opt for employee payment if he or she becomes disabled during the year. However, if all the facts about such a plan were known to the IRS, it would probably be viewed as a sham—that is, treated as an employer-paid plan if an employee becomes disabled.

However, the following plan design would probably pass muster for tax purposes: the plan provides for the employee to choose (in advance) cost-sharing of premiums each year from zero to 100%. Just before the beginning of each year the employee would choose whatever share was appropriate under the circumstances. If the employee was in poor health, he could choose 100% employee-paid coverage for the following year, so that benefits under the plan, if he becomes disabled during that year, would be tax-free. Since there is no certainty that the employee will actually become disabled, the employee's election is subject to a real economic risk and should be valid for tax purposes.[8]

### FOOTNOTES

1. IRC Section 106(a).
2. IRC Sections 104(a)(3), 105(a); Treas. Reg. §1.105-1(d).
3. Treas. Regs. §§1.105-1(d), 1.105-1(e).
4. IRC Section 22.
5. IRC Sections 3121(a)(2), 3306(b)(2).
6. IRC Section 3402(o).
7. IRC Section 3121(a)(4).
8. See PLR 2003-12001, Nov. 13, 2002.

# Chapter 47

# HEALTH REIMBURSEMENT ARRANGEMENT (HRA)

## WHAT IS IT?

Under a health reimbursement arrangement, or HRA, an employer reimburses covered employees for specified medical (health and accident) expenses. These reimbursements come directly from corporate funds rather than from a third party insurer.

An HRA is used (1) as a substitute for health insurance (see Chapter 39); (2) as a supplement to provide payments for medical expenses not covered under the company's health insurance plan (such as dental expenses); or (3) to pay for medical expenses in excess of the limits in the company's health insurance plan. The tax objective of the plan is to provide tax-free benefits to the covered employees and obtain a corresponding employer tax deduction for the benefits paid.

HRAs were often used in the past to provide extra benefits for selected groups of executives. However, current tax law denies tax benefits to highly compensated employees if a "self-insured" plan does not meet the nondiscrimination tests of Code section 105(h), as described below.

## WHEN IS IT INDICATED?

1.  Where a corporation is closely held and shareholders and their family members are the primary or only employees.

2.  In a professional corporation, where the only employee is a professional in a high income tax bracket, or where there are few other employees.

3.  Where an employer would like to provide employees with medical benefits beyond those provided by the basic medical coverage already in force.

## DESIGN FEATURES

Basically, an HRA is simple. The company adopts a plan by corporate resolution specifying (1) the group of employees covered; (2) the types of medical expenses that will be reimbursed; and (3) any limits or conditions on payment by the company. When an employee incurs medical expenses subject to reimbursement the employee submits a claim to the employer. The employer then reimburses the employee, provided that the claim is covered under the plan.

The plan's objective is to provide tax-free benefits to employees. Benefits will be tax free if (1) they qualify as medical expenses under the Code; and (2) (for a highly compensated employee) the plan is nondiscriminatory under Code section 105(h), as discussed below under "Tax Implications."

A broad range of expenses can qualify as medical expenses under an HRA. This is one of the advantages of these plans—the plan can cover expenses often not available under health insurance plans. For example, an HRA can cover full dental expenses including orthodontia, and even items such as swimming pools prescribed by a physician for treatment of a condition such as arthritis. Any expense that could be deducted by an individual as an itemized medical expense under Code section 213 is eligible for tax free reimbursement under an HRA. See Figure 47.1 at the end of this chapter for a partial list of items that have been approved for deduction under Section 213, and, thus, are eligible for tax free reimbursement under an HRA. Note that Section 213 has some specific exclusions; in particular, cosmetic surgery.

The plan can be fully funded and administered by the employer, or the employer can obtain an insurance contract to provide one or more features. Insurance contracts can help to make plans more workable by providing (1) administrative services; (2) claims evaluation; or (3) insurance against large claims—known as "stop loss" coverage.

Stop loss coverage is generally very important if the employer is small and the HRA could become potentially liable for a large medical expense.

---

*Example:* Suppose Mullions, P.C., an architectural firm, has an HRA for its sole shareholder-employee Ornate Mullions and its two employees. The HRA supplements the company's health insurance. In some years, there have been no claims at all against the plan. However, suppose an employee has cosmetic surgery that results in complications and $90,000 in hospital and doctors' bills in one year. Such a payment could bankrupt a small company.

---

An insurance stop loss contract could be obtained that would prevent this disaster by limiting the company's exposure in any one year to some specified amount that the company considers within its means. The premiums for stop loss coverage are usually relatively low because medical catastrophes are rare events.

## TAX IMPLICATIONS

1.  The employer may deduct 100% of the cost of benefits paid to employees under the plan. Plan administrative expenses, and the cost of any insured stop loss coverage, are also fully deductible.[1]

2.  Deductions for prefunding medical benefits (that is, setting funds aside and deducting amounts for medical benefits to be paid in future years) are limited under rules set out in Code sections 419 and 419A. Generally, for a given year, an employer can deduct expenditures for medical benefits up to a limit equal to the total of (a) the direct costs of the plan for the year—claims paid plus administrative costs, plus (b) contributions to an asset account up to 35% of the preceding year's direct costs.

3.  The employee does not have taxable income when benefits are paid. Benefits are tax-free when medical expenses are paid directly to doctors or hospitals, or when the plan reimburses the employee for covered expenses.[2] Highly compensated employees may have to pay taxes on the reimbursements to the extent that the plan is discriminatory under the Section 105(h) rules described below. See the "Questions and Answers" for further discussion.

4.  The employee is eligible for an itemized medical expense deduction under Code section 213 for any medical expenses not covered by the HRA or other employer health insurance plan. The Section 213 deduction is available only if the taxpayer itemizes deductions on the tax return. The deduction is limited to the amount by which the total of all eligible medical expenses exceeds 7.5% of the taxpayer's adjusted gross income.

## Nondiscrimination Rules

Health reimbursement arrangements that are funded on a "pay as you go" basis are generally considered "self insured" for tax purposes, and therefore are governed by nondiscrimination rules found in Code section 105(h). Failure to comply with these rules means that plan benefits will be taxable to "highly compensated" employees. Code section 105(h) defines a highly compensated employee as one who is (1) one of the five highest paid officers; (2) a shareholder who owns more than 10% of the company's stock; or (3) is among the highest paid 25% of all employees. Nonhighly compensated employees receive benefits tax-free even in a discriminatory plan. The nondiscrimination rules are as follows:

### Coverage Test

The plan must:

*   benefit 70% or more of all employees;

*   benefit 80% or more of all employees who are eligible to participate in the plan if at least 70% of all employees are eligible to participate; or

*   benefit a classification of employees, established by the employer, that does not discriminate in favor of highly compensated employees.

### Benefits Test

All benefits provided for highly compensated employees under the plan must be provided for all plan participants.

### Who Can Be Excluded

In applying the coverage tests, the following can be excluded:

*   employees who have not completed three years of service

*   employees who have not attained age 25

*   part-time or seasonal employees

- employees in a collective bargaining unit if there has been good faith bargaining on the health plan issue

- nonresident alien employees who received no U.S. income

## Internal Revenue Code Eligibility and Coverage Requirements

The tax law provides certain requirements for group health plan coverage subject to a penalty for noncompliance. "Group health plan" is broadly defined and apparently includes HRAs.[3] Broadly, the requirements are:

- Exclusion of participants for pre-existing conditions is limited to: (1) conditions for which medical advice or treatment was recommended or received within the 6-month period ending on the enrollment date; and (2) the exclusion extends for no more than 12 months. Credit must be given against this period for previous coverage.[4]

- Participants may not be excluded (or required to pay an extra premium) on the basis of: (1) health status; (2) medical condition, whether physical or mental; (3) claims experience; (4) receipt of health care; (5) medical history; (6) genetic information; (7) evidence of insurability; or (8) disability.[5]

- The plan may not restrict benefits for any hospital length of stay in connection with childbirth for the mother or newborn child to less than 48 hours (96 hours for caesarean births).[6]

- Limits on benefits for mental illness must be no more restrictive than those for medical or surgical benefits. (This provision expires for services furnished on or after December 31, 2003.)[7]

These provisions do not apply to governmental plans or to plans that have fewer than two participants who are current employees. Other complex exclusions also apply.[8]

The penalty for noncompliance with these provisions is generally $100 per day for each individual up to a total of the lesser of: (1) 10% of the employer's payments under group health plans in the previous year; or (2) $500,000.[9] This is the same penalty amount that applies to COBRA violations (see below).

## COBRA Continuation of Coverage

An employer's adoption of any kind of health plan for employees results in an additional and typically unexpected cost due to certain provisions in the Consolidated Omnibus Budget Reconciliation Act of 1985 (COBRA), under which the employer is subject to penalties unless the plan makes available continuation of health plan benefits for certain employees and their dependents after termination of employment and certain other qualifying events.[10] There is an exemption for small employers—the COBRA continuation provisions apply for a given year only if the employer had 20 or more employees on a typical business day in the preceding year. Final regulations provide that an employer is considered to have employed fewer than 20 employees during a calendar year if it had fewer than 20 employees on at least 50% of its typical business days during that year.[11] Only common law employees are taken into account for purposes of the small-employer exception. Self-employed individuals, independent contractors, and directors are not counted.[12] In the case of a multiemployer plan, a small-employer plan is a group health plan under which each of the employers contributing to the plan for a calendar year normally employed fewer than 20 employees during the preceding calendar year.[13] Government and church plans are also exempt.

In general, under COBRA, the employer must provide the option to continue an employee's existing health plan coverage (including dependent coverage) for 36 months after the following qualifying events:

- death of the employee;

- divorce or legal separation of the covered employee (coverage continues for the former spouse and dependents);

- the employee's entitlement to Medicare benefits;

- a bankruptcy proceeding under the United States Code where the employee retired from the employer; and

- a child ceasing to be a dependent for plan purposes.

Health plan coverage must be continued for 18 months after termination of employment or reduction in hours of employment, other than for "gross misconduct."[14] If termination is for disability, coverage must be continued for 29 months.

If an employee is on leave under the Family and Medical Leave Act of 1993 (FMLA) and does not return to work, the COBRA qualifying event generally is deemed to take place on the last day of the FMLA leave.[15]

Continuation coverage can be terminated before the 36, 29, or 18 month period if:

- the employer terminates its health plan for all employees;

- the beneficiary fails to pay his or her share of the premium; or

- the beneficiary becomes covered under any other plan providing medical care. However, if the new plan excludes a pre-existing condition, the employee must be allowed to continue coverage for the full COBRA period.

The employer can require the former employee or beneficiary to pay part of the cost of continuation coverage. However, this former employee or beneficiary's share cannot be more than 102% of the cost to the plan of coverage for similarly situated beneficiaries with respect to whom a qualifying event has not occurred. This is true whether the cost is paid by the employer or employee. The premium for an employee disabled at the time of his termination or reduction in hours may be as much as 150% of the plan cost after the 18th month of continuation coverage.

The penalty for noncompliance with these requirements is, generally, a tax of $100 a day during the period that any failure with respect to a qualified beneficiary continues.

The COBRA continuation requirements are discussed further in Chapter 39.

## ERISA AND OTHER REQUIREMENTS

An employer's HRA is a "welfare benefit plan" subject to the ERISA requirements discussed in Appendix A. For Form 5500 filing purposes, stop loss insurance is not a "plan asset" that must be reported on Schedule A, Form 5500.[16]

## WHERE CAN I FIND OUT MORE ABOUT IT?

1. Beam, Burton T., Jr. and John J. McFadden, *Employee Benefits,* 6th ed. Chicago, IL: Dearborn Financial Publishing, Inc., 2000.

2. *Tax Facts 1*, Cincinnati, OH: The National Underwriter Co. (revised annually).

3. Leimberg, Stephan R., et al., *The Tools and Techniques of Estate Planning,* 11th ed. Cincinnati, OH: The National Underwriter Co., 1998.

4. Cady, Donald F., *Field Guide to Estate Planning, Business Planning, & Employee Benefits,* Cincinnati, OH: The National Underwriter Co., (revised annually).

## QUESTIONS AND ANSWERS

**Question** — Is it possible to design an HRA that excludes rank and file employees by funding the HRA with a health insurance contract?

*Answer* — Yes. Insured HRAs are exempt from the nondiscrimination requirements of Code section 105(h). However, a plan is not considered insured just because an insurance company is somehow involved by paying claims or providing administrative services. There must be an actual "shifting of risk" for the payment of health benefits from the employer to the insurance company.[17]

**Question** — Is there ever any advantage in designing an HRA that discriminates by covering only specific executives?

*Answer* — The consequence of not meeting the nondiscrimination requirements is only that:

(1) part or all of plan reimbursements (the excess reimbursements, as computed under the complex Section 105(h) rules) are taxable to highly compensated employees;

(2) taxable excess reimbursements must be reported by the employer on the employee's Form W-2.

The employer does not lose any part of its deduction for a discriminatory plan.

The excess reimbursement in a discriminatory plan is either:

(1) if the plan provides a benefit to a highly compensated employee but not to other participants, the excess reimbursement is the amount of such benefit that is reimbursed; or

(2) if the benefit is provided to both nonhighly and highly compensated employees but on a discriminatory basis, the excess reimbursement is the amount reimbursed to the highly compensated participant, multiplied by the total amount reimbursed to all highly compensated participants for the year, over the total amount reimbursed to all employees for the year.[18]

---

*Example:* Suppose that a plan provides eligibility for medical reimbursement immediately upon hire to Hal Gall, a highly compensated executive, but under the plan all other employees must be employed for four years before they are covered. In 2003, Hal is reimbursed $6,000 for hospital and surgical expenses for his knee surgery. In 2003, amounts reimbursed under the plan to all highly compensated participants totaled $30,000 out of a total of $90,000 of reimbursements. Hal's excess reimbursement for 2003 is

$$\$6,000 \quad X \quad \frac{\$30,000}{\$90,000} \quad = \quad \$2,000$$

Thus, for 2003, Hal must report $2,000 of the $6,000 reimbursement as additional taxable income. The remaining $4,000 of the reimbursement is tax free.

---

If there is a case where these consequences are not objectionable, a discriminatory plan may be useful. The consequences of a discriminatory plan can be alleviated by paying bonuses to highly compensated employees—taxable to employees and deductible to the employer—to cover the amount of tax generated by "excess reimbursements" taxed to the employee. Such a plan may still provide some tax advantage, if the employer's outlay exceeds the employee's tax cost. And the cost may be substantially less than providing the benefit on a nondiscriminatory basis.

**Question** — Can a partnership provide HRA benefits to a partner on a favorable tax basis?

*Answer* — In a Technical Advice Memorandum (TAM), the IRS took a very unfavorable position with respect to HRAs for the self-employed. Based on a technical reading of the various relevant Code provisions, the IRS asserted that the HRA did not constitute "insurance," and therefore implied that the benefit *payments* were taxable income.[19] Under this view, a partner receiving reimbursement for a serious medical condition might have hundreds of thousands of dollars of additional taxable income in a year during which the partner spent mostly in the hospital or otherwise out of service.

## FOOTNOTES

1. Treas. Reg. §1.162-10(a).
2. IRC Section 105(b).
3. IRC Sections 9832(a), 5000(b)(1).
4. IRC Section 9801.
5. IRC Section 9802.
6. IRC Section 9811.
7. IRC Section 9812.
8. IRC Section 9831.
9. IRC Section 4980D.
10. IRC Section 4980B.
11. Treas. Reg. §54.4980B-2, A-5.
12. Treas. Reg. §54.4980B-2, A-5.
13. Treas. Reg. §54.4980B-2, A-5.
14. The definition of "gross misconduct" is not provided under COBRA, but has been developed through case law, often based on state law definitions.
15. Notice 94-103, 1994-2 CB 569.
16. DOL Adv. Op. 92-02A.
17. Treas. Reg. §1.105-11.
18. IRC Section 105(h)(7).
19. TAM 9320004.

**Figure 47.1**

## DEDUCTIBLE MEDICAL EXPENSES

- Professional Services of
  - Christian Science Practitioner
  - Oculist
  - Unlicensed practitioner if the type and quality of his services are not illegal
- Equipment and Supplies
  - Abdominal supports
  - Air conditioner where necessary for relief from an allergy or for relieving difficulty in breathing
  - Arches
  - Autoette (auto device for handicapped person), but not if used to travel to job or business
  - Back supports
  - Contact lenses
  - Cost of installing stair-seat elevator for person with heart condition
  - Elastic hosiery
  - Eyeglasses
  - Fluoridation unit in home
- Medical Treatments
  - Acupuncture
  - Diatheray
  - Healing services
  - Hydrotherapy (water treatments)
- Medicines
  - Drugs
  - Patient medicines
- Miscellaneous
  - Birth control pills or other birth control
  - Braille books —excess cost of braille books over cost of regular editions
  - Clarinet lessons advised by dentist for treatment of tooth defects
  - Convalescent home — for medical treatment only
  - Face lifting operation, even if not recommended by doctor
  - Fees paid to health institute where the exercises, rubdowns, etc., taken there are prescribed by a physician as treatments necessary to alleviate a physical or mental defect or illness
  - Hair transplant operation

- Miscellaneous (cont'd)
  - Practical or other non-professional nurse for medical services only; not for care of a healthy person or a small child who is not ill
  - Costs for medical care of elderly person, unable to get about, or person subject to spells
  - Hearing aid
  - Heating devices
  - Invalid chair
  - Orthopedic shoes
  - Reclining chair if prescribed by doctor
  - Repair of special telephone equipment for the deaf
  - Sacroiliac belt
  - Special mattress and plywood bed boards for relief of arthritis of spine
  - Truss
  - Wig advised by doctor as essential to mental health of person who lost all hair from disease
  - Navajo healing ceremonies ("sings")
  - Sterilization
  - Vasectomy
  - Whirlpool baths
  - Vitamins, tonics, etc., prescribed by doctor — but not if taken as food supplement or to preserve your general health
  - Kidney donor's or possible kidney donor's expenses
  - Legal fees for guardianship of mentally ill spouse where commitment was necessary for medical treatment
  - Nurse's board and wages, including social security taxes you pay on wages
  - Remedial reading for child suffering from dyslexia
  - Sanitarium and similar institutions
  - "Seeing-eye" dog and its maintenance
  - Special school costs for physically and mentally handicapped children
  - Wages of guide for a blind person
  - Telephone-teletype costs and television adapter for closed caption service for deaf person

* A partial list of items which the IRS or the courts have held to constitute deductible medical expenses.

**Figure 47.1 (continued)**

## NONDEDUCTIBLE MEDICAL EXPENSES

- Antiseptic diaper service
- Athletic club expenses to keep physically fit
- Babysitting fees to enable you to make doctor's visits
- Boarding school fees paid for healthy child while parent is recuperating from illness. It makes no difference that this was done on a doctor's advice
- Bottled water bought to avoid drinking fluoridated city water
- Cost of divorce recommended by psychiatrist
- Cost of hotel room suggested for sex therapy
- Cost of trips for a "change of environment" to boost morale of ailing person. That doctor prescribed the trip is immaterial
- Dance lessons advised by doctors as physical and mental therapy or for the alleviation of varicose veins or arthritis; however, the cost of a clarinet and lessons for the instrument were allowed as deduction when advised as therapy for a tooth defect
- Deductions from your wages for a sickness insurance under state law
- Domestic help — even if recommended by doctor because of spouse's illness. But part of cost attributed to any nursing duties performed by the domestic is deductible
- Funeral, cremation or burial, cemetery plot, monument, mausoleum
- Health programs offered by resort hotels, health clubs and gyms
- Illegal operation and drugs
- Marriage counseling fees
- Maternity clothes
- Premiums, in connection with life insurance policies, paid for disability, double indemnity or for waiver of premium in event of total and permanent disability or policies providing for reimbursement of loss of earnings or a guarantee of a specific amount in the event of hospitalization
- Scientology fees
- Special food or beverage substitutes — but excess cost of chemically uncontaminated foods over what would have ordinarily been spent on normal food was deductible for allergy patients
- Toothpaste
- Transportation costs of a disabled person to and from work
- Traveling costs to look for a new place to live on doctor's advice
- Travel costs to favorable climate when you can live there permanently
- Tuition and travel expenses to send a problem child to a particular school for a beneficial change in environment
- Veterinary fees for pet; pet is not a dependent
- Weight reduction or stop smoking programs undertaken for general health, not for specific ailments
- Your divorced spouse's medical bills. You may be able to deduct them as alimony

* A list of some expenses which have been held *not* deductible.

# Chapter 48

# MOVING EXPENSE REIMBURSEMENT

## WHAT IS IT?

Many companies reimburse employees' moving expenses connected with changes in job location. While the reimbursements are taxable income to the employee, the moving expenses may be deductible from the employee's gross income. Moving expense reimbursement, therefore, not only helps employees bear a major expense but can be a form of tax-free compensation for employees.

## WHEN IS IT INDICATED?

Because of the major benefits of a moving expense reimbursement to employees, employers should consider it whenever it is consistent with their recruitment and staffing needs.

## ADVANTAGES

1. A company may have to recruit executives and employees from a wide geographical area; reimbursing moving expenses can help induce a prospective employee to change jobs.

2. Larger companies with more than one geographical location can encourage mobility of their employees among company locations by adopting a moving expense reimbursement policy.

3. A moving expense reimbursement can be a tax-free form of compensation for employees.

4. Employers have complete flexibility in designing moving reimbursement plans. Reimbursement can be offered only to selected employees or even a single employee. Amounts and terms of reimbursement can be varied from employee to employee, and reimbursement can be offered as needs arise without having to adopt a formal plan in advance.

## DISADVANTAGES

1. The *distance* test (see below) requires an employee's new main job location to be at least 50 miles farther from the employee's former home than the old main job location was in order to deduct moving expenses.

2. An employee may not deduct expenses for house hunting or expenses for selling, buying, or leasing a residence.

## TAX IMPLICATIONS

*Employer tax treatment*

1. Moving expense reimbursements to employees or to third parties (moving companies, etc.) on behalf of employees are deductible by the employer as compensation expenses if, together with all other forms of compensation, the amount is reasonable (the "reasonable compensation" test).

2. Reimbursement amounts must be reported as compensation on the employee's Form W-2 for the year. The employer does not have to withhold taxes if it reasonably believes that the employee will be entitled to an offsetting deduction; however, withholding is required on nondeductible moving expense reimbursements.[1]

3. There are no coverage or nondiscrimination rules that limit employer and employee deductions for moving expenses to "nondiscriminatory" plans. Reimbursement can be provided for whatever employee the employer chooses, and in whatever amounts the employer considers appropriate.

*Employee tax treatment*

Employees can deduct moving expenses as an above-the-line deduction (subtracted from gross income), if certain requirements are met.[2] The deduction is subject to a variety of typically complex rules and limitations:

1. the *distance* test

2. the *time* test

3. limitations on the *types of expenses* that are deductible

There are no dollar limits on otherwise deductible expenses.

*Distance test.* A move meets the distance test if the new main job location is at least 50 miles farther from the employee's former home than the old main job location was. For example, if the employee's old job location was 10 miles from his home, the distance test is satisfied if the new job location is at least 60 miles from the old home. Distances are measured by the shortest of the more commonly traveled routes.[3]

*Time test.* To deduct moving expenses, the employee must work full time for at least 39 weeks during the first 12 months after arriving at the new job location. The regulations contain numerous complex exceptions to and variations on this rule.[4]

*Types of expenses deductible.* Deductible moving expenses include only the reasonable costs of the following[5]:

(a) packing, crating, and moving household goods and personal effects (personal effects include a car and household pets; moving expenses include the costs of connecting and disconnecting utilities);

(b) storage and insurance within any consecutive 30-day period after moving out of the former home and before delivery to the new home;

(c) traveling to the new home — a 12 cents/mile allowance for 2003 can be used for travel in the employee's own car.[6] The cost of meals is *not* deductible as a moving expense.

*Nondeductible expenses.* The following expenses are *not* deductible as moving expenses[7]:

- home improvements to help sell the old home

- loss on sale of the old home

- mortgage penalties

- forfeiture of club dues or entry fees

- any part of the purchase price of the new home

- real estate taxes

- car registration or driver's license fees

- reinstalling carpets or draperies

- storage charges other than as described earlier

- expenses for house hunting and expenses for selling, buying, or leasing a residence

*Reporting by Employee.* An employee claiming a moving expense deduction, whether or not the employer provided any reimbursement, must file Form 3903; copies of this form and instructions are reproduced at the end of this chapter.

## ERISA AND OTHER IMPLICATIONS

A moving expense reimbursement plan does not appear to fall within the definition of either a pension or welfare benefit plan for ERISA purposes.[8] Consequently, there is no reporting requirement (so no Form 5500 needs to be filed), nor do any other ERISA provisions apply.

## WHERE CAN I FIND OUT MORE ABOUT IT?

IRS Publication 521, *Moving Expenses*, is available without charge from the IRS.

## QUESTIONS AND ANSWERS

**Question** — Suppose you change jobs to a more distant location and try commuting from your old home for several years, then decide it is too difficult and move closer to the new job. Are moving expenses deductible then?

*Answer* — The IRS position is that moving expenses are not closely related to work at the new job location (and therefore not deductible) unless they are incurred within one year from the date the employee first reported to work at the new job. However, the expenses can be deducted if the employee can show that circumstances did not permit a move within one year, such as the need for children to complete high school in the old location. The IRS probably would not view the circumstances in the question as justifying a moving expense deduction.[9]

**Question** — If an employer wants to protect an employee against obtaining an inadequate price on the forced sale of a residence when moving, what is the best way to do it?

*Answer* — If the employer simply reimburses the employee for any reduction in house/sale proceeds, the reimbursement is taxable income to the employee, and it is not offset by any moving expense or other tax deduction. (Capital losses on the sale of a personal residence by an individual are nondeductible.[10])

It is better from a tax standpoint for the employer to actually buy the house from the employee. Any capital gain (up to $250,000 per taxpayer, if certain requirements are met) that the employee realizes on the sale will generally be excludable under Code section 121. The sale price should be the fair market value as determined by an independent real estate appraiser. Although this price may legitimately be higher than a "forced sale" price, it should not exceed the fair market value, as any excess over fair market value could be deemed to be additional compensation income to the employee.

## FOOTNOTES

1. IRC Section 3401(a)(15).

2. IRC Section 62(a)(15).

3. IRC Section 217(c). However, if the *new* home is farther from the new job location than the old home was, the moving expenses are not deductible on the ground that the move is not related to starting work. Treas. Reg. §1.217-2(a)(3). For example, suppose the old home was 5 miles from the old job. You change job locations to a location 55 miles from the old home. You then move to a new home 60 miles from the new job. The distance test is met because the new job location is at least 50 miles farther from your old home, but moving expenses are not deductible because the move actually produces a longer commute than if you had stayed put. However, you can deduct the moving expenses if you can show that the 60-mile commute takes less time and money than the 55-mile commute from your old home, or if you are required as a condition of employment to live in the new home.

4. IRC Section 217(c)(2); see also, Treas. Reg. §1.217-2(c)(4).

5. The list given here is a summary of the rules in IRC Section 217(b), Treas. Reg. §1.217-2(b), and IRS Pub. 521.

6. News Release 2002-100, September 18, 2002.

7. Treas. Reg. §1.217-2(b)(3); see also, IRS Pub. 521.

8. See DOL Reg. §2510.3-1.

9. See Treas. Reg. §1.217-2(a)(3), Ex. (2).

10. Treas. Reg. §1.165-9(a). If a corporation purchases the house from an employee and later sells it at a loss, the loss is treated by the corporation as a capital loss. *Azar Nut Co. v. Comm.*, 931 F.2d 314 (5th Cir. 1991).

Form **3903**
(Rev. October 2002)
Department of the Treasury
Internal Revenue Service

# Moving Expenses

▶ **Attach to Form 1040.**

OMB No. 1545-0062

Attachment
Sequence No. **62**

Name(s) shown on Form 1040

Your social security number

**Before you begin:** √ See the **Distance Test** and **Time Test** in the instructions to find out if you can deduct your moving expenses.

√ If you are a member of the armed forces, see the instructions to find out how to complete this form.

**1** Enter the amount you paid for transportation and storage of household goods and personal effects (see instructions) . . . . . . . . . . . . . . . . . **1**

**2** Enter the amount you paid for travel and lodging expenses in moving from your old home to your new home. **Do not** include the cost of meals (see instructions) . . . . . . . . . **2**

**3** Add lines 1 and 2 . . . . . . . . . . . . . . . . . **3**

**4** Enter the total amount your employer paid you for the expenses listed on lines 1 and 2 that is **not** included in the wages box (box 1) of your W-2 form. This amount should be identified with code **P** in box 12 of your W-2 form . . . . . . . . . . . . . **4**

**5** Is line 3 **more than** line 4?

☐ **No.** You **cannot** deduct your moving expenses. If line 3 is less than line 4, subtract line 3 from line 4 and include the result on the "Wages, salaries, tips, etc." line of Form 1040.

☐ **Yes.** Subtract line 4 from line 3. Enter the result here and on the "Moving expenses" line of Form 1040. This is your **moving expense deduction** . . . . . . . . . . . . . **5**

## General Instructions

### A Change To Note

For 2002, the standard mileage rate for using your vehicle to move to a new home is 13 cents a mile. Beginning in 2003, the standard mileage rate for using your vehicle to move to a new home is 12 cents a mile.

### Purpose of Form

Use Form 3903 to figure your moving expense deduction for a move related to the start of work at a new principal place of work (workplace). If the new workplace is outside the United States or its possessions, you must be a U.S. citizen or resident alien to deduct your expenses.

If you qualify to deduct expenses for more than one move, use a separate Form 3903 for each move.

For more details, see **Pub. 521,** Moving Expenses.

### Who May Deduct Moving Expenses

If you move to a new home because of a new principal workplace, you may be able to deduct your moving expenses whether you are self-employed or an employee. But you must meet both of the tests explained next.

### Distance Test

Your new principal workplace must be at least 50 miles farther from your old home than your old workplace was. For example, if your old workplace was 3 miles from your old home, your new workplace must be at least 53 miles from that home. If you did not have an old workplace, your new workplace must be at least 50 miles from your old home. The distance between the two points is the shortest of the more commonly traveled routes between them.

 *To see if you meet the distance test, you can use the worksheet below.*

## Distance Test Worksheet

*Keep a Copy for Your Records*

**TIP** *Members of the armed forces may not have to meet this test. For details, see the instructions on the back of this form.*

1. Enter the number of miles from your **old home** to your **new workplace** . . . . . . . . . . . . **1.** _____ miles

2. Enter the number of miles from your **old home** to your **old workplace** . . . . . . . . . . . . **2.** _____ miles

3. Subtract line 2 from line 1. If zero or less, enter -0- . . . . . . . . . . **3.** _____ miles

**Is line 3 at least 50 miles?**
☐ **Yes.** You meet this test.
☐ **No.** You do not meet this test. You **cannot** deduct your moving expenses. **Do not** complete Form 3903.

**For Paperwork Reduction Act Notice, see back of form.**　　Cat. No. 12490K　　Form **3903** (Rev. 10-2002)

# Moving Expense Reimbursement

Form 3903 (Rev. 10-2002)

## Time Test

If you are an employee, you must work full time in the general area of your new workplace for at least 39 weeks during the 12 months right after you move. If you are self-employed, you must work full time in the general area of your new workplace for at least 39 weeks during the first 12 months and a total of at least 78 weeks during the 24 months right after you move.

**What If You Do Not Meet the Time Test Before Your Return Is Due?** If you expect to meet the time test, you may deduct your moving expenses in the year you move. Later, if you do not meet the time test, you must either:

● Amend your tax return for the year you claimed the deduction by filing **Form 1040X,** Amended U.S. Individual Income Tax Return or

● For the year you cannot meet the time test, report as income the amount of your moving expense deduction that reduced your income tax for the year you moved.

If you do not deduct your moving expenses in the year you move and you later meet the time test, you may take the deduction by filing an amended return for the year you moved. To do this, use Form 1040X.

**Exceptions to the Time Test.** You do not have to meet the time test if any of the following apply.

● Your job ends because of disability.

● You are transferred for your employer's benefit.

● You are laid off or discharged for a reason other than willful misconduct.

● You are in the armed forces and the move is due to a permanent change of station (see below).

● You meet the requirements (explained later) for retirees or survivors living outside the United States.

● You are filing this form for a decedent.

**More Information.** For more information on the time test, see Pub. 521.

## Members of the Armed Forces

If you are in the armed forces, you do not have to meet the **distance** and **time tests** if the move is due to a permanent change of station. A permanent change of station includes a move in connection with and within 1 year of retirement or other termination of active duty.

### How To Complete the Form

**Do not** include on lines 1 and 2 any expenses for moving services that were provided by the government. If you and your spouse and dependents are moved to or from different locations, treat the moves as a single move.

On line 4, enter the total reimbursements and allowances you received from the government in connection with the expenses you claimed on lines 1 and 2. **Do not** include the value of moving services provided by the government. Complete line 5 if applicable.

## Retirees or Survivors Living Outside the United States

If you are a retiree or survivor who moved to a home in the United States or its possessions and you meet the following requirements, you are treated as if you moved to a new principal workplace located in the United States. You are subject only to the distance test.

### Retirees

You may deduct moving expenses for a move to a new home in the United States when you actually retire if both your old principal workplace and your old home were outside the United States.

### Survivors

You may deduct moving expenses for a move to a home in the United States if you are the spouse or dependent of a person whose principal workplace at the time of death was outside the United States. In addition, the expenses must be for a move **(a)** that begins within 6 months after the decedent's death and **(b)** from a former home outside the United States that you lived in with the decedent at the time of death.

## Reimbursements

You may choose to deduct moving expenses in the year you are reimbursed by your employer, even though you paid the expenses in a different year. However, special rules apply. See **How To Report** in Pub. 521.

## Filers of Form 2555

If you file **Form 2555,** Foreign Earned Income, to exclude any of your income or housing costs, report the full amount of your deductible moving expenses on Form 3903 and on Form 1040. Report the part of your moving expenses that is not allowed because it is allocable to the excluded income on the appropriate line of Form 2555. For details on how to figure the part allocable to the excluded income, see **Pub. 54,** Tax Guide for U.S. Citizens and Resident Aliens Abroad.

## Specific Instructions

You may deduct the following expenses you paid to move your family and dependent household members. Do not deduct expenses for employees such as a maid, nanny, or nurse.

### Line 1

**Moves Within or to the United States or its Possessions.** Enter the amount you paid to pack, crate, and move your household goods and personal effects. You may also include the amount you paid to store and insure household goods and personal effects within any period of 30 days in a row after the items were moved from your old home and before they were delivered to your new home.

**Moves Outside the United States or its Possessions.** Enter the amount you paid to pack, crate, move, store, and insure your household goods and personal effects. Also, include the amount you paid to move your personal effects to and from storage and to store them for all or part of the time the new workplace continues to be your principal workplace.

 *You do not have to complete this form if **(a)** you moved in an earlier year, **(b)** you are claiming only storage fees during your absence from the United States, and **(c)** any amount your employer paid for the storage fees is included in the wages box of your W-2 form. Instead, enter the storage fees on the "Moving expenses" line of Form 1040, and write "Storage" next to the amount.*

### Line 2

Enter the amount you paid to travel from your old home to your new home. This includes transportation and lodging on the way. Include costs for the day you arrive. Although not all the members of your household have to travel together or at the same time, you may only include expenses for one trip per person.

If you use your own vehicle(s), you may figure the expenses by using either:

● Actual out-of-pocket expenses for gas and oil or

● Mileage at the rate of 13 cents a mile (12 cents a mile for 2003).

You may add parking fees and tolls to the amount claimed under either method. Keep records to verify your expenses.

**Paperwork Reduction Act Notice.** We ask for the information on this form to carry out the Internal Revenue laws of the United States. You are required to give us the information. We need it to ensure that you are complying with these laws and to allow us to figure and collect the right amount of tax.

You are not required to provide the information requested on a form that is subject to the Paperwork Reduction Act unless the form displays a valid OMB control number. Books or records relating to a form or its instructions must be retained as long as their contents may become material in the administration of any Internal Revenue law. Generally, tax returns and return information are confidential, as required by Internal Revenue Code section 6103.

The time needed to complete and file this form will vary depending on individual circumstances. The estimated average time is: **Recordkeeping,** 33 min.; **Learning about the law or the form,** 9 min.; **Preparing the form,** 15 min.; and **Copying, assembling, and sending the form to the IRS,** 13 min.

If you have comments concerning the accuracy of these time estimates or suggestions for making this form simpler, we would be happy to hear from you. See the Instructions for Form 1040.

# Chapter 49

# RESTRICTED STOCK PLAN

## WHAT IS IT?

A restricted stock plan is an arrangement to compensate executives by giving them shares of stock subject to certain restrictions or limitations. Usually, the stock used in such plans is stock of the employer corporation or its subsidiary.

Company stock is attractive to executives as an element of compensation, because it allows sharing in company growth. To the employer, the use of stock is attractive as a "double incentive" plan for executives, because the terms of the plan can be based on executive performance, and, in addition, increases in the value of the stock may reflect, to some extent, the executive's performance.

Employers often adopt stock plans with restrictions designed to help retain employees or discourage conduct that the employer deems undesirable, such as going to work for a competitor. These restrictions can also serve the employee's interest, by postponing taxation of compensation to the employee.

For an outline of some advanced types of stock and other plans used for compensating executives, particularly in large corporations, see Appendix D.

## WHEN IS IT INDICATED?

1. When the employer is willing to create new shareholders of the company. Shareholders of a closely held corporation often do not want to share company stock and potential control of the business outside of the existing group of shareholders.

2. When a corporation wants to provide an executive with an incentive-based form of compensation. In restricted stock plans, the ultimate amount the executive receives generally depends on the value of the stock. If the plan is well designed, the value of company stock will reflect the executive's performance, at least to some extent.

3. When an employer wants to use a compensation arrangement as a way of discouraging certain specified conduct, such as leaving employment within a short time or going to work for a competitor.

4. When an executive wants an "equity-based" form of compensation—that is, compensation based on the value of the company's stock. Equity-based compensation allows an executive to share in the upside potential of a company's growth. This type of compensation is particularly useful in the start-up phase of a high technology company, where growth can be very significant.

## ADVANTAGES

1. Restricted stock plans can allow deferral of taxation to the employee until the year in which the restricted stock becomes "substantially vested." Essentially, this means nonforfeitable, as discussed below under "Tax Implications."

2. A stock plan allows employees an interest in the increase in value of a company's stock. This type of payment, especially when coupled with deferral of taxation, can be much more valuable than straight cash compensation.

3. A restricted stock plan allows an employer to grant an executive an equity interest in the company, but withdraw it if the executive leaves prematurely or goes to work for a competitor.

4. For non-tax purposes, an executive has all the advantages of stock ownership, such as voting rights, dividends, and appreciation potential, but is not taxed on receipt of the stock to the extent it is not substantially vested.

## DISADVANTAGES

1. The employer does not receive a tax deduction for a restricted stock plan until the year in which the property becomes substantially vested, and therefore taxable to the executive (unless the executive elects to be taxed earlier under Section 83(b), as discussed under "Tax Implications," below).

2. The possibility of a Section 83(b) election by the executive means that the employer may not have control of the amount or timing of its tax deduction.

3. S corporations must be certain that the restrictions do not create a second class of stock, which would violate the S corporation one-class-of-stock rule. An S corporation that violates this rule will terminate its S election, thus subjecting all corporate income to taxation at ordinary corporate rates.

Generally, an S corporation will not be treated as having more than one class of shares so long as all shares confer identical rights to liquidation and distribution proceeds. Thus, guaranteed distributions following a vesting period may violate the rule unless all shares enjoy the same guaranteed distributions. Ordinary contractual arrangements, such as employment agreements, will not be deemed to affect distribution and liquidation proceeds, unless a principal purpose of the arrangement is to circumvent the one-class rule.

4. Issuing new shares of restricted stock tends to dilute ownership of the corporation. This may be particularly undesirable for closely held corporations. Shareholders of these corporations seldom want to share control or profits, or share company assets upon sale or liquidation of the business.

5. If the change (up or down) in value of the stock is not consistent with the executive's performance, this can be disadvantageous to both employer and executive. If the stock goes up with little or no effort by the executive, other shareholders will be resentful. If the stock drops in value in spite of excellent executive performance, the incentive element of the plan is lost or diminished.

## WHAT CAN BE ACCOMPLISHED WITH RESTRICTIONS ON STOCK

The types of restrictions used in restricted stock plans can be tailored to meet employer and employee objectives.

### Employee Retention

Employers often use stock plans to tie key employees to the company. With this type of objective, for example, stock might be transferred to an employee subject to a restriction that it cannot be sold or otherwise transferred by the employee during a specified period—such as five years. If the employee quits before this time, the stock must be returned to the company. This simple form of restriction can also be used as a way of keeping retirees tied to the company and providing them with some useful deferral of income. The stock can be transferred to an executive retiree, subject to a provision that the retiree remain available for consulting services to the employer during a specified time, such as five years.

### Discouraging Misconduct

Restrictions can also be associated with specific employee conduct that the company wants to discourage. For example, a restricted stock plan might provide that stock must be returned to the employer if, during a period of five years, the employee is discharged by the company for cause, or discharged for some specific reason, such as embezzlement or disclosure of trade or marketing information. In certain industries, typically high technology industries, stock in restricted stock plans is forfeitable if the employee engages in competition with the employer—for example, starts a competitive business or goes to work for a competitor.

From a contractual point of view, restrictions involving noncompetition agreements may be unenforceable in the courts if they go beyond reasonable limits. However, the courts generally will enforce a noncompetition provision if it is *reasonable* with respect to: (1) the geographic area to which it applies; and (2) the period of time to which it applies.

---

*Example:* Suppose Apex Industries operates a plumbing fixture business only on the east coast, and has no plans to expand geographically. Apex's restricted stock agreement with employee Hank, aged 35, provides a forfeiture of stock if Hank works in a competing business anywhere in the country. Hank quits and starts a plumbing fixture business in California. If Apex tries to enforce the noncompetition provision, the courts are likely to deem it unreasonable and unenforceable because it goes beyond a reasonably broad geographic area. The same result would probably apply if the plan restricted Hank from competing in the immediate geographic area "for the rest of his life."

---

## Incentives

Restricted stock plans can be designed as incentive plans, similar to bonus plans. For example, a restricted stock plan might give an executive 1,000 shares of company stock, subject to a forfeiture if gross sales in the executive's division do not increase by at least 20% within five years. When sales reach the targeted level, the forfeitability restrictions would end. The stock would then belong to the executive without restriction. The advantage of this arrangement over a cash bonus is simply that it increases the security of the benefit to the employee, compared with the employer's mere promise to pay a cash bonus. However, there are some risks, from the employee's point of view, when compared with the stated contingent bonus amount, because the value of the stock could very well go down, even though the employee works effectively and meets or exceeds the designated target sales level.

## TAX IMPLICATIONS

1.  Under Section 83 of the Internal Revenue Code, an employee is not subject to tax on the value of restricted property received as compensation from the employer until the year in which the property becomes "substantially vested" (unless the employee makes a "Section 83(b) election" to include it in income in the year received, as discussed in Section 2, below).

    The definition of substantial vesting in Section 83 and the regulations thereunder is of great significance in designing restricted stock plans. These plans are obviously much less attractive to employees if they are not carefully designed to provide tax deferral within the rules of Section 83.

    ---

    *Example:* If an employee receives restricted stock in 2003 that is deemed (for tax purposes) to be substantially vested in 2003, the employee will pay tax in that year (and the corporation will get a corresponding deduction; see below), even if, under state law, the employee does not completely own the stock. In spite of the taxability to the employee, the restrictions on the stock received may still be legally effective under state property law, so that the employee cannot sell the stock in 2003 and realize any cash at that time.

    ---

    *Substantial vesting.* Under Section 83, property is not considered substantially vested, so long as it is subject to a "substantial risk of forfeiture" and is not transferable by an employee to a third party free of this risk of forfeiture.

    The question of whether a substantial risk of forfeiture exists depends on the facts and circumstances in each case. The regulations under Section 83 contain various examples and guidelines.

    • Generally, a substantial risk of forfeiture is considered to exist if the employee must return the property unless a specified period of service for the employer is completed.[1]

    • In general, a forfeiture that occurs only as a result of some event that is relatively unlikely would not constitute a substantial risk of forfeiture. For example, the plan might provide that an employee must return the stock if he commits embezzlement within a specified period of time. This unlikely event, which furthermore is within the control of the employee, probably would not constitute a substantial risk of forfeiture,[2] and the executive would therefore be taxed immediately upon receipt of the stock.

    • A forfeiture that occurs as a result of a failure to meet certain incentive targets, such as a certain level of sales, generally is a substantial risk of forfeiture.[3]

    • A forfeiture that occurs as a result of going to work for a competitor constitutes a substantial risk if the employee has scarce skills in an active job market.[4]

    Where an employee is an owner or major shareholder of a company, forfeiture provisions of almost any type are likely to be challenged by the IRS as being insubstantial, because the employee's control or influence over the company can render them relatively ineffective.[5]

    As indicated above, property will not be considered subject to a substantial risk of forfeiture if it can be transferred by the employee to another person or entity free of the risk of forfeiture. When employer stock is used in a restricted stock plan, this requirement is usually met by a "legend" or statement imprinted on share certificates indicating that transfer and ownership of the shares are subject to a restricted property plan. This notifies any prospective buyer or other recipient that the employee is not free to sell, give away, or otherwise transfer the shares without restrictions.

2. Under Section 83(b), an executive can elect to recognize income as of the date when he receives the restricted property, rather than waiting until it becomes substantially vested. This election must be made within 30 days of receiving the property and must comply with requirements in the IRS regulations.

The amount included in income under this Section 83(b) election is the excess, if any, of the fair market value of the property at the time of transfer (determined without regard to any restrictions other than "non-lapse" restrictions—see below) over any amount the executive paid for the property. For example, if the stock is worth $60 per share at the time of receipt and the executive pays nothing for it, under a Section 83(b) election, the executive would report ordinary income of $60 per share in the year of receipt.

Why would an executive make a Section 83(b) election? Because if a Section 83(b) election is made, any subsequent appreciation in value of the property is treated as capital gain and taxed at lower capital gain rates. That gain is not subject to tax until the stock is sold. This can be a major consideration in deciding whether to make a Section 83(b) election. Section 83(b) elections may also be advantageous in special situations; for example, where the executive wants to maximize taxable income in a particular year in order to offset deductible losses.

When an executive includes an amount in income under a Section 83(b) election, the employer gets a tax deduction at that time for the same amount. The employer gets no further tax deduction if the property subsequently increases in value in the hands of the executive, whether or not the executive sells the property. Another disadvantage of the Section 83(b) election is that if the stock is forfeited for any reason, no deduction is allowed to the executive for the loss.

The executive making a Section 83(b) election is therefore gambling that the stock will increase substantially in value from the date of the election and that the stock will not be forfeited before the executive is able to sell or dispose of it without restriction.

3. Sometimes the stock received does not have a forfeiture provision as such, but rather has a restriction that reduces the value of the stock to the employee. In that case, the value of the stock is includable in income when received. But the amount includable is less than the full market value.

---

*Example:* A plan may provide an employee with a fully vested interest in the stock, but with a provision that the employee cannot re-sell the stock without first offering it back to the company at a specified price. In that case, because of the "first offer" provision, the value of the stock in the hands of the executive would not be its unfettered market value, but rather a reduced value reflecting the restriction.

---

A restriction will be taken into account for valuation purposes only if it is a "non-lapse restriction"—a restriction that, by its terms, will never lapse.[6] The first offer requirement of the type described in the example above would probably qualify as a non-lapse restriction. Whether a restriction constitutes a non-lapse restriction is a facts and circumstances determination. The IRS takes a restrictive view in its regulations and rulings, so non-lapse restrictions are difficult to design.

4. When an employee has become substantially vested in restricted property, its value is taxed in that year as compensation income.[7] Gain on any subsequent sale of the property is generally taxed as capital gain, as in the case of similar property acquired by any other means.

5. The employer's tax deduction for compensation income to the executive under a restricted stock plan is deferred until the year in which the employee is substantially vested and includes the amount in income. Technically, the employer's tax deduction occurs in the employer's taxable year in which, or with which, the taxable year of the employee in whose income the amount is includable ends.[8] This is the usual rule for the timing of an employer's deduction for deferred compensation payments, as discussed in Chapter 30. As with other types of compensation, the employer is required to withhold and pay tax and in order to meet certain informational requirements. However, the IRS has withdrawn a provision that conditioned the employer's deduction upon the employer's actually withholding and paying tax.[9]

## WHERE CAN I FIND OUT MORE ABOUT IT?

1. Leimberg, Stephan R. et al., *The Federal Income Tax Law*. Warren, Gorham, and Lamont, 1997.

2. Graduate Course: Executive Compensation (GS 842), The American College, Bryn Mawr, PA.

## QUESTIONS AND ANSWERS

**Question** — How does a restricted stock plan affect an employer's accounting statements?

*Answer* — If stock is issued with restrictions based only on continued employment, the excess of the stock's fair market value when issued over the amount paid for it by the executive is a compensation expense for accounting purposes and is charged to earnings on a systematic basis over the related period of employment—the period during which the restrictions are in effect. If restrictions are based on contingent factors such as executive or company performance, the charge to expense can be delayed until the result is known for certain. These rules are set out in the currently effective official accounting statement, APB 25. The accounting profession is currently reconsidering the treatment of many executive compensation arrangements and some changes may appear in the future.

**Question** — Do federal securities laws apply to restricted stock, and what is their effect?

*Answer* — Federal securities registration is not generally required if stock is issued without cost, because no "sale" is deemed to occur for securities law purposes. However, the SEC (Securities Exchange Commission) views stock issued to executives as compensation to have been bargained for and thus sold, so the securities laws may apply. Many restricted stock arrangements qualify for one or more of the exemptions from securities registration, typically the "private placement" exemption, whereby registration is not required where securities are issued to a limited number of persons.

Planners must also determine whether executives are restricted under the federal securities laws from re-selling stock acquired under the plan. SEC Rule 144 includes conditions under which such stock can be resold freely. Executives holding stock in a restricted stock plan may also be subject to the anti-fraud provisions of the securities law, such as the insider trading restrictions.

## FOOTNOTES

1. Treas. Reg. §1.83-3(c)(1).
2. Treas. Reg. §1.83-3(c)(2).
3. Ibid.
4. Ibid.
5. Treas. Reg. §1.83-3(c)(3).
6. Treas. Regs. §§1.83-5(a), 1.83-3(h).
7. IRC Section 83(a).
8. Treas. Reg. §1.83-6(a)(1).
9. Treas. Reg. §1.83-6(a)(2).

# Chapter 50

# SEVERANCE PAY PLAN

## WHAT IS IT?

A severance pay plan is an agreement between employer and employee to make payments after the employee's termination of employment.

Severance pay arrangements are almost completely flexible if characterization as an ERISA pension plan is avoided (see below). If ERISA's pension plan rules do not apply, the plan can cover any group of employees or even a single employee, on any terms and conditions that the employer considers appropriate. For example, provided that ERISA's pension plan rules do not apply to a severance pay arrangement, payments thereunder can be withheld if the employee's service is severed due to misconduct. Severance agreements can be, and often are, negotiated individually with executives.

For a discussion of additional considerations that apply where severance pay is contingent upon a change in corporate ownership, see Chapter 37, Golden Parachute Plan. See also Chapter 54, Welfare Benefit Trusts and VEBAs, for plans that pay severance benefits from prefunded trust arrangements.

## TAX IMPLICATIONS

1.  Severance payments are deductible by the employer if: (a) the payments are compensation for services previously rendered by the employee, and (b) the payments are reasonable in amount.[1]

    Severance payments made pursuant to a written plan or agreement, which is entered into while the employee is still actively at work, should be considered compensation for services in most cases. The promised severance benefits in such a case are considered part of the employer's pay/benefit package, which compensates the employee for services. However, if there is no written plan or agreement in place prior to termination of employment, the IRS could argue that the payment is something other than compensation—such as a gift, a dividend, a "buy out" payment for the employee's interest in the business, or whatever other characterization

might fit the particular facts of the situation. Planners should counsel clients to try to avoid this result by adopting formal severance plans, policies, or agreements.

The "reasonableness" test which applies to severance pay arrangements is the same test that applies to all forms of compensation payments. (See the discussion in Chapter 30, Cash Compensation Planning.)

2.  *Unfunded Plan.* If the severance pay plan is unfunded (i.e., no assets are placed beyond the reach of the employer's creditors), severance payments are taxable to the recipient as compensation income in the year actually or constructively received.[2]

    Employers should be aware of the constructive receipt issue concerning severance payments.

    *Example.* Suppose employee Bob Cratchit is terminated on December 24, 2003 and is entitled to an immediate severance benefit of $350 (two weeks' pay). Bob asks his employer to give him a tax break by paying the severance benefit on January 2, 2004, and the employer does so. Technically, Bob has run afoul of the constructive receipt doctrine (see Chapter 15 for discussion); he should report the $350 severance benefit in 2003, because he had an unrestricted right to receive the payments in 2003.

    While the IRS may sometimes overlook small "constructive receipt" issues in situations like the Cratchit example, they will be alert to constructive receipt where substantial amounts are involved.

    *Example.* Suppose an executive severance pay plan provides a severance benefit of 1½ years' salary, payable over a 2-year period. If the executive has no option but the 2-year payment, the payments will be included in income as they are received. However, if the executive can choose, at the time when he severs employment or thereafter, to accelerate the payment schedule to one year (without risk of forfeiting the benefit), then the entire amount must be reported as received in that one year, even if the executive actually chooses to and does receive it over a 2-year period. Careful drafting of the agreement is essential to avoid such unexpected tax results.

---

*Funded Plan.* A severance pay plan is considered to be funded if assets are set aside beyond the reach of the employer's creditors (typically in a trust) solely to pay plan benefits to employees. (The concept of funding is discussed at length in Chapter 15.) Severance pay plans funded through welfare benefit trusts or voluntary employees' beneficiary associations (VEBAs) are of current interest among compensation planners; these are discussed in Chapter 54. If severance pay benefits are funded, the value of the benefit is taxable to the employee in the first year in which he no longer has a substantial risk of forfeiting the benefit. This could result in taxation before the employee has actual or constructive receipt of the benefits. For example, suppose a funded plan provides severance benefits, payable in two equal annual installments, upon the employee's involuntary termination, death, or disability. Unless the plan provides a substantial risk of forfeiture that continues after termination, death, or disability, the full value of the benefits will be taxable in the year in which the employee terminates, dies, or becomes disabled, even if actual payment is spread over two years.

3. If the severance payment is characterized as a "parachute payment," the employer's deduction may be limited and the employee may be subject to penalty. In general, parachute payments are severance payments that take effect upon changes in business ownership. The parachute rules are discussed in Chapter 37.

4. In general, the tax consequences of a severance pay plan (whether or not it is governed by ERISA, as discussed below) are similar to those of a nonqualified deferred compensation plan. Refer to Chapter 15 for a discussion of further tax considerations.

5. Final regulations provide guidance on the Social Security tax treatment of nonqualified deferred compensation.[3] According to the final regulations, certain welfare benefits are not treated as deferred compensation for FICA purposes. In particular, the IRS believes that severance pay in general is not subject to the special timing rule[4] for nonqualified deferred compensation, which provides that any amount deferred shall be taken into account for FICA purposes, as of the later of: (1) when the services are performed; or (2) when there is no substantial risk of forfeiting the rights to the amount deferred.[5]

## ERISA IMPLICATIONS

1. Labor Department regulations provide that a severance pay plan will not be considered a "pension plan," for ERISA purposes, if the following requirements are met:[6]

   • Payments are not contingent, directly or indirectly, upon retirement;

   • The total payments do not exceed twice the employee's annual compensation for the year immediately preceding the termination of employment; and

   • All payments are completed within 24 months after termination of employment (or, in the case of a "limited program of terminations," within the later of 24 months after termination or 24 months after the employee reaches normal retirement age).

   If these conditions are met, the plan will be considered a "welfare benefit plan" for ERISA purposes. See Appendix A for the reporting requirements applicable to welfare plans.

2. If a severance pay plan does not meet the ERISA "pension plan" exemption described above, it will be treated essentially as a nonqualified deferred compensation plan for ERISA purposes. Unfunded plans for a select group of executives may be eligible for the ERISA "top hat" limited exemption, as discussed in Chapter 15. See also the discussion of this issue in Chapter 54.

3. If the plan covers only a single person and was individually negotiated, some courts have found that ERISA is not applicable because there is no "plan for employees."[7] Therefore, for example, there would be no reporting requirements. However, many employers might want to file "protective" ERISA filings to avoid possible penalties.

## FOOTNOTES

1. Treas. Reg. §1.162-7.
2. Treas. Reg. §1.61-2(a).
3. Treas. Reg. §31.3121(v)(2)-1.
4. IRC Section 3121(v)(2)(A).
5. See Treas. Reg. §31.3121(v)(2)-1(b)(4)(iv).
6. Labor Reg. §2510.3-2(b).
7. See, e.g., *Motel 6, Inc. v. Superior Court*, 195 Cal. App. 3d 1464; 241 Cal. Rptr. 528 (1987). The leading case on this issue is *Fort Halifax Packing Co. v. Coyne*, 48 U.S. 1 (1987).

# Chapter 51

# SICK PAY (SHORT TERM DISABILITY)

## WHAT IS IT?

A sick pay or short term disability plan is a plan that continues employees' salary or wages for a limited time during periods of illness or other disability. Generally, sick pay or short term disability payments do not extend beyond about six months. Programs covering disabilities lasting longer than six months are generally considered long term disability programs, and are discussed in Chapter 46.

## WHEN IS IT INDICATED?

1. Almost all employers have a broad based program providing some sick pay for short absences from work. This is a "high visibility" benefit that employees count on and appreciate.

2. An employer may want to provide special favorable short term disability programs for selected executives. Under current law, such plans can be provided on a discriminatory basis. That is, the employer can choose (1) who will be covered; (2) the level of benefits, which can vary from employee to employee; and (3) the terms and conditions of coverage.

## DESIGN FEATURES

Most planners divide short term coverage into two types of plans: (1) sick pay; and (2) short term disability plans. Although there is some overlap in these concepts, *sick pay* generally refers to uninsured continuation of salary or wages (usually 100% replacement) for a short period of time beginning on the first day of illness or disability. A *short term disability plan* is one that goes into effect when the employee's sick pay benefits run out and extends until the six month limit has been reached, when the employer's long term disability plan (if any) and Social Security disability go into effect. Short term plans, as defined this way, can be and often are insured.

## Sick Pay

Sick pay benefits are usually provided for a broad group of employees. However, an employer can have a plan for selected executives only, or a plan with more favorable benefits for executives.

Usually, only full-time employees are covered under sick pay plans. The employer can define the term "full-time" for this purpose in any reasonable manner; the 1,000 hour "year of service" definition applicable to qualified plans does not apply.

The duration of sick pay benefits is often tied to the length of an employee's service. For example, there may be no benefits until an employee has completed three months of service, then the plan will provide full benefits. Or, duration of benefits can be graded, based on service. For example, employees may be entitled to 20 days of sick pay annually after 10 years of service, with the number of days of sick pay reduced for shorter service. One danger in providing increasingly generous sick pay as a "benefit" is that employees may come to believe that they are expected to take advantage of such sick days and abuse the benefit.

Some sick pay plans allow "carryover" of unused benefits. For example, if an employee is entitled to 10 days of sick pay in 2003 and uses only five of them, then the plan could allow the employee to carry over these five days to 2004, thus having 15 days of sick pay available in 2004. Plans allowing carryovers usually provide some maximum limit on the sick pay available for any one year. Usually, no more than six months of sick pay can be accumulated.

If long periods of sick pay are allowed, benefits are often reduced below 100% of salary after a specified period of time (such as 30 days). This reduces employer costs and helps to "phase in" the long term benefits available, which usually do not provide 100% salary replacement.

Preventing sick pay abuse is a major management problem in many organizations. Some employers require a physician's certificate to obtain sick pay, particularly if the employee's absence is longer than one week. In some organizations, management simply accepts the idea that employees will take whatever "sick days" are available and limits them accordingly. Generally speaking, absenteeism is a symptom of management problems that cannot be solved simply by the design of employee benefit programs.

### Short Term Disability Plans

A short term disability plan fills the gap between sick pay and the employer's long term disability plan, if any. These plans are often insured, particularly for smaller employers, since the employer's liability to continue a disabled employee's salary for six months or so can be a considerable burden.

The design of short term plans, particularly if they are insured, is similar to the long term plans discussed in Chapter 46. However, there are some significant differences:

- Short term plans often have broader coverage than long term plans. An employer's long term plan may be limited to selected executives.

- Short term plans often require less service for coverage. Long term plans may be reserved for career employees, such as those with five or more years of service.

- The definition of disability is typically more generous (i.e., easier to meet) in a short term plan than in a long term plan. Usually the "regular occupation" definition is used. That is, disability in a short term plan is typically defined as "the total and continuous inability of the employee to perform any and every duty of his or her regular occupation."

Coverage exclusions in insured short term plans are similar to those in long term plans, as discussed in Chapter 46. As with long term plans, the Civil Rights Act of 1964 prohibits exclusion of pregnancy-related disabilities if the employer has 15 or more employees. (State civil rights laws may apply even to smaller employers.)

### TAX IMPLICATIONS

1. The employer can deduct payments made directly to employees under a sick pay or short term disabil-

ity plan, as compensation to employees. The employer can also deduct premium payments made under an insured plan. Like all compensation deductions, these payments are subject to the "reasonableness" requirement described in Chapter 30.

2. In some insured plans, employees pay part of the cost of the plan, usually through payroll deductions. These payments are not tax deductible by the employee.

3. Employer payments of premiums under an insured disability plan do not result in taxable income to the employee.[1]

4. Benefit payments under an employer-paid plan are fully taxable to the employee as received (subject to the credit described below) if the plan was fully paid for by the employer. If the employer paid only part of the cost, then only a corresponding part of the benefit is taxable, again subject to the credit. For example, if the employer paid 75% of the disability insurance premiums and the employee paid the remaining 25%, only 75% of the disability benefit received by the employee would be taxable.[2]

   IRS regulations specify the time over which the employer and employee percentages are to be measured for this purpose. For group disability insurance, generally, payments over the three year period prior to the disability are taken into account in determining the percentages paid by employer and employee.[3]

5. *Disability credit.* If an employee receiving benefits meets the "total and permanent" disability definition, a limited tax credit reduces the tax impact of disability payments for lower-income recipients.[4] Because of this definition, the credit has little or no impact on most employees receiving sick pay or short term benefits, but it may come into effect for more serious or long term conditions.

   "Total and permanent disability" (the Social Security definition) means a condition under which the individual "is unable to engage in any substantial gainful activity by reason of any medically determinable physical or mental impairment which can be expected to result in death or which has lasted or can be expected to last for a continuous period of not less than 12 months."[5] This is the strictest disability definition that is commonly used for any purpose.

Generally, the disability credit is calculated by taking the maximum amount subject to the credit (see below) and subtracting one half of the amount by which the taxpayer's adjusted gross income exceeds the AGI limits (see below). The credit is equal to 15% of this amount. Thus, the maximum annual tax credit is $1,125 for a joint return as indicated below. The chart below shows the maximum amounts eligible for the credit, the maximum credit that may be obtained and the limitations to adjusted gross income (AGI):

### MAXIMUM AMOUNT SUBJECT TO CREDIT

| | |
|---|---|
| Single Person | $5,000 |
| Joint Return (where one spouse is a qualified individual) | $5,000 |
| Joint Return (where both spouses are qualified individuals) | $7,500 |
| Married Filing Separately | $3,750 |

### MAXIMUM CREDIT

| | |
|---|---|
| Single Person | $750 |
| Joint Return (where one spouse is a qualified individual) | $750 |
| Joint Return (where both spouses are qualified individuals) | $1,125 |
| Married Filing Separately | $562.50 |

### ADJUSTED GROSS INCOME LIMITS

| | |
|---|---|
| Single Person | $7,500 |
| Married Filing Jointly | $10,000 |
| Married Filing Separately | $5,000 |

*Example:* If a disabled employee has adjusted gross income (from all sources, including taxable disability income) of $14,000, and is married, filing jointly, the amount on which his disability tax credit is calculated would be $5,000 (the maximum amount for a joint return where only one spouse receives disability income payments) less $2,000 (½ of the amount by which the taxpayer's AGI exceeds $10,000). In short, this is $5,000 - $2,000, or $3,000. The taxpayer's credit is equal to 15% of $3,000, or $450. Accordingly, the employee's income tax bill for the year is reduced by $450. Note that, to receive this credit, the employee must meet the Social Security total and permanent definition of disability. An employee might receive benefits under some employer plans without meeting this strict definition of disability, as discussed above.

This tax credit is even further reduced by 15% of any tax-free income received by the employee from a pension, annuity, or disability benefit, including Social Security. Since most disability plans are integrated with Social Security benefits, this further reduction makes the credit even less valuable.

In view of all the reductions applicable to this credit, and the extremely low AGI limits on full availability, the credit is a minor factor in the design of disability benefits, and plays practically no part in designing benefits for executives.

6. Disability insurance premiums paid by the employer under the plan are not considered wages subject to employment taxes (FICA—Social Security—and FUTA—federal unemployment).[6] Generally, disability insurance premiums are not subject to state employment taxes either, but individual state laws should be consulted.

7. Disability benefits are subject to federal income tax withholding if paid directly by the employer. If paid by a third party, such as an insurance company, withholding is required only if the employee requests it.[7]

8. Disability benefits attributable to employer contributions are subject to Social Security taxes for a limited period at the beginning of a disability. Thereafter, they are not considered wages subject to Social Security tax.[8]

## ERISA REQUIREMENTS

A sick pay or short term disability income plan is considered a welfare benefit plan under ERISA (see Appendix A). Such plans require a written summary plan description, the naming of a plan administrator, and a formal written claims procedure by which employees can make benefit claims and appeal denials. The plan is not subject to the eligibility, vesting, or funding requirements of ERISA. The plan administrator must provide plan participants with a summary plan description (SPD).

## WHERE CAN I FIND OUT MORE ABOUT IT?

1. Beam, Burton T., Jr. and John J. McFadden, *Employee Benefits*, 6th ed. Chicago, IL: Dearborn Financial Publishing, Inc., 2000.

2. *Tax Facts 1.* Cincinnati, OH: *The National Underwriter Company.* Revised annually.

## FOOTNOTES

1. IRC Section 106(a).
2. IRC Sections 104(a)(3), 105(a); Treas. Reg. §1.105-1(d).
3. Treas. Regs. §§1.105-1(d), 1.105-1(e).
4. IRC Section 22.
5. IRC Section 22(e)(3).
6. IRC Sections 3121(a)(2), 3306(b)(2).
7. IRC Section 3402(o).
8. IRC Section 3121(a)(4).

# Chapter 52

# SPLIT DOLLAR LIFE INSURANCE

## WHAT IS IT?

Split dollar life insurance is an arrangement, typically between an employer and an employee, in which there is a sharing of the costs and benefits of the life insurance policy. (Split dollar plans can also be adopted for purposes other than providing an employee benefit—for example between a parent corporation and a subsidiary, or between a parent and a child or in-law.) Usually split dollar plans involve a splitting of premiums, death benefits, and/or cash values, but they may also involve the splitting of dividends or ownership.

Under the classic approach, the employer corporation pays that part of the annual premium which equals the current year's increase in the cash surrender value of the policy. The employee pays the balance, if any, of the premium. In the long run this provides a low outlay protection incentive for selected employees to stay with the employer. If the insured employee dies, the corporation recovers its outlay (an amount equal to the cumulative cash value) and the balance of the policy proceeds is paid to the beneficiary chosen by the employee.

New regulations governing split dollar plans were proposed in 2002 and could be finalized in 2003. As discussed below, these proposed regulations extensively change the federal income tax rules applicable to split dollar plans. Most planners believe that the new rules will make split dollar plans less attractive than they were in the past.

## WHEN IS IT INDICATED?

1.  When an employer wishes to provide an executive with a life insurance benefit at low cost and low outlay to the executive. Split dollar plans are best suited for executives in their 30's, 40's, and early 50's because the plan requires a reasonable duration in order to build up adequate policy cash values and the cost to the executive (the P.S. 58 or Table 2001 cost—see below) can be excessive at later ages.

2.  When a preretirement death benefit for an employee is a major objective, split dollar can be used as an alternative to an insurance-financed nonqualified deferred compensation plan.

3.  When an employer is seeking a totally selective executive fringe benefit. An employer can reward or provide incentives for employees on a "pick and choose" basis. Neither the coverage, amounts, nor the terms of the split dollar arrangement need to meet nondiscrimination rules that add cost and complexity to many other benefit plans.

4.  When an employer wants to make it easier for shareholder-employees to finance a buy out of stock under a cross purchase buy-sell agreement or make it possible for non-stockholding employees to effect a one way stock purchase at an existing shareholder's death. This helps establish a market for what otherwise might be unmarketable stock while providing an incentive for bright, creative, productive employees to remain with the company and increase profits.

## ADVANTAGES

1.  A split dollar plan allows an executive to receive a benefit of current value (namely, life insurance coverage) using employer funds, with minimal or no tax cost to the executive.

2.  In most types of split dollar plans, the employer's outlay is at all times fully secured. At the employee's death or termination of employment, the employer is reimbursed from policy proceeds for its premium outlay. The net cost to the employer for the plan is merely the loss of the net after-tax income the funds could have earned while the plan was in effect. If a split dollar plan is treated as a loan, the employer may recognize taxable income as part of the transaction.

3.  Many types of split dollar design are possible so the plan can be customized to meet employer and employee objectives and premium paying abilities.

## DISADVANTAGES

1. The employer receives no tax deduction for its share of premium payments under the split dollar plan.

2. The employee must pay income taxes each year on the current cost of life insurance protection under the plan (less any premiums paid by the employee). This cost may be determined by using either P.S. 58 rates or one-year term insurance rates published by the insurance company, or Table 2001 rates, as discussed below.

3. The plan must remain in effect for a reasonably long time—10 to 20 years—in order for policy cash values to rise to a level sufficient to maximize plan benefits.

4. The plan must generally be terminated at approximately age 65, because the employee's tax cost for the plan rises sharply at later ages.

5. Plans that provide for an employee share in the policy's cash value—equity-type split dollar plans—have been attractive in the past because they provide a savings or investment benefit for the employee, but under new regulations the tax treatment of these plans is unfavorable.

## DESIGN FEATURES

In a split dollar arrangement between employer and employee, at least three aspects of the policy can be subject to different types of "split": (1) the premium cost, (2) the cash value, and (3) the policy ownership. Following is a brief discussion of these variations, their advantages and disadvantages, and when they are used.

### Premium Cost Split

There are four major categories of premium split:

(a) the classic or *standard* split dollar plan under which the employer pays a portion of the premiums equal to the increase in cash surrender value of the policy for the year, or the net premium due, if lower. (See Figure 52.1.) The employee pays the remainder of the premium.

Advantages of this approach are that the employer's risk is minimized (because the cash value is enough to fully reimburse its outlay even if the plan is terminated in the early years) and the plan is (arguably) simple to design and explain.

The principal disadvantages are that the employee's outlay is very high in the initial years of the plan, when cash values increase slowly, and the tax benefits available are not maximized under this option, as discussed in "Tax Implications," below.

(b) the *level premium* plan, under which the employee's premium share is leveled over an initial period of years, such as 5 or 10. (See Figure 52.2.) This alleviates the large initial premium share required of the employee under the standard arrangement. If the plan stays in existence long enough the employee and employer ultimately pay nearly the same total amount as under the standard arrangement.

The disadvantage of the level premium plan is that if the plan is terminated in the early years, the policy cash value is not sufficient to fully reimburse the employer for its total premium outlay. This possibility should be considered in drafting the split dollar agreement.

(c) the *employer pay all* arrangement, with the employer paying the entire premium and the employee paying nothing. (See Figure 52.3.) This arrangement is used when the employee's funds to pay for the plan are severely limited. The employee's cost in this arrangement is limited to the P.S. 58 or Table 2001 cost of pure insurance coverage that must be reported by the employee as taxable income. If the split dollar plan is treated as a loan, the reportable income by the employee is measured under Section 7872, as discussed below under "Tax Implications."

As with the level premium plan, if the plan is terminated early, the policy cash value will not fully reimburse the employer outlay; again, the agreement between the employer and employee should address this problem.

(d) the *"P.S. 58" offset* plan, under which the employee pays an amount equal to the P.S. 58 cost (or, after 2001, the Table 2001 cost, if applicable) for the coverage (or if less, the net premium due) each year. The employer pays the balance of the premium. (See Figure 52.4.) The purpose of this

Figure 52.1

| | | “STANDARD” PLAN | | | |
|---|---|---|---|---|---|
| | | WHOLE LIFE<br>FACE AMOUNT: $100,000<br>DIVIDENDS APPLIED TO BUY ONE-YEAR TERM INSURANCE,<br>REMAINDER TO REDUCE PREMIUM<br>MALE AGE: 40<br>FIRST-YEAR PREMIUM = $2,298.00 | | | |
| | | Premium Split | | Payment on Death | |
| Year | Guar.<br>Cash<br>Value | Paid<br>By<br>Employer | Paid<br>By<br>Employee | To<br>Employer | To<br>Employee's<br>Beneficiary |
| 1 | 0 | 0 | 2,298 | 0 | 100,000 |
| 2 | 1,700 | 1,700 | 598 | 1,700 | 98,300 |
| 3 | 3,600 | 1,900 | 219 | 3,600 | 100,000 |
| 4 | 5,500 | 1,900 | 189 | 5,500 | 100,000 |
| 5 | 7,500 | 2,000 | 60 | 7,500 | 100,000 |
| 6 | 9,500 | 2,000 | 32 | 9,500 | 100,000 |
| 7 | 11,500 | 2,000 | 0 | 11,500 | 100,000 |
| 8 | 13,600 | 1,974 | 0 | 13,474 | 100,126 |
| 9 | 15,700 | 1,948 | 0 | 15,421 | 100,279 |
| 10 | 17,800 | 1,926 | 0 | 17,347 | 100,453 |
| Total | | 17,347 | 3,396 | | |
| Average | | 1,735 | 340 | | |
| 11 | 20,000 | 1,905 | 0 | 19,252 | 100,748 |
| 12 | 22,200 | 1,888 | 0 | 21,141 | 101,059 |
| 13 | 24,400 | 1,864 | 0 | 23,004 | 101,396 |
| 14 | 26,700 | 1,869 | 0 | 24,874 | 101,826 |
| 15 | 29,000 | 1,866 | 0 | 26,740 | 102,260 |
| Total | | 26,740 | 3,396 | | |
| Average | | 1,783 | 226 | | |
| 16 | 31,300 | 1,870 | 0 | 28,609 | 102,691 |
| 17 | 33,700 | 1,879 | 0 | 30,488 | 103,212 |
| 18 | 36,000 | 1,895 | 0 | 32,383 | 103,617 |
| 19 | 38,400 | 1,926 | 0 | 34,309 | 104,091 |
| 20 | 40,900 | 1,969 | 0 | 36,278 | 104,622 |
| Total | | 36,278 | 3,396 | | |
| Average | | 1,814 | 170 | | |

**Figure 52.2**

| | | "LEVEL PREMIUM" PLAN | | | |
|---|---|---|---|---|---|

WHOLE LIFE
FACE AMOUNT: $100,000
DIVIDENDS APPLIED TO BUY ONE-YEAR TERM INSURANCE,
REMAINDER TO REDUCE PREMIUM
MALE AGE: 40
FIRST-YEAR PREMIUM = $2,298.00

| Year | Guar. Cash Value | Premium Split | | Payment on Death | |
|---|---|---|---|---|---|
| | | Paid By Employer | Paid By Employee | To Employer | To Employee's Beneficiary |
| 1 | 0 | 2,004 | 294 | 2,004 | 97,996 |
| 2 | 1,700 | 2,004 | 294 | 4,008 | 95,993 |
| 3 | 3,600 | 1,824 | 294 | 5,832 | 97,768 |
| 4 | 5,500 | 1,795 | 294 | 7,626 | 97,874 |
| 5 | 7,500 | 1,766 | 294 | 9,392 | 98,108 |
| 6 | 9,500 | 1,738 | 294 | 11,130 | 98,370 |
| 7 | 11,500 | 1,706 | 294 | 12,836 | 98,664 |
| 8 | 13,600 | 1,680 | 294 | 14,515 | 99,085 |
| 9 | 15,700 | 1,653 | 294 | 16,169 | 99,531 |
| 10 | 17,800 | 1,631 | 294 | 17,800 | 100,000 |
| Total | | 17,800 | 2,943 | | |
| Average | | 1,780 | 294 | | |
| 11 | 20,000 | 1,905 | 0 | 19,705 | 100,295 |
| 12 | 22,200 | 1,888 | 0 | 21,594 | 100,606 |
| 13 | 24,400 | 1,864 | 0 | 23,457 | 100,943 |
| 14 | 26,700 | 1,869 | 0 | 25,327 | 101,373 |
| 15 | 29,000 | 1,866 | 0 | 27,193 | 101,870 |
| Total | | 27,193 | 2,943 | | |
| Average | | 1,813 | 196 | | |
| 16 | 31,300 | 1,870 | 0 | 29,062 | 102,238 |
| 17 | 33,700 | 1,879 | 0 | 30,941 | 102,759 |
| 18 | 36,000 | 1,895 | 0 | 32,836 | 103,164 |
| 19 | 38,400 | 1,926 | 0 | 34,762 | 103,638 |
| 20 | 40,900 | 1,969 | 0 | 36,731 | 104,169 |
| Total | | 36,731 | 2,943 | | |
| Average | | 1,837 | 147 | | |

Figure 52.3

| | | "EMPLOYER PAY ALL" PLAN | | | |
|---|---|---|---|---|---|
| | | WHOLE LIFE<br>FACE AMOUNT: $100,000<br>DIVIDENDS APPLIED TO BUY ONE-YEAR TERM INSURANCE,<br>REMAINDER TO REDUCE PREMIUM<br>MALE AGE: 40<br>FIRST-YEAR PREMIUM = $2,298.00 | | | |
| | | Premium Split | | Payment on Death | |
| Year | Guar.<br>Cash<br>Value | Paid<br>By<br>Employer | Paid<br>By<br>Employee | To<br>Employer | To<br>Employee's<br>Beneficiary |
| 1 | 0 | 2,298 | 0 | 2,298 | 97,702 |
| 2 | 1,700 | 2,298 | 0 | 4,596 | 95,404 |
| 3 | 3,600 | 2,119 | 0 | 6,715 | 96,885 |
| 4 | 5,500 | 2,089 | 0 | 8,804 | 96,696 |
| 5 | 7,500 | 2,060 | 0 | 10,864 | 96,636 |
| 6 | 9,500 | 2,032 | 0 | 12,896 | 96,604 |
| 7 | 11,500 | 2,000 | 0 | 14,896 | 96,604 |
| 8 | 13,600 | 1,974 | 0 | 16,870 | 96,730 |
| 9 | 15,700 | 1,948 | 0 | 18,817 | 96,883 |
| 10 | 17,800 | 1,926 | 0 | 20,743 | 97,057 |
| Total | | 20,743 | 0 | | |
| Average | | 2,074 | 0 | | |
| 11 | 20,000 | 1,905 | 0 | 22,649 | 97,351 |
| 12 | 22,200 | 1,888 | 0 | 24,537 | 97,663 |
| 13 | 24,400 | 1,864 | 0 | 26,400 | 98,000 |
| 14 | 26,700 | 1,869 | 0 | 28,270 | 98,430 |
| 15 | 29,000 | 1,866 | 0 | 30,136 | 98,864 |
| Total | | 30,136 | 0 | | |
| Average | | 2,009 | 0 | | |
| 16 | 31,300 | 1,870 | 0 | 32,005 | 99,295 |
| 17 | 33,700 | 1,879 | 0 | 33,884 | 99,816 |
| 18 | 36,000 | 1,895 | 0 | 35,779 | 100,221 |
| 19 | 38,400 | 1,926 | 0 | 37,705 | 100,695 |
| 20 | 40,900 | 1,969 | 0 | 39,674 | 101,226 |
| Total | | 36,674 | 0 | | |
| Average | | 1,984 | 0 | | |

arrangement is to "zero out" the employee's income tax cost for the plan, as discussed below.

As a further refinement, the employer can reduce the employee's out-of-pocket cost for this arrangement by paying a tax deductible "bonus" to the employee equal to the employee's payment under the split dollar plan. The employer might want to go a step further and pay an additional amount equal to the tax on the first bonus as a "double bonus."

The offset arrangement is an advantageous one that is commonly used. However, as with most variations on the standard plan, the employer remains exposed to some risk if the plan is terminated early, because the cash value will be less than the employer's outlay in some cases. The split dollar agreement should deal with this issue.

## Cash Value and Death Proceeds Split

The purpose of the split of cash value or death proceeds is to reimburse the employer, in whole or in part, for its share of the premium outlay, in the event of the employee's death or termination of the plan.

At the employee's death, any policy proceeds not used to reimburse the employer go to the employee's designated beneficiary. This provides a significant death benefit in the early years of the plan, one of the principal objectives of a split dollar plan.

Most plans are designed to provide cash value growth sufficient to reimburse the employer after a number of years. The excess cash value can also benefit the employee, by allowing the plan to provide an attractive investment element (in a sense, a "deferred compensation" or "pension" element) in addition to the death benefit. Some plans are designed primarily to maximize this element. The "equity" type plan, described below, is one example.

The following are commonly used cash value/death proceeds split arrangements:

(a) the employer's share is the *greater* of (i) the aggregate premiums it has paid or (ii) the policy's cash value;

(b) the employer can recover only up to the amount of its aggregate premiums paid (a feature of the "equity" split dollar plan described below); or

(c) the employer is entitled to the entire cash value.

If a plan terminates early—usually when the employee terminates employment before the plan has matured—the cash value of the policy may not be sufficient to fully reimburse the employer for the aggregate premium payments it has made. The plan can provide that the employee is personally responsible to reimburse the employer in that event. As a practical matter, however, it may be difficult to enforce such a requirement, particularly if the amount is insufficient to justify the costs of a lawsuit. (A practical suggestion is to make sure that the company's severance pay arrangement, if any, allows recovery of any such amount out of severance pay otherwise due.)

## Policy Ownership

There are two methods of arranging policy ownership under a split dollar plan: the "endorsement method" and the "collateral assignment method."

Under the *endorsement* method, the employer owns the policy and is primarily responsible to the insurance company for paying the entire premium. The beneficiary designation provides for the employer to receive a portion of the death benefit equal to its premium outlay (or some alternative share), with the remainder of the death proceeds going to the employee's designated beneficiary. An endorsement to the policy is filed with the insurance company under which payment to the employee's beneficiary cannot be changed without consent of the employee (or, in some cases, a designated third person where the employee wishes to avoid incidents of ownership for estate tax purposes).

Advantages of the endorsement method are:

(1) greater control by the employer over the policy.

(2) simpler installation and administration; the only documentation required (except for possible ERISA requirements described below) is the policy and endorsement.

(3) avoidance of any formal arrangement that might be deemed to constitute a "loan" under current regulations, general tax principles, or for purposes of state laws prohibiting corporate loans to officers and directors.

(4) if the company owns an existing key employee policy on the employee, it can be used directly in

**Figure 52.4**

| | | "P.S. 58 OFFSET" PLAN | | | |
|---|---|---|---|---|---|

WHOLE LIFE
FACE AMOUNT: $100,000
DIVIDENDS APPLIED TO BUY ONE-YEAR TERM INSURANCE,
REMAINDER TO REDUCE PREMIUM
MALE AGE: 40
FIRST-YEAR PREMIUM = $2,298.00

| Year | Guar. Cash Value | Premium Split | | Payment on Death | |
|---|---|---|---|---|---|
| | | Paid By Employer | Paid By Employee | To Employer | To Employee's Beneficiary |
| 1 | 0 | 1,864 | 434 | 1,864 | 98,136 |
| 2 | 1,700 | 1,842 | 456 | 3,706 | 96,294 |
| 3 | 3,600 | 1,628 | 490 | 5,334 | 98,266 |
| 4 | 5,500 | 1,565 | 524 | 6,899 | 98,601 |
| 5 | 7,500 | 1,499 | 561 | 8,398 | 99,102 |
| 6 | 9,500 | 1,420 | 612 | 9,818 | 99,682 |
| 7 | 11,500 | 1,344 | 656 | 11,500 | 100,000 |
| 8 | 13,600 | 1,268 | 706 | 13,600 | 100,100 |
| 9 | 15,700 | 1,188 | 760 | 15,700 | 100,000 |
| 10 | 17,800 | 1,106 | 820 | 17,800 | 100,000 |
| Total | | 14,724 | 6,019 | | |
| Average | | 1,472 | 602 | | |
| 11 | 20,000 | 1,022 | 883 | 20,000 | 100,000 |
| 12 | 22,200 | 936 | 952 | 22,200 | 100,000 |
| 13 | 24,400 | 848 | 1,015 | 24,400 | 100,000 |
| 14 | 26,700 | 759 | 1,110 | 26,700 | 100,000 |
| 15 | 29,000 | 665 | 1,201 | 29,000 | 100,000 |
| Total | | 18,956 | 11,180 | | |
| Average | | 1,264 | 745 | | |
| 16 | 31,300 | 570 | 1,300 | 31,300 | 100,000 |
| 17 | 33,700 | 470 | 1,408 | 33,700 | 100,000 |
| 18 | 36,000 | 367 | 1,527 | 36,000 | 100,000 |
| 19 | 38,400 | 268 | 1,658 | 38,400 | 100,000 |
| 20 | 40,900 | 167 | 1,802 | 40,900 | 100,000 |
| Total | | 20,799 | 18,875 | | |
| Average | | 1,040 | 943 | | |

*Note:* After 2001, P.S. 58 rates may no longer be used to measure the value of life insurance protection.

the split dollar plan without change of owner-ship. (Using an existing policy may be important if the employee has developed health problems since the policy was issued.)

Under the *collateral assignment* method, the employee (or a third party) is the owner of the policy and is responsible for premium payments. The employer then makes interest free loans of the amount of the premium the employer has agreed to pay under the split dollar plan (these may or may not be treated as loans for income-tax purposes). To secure these loans the policy is assigned as collateral to the employer. At the employee's death, the employer recovers its aggregate premium payments from the policy proceeds, as collateral assignee. The remainder of the policy proceeds are paid to the employee's designated beneficiary. If the plan terminates before the employee's death, the employer has the right to be reimbursed out of policy cash values; the employee continues as the owner of the policy.

Some advantages of the collateral assignment method are:

(1) it arguably gives more protection to the employee and the employee's beneficiary; and

(2) it is easier to implement using existing insurance policies owned by the employee.

## SPLIT DOLLAR PLAN VARIATIONS

In recent years, changes in the tax law have resulted in a need for new kinds of tax planning. Because of the inherent flexibility of the split dollar concept, planners have been able to devise variations on these plans that meet tax and financial objectives for executives in the changing investment and tax climate. Following is a brief description of some of these variations.

### Equity Split Dollar

In the equity split dollar arrangement the employer's interest in the policy cash value is limited at all times to the aggregate premiums it has paid. Thus, after the policy cash value reaches the level of the aggregate employer premium payments, the employee begins receiving a gradually-increasing interest in the investment build-up in the policy. The ability to receive an increasing interest in the cash value makes this plan what is referred to as an "equity split dollar plan."

As discussed in "Tax Implications" below, under the proposed split dollar regulations, an endorsement-type equity plan will result in taxable income to the employee each year reflecting the buildup in the employee's interest in the cash value. If the plan is a collateral-assignment arrangement, the arrangement will be treated as a series of loans to the employee to pay premiums, without any taxation of the equity as such. In neither case is the tax treatment of equity plans particularly favorable.

### Reverse Split Dollar

A "reverse split dollar" plan is one in which the *employee* has the right to policy cash values up to the aggregate of his premium payments. The employer is beneficiary of the death proceeds in excess of the employee's share. In other words, as its name implies, a reverse split dollar plan is the reverse of the usual arrangement. A Notice put out by the IRS in 2002 has generally ended the viability of reverse split dollar.

In Notice 2002-59, 2002-36 IRB 481, the IRS states that a party to a split dollar arrangement may use Table 2001 or the insurer's rates only to value current life insurance protection when the protection is conferred as an economic benefit by one party on another party, determined without regard to consideration or premiums paid by the other party. Thus, if one party has the right to current life insurance protection, neither Table 2001 not the insurer's rates can be used to value that party's insurance protection to establish the value of policy benefits that another party may be entitled.

Notice 2002-59 provides an example where the premium rates are properly used and an example where they are not properly used. In one example, a donor pays premiums on a life insurance policy that is part of a split dollar arrangement between the donor and a trust, with the trust having the right to the current life insurance protection. The current life insurance protection has been conferred as an economic benefit by the donor on the trust and the donor is permitted to value the life insurance protection using either Table 2001 or the insurer's lower term rates.

However in the second example, if the donor or the donor's estate has the right to the current life insurance protection, neither Table 2001 nor the insurer's lower term rates may be used to value the donor's current life insurance protection to establish the value of economic benefits conferred upon the trust. Results will be similar if the trust pays for all or a portion of its share of benefits provided under the life insurance arrangement.

Notice 2002-59 does not contain an effective date, which indicates that the IRS does not consider it "new" guidance, but a restatement of current law. If that is the case, it will affect reverse split dollar arrangements that were in place before the notice was issued.

## TAX IMPLICATIONS

1. Tax treatment of split dollar arrangement prior to the proposed regulations.

In order to understand split dollar planning fully, a brief history of the tax treatment is helpful. Also, prior tax treatment still applies on a transitional basis (see "What are the transition rules for the proposed regulations" in Questions and Answers below).

Before 1964, the tax treatment of split dollar plans was unsettled. The IRS then ruled (in Rev. Rul. 64-328[1]) that the tax consequences of a split dollar plan would be the same regardless of whether the collateral assignment or the endorsement arrangement was used. In effect this ruling held that after 1964 the IRS would not treat a split dollar plan was an interest-free loan. In 1964, interest-free loans were not subject to income tax.

Under Rev. Rul. 64-328, the employee is considered to be in receipt each year of an amount of taxable "economic benefit." This taxable amount for the basic insurance coverage was equal to the P.S. 58 rate for the insurance protection under the plan less the premium amount paid by the employee. As an alternative, the annual renewable term insurance rates of the company issuing the split dollar policy could, under prior law, be substituted for the P.S. 58 rates if the term rates are lower than the P.S. 58 rates.[2] (Note that under the 2002 proposed regulations in the case of an endorsement-type plan or non-equity collateral assignment plan this tax treatment still applies, in effect.) The application of policy dividends further affected the employee's income tax consequences.

Prior law did not provide any specific treatment of equity-type plans. In the absence of specific rules, many practitioners took the position that increases in the employee's share of the cash value were not taxable to the employee, or taxable only when the plan was terminated and the policy "rolled out" to the employee.

Under both current and prior law, the employer cannot deduct any portion of its premium contribution. The IRS does not allow a deduction even for the part of the employer's contribution that results in taxable income to the employee.[3]

2. Treatment of split dollar arrangements under the proposed regulations.

These proposed regulations would significantly change the treatment of split dollar plans. At this writing, the shape of the final regulations is unclear, and it is difficult to provide specific rules for planning split dollar arrangements currently and in the future. However, at least the general outlines of the provisions in the proposed regulations may be assumed to be applicable in the near future, with regulations probably made final in 2003 or early 2004. Transitional rules are discussed in Questions and Answers, below.

Under the proposed regulations, a split dollar arrangement is "any arrangement between an owner and a non-owner of a life insurance contract" that satisfies three criteria:

1. Either party pays premiums, including a payment by means of a loan secured by the life insurance contract;

2. One of the parties can recover a portion of the premiums paid from the contract (or payment is secured by the contract); and

3. The arrangement is not part of a Section 79 group-term life insurance plan.

The proposed regulations provide that if (a) the plan is a "compensatory arrangement" (essentially one in which the beneficiary is a person or entity the employee "would reasonably be expected to designate as the beneficiary") and (b) the employer pays any part of the premium, then the plan is deemed a split dollar plan, regardless of the criteria listed above. There is a similar provision for split dollar plans for shareholders and corporations.[4]

This broad definition covers most normal compensation-planning split dollar arrangements between an employer and employee. It also covers the types of plans sometimes referred to as "private split dollar" that are used among individuals for business continuation or estate planning purposes. This chapter focuses on compensatory arrangements.

In general, the proposed regulations provide two "mutually exclusive regimes for taxing split dollar life insurance arrangements"-the *economic benefit* regime, and the *loan* regime. Each regime has different tax consequences.

A preliminary issue in determining which regime applies is to ascertain who is the owner of the insurance policy. The rules are generally as follows:

- The person named as the policy owner is generally treated as the owner for purposes of the proposed regulations.

- If two or more persons are named as owners and all named owners have all the incidents of ownership with respect to an undivided interest in the contract, each person is treated as owner of a separate contract.

- If two or more persons are named as owners and each does not have all incidents of ownership, the first-named owner is considered the owner for purposes of the proposed regulations.

A special rule provides that if the arrangement is a non-equity plan (one where the only benefit to the employee or service provider is current life insurance protection) then the employer or service recipient is treated as the owner of the life insurance contract.[5] This special rule would appear to place collateral-assignment non-equity plans under the economic benefit treatment, as well as endorsement non-equity plans.

*Economic benefit treatment.* Under the economic benefit regime, "the owner of the life insurance contract is treated as providing economic benefits to the non-owner of the contract." This approach is similar to the rules governing split dollar plans under Rev. Rul. 64-328, with some significant differences. That is, the value of the life insurance coverage or other benefit provided to an employee under a split dollar plan is valued and taxed to the employee as additional taxable income. Under the regulations, the economic benefit regime essentially applies to two types of plans:

a. An "endorsement" type of plan under which the employer is the owner of the life insurance contract and endorses a portion of the death benefit to the employee.

b. Any split dollar plan entered into in connection with the performance of services, where the employee or service provider is not the owner of the contract. (Similar provisions apply to donor-donee plans).[6]

Under the economic benefit regime, economic benefits must be "fully and consistently" accounted for by owner and nonowner. The value of the economic benefits, reduced by any consideration paid by the non-owner to the owner, is treated as transferred from the owner to the non-owner. In the case of an employment relationship, this amount is treated as compensation. Other types of relationships result in a different tax treatment, accordingly.[7]

If the plan is a non-equity arrangement (the economic benefit consists only of current life insurance protection), this economic benefit is to be valued in accordance with a table or method to be furnished in the future. For many years, the "P.S. 58" table was used for this purpose. This was a table based on mortality rates in the 1940s and generally provided for high insurance costs. A new Table 2001 was announced in Notices 2001-10 and 2002-8 (see Transitional Rules below). The Table 2001 rates are much lower than the P.S. 58 rates. Presumably Table 2001 will ultimately be replaced by a new table around the time the final regulations are published.

---

*Example* (from Preamble to the proposed regulations): Employer R owns a $1,000,000 policy that is part of a split dollar arrangement with Employee E. R pays all premiums and is entitled to receive the greater of its premiums or the cash surrender value of the contract when the arrangement terminates or E dies. In Year 10 the cost of term insurance for E (under appropriate IRS table, yet to be furnished) is $1.00 per $1,000 of insurance and the cash surrender value of the contract is $200,000. In Year 10, E must include in compensation income $800 ($1,000,000 - $200,000 payable to R, or $800,000, multiplied by .001 (E's premium rate factor)). If E had paid $300 of the premium, E would include $500 in compensation income.

---

If the plan is an equity-type arrangement (a plan providing the non-owner something other than just current life insurance protection) then "any right in, or benefit of, a life insurance contract (including, but not limited to, an interest in the cash surrender value) provided during a taxable year to a non-owner...is an economic benefit"[8]....

In other words, current life insurance protection as well as any other benefit received by the employee during the year, including increases in the employee's vested interest in the policy's cash value, constitute taxable compensation income under these proposed regulations.

*Rollout* (transfer of contract). The proposed regulations specifically provide that when a contract is transferred to a non-owner (transferee), the transferee has income equal to the fair market value of the contract over the sum of:

- The amount paid by the transferee to the transferor

- The amount that the transferee took into income as an economic benefit under an equity split dollar arrangement, less (a) the economic benefit attributable to current life insurance protection and (b) any amount paid by the transferee for the pure equity element.[9]

Fair market value for this purpose is the cash surrender value and the value of all other rights under the contract other than current life insurance protection. The possibility of an artificially low cash value—the "springing cash value" issue is not alluded to in the proposed regulation.[10]

Unlike prior rules for split dollar plans, no amounts paid by the employee toward the premium are includible in the employee's basis.[11] These amounts are included in the owner's (employer's) gross income and included in the owner's basis for the contract.[12] This tends to discourage the use of contributory plans.

*Policy valuation at rollout.* Rollouts often involve the springing cash value issue. Insurance policies can be designed to specify very low cash values for a period of time, followed by a rapid increase in cash value. If rollout occurs when the cash value is low, the argument can be made that the tax consequence to the employee on distribution of the policy (or the cost for the employee to buy the policy) is low because of the low cash value at that time. However, the IRS position in general is that the tax consequences are based on the policy's "fair market value" and not the stated cash value alone. The fair market value is based on what the policy would be worth to a buyer or recipient in an arms-length transaction. Policy reserves used for purposes of insurance company income taxation can be used for this purpose.[13]

*Sec. 83.* For a compensatory arrangement (employer-employee) the rules under this heading (Rollout) do not apply until the amount is taxable under Section 83 of the Code. That is, taxation to the employee could be delayed to a year later than the year of rollout if the contract is subject to a substantial risk of forfeiture. The amount would not be taxable until the year in which the contract is no longer subject to a risk of forfeiture (becomes substantially vested).[14]

*Loan treatment.* Under the loan regime,[15] the non-owner of the life insurance contract is treated as lending premium payments to the owner. The loan regime is the default treatment for split dollar plans that do not meet the specific requirements for the economic benefit regime. Thus, loan treatment will apply to plans of the type that have been referred to as "collateral assignment" plans where the employee or the employee's trust or beneficiary is the owner of the contract. However, it appears that loan treatment would not apply to a non-equity collateral assignment contract.

A payment under a split dollar arrangement is treated as a loan for federal tax purposes if the arrangement is like the traditional collateral assignment arrangement; specifically if:

1. The payment is made by the nonowner directly or indirectly to the owner or the insurance company;

2. The payment is a loan under general principles of federal tax law or if a reasonable person would expect the payment to be repaid in full to the non-owner; and

3. The payment is made from or secured by either the death benefit or the cash surrender value.[16]

If the loan is an interest-free or below-market loan (as it generally would be), Section 7872 applies to determine the amount of resultant additional compensation that is taxed to the employee. Generally, except possibly where the employee is significantly advanced in age, Section 7872 will result in more income inclusion than the application of the economic benefit approach, although this will depend on the final IRS table replacing P.S. 58 and Table 2001.

If the arrangement carries no stated interest rate, and is considered a "demand loan" (an issue that needs IRS clarification) it would be treated under Code Section 7872 as follows:

- Employer is treated as if it paid additional compensation income to the employee equal to the "applicable federal rate." This amount is taxable to the employee and deductible by the employer.

- Employee is treated as if he paid this additional amount back to the employer. This amount is additional taxable income to the employer, and is generally not deductible to the employee (unless it can be characterized as some kind of deductible interest such as home mortgage interest).

If the loan is a term loan (a loan payable at a certain date), the amount of the loan in excess of the present value of the scheduled payments (if any) is immediately taxable to the executive (see Chapter 44, Loans to Executives, for discussion).

*Effective Date.* The proposed regulations apply to arrangements entered into or materially modified after date of final regulations. Final regulations could appear in the later half of 2003 or early 2004.

The proposed regulations provide that the transitional rules in Notice 2002-8 will continue to apply (see Questions and Answers below) for arrangements entered into on or before the effective date of the final regulations. Alternatively, taxpayers are allowed to apply the proposed regulations immediately to existing and new arrangements, if all parties treat the arrangement consistently.

3. Death benefits from a split dollar plan—both the employer's share and the employee's beneficiary's share—are generally income tax free.[17]

   The tax-free nature of the death proceeds is lost if the policy has been "transferred for value" in certain situations. The transfer for value trap should be carefully avoided in designing split dollar plans.[18]

   The following transfers of insurance policies are exempt from the transfer for value rules—in other words, they will not cause the loss of the death proceed's tax-free nature:

   (a) a transfer of the policy to the insured;

   (b) a transfer to a partner of the insured or to a partnership of which the insured is a partner;

   (c) a transfer to a corporation of which the insured is a shareholder or officer; and

   (d) a transfer in which the transferee's basis is determined in whole or in part by reference to the transferor's basis (i.e., a "substituted" or "carryover" basis).

Some examples of potential transfer for value situations to be avoided in split dollar plans are:

- Do not initiate the plan by transferring an existing corporate-owned key employee policy to a third party beneficiary;

- Do not start the plan by transferring an employee-owned policy to the corporation unless the employee is a shareholder or officer;

- At termination of the plan, do not transfer the corporation's interest in the policy to a third party beneficiary; although there are some arrangements where this presents no problem, it is better to make such a transfer to the insured.

4. If the employee had no "incidents of ownership" in the policy, the death benefit is not includable in the employee's estate for federal estate tax purposes unless the policy proceeds are payable to the employee's estate.[19] If an employee is potentially faced with a federal estate tax liability, all incidents of ownership in the policy should therefore be assigned irrevocably to a third party—a beneficiary or a trust. Proceeds generally should be payable to a named personal beneficiary and not to the employee's estate.

   If the employee is a controlling shareholder (more than 50 percent) in the employer corporation, the *corporation's* incidents of ownership in the policy will be attributed to the majority shareholder. The current IRS position is that even if the corporation has only the right to make policy loans against its share of the cash value, this is an incident of ownership that will be attributed to the controlling shareholder and cause estate tax inclusion of the policy death proceeds.[20]

   For a majority shareholder, the only way to avoid estate tax inclusion is for not only the employee but also the employer to get rid of the incidents of ownership. The corporation can avoid such incidents by retaining no rights of ownership in the policy, including any policy contract provisions or riders relating to the split dollar agreement. One procedure for accomplishing this is for the employee's personal beneficiary to be the original purchaser of the policy, and the beneficiary to enter into the split dollar agreement with the corporation on a collateral assignment basis.

5. There may be federal gift tax consequences if a person other than the employee owns the insurance policy used in a split dollar plan. The transfer of the policy from the employee to another party is a gift subject to tax. In addition, there is a continuing annual gift if the employee pays the premiums. There is also a continuing annual gift by the employee if the *employer* pays premiums, because this employer payment represents compensation earned by the employee that is indirectly transferred to the policyowner.[21] Such potentially taxable gifts may avoid taxation if they qualify for the annual gift tax exclusion ($11,000, as indexed for 2003). Gifts made directly to beneficiaries generally qualify, while gifts to insurance trusts may be considered "future interests" that do not qualify for the gift tax exclusion.

## ERISA REQUIREMENTS

A split dollar plan is considered an "employee welfare benefit plan" and is subject to the ERISA rules applicable to such plans, as discussed in Appendix A.

A welfare plan can escape the ERISA reporting and disclosure requirements, including the Form 5500 filing and the summary plan description (SPD) requirement, if it is an "insured" plan maintained for "a select group of management or highly compensated employees."[22] Most split dollar plans qualify for this exception. If the plan covers more than a select group, it must provide SPDs to participants. (If the plan covers fewer than 100 participants, the SPD need not be filed with the DOL.[23])

ERISA further requires a written document, a "named fiduciary," and a formal claims procedure for split dollar plans.[24]

## WHERE CAN I FIND OUT MORE ABOUT IT?

1. Graduate Course: Executive Compensation (GS 842), The American College, Bryn Mawr, PA.

## QUESTIONS AND ANSWERS

**Question** — What is the impact of a split dollar plan on corporate earnings for accounting purposes?

*Answer* — Many corporate managers, particularly in publicly held corporations, are concerned that adoption of various executive compensation plans may cause a charge to corporate earnings for financial reporting purposes. The tendency in the accounting profession is toward requiring charges to earnings for most types of executive compensation, and the Financial Accounting Standards Board (FASB) is currently considering new accounting rules in this area.

Under the rules currently in effect, however, there would not be a charge to earnings under a "standard" split dollar plan such as that in Figure 52.1, because the corporation controls the cash value of the policy and the premium outlay is always balanced by a cash value increase owned by the corporation.

**Question** — Is split dollar a useful compensation technique for a partner, proprietor, or shareholder employee of an S corporation?

*Answer* — Generally, split dollar does not work as a way of using "corporate dollars" for owners of S corporations or unincorporated entities. For example, suppose an S corporation earns $50,000 after paying a $100,000 salary to its sole shareholder-employee Lionel. The corporation proposes to pay $10,000 of this as premiums for a split dollar insurance program for Lionel. Lionel's taxable income *with* the split dollar plan: $150,000 (plus possible P.S. 58/Table 2001 costs, although it is not clear that double taxation is required). *Without* the split dollar plan, Lionel's taxable income is also $150,000. At best, the split dollar plan risks taxation on the premium plus the P.S. 58/Table 2001 costs, and using the corporation in this manner provides no advantage over holding the insurance personally.

More generally, with an S corporation split dollar plan on several shareholder-employees, the effect is to reallocate the cost of the plan toward the majority shareholder. Most majority shareholders will not be interested in such an arrangement. The results are generally the same for partners and proprietors.

Split dollar can sometimes work in unincorporated businesses. First, it does work for key (nonshareholder) employees of an S corporation or unincorporated business, because they are not subject to the income pass-through that applies to owners.

Split dollar may also work for owners where an S corporation's taxable income is reduced to zero through carryovers, depreciation, etc. Then the use of corporate funds for split dollar insurance for a shareholder-employee does not affect taxable income.

Another possible use for split dollar for a shareholder of an S corporation applies where saving gift taxes, not income taxes, is the object. For example, suppose an S corporation shareholder-employee wants to set up an irrevocable insurance trust for his children. He will make gifts to the trust to pay premiums, which puts the entire premium into his gift tax base and to the extent the annual exclusion is exceeded, this will reduce his lifetime exclusion or result in gift taxes. If, however, the plan is set up as a split dollar arrangement between the trust and the S corporation, the shareholder-employee's annual gift will be equal only to his P.S. 58/Table 2001 or one-year term premium costs. This will be below the annual exclusion ceiling for considerable amounts of insurance for many years in some cases.

**Question** — What are the transition rules currently in effect for split dollar plans as a result of the shift from the old rules to the pending new rules?

*Answer* — The transitional rules (from Notice 2002-8) are as follows:

- Arrangements entered into before the date of publication of final regulations will have no current tax on the equity buildup. This provision removes a threat that was implicit in earlier IRS pronouncements. However, the proposed regulations appear to provide for current taxation of equity buildup, as discussed above.

- Arrangements entered into before the date of publication of final regulations will not be treated as terminated with a rollout and transfer of property subject to Section 83 as long as life insurance protection continues to be treated as an economic benefit to the employee.

- For arrangements entered into before the date of publication of final regulations, the parties will have the option of treating premium payments as loans under any reasonable effort to comply with Section 7872.

- For a split dollar arrangement entered into before January 28, 2002, and which is terminated with a rollout before January 1, 2004, there will be no Section 83 taxation of the rollout. This grandfathering provision is particularly welcome, because many of these arrangements have been sold to clients with representations that the rollout would not be a taxable event.

Notice 2002-8 retains Table 2001, which replaced the P.S. 58 table for valuing economic benefit. No such table was included in the proposed regulations, so it is believed that Table 2001 will be replaced at the time final regulations are published. This change is also accompanied with a series of transitional rules:

- Arrangements entered into before January 28, 2002, can continue to use the P.S. 58 rates if those rates are stated in the split dollar plan. Since the Table 2001 rates are lower than the P.S. 58 rates, this is useful only for limited purposes.

- Arrangements entered into "before the effective date of future guidance" can use Table 2001.

- Arrangements entered into before the effective date of future guidance can use an insurer's lower term premium rate in lieu of P.S. 58 or Table 2001 rates. However, after December 31, 2003, the published insurer rates may not be used "(i) unless the insurer generally makes the availability of such rates known to persons who apply for term insurance coverage from the insurer, and (ii) the insurer regularly sells term insurance at such rates to individuals who apply for term insurance coverage through the insurer's normal distribution channels."

## FOOTNOTES

1. Rev. Rul. 64-328, 1964-2 CB 11.
2. Rev. Rul. 66-110, 1966-1 CB 12
3. IRC Section 264(a)(1).
4. Prop. Reg. Sec. 1.61-22(b).
5. Prop. Reg. Sec. 1.61-22(c), (d)(2).
6. Prop. Reg. Sec. 1.61-22(b)(3).
7. Prop. Reg. Sec. 1.61-22(d)(1).
8. Prop. Reg. Sec. 1.61-22(d)(3).
9. Prop. Reg. Sec. 1.61-22(g)(1).
10. Prop. Reg. Sec. 1.61-22(g)(2).
11. Prop. Reg. Sec. 1.61-22(g)(4)(D)(iii).
12. Prop. Reg. Sec. 1-61(f)(3).
13. Notice 89-25, 1989-1 CB 662.
14. Prop. Reg. Sec. 1.61-22(g)(3).
15. Prop. Reg. Sec. 1.7872-15.
16. Prop. Reg. Sec. 1.7872-15(a)(2).
17. IRC Section 101(a)(1).
18. IRC Section 101(a)(2).
19. IRC Section 2042.
20. Rev. Rul. 82-145, 1982-2 CB 213.
21. Rev. Rul. 78-420, 1978-2 CB 67.
22. Labor Reg. §2520.104-24.
23. Labor Reg. §2520.104-20.
24. ERISA Section 402(a).

# Chapter 53

# STOCK OPTION

## WHAT IS IT?

A stock option is a formal, written offer to sell stock at a specified price, within specified time limits. Employers often use stock options for compensating executives. Such options are generally for stock of the employer company or a subsidiary.

Options are typically granted to an employee as additional compensation, at a favorable price, either below or near the current market value, with an expectation that the value of the stock will rise, making the option price a bargain beneficial to the executive. Options typically remain outstanding for a period of 10 years. If the price of the stock goes down, the executive will not purchase the stock, so the executive does not risk any out-of-pocket loss.

The executive is generally not taxed upon the grant of an option; taxation is deferred to the time when the stock is purchased, or later. Thus, stock options are a form of deferred compensation, with the amount of compensation based upon increases in the value of the company's stock. This "equity" form of compensation is popular with executives, because it gives them some of the advantages of business ownership.

There are two main types of stock option plans used for compensating executives: (1) incentive stock option (ISO) plans; and (2) nonstatutory stock options. ISOs are a form of stock option plan with special tax benefits; these are discussed in Chapter 41. Nonstatutory stock options will be discussed here.

For an outline of some advanced types of stock option and other plans used for compensating executives, particularly in large corporations, see Appendix D of this book.

## WHEN IS IT INDICATED?

1. When an employer is willing to compensate employees with shares of company stock. Many family corporations or other closely held corporations do not want to share ownership of the business in this manner. Option plans are most often used by corporations whose ownership is relatively broad, and are common in large corporations whose stock is publicly traded.

2. Where an employer wishes to reward executive performance by providing equity-type compensation—that is, compensation that increases in value as the employer stock increases in value. This has generally been viewed as the perfect incentive for executives, since the executives' interests will be the same as those of shareholders—to increase the value of the corporation. However, recent financial scandals suggest that, at least for CEOs and high executives of large corporations, stock-based compensation may tempt executives to engage in short-term manipulation of the stock price to the detriment of regular shareholders. Executive compensation arrangements should be designed with this caution in mind.

## ADVANTAGES

1. Nonstatutory stock option plans can be designed in virtually any manner suitable to an executive or to the employer. There are few tax or other government regulatory constraints. For example, a stock option plan can be provided for any group of executives, or even a single executive. Benefits can vary from one executive to another without restriction. There are no nondiscrimination coverage or benefit rules.

2. Stock options are a form of compensation with little or no out-of-pocket cost to the company. The real cost of stock options is that the company forgoes the opportunity to sell the same stock on the market and realize its proceeds for company purposes.

3. Stock options are a form of compensation on which tax to the employee is deferred. As discussed under "Tax Implications," below, tax is generally not payable at the time when a stock option is granted to the executive. Taxation to the employee generally occurs when the option is exercised; however, it may

be possible to further defer taxation by combining the option with a nonqualified deferred compensation agreement, under which the tax at exercise is further deferred, by restricting or limiting access to the required stock (or stock value) for a period of time or until retirement.[1]

## DISADVANTAGES

1. The executive bears the market risk of this kind of compensation. If the market value of stock goes below the option price while the option is outstanding, the employee does not have any actual out-of-pocket loss; however, since the executive will not purchase the stock, there is no additional compensation received. And, after an option is "exercised" (i.e., company stock is purchased by the executive), the executive bears the full market risk of holding company stock.

2. The executive must have a source of funds to purchase the stock (and pay taxes due in the year of exercise) in order to benefit from the plan. Executives often borrow money with the anticipation that dividends from the stock purchased, plus immediate resales of some stock, will be sufficient to pay part or all of the interest on the borrowed funds. However, it must be remembered that investment interest in excess of investment income is not deductible.

3. Fluctuation in the market value of the stock may have little or no relation to executive performance. This factor weakens the value of a stock option plan as a performance incentive.

4. As discussed under "Tax Implications," below, the employer's tax deduction is generally delayed until the executive exercises the option and purchases stock. Furthermore, the employer generally gets no further deduction, even if the executive realizes substantial capital gains thereafter.

## TAX IMPLICATIONS

1. If an option has no readily ascertainable fair market value (see below) at the time it is "granted" (i.e., transferred to the executive), there is no taxable income to the executive at the date of the grant.[2]

2. The employee has taxable compensation income (ordinary income) in the year when shares are actu- ally purchased under the option. The amount of taxable income to the employee is the "bargain element"—the difference between the fair market value of the shares at the date of purchase and the option price (the amount the executive actually pays for these shares).[3] The employer must withhold and pay federal income tax with respect to this compensation income.

3. The employer does not get a tax deduction at the time an option is granted. The employer receives a tax deduction in the same year in which the employee has taxable income as a result of exercising the option and purchasing shares. The amount of the deduction is the same as the amount of income the employee must include.[4]

---

*Example.* Executive Lee was given an option in 2002 to purchase 1,000 shares of Employer Company stock at $100 per share, the 2002 market price. The option can be exercised by Lee at any time over the next five years. In 2004, Lee purchases 400 shares for a total of $40,000. If the fair market value of the shares in 2004 is $60,000, Lee has $20,000 of ordinary income in 2004. Employer Company gets a tax deduction of $20,000 in 2004 (assuming that Lee's total compensation meets the reasonableness test), which is the same amount as Lee's compensation income. If Lee re-sells this stock at a gain in a later year, he has capital gain income. Employer Company gets no further tax deduction, even though Lee realizes and reports capital gain income from selling the stock.

---

4. The executive's basis in shares acquired under a stock option plan is equal to the amount paid for the stock, plus the amount of taxable income reported by the executive at the time the option was exercised.[5] In the example in paragraph 3 above, Lee's basis for the 400 shares purchased in 2004 is $60,000—the $40,000 that Lee paid, plus the $20,000 of ordinary income that he reported in 2004. Therefore, if Lee sells the 400 shares in 2005 for $90,000, he must report $30,000 of capital gain in 2005 (the selling price of $90,000, less his basis of $60,000). Employer Company gets no additional tax deduction in 2005.

5. If the option has a readily ascertainable fair market value at the time of the grant, paragraphs (1) through (4) above do not apply. An option will be deemed to

have a readily ascertainable fair market value if: (a) the option has a value that is determinable as of the time of the grant, *and* (b) the option can be traded on an established market.[6]

The tax rules that apply are:

(a) If an option meets these rules, it is taxed at the time of the grant, and the employer receives a corresponding tax deduction at that time.

(b) The employee has no further taxable compensation income when the option is later exercised.

If the employer stock is expected to increase in value substantially, there is an advantage in designing an option plan so that it is taxed at the time of the grant. However, this approach can be used only where options can be traded on an established market.

## WHERE CAN I FIND OUT MORE ABOUT IT?

1. Leimberg, Stephan R., et al., *The Federal Income Tax Law*, Warren, Gorham, and Lamont, 1995.

2. Graduate Course: Executive Compensation (GS 842), The American College, Bryn Mawr, PA.

3. Kroll, "Emerging Trends in Executive Compensation," *Journal of Deferred Compensation*, Spring 1997.

## QUESTIONS AND ANSWERS

**Question** — What is the effect of federal securities laws on stock option plans?

*Answer* — From the employer viewpoint, it is necessary to determine whether the stock is subject to the registration requirements of federal securities law. Various exemptions from registration may apply to stock provided only to selected executives for compensation purposes, but the existence of such an exemption must be verified. State securities laws may also apply.

Advisors to the executive must determine if any of the resale restrictions of federal securities law apply to the sale of stock acquired under the plan. In addition, the executive may be considered an "insider," and subject to the insider trading restrictions upon the resale of stock.

## FOOTNOTES

1. See Brisendine, "Deferring Tax On Gain From Stock Option Exercises: Does It Work?" *Benefits Law Journal*, Summer 1997. The author's comments in this article are particularly authoritative because he is a former IRS official familiar with IRS positions in this area.
2. IRC Section 83(e)(3).
3. IRC Section 83(a).
4. IRC Section 83(h).
5. Treas. Regs. §§1.61-2(d)(2); 1.83-4(b).
6. Treas. Reg. §1.83-7(b).

# Chapter 54

# VEBA WELFARE BENEFIT TRUST

## WHAT IS IT?

A VEBA is not a benefit plan as such — it is a type of fund into which employers make deposits that will be used to provide specified employee benefits in the future. For example, an employer can contribute funds on a regular basis to a VEBA that provides covered employees with a death benefit payable to their named beneficiary.

A VEBA can be either a trust or a corporation, but is generally a trust. It is set up by an employer unilaterally or through collective bargaining to hold funds used to pay benefits under specific employee benefit plans.[1] Income of the VEBA is exempt from regular income tax if the VEBA meets the requirements of Section 501(c)(9).

## WHEN IS IT INDICATED?

1. When an employer wants to provide benefit security for all covered employees by placing funding amounts in trust, for the exclusive benefit of employees and beyond the reach of corporate creditors.

2. When an employer wants to accelerate deductibility of employee benefit costs by prefunding those costs. Accelerated deductions are available only in limited situations — see *Questions and Answers* regarding 419A(f)(6) plans.

## ADVANTAGES

1. The IRS has approved the use of employer-funded whole life insurance policies meeting certain guidelines to fund a death benefit in a VEBA.[2] However, the Department of Labor (DOL), and some state insurance regulators, may challenge the propriety of using whole life insurance for such purposes.[3]

2. Benefit security for individual employees is enhanced by using VEBA, since there is an irrevocable trust for the exclusive benefit of employees and protection against reversion of funds to the employer.

## DISADVANTAGES

1. Installing and administering a VEBA can be relatively complex and costly. Smaller employers will find these plans feasible only if they use a vendor of "packaged" plans provided to groups of employers.

2. Use of a multiple-employer plan, which is often the only practical way to utilize a VEBA, means that the employer loses some degree of control over the plan's design, investments, and even, to some extent, the tax consequences of the plan.

3. A reversion of assets to the employer is effectively prohibited[4] (in contrast to qualified pension and profit-sharing plans, where reversions are allowed subject to a penalty). This means that the plan must be carefully designed to avoid overfunding and potential losses of funding intended for owner-employees.

## VEBA DESIGN ISSUES

### Who Must Be Covered?

1. A plan funded through a VEBA must generally cover more than one employee.[5]

2. Coverage generally must be broad. It is possible to design VEBA-funded plans that do not cover all employees, but excluding employees brings the planner into a fearsome thicket of overlapping, complex, and unclear rules designed to prevent discrimination. In summary, these are as follows:

   - Provisions in the Section 501(c)(9) regulations that result in a loss of the VEBA's tax exemption if violated.[6]

   - A separate code section providing specific non-discrimination rules for VEBA-funded plans.[7] Full regulations under this section have not yet been issued by the IRS.

- Nondiscrimination provisions in the Code applicable to each separate benefit plan included in the VEBA plans. For example, a group term life insurance plan funded through a VEBA must meet the provisions of Section 79.[8]

In many cases these rules require such broad coverage that relatively few employees can be excluded from VEBA plans. Because the savings to be gained through excluding employees often do not outweigh the tax risks and expense of compliance with these rules, many VEBA plans simply cover all employees.

3. The direct result of failing to meet the nondiscrimination rules is loss of tax exemption of the VEBA, which may not be a severe sanction if the VEBA has relatively little taxable income (by having invested in life insurance or tax-free bonds, for example). However, plans that are funded through the VEBA may have their own coverage requirements with various consequences for failure to have broad enough coverage.

4. Under the VEBA rules, generally, a plan providing a disproportionate share of benefits to owner-employees will not be tax exempt.[9]

### What Kinds of Benefits Can Be Provided?

The VEBA regulations list the following as permitted VEBA benefits:[10]

- life insurance before and after retirement;

- other survivor benefits;

- sick and accident benefits; and

- other benefits, including vacation and recreation benefits, severance benefits paid through a severance pay plan discussed below, unemployment and job training benefits, and disaster benefits.

The following are among items specifically *prohibited* as VEBA benefits: savings, retirement, or deferred compensation plans; coverage of expenses, such as commuting expenses accident or homeowners' insurance covering damage to property, and other items unrelated to maintenance of the employee's earning power.[11]

Any plan funded through a VEBA, in addition to being subject to whatever nondiscrimination rules apply to that type of plan (for example, Section 79 rules for group term life insurance, etc.) is also subject to the VEBA benefit nondiscrimination rules of Section 505. In particular, Section 505(b)(7) limits compensation used in the plan's benefit formula to $200,000 annually (as indexed for 2003). This is the same compensation limit that applies to qualified plans under Section 410(a)(17). For example, if a plan provided a death benefit of 2 times compensation for all employees, the death benefit for an employee earning $500,000 would be limited to $400,000 (in 2003) rather than $1,000,000.

## TAX IMPLICATIONS

### Taxation of Employees

Premium payments or other funding deposits to the fund by the employer are generally not taxable to employees; that is, they are treated the same as if there was no VEBA and the employer maintained the plan without a VEBA.

Benefits payable to employees or beneficiaries are, in general, subject to the same income tax treatment as if they were paid directly by the employer.

*Life Insurance.* If the VEBA includes a life insurance (death benefit) plan, the value of life insurance protection is taxable (measured either by the Table 2001 rates or some other measure, as applicable — see Chapter 13). If the plan qualifies as a group term plan under the rules of Section 79, the cost of the first $50,000 of protection is tax-free to the employees and additional insurance coverage is taxed under the Table 2001 rates.

Life insurance proceeds paid directly by a commercial insurer to a beneficiary on group term policies held by a VEBA are income tax free to beneficiaries.[12] It is unclear whether proceeds paid under a whole life policy are entirely income tax free or are taxed similarly to life insurance proceeds received under a qualified plan (see Chapter 13).

For federal estate tax purposes, life insurance held by a VEBA can be kept out of the participant's estate by avoiding incidents of ownership, just as with personally owned insurance. If an irrevocable beneficiary designation is made at least 3 years before death, the policy proceeds will not be includible in the estate.

## Taxation of the VEBA

Income of a VEBA is exempt from regular income tax if all the requirements of Section 501(c)(9) and Section 505 are met, as discussed above.

An organization will not be treated as a tax-exempt VEBA unless it notifies the IRS.[13] This is generally accomplished by filing within 15 months from the end of the month in which the VEBA was organized an application for recognition of exempt status (Form 1024).[14]

Generally, VEBA income set aside (to provide for appropriate benefits and reasonable costs of administering those benefits) in excess of the Section 419A account limits (calculated without reference to any reserve for postretirement medical benefits) is subject to taxation as "unrelated business taxable income (UBTI)" under Code Sections 511 and 512. (Any VEBA income derived from an unrelated trade or business regularly carried on by the VEBA is also subject to such taxation.)

These rules relating to UBTI are applicable even if the VEBA is part of a 10-or-more-employer plan under Section 419A(f)(6).[15] Since maximum tax deduction benefits derive from funding 419A(f)(6) plans far in excess of the Section 419A limits (discussed in the Questions and Answers), to some extent this UBTI exposure nullifies the advantage of the tax-exempt status of the VEBA for purposes of funding a 419A(f)(6) plan. Funding with life insurance or tax-free investment vehicles can eliminate or minimize UBTI exposure.

## Employer's Deduction

In general, an employer can deduct actuarially reasonable contributions to a VEBA that are designated to fund the benefits provided through the VEBA. Deductions are generally subject to the same limits as if the benefit were provided directly; these are found in Code Sections 419 and 419A. These sections provide that deductions are generally limited to the current annual cost of benefits, with a small reserve provision for benefits or claims incurred but not paid.

## ERISA AND OTHER REQUIREMENTS

ERISA treatment of benefits funded through a VEBA is the same as the treatment of any individual benefit plan funded by any other means. The use of a VEBA does not create or remove any reporting and disclosure,

fiduciary, or other requirement otherwise applicable to the benefit plan.

A VEBA is subject to the filing requirement discussed in "Taxation of the VEBA," above.

## WHERE CAN I FIND OUT MORE ABOUT IT?

1. Amoroso, "Computing Deduction Limits for Contributions to Welfare Benefit Plans," *Journal of Taxation*, September 1992.

2. Stiefel and Roth, "VEBAs Revisited as Funding Mechanisms — After DEFRA," *Benefits Law Journal*, Winter 1989/1990.

3. Weiss, "The Multiple Employer Welfare Benefit Trust," *Journal of the American Society of CLU & ChFC*, March 1990.

## QUESTIONS AND ANSWERS

**Question**—Can whole life or other cash value life insurance products be used to fund a death benefit in a VEBA?

*Answer*—The IRS has approved the use of whole life insurance by a VEBA to fund a death benefit plan for employees.[16] The premium schedule under the insurance policies apparently provides an actuarially sound method of funding the death benefit. This in effect provides some acceleration of funding of death benefits as compared with payment and deduction of term premiums only. However, the Department of Labor may challenge the use of whole life insurance to fund death benefits.[17] See also Question and Answer below relating to 419A(f)(6) plans.

**Question**—Can an employer recover excess assets in a VEBA when it terminates after paying out all benefits due to participants?

*Answer*—No, the VEBA regulations effectively provide that when a VEBA is terminated, all excess assets must be paid out to covered employees.[18] Also, under Section 4976, there is generally a 100% penalty tax imposed when a portion of a welfare benefit fund reverts to an employer. What this means in practice is that an employer must avoid overfunding a plan funded through a VEBA.

**Question**—How are VEBA assets allocated when a plan terminates?

*Answer*—As indicated in the preceding question, plan assets cannot revert back to the employer. A VEBA must include a nondiscriminatory formula under which excess assets are allocated to plan participants.[19] For example, assets could be allocated under a formula as follows:

$$\text{Participant's share} = \frac{\text{Participant's compensation during period of participation}}{\text{Total compensation of all participants for all plan years}} \times \text{Excess Plan Assets}$$

Since this formula would tend to increase the share of long-term key employees, consideration should be given to restricting the number of years of participation used in the numerator — to five years, for example.

**Question**—Can plan participants borrow from a VEBA?

*Answer*—Loans from VEBAs are not permitted except in times of "distress," which appears to be strictly interpreted by the IRS.[20]

**Question**—What is a 419A(f)(6) plan and its relationship to a VEBA?

*Answer*—A 419A(f)(6) is a multi-employer (noncollectively bargained) welfare benefit trust arrangement. It can be funded through a VEBA or through a taxable trust. Its advantage is that the usual deduction limitations under Sections 419 and 419A do not apply. In recent years, this provision has been used to provide severance and death benefit plans, usually covering primarily highly compensated employees.

The basic requirements for a deduction under Section 419A(f)(6) are:

1. the plan must be a "welfare benefit";

2. the plan must be a "10 or more employer plan" (defined as a plan to which more than one employer contributes and to which no employer normally contributes more than 10% of the total); and

3. the plan must not maintain "experience-rating arrangements with respect to individual employers."[21]

Because of perceived abuses in the use of this provision, the IRS issued proposed regulations in 2002 that most planners believe will significantly cut back the practicality of using 419A(f)(6) plans. The proposed regulations have the following major provisions:[22]

- An extensive definition of "experience rating" and examples illustrating it. In general, these rules require plans to pool funds of all participating employers and do not allow for experience-adjusted contributions for individual employers based on the experience of their employees only. The use of individual level-premium life insurance contracts, with each employer making an annual contribution equal to the total premiums for its employees, is considered experience-rating. The cash values in the policies are deemed "proxies" for the employer's experience.[23]

- A provision to the effect that insurance contracts are treated as fund assets, with the implications indicated in the preceding paragraph.

- A list of bad characteristics, any one of which will "poison" the plan (but the absence of which does not necessarily guarantee compliance).[24] These are:

  - *Allocation of plan assets* to a specific employer within the fund.

  - *Differential pricing* for different employers in the plan unrelated to standard actuarial factors such as age of the employees covered, number of dependents, etc.

  - *No fixed welfare benefit package.* That is, the plan must provide fixed welfare benefits for a fixed period for a fixed cost. (The implication is that benefits must not be based on fund balances as such).

  - *Unreasonably high cost.*

  - *Nonstandard benefit triggers.* Payments can be made only for illness, personal injury, death, or the employee's involuntary separation from employment. Payments cannot be made to employees when the employer withdraws from the plan.

## FOOTNOTES

1. See Treas. Regs. §§1.501(c)(9)-2(a)(1), 1.501(c)(9)-2(c)(1), 1.501(c)(9)-3.

2. GCM 39440 (1985).

3. On occasion, the DOL has objected to the use of whole life insurance products in ERISA employee benefit plans. The DOL does not have a hard and fast rule prohibiting the sale of whole life insurance to or the purchase of whole life insurance by ERISA plans. Rather, the DOL's position seems to be that the propriety of whole life insurance is judged just as the propriety of other investments is judged — on a facts and circumstances basis. Alternatives, such as term insurance, must be presented, considered, and analyzed. See, e.g., *Reich v. McDonough*, Civ. Action No. 91-12025 H (D. Mass. Dec. 10, 1993) (consent judgment and order settling the case of *Martin v. Feingold*, Civ. Action No. 91-12025 H (D. Mass. filed July 31, 1991)).

4. Generally, an organization will not be a tax-exempt VEBA if the written instrument creating the organization provides for the distribution of its assets upon dissolution to the contributing employers or if state law (in the state in which the organization was created) provides for such distribution. Treas. Reg. §1.501(c)(9)-4(d). Additionally, Code Section 4976 generally imposes a 100% penalty tax when a portion of a welfare benefit fund reverts to an employer.

5. Relevant parts of the Code's definition of a welfare benefit fund are written in the plural: a welfare benefit fund is, in part, a fund providing welfare benefits to "employees or their beneficiaries." Language describing VEBAs in a similarly plural fashion has been held to require that a VEBA provide benefits to more than one employee. IRC Sec. 419(e)(1)(b). See also Rev. Rul. 85-199, 1985-2 CB 163.

6. See Treas. Regs. §§1.501(c)(9)-2(a)(2), 1.501(c)(9)-4(b).

7. IRC Sec. 505(b).

8. See IRC Sec. 505(b)(3).

9. Treas. Regs. §§1.501(c)(9)-2,(a)(2), 1.501(c)(9)-4(b). See also GCMs 39818 (1990), 39801 (1989)

10. Treas. Reg. §1.501(c)(9)-3.

11. Treas. Reg. §1.501(c)(9)-3(f).

12. See, e.g., Let. Ruls. 8534048, 8352022, 8035066, and 8025100.

13. IRC Sec. 505(c).

14. Temp. Treas. Reg. §1,505(c)-1T, Q&A-3, Q&A-4, Q&A-5, and Q&A-6.

15. IRC Sec. 512(a)(3)(E)(i); Temp. Treas. Reg. §1.512(a)-5T, Q&A-3.

16. GCM 39440 (1985).

17. See note 3, above.

18. See Treas. Reg. §1.501(c)(9)-4(d).

19. Ibid.

20. Treas. Reg. §1.501(c)(9)-3(f). This regulation provides that permissible VEBA benefits do not include "the provision of loans to members except in times of distress (as permitted by section 1.501(c)(9)-3(e))." That regulation provides examples of acceptable VEBA benefits, but only explicitly mentions loans once: stating that VEBAs may provide "temporary living expense loans . . . at times of disaster (such as fire or flood) . . . ." Treas. Reg. §1.501(c)(9)-3(e). On a different but related issue, an IRS General Counsel's Memorandum has suggested that a loan from a VEBA to the employer might jeopardize the VEBA's tax-exempt status. GCM 39884 (1992).

21. IRC Sec. 419A(f)(6).

22. Prop. Treas. Reg. §1.419A(f)(6)-1; 67 Fed. Reg. 45933 (7-11-2002).

23. Prop. Treas. Regs. §§1.419A(f)(6)-1(b), 1.419A(f)(6)-1(f), Example 4.

24. Prop. Treas. Reg. §1.419A(f)(6)-1(c).

# ERISA REPORTING AND DISCLOSURE FOR PENSION AND WELFARE PLANS

The Employee Retirement Income Security Act of 1974—ERISA—imposes extensive reporting and disclosure requirements on a broad range of employee benefit plans.

These provisions require various forms and information to be disclosed to plan participants and/or filed with the IRS or the Department of Labor.

Under ERISA, employee benefit plans are divided into two types—pension plans and welfare plans. These terms are defined broadly enough that it generally makes sense to think of them in terms of their exceptions rather than their definitions. That is, an employee benefit plan should be considered covered by the provisions of ERISA unless there is a specific exemption in ERISA or the regulations interpreting ERISA.

## PLANS EXEMPT FROM ERISA

ERISA Section 4(b) contains an exemption from most or all ERISA provisions, including the reporting and disclosure requirements, for certain types of employer plans (both pension and welfare plans). These ERISA-exempt employer plans are:

- plans of state, federal, or local governments or governmental organizations.

- plans of churches, synagogues, or related organizations. (These plans, however, can elect to be covered under ERISA.)

- plans maintained outside the United States for nonresident aliens.

- unfunded excess benefit plans. (These are one type of nonqualified deferred compensation plan, as described in Chapter 14.)

- plans maintained solely to comply with workers' compensation, unemployment compensation, or disability insurance laws.

## "PENSION PLANS" UNDER ERISA

ERISA Section 3(2) defines an "employee pension benefit plan" and "pension plan" as any plan, fund, or program which is established or maintained by an employer or by an employee organization (such as a labor union), or by both, to the extent that by its express terms or as a result of surrounding circumstances such plan, fund, or program (1) provides retirement income to employees, or (2) results in a deferral of income by employees for periods extending to the termination of covered employment or beyond, regardless of the method of calculating the contributions made to the plan, the method of calculating the benefits under the plan, or the method of distributing benefits from the plan.

This definition includes all qualified pension, profit sharing, stock bonus, and similar qualified plans. It also includes some nonqualified deferred compensation plans. (These may, however, be eligible for exemption from ERISA's strict reporting and disclosure requirements—see Chapter 14, at "ERISA REQUIREMENTS.") In general, an ERISA pension plan is any employee benefit plan that involves deferral of an employee's compensation to his or her retirement date or later.

### Regulatory Exemptions — Pension Plans

In addition to these exemptions in ERISA itself, Section 2510.3-2 of the Labor regulations gives partial exemption or special treatment for certain pension-like plans. These special regulatory exemptions include the following:

- A *severance pay plan* is not treated as a pension plan if:

    (1) payments do not depend directly or indirectly on the employee's retiring;

    (2) total payments under the plan do not exceed twice the employee's annual compensation

during the year immediately preceding the separation from service; and

(3) all payments to any employee are generally completed within 24 months of separation from service.

A severance pay plan meeting these criteria need not comply with the reporting and disclosure requirements for pension plans, but must meet the more limited reporting and disclosure requirements for welfare plans discussed below. For example, welfare plans with fewer than 100 participants need not file an annual report (Form 5500 series) if benefits are fully insured or are paid by the employer out of its general assets.

- *Supplemental payment plans* that provide extra benefits to retirees to counteract inflation are exempt from numerous ERISA requirements under Department of Labor regulations.

- *Employer-facilitated IRAs, simplified employee pensions (SEPs), SIMPLEs, and Section 403(b) TDA plans* are, in some cases, either exempt from ERISA's reporting and disclosure requirements or subject to reduced ERISA reporting and disclosure requirements.[1] For details, see the chapters in the main text relating to these plans.

## Pension Plan Reporting and Disclosure

Pension plans must meet the reporting and disclosure requirements described in the chart at the end of this Appendix, with certain exceptions.

At the end of this Appendix is a compliance chart indicating the major reporting and disclosure requirements of ERISA and the timetables for filing or reporting. Copies of Forms 5500 and 5500EZ are also included. Current versions of these forms, as well as the schedules, may be obtained from the local IRS office, or online from the IRS website (http://www.irs.ustreas.gov). Downloaded forms may not be used for filing in some cases.

The following brief explanation of the most important of these reporting and disclosure requirements for pension plans should be helpful in interpreting the significance of these requirements. The major elements of reporting and disclosure are as follows:

1. *The Summary Plan Description (SPD)*. The SPD is intended to describe the major provisions of the plan to participants in plain language. An SPD must be furnished automatically to participants within 120 days after the plan is established or 90 days after a new participant enters an existing plan.[2] If plan provisions change, supplements to the SPD generally must be provided to participants. The contents of the SPD are prescribed by Labor Department regulations, but there is no government form for SPDs. Plans are only required to file a copy of their SPD with the Labor Department if requested to by the Labor Department.

2. *The Annual Report (Form 5500 series)*. This annual financial reporting form must be filed with the IRS each year by the end of the seventh month after the plan year ends.[3] In addition to balance sheets and income statements, an actuary's report (Schedule B, Form 5500) must be included if the plan is a defined benefit plan, and information about any insurance contracts held by the plan must be included on Schedule A, Form 5500.

   The Form 5500 is required to be filed with the Department of Labor. The Form 5500 was revised beginning with the 1999 filing year. Under the revised format there are 13 schedules that accompany the new Form 5500. A plan is only required to file only those schedules that apply to its circumstances.

3. *Summary Annual Report*. The summary annual report is a brief summary of financial information from the Annual Report (Form 5500 series) that must be provided to plan participants each year within nine months of the end of the plan year.[4] Labor regulations have essentially reduced this report to a formality. Participants have a right to see the full Annual Report if they need information about the plan's financial status.

4. *Individual Accrued Benefit Statement*. If a plan participant requests a statement of his or her individual benefits under the plan, the plan administrator must provide it within 30 days. Only one such statement each year needs to be provided to a participant.[5] However, it is good policy to provide an annual individual benefit statement to plan participants, since this helps to communicate the plan's benefits and give them greater impact.

## Title IV Reporting and Disclosure Requirements

Title IV of ERISA, the plan termination insurance provisions, imposes various reporting and disclosure obligations on certain defined benefit pension plans in an effort to help the Pension Benefit Guaranty Corporation insure and protect pension benefits. While a review of these requirements is beyond the scope of this appendix, it should be noted that these requirements were significantly amended in the Uruguay Round Agreements Act of 1994 (popularly referred to as the GATT legislation).

## "WELFARE PLANS" UNDER ERISA

A welfare plan (also called a "welfare benefit plan") is defined in Section 3(1) of ERISA as any plan, fund, or program established or maintained by an employer or by an employee organization, or by both, for the purpose of providing for its participants or their beneficiaries, through the purchase of insurance or otherwise, medical, surgical, or hospital care or benefits, or benefits in the event of sickness, accident, disability, death or unemployment, or vacation benefits, apprenticeship or other training programs, or day care centers, scholarship funds, or prepaid legal services. Certain other plans described in federal labor law are also included.

## Regulatory Exemptions — Welfare Plans

For welfare plans, Section 2510.3-1 of the Labor regulations provides exemptions and limitations from the applicability of ERISA. The following employment practices and benefits are among those that have been declared by regulation to be exempt from the ERISA reporting and disclosure requirements:

- overtime pay, shift pay, holiday premiums, and similar compensation paid for work done other than under normal circumstances.

- compensation for absence from work due to sickness, vacation, holidays, military duty, jury duty, or sabbatical leave or training programs, if paid out of the general assets of the employer (i.e., not funded in advance).

- recreational or dining facilities or first aid centers on the employer's premises.

- holiday gifts.

- group insurance programs offered to employees by an insurer under which no contribution is made by the employer, participation is voluntary, and the program is not actively sponsored by the employer.

- unfunded tuition reimbursement or scholarship programs (other than Section 127 educational assistance plans—see Chapter 33) that are paid out of the employer's general assets.

## Welfare Plan Reporting and Disclosure

All other welfare plans are subject to ERISA reporting and disclosure requirements. However, in general, these are less onerous than those applicable to pension plans.

*Small welfare plan exemption.* One special rule provides that welfare plans with fewer than 100 participants need not file an annual report (Form 5500 series) if they are fully insured or are paid out of the general assets of the employer on a pay-as-you-go basis. These plans also do not need to file a Summary Plan Description.[6]

At the end of this Appendix there is a compliance chart indicating major forms that must be filed with the IRS or Department of Labor or disclosed to participants. Copies of Forms 5500 and 5500EZ are also included. Current versions of these forms, as well as the schedules, may be obtained from the local IRS office or online from the IRS website (http://www.irs.ustreas.gov). Downloaded forms may not be used for filing in some cases.

## FOOTNOTES

1. See also Labor Regs. §§2520.104-48, 2520.104-49 (SEPs); see also IB 99-1, 64 Fed. Reg. 32999 (6-18-99).

2. ERISA Section 104(b)(1).

3. ERISA Sections 103(a)(1)(A), 104(a)(1)(A); IRC Section 6058(a).

4. Labor Reg. §2520.104b-10(c).

5. ERISA Section 105.

6. Labor Reg. §2520.104-20. These plans are relieved of a variety of other reporting and disclosure requirements. For details, see Labor Reg. §2520.104-20.

**Figure A.1**

## MAJOR REPORTING AND DISCLOSURE REQUIREMENTS FOR PENSION PLANS

### I. Government Filings

| Form | Description | Who Must File | When to File | Where to File |
|---|---|---|---|---|
| 5500 | Annual Return/Report of Employee Benefit Plan. | Plan administrator. | On or before last day of seventh month after available — file Form 5558.) | Address indicated in instructions to Form 5500. |
| 5500EZ | Annual Return of One-Participant (Owners and Their Spouses) Plans. | Plan administrator. May be filed for plans that cover only an individual or an individual and spouse who are the owners of a business. May also be filed for partnership plans that cover only partners or partners and their spouses. | Same as Form 5500. | Address indicated in instructions to Form 5500EZ. |
| Schedule A (Form 5500) | Insurance Information. | Plan administrator, where any plan benefits are provided by an insurance company or similar organization. | Attachment to Form 5500. | Same as Form 5500. |
| Schedule B (Form 5500) | Actuarial Information. | Plan administrator of defined benefit plan subject to minimum funding standards. | Attachment to Form 5500. | Same as Form 5500. |
| Schedule C (Form 5500) | Service Provider and Trustee Information. | Plan administrator. | Attachment to Form 5500. | Same as Form 5500. |
| Schedule E (Form 5500) | ESOP Annual Information. | Plan administrator. | Attachment to Form 5500. | Same as Form 5500. |
| Schedule G (Form 5500) | Financial Schedules. | Plan administrator. | Attachment to Form 5500. | Same as Form 5500. |
| Schedule P (Form 5500) | Annual Return of Fiduciary of Employee Benefit Trust. | Trustee or custodian of qualified trust or custodial account. (Begins running of statute of limitations.) | Attachment to Form 5500. | Same as Form 5500. |

**Figure A.1 (continued)**

## MAJOR REPORTING AND DISCLOSURE REQUIREMENTS FOR PENSION PLANS

### I. Government Filings (continued)

| Form | Description | Who Must File | When to File | Where to File |
|------|-------------|---------------|--------------|---------------|
| Schedule SSA (Form 5500) | Annual Registration Statement Identifying Separated Participants with Deferred Vested Benefits. | Plan administrator, if plan had participants who separated with deferred vested benefits during the plan year. | Attachment to Form 5500. | Same as Form 5500. |
| Schedule T (Form 5500) | Qualified Pension Plan Coverage Information. | Plan administrator. | Attachment to Form 5500. | Same as Form 5500. |
| PBGC Form 1-ES | Estimated Premium Payment (Base premiums for plans with 500 or more participants). | Plan administrator or sponsor of defined benefit plan (with 500 or more participants) subject to PBGC provisions. | Within two months after the end of the prior plan year. | Pension Benefit Guaranty Corporation P.O. Box 7247-7426 Philadelphia, PA 19170-7426 |
| PBGC Form 1 | Annual Premium Payment. | Plan administrator or sponsor of defined benefit plan subject to PBGC provisions. | Within 8½ months after the end of the prior plan year. | Pension Benefit Guaranty Corporation P.O. Box 7247-7426 Philadelphia, PA 19170-7426 |

### II. Disclosure to Pension Plan Participants

| Item | Description | Who Must Provide | When Provided |
|------|-------------|------------------|---------------|
| Summary Plan Description | Summary of the provisions of the plan in plain language; includes statement of ERISA rights. | Plan administrator. | New plans: within 120 days after effective date. Updated SPD must be furnished within 210 days of every fifth plan year for plans that have been amended; otherwise SPD must be redistributed every 10 years. New participants: within 90 days after becoming a participant or benefits commence (in the case of beneficiaries). |
| Summary of Material Modification | Summary of any material modification to the plan and any change in information required to be in summary plan description. | Plan administrator. | Within 210 days after the close of the plan year in which the modification was adopted unless changes or modifications are described in a timely distributed summary plan description. |
| Summary Annual Report | Summary of annual report Form 5500. | Plan administrator. | Nine months after end of plan year, or within two months after close of extension period for filing plans filing that form.) |

**Figure A.1 (continued)**

| | | | |
|---|---|---|---|
| **MAJOR REPORTING AND DISCLOSURE REQUIREMENTS FOR PENSION PLANS** | | | |
| **II. Disclosure to Pension Plan Participants (continued)** | | | |
| **Item** | **Description** | **Who Must Provide** | **When Provided** |
| Notice of Preretirement Survivor Benefit | Written explanation of preretirement survivor annuity, participant's right to make an election (or revoke election) to waive the annuity, spouse's rights, and effect of election or revocation. | Plan administrator of plan required to provide (see Chapter 24). | Within period beginning on first day of plan year in which participant attains age 32 and ending with close of plan year in which participant attains age 34. Election must be made within the period beginning on the first day of the plan year in which the participant attains age 35 and ending with the participant's death. For individuals who become participants after age 32, plan must provide explanation within three years of first day of plan year they become participants. |
| Notice of Joint and Survivor Benefit | Written explanation of joint and survivor annuity, right to make election to waive the annuity, right to revoke waiver, effect of election or revocation, and rights of the spouse. | Plan administrator of plan required to provide (see Chapter 24). | Within reasonable period before annuity starting date. Election must be made no sooner than 90 days before the annuity starting date. |
| Notice to Terminated Vested Participants | Same information as provided to IRS on Schedule SSA (Form 5500) concerning participant's accrued benefit. Statement must include notice if certain benefits may be forfeited if the participant dies before a particular date. | Plan administrator. | No later than due date for filing Schedule SSA (Form 5500). |
| Individual Accrued Benefit Statement | Statement of participant's benefit accrued to date based on the latest available data. Statement must include notice of certain benefits may be forfeited if the participant dies before a particular date. | Plan administrator. | Within 30 days of participant's request. Need not be provided more than once in a 12-month period. |

**Figure A.2**

## MAJOR REPORTING AND DISCLOSURE REQUIREMENTS FOR WELFARE PLANS

### I. Government Filings

| Form | Description | Who Must File | When to File | Where to File |
|------|-------------|---------------|--------------|---------------|
| 5500 | Annual Return/Report of Employee Benefit plan. | Plan administrator. | On or before the last day of the seventh month extension available — file Form 5558.) | Adress indicated in instructions to Form 550. |
| Schedule A (Form 5500) | Insurance information. | Plan administrator, where any benefits under the plan are provided by insurance company or similar organization. | Attachment to Form 5000. | Same as Form 5500. |

### II. Disclosure to Welfare Plan Participants and Beneficiaries

| Item | Description | Who Must Provide | When Provided |
|------|-------------|------------------|---------------|
| Summary Plan Description | Summary of the provisions of the plan in plain language; includes statement of ERISA rights. | Plan administrator. | New plans: within 120 days after effective date. Updated SPD must be furnished within 210 days of every fifth plan year for plans that have been amended. Otherwise, SPDs must be redistributed every 10 years. New participants: within 90 days after becoming a participant or benefits commence (in the case of beneficiaries). |
| Summary of Material Modifica- | Summary of any material modification to the plan and any distributedtions required to be in summary plan description. | Plan administrator. | Within 210 days after the close of the plan year in which the modification was adopted unless changes or modifications are described in a timely change in information summary plan description. |
| Summary Annual Report | Summary of annual report Form 5500. | Plan administrator. | Nine months after end of plan year or within two months after close of extension period for filing annual report, if applicable. |

**Form 5500**

Department of the Treasury
Internal Revenue Service

Department of Labor
Pension and Welfare Benefits
Administration

Pension Benefit
Guaranty Corporation

## Annual Return/Report of Employee Benefit Plan

This form is required to be filed under sections 104 and 4065 of the Employee Retirement Income Security Act of 1974 (ERISA) and sections 6047(e), 6057(b), and 6058(a) of the Internal Revenue Code (the Code).

▶ **Complete all entries in accordance with the instructions to the Form 5500.**

Official Use Only
OMB Nos. 1210-0110 / 1210-0089

**2002**

**This Form is Open to Public Inspection.**

### Part I    Annual Report Identification Information

For the calendar plan year 2002 or fiscal plan year beginning MM / DD / YYYY    and ending MM / DD / YYYY

**A**    This return/report is for:    **(1)** ☐ a multiemployer plan;    **(3)** ☐ a multiple-employer plan; or

**(2)** ☐ a single-employer plan (other than a multiple-employer plan);    **(4)** ☐ a DFE (specify) ................... ☐

**B**    This return/report is:    **(1)** ☐ the first return/report filed for the plan;    **(3)** ☐ the final return/report filed for the plan;

**(2)** ☐ an amended return/report;    **(4)** ☐ a short plan year return/report (less than 12 months).

**C**    If the plan is a collectively-bargained plan, check here ................................................................ ▶ ☐

**D**    If filing under an extension of time or the DFVC program, check box and attach required information. (see instructions) .................... ▶ ☐

### Part II    Basic Plan Information -- enter all requested information.

**1a**    Name of plan

**1b**    Three-digit plan number (PN) ▶            **1c**    Effective date of plan    MM / DD / YYYY

**Caution:** *A penalty for the late or incomplete filing of this return/report will be assessed unless reasonable cause is established.*

Under penalties of perjury and other penalties set forth in the instructions, I declare that I have examined this return/report, including accompanying schedules, statements and attachments, as well as the electronic version of this return/report if it is being filed electronically, and to the best of my knowledge and belief, it is true, correct and complete.

**Signature of plan administrator**

**SIGN HERE** ▶ _____    Date    MM / DD / YYYY

Type or print name of individual signing as plan administrator

**a**

**Signature of employer/plan sponsor/DFE**

**SIGN HERE** ▶ _____    Date    MM / DD / YYYY

Type or print name of individual signing as employer, plan sponsor or DFE

**b**

For Paperwork Reduction Act Notice and OMB Control Numbers, see the instructions for Form 5500.    Cat. No. 13500F    Form **5500** (2002)

0 1 0 2 0 0 0 1 0 4

v5.0

Form 5500 (2002)                                                    Page **2**

**2a** Plan sponsor's name and address (employer, if for single-employer plan) (Address should include room or suite no.)

1) Name

2) **c / o**

3) Street

4) City

**2b** Employer Identification Number (EIN)

5) State  Zip Code

6) Foreign Routing Code

**2c** Sponsor's telephone number

7) Foreign Country

**2d** Business code (see instructions)

8) D/B/A

9) Location Address (if different than Street)

Location Address, City, State, Zip (if different than above)

**3a** Plan administrator's name and address (If same as plan sponsor, enter "Same")

1) Name

2) **c / o**

3) Street

4) City

**3b** Administrator's EIN

5) State  Zip Code

6) Foreign Routing Code

**3c** Administrator's telephone number

7) Foreign Country

**4** If the name and/or EIN of the plan sponsor has changed since the last return/report filed for this plan, enter the name, EIN and the plan number from the last return/report below:

**a** Sponsor's name

**b** EIN                    **c** PN

0 1 0 2 0 0 0 2 0 5

Form 5500 (2002)                                                                 Page **3**

**5** Preparer information (optional)

**a** Name (including firm name, if applicable) and address

1) Name

2) Street

3) City

4) State   Zip Code

5) Foreign Postal Code

6) Foreign Country

**b** EIN

**c** Telephone number

**6** Total number of participants at the beginning of the plan year .................................................

**7** Number of participants as of the end of the plan year (welfare plans complete only lines **7a**, **7b**, **7c**, and **7d**)

  **a** Active participants ...................................................................................................

  **b** Retired or separated participants receiving benefits.............................................

  **c** Other retired or separated participants entitled to future benefits........................

  **d** Subtotal. Add lines **7a**, **7b**, and **7c** ...................................................................

  **e** Deceased participants whose beneficiaries are receiving or are entitled to receive benefits ...........................

  **f** Total. Add lines **7d** and **7e** .....................................................................................

  **g** Number of participants with account balances as of the end of the plan year (only defined contribution plans complete this item) ...........

  **h** Number of participants that terminated employment during the plan year with accrued benefits that were less than 100% vested ...........

  **i** If any participant(s) separated from service with a deferred vested benefit, enter the number of separated participants required to be reported on a Schedule SSA (Form 5500) ...........

0102000306

Form 5500 (2002)                                                                 Page **4**

**8**  Benefits provided under the plan (complete **8a** and **8b**, as applicable)

**a**  ☐  Pension benefits  (check this box if the plan provides pension benefits and enter below the applicable pension feature codes from the List of Plan Characteristics Codes printed in the instructions):

☐ ☐ ☐ ☐ ☐ ☐ ☐ ☐ ☐ ☐ ☐

**b**  ☐  Welfare benefits  (check this box if the plan provides welfare benefits and enter below the applicable welfare feature codes from the List of Plan Characteristics Codes printed in the instructions):

☐ ☐ ☐ ☐ ☐ ☐ ☐ ☐ ☐ ☐ ☐

**9a**  Plan funding arrangement (check all that apply)

   **(1)**  ☐  Insurance

   **(2)**  ☐  Code section 412(i) insurance contracts

   **(3)**  ☐  Trust

   **(4)**  ☐  General assets of the sponsor

**9b**  Plan benefit arrangement (check all that apply)

   **(1)**  ☐  Insurance

   **(2)**  ☐  Code section 412(i) insurance contracts

   **(3)**  ☐  Trust

   **(4)**  ☐  General assets of the sponsor

**10**  Schedules attached (Check all applicable boxes and, where indicated, enter the number attached. See instructions.)

**a  Pension Benefit Schedules**

   **1)**  ☐  **R**  (Retirement Plan Information)

   **2)**  ☐ ☐☐☐  **T**  (Qualified Pension Plan Coverage Information)

       If a Schedule T is not attached because the plan is relying on coverage testing information for a prior year, enter the year ........ ▶  ☐YYYY☐

   **3)**  ☐  **B**  (Actuarial Information)

   **4)**  ☐  **E**  (ESOP Annual Information)

   **5)**  ☐  **SSA**  (Separated Vested Participant Information)

**b  Financial Schedules**

   **1)**  ☐  **H**  (Financial Information)

   **2)**  ☐  **I**  (Financial Information--Small Plan)

   **3)**  ☐ ☐☐☐  **A**  (Insurance Information)

   **4)**  ☐  **C**  (Service Provider Information)

   **5)**  ☐  **D**  (DFE/Participating Plan Information)

   **6)**  ☐  **G**  (Financial Transaction Schedules)

   **7)**  ☐ ☐☐☐  **P**  (Trust Fiduciary Information)

0 1 0 2 0 0 0 4 0 7

Form **5500-EZ**

Department of the Treasury
Internal Revenue Service

**Annual Return of One-Participant
(Owners and Their Spouses) Retirement Plan**

This form is required to be filed under
section 6058(a) of the Internal Revenue Code.

▶ **Complete all entries in accordance with
the instructions to the Form 5500-EZ.**

Official Use Only

OMB No. 1545-0956

**2002**

This Form is Open to
Public Inspection.

---

**Part I**    **Annual Return Identification Information**

For the calendar plan year 2002
or fiscal plan year beginning    MM / DD / YYYY      **and ending**    MM / DD / YYYY

**A**   This return is:    **(1)** ☐   the first return filed for the plan;    **(3)** ☐   the final return filed for the plan;

                  **(2)** ☐   an amended return;    **(4)** ☐   a short plan year return
                                                        (less than 12 months).

**B**   If filing under an extension of time, check box and attach required information. (see instructions) ............................ ▶ ☐

---

**Part II**    **Basic Plan Information --** enter all requested information.

**1a**   Name of plan

**1b**   Three-digit plan number (PN) ▶   ☐☐☐

**1c**   Date plan first
became effective    MM / DD / YYYY

**Caution:** *A penalty for the late or incomplete filing of this return will be assessed unless reasonable cause is established.*

Under penalties of perjury and other penalties set forth in the instructions, I declare that I have examined this return, including accompanying schedules, statements and attachments, as well as the electronic version of this return if it is being filed electronically, and to the best of my knowledge and belief, it is true, correct and complete.

**Signature of employer or plan administrator**

**SIGN HERE** ▶                                Date    MM / DD / YYYY

Type or print name of individual signing as employer or plan administrator

For Paperwork Reduction Act Notice, see the instructions for Form 5500-EZ.      Cat. No. 63263R      Form **5500-EZ** (2002)

0 3 0 2 0 0 0 1 0 6

v5.0

---

Form 5500-EZ (2002)                                                        Page **2**

Official Use Only

**2a**  Employer's name and address (Address should include room or suite no.)

1)  Name

    Name Continued

2)  c / o

3)  Street

4)  City

5)  State    Zip Code

6)  Foreign Routing Code

7)  Foreign Country

8)  D/B/A

9)  Location Address if different than Street

    Location Address if different than (4) or (5)

**2b**  Employer Identification Number (EIN)
     (Do not enter your Social Security Number)

**2c**  Employer's telephone number

**2d**  Business code (see instructions)

**3a**  Plan administrator's name and address (If same as employer, enter "Same")

1)  Name

    Name Continued

2)  c / o

3)  Street

4)  City

5)  State    Zip Code

6)  Foreign Routing Code

7)  Foreign Country

**3b**  Administrator's EIN

**3c**  Administrator's telephone number

**4**  If the name and/or EIN of the employer has changed since the last return filed for this plan, enter the name, EIN and the plan number from the last return below:

a  Employer's name

b  EIN                              c  PN

0 3 0 2 0 0 0 2 0 7

Form 5500-EZ (2002)                                      Page **3**

Official Use Only

**5**   Preparer information (optional)

**a**   Name (including firm name, if applicable) and address

**1)**   Name

     Name Continued

**2)**   Street

**3)**   City                                               **b**   EIN

**4)**   State   Zip Code

**5)**   Foreign Routing Code                               **c**   Telephone number

**6)**   Foreign Country

**6**   Type of plan:   **(a)**  ☐  Defined benefit pension plan (other than a plan described in Code section 412(i))   **(d)**  ☐  Profit-sharing plan

                    **(b)**  ☐  Defined benefit pension plan described in Code section 412(i)   **(e)**  ☐  Stock bonus plan

                    **(c)**  ☐  Money purchase pension plan (see instructions)   **(f)**  ☐  ESOP plan (attach Schedule E (Form 5500))

**7a**  If this is a master/prototype, or regional prototype plan, enter the opinion/notification letter number ..........  ▶

  **b**  Check if this plan covers:

     **(1)**  ☐  Self-employed individuals,   **(2)**  ☐  Partner(s) in a partnership, or   **(3)**  ☐  100% owner of corporation

**8a**  Enter the number of qualified pension benefit plans maintained by the employer (including this plan) ........................  ▶

  **b**  Check here if you have more than one plan and the total assets of all plans are more than $100,000 (see instructions) ........  ▶

**9**   Enter the number of participants in each category listed below:   **Number**

  **a**  Under age 59 1/2 at the end of the plan year ...................................................................................

  **b**  Age 59 1/2 or older at the end of the plan year, but under age 70 1/2 at the beginning of the plan year ......................

  **c**  Age 70 1/2 or older at the beginning of the plan year ..................................................................

0 3 0 2 0 0 0 3 0 8

Form 5500-EZ (2002)                                          Page **4**

Official Use Only

**10a** *(1)* Is this a fully insured pension plan which is funded entirely by insurance or annuity contracts? ▶          ☐ Yes          ☐ No

If "Yes," complete lines 10a*(2)* through 10f and skip lines 10g through 13d.

*(2)* If 10a*(1)* is "Yes," are the insurance contracts held: ............................................. ▶ **(1)**          ☐ under a          **(2)** ☐ with no
trust                    trust

**b** Cash contributions received by the plan for this plan year ......................................          00

**c** Noncash contributions received by the plan for this plan year ...................................          00

**d** Total plan distributions to participants or beneficiaries (see instructions) .................          00

**e** Total nontaxable plan distributions to participants or beneficiaries ...........................          00

**f** Transfers to other plans ......................................................................................          00

**g** Amounts received by the plan other than from contributions ..................................          00

**h** Plan expenses other than distributions ...............................................................          00

|  | **(a)** Beginning of Year | **(b)** End of Year |
|---|---|---|
| **11a** Total plan assets ........ | 00 | 00 |
| **b** Total plan liabilities ..... | 00 | 00 |

**12** **Specific Assets:** If the plan held assets at any time during the plan year in any of the following categories, check "Yes" and enter the current value of any assets remaining in the plan as of the end of the plan year. Otherwise, check "No."

|  | Yes | No | Amount |
|---|---|---|---|
| **a** Partnership/joint venture interests ............................................... | ☐ | ☐ | 00 |
| **b** Employer real property.................................................................. | ☐ | ☐ | 00 |
| **c** Real estate (other than employer real property) ........................... | ☐ | ☐ | 00 |

0 3 0 2 0 0 0 4 0 9

Form 5500-EZ (2002)                                                    Page **5**

| | Yes | No | Amount |
|---|---|---|---|
| **d** Employer securities ......................................................... | ☐ | ☐ | .00 |
| **e** Participant loans (see instructions) ................................ | ☐ | ☐ | .00 |
| **f** Loans (other than to participants) ................................... | ☐ | ☐ | .00 |
| **g** Tangible personal property ............................................. | ☐ | ☐ | .00 |

**13** Check "Yes" and enter amount involved if any of the following transactions took place between the plan and a disqualified person during this plan year. Otherwise, check "No."

| | Yes | No | Amount |
|---|---|---|---|
| **a** Sale, exchange, or lease of property ............................. | ☐ | ☐ | .00 |
| **b** Payment by the plan for services ................................... | ☐ | ☐ | .00 |
| **c** Acquisition or holding of employer securities ................. | ☐ | ☐ | .00 |
| **d** Loan or extension of credit ........................................... | ☐ | ☐ | .00 |

| | | Yes | No |
|---|---|---|---|
| **14a** Does your business have any employees other than you and your spouse (and your partners and their spouses)? ....................................................................................................................... ▶ | | ☐ | ☐ |
| If 14a is "No," do not complete line 14b or line 14c. See the specific instructions for line 14b and line 14c. | | | |
| **b** Total number of employees (including you and your spouse and your partners and their spouses) ............ ▶ | | | |
| **c** Does this plan meet the coverage requirements of Code section 410(b)? .......................................... ▶ | | ☐ | ☐ |
| **15a** Did the plan distribute any annuity contracts this plan year? ........................................................ ▶ | | ☐ | ☐ |
| **b** During this plan year, did the plan make distributions to a married participant in a form other than a qualified joint and survivor annuity or were any distributions on account of the death of a married participant made to beneficiaries other than the spouse of that participant? ................................................................. ▶ | | ☐ | ☐ |
| **c** During this plan year, did the plan make loans to married participants? .......................................... ▶ | | ☐ | ☐ |

0 3 0 2 0 0 0 5 0 A

## COMMONLY CONTROLLED EMPLOYERS

In designing qualified plans and other employee benefit plans, the plan designer often deals with employer organizations (incorporated or unincorporated) that are owned or controlled in common with other such organizations. Plan coverage must then sometimes be coordinated among members of the commonly controlled group of employers.

Common control must be taken into account in identifying the "employer" in an employee benefit plan under a variety of complex rules in the Internal Revenue Code. The objective of these rules is to prevent a business owner from getting around the coverage and nondiscrimination requirements for qualified plans by artificially segregating employees to be benefited from a plan into one organization, with the remainder being employed by subsidiaries or organizations with lesser plan benefits or no plan at all. While this is still technically possible, the controlled group rules restrict this practice considerably.

### Overview of Controlled Group Rules

The common control rules are inherently complicated, because the forms in which businesses can be owned are complicated. Complexity in the ownership structure of a business reflects many non-tax considerations such as capital structure and administrative needs; consequently these common control rules probably will always be complicated. There are four sets of these common control rules:

1. Under IRC Section 414(b), all employees of all corporations in a *controlled group* of corporations are treated as employed by a single employer for purposes of IRC Sections 401, 408(k), 408(p), 410, 411, 415, and 416. The major impact of this comes from the participation rules of Section 410, which, in effect, require the participation and coverage tests to be applied to the entire controlled group, rather than to any single corporation in the group. IRC Section 414(c) provides similar rules for commonly controlled partnerships and proprietorships.

2. IRC Section 414(m) provides that employees of an *affiliated service group* are treated as employed by a single employer. This requirement similarly has its major impact in determining participation in a qualified plan, but it applies to other employee benefit requirements as well.

3. A *leased employee* is treated as an employee of the lessor corporation under certain circumstances under IRC Section 414(n).

Some examples will give a general idea of the impact of these provisions on plan design; these are discussed in detail later. *Note:* The common thread of these examples is that the related organization's employees must be *taken into account* in applying the participation rules. This does not mean that these employees must necessarily be covered.

---

*Example:* Alpha Corporation owns 80% of the stock of Beta Corporation. Alpha and Beta are members of a parent subsidiary-controlled group of corporations. In applying the participation and coverage rules of IRC Section 410, Alpha and Beta must be considered as a single employer.

---

*Example:* Bert and Harry own stock as follows:

| Owner | Corporation A | Corporation B |
|-------|---------------|---------------|
| Bert  | 60%           | 60%           |
| Harry | 30            | 30            |
|       | 90%           | 90%           |

---

Corporations A and B are a brother-sister controlled group. Thus, A and B must be considered as a single employer for purposes of IRC Section 410 and most other qualified plan rules.

*Example:* Medical Services, Inc., provides administrative and laboratory services for Dr. Sam and Dr. Joe, each of whom is an incorporated sole practitioner. Dr. Sam and Dr. Joe each own 50% of Medical Services, Inc. If either Dr. Sam or Dr. Joe adopts a qualified plan, employees of Medical Services, Inc., will have to be taken into account in determining whether plan coverage is nondiscriminatory.

*Example:* Calculators Incorporated, an actuarial firm, contracts with Temporary Services, Inc., an employee-leasing firm, to lease employees on a substantially full-time basis. The leased employees will have to be taken into account in determining nondiscrimination in any qualified plan of Calculators, unless Temporary maintains a minimum (10% nonintegrated) money-purchase pension plan for the leased employees.

## CONTROLLED GROUPS OF CORPORATIONS AND OTHER BUSINESS ORGANIZATIONS

Under IRC Sections 414(b) and 414(c), all employees of members of a controlled group of corporations or controlled group of trades or businesses (whether or not incorporated) that are under common control are treated as employed by a single employer for purposes of Sections 401, 408(k), 408(p), 410, 411, 415, and 416. This covers most provisions of the qualified plan law. The most important impact relates to the coverage requirements of IRC Section 410. Thus, all employees of employers in a controlled group must be taken into account when determining whether a qualified plan maintained by any employer in the controlled group satisfies the percentage participation tests or the discriminatory tests.

The existence of a controlled group is determined by applying the rules of IRC Section 1563(a), a section originally designed to inhibit corporations from breaking up into smaller units to take advantage of the graduated corporate tax rates. Under this provision, there are three types of controlled groups: parent-subsidiary controlled groups, brother-sister controlled groups, and combined groups.

### Parent–Subsidiary Controlled Group

A parent-subsidiary controlled group is one or more chains of corporations connected through stock ownership with a common parent corporation if, with respect to the stock of each corporation (except the parent corporation):

At least 80% of the total combined voting power of all classes of stock entitled to vote or at least 80% of the total value of shares of all classes of stock is owned by one or more corporations in the group and the common parent corporation satisfies the same 80% test with at least one other corporation in the group. Stock owned directly by any other corporation in the group is excluded in determining the parent corporation's ownership.

In applying this test to unincorporated trades or businesses, the 80% test is applied to an interest in profits or to a capital interest.

*Example*: Suppose Alpha Corporation owns 80% of the total combined voting power of all classes of stock entitled to vote of Beta Corporation. Beta Corporation owns stock that possesses at least 80% of the total value of shares of all classes of stock of Gamma Corporation. Alpha is the common parent, and the parent-subsidiary controlled group consists of Alpha, Beta, and Gamma.

### Brother–Sister Controlled Group

A brother-sister controlled group consists of two or more corporations in which five or fewer individuals, estates, or trusts own (with attribution, as described below) stock possessing:

At least 80% of the total combined voting power or value of all classes of stock (excluding nonvoting stock which is limited and preferred as to dividends) of each corporation, and more than 50% of the total combined voting power or value of all classes of stock (excluding nonvoting stock that is limited and preferred as to dividends) of each corporation, taking into account the stock ownership of each owner only to the extent that the owner's interest is identical in each corporation.

*Example:* Corporations M, N, and O have only one class of stock, which is owned by five unrelated individuals as follows:

| | Percentage of Ownership in | | | Identical Ownership in |
|---|---|---|---|---|
| Investor | M | N | O | MNO |
| Alex | 20% | 10% | 20% | 10 % |
| Bartley | 20 | 30 | 10 | 10 |
| Clay | 20 | 20 | 30 | 20 |
| Davis | 20 | 20 | 20 | 20 |
| Ensley | 20 | 20 | 20 | 20 |
| Total | 100% | 100% | 100% | 80 % |

Corporations M, N, and O constitute a brother-sister controlled group.

---

*Example:* Three corporations, Q, S, and T are owned by four unrelated individuals as follows:

| | Percentage of Ownership in | | | Identical Ownership in | | |
|---|---|---|---|---|---|---|
| Investor | Q | S | T | Q-S | Q-T | S-T |
| Walt | 50 % | 25 % | 25.5 % | 25 % | 25.5 % | 25.0 % |
| Xavier | 50 | 25 | 25.5 | 25 | 25.5 | 25.0 |
| Yolanda | 0 | 25 | 24.5 | 0 | 0.0 | 24.5 |
| Zorba | 0 | 25 | 24.5 | 0 | 0.0 | 24.5 |
| Totals | 100 % | 100 % | 100 % | 50 % | 51 % | 99 % |

Corporation Q and S do not constitute a brother-sister controlled group, because, although four individuals together own 100% of each, taking only identical ownership into account, there is only 50% common control. Although identical ownership in Q and T adds up to 51%, they are not a brother-sister group—see the next example. Finally, S and T constitute a brother-sister controlled group, with identical ownership adding up to a total of 99%.

---

At one time, the IRS included an example in the regulations which, somewhat simplified, went as follows:

| | Percentage of Ownership in | | | Identical Ownership in | | |
|---|---|---|---|---|---|---|
| Investor | A | B | C | AB | AC | BC |
| 1 | 100 % | 60 % | 60 % | 60 % | 60 % | 60 % |
| 2 | 0 | 40 | 0 | 0 | 0 | 0 |
| 3 | 0 | 0 | 40 | 0 | 0 | 0 |
| Total | 100 % | * | * | 60 % | 60 % | 60 % |

*100% under prior regulations; 60% under current regulations. See below.

---

Prior regulations asserted that AB, AC, and BC constituted brother-sister controlled groups, even though some of the owners held no interest at all in A, B, or C. This interpretation was declared invalid by the U.S. Supreme Court in *U.S. v. Vogel Fertilizer Company.*[1] Current regulations now reflect this by providing that each person whose stock ownership is taken into account for purposes of the 80% requirement also must be a person whose stock ownership is counted toward the 50% requirement.[2] Under this interpretation, there are no brother-sister groups in this situation.

## Combined Group

A combined group is three or more corporations each of which is a member of a parent-subsidiary group or a brother-sister group and one of which is a common parent of a parent-subsidiary group and also is included in a brother-sister group.

---

*Example*: Ken, an individual, owns 80% of the total combined voting power of all classes of stock of Steel Corporation and Lint Corporation. Lint Corporation owns 80% of the total combined voting power of all classes of the stock of Octopus Corporation. Steel and Lint are members of a brother-sister controlled group. Lint and Octopus are members of a parent-subsidiary group. Lint is the common parent of the parent-subsidiary group and also a member of the brother-sister group. Therefore, Steel, Lint, and Octopus constitute a combined group.

---

## Stock Not Taken into Account in Controlled Group Determination

Certain stock is excluded from consideration in computing the percentages in the controlled group tests.[3] In general, note that excluding stock from consideration makes it more likely that the tests will be met, because the target shareholder's stock will be a larger percentage of the amount outstanding. This is the purpose of these exclusionary rules; in general, they are designed to thwart attempts to get around controlled group tests by transferring stock to various trusts or other entities, as the rules indicate.

First of all, nonvoting preferred stock and treasury stock are not taken into account.

In addition, if the parent owns 50% or more of the total combined voting power or value of all classes of stock in the potential subsidiary corporation, the following are not taken into account in determining the existence of a parent-subsidiary controlled group:

Stock in a subsidiary held by a trust that is part of a plan of deferred compensation for the benefit of the employees of the parent or the subsidiary.

Stock in the subsidiary owned by an individual who is a principal shareholder (5% or more of voting power or total value) or an officer of the potential parent.

Stock in the subsidiary owned by an employee of the subsidiary, if the stock is subject to conditions that run in favor of the parent or subsidiary and that substantially restrict the right to dispose of such stock. Stock subject to the typical buy-sell agreement generally would fall within this provision.

Stock in the subsidiary owned by a tax-exempt organization that is controlled directly or indirectly by the parent or subsidiary or by an individual, estate, or trust that is a principal shareholder of the parent, by an officer of the potential parent, or by any combination of the above.[4]

For purposes of the brother-sister controlled group tests, the following stock is excluded whenever five or fewer potential common owners own at least 50% of the total combined voting power or value of all classes of stock:

Stock held for the benefit of the employees of the corporation by a qualified retirement plan trust.

Stock owned by an employee of the corporation, if the stock is subject to restrictions that run in favor of any of the common owners of the corporation and that substantially restrict the right to dispose of the stock (with an exception for a bona fide reciprocal stock-purchase agreement).

Stock owned by a tax-exempt organization that is controlled directly or indirectly by the corporation, by an individual, estate, or trust that is a principal shareholder of the corporation, by an officer of the corporation, or by any combination of these.[5]

## Constructive Ownership (Attribution) Rules

In determining the existence of a controlled group, an individual may be deemed to own not only stock owned directly but also stock owned by certain related parties.[6]

The following rules apply for both parent-subsidiary and brother-sister determinations[7]:

An option to acquire stock causes the option holder to be treated as owning the stock.

Stock owned directly or indirectly by or for a partnership is considered owned by any partner having an interest of 5% or more in capital or profits, in proportion to the partner's interest in capital or profits (whichever is greater).

Stock owned directly or indirectly by an estate or trust (excluding a qualified trust) is considered owned by a beneficiary who has an actuarial interest of 5% or more in such stock, to the extent of the actuarial interest.

Stock owned directly or indirectly by or for any portion of a grantor trust is considered owned by the grantor.

Further attribution rules apply in the brother-sister situation.[8] These are:

Stock owned directly by or for a corporation is considered owned by any person who owns 5% or more in value of its stock in proportion to the percentage of corporate value owned by the person.

An individual is considered to own stock in a corporation owned directly or indirectly by or for his spouse (if not legally separated under a decree of divorce or separate maintenance), unless the person's ownership satisfies certain standards of remoteness set out in Section 1563(e)(5).

A parent is deemed to own stock owned directly or indirectly by or for his children, including legally adopted children, who are less than 21 years of age, and an individual less than 21 years old is deemed to own stock owned directly or indirectly by or for his parents, including legally adoptive parents.

If an individual owns more than 50% of the total combined voting power or value of all classes of stock in a corporation, the individual is considered as owning stock in the corporation owned directly or indirectly by or for his parents, grandparents, grandchildren, and children who have attained age 21.

The above attribution rules all can be used to provide reattribution to another owner, except that stock attributed under the family attribution rules is not reattributed.[9] This can result in very complex attribution patterns, in some cases.

## Consequences of Controlled Group Status

Once again, all employees of all corporations that are members of a controlled group of corporations are treated as employed by a single employer for various purposes, specified in IRC Section 414(b). Probably the most significant of these consequences is the application of the coverage tests of IRC Section 410. All three tests will be applied to the group as a whole, except to the extent that the tests can be applied to a subgroup constituting a separate line of business under IRC Section 414(r). This does not necessarily mean that a plan cannot qualify if it involves employees of only one member of a controlled group. The plan for a single company in the controlled group could qualify if it meets one of the three tests, such as the average-benefit test in particular.

It is also possible that the controlled group aggregation rules can be applied to the advantage of the employer. For example, a plan for a controlled group might meet the average-benefit test, even though in a given corporation included in the group there might be only one or two participants, both among the highest paid employees of that corporation. Considered separately, the plan for that corporation would fail to qualify.

## AFFILIATED SERVICE GROUP

The purpose and effect of the affiliated service group rules of IRC Section 414(m) are best understood by looking at the loophole that this provision was designed to close. This loophole typically involved professional corporations or partnerships that desired to exclude rank-and-file employees from qualified plans maintained for the professional owners.

*Example*: Consider a situation in which two physicians enter into an equal partnership for the practice of medicine. A similar alternative practice was for each doctor to form a one-person professional corporation and then have the professional corporation enter into a partnership. The partnership could then form a separate support business to provide all support services for the medical practice, and the support business would become the employer of all the support employees. Each of the doctors would own just 50% of the support organization. Under all the other aggregation rules discussed here, except for the affiliated service group rules, the doctors could each adopt a qualified plan covering only themselves and none of the regular employees. The affiliated service group rules basically eliminate this type of planning or restrict it severely.

---

The affiliated service group provisions provide complex rules under which the employees of an *affiliated service group* must be included in any qualified plans that benefit the owners. An affiliated service group includes the *service organization* and the professional organization itself. For purposes of most of the pension provisions, including the coverage and nondiscrimination rules, all employees of an affiliated service group are treated as being employed by a single employer.

An affiliated service group means a service organization and one or more organizations that meet one of the following two tests[10]:

1. A service organization that is a shareholder or partner in the first organization and regularly performs services for the first organization or is regularly associated with the first organization in performing services for third persons.

2. An organization in which a significant portion of its business is the performance of services of a type historically performed for the first organization or for a service organization that is the shareholder or partner in the first organization. However, this applies only if 10% or more of the organization is owned by highly compensated employees (as defined in Chapter 25) of the first organization or any service organization that is a shareholder or partner in the first organization.

In addition, an affiliated service group also consists of a service recipient and an organization that performs management functions for the recipient.[11]

Under the proposed regulations, the rules apply primarily to service organizations of the type that provide professional services in the field of health, law, engineering, architecture, accounting, actuarial science, performing arts, consulting, or insurance. However, this list can be further expanded through regulations.[12]

*Example*: As an example of the operation of the affiliated service group rules, suppose Dr. VanDerslice incorporates and the corporation becomes a partner with the professional corporations of other doctors. Doctor VanDerslice's corporation regularly associates with the other professional corporations in performing services for a third person—individual patients, a hospital, and the like. Each corporation and the partnership of these corporations constitutes an affiliated service group, because the corporation is a service organization that is a partner with the others and is regularly associated with the partnership in performing services for third persons.

As is readily apparent, the affiliated service group rules go considerably beyond the loophole they were initially intended to close. Furthermore, the complexity of these rules is such that it is often difficult to determine whether they apply. Furthermore, many of the affiliated service group provisions involve a degree of subjective judgment—that is, ultimately they are up to the discretion of the IRS—unlike the controlled group rules which, though complex, are relatively mechanical. Thus, in doubtful cases, it is advisable to obtain a ruling from the IRS about whether an organization is a member of an affiliated service group.[13]

## EMPLOYEE LEASING

The leased employee provisions of IRC Section 414(n) were designed to reduce the discrimination potential from an employer's choosing to lease employees from an independent employee leasing organization, rather than employ them directly. The purpose of this practice is to keep the employees technically off the payroll of the lessee business and, thus, outside the coverage of its qualified plans.

This practice is limited under current law. A leased employee is considered an employee of the lessee organization for which the services are performed if:

The employee has performed services on a substantially full-time basis for at least one year, and the services are "performed under the primary direction or control by the recipient."[14]

This rule does not apply if the leasing organization itself maintains a "safe-harbor" plan for the leased employees meeting certain minimum requirements:

The plan must be a nonintegrated money-purchase plan with an employer contribution rate of at least 10% of compensation, and the plan must provide immediate participation and full and immediate vesting; and

All employees of the leasing organization with compensation of $1,000 or more over the past four years must be covered.

The safe-harbor exemption may not be used if leased employees constitute more than 20% of the recipient's (lessor's) nonhighly compensated work force.

Since 10% is a relatively modest plan contribution level, many leasing organizations adopt this approach. Thus, employee leasing remains a viable method for minimizing plan benefits and contributions for low-level employees, even with the restrictions of IRC Section 414(n).

Because of the 1-year requirement, the leasing provision has no impact on most short-term temporary help. Attempts to technically avoid this requirement by rotating leased employees may not be effective, because the 1-year requirement is determined on the basis of cumulative service for the recipient. The requirement of treating the leased employee as an employee of the recipient does not begin until the leased employee has met the 1-year service requirement.

Because of the relatively low safe-harbor provision, some employers might be tempted to convert all their employees to leased employees through some arrangement with a leasing organization. However, the IRS has taken the position that the Code provision applies only to bona fide employee leases. If the lease is not deemed bona fide, the employees will be treated for qualified plan purposes as if they were employed directly.

## FOOTNOTES

1. 102 S.Ct. 821 (1982).
2. Treas. Reg. §1.1563-1(a)(3).
3. IRC Section 1563(c).
4. IRC Section 1563(c)(2)(A).
5. IRC Section 1563(c)(2)(B).
6. IRC Section 1563(e).
7. IRC Section 1563(d).
8. IRC Section 1563(d)(2).
9. IRC Section 1563(f)(2).
10. IRC Section 414(m)(2).
11. IRC Section 414(m)(5).
12. Prop. Treas. Reg. §1.414(m)-2(f).
13. A ruling can be obtained pursuant to Rev. Proc. 92-6, Sec. 14, 1992-1 CB 611.
14. See IRC Section 414(n).

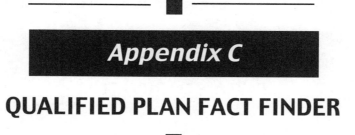

# Appendix C

## QUALIFIED PLAN FACT FINDER

### APP FORM 101

### RETIREMENT PLAN DATA AND ABSTRACT FORM

Prepared for _____

By _____

Date _____

## SECTION I — RETIREMENT PLAN DATA

## PART A — CLIENT PROFILE

A-1. Legal Name _____

Address _____

_____ Zip _____

Telephone Number _____

Contact _____

A-2. Employer (Taxpayer) Identification Number _____

A-3. Nature of Enterprise (Check Appropriate Line)

| | | | |
|---|---|---|---|
| 3.1 _____ Sole proprietorship | | 3.6 _____ Municipal corp. or government agency |
| 3.2 _____ Partnership | | 3.7 _____ Professional corporation |
| 3.3 _____ Business corporation | | 3.8 _____ Business or real estate trust |
| 3.4 _____ S corporation | | 3.9 _____ Other: specify |
| 3.5 _____ Exempt org. (Sec. _____) | | _____ |

A-4. Nature of Business (Principal Business Activity)

_____

_____

IRS business code number _____

A-5. Accounting Method (Check One)

_____ Cash          _____ Accrual

A-6. Fiscal Year Ends _____
          (Month)                              (Day)

A-7. Date of Incorporation or Establishment

_____ (Month and Year)

A-8. State of Incorporation or Domicile _____

A-9. Related Corporation or Unincorporated Entities, including Affiliated Service Groups (Names, Nature of Enterprises, Ownership Percentages of Related Enterprises)

_____

_____

_____

_____

A-10. Predecessor Entities

    10.1 Name _____

    10.2 Nature of Entity _____

    10.3 Date of Establishment _____

    10.4 Date of Transfer _____

A-11. What is the Approximate Rate of Employee Turnover as a Percent of the Active Group for the Past Five Years?

    19____        _____%

    19____        _____%

    19____        _____%

    19____        _____%

    19____        _____%

A-12. Client Motives (For a New Benefit Program)

_____

_____

_____

A-13. Employee Groups under Consideration (For a New Benefit Program)

    13.1 _____ Salaried Employees

    13.2 _____ Hourly Employees

    13.3 _____ Collective-Bargaining Unit Employees

    13.4 _____ Leased Employees

    13.5 _____ Other

A-14. Competitors in Industry (Details as to Their Compensation Programs)

_____

_____

_____

A-15. Local Nonindustry Employers (Details as to Their Compensation Programs)

_____

_____

_____

_____

## PART B — FINANCIAL DATA

B-1.  Attach Balance Sheets (Last Two or Three Years) and Summarize

_____

_____

B-2.  Attach Profit and Loss Statements and Summarize

_____

_____

_____

_____

_____

B-3.  Summarize Earnings Projections

_____

_____

B-4.  What Type of Cost Commitment Can Be considered for a Pension or a Profit-Sharing Plan or Both?

4.1  _____% of payroll

4.2  _____% of profit

4.3  _____% of profit in excess of $_____

4.4  $_____ Flat dollar amount

4.5  Other _____

_____

# PART C — CLIENT'S OTHER BENEFIT PROGRAMS

C-1.  Nonqualified Retirement Plans

    1.1   Plans of general application _____

          _____

          _____

          _____

    1.2   Personal plans (for individuals)

          _____

          _____

          _____

C-2.  Group Life Insurance

    2.1   How much _____

    2.2   Who is covered _____

    2.3   Beneficiary _____

    2.4   Premiums paid by

          (a) _____ Employer

          (b) _____ Employee

               _____ Payroll deduction

               _____ Other (specify) _____

    2.5   Carrier _____

C-3.  Accidental Death and Dismemberment

    3.1   How much _____

    3.2   Who is covered _____

    3.3   Beneficiary _____

    3.4   Premiums paid by

          (a) _____ Employer

          (b) _____ Employee

               _____ Payroll deduction

               _____ Other (specify) _____

    3.5   Carrier _____

    3.6   Workmen's compensation offset

          _____ Yes         _____ No      Explain _____

3.7    All accidents covered

_____ Yes                    _____ No              Explain _____

C-4.   Long-Term Disability Coverage

4.1    How much _____            How long _____

4.2    Who is covered _____            Waiting period _____

4.3    Premiums paid by

_____    Employer

_____    Employee

_____ Payroll deduction

_____ Other (specify) _____

4.4    Carrier _____

4.5    All causes

_____ Yes                    _____ No              Explain _____

4.6    Offsets

_____ Yes                    _____ No              Explain _____

4.7    Definition of disability _____

_____

_____

C-5.   Existing Qualified Retirement Plans (list the following for each plan—use additional sheets if necessary)

5.1    Name of plan _____

5.2    Circle type of plan:    Defined-Benefit  Money-Purchase  Target       Profit-Sharing

5.3.   a. Collectively bargained plan?_____No _____Yes (attach relevant portions of collective bargaining agreement)

b. Multiemployer plan? _____No _____Yes

5.4    Eligibility: a. age _____  b. Waiting period _____  c. employee classification _____

5.5    Contribution rate: By employer _____         By employee

5.6    Benefit structure _____

5.7    Normal retirement benefit _____ At Age _____

5.8    Early retirement benefit _____ At Age _____

5.9    Death benefit _____

5.10   Disability benefit _____

Definition of disability _____

5.11   Vesting rate _____

5.12   Number of employees covered _____

5.13   Are there any employees who are covered by this plan to be covered by new plan? _____

If so, are there to be offset provisions? _____

## PART D – EMPLOYEE CENSUS DATA

| Name | Sex | Date of Birth (or Age) | Date Hired (or Years of Service) | Position | Highly Compensated (HC) or Key (K) Employee? | Percent of Voting Stock | Annual Nondeferred Compensation | | | | Social Security Number |
|------|-----|------------------------|----------------------------------|----------|----------------------------------------------|-------------------------|--------|-------|----------|-------|------------------------|
| | | | | | | | Basic | Bonus | Overtime | Total | |
| | | | | | | | | | | | |
| | | | | | | | | | | | |
| | | | | | | | | | | | |
| | | | | | | | | | | | |
| | | | | | | | | | | | |
| | | | | | | | | | | | |
| | | | | | | | | | | | |
| | | | | | | | | | | | |
| | | | | | | | | | | | |
| | | | | | | | | | | | |
| | | | | | | | | | | | |
| | | | | | | | | | | | |
| | | | | | | | | | | | |

## SECTION II — RETIREMENT PLAN ABSTRACT

## PART E — PLAN CHARACTERISTICS AND PROVISIONS

E-1.  Name of Plan _____

E-2.  Type of Plan

     2.1  _____Defined-benefit: _____ Unit-benefit _____ Flat-benefit _____ Fixed-benefit

     2.2  _____Defined-contribution money purchase

     2.3  _____Target (assumed-benefit)

     2.4  _____Profit-sharing

     2.5  _____Thrift (savings)

     2.6  _____Section 401(k)

     2.7  _____Stock bonus

     2.8  _____ESOP

     2.9  _____Tax-deferred annuity (Section 403(b))

     2.10_____Other or combination of types (specify _____

E-3.  Effective Date _____

E-4.  Anniversary Date _____

E-5.  Formal Name of Plan _____

E-6.  Eligibility Requirements

     6.1  Minimum age _____

     6.2  Waiting period _____

     6.3  Entry dates (explain) _____

     6.4  Employee classification _____

     _____

6.5 Other (specify) _____

_____

_____

E-7. Past Service: Is Past Service with Prior Employer(s) to Count as Service with Company for Eligibility Purposes?

_____

For benefit computation purposes? _____

If yes, name prior employer(s) _____

_____

_____

_____

E-8. Integration

8.1 _____ Nonintegrated

8.2 _____ Social security (OASDI)

8.3 _____ Railroad retirement act

E-9. Type of Integration

9.1 _____ Excess (stepped up)

9.2 _____ Offset

E-10. Integration Level

10.1 _____ Uniform integration break point $_____

10.2 _____ Covered compensation table I

10.3 _____ Covered compensation table II

10.4 _____ Other _____

_____

E-11. Integration Benefit Formula _____

_____

_____

_____

E-12. Other Offsets: Indicate the Contributions to or Benefits from Other Plans Which Are to be Used as Offsets to This Plan and Whether or Not Such Other Plans Are Qualified Plans under the Internal Revenue Code.

_____

_____

_____

_____

E-13. Normal Retirement Benefit

    13.1    Formula

    13.2    Age _____

    13.3    Minimum years of service _____

    13.4    Minimum years of plan participation _____

    13.5    Other _____

E-14. Early Retirement Benefit

    14.1    Formula

    14.2    Age _____

    14.3    Minimum years of service _____

    14.4    Minimum years of plan participation _____

    14.5    Other _____

E-15. Deferred Retirement Benefit

    15.1    Formula

    15.2    Maximum age _____

    15.3    Minimum years of service _____

    15.4    Minimum years of plan participation _____

    15.5    Other _____

E-16. Disability Retirement

    16.1    Formula

    16.2    Minimum age _____

    16.3    Minimum years of service _____

    16.4    Minimum years of plan participation _____

    16.5    Benefit commencement date _____

    16.6    Definition of disability _____

            (a) _____ Disability for social security purposes

            (b) _____ Other (specify) _____

E-17. Death Benefits

    17.1    Preretirement _____

    17.2    Postretirement _____

E-18.    Emergency Distributions _____

E-19. Describe Deferral or Salary Reduction Option (Section 401(k) Plan) _____

E-20. Withdrawal of Participant Contributions

    20.1    When _____

    20.2    How much _____

    20.3    Earnings on contributions _____

20.4    Penalty _____

20.5    Notice requirement _____

E-21. Loans to participants

    21.1    Maximum (if other than §72(p) limit ($50,000, ½ vested benefit, $10,000)) _____

    21.2    Minimum _____

    21.3    Interest rate _____

    21.4    Duration _____

E-22. Other Benefits (specify) _____

_____

_____

E-23. Contributions

    23.1    Rate of employer contributions

        (a) _____    Discretionary

        (b) _____    As actuarially determined

        (c) _____    Formula (state formula)

    23.2    Rate of Participant Contributions

        (a) _____    Voluntary

        Minimum _____

        Maximum _____

        (b) _____    Required

             Amount of rate _____

             Method of collection

             _____ Payroll withholding

             _____ Other (specify) _____

             _____

    23.3    Employer Contributions To Be In

        (a) _____    Cash

        (b) _____    Stock

        (c) _____    Other

E-24. Use of Forfeitures (If Any)

    24.1_____To reduce subsequent employer contributions

    24.2_____Reallocated among plan participants (defined-contribution only) state reallocation basis: _____

    _____

E-25. Employer Contribution Allocation Formula

    25.1_____None. Unallocated funding

    25.2_____Prorate according to compensation

    25.3_____Prorate according to service

    25.4_____Prorate according to compensation and service

    25.5_____According to amounts contributed by employees

    25.6_____Other (specify) _____

    _____

E-26. Vesting Schedule (Employer Contributions, Amounts Attributable to Employer Contributions, or Benefits Purchased with Employer Contributions)

    26.1    5-year vesting _____

    26.2    3- to 7-year vesting _____

    26.3    100% vesting with 2-year eligibility period _____

    26.4    Other basis (specify) _____

    _____

    26.5    Set forth the vesting schedule in space below

    _____

    _____

    _____

    _____

    _____

    _____

E-27. Full and Immediate Vesting Is Required for Amounts, Earnings, and Benefits Derived from Employee Contributions.

E-28. Special Provisions Relating to Vesting in Individual Insurance Contracts _____

_____

_____

_____

_____

E-29. Definition of "Compensation" and "Hour of Service" for Plan Purposes (Indicate Status of Commissions, Bonuses, Overtime, etc., and for Defined-Benefit Plan Indicate Career Average, Final Average, or Other Basis for Determining Benefits)

_____

_____

_____

_____

E-30. Definition of "Net Income" or "Net Profits" for Plan Purposes (If Applicable)

30.1 _____ Profits for federal income tax purposes, but prior to reduction for contributions under (a) _____ this plan or (b) _____ qualified plans including this plan, but excluding

_____

(state plans to be excluded) sponsored by employer

30.2 _____ Other (specify)

_____

E-31. Beneficiary Designations

31.1 _____ None

31.2 _____ Automatic to spouse, if surviving, otherwise to estate of (a) _____ deceased participant or

(b) _____ deceased spouse

31.3 _____ Automatic to estate of deceased participant

31.4 _____ As per designation by employee

E-32. Earmarking of Contributions (Directed Investments)

32.1 _____ Yes

32.2 _____ No

If yes, indicate investment options and limitations _____

_____

_____

_____

E-33. Mode of Distribution of Benefits (Normal Retirement)

33.1 _____ Joint life, participant and spouse (at least 50% to spouse)

33.2 _____ Full range of options (see below)

33.3 _____ Limited range of options (indicate which options are available below)

33.4 _____ Range of options

    (a) _____ Life of participant only

    (b) _____ Life of participant, 5 years certain

    (c) _____ Life of participant, 10 years certain

    (d) _____ Joint life, participant and spouse (at least 50% to spouse)

    (e) _____ Joint life, participant and dependent

    (f) _____ Joint life, participant and designated joint annuitant

    (g) _____ Installments for 3 years

    (h) _____ Installments for 5 years

    (i) _____ Installments for 10 years

    (j) _____ Installments for 15 years

    (k) _____ Lump sum

    (l) _____ Other (specify) _____

_____

33.5    Method of determining actuarial equivalence _____

_____

_____

33.6    How options are elected _____

_____

E-34. Timing of Distribution of Benefits

34.1    Normal retirement benefits

    (a) _____ First day of month following normal retirement date

    (b) _____ Other (specify) _____

_____

34.2    Early Retirement Benefits

    (a) _____ First day of month following early retirement date

    (b) _____ First day of month following normal retirement date

    (c) _____ First day of any month after early retirement date but not later than first day of month following normal retirement date

    (d) _____ Combination of (b) & (c) above at employee's option

34.3    Disability benefits

(a) _____ First day of month following disability

(b) _____ First day of month following normal retirement date

(c) _____ First day of month following early retirement date after disability and before normal retirement date

(d) _____ Other (specify) _____

_____

(e) _____ Combination of (b) & (c) above at

_____ Employee's option

34.4    Preretirement death benefits

(a) _____ As promptly as practicable following death

(b) _____ Other (specify) _____

_____

34.5    Postretirement death benefits

(a) _____ As promptly as practicable following death

(b) _____ Pursuant to mode of retirement benefit election

(c) _____ Other (specify) _____

_____

34.6    Severance benefits

(a) _____ As promptly as practicable following termination of employment
(not later than 60th day after close of plan year)

(b) _____ At normal retirement date

(c) _____ 10 years after plan participation

(d) _____ (a) or (c) at option of plan participant

E-35. Plan Administration

35.1    Plan administrator _____ Employer _____ Other (specify)

_____

35.2    Plan administrator to have investment power? _____ Yes _____ No

E-36. Insurance Provision and Restrictions _____

_____

_____

_____

E-37. Should There be Provisions in Plan and Trust Specifying That Insurance Company is Not a Party?

_____ Yes                    _____ No

E-38. Other Special Features and Notes as to Plan Provisions (Attach Additional Sheets if Necessary)

_____

_____

_____

_____

_____

## PART F — PLAN CENSUS DATA

Data for test under Section 410(b)(1) of the Internal Revenue Code

F-0.   Is this data being provided for a separate line of business under Code Sec. 414(r)?

☐   Yes, eligible (describe)          _____

☐   No, not eligible

☐   No separate line of business

F-1.   Total number of employees          _____

F-2.   Number of employees in collective-bargaining unit
(retirement benefits were subject to good faith bargaining)
(Code Sec. 410(b)(3)(A))          _____

F-3.   Number of employees who have not yet satisfied
proposed plan eligibility waiting period* and
minimum age requirements (Code Sec. 410(b)(4))          _____

F-4.   Number of employees excluded under Code Secs. 410(b)(3)(B)-(C)          _____

F-5.   Total Lines F-2 through F-4          _____

F-6.   Difference = Line F-1 minus Line F-5          _____

F-6.1. Number of employees included in F-6 who are highly compensated
(Code Sec. 414(q))          _____

*NOTE:*      *If plan excludes part-time or seasonal employees, defined as other than employment for fewer than*
*1,000 hours per year, indicate here the definition used in the plan*

_____

_____

F-7.   Employees excluded from coverage*

7.1   Ineligible due to being salaried          _____

7.2   Ineligible due to being hourly paid          _____

7.3   Ineligible due to job classification          _____

7.4   Ineligible due to being covered in another qualified plan          _____

7.5   Ineligible due to geographic location          _____

7.6   Ineligible for other reasons (specify)          _____

_____          _____

_____          _____

_____          _____

7.8   Total excluded under F-7          _____

*NOTE: No excluded employee should be counted in more than one category above.*

F-8.   Number of employees presently eligible to participate in plan
(F-6 minus F-7.8)          _____

F-9.   Number of employees actually participating in plan          _____

F-10.  Number of plan participants who are highly compensated          _____

Percentage test

F-11. Percentage of non-highly compensated employees participating—100 times

$$\left( \frac{\text{line F-9 minus line F-10}}{\text{line F-6 minus line F-6.1}} \right)$$

_____%*

Ratio test

F-12. Percentage of highly compensated employees participating—100 times
   (line F-10 divided by F-6.1)

_____%

F-13. 0.7 times line F-11

_____%

F-14. Percentage of non-highly compensated employees participating—100 times

$$\left( \frac{\text{line F-9 minus line F-10}}{\text{line F-6 minus line F-6.1}} \right)$$

_____%**

Average Benefits Test

F-15. Describe nondiscriminatory classification of employees _____

F-16. Average benefit percentage _____

_____

\*    If F-11 is 70 or greater, the plan's coverage meets the percentage test and no further computation is required.

\*\*   If F-14 is equal to or greater than F-13, the plan meets the ratio test and no further compensation is required.

## PART G — FUNDING

G-1.  Type of Instrument

    1.1 _____ Self-administered trust

    1.2 _____ Group DA

    1.3 _____ Group IPG

    1.4 _____ Group annuity

    1.5 _____ Individual policy (fully insured)

    1.6 _____ Individual policy and investment fund

    1.7 _____ Other (specify) _____

    _____

G-2.  Actuarial Assumptions and Cost Method

    2.1  Actuarial assumptions

        (a) _____ Interest _____

        (b) _____ Turnover _____

        (c) _____ Annuity form to be funded _____

        (d) _____ Annuity purchase rate (dollar amount needed to purchase benefit of $10.00 per month at normal retirement)

            Male _____        Female _____

                    or

        (Dollar amount of monthly retirement income that can be purchased at normal retirement by $1,000)

            Male _____        Female _____

        (e) _____ Preretirement mortality _____

        (f) _____ Salary scale _____

        (g) _____ Other (specify) _____

        _____

    2.2  Actuarial cost method _____

    _____

G-3.  Type of Fiduciary Arrangement

    3.1 _____ Bank trustee

    3.2 _____ Individual trustee(s)

    3.3 _____ Insurance or annuity contracts

    3.4 _____ Custodial account

    3.5 _____ U.S. retirement bonds

    3.6 _____ Other (specify) _____

    _____

G-4. Annual Asset Valuation Date _____

G-5. Trust (or Other) Fiscal Year _____

G-6. Fund (Trust, Custodial Account, Annuity Plan) Identification Number _____

G-7. SS-4 Needed? _____ Yes _____ No

G-8. Full Name and Address of Trustee or Other Fiduciary (Named Fiduciary) _____

_____

_____

_____

G-9. Is Trustee or Other Fiduciary Subject to Instruction by or Consent of Plan Committee, Advisor, or Other Party as to Acquisition, Retention, or Disposition of Investment Assets? _____

If so, specify name and address of party whose consent is needed and acts for which consent is needed.

_____

_____

_____

G-10. Situs of Trust _____

G-11. Who Will Prepare and File Plan/Trust Returns and Reports with Internal Revenue Service and Department of Labor?

11.1 Form 5500 (or 5500-C or 5500-R—indicate which) _____

11.2 Schedule A Form 5500 _____

11.3 Schedule B Form 5500 _____

11.4 Other reports _____

_____

_____

_____

G-12. Unusual Trust Agreement Provisions (Or Unusual Provisions to Be Included in Agreements Used in Lieu of or in Addition to Trust Agreement) _____

_____

_____

_____

G-13. Fiduciary Employer (Taxpayer) Identification Number _____

G-14. Plan Administrator (If Other Than Employer) Identification Number _____

## PART H — AGENCY FILING RECORDS

H-1. Internal Revenue Service

1.1 Who will file for "Letter of Determination" _____

_____

_____

_____

1.2 Indicate forms needed and date filed*

| Needed | Form No. | Date Filed | Response Received |
|--------|----------|------------|-------------------|
| (a) _____ | SS-4 (Employer) | _____ | _____ |
| (b) _____ | SS-4 (Plan Administrator | _____ | _____ |
| (c) _____ | 2848 or 2848-D | _____ | _____ |
| (d) _____ | 5300 | _____ | _____ |
| (e) _____ | 5302 | _____ | _____ |
| (f) _____ | 5303 | _____ | _____ |
| (g) _____ | 5307 | _____ | _____ |
| (h) _____ | 5309 | _____ | _____ |
| (i) _____ | 5310 | _____ | _____ |

*Form Index:

    (a)/(b)  SS-4—Application for employer (taxpayer) or plan administrator identification number

    (c)  2848 or 2848-D—Power of attorney or authorization and declaration

    (d)  Form 5300—Application for determination

    (e)  5302—Employee census

    (f)  Form 5303—Application for determination for collectively bargained plan

    (g)  Form 5307—Short form application for determination for employee benefit plan

    (h)  Form 5309—Application for determination of employee stock ownership plan

    (i)  5310—Application for determination upon termination—notice of merger, consolidation or transfer of plan assets or liabilities

    Where Letters of Determination are issued, indicate date of issuance and symbols in "response received" column.

H-2. State Government Filings (Preempted by Federal Law in Most Cases)

| Filings Required | Forms to Be Submitted | Parties to Do Filing | Dates of Filing | Responses Received |
|---|---|---|---|---|
| | | | | |
| | | | | |
| | | | | |
| | | | | |
| | | | | |
| | | | | |
| | | | | |

H-3. Securities and Exchange Commission _____

_____

_____

_____

H-4. Other _____

_____

_____

## PART I — OTHER PROFESSIONALS

(Insert names, addresses, telephone numbers, and tax numbers)

I-1.   Company's Accountant _____

_____

_____

_____

I-2.   Company's Counsel _____

_____

_____

_____

I-3.   Actuary _____

_____

_____

_____

I-4.   Consultant _____

_____

_____

_____

I-5.   Fiduciary _____

_____

_____

_____

I-6.   Insurance Consultants (Indicate Lines of Coverage) _____

_____

_____

_____

I-7.   Union Representatives _____

_____

_____

_____

I-8. Others (Specify) _____

_____

_____

_____

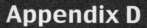
# Long–Term Incentives:

# A Comparative Analysis

## Non-Qualified Stock Options (NQSOs)
## Public Companies

### Description & Common Features

A right to purchase shares of company stock at a stated price ("option price") for a given period of time, frequently ten years.

Option exercise price normally equals 100% of the stock's fair market value on date of grant, but may be set below or above this level (i.e., "discount" or "premium"). However, recipients normally must wait a period of time (a "vesting period" of often one to four years) before they can exercise options, although vesting may be accelerated in certain circumstances (e.g., upon change in control). The option term may be shortened if the recipient's employment terminates before exercise.

NQSOs may be exercised by cash payment or by tendering previously owned shares of stock, depending on plan terms. NQSOs may be granted in tandem with stock appreciation rights or other devices.

## Incentive Stock Options (ISOs)
## Public Companies

### Description & Common Features

Option to purchase shares of com- pany stock at 100% (or more) of stock's fair market value on date of grant ("option price") for a period of up to ten years, and designed to meet various other statutory require- ments to qualify for ISO tax treatment, for example:

• $100,000 annual vesting limitation required.

• Stock must be held for at least two years after option grant and one year after exercise. Any sales before this time frame cause exercise to be taxed as nonqualified stock option.

• Post-termination exercise is limited (e.g., one year after disability terminations, three months after other terminations except for death). Any exercises after this time frame are taxed as nonqualified stock options.

• Shareholder approval re- quired.

• ISO can only be granted to a company's employees, not to outside directors, contractors or consultants.

## Incentive Stock Options (ISOs) Public Companies (cont'd)

### Description & Common Features

• ISO must be repriced when ISO is materially amended after the grant (with the exercise price adjusted to at least the stock's fair market value on the amendment date).

Recipients normally must wait a period of time (a "vesting period" of often one to four years) before they can exercise options, although vesting may be accelerated in certain circumstances (e.g., upon change of control). The option term may be shortened if the recipient's employment terminates before exercise.

ISOs may be exercised by cash payment or by tendering previously owned shares of stock, depending on plan terms. ISOs may be granted in tandem with stock appreciation rights that have identical terms.

## Phantom Stock/ Deferred Stock Units — Public Companies

### Description & Common Features

Units analogous to company shares, with a value generally equal to the full value of the underlying stock.

Units can be settled in cash and/or stock with the settlement date or event (e.g., termination of employment) fixed in advance and not controlled by the individual.

Note: The term "phantom stock" is used in other contexts (e.g., formula or appraised value stock for non-public companies or divisions). It also may be used to describe an arrangement like an SAR with a fixed exercise date. The treatments described here reflect only the definition given above.

## Restricted Stock —
## Public Companies

### Description & Common Features

An award of company stock with no or nominal cost that is non-transferable and subject to a substantial risk of forfeiture. As owners of the shares, holders normally have voting and dividend rights even while shares are subject to restrictions. These restrictions typically lapse over a period of three to five years.

Some companies grant restricted stock "units" under which shares of company stock will be granted when restrictions lapse. Such units have the same tax and expensing treatment as restricted stock; however, individuals do not have voting rights or beneficial ownership until actual shares are issued and balance sheet consequences will be different.

## Performance Units/
## Performance Cash
## Public Companies

### Description & Common Features

A grant of a contingent number of units or a contingent cash award. Units may have a fixed dollar value, with the *number* earned varying with performance. Alternatively, a fixed number of units may be granted, with the *value* varying on the basis of performance.

Duration of performance cycle varies, but three to five years is typical. Financial objectives may relate to such measures as cumulative growth in earnings or improvements in rates of return.

At end of cycle, awards are paid in cash and/or stock according to the plan's earnout provisions and actual company performance.

## Performance Shares — Public Companies

### Description & Common Features

A contingent grant of a fixed number of common shares at the beginning of a performance cycle, with the *number* of shares payable at the end of the cycle dependent on how well performance objectives are achieved. The ultimate *value* of the performance shares depends on both the number of shares earned and their market value at the end of the cycle.

Duration of performance cycles varies, but three to five years is typical. Financial objectives may relate to such measures as cumulative growth in earnings or improvement in rates of return.

At end of cycle, awards are paid in cash and/or stock according to the plan's earnout provisions and actual company performance.

## Stock Appreciation Rights (SARs) — Public Companies

### Description & Common Features

Rights, normally granted in tandem with stock options, that permit the individual to receive a payment equal to the excess of the stock's value at exercise over the option price, in lieu of exercising the underlying stock option.

SARs may be attached to incentive stock options or nonqualified stock options or may be granted on a "free-standing" or "independent" basis without a tandem option.

SARS may be settled in cash, and/or stock.

Companies rarely grant SARs because individuals can enjoy the same economic benefits with cashless option exercises using broker loans without adverse variable accounting to the company.

# ACCOUNTING FOR BENEFIT PLANS

Accounting rules, including those affecting employee benefit plans, are promulgated by the Financial Accounting Standards Board (FASB). The FASB is a private organization designated by the accounting profession to promulgate general principles, practices and standards for accounting and financial disclosure. These FASB rules do not have the force of law as such, but they represent, de facto, the standards expected by shareholders, investors, and the government in financial reports of businesses, and they are generally followed by independent accountants for purposes of certifying financial statements. They are, therefore, quasi-regulatory in effect and should be considered along with state and federal government regulations in the design of executive benefit plans.

## PENSION PLANS

The accounting rules for deferred compensation make no distinction between qualified and nonqualified plans as such. Instead, the applicable accounting rule depends on whether the plan constitutes one or more "individual deferred compensation contracts" on the one hand, or a "pension plan" on the other. While the balance sheet result is about the same either way, individual deferred compensation contracts are governed by the older Accounting Principles Board (APB) Opinion No. 12, as amended by FAS 106. Pension plans, however, are governed by FAS 87.

Whether a plan is one or the other is to some extent a matter of the accountant's discretion. In general, if one or only a few executives are covered, APB No. 12 would be applied, while if the plan is a defined benefit plan or a pension plan as defined in ERISA, FAS 87 would apply.[1]

Under APB No. 12, the benefits accrued under a deferred compensation contract are charged to expense and spread ratably over the period of the executive's service. As amended by FAS 106, the period of service to be used is the period between the time the contract is entered into and the first year in which the executive is eligible for benefit payments (even if the executive might choose to further defer actual payment). Accrued benefits are charged to expense at their present value; the discount rate is not specified in APB No. 12 but accountants are likely to use current rates of return on high quality fixed-income investments. No funding method is specified in APB No. 12, but apparently either a level funding or accrued benefit approach can be used.

FAS 87, "Employers' Accounting for Pensions," was put in final form in 1985. Highlights of FAS 87 are:

1. Annual pension cost—the periodic cost charged against earnings, referred to as the "net periodic pension cost"—is determined under a uniform method prescribed by FAS 87. The employer may not simply charge the amount actually contributed to the plan to expense for the accounting year.

2. Generally, the unit credit (accrued benefit) method is used in determining the net periodic pension cost, regardless of the actuarial method used by the plan.

3. If the net periodic pension cost differs from the employer's actual plan contribution for the year, the difference will be shown as an asset or liability on the balance sheet.

4. If the plan's past service costs (accumulated benefit obligation) exceed the fair market value of plan assets, a liability referred to as the *unfunded accumulated-benefit obligation* must be reflected on the balance sheet. This liability is balanced by an intangible asset on the balance sheet.

5. A specific format is prescribed for various financial statement footnotes relating to the pension plan, such as the fair market value of plan assets and any unamortized prior service costs.

For a plan that is terminating during the year, FAS 88, "Employers' Accounting for Settlements and Curtailments of Defined Benefit Pension Plans and Termination Benefits," provides rules for dealing with special accounting problems in plan termination.

Nonqualified and qualified plans must be reported separately by employers, since assets of qualified and nonqualified plans cannot be mingled. If a nonqualified plan is informally funded or financed—as such plans usually are (see Chapter 15)—the plan is considered to have no assets for accounting purposes, a fact which will increase the magnitude of the reported liabilities. The assets used for informal financing are corporate assets, not plan assets.

These accounting rules increase the balance sheet "visibility" of nonqualified plans, as compared with qualified plans, because of the fact that the liability will generally rise steadily in a plan that is not formally funded. Planners can generally mitigate this disadvantage by using an informal funding mechanism that produces a steadily increasing corporate asset, such as the cash value of an insurance policy; this asset can be pointed to as evidence of the company's financial responsibility with regard to the nonqualified plan liability.

## CORPORATE–OWNED LIFE INSURANCE

Corporate-owned life insurance, whether held as an informal financing asset for a nonqualified pension plan (see above) or for other corporate or employee benefit purposes, is accounted for in accordance with FASB Technical Bulletin 85-4. The charge to corporate earnings is the premium less the cash value increase. Generally, this produces a charge to earnings only in the first few years of the policy, after which there is a profit. The policy's cash value appears as an asset on the balance sheet.

FASB Statement No. 109 (1992), superseding FAS 96 (1987), requires corporations to create a balance sheet liability to reflect taxes anticipated to be payable in the future (deferred taxes). If the corporation holds property with unrealized gain, it must generally show a liability for taxes on that gain, even if the gain is not realized during the accounting year. This rule potentially has an impact on corporate-owned life insurance, such as that held in a split-dollar plan, informally funded deferred compensation plan, or other plan. If the corporation's share of the cash value exceeds the corporation's basis, there is a potentially taxable gain. However, in the great majority of plans using corporate-owned life insurance, the corporation intends to hold the policy until the insured dies, at which point the corporation's realized gain will be nontaxable, except for possible alternative minimum tax liability.

FASB's previous statement on accounting for income taxes, FAS 96, stated the requirement of creating a tax liability in an inflexible way that appeared to apply to all insurance policies, regardless of whether the policy was likely to actually generate taxable income. However, FAS 109, which supersedes FAS 96, states that the difference between basis and cash value of a corporate-owned policy does not create a reportable liability if "the asset is expected to be recovered without tax consequence upon the death of the insured (there will be no taxable amount if the insurance policy is held until the death of the insured)."

FAS 109 does not directly discuss whether possible AMT on the death proceeds must be reflected as a balance sheet liability. However, it can be argued that the principles of the FAS would require the potential AMT to be so reported. As discussed in Chapter 42, the receipt of a death benefit, even though regular income-tax free, can result in an AMT liability.

## HEALTH AND OTHER WELFARE BENEFIT PLANS

Health and life insurance benefit plans generally involve no significant accounting issues so long as the plans provide simply the usual year-to-year benefit and premium payment obligations. However, where employers provide benefits after employees retire, the FASB has recognized that there is a question as to how this obligation should be recognized for accounting purposes. The issue has become more important in light of recent court cases that restrict an employer's right to unilaterally modify or rescind benefits provided to retirees.

The FASB in 1989 issued an "exposure draft" of rules in this area, which was formalized as FAS 106, effective generally for fiscal years beginning after December 15, 1992, with a later date for certain small (under 500) nonpublic plans.

FAS 106 is based on the premise that post-retirement benefits of all types are, like pension benefits, a form of deferred compensation that is earned year by year by employees while they are actively working for the employer. Accordingly, FAS 106 requires an accrual of such benefits as they are earned, rather than as they are paid. This accrual will create a charge to earnings, and unfunded accrued benefits will create a growing balance sheet liability.

FAS 106 covers medical and life insurance, tuition assistance, day care, legal services, and housing subsidies, as well as other benefits provided during retirement in return for prior employment services. Retiree medical benefits have by far the greatest potential financial impact. FAS 106 includes specific guidelines for valuing post-retirement medical benefits.

This potential balance sheet liability will cause employers to seek to provide either funded plans or asset reserves or other financing assets such as life insurance contracts to cover the liabilities created by post-retirement benefits.

Under FAS 106, if assets are not segregated into a trust specifically for the purpose of funding the post-retirement benefits, they are not "plan assets" that directly reduce the balance sheet liability for post-retirement benefits. Thus, typical corporate-owned life insurance policies or asset reserves would not qualify as plan assets, nor would a Section 501(c)(9) trust (VEBA) if the VEBA included assets to fund benefits for active employees. However, Section 401(h) medical accounts (see Chapter 39) probably would qualify.

Although informal financing of retiree benefits will not reduce the balance sheet liability, the existence of assets can help to demonstrate the corporation's financial responsibility in planning to meet the projected liability. Corporate-owned life insurance can be used favorably for this purpose. Methods of financing retiree medical benefits are discussed further in Chapter 39.

## FOOTNOTES

1. See *Tax Management Portfolio 393-2nd*, "Accounting for Pensions and Deferred Compensation," Bureau of National Affairs, Inc., Washington, D.C., (2001), page 11 for authors' views on how this distinction is made. According to their rationale, it would appear that most accountants would not apply FAS 87 to an unfunded plan, but this is not clear from FAS 87 itself.

# THE UNAUTHORIZED PRACTICE OF LAW IN THE EMPLOYEE BENEFIT AREA

It is often difficult to draw the boundaries of professional responsibility in areas as complex, sophisticated, and rapidly changing as employee benefit and retirement planning. Special skills and learning are necessary prerequisites—not only to the attorney—but also to the CPA, CLU, CFP, ChFC, or any other individual serving a client in an advisory capacity.

## WHY ONLY ATTORNEYS?

Yet it is clear that regardless of how knowledgeable an advisor is, only the attorney may "practice law." This regulation and limitation on the practice of law is in the public interest and is intended to provide reasonable protection for the clients being advised. Among the specific reasons for the prohibition are these:

(1) The public needs and deserves protection against advice by self-styled advisors who have not been trained, examined, or licensed by a recognized and accredited educational body or by governmental authorities.

(2) Even a non-lawyer who is highly skilled in specific areas of tax law may lack the broader viewpoint and depth provided by a good law school.

(3) The lawyer-client relationship is one of confidentiality, relative objectivity, and impartiality. It is impossible for the non-lawyer to match the protection afforded by the law to the "attorney-client" relationship. Although no professional is completely objective (attorneys and accountants sell their time and expertise), the attorney is generally in a position to be more objective than a professional selling a product. Certainly, when the time comes to make a choice between competing vendors or competing products, the attorney is more likely to be impartial (although not necessarily more knowledgeable) than either of the parties selling the products.

## THE ROLE OF THE SPECIALIST

None of these points, however, imply that the non-attorney has no viable or vital part in the planning process. Much to the contrary, the employee benefit and retirement planning specialist can add immensely to the end result. In fact, it is often the non-attorney specialist who introduces the tool or technique to the client, motivates the client, and follows through to make sure the employee benefit or retirement plan is fully implemented.

If moving the process along were the only role and utility of the non-attorney, that alone would be enough to warrant a place on the planning team. But the non-attorney specialist does so much more. Few attorneys are experts in employee benefit and retirement planning. But even those that are can learn a great deal from the specialist about the available products, the actuarial assumptions and implications, and how these factors interact with each other and can be best utilized in meeting the client's objectives.

## NO ONE PROFESSION (OR PROFESSIONAL) IS ENOUGH

The key point is that no single professional is competent to know everything or single-handedly complete the entire employee benefit or retirement planning process. Each member of the planning team should serve the client with his or her own essential and very special skills. If any member of the team usurps the rightful province of another, it is the client who loses. Stated in a more positive way, the client is best served if the attorney and non-attorney specialists work together to formulate, implement, qualify, and maintain a plan which best meets the client's needs.

## THE UNAUTHORIZED PRACTICE OF LAW—WHAT IS IT NOT?

There is consensus that certain activities are not the unauthorized practice of law. Even the most conservative authorities[1] generally agree that the following would not be considered the unauthorized practice of law in the field of employee benefit and retirement planning:

(1) Promoting, marketing, and selling the plan. This assumes the specialist does not hold himself out as an attorney or as a provider of services that constitute the practice of law.

(2) Explaining alternatives generally available to the public. This means the planner can safely:

A. review the different types of tools or techniques available;

B. describe which classes of employees are required to be covered under federal and state law;

C. explain the costs of benefits provided to employees;

D. illustrate the amounts of contributions to the plan; and

E. discuss general legal principles.

(3) Gather client data. A non-attorney can:

A. assemble employee census data;

B. obtain information on the employer's resources and objectives; and

C. ascertain the costs and liabilities associated with the plan's operation and various plan options.

(4) Perform certain form completion. A non-attorney can:

A. complete the annual returns and reports for the plan;

B. complete and file the SPD (Summary Plan Description);

C. decide upon the elections, consents, and waivers to be used in the administration of the plan—to the extent federal rules and regulations specifically state that such can be completed by a non-lawyer;

D. present a plan to the IRS for "qualification"— if a federal law or regulation specifically authorizes such an action; and

E. administer a plan and deal with regulators— if, when a situation arises that requires legal advice, the administrator advises the client to seek legal advice.

If an employee benefits/retirement planning firm hires an attorney as an employee, that attorney can draft a master or prototype plan for the employer. Upon the request of the client's attorney (an attorney independently selected by the client), he or she may also assist that attorney in drafting plan documents.

## THE UNAUTHORIZED PRACTICE OF LAW—WHAT IT IS (MAYBE)

Almost everyone will agree that the actual drafting of a specific employer's plan document, the preparation of the instruments and contracts by which legal rights are secured, is the practice of law. The odds are very high that he who drafts such documents is practicing law.

Beyond this point, however (and in the minds of some, even at this point) things become hazy. Each state has the right to decide independently from all others what is meant by "unauthorized practice of law."

Will the following constitute the unauthorized practice of law?

You review a plan document and advise a client that—in his particular circumstance—that document will—or will not—have specific legal implications or that the instrument in question is "right" or "not right" for them.

After analyzing client information, you decide on the type of plan the client should have and select the specific provisions that should be inserted into the plan documents.

You make "bottom line recommendations" as to which format and plan provisions would be most suitable to a client's needs.

The employer has decided to adopt a master or prototype plan. You advise the employer as to which plan options would best meet the firm's needs and objectives.

You draft amendments to an already existing plan or to incorporate documents adopting the plan.

You do the initial draft of a plan document but submit it for review, approval, and adoption by the client's lawyers.

You apply to the IRS, on behalf of the employer, for qualification of the plan.

The employer wants to terminate a plan. You prepare all papers and submit them to the IRS.

You give advice regarding the tax laws and other laws on the plan and its participants.

If these actions are the unauthorized practice of law, is the client denied the benefit of receiving advice from accountants, actuaries, and plan specialists who are experts in their fields? Would prohibiting such actions by these experts amount to a questionable restraint on interdisciplinary competition? Is it not only possible but highly likely that the non-attorney expert is better suited than the attorney in matters such as product choice and design? Would thwarting the non-attorney from performing these vital roles significantly increase the cost of plan creation and administration (or further discourage the use of plans vital to the security of millions of employees)?

A strong working knowledge of law is essential to professionals in the employee benefits and retirement planning field. Generally, the protection of the public can be achieved without hampering or unduly burdening professionals with impractical and technical restrictions which have no reasonable justification. To say that non-attorneys cannot discuss any pertinent legal principles with a client would be so unreasonable and narrow as to be absurd.

## THEORIES AND MYTHS

Where are the boundaries? In most states they are decided on a case by case basis. Here are some guidelines that will provide a continuum of risk, if not answers:

*The General-Specific Test*: Where a statute or legal interpretation has become so well known and settled that no further legal issue is involved, there should be no problem in suggesting its simple application on a general basis. No violation should arise from the sharing of legal knowledge which is either generally informative or, if specific, so obvious as to be common knowledge. But it is when the advice moves from the general and obvious to the specific and uncertain that the line is approached. Providing advice involving the application of legal principles to a specific fact situation is clearly the "practice of law" under the "general-specific" test.

*The "Complexity" Theory*: This theory states that the non-attorney should not answer "difficult" or "complex" questions of law. One court said that an issue is "difficult" or "complex" when the advice that is given or the service that is rendered requires the use of any degree of legal knowledge or skill. Perhaps a "judgment" theory should be applied instead. Rather than focus on difficulty or complexity, the focus should be on the extent to which legal judgment is required with respect to controversial or uncertain questions of law in an actual case.

*The "Expert/Specialist" Theory*: No safety can be found in proving that the non-lawyer is both a specialist and an acknowledged expert in the field. The rationale for this seemingly harsh stand is that the interest of the public is not protected by narrow specialization of a person who lacks the broad perspective and orientation of a state licensed attorney. That dimension of skill and knowledge comes only from a thorough understanding of legal concepts, processes, and the interaction of all the branches of law. In other words, according to this theory, the rules may have been learned by the non-lawyer but often the full meaning and import of the rule and its components—and the impact of that rule on other seemingly unrelated rules—may not be fully understood by even a highly competent specialist who is an expert in his or her field but who is not a state licensed attorney.

*The "No Fee" Theory*: A study of the unauthorized practice cases shows that a non-attorney is not protected by merely refraining from charging fees for legal advice. Most courts had little trouble finding violations where clients relied on advice or were provided with legal services regardless of whether or not fees were charged.

*The "Practices of the Past" Theory*: Custom and tradition long acquiesced to by the local bar association will not make proscribed activities any less the practice of law. Practices of the past, therefore, provide little defense in the present.

## THE BOTTOM LINE

*The Tools and Techniques of Employee Benefit and Retirement Planning* is not designed to help the non-lawyer eliminate the need for an attorney. To the contrary, it is a text (widely used by attorneys and in law schools throughout the country) designed for all the members of the employee benefit and retirement planning team to help delineate the large number of alternative solutions to general problem areas. Definitive solutions, the choice of which specific tools and techniques to use in a given case or how they should be used should be considered by the client together with his or her attorney and plan specialists. The drafting or adopting of plan documents needed to execute the techniques or utilize the tools discussed in this text is exclusively the province of the lawyer.

Every member of the planning team is obligated to be aware of the alternative tools and techniques, to understand their limitations as well as their problem-solving potential, and to be knowledgeable enough to discuss them in general terms with clients and other advisors.

## FOOTNOTES

1.  The Florida Bar Association issued a proposed advisory opinion filed with the Florida Supreme Court (Case Number 74-479) that sought to restrict non-attorneys to a severe and unprecedented degree in connection with the design and installation of pension plans. The Florida Supreme Court rejected this proposal, however. In any event, most of the items listed here would be permissible for non-attorneys even under this restrictive advisory opinion.

    More recently, in 2002 the Authorized Practice Committee of the North Carolina State Bar challenged the retirement plan services provided by a large financial institution and a smaller plan administration firm. The Committee asserted that the following constituted unauthorized practice of law: (1) advising, counseling, or recommending to any entity that a particular profit sharing, deferred compensation, pension, or other retirement plan is appropriate to that entity's particular circumstances or that it should adopt and implement such a plan; or (2) preparing, drawing, drafting, amending, restating, or aiding in such processes of any documents necessary to implement such a plan. This is a very broad assertion similar to the Florida case. The North Carolina situation is scheduled for a hearing and will ultimately be determined by the North Carolina courts.

# ETHICS: WHAT THE EMPLOYEE BENEFIT AND RETIREMENT PLANNER MUST KNOW A Practical Guideline

## WHY ETHICS?

Ethics are standards of an aspirational and inspirational nature reflecting commitments to model standards of exemplary professional conduct.[1] Every major profession[2] has adopted some form of "near law"—a Code, Canon, or set of guidelines to what the profession expects of its members.[3] This discussion is meant to provide a checklist for the practitioner in the employee benefit and retirement planning field. It is not intended to be anything more than what its title implies, a "practical guideline," a self-monitoring device to help employee benefit and retirement planners.

Why do professional organizations need such codes of conduct? Why do planners need a practical code of ethics?

First, ethics are a means of creating standards by which conduct can be measured both by the member and by the group itself. Second, ethics serve as a way to acknowledge an obligation to society, to the professional group, and to the client. Third, a code of ethics increases the likelihood that the profession will be governed by high standards. Fourth, ethics are a means of examining priorities and building a tradition based on integrity.

A fifth reason for ethics is as a limitation on power. It is the "power of the experts" that ethics help to control; the attorney, accountant, trust officer, and the employee benefit and retirement planning expert all know things the client does not.[4] This special knowledge gives the professional a Kafkaesque power over a layman who must put great faith and trust in (and take great risk in the accuracy and appropriateness of) what he is told. The client cannot possibly know the full extent of the problems, possibilities, and consequences without the assistance of the planner.

The premise upon which practical ethics must be based is that power must be exercised in the interest of those for whose benefit it was entrusted rather than abused for the self aggrandizement of the planner. The limitations and restrictions on the planner must not, however, be so unenforceable, unrealistic, and impractical as to be counter productive. Practical ethics, therefore, must strike a balance. The questions that follow are designed to help the reader do just that.

*Honesty*: Have you engaged in any business or professional activity which involved an act (or omission) of a dishonest, deceitful, or fraudulent nature?

Have you used your license, degree, or designation to attribute to yourself a depth or scope of knowledge, skills, and professional capabilities you do not, in fact, possess?

Have you been fair and honest in your dealings with the IRS and in fostering confidence in the system?[5]

*Competency*: Do you have the requisite legal knowledge and practical skill, and have you exercised thoroughness?

Have you undertaken a role that entails responsibilities in addition to that inherent to your profession and—if so—are you properly trained and equipped (and willing and otherwise able) to perform them in a competent and efficient manner?

Have you done the proper preparation? In other words, are you qualified to perform the services requested and do you know enough to perform the services required beyond those requested?

What have you done to understand the specific facts and circumstances of the client, the company, its employees, and their needs and objectives?[6]

Do you keep abreast of changing economic and legislative conditions that may affect the client's plan?[7]

*Representation*: Have you established the boundaries of your relationship so that the client knows what you will or will not do?

Have you specified those limits in writing for all parties concerned?

Have you—in any way—denied the client the benefit of the knowledge and skill of another professional who could assist in serving the client?

*Diligence*: Did you do what was required in a reasonably prompt manner?

If you are responsible for preparing IRS forms, documents, affidavits, or other papers for the client, did you do so in a timely manner?

Did you advise a client promptly of any noncompliance, error, or omission having to do with a state or federal tax return or other document the client was required by law to complete?

*Communication*: Did you return phone calls or answer letters promptly? Do you keep the client (and other professionals) informed on a regular basis of economic and legal changes that may have an impact upon the client's plans?[8]

*Confidentiality*: Did you keep client information confidential (except to the extent specifically authorized by the client to disclose it)?[9]

*Fees*: Did you charge fees that were reasonable based on (a) the amount of work performed or the number of hours it took to do the work, (b) the difficulty and judgment involved in the problems that had to be solved, (c) the importance of the problem, and (d) your professional expertise, skill, and standing?

Did you communicate, in writing, the formula by which fees or other charges would be based?

Have you billed only after performing services in a satisfactory manner?

Have you refunded any advance fee that has not been fully earned?

*Conflict of Interest*:[10] Did you inform the parties you are representing of their respective rights and the pros and cons of the proposed action (or inaction) on each party?

Have you used the special knowledge you have in any manner that would operate to the detriment of the client?[11]

Do you represent two parties who have or are likely to have conflicting interests? (This problem is known as "simultaneous representation."). If so, are you satisfied that you can represent both parties adequately and have you made full disclosure to and obtained consent from both parties?

Have you, in any way, allowed the pursuit of financial gain or any other personal benefit to interfere with the exercise of sound professional judgment and skills?[12]

Have you made full disclosure of any conflicts of interest in writing to your client?

*Disclosure*: Have you, in any other way, breached your duty of loyalty to your client (or your associates, partners, or employer) by failing to disclose information?

Have you withheld information from another professional or governmental official that is important and appropriate for that person to know?

Have you misrepresented the benefits, costs, or limitations of any employee benefit and retirement planning tool or technique or failed to fully explain the advantages and disadvantages of viable alternatives?[13]

*Direct Relations*: Have you obtained information directly from the client or did you obtain it second or third hand from another party or advisor acting as a conduit?[14]

*Courtesy*: Has your courtesy extended, not only to your client, but also to the other professionals who seek to serve that person?[15]

*Public Regard*: Have you followed the laws applicable to your business and professional activities?[16]

Have you done what you can to raise the level of integrity and professionalism and avoided activities that detract from the opinion the public places on your profession?

Have you impaired the reputation of another practitioner?

Have you competed unfairly?

Have you used your degree or designation in less than a responsible or dignified or appropriate manner?

Do you avoid associating with those who are not ethical?

Have you provided the public with useful and objective information concerning potential problems, possible solutions, and impartial advisory opinions?

Have you attempted—in all your dealings with the public—to avoid the appearance of impropriety?

*Mentoring*: Have you helped others enter the profession? Have you helped them attain and retain competence?[17]

Have you encouraged and assisted others in obtaining higher levels of professional competence?

It is not enough merely to avoid advocating, sanctioning, participating in, or carrying out an unethical act. Professional ethics forbid condoning the unethical act of another and require taking positive action to maintain an exemplary level of conduct. For instance, the *Code of Ethics of the International Association for Financial Planning* directs its members to

"Oppose those who are deficient in moral character or professional competence, whose actions may cause financial harm to their clients."

Ethics are a reminder that the client sees the professional in this area as much as a counselor as an advocate, more of an advisor than a scholar. Ethics reinforce the importance of the role of all the members of the planning team as intermediaries and protectors who look out for the overall best interests of the business in recommending a course of action.

Ethical standards do not demand absolute, unreasoning, and undivided loyalty to a single client nor do they demand saint-like perfection in any other area. But being ethical has its (generally quite affordable) price; professional honesty, integrity, and competence compatible with the realities of modern practice. In fact, the increased pride and respect gained from others (and oneself) is well worth the price. Can any planner afford not to pay it?

## FOOTNOTES

1. See the *Code of Professional Ethics of the Chartered Property Casualty Underwriters.*

2. See "For the Long Term—Professional Ethics and The Life Underwriter," *Life Association News*, December 1985, for an excellent discussion on that subject. Dr. Clarence C. Walton, the author of that article, states that among the characteristics of a mature professional are:

    A. Primary commitment to the interest of the client,

    B. Possession of expert knowledge,

    C. Self regulation, and

    D. Awareness of the long term consequences of his or her action

    Dr. Walton provides excellent guidelines for organizations that sincerely wish to promote and enforce a code of ethics.

3. Information on the Code of conduct for your profession should be obtained by writing to the appropriate national organization to which you belong. For information on The ABA's Model Rules of Professional Conduct, attorneys should write to the American Bar Association, P.O. Box 10892, Chicago, Ill 60610-0892. The American Bar Association can also be reached by calling 1-800-285-2221.

4. See "Estate Planners: Where Do Your Loyalties Lie?," *Trusts and Estates*, May 1977, p. 356.

5. The duties of a professional to the IRS are spelled out in IRS circular 230, which embraces, under a uniform standard, many of the traditional ethical and professional standards common to national professional organizations. See "Regulations Within The IRS," *Trusts and Estates*, April 1990, p. 30.

6. The *Code of Ethics of the Society of Financial Service Professionals* states, "The member must make a conscientious effort to ascertain and to understand all relevant circumstances surrounding the client."

7. The *Code of Ethics of the Society of Financial Service Professionals* states, "A member shall continue his education throughout his professional life." Its interpretive comment adds, "A member must continue to maintain and to improve his professional abilities. Continuing education includes both the member adding to his knowledge of the practice of his profession; and, the member keeping abreast of changing economic and legislative conditions which may affect the financial plans of the insuring public."

8. The *Code of Ethics of the Society of Financial Service Professionals* states, "A member shall render continuing advice and service." Its interpretive comment provides, "Advice and service, to be competent, must be ongoing as the client's circumstances change and as these changes are made known to the member."

9. The *Code of Ethics of the Society of Financial Service Professionals* states, "A member shall respect the confidential relationship existing between client and member."

10. The *Code of Ethics of the International Association for Financial Planning* states, "The reliance of the public and the business community on sound financial planning and advice imposes on the financial planning profession an obligation to maintain high standards of technical competence, morality, and integrity. To this end, members of the International Association for Financial Planning, Inc. shall at all times maintain independence of thought and action..." The *Code of Ethics of the Society of Financial Service Professionals* states, "In a conflict of interest situation the interest of the client must be paramount."

11. The *Code of Ethics of the Society of Financial Service Professionals* states, "A member possessing a specific body of knowledge which is not possessed by the general public has an obligation to

use that knowledge for the benefit of the client and to avoid taking advantage of that knowledge to the detriment of the client."

12. See the *Code of Professional Ethics of the American Institute of the Chartered Property Casualty Underwriters*.

13. Each professional must ask himself or herself three questions:

1) What are the pros and cons of the viable alternatives?

2) Which alternatives offer the client the greatest financial security and the least overall cost?

3) What if the client does nothing?

Then these three issues must be shared with the client's other advisors and with the client.

14. Only through direct relations can a professional be sure that he or she has all of the relevant facts including an understanding of the client's objectives and fears and can make sure both parties fully understand each other.

15. The *Code of Ethics of the Society of Financial Service Professionals* states, "A member is to accord due courtesy and consideration to those engaged in related professions who are also serving the client."

16. The *Code of Ethics of the Society of Financial Service Professionals* states, "A member has a legal obligation to obey all laws applicable to his business and professional activities. The placement of this Guide within the Code raises this obligation to the level of an ethical obligation."

17. The *Code of Ethics of the Society of Financial Service Professionals* states, "Encouraging others who might be qualified to enter into a practice is one hallmark of a professional."

# MALPRACTICE IN COMPENSATION PLANNING
# HOW TO AVOID IT — AND THE LAWSUIT THAT COMES WITH IT

Errors in pension and employee benefit design and administration are an increasingly common source of malpractice claims.

Reducing the risk of a malpractice suit and enhancing available defenses are the subjects of this discussion.

## "TARGET OF OPPORTUNITY" — WHY ME?

Those professionals wise enough to know that malpractice is a disease that may attack anyone do not ask the question, "Why Me?" Instead, they ask, "When?" Malpractice claims are made uncomfortably often against those who—out of ignorance, arrogance, or incompetence—thought it could not happen to them. Suits are also brought against planners with fine reputations who honestly thought they had done everything right. It is a dangerous misconception to think that only those who are clearly sloppy and unethical encounter malpractice claims.[1]

Mere good faith and honest intent will not protect the practitioner who has caused a client loss. It may be true that a planner will not be held liable for the failure to foresee the ultimate resolution of a debatable point of law or for an error in judgment if he acts in good faith and in an honest belief that his advice and acts are well founded and in the best interest of his clients.[2] But such a planner can still be sued and still incur most of the costs of someone who in fact is guilty of malpractice.

Who are likely "targets of opportunity"?

*"DEEP POCKETS."* When clients sue, they sue everyone in sight. But the bulk of the litigation effort is understandably against those from whom recovery is most likely. The appearance of success is a magnet.

*INSURANCE.* Certainly one contributing factor is the common knowledge that professionals carry insurance for malpractice. Some plaintiffs feel they are not suing the professional, but that they are suing the insurer.

*TOUTED EXPERIENCE, SKILL, AND KNOWLEDGE.* In general, professionals who obtain or retain clients by holding themselves out as possessing a higher level of skill than other practitioners will be held to that higher level. If an advisor's business card says, "Compensation Planner" or "Tax Specialist" or he has an advanced degree or a CFP, CLU, or ChFC designation or otherwise advertises greater expertise or skill than an ordinary practitioner, he is expected to exercise that expertise or skill.[3]

*IMPERSONAL.* It is far easier to sue a party perceived as a "giant institution guided by computers rather than people" than to sue a long time advisor who has served with warmth, openness, compassion and has provided substantial personal attention in a respectful manner. This public image of banks, insurance companies, large law firms, and other institutions as impersonal money machines can best be changed from the top down by an insistence on courtesy and attention to the client from everyone in the firm.

*"BIG GUY vs. LITTLE GUY."* There is a feeling in this country, right or wrong, that the "Big Guys" are using their weight to beat up the "Little Guys." So when the little guy gets into the judicial system a jury may feel sympathetic and tend to punish the big guy with an angry vengeance.

*FRUSTRATION WITH THE LAW(S).* The potential for malpractice increases in proportion to the complexity, speed of change, and labyrinthine interrelationship of various federal and state corporate, tax, labor, and securities laws—and to clients' confusion and frustration. From the planner's point of view, the combination is a nightmare. If the planner feels this way, think of how angry clients must be when told that last year's law is now out and substantial time, money, and emotional energy must be invested all over again. Consider, for example, that a compensation planner for a client having employees in many states may have to consider variations in benefit plans to meet each state's requirements. Furthermore, a malpractice claim might be converted into an unfair trade practice claim in order to gain the advantage of a longer statute of limitations.[4]

## TO WHOM IS ONE LIABLE?

This question is not always as easy to answer as it sounds. The simple answer is, one is liable to those who employ him. The general rule is that a duty is owed only to the person with whom he contracts, his client. But liability may extend to others as well.[5]

An advisor is not liable—even for an act of negligence—to someone to whom he owes no duty.[6] The legal term is "privity." But the defense that there is no privity, no duty to an injured party, can easily be forfeited and is currently being eroded in the courts.[7]

This six-pronged test may be used to determine privity[8]:

1. To what extent is the transaction intended to benefit the third person?

2. Can harm to that third person be foreseen?

3. How likely is it that the third person will suffer real injury?

4. How close is the connection between the advisor's conduct and the injury that the third party could suffer?

5. How "morally wrong" is the advisor's action?

6. Would future harm to this or some other client be served by finding privity here?

At least one state will grant "standing" (the right to sue) to a narrow class of third party beneficiaries where it is clear that the client intended to benefit that party and the client is unable to enforce the contract.[9] Generally, for a third party to collect, written evidence must show that the client's intent must be frustrated and the client's loss must be a direct result of the planner's negligence.

## WHAT CAN GET THE ADVISOR INTO TROUBLE?

*IF HE SAYS HE KNOWS, HE'D BETTER.* Compensation and retirement planning is too complex to be a sideline. Failure to exercise reasonable care and skill in performing duties for a person induced to rely on an advisor because of his professed skills, knowledge, or experience ("John Jones, Benefit Consultant") can result in liability for loss incurred.[10] If one holds himself out as an expert and directly or indirectly promises to provide a product or service to serve a specific purpose or accomplish a particular objective, he assumes the liability for the achievement of that purpose or objective.[11] The skill, knowledge, diligence, and care used must equal or exceed that standard ordinarily exercised by others in the same profession.[12] In short, if one calls himself a professional (or by action or inaction allows others to rely on him as such), he must assume the responsibilities and duties generally associated with such a status—or be held liable for the client's loss.

*NOT KNOWING WHO THE CLIENT IS.* Is the client the employer or an executive negotiating for benefits and compensation? If there is any question or inherent conflict in their positions, separate advisors for each may be best.

There are many cases where the planner never or seldom meets the client. For instance, suppose that a benefit advisor prepares a form and explanatory material for a wife to waive spousal benefits under a pension plan. If the advisor never met the wife, how can it be argued that she has been properly advised or that she understood what she signed? The situation is a "lack of informed consent" case in the making.

*IF HE SAYS HE WILL, HE'D BETTER.* An advisor should never create false expectations by making promises he has no intention of keeping or by promising results he does not know he can deliver. He may be held liable to clients if he promises to keep them informed of significant developments and then does not.[13] He has an obligation to finish substantially the task he has begun for a client, decline the appointment, or, with the client's consent, accept the employment and associate a lawyer who is competent. He must also prepare adequately for and give appropriate attention to the work he has accepted.

*OVERNIGHT EXPRESS.* Clients often want various plans implemented almost overnight—just before government filing deadlines or when they are about to leave on an extended vacation or business trip. This means there is insufficient time to collect, analyze, and act upon complete information. One should refuse to be rushed (but be prepared to work quickly).

## HOW DOES ONE STAY OUT OF TROUBLE?

*"HIRING — AND FIRING — THE CLIENT."* The advisor should ask why the client has chosen him. It's flattering to think one has been selected because of one's expertise or reputation, but the reason may be that another practitioner decided not to represent the client. One should obtain as much information about the client's background with other professionals as possible before agreeing to work with the client. The first interview should be considered a primary opportunity to screen and qualify the client. Perhaps the potential client should be discarded if he seems to be a perfectionist, unrealistic, hurried, angry, overly optimistic, overly fee-conscious, or if he wants services one is not positive he can provide cost effectively.[14] One should beware of clients who are wealthy but in constant cash flow difficulty, seem immature, refuse to accept responsibility for their own actions, or appear constantly ambivalent.[15] These personality types are likely to present a future litigation problem.

*TRUST INSTICTS.* One should turn down a client who requests something that is not quite right. If a client has outgrown the advisor's capacity, he should either recommend another firm or bring a specialist in to work with the client. If an advisor feels the client cannot be trusted, he should refuse to work with the client.

*RISK—TAKING PROPENSITY.* One of the biggest causes of claims is that the professional misjudges or never considers or does not reevaluate the risk— taking propensity of the client as his circumstances change. The solution is constant communication.

*EXPERTISE BOUNDARIES.* The advisor should do only those things he is competent (and licensed) to do— and do those things competently. Should a life insurance agent review a pension plan? Should an attorney or accountant judge the adequacy or appropriateness of a client's life insurance portfolio? Should a trust company review documents? Should a financial planner serve as trustee?[16]

Document examination exposure is real. Should one disclaim any liability for review of document viability or efficacy? Incompetent, inconsistent, and informal review is a formula for disaster. If the task is undertaken, it should be done by a person with the appropriate training, expertise, and time to do the job competently and enthusiastically. "You assume an obligation to your client to undertake reasonable research in an effort to ascertain relevant legal principles and to make an informed decision as to a course of action based on an intelligent assessment of the problem."[17]

Furthermore, the planner has a duty either to avoid involving a client in "murky" areas of the law if there are viable alternative tools or techniques that are available, or to inform the client of the risks and let the client make the decision.[18]

Lack of specialized investment knowledge on the part of the planner or fiduciary often results in investment problems. Numerous trust funds are managed by individuals who adopt a passive and simplistic approach. The need for professional investment management and the complexity of modern portfolio theory is ignored or overlooked and too little time is spent in making investment decisions or addressing overall investment policy and asset allocation.[19]

*RESOURCE LIMITS.* The advisor should not accept engagements that will require resources beyond what he can cost-effectively deliver. For example, if his operation does not have the backup personnel to properly service a high number of clients, he should not agree to do deferred compensation and benefit planning for a firm's top 100 executives.

*OUTSIDE EXPERTS.* An advisor should seek help before it is needed. When appropriate, he should recommend that another professional be used, either in his place or together with him. If he makes a specific recommendation, he may be held liable for the actions of that professional. One way to protect himself is by giving out the names of at least three qualified professionals (make sure the criteria for "qualified" extend beyond mere reputation), or stay involved with the representation.

## THE "ENGAGEMENT LETTER"

The engagement letter is the first and primary step in insulating yourself from a successful malpractice suit. An engagement letter should be obtained in every client relationship at the first possible time. The letter spells out the extent and limits of the services to be performed. The following are critical elements of such a letter:

Scope of services and description of work product;

Period of time covered;

Responsibilities undertaken;

Responsibilities the client is expected to assume;

Fee arrangements—amount, terms, and frequency of billing;

Arrangements for update and extension of service;

List of parties represented—and exclusion of those not represented;

Intended use and potential distribution (or restriction) of the advisor's work product[20]; and

Client's acceptance signature and date.

## PUT IT (ALL) IN WRITING

Protecting one's self means meticulous record keeping starting at the onset of the relationship. Changes in risk—taking propensity or attitude of the client or his family, comments at meetings, phone conversations, and other special instructions should be noted. The advisor's files should clearly reflect and support his recollection of events and should be dictated and transcribed as soon as possible after the occurrence (preferably, contemporaneous with the events). The more complete and organized the files, the more likely the judge, jury, or board of arbitrators will consider the advisor's word persuasive (assuming, of course, the files corroborate what he is now saying).

Whenever possible, quote the client's exact words.[21] This is particularly important whenever a client—or one of his other advisors—decides to pursue an aggressive tax policy or take an investment risk (and doubly important if you have advised against that course of action). For instance, if an attorney tells a client that the business does not need all of the life insurance the agent is suggesting, the agent should attempt to take down as accurately as possible the exact words of the attorney. The attorney should do the same.

Contemporaneous and near verbatim notes should also be taken if the client asks that the advisor not do a service (or anything) he would normally do or if the client asks him to attempt a service that he ordinarily would not do.

Detailed notes are particularly important if the client seems uncooperative or unwilling to provide the information or documents that are necessary to do the job properly.

*FEES.* Fees should not be set at levels that will require cutting corners or operating at a loss for this engagement. The fee must be large enough to justify internally the time that should be invested in a case—or the case should be turned down. Fees should include the costs that will be incurred to meet high ethical standards and avoid malpractice by implementation of systematic quality control and other appropriate courses of action.

A fee dispute which results in litigation with a client may trigger a malpractice case. The solution is to secure a written agreement as to fees and billing procedures at the onset of the relationship with the client. One should think carefully about the wisdom of suing the client and the likelihood and expense of a malpractice lawsuit by the client. It is wise to communicate clearly the basis or rate of fee or other method of compensation to a new client in writing before or as soon as possible after the relationship begins. The client should be billed periodically and provided detailed information about the services rendered and the time invested.

*DATA FORMS.* Many times the error or omission of the planner is due to an incomplete or incorrect understanding of the facts. The advisor should obtain comprehensive and accurate data by developing a data gathering system (see Appendix C). Some planners feel they can gather data without forms or checklists but inevitably forget to ask basic questions. One must be sure to confirm with the client the facts gathered—before acting upon them.

A client's existing compensation arrangements should be verified from the documents themselves. It is astounding how often otherwise competent attorneys draft plans that do not match the facts. One needs to check benefit plan documents, insurance contracts, and employee benefit booklets and summary plan descriptions rather than rely on the client's memory. Current insurance policy information should be confirmed by writing to the insurer.

## LIMITS OF THE RELATIONSHIP

The client's instructions must be followed—correctly. This entails first truly understanding what those instructions are. Then it requires a written memorandum (preferably signed by the client). Meticulous records of all conversations should be made and kept. If investments are or will be involved in the relationship, an investment policy should document agreed-upon investment objectives, risk parameters, return targets, volatility tolerance, and asset allocation ranges.

A written consent should be obtained for actions outside the scope of the relationship as contained in the engagement letter.

## RECORDS AND SYSTEMS

*THE RIGHT STUFF.* Keep research documents that indicate decisions were made in a methodical and logical manner and that a deliberate investigation preceded and supported each suggestion. Retain documents which illustrate the tax law as it existed at the time tax decisions were made.[22] Memos to the file, prepared contemporaneously with conversations with a client and decision making, are highly useful in establishing the background and intent at the time an action was taken. Make controversial decisions only with the informed knowledge and written consent of the client. Document any oral advice immediately.

Develop and use a presentation system that will prove that regular discussions covering all of the important areas of benefit planning with a client took place.[23] A checklist should be incorporated into that system in order to demonstrate that these issues have been discussed with the client and reflect the client's circumstances and objectives.

A retrieval system should be established to locate documents or plans that need updating for specific changes. For example, all qualified plans, active or inactive, must be regularly amended to reflect changes in the law.

*"TRIGGER SYSTEM."* A checklist of follow-up procedures should be developed so that time-sensitive responsibilities will be met by the appropriate parties and unreasonable delays in the preparation and implementation of the plan can be avoided. Set deadlines, establish priorities, and specify responsibilities. Create a "tickler" file (i.e., a docketing system) to meet all deadlines, statutes of limitations, and filing and payment deadlines. Set up a centralized system to personally remind the party responsible for action and review at given times or events. Incorporate into the system a series of client reminders (e.g., "Major new tax law changes suggest we should review your qualified plans as soon as possible").

## QUALITY CONTROL

An advisor is responsible for the errors or omissions of his partners, associates, and employees. Quality control is therefore not a luxury; it is a business necessity.

*UNDERSTANDING OF ETHICAL ISSUES.* The planner should discuss with colleagues the danger when a breach of ethics is coupled with an angry or disgruntled client or family member.

*WHO IS THE "QUARTERBACK?"* In any operation larger than a one-person firm, it is essential that the activities of the entire staff be co-ordinated by a "quarterback" who accepts responsibility. This person must be sure that all staff members are kept informed and that there is a logical and automatic flow of necessary information, that no tasks have been overlooked, and that no efforts are duplicated. He must also be sure that information received by staff members is properly recorded and relayed to him and to the central file on each client.

*INDEPENDENT REVIEW.* An effective method of quality control is to have the final product reviewed by a well qualified associate before it is shared with a client.

*REVIEW OF STAFF COMPETENCE, EXPERIENCE, QUALIFICATIONS.* Compensation planning, almost by definition, requires the input of many professionals. Most planners not only must cooperate with other planners outside their offices but must also rely on associates within their offices. Staff members must be currently competent, and they must be well trained in and conform to standardized office procedures, policies, and proper file management techniques. Appropriate supervision for all levels of staff should be built in. Continuing education should be a part of any firm's ongoing business plan.

## EXTERNAL COMMUNICATIONS

Almost every authority who speaks and every article that is written on malpractice states that many lawsuits could probably have been avoided by a simple solution: "Communicate, Communicate, Communicate!"[24]

Many, or even most, of the grievance complaints and malpractice actions can be headed off if the advisor will:

*MAKE IT CLEAR AND MAKE IT OFTEN.* The planner should avoid technical jargon. He should not assume lay persons understand what he means by such terms as a "qualified plan," a "QDRO," or an "ESOP." He can use word pictures, graphs, flow charts, or diagrams to illustrate his points—and give the clients copies to take home.[25]

He should continually inform clients of all actions he and his staff have taken (or not taken);

forward to clients copies of documents he sends to other professionals; provide the client with periodic written reports even if a particular report merely explains why no progress has been made since the last report; and confirm in writing all transactions, expenses, fees, income, or other events of importance.

He should inform the client of any changes in the relationship or responsibilities of the parties; make sure reports are understandable; and use graphs, charts, and checklists to show the progress he has made.

He should confirm objectives, responsibilities, and timetables through a series of scheduled meetings among the client and other advisors.

A newsletter is a good way to keep in touch with clients on a regular basis.

The advisor should schedule regular reviews and give special emphasis to contacting clients from whom he has not heard or had contact with in a given period of time. He should document his attempt to contact those who do not respond.

He should keep copies of all correspondence and conversations with other professionals who are working with his client.

He should study the client's verbal and body language to be sure he is understood and encourage the client to call or write to him after the meeting to ask questions if "he has not made himself understood."

*AVOID CASUAL OR INFORMAL ADVICE.* The advisor should not give advice at cocktail parties or other social events.[26] Liability can be imposed even though no fee has been charged for services if a client relies on information he has been provided.

*CALL BACK — PROMPTLY.* A careful advisor will return telephone calls promptly. If this is impossible, his secretary or an associate should do it for him so the client does not feel ignored.

*AVOID "HEEL COOLING."* A planner should not keep clients waiting on the phone or in his office. He should be sure he receives messages promptly—and accurately. He should not allow a phone call to interrupt a meeting with a client. It is a good idea to reward staff members for being extra polite. In short, give the client respect and common courtesy.

## AVOIDING (OR NEUTRALIZING) CONFLICT OF INTEREST PROBLEMS

*CONFLICTS WITH EXISTING CLIENTS.*[27] The duty of loyalty requires any planner to be extremely cautious about serving a client in more than one capacity. For instance, the client of an attorney or CPA may want that person to serve as an executor or trustee — while at the same time desiring that person to continue to provide planning advice and other services to various family members. Can the advice be disinterested and objective? Can the professional ethically charge fees for both services? Can those fees honestly be set at "arm's-length"?

Although there is no legal prohibition against representing more than one client in a single transaction, planners should be particularly alert for situations in which there is an obvious or potential difference in their interests. For instance, a defined benefit plan typically favors older long service employees while profit sharing and defined contribution pension plans usually are to the benefit of younger employees.

Another conflict of interest problem that often occurs where more than one person is represented is the disclosure of confidential information. Can a planner freely tell a wife what her husband has disclosed? Can a planner share information from one shareholder with others? The planner needs to inform all parties that information may not be privileged or confidential as to other members of the group unless specific direction is given.

Any possible conflicts of interest should be disclosed—in writing—to the client as quickly as possible or the planner should withdraw without disclosure if confidential information is involved. Recognition of disclosure and acceptance of its consequent risks should be acknowledged in any instrument signed by the client.

The planner should avoid or treat extremely carefully any financial involvement in a client's business or in a business venture.

*CONFLICTS WITH FUTURE CLIENTS.* A planner should ask himself whether acceptance of a client will create a conflict with respect to more desirable work with another client in the future?[28]

*RED FLAG PROCEDURES.* It is important for the planner to train himself and his staff to recognize "red flags." A procedure for identifying problems and quickly dealing with them is essential.

*DEALING WITH PROBLEMS.* The planner must routinely review and deal with problems promptly. If a problem occurs, he must call or write the client immediately and explain the problem and the potential consequences and alternatives. If a client is angry or dissatisfied, he ought to take immediate action—talk to the client and resolve the problem. He cannot safely assume the problem will go away or that the client will forget it.

*THE PROBLEM TEAM.* A good idea is to create a "Problem Team" in the firm which meets immediately every time the potential for a dissatisfied client is recognized. That team should not only review the file in the case in point but also any other procedures, activities, omissions, or oversights which may trigger future problems that could develop into litigation.

*EARLY, ACTIVE REMEDIAL CONCILIATORY EFFORTS.* The quicker an attempt is made to resolve the problem to the client's satisfaction, the less likely there will be litigation. Providing a large apology might avoid writing a small check. Writing a small check might avoid defending a large lawsuit. One litigation attorney put it this way: "The good will that can be generated by such an act and accompanying attitudes might be much cheaper and better in the long run than paying expensive attorneys for years of litigation with an uncertain outcome."[29] Sometimes, assigning a new person to speak to the client will serve to quell the objection.

## ABOUT MALPRACTICE INSURANCE

*SUFFICIENT LEVELS OF COVERAGE.* The first step in evaluating current insurance is to see if there is enough insurance to cover any likely risk. But this is only a first step.

*"CLAIMS MADE" POLICIES.* Most malpractice coverage is sold on a "claims made" basis. This means the policy covers only claims which are first asserted and reported to the insurer within the policy year.

*"PRIOR ACTS" COVERAGE.* The action alleging malpractice often does not occur until years after the alleged negligence occurred. If the policy has a "prior acts" coverage, it covers a claim asserted during a policy year even though the negligence giving rise to the claim occurred in some prior year.[30] If a policy lacks or excludes prior acts or limits prior acts coverage, it is likely that there will be a "coverage gap." There will be no coverage under the policy in effect when the alleged negligence occurred because the claim was not made in that policy year. The current policy will not cover the alleged negligence because negligence alleged to have occurred before the present policy year is excluded or omitted from the coverage.

*THE "TAIL."* A tail is an extended reporting option somewhat related to prior acts coverage. If one purchases a tail, he is permitted (usually at the end of each policy year or earlier if the policy is canceled during the term) to convert "claims made" coverage to "occurrence" coverage for any negligence allegedly committed—but not yet reported—up to the end of that policy year. The extended reporting of claims option available through a tail is expensive. The premium is a multiple of the regular annual premium. Tails should be considered by retiring planners who will no longer keep their full malpractice coverage in force or by attorneys who are forced to switch malpractice insurance carriers because of a cancellation or a refusal of a carrier to renew coverage (typically due to claims made) if the new carrier refuses to provide prior acts coverage. Tails are "cut off" after some period of time unless the tail is unlimited. Under an unlimited tail, the insurer remains liable for negligence occurring before the policy period expires regardless of when the claim is asserted.

*THE DEDUCTIBLE.* Most planners opt for a higher deductible in order to reduce the premium outlay. But one should check to see if legal costs he would incur in a malpractice suit apply against his share of the deductible. Does the deductible apply "per claim" or "per policy year"? Where there is more than one claim in a given policy year, a per claim deductible becomes a hidden cost: a second deductible must be satisfied in the event of a second claim within a year. A per year deductible means the deductible amount need be paid only once in a given year regardless of the number of claims. Because when it rains, it pours, a per claim provision might prove quite costly.

*THE SETTLEMENT.* Some policies give the insurer the right to limit its exposure through a provision entitled "Settlement." This means the insurer can force a settlement with the plaintiff (regardless of the insured's wishes) because of the cost. Some settlement provisions state that if one does not wish to settle under specified terms, the insurer will limit its payment to the amount specified in a settlement agreement at which point all other exposure (including defense cost) becomes the insured's obligation. Why might an insured not want to settle—even though economically it might make sense? The psychological cost of admitting wrongdoing or malpractice—coupled with the loss in reputation—are strong reasons why he may want to maintain the right to say "NO" to a settlement. One should be sure that right does not expose him to a loss of coverage above the limits in the proposed settlement.

*DUTY TO DEFEND vs. DUTY TO INDEMNIFY.* A "duty to defend" policy requires the insurer to appoint defense counsel and pay that attorney's fee as billed. An "indemnification" policy allows the insured to select counsel but he must fund his defense unless he can reach an interim fee agreement.[31] He will not be reimbursed for defense costs until the case is concluded. Obviously, interim funding can be a problem.

*DEFINITION OF "DAMAGES."* The way covered damages is defined is crucial. One may be exposed to fines, penalties, and punitive, or even treble, damages. Check with the insurance agent to clarify how broadly or narrowly the policy construes the term "damages."

*INNOCENT PARTNER COVERAGE.* Does the policy provide coverage for the defalcations of another member of the firm? One is liable for his partner's embezzlement even if he has not benefited by it. The insurer will deny a claim based on the partner's fraud and/or criminal activity unless there is "innocent partner" coverage.

*OTHER KEY PROVISIONS.* A malpractice policy ideally will provide coverage for the defense costs if it is claimed the insured is guilty of intentional conduct (even though the policy does not indemnify the costs of the intentional conduct). Does the policy cover libel or slander or defense of RICO claims?

*INSURER'S STABILITY.* It is important to check the financial stability of the insurer and to be sure the insurer has a solid reputation for integrity and responsiveness. It is worth finding out if the insurer itself has been involved in litigation with its own insureds. The lowest premium will not compensate for the aggravation and other costs of suing the carrier to get it to defend properly a malpractice case.

*HANDLING A CLAIM.* A detailed discussion of malpractice claims procedures is beyond the scope of this article. However, the following steps will help in the defense of a malpractice suit:

1. Notify the insurer immediately no matter how small the suit is.

2. Once the insured has been notified formally that he is being sued, say as little as necessary to the suing client.

3. Secure all work product immediately.

4. Inform the entire staff of the problem and the action game plan.

5. Do whatever is necessary to assist in the defense of the case.

## THE TOTAL COST

The frequency of malpractice actions in the year 2000 and afterward can be expected to increase many times what it was in the 1990s. No profession in the compensation planning team will escape unscathed. There are no conclusive signs that this trend is reversing.[32]

*DIRECT COSTS.* Malpractice premiums for compensation planning are in the highest classification—along with corporate securities work—for a very good reason. The dollars at risk are substantial.

*LOSS OF REPUTATION.* The cost of a malpractice suit cannot be measured merely in terms of the court judgment or out of court settlement or the cost of attorneys. The cost to a professional's reputation (win or lose) may be staggering. For instance, it would be difficult to attract new partners or new associates if one has been successfully sued for malpractice.

*LOSS OF STANDING WITH PEERS.* Compensation planning is a process based partially on knowledge and largely on trust. A malpractice suit calls into question competence which in turn destroys confidence, not only of current and potential clients but also the confidence of other members of the planning team with whom one must deal.

*THE PSYCHOLOGICAL TRAUMA.* A planner who becomes a defendant in a lawsuit must deal with the incredible pressure and emotional trauma of being sued.[33] Often, the planner (and perhaps office associates, partners, and friends) will see the action taken by the client as an attack on his professional ability, integrity, or judgment. This cannot help the practitioner's morale and will probably result in adverse fallout on other projects. This psychological strain is compounded by time; the legal process is typically long and drawn out over a period of years even if the claim is unfounded.

*HIDDEN ECONOMIC COSTS.* Colleagues from whom the practitioner received referrals and the general public may hear about the lawsuit. This will cause almost certain financial damage. Furthermore, the planner is required to participate in his own defense whether or not he is adequately insured. This, in turn, translates into dozens, sometimes hundreds, of unbillable hours spent gathering facts and records and recreating the facts, giving depositions, briefing defense attorneys, and testifying at trial.

*CUT AND RUN?* If it appears a matter cannot be resolved by the procedures discussed above, it may be prudent to consider "discharging the client." Obviously, this is a last resort but it should not be overlooked in a "heads they win—tails we lose situation."

## SUMMARY

Creating and maintaining a successful compensation planning practice requires a methodical, systematic approach to risk management. Planners are vulnerable to litigation no matter how careful they are. But the risk of a claim and the potential for a successful claim can be substantially reduced through continuing a vigorous and systematized policy of internal and external positive communication, common sense courtesy, quality control, and a strong emphasis on high quality continuing education of every member of the firm.

A planner should check that he has:

- Established and improved client relationships.

- Controlled the management of client relationships.

- Improved office practices.

- Identified problem areas.

- Corrected problems before they occur.

Looking at everything in this discussion positively, the "action suggestions" described here can be thought of not only as defensive but as the blueprint for a vigorous office organizing and client market building campaign.

## FOOTNOTES

1. Compare "Avoiding Malpractice Suits: Some Sound Advice," *Trusts and Estates*, April 1990, p. 12.

2. This is called the "best judgment" or "good faith" defense.

3. Compare *Killey Trust*, 457 Pa. 474 (1974). Large corporate planners such as banks and trust companies will likely be held to a higher level of competence than others because of their access to information and expertise.

On the other hand, the sophistication, education, and expertise of the client is not a defense. See *Blankenheim v. E.F. Hutton and Co.*, 217 Cal. App. 3d 1463 (1990), which held that the relationship between a stockbroker and his customer is fiduciary in nature, imposing on the former the duty to act in the highest good faith toward his customer. The court held that the plaintiff's concession that they were experts in the accounting and taxation area and any experience the plaintiff may have acquired following his investment was irrelevant to reliance on the broker's representations at the time of the sale.

4. In one case the attorney drafted a trust that failed to qualify for the marital deduction. This action was barred by a 3-year statute of limitations. So the plaintiff also sued for a violation of the state's Unfair Trade Practices Act, which had a much longer statute of limitations and allowed a suit by "any person who purchases or leases goods, services, or property." The estate successfully alleged that the will draftsman had engaged in an unfair and deceptive act and practice by holding himself out as an attorney reasonably skilled in the preparation and drafting of last wills and testaments and in his ability to comply with the decedent's wishes and to minimize the tax obligations of her estate.

5. See "Court Decisions Reinforce the Idea That an Insurance Agent Who Holds Himself Out to Have Great Expertise will be Bound to the Exercise of It," *Trusts and Estates*, Oct. 1988, p. 55.

6. Compare *Bell v. Manning*, 613 S.W.2d 335 (1981).

7. *Lucas v. Hamm*, 15 Cal. Rptr. 821 (1961), *cert. denied*, 368 U.S. 987 (1962).

8. The California Supreme Court used this test in *Biakanja v. Irving*, 49 Cal. 2d 647, 320 P.2d 16 (1958).

   Although there is a trend toward relaxing the requirement of privity, New York and Texas are staunch supporters of the rule. See *Victor v. Goldman*, 344 N.Y.S.2d 672 (1973), *aff'd*, 351 N.Y.S.2d 956 (2d Dept. 1974) and *Dickey v. Jansen*, 731 S.W.2d 581 (1987).

9. *Guy v. Liederbach*, 459 A.2d 744 (Penn. 1983).

10. See *Bogley v. Middleton Tavern, Inc.*, 421 A.2d 571 (1980). Of course, the knee jerk defense is, "The insurance was purchased in an arm's-length transaction involving no confidential or fiduciary relationship between the insured and the agent." This tactic might work if the agent never professed to be anything other than a salesperson. See *Lazovick v. Sun Life Ins. Co. of America*, 586 F. Supp. 918 (E.D. Pa. 1984). This defense probably would not hold up for most readers of this text who typically hold themselves out as having significantly greater expertise than the average life insurance agent.

11. *Wright Body Works, Inc. v. Columbus Interstate Ins. Agency*, 210 S.E.2d 801 (1974).

12. *State Farm Life Ins. Co. v. Fort Wayne National Bank*, 474 N.E.2d 524 (Ind. Ct. App. 1985).

13. *Morales v. Field, DeGoff, Huppert and MacGowan*, 99 Cal. App. 3d 307 (1979).

14. See "Does This Prospect Mean Trouble?," *Practical Financial Planning*, Oct./Nov. 1988, p. 23.

15. See "Reducing the Risk of Estate Planning Malpractice," *Tax Management Estates, Gifts, and Trusts Journal*, (BNA) March/April 1984, p. 36.

16. See "How Not to be a Trustee," *Financial Planning*, May 1990, p. 69.

17. *Horne v. Peckham*, 97 Cal. App. 3d 404 (1979).

18. Where there is reasonable doubt among well informed practitioners, there should be no liability. But this assumes a diligent quest for answers was made. Failure to research an issue or fully understand the facts will result in a denial of the "unsettled law" defense. See *Smith v. Lewis*, 530 P.2d 589 (1975).

19. See "Steps to Protect the Fiduciary from Liability for Investment Decisions," *Estate Planning*, July/August, 1989, p. 228.

20. In "Taming the Liability Monster," *L&H Perspective*, V. 15, No. 1/1989, p. 38, the author states that "A nightmare for the professional is reliance by unknown third parties on their work product."

21. As one attorney was interviewing a couple, he would pause from time to time to "capsulize" their thoughts into a dictaphone. Before he did, he would remind them each time, "Be sure to stop me if this isn't exactly what you want or if I've misunderstood what you've just said."

22. You may have to prove that, at the time you were making the decision, the available information was much different from what it is at the time litigation occurs. See "How to Manage a Growing Tax Practice," *The Practical Accountant*, May 1990, p. 27.

23. See "Avoiding and Handling Malpractice Claims Against Estate Planners," *Estate Planning*, Sept./Oct. 1989, p. 267.

24. Compare "Coping with Administrative Problems: There's More to Life and Death than Taxes," 21 U. of Miami Institute on Estate Planning, Chapter 17 (1987).

25. Some attorneys use commercially written brochures to make their points or to give clients something to take home that will help them understand more complex concepts. A number of highly useful client-oriented brochures are available from Leimberg & LeClair, Inc., P.O. Box 1332, Bryn Mawr, Pa. 19010 (610-527-5216).

26. See *Newton Estate*, T.C. Memo 1990-208, for an example of the damage a well intended but offhand remark can do. The executor's reliance on the statement of an attorney as to the filing deadline did not constitute reasonable cause for the filing delay where the attorney admittedly had not been retained to render advice on federal estate tax matters, was not paid any fee for the advice, did not normally practice in that area of the law, and had advised the executor to verify any information with a tax practitioner. The "offhand remark" may not result in a malpractice case for this attorney — but it certainly would not result in a good relationship with the client either.

27. Consider an index which includes data on clients and other parties to transactions with which the firm is involved. Include a procedure through which the system automatically updates the files to add the names of new family members, business associates, or others related to the client.

28. Obtain a "Waiver of Conflict" letter with respect to one-time consulting arrangements. Obtain advance written consent to future simultaneous adverse representation on any matter not substantially related to the matter undertaken for a new client.

29. "Protecting the Corporate Fiduciary's Tender Backside," *Trusts and Estates*, Feb. 1988, p. 72.

30. See "About Your Malpractice," *Lawyer's Digest*, Pa., May 1988, p. 11.

31. "How the Accountant/Financial Planner Can Reduce Exposure to Liability Claims," *The Practical Accountant*, Feb. 1990, p. 15.

32. See "Taming the Liability Monster," *L&H Perspective*, Vol. 15/No. 1, 1989, p. 37.

33. See "Strategies to Avoid Malpractice," *Practical Financial Planning*, Vol. 2, No. 3, April/May 1989, p. 29.

# AGE AND SEX DISCRIMINATION

## I. AGE DISCRIMINATION

### A. Pension Plans

#### Age Discrimination in Employment Act

The federal Age Discrimination in Employment Act (ADEA), as amended in 1978, 1986, 1990, and 1996 provides that it is unlawful for an employer

(1) to fail or refuse to hire or to discharge any individual or otherwise discriminate against any individual with respect to his compensation, terms, conditions, or privileges of employment, because of such individual's age;

(2) to limit, segregate, or classify its employees in any way which would deprive or tend to deprive any individual of employment opportunities or otherwise adversely affect his status as an employee, because of such individual's age; or

(3) to reduce the wage rate of any employee in order to comply with [ADEA].[1]

ADEA applies to workers and managers of any business that engages in interstate commerce (which the courts have defined very broadly) and employs at least 20 persons for each working day in each of 20 or more calendar weeks in the current or preceding calendar year.[2]

State laws are not preempted by ADEA. Therefore it is possible that benefit discrimination allowed under ADEA might be prohibited under applicable state law.

The primary impact of ADEA on pension plans is that the language quoted above prohibits mandatory retirement at any age. However, mandatory retirement at age 65 is specifically permitted for an individual who has been in a "bona fide executive or high policy making position" for at least two years before retirement and who is entitled to a minimum fully vested pension of $44,000 annually calculated as a straight life annuity.[3]

Beyond the issue of compulsory retirement, the language of ADEA is general and does not provide specific guidance regarding its application to pension plans, qualified or nonqualified. The Equal Employment Opportunities Commission (EEOC) has issued some regulations in this area, but in light of the *Betts* case discussed below, the current validity of prior ADEA interpretations may be questionable.

For qualified plans, there are specific age discrimination provisions in the Internal Revenue Code, as discussed below, that are not affected by any controversy regarding ADEA.

#### IRC Age Discrimination Provisions for Qualified Plans

Under Code section 411(b)(2), a *defined contribution* plan cannot reduce allocations (or the rate of allocations) of employer contributions, forfeitures, or income, gains or losses, in a participant's account because of the participant's age. However, the plan can have a "cap" on the number of years during which employer contributions and forfeitures will be allocated, or the total amount of contributions or forfeitures, provided that it is not based on age as such. For example, a plan can provide that employer contributions and forfeitures will be allocated only over the participant's first 25 years of service. Few plans use this approach.

Correspondingly, under Code section 411(b)(1)(H), in a *defined benefit* plan, the benefit formula cannot cutoff accruals at a specified age, but it can provide that benefits are accrued fully after a specified number of years of service, such as 25. Plans can continue to use age 65 as the "normal retirement age" for funding and benefit accrual purposes. If employees work past age 65, the regulations provide alternative methods for benefit payment and/or accrual.[4]

### B. Welfare Benefit Plans

Prior to the *Betts* case discussed below, in applying ADEA to benefit plans, an "equal cost" approach was developed in court cases and in EEOC regulations. That is, an employer was not required to provide exactly the same benefits to older as to younger employees, but rather to provide benefits having the same cost level. Thus, for example, amounts of life insurance coverage (amounts of death benefit) could be reduced for older employees to reflect the increasing premium cost. EEOC regulations allowed the use of up to 5-year age brackets for computing benefit costs. Costs were to be determined on a benefit by benefit basis under the EEOC regulations.[5]

ADEA contains a provision allowing an employer to "observe the terms of a bona fide employee benefit plan...that is a voluntary early retirement incentive plan consistent with the relevant purpose or purposes of [the ADEA]."[6] For many years the courts and the regulatory agencies have interpreted this as an authorization for adopting rules such as the EEOC regulations.

However, in 1989 the U.S. Supreme Court decided *Public Employees Retirement System of Ohio v. Betts*.[7] Specifically, the *Betts* case involved a disability retirement benefit that was not available to employees who retired after age 59. While the Court found that this benefit did not violate ADEA, it also ruled broadly that ADEA exempts all provisions of bona fide employee benefit plans, unless the plan is a subterfuge for discrimination in non-fringe benefit aspects of the employment relationship. In so holding, the Supreme Court invalidated the EEOC's "equal cost" regulation referred to above.

After the decision in the *Betts* case, Congress took up the age discrimination issue fairly quickly, and in 1990 passed corrective legislation that essentially restores and codifies the DOL's "equal benefit or equal cost" rule. Highlights of this legislation include:

1. The equal benefit or equal cost principle under prior EEOC regulations discussed above has now been adopted legislatively.

2. The law establishes minimum standards for employee waivers of rights under limited early retirement "window" provisions in which employees must decide whether or not to accept the program during a limited time period. If an employer adopts an early retirement incentive plan to encourage older employees to retire, employees must be given at least three weeks to decide if they want to accept the plan and must be advised in writing to consult a lawyer before accepting.

3. The law does not apply retroactively.

4. Like the original Age Discrimination in Employment Act, the amended Act applies to businesses that employ at least 20 persons during the year.

## II. SEX DISCRIMINATION

Sex discrimination in employee benefit plans is governed primarily by the federal Civil Rights Act of 1964, which provides as follows:

(a) It shall be an unlawful employment practice for an employer—

(1) to fail or refuse to hire or to discharge any individual, or otherwise to discriminate against any individual with respect to his compensation, terms, conditions, or privileges of employment, because of such individual's race, color, religion, sex, or national origin; or

(2) to limit, segregate, or classify its employees or applicants for employment in any way which would deprive or tend to deprive any individual of employment opportunities or otherwise adversely affect his status as an employee, because of such individual's race, color, religion, sex, or national origin.[8]

The Civil Rights Act covers all employers in interstate commerce who have at least 15 employees for each working day in at least 20 calendar weeks in the current or preceding calendar year.[9]

There are no provisions in the Internal Revenue Code or ERISA directly dealing with sex discrimination, so court decisions and regulations under the Civil Rights Act are the primary source of authority in the benefits area.[10]

In the area of wage and benefit discrimination, the Civil Rights Act provisions overlap with another federal statute, the Equal Pay Act of 1963.[11] For most benefit purposes, it is adequate to discuss only the Civil Rights Act, since there are few, if any, benefit practices permitted by the Civil Rights Act that are prohibited by the Equal Pay Act. However, there is an important difference that affects smaller employers: the Equal Pay Act has *no small employer exception*.[12]

Sex discrimination raises obvious issues in employee benefits because so many common benefits involve actuarial differences in cost between men and women—life insurance, annuities (pensions), and health insurance, particularly with regard to coverage for pregnancy. The issues involved have been fought over in the courts and the regulatory agencies; the history will not be rehashed here, but instead the result—the state of current law—will be summarized as well as possible.

*Pension plans.* Pension plans raise the issue of whether the law requires employers to make equal *contributions* or provide equal *benefits.* The court cases on this issue are not entirely clear, but the weight of Supreme Court decisions has convinced most commentators that an equal-benefit approach is required.[13] Specifically,

- A defined benefit plan should offer the same benefit for men and women retirees similarly situated (most always have done so).

- Employers with defined benefit plans can use sex-based actuarial assumptions for funding purposes, since this does not affect employees' benefits.

- If a retirement plan includes an incidental life insurance benefit, the same amount of life insurance must be provided to men and women employees with the same retirement benefits. If the plan is contributory, contributions must be based on unisex tables.

- If a defined contribution plan offers an annuity form of payout, either exclusively or as an option, unisex annuity rates must be used within the plan itself. (This will not prevent male retirees from taking a lump sum distribution and using the money to purchase a sex-based annuity providing higher monthly payments from an insurance company.)

*Life insurance.* The same Supreme Court cases cited for pension plans have convinced most commentators that the courts will uphold prohibitions against sex-based life insurance benefits in an employer plan.[14] Therefore, any life insurance plan should provide the same amount of insurance to any participant, male or female, who is otherwise similarly situated (same compensation, same job classification, etc.). If plan participants must contribute to the plan (as in supplemental group coverage, for example) unisex premium rates must be used.

*Health insurance.* In the area of health insurance, certain controversies have been settled only by federal legislation. Congress in 1978 added Section 701(k) to the Civil Rights Act to indicate that distinctions among employee benefits based on pregnancy or childbirth are considered sex-related. EEOC interpretive guidelines based on this Act[15] require pregnancy and childbirth-related medical expenses of employees to be treated the same as other medical expenses. Also, the EEOC guidelines require pregnancy benefits to be provided to spouses of male employees if spouses of female employees also receive health benefits.

Other EEOC regulations prohibit restricting spousal and family benefits to employees who are deemed "head of household" and also prohibit plans that provide benefits to spouses of male employees that are not available to female employees.[16]

## FOOTNOTES

1. ADEA, §4(a); 29 USC §623(a).
2. 29 USC §630(b).
3. ADEA, §12(c)(1), 29 USC §631(a); 29 CFR (EEOC Reg.) §1627.17.
4. Prop. Reg. §1.411(b)-2(b)(4).
5. 29 CFR (EEOC Reg.) §1625.10.
6. ADEA, §4(f)(2)(B), 29 USC §623(f)(2)(B). This exception does not permit involuntary retirement because of age or failure to hire because of age.
7. *Public Employees Retirement System of Ohio v. Betts*, 492 U.S. 158 (1989).
8. Civil Rights Act of 1964, §703(a), 42 USC §2000e-2(a).
9. 42 USC §2000e(b).
10. Some commentators have theorized that the fiduciary provisions of ERISA require impartial dealing with plan participants.
11. 29 USC §206.
12. Certain types of business are excepted, however, such as retail sales, fishing, agriculture, and newspaper publishing. 29 USC §§203(s), 213(a).
13. *Los Angeles Department of Water and Power v. Manhart*, 435 U.S. 702 (1978), involved a contributory pension plan of a municipality. The Court held that the plan could not require women to pay higher contributions than men to receive equal periodic benefits upon retirement. *Arizona Governing Committee v. Norris*, 463 U.S. 1073 (1983), involved a Section 457 deferred compensation plan (see Chapter 11) of a municipality. The plan provided a sex-based annuity table for retirees, so that for a given account balance, a female participant received a smaller monthly retirement payment. In both these cases, the Supreme Court found a violation of the Civil Rights Act.
14. Existing EEOC regulations prohibit sex discrimination in all fringe benefits. 29 CFR §§1604.9(b), 1620.4, 1604.9(e).
15. 44 Federal Register 23804 (April 20, 1979). The provision of these guidelines requiring pregnancy benefits to spouses of male employees was upheld by the Supreme Court in *Newport News Shipbuilding and Dry Dock Co. v. EEOC*, 462 U.S. 669 (1983).
16. 29 CFR §§1604.9(c), 1604.9(d).

# ESTATE AND RETIREMENT PLANNING WITH QUALIFIED PLANS AND IRAs

Tax and retirement planners are seeing increasing numbers of a certain type of client who is facing a potential retirement tax disaster. The typical client profile is of an older business owner or executive with a large qualified plan balance (or rollover IRA balance), as well as substantial other assets that will be includable in his estate for federal estate tax purposes.

The reason for the potential disaster is the heavy potential tax impact on retirement plan assets. The combination of regular federal (35%, as amended by JGTRRA 2003), state, and local (another 10% or more in some areas) income taxes; and federal estate taxes (49% in 2003) can practically confiscate a qualified plan distribution unless something is done to avoid this result. In a worst-case scenario, the tax rate on $1,000,000 of qualified plan assets included in a decedent's estate could reach a rate of more than 75%.

In addition, planners must make sure that frighteningly complex technical rules are complied with so that a client's qualified plan assets will actually go where they were intended to go, with the intended tax results. For example, in one private letter ruling, the IRS determined that the marital deduction was not available where a decedent designated a marital trust as an IRA beneficiary, using standard bank forms. The reason? The IRS stated that the bank standard forms did not comply with the technical requirements for a marital deduction, and the situation could not be cured by a postmortem amendment of the beneficiary designation.[1]

The courts have generally indicated no inclination to give planners the benefit of the doubt in this complex area. For example, in *Oddi v. Ayco Corp*,[2] a planner erroneously advised taking an immediate taxable distribution from a qualified plan instead of leaving money in and withdrawing (and deferring taxes) over a period of years, and the client was awarded over $400,000 from the planner.

## AN ISSUE AT RETIREMENT: ROLLOVER VS. KEEPING IT IN PLAN

For some clients nearing retirement who have large profit sharing accumulations, or otherwise have the option of receiving a lump sum distribution, a preliminary consideration is whether the plan accumulation should be kept in a qualified plan or rolled over to an IRA. There are advantages in each approach. Often a rollover is the appropriate thing to do, but it should not be chosen without considering the options.

### Advantages of a Rollover

- If the plan participant is a controlling owner, a rollover may allow him or her to simply terminate the qualified plan, which would then require no further contributions. There is also no further plan administration (filing Form 5500s, etc.) if the plan terminates.

- In an IRA, there may be more investment flexibility in practice since the IRA owner is not dependent on plan trustees and can shop for the best and most flexible IRA arrangement.

- If the plan is subject to the qualified joint and survivor annuity requirement (see below), consent of the participant's spouse is required for the initial rollover, but is not required for subsequent changes in IRA beneficiary designations.

### Advantages of Keeping it in a Qualified Plan

- Plan loans may be available, up to the $50,000 maximum limit.

- The plan can invest in life insurance.

- The participant may be able to use 10-year averaging (available only to certain plan participants born before 1936; see Chapter 26) on a lump sum distribution.

- Qualified plans have better protection against creditors because of ERISA's anti-alienation rule. The U.S. Supreme Court has clarified this somewhat;[3] however, this subject is complex. The ERISA protection probably does not apply to business owners as such, particularly in plans like Keogh plans where the owner is the only plan participant.[4] Note, however, that whatever the status of federal protections, state laws protecting pensions, annuities, insurance, etc., may be available in many states.[5] Many states also explicitly protect IRAs, which are not protected by ERISA.

- If the plan is a defined benefit plan, PBGC insurance may be applicable within its dollar limits ($3,664.77 in 2003). PBGC insurance is not available to a plan "exclusively for substantial owners" or to a plan of a professional service employer that does not at any time have more than 25 active participants.[6]

- From the standpoint of the nonparticipant spouse, a qualified plan provides better protection.

## Converting to a Roth IRA

A Roth IRA presents unique opportunities for retirement, tax and estate planning. In many situations, an existing IRA can be rolled over to a Roth IRA; the planner must consider whether this rollover is available to the client and whether it is a good idea.

Some basic aspects of Roth IRAs (see Chapter 17) must be considered:

- Conversion is not permitted in a year when the modified AGI of the IRA account holder (the IRS views this as joint AGI for married individuals) exceeds $100,000 (not including the rolled over IRA amount).

- Conversion is not permitted if the account holder is married and filing separately.

- There is no limit on the rollover, and it can be a total or partial rollover of an existing IRA.

- The amount rolled over is included in gross income of the IRA account holder for federal income tax purposes.

- Distributions (principal and interest) from the Roth IRA are received tax free if (1) they are made after a 5-year holding period, and (2) they are made after age 59½, death, disability, or for a first-time home purchase.

- No minimum distribution rules apply except at death (i.e., at death the beneficiary must take minimum distributions, which are still income tax free, but which lose their Roth IRA character when distributed).

### The Economics of the Conversion

- A Roth IRA conversion would be a *wash* if (a) taxes had to be paid out of the IRA, (b) only the net amount were going to actually end up in the Roth IRA, and (c) income tax rates were not expected to change, because all factors act equally on the gross IRA amount or the net Roth IRA amount when looking at the net effect of the transaction at any point in the future. *However*, the fact that an income tax reduction has just been implemented in mid-2003[7] may favor making a conversion sooner, rather than later.

- For older clients who will have to start minimum distributions soon, the fact that taxes will have to be paid soon on the traditional IRA minimum distributions makes traditional IRAs less attractive. Since no lifetime minimum distribution requirements apply to Roth IRAs, the distributions and tax on them may be deferred until after death.

- If tax dollars can be found from non-IRA sources (without incurring further income taxes) and the full IRA amount is rolled over to the Roth IRA (without pushing up the owner's tax bracket), the Roth conversion is beneficial because the earnings of the Roth IRA are not subject to income tax.

### Why Should a Roth IRA Conversion be Considered (if the Client is Eligible)

- The basic economics of the conversion (see above) can be attractive.

- Conversion reduces taxes at death (since income taxes are already paid).

- Conversion provides a source for the unified credit amount at death ($700,000 in 2003; see below). A Roth IRA is better for this purpose than a traditional IRA or qualified plan interest, since a Roth IRA is not an IRD asset (see below).

| Year | Unified Credit |
|------|----------------|
| 2000 | 675,000 |
| 2001 | 675,000 |
| 2002 | 700,000 |
| 2003 | 700,000 |
| 2004 | 850,000 |
| 2005 | 950,000 |
| 2006 & later | 1,000,000 |

### Negatives of a Roth IRA Conversion

- To get the full benefit from a conversion, the client must come up with non-IRA funds to pay the taxes in the year of conversion.

- While the 2003 reductions in federal income tax rates might make many conversions more advantageous, the possible effect of more dramatic future tax reform could be adverse. For example, suppose the "flat tax" is enacted, with no taxes on investment earnings? Or income tax is replaced with a consumption tax? Nobody can predict these contingencies.

### Nonparticipant Spouse's Rights

The rights of a nonparticipant spouse in qualified plan accumulations is a critical issue. In addition to any rights that exist under state law (these may vary between community property and common law jurisdictions) federal law (under the Retirement Equity Act of 1984, or REA) provides specific rights to the spouse:

- If the plan is subject to the "qualified joint and survivor annuity" requirement (see Chapter 26), among other requirements, the nonparticipant spouse's consent is required for any change in the beneficiary that reduces the spousal benefit. If the benefit from such a plan is rolled over to an IRA, spousal consent to the rollover is required. However, after the benefit has been rolled over to an IRA, no further spousal consent is required under federal law for any disposition of the IRA assets. If there is a rollover, this emphasizes the significance of the initial spousal consent; spouses in this situation should be fully informed of this significance and of their legal rights. It may be advisable for the spouse to have a separate financial or legal advisor in order to prevent later claims that the consent was not an informed one.

- A stock bonus plan, profit sharing plan, or ESOP does not have to meet the joint and survivor requirement if the participant's nonforfeitable account balance is payable as a death benefit to the spouse.[8] Thus, the spouse must consent to any change in the beneficiary of the death benefit. However, the plan participant can bypass this consent requirement by taking a lump sum distribution (spousal consent is not required at that point) and then disposing of the lump sum in any desired arrangement, also without spousal consent. Similarly, amounts in these plans can be rolled over to an IRA without spousal consent (but some plans administratively require spousal consent here, however, to avoid later claims) and the IRA owner is then free to apply IRA assets without spousal consent. Again, particularly where spousal rights are so limited, this situation emphasizes the importance of spouses being informed of their rights and exercising those rights in a prudent manner.

### Using a "Frozen" Plan

A frozen plan is one that has been amended to terminate future employer contributions and new plan entrants, but otherwise continues to exist for the benefit of existing participants. For a business-owner retiree, however, using a frozen plan may not be feasible. First, the IRS view is that if the plan continues to exist, the plan sponsor must continue to exist. For many small businesses, the business is likely to end with the retirement of the owner. In addition, Form 5500 must continue to be filed even for a frozen plan, and the plan must be amended to reflect any changes in the law, so administrative costs for a frozen plan can be considerable.

## PLANNING RETIREMENT DISTRIBUTIONS

*Lump sum or periodic payments.* For clients with relatively large account balances, it almost never makes sense to take all the money out and pay taxes on it immediately. The remaining 10-year averaging provision does not provide significantly lower tax rates for large distributions. The primary income tax benefit available from qualified plan and IRA accumulations is the potential for long-term tax deferral.

*Tax deferral as the basic goal.* The current rules for required minimum distributions permit significant long-term tax deferral for qualified accumulations. Attaining maximum tax deferral should be the primary consideration for the planner unless there are compelling nontax reasons for taking distributions faster than required.

The potential for tax deferral can extend over as many as three life expectancies. During the plan participant's lifetime, minimum distributions are calculated over what amounts to a joint life expectancy (see Chapter 26). If the participant is married and dies before the spouse, the spouse can roll the remaining balance into the spouse's own IRA, and name a younger beneficiary. At the spouse's death, the younger beneficiary can continue payments over the beneficiary's life expectancy. To understand how to achieve maximum deferral (as well as the alternative results), it's important to understand the minimum distribution rules under Code Section 401(a)(9), and in particular the final regulations under this section.[9] These are complex and the following is only a summary — often the regulations themselves and IRS rulings must be consulted to resolve questions that arise.

The lifetime minimum distribution requirements were significantly simplified by reproposed regulations in 2001 and final regulations in 2002. These rules are explained in Chapter 26. For an individual's lifetime distributions, the life expectancies in Figure J.1 must be used to determine distribution for 2003 and later years.

For complete estate and retirement planning purposes, the rules applicable at the participant's death are also important. The rules for after-death distributions depend on whether the participant dies before or after the required beginning date (RBD) for minimum distributions. As discussed in Chapter 26, the RBD is generally April 1 of the year following the later of the (i) attainment of age 70½ or (ii) actual retirement; however, the "actual retirement" option is not available to an owner of more than 5% of the business sponsoring the qualified plan, nor to IRAs.

## Beneficiary is the Participant's Spouse

- *Rollover to IRA.* If the surviving spouse makes a spousal rollover to an IRA, minimum distributions

**Figure J.1**

| Uniform Lifetime Table (2002 Final Regulations) | | | | | |
|---|---|---|---|---|---|
| Age of Employee | Distribution Period | Age of Employee | Distribution Period | Age of Employee | Distribution Period |
| 70 | 27.4 | 86 | 14.1 | 101 | 5.9 |
| 71 | 26.5 | 87 | 13.4 | 102 | 5.5 |
| 72 | 25.6 | 88 | 12.7 | 103 | 5.2 |
| 73 | 24.7 | 89 | 12.0 | 104 | 4.9 |
| 74 | 23.8 | 90 | 11.4 | 105 | 4.5 |
| 75 | 22.9 | 91 | 10.8 | 106 | 4.2 |
| 76 | 22.0 | 92 | 10.2 | 107 | 3.9 |
| 77 | 21.2 | 93 | 9.6 | 108 | 3.7 |
| 78 | 20.3 | 94 | 9.1 | 109 | 3.4 |
| 79 | 19.5 | 95 | 8.6 | 110 | 3.1 |
| 80 | 18.7 | 96 | 8.1 | 111 | 2.9 |
| 81 | 17.9 | 97 | 7.6 | 112 | 2.6 |
| 82 | 17.1 | 98 | 7.1 | 113 | 2.4 |
| 83 | 16.3 | 99 | 6.7 | 114 | 2.1 |
| 84 | 15.5 | 100 | 6.3 | 115 | 1.9 |
| 85 | 14.8 | | | | |

for the surviving spouse's life expectancy do not have to begin until April 1 of the year following the year the *surviving spouse* attains age 70½. The surviving spouse is then subject to the same minimum distribution options as if the surviving spouse were the participant (see Chapter 26). The minimum distribution at that time is based on the table set forth in 2002 final regulations (Figure J.1), Furthermore, the surviving spouse can name a new beneficiary, such as a child.

---

*Example:* Christopher dies at age 80 having named his spouse, Patricia, aged 77, as the beneficiary of his IRA. Patricia rolls the benefit into her own IRA and names their only child, Andy, as beneficiary. During Patricia's lifetime, the same lifetime table (see Figure J.1) used during Christopher's lifetime is used to calculate the minimum distribution for each year during Patricia's lifetime. For example, in the year following Christopher's death, Patricia's age will be 78; thus, the distribution period is 20.3 years. After Patricia's death, minimum distributions to Andy are determined based on his single life expectancy (see Figure J.2), assuming that he is still the beneficiary at that time.

---

- *No rollover.* If the beneficiary is the surviving spouse, but rollover treatment is unavailable or not chosen, distributions must begin by December 31 of the year following the participant's death; but if the deceased participant had not reached age 70½, the distributions can be deferred to December 31 of the year the *deceased participant* would have been 70½.

- If the surviving spouse survives until the date when the participant was or would have been 70½, minimum distributions are determined over the remaining life expectancy of the surviving spouse. This life expectancy is not a fixed period but is newly determined (recalculated) each year that the spouse survives. This has the effect of reducing the annual required minimum distribution compared with a fixed life expectancy. After the surviving spouse dies, the distribution period reverts to a fixed period based on the spouse's life expectancy, determined in the year of death and reduced by one for each year thereafter.

- If the surviving spouse dies before the participant would have been 70½, there is a special rule that treats the spouse as if the spouse were the partici-

pant (except that if the spouse has remarried and then dies, the surviving spouse will not be permitted the spousal rollover described above).

## Nonspouse Individual Beneficiary

- If the beneficiary is an individual who is not the spouse, minimum distributions must begin as of the end of the year following death, and the amounts are based on the individual beneficiary's life expectancy, determined based on his birthday in the year after the death (using the single life expectancy table; see Figure J.2). In subsequent years, the applicable distribution period is the life expectancy from the previous year, minus one. In other words, the distribution is made over a fixed period (no recalculation). The same fixed period continues in effect even if the person named as beneficiary at the time of death subsequently dies and leaves the benefit to another heir.

---

*Example:* Jack dies at age 76 owning an IRA account that is valued at $840,000 as of the end of the year of his death. The sole beneficiary is Sarah his niece, who reaches age 54 in the year after Jack's death. The minimum distribution is $840,000/30.5 (Sarah's single life expectancy) = $27,541. The remaining distribution period is now fixed. In the next year, the applicable distribution period is 29.5 (30.5 - 1; see Figure J.2) and so on in future years. In total, distributions can continue for 30.5 years after the death of the participant. This is true even if Sarah dies before the end of the period and leaves the benefit to her heirs.

---

- If distributions are not begun as of the end of the year following death over the beneficiary's life expectancy, generally the only option is that distributions must be completed by December 31 of the fifth year following the participant's death. Under the 5-year rule, there are no minimum distribution requirements for any year other than the fifth year.

## No Individual Beneficiary

- *Death before the RBD.* If the participant dies before the RBD, and there is no designated beneficiary as of the end of the year after the employee's death (which would be the case if a nonindividual such as a charity or the estate were named as beneficiary), the entire

**Figure J.2**

| | Single Life Table | | | | |
|---|---|---|---|---|---|
| **Age** | **Life Expectancy** | **Age** | **Life Expectancy** | **Age** | **Life Expectancy** |
| 0 | 82.4 | 38 | 45.6 | 75 | 13.4 |
| 1 | 81.6 | 39 | 44.6 | 76 | 12.7 |
| 2 | 80.6 | 40 | 43.6 | 77 | 12.1 |
| 3 | 79.7 | 41 | 42.7 | 78 | 11.4 |
| 4 | 78.7 | 42 | 41.7 | 79 | 10.8 |
| 5 | 77.7 | 43 | 40.7 | 80 | 10.2 |
| 6 | 76.7 | 44 | 39.8 | 81 | 9.7 |
| 7 | 75.8 | 45 | 38.8 | 82 | 9.1 |
| 8 | 74.8 | 46 | 37.9 | 83 | 8.6 |
| 9 | 73.8 | 47 | 37.0 | 84 | 8.1 |
| 10 | 72.8 | 48 | 36.0 | 85 | 7.6 |
| 11 | 71.8 | 49 | 35.1 | 86 | 7.1 |
| 12 | 70.8 | 50 | 34.2 | 87 | 6.7 |
| 13 | 69.9 | 51 | 33.3 | 88 | 6.3 |
| 14 | 68.9 | 52 | 32.3 | 89 | 5.9 |
| 15 | 67.9 | 53 | 31.4 | 90 | 5.5 |
| 16 | 66.9 | 54 | 30.5 | 91 | 5.2 |
| 17 | 66.0 | 55 | 29.6 | 92 | 4.9 |
| 18 | 65.0 | 56 | 28.7 | 93 | 4.6 |
| 19 | 64.0 | 57 | 27.9 | 94 | 4.3 |
| 20 | 63.0 | 58 | 27.0 | 95 | 4.1 |
| 21 | 62.1 | 59 | 26.1 | 96 | 3.8 |
| 22 | 61.1 | 60 | 25.2 | 97 | 3.6 |
| 23 | 60.1 | 61 | 24.4 | 98 | 3.4 |
| 24 | 59.1 | 62 | 23.5 | 99 | 3.1 |
| 25 | 58.2 | 63 | 22.7 | 100 | 2.9 |
| 26 | 57.2 | 64 | 21.8 | 101 | 2.7 |
| 27 | 56.2 | 65 | 21.0 | 102 | 2.5 |
| 28 | 55.3 | 66 | 20.2 | 103 | 2.3 |
| 29 | 54.3 | 67 | 19.4 | 104 | 2.1 |
| 30 | 53.3 | 68 | 18.6 | 105 | 1.9 |
| 31 | 52.4 | 69 | 17.8 | 106 | 1.7 |
| 32 | 51.4 | 70 | 17.0 | 107 | 1.5 |
| 33 | 50.4 | 71 | 16.3 | 108 | 1.4 |
| 34 | 49.4 | 72 | 15.5 | 109 | 1.2 |
| 35 | 48.5 | 73 | 14.8 | 110 | 1.1 |
| 36 | 47.5 | 74 | 14.1 | 111 | 1.0 |
| 37 | 46.5 | | | | |

balance must be distributed by December 31 of the fifth year following the participant's death. Under this option, there are no minimum distribution requirements for any year other than the fifth year.

- *Death on or after the RBD.* If the participant dies on or after the RBD and there is no designated beneficiary as of the end of the year after the employee's death, the distribution period is the participant's life expectancy calculated in the year of death and reduced by one for each subsequent year (again,

recalculation is no longer available to determine the required distribution after the participant's death).

---

*Example:* Cookie dies at age 80, having named her estate as the beneficiary of her IRA. Her account balance at the end of the year of her death is $240,000 and her life expectancy is 9.2 (10.2 - 1) in the year following death. The required distribution in the year following death is $26,087 ($240,000/9.2). In each of the following years, the applicable distribution period is reduced by one, until all amounts are distributed after 9 years.

---

If the participant dies after the required beginning date, in the year of death, the heirs must take the decedent's required distribution (if this distribution was not taken before death) based on the method under which the decedent had been taking distributions. In subsequent years, the required distributions will depend upon who is the chosen beneficiary.

### Beneficiary Designation

Under the final regulations, the beneficiary for purposes of determining the required distribution is the beneficiary who actually inherits the benefit. Technically, it is the beneficiary determined as of September 30 of the year following death. A "designated beneficiary" must be an individual (that is, not a charity or the participant's estate) if minimum distributions are to be based on the beneficiary's life expectancy. The beneficiary of a trust will not be treated as a designated beneficiary unless the trust satisfies certain requirements (see below).

If there are multiple designated beneficiaries as of September 30 of the year following death (and separate accounts for each participant have not been established), the life expectancy of the oldest beneficiary (with the shortest life expectancy) is used for determining the required distributions. If one of those beneficiaries is a nonindividual, then the participant is deemed to have no designated beneficiary. If there are multiple designated beneficiaries and separate accounts exist, the minimum distributions are calculated separately for each account and taken by each beneficiary over his or her fixed-term life expectancy.

### Trust as a Designated Beneficiary

It is often useful in estate planning to designate a trust as beneficiary of an IRA or qualified plan benefit, perhaps to use the optimal marital deduction—unified credit formula approach—with respect to the retirement plan assets. If certain requirements of the 2002 final regulations are met by the trust, a trust beneficiary can qualify as a designated beneficiary, so that the beneficiary's life expectancy can be used to determine the minimum distributions after the participant's death. If the trust has multiple beneficiaries, the age of the oldest beneficiary will be used to determine the minimum distribution.

The final regulations set forth the following requirements for a beneficiary of the trust to be treated as designated beneficiary under the minimum distribution rules:

- Beneficiaries of the trust must be identifiable from the trust instrument.

- The trust must be a valid trust under state law— or would be a valid trust except that there is no corpus. The final rules make it clear that the IRS believes that the trust could be a living or testamentary trust.

- The trust must be either be irrevocable, or become irrevocable upon death (i.e., it can be revocable only until the participant's death).

- Certain documentation of the trust provisions (such as a copy of the trust instrument, or a list and description of the beneficiaries), must be provided to the plan administrator.

Under these rules, the usual estate planning trusts (either living or testamentary) that create a marital deduction and unified credit shelter/bypass share at a participant's death can be used as the designated beneficiary of the retirement plan benefits without jeopardizing the use of a beneficiary's life expectancy for the purpose of determining a minimum distribution. However, complex questions remain on this issue.

## ESTATE PLANNING FOR QUALIFIED PLAN AND IRA ACCUMULATIONS

*Outright gift to spouse.* Whenever possible, participants should leave qualified plan or IRA balances to their spouses. This has several advantages:

(a) it eliminates federal estate tax at the participant's death through use of the marital deduction.

(b) the spouse pays income taxes as distributions are made, thus preserving income tax deferral at least for the spouse's life. If the benefit comes from an IRA, or if the spouse rolls over the benefit into his or her own IRA, the spouse can then choose a beneficiary and extend income tax deferral beyond death and possibly over the lifetime of the beneficiary.[10] However, estate taxes due at the spouse's death may require the estate to dip into retirement plan funds and therefore the amount available for further income tax deferral may be reduced or eliminated.

*Leaving as QTIP.* An outright transfer of a qualified plan balance to the spouse at the participant's death may be unsuitable for various reasons:

- the participant desires to provide for ultimate beneficiaries (e.g., children from a prior marriage) that the spouse would not necessarily provide for,

- the spouse is not considered financially competent, or

- the spouse is not a U.S. citizen and the marital deduction is not available unless a qualified domestic trust receives the assets.[11]

The use of a QTIP versus an outright gift adds complications. The basic problem is that fund *earnings* cannot accumulate tax-free in a QTIP; QTIP income must be distributed to the spouse.[12] The amount that has to be distributed may be more than is required under the applicable minimum distribution rules. Investment primarily in nonincome producing property to circumvent this rule probably will not work; the trust then might not qualify as a QTIP, and moreover the spouse can force trust property to be made more productive.[13] The IRS has published rules for QTIPs as beneficiaries of qualified plan accumulations;[14] these must be carefully followed or the estate might not qualify for the marital deduction.

*Bypass trust.* Qualified plan or IRA benefits should generally be paid to a bypass trust *only* if there are no other assets to fund the bypass trust. Reasons:

- Income taxes must be paid on the qualified plan benefits, so part of the unified credit is therefore wasted. For example, if an IRA account worth $700,000 is paid into a bypass trust, the recipients must pay about $200,000 or more of this in income taxes. Therefore they receive not the full $700,000 (in 2003) that potentially can be passed to them free of transfer taxes, but only about $500,000.

- The unified credit should be reserved for assets that are most likely to appreciate in value.

This is a way of transferring the future appreciation free of transfer taxes. For qualified plan and IRA benefits, the fund will only decline in value as income-taxable minimum distributions are made.

- The spouse cannot treat the amount as his/her own IRA (since amounts designed to use the unified credit are not paid to the spouse). This means that one of the best means of extending income tax deferral (over the life of the spouse and the spouse's designated beneficiary) is not available.

Note that "waste" of the credit can be avoided by having the estate named as residual beneficiary (possibly using disclaimers, see below), and making a pecuniary bequest of $700,000 (in 2003) to the bypass trust. The estate then pays income taxes, and the bypass trust gets a full $700,000. But the other disadvantages listed above still apply to this approach.

## SUMMARY

Considerable tax deferral is theoretically possible with qualified plan accumulations. All other things being equal, the goal of the retirement and estate planner in dealing with these accumulations should be to maximize this unique tax benefit by maximizing income tax deferral. As indicated above, deferral can be extended through two deaths by naming the participant's spouse as beneficiary, provided the spouse survives the participant and elects to roll over the amount to his/her own IRA, with a younger child or other heir as beneficiary.

However, as an actual blueprint for planning, this has some deficiencies. The desired result—maximum tax deferral—is contingent on (1) the spouse's actually surviving the participant and (2) the possible impact of estate taxes at death; often these cannot be paid without using up the potentially tax-deferrable qualified plan funds.

Possible approaches include:

- Use a pure "game-theory" planning technique; that is, investigate health, genetics, etc., as applied to the participant and spouse, determine probable dates of death and design a distribution plan that minimizes taxes in this "most likely" contingency; or

- Provide a hedge for the plan using life insurance. Use part of the plan balance during the lifetimes of the participant and spouse to purchase life insurance. Second-to-die insurance would be used if both spouses are living and the nonparticipant spouse is the beneficiary; single life insurance on the participant's life would be used otherwise. The insurance generally would be placed in an irrevocable life insurance trust for the benefit of the children or other ultimate beneficiaries. The purpose of this "wealth replacement trust" is to replace the assets lost to federal estate taxation upon the death of the participant or spouse.

## WHERE CAN I FIND OUT MORE ABOUT IT?

1. Choate, Natalie "Understanding the New Minimum Distribution Rules," http://www.ataxplan.com/articles (2002).

2. Tax Facts 1 (2003), The National Underwriter Co. Cincinnati, OH, www.nationalunderwriter.com.

## FOOTNOTES

1. See Let. Rul. 9220007.
2. 947 F.2d 257 (7th Cir. 1992).
3. *Patterson v. Shumate*, 112 S.Ct. 2242 (1992).
4. See, e.g., *Kelly v. Blue Cross*, No. 91-0005L (D.RI 1993), which held that the sole owner of a corporation was not an employee for ERISA purposes, relying on other cases in the First and Sixth Circuits.
5. See *In re Schlein*, 1993 U.S. App. LEXIS 31333, (11th Cir. 1993) holding that ERISA does not preempt state bankruptcy law exemption of pension benefits.
6. ERISA Section 4021(b).
7. IRC Section 1, as amended by JGTRRA 2003. Note that this tax rate reduction remains subject to the sunset provisions of EGTRRA 2001, beginning after December 31, 2010. JGTRRA 2003, Sec. 107.
8. IRC Section 401(a)(11).
9. Treas. Regs. §§1.401(a)(9)-9; 1.403(b)-3; and 1.408-8. These are effective for distributions for calendar years beginning on or after January 1, 2003. Distributions prior to 2003 were subject to different rules.
10. IRC Section 408(d). In the case of an IRA, the spouse would treat the IRA as his or her own; in the case of a qualified plan, the spouse would receive a lump sum distribution and roll it over into the spouse's own IRA. IRC Section 402(c)(9). However, according to final required minimum distribution regulations, a surviving spouse cannot treat an IRA as his or her own if a trust is named as beneficiary of the account, even if the spouse is the sole beneficiary of the trust. Reg. §1.408-8, A-5(a).
11. IRC Section 2056(d).
12. IRC Section 2056(b)(7)(B); Rev. Rul. 2000-2, 2000-1 CB 305.
13. Treas. Reg. §20.2056(b)-5(f)(4).
14. See Rev. Rul. 2000-2, 2000-1 CB 305.

## Joint and Last Survivor Table - Life Expectancy

| Ages | 35 | 36 | 37 | 38 | 39 | 40 | 41 | 42 | 43 | 44 | 45 | 46 | 47 | 48 | 49 | 50 |
|---|---|---|---|---|---|---|---|---|---|---|---|---|---|---|---|---|
| 35 | 55.2 | 54.7 | 54.3 | 53.8 | 53.4 | 53.0 | 52.7 | 52.3 | 52.0 | 51.7 | 51.5 | 51.2 | 51.0 | 50.8 | 50.6 | 50.4 |
| 36 | 54.7 | 54.2 | 53.7 | 53.3 | 52.8 | 52.4 | 52.0 | 51.7 | 51.3 | 51.0 | 50.7 | 50.5 | 50.2 | 50.0 | 49.8 | 49.6 |
| 37 | 54.3 | 53.7 | 53.2 | 52.7 | 52.3 | 51.8 | 51.4 | 51.1 | 50.7 | 50.4 | 50.0 | 49.8 | 49.5 | 49.2 | 49.0 | 48.8 |
| 38 | 53.8 | 53.3 | 52.7 | 52.2 | 51.7 | 51.3 | 50.9 | 50.4 | 50.1 | 49.7 | 49.4 | 49.1 | 48.8 | 48.5 | 48.2 | 48.0 |
| 39 | 53.4 | 52.8 | 52.3 | 51.7 | 51.2 | 50.8 | 50.3 | 49.9 | 49.5 | 49.1 | 48.7 | 48.4 | 48.1 | 47.8 | 47.5 | 47.3 |
| 40 | 53.0 | 52.4 | 51.8 | 51.3 | 50.8 | 50.2 | 49.8 | 49.3 | 48.9 | 48.5 | 48.1 | 47.7 | 47.4 | 47.1 | 46.8 | 46.5 |
| 41 | 52.7 | 52.0 | 51.4 | 50.9 | 50.3 | 49.8 | 49.3 | 48.8 | 48.3 | 47.9 | 47.5 | 47.1 | 46.7 | 46.4 | 46.1 | 45.8 |
| 42 | 52.3 | 51.7 | 51.1 | 50.4 | 49.9 | 49.3 | 48.8 | 48.3 | 47.8 | 47.3 | 46.9 | 46.5 | 46.1 | 45.8 | 45.4 | 45.1 |
| 43 | 52.0 | 51.3 | 50.7 | 50.1 | 49.5 | 48.9 | 48.3 | 47.8 | 47.3 | 46.8 | 46.3 | 45.9 | 45.5 | 45.1 | 44.8 | 44.4 |
| 44 | 51.7 | 51.0 | 50.4 | 49.7 | 49.1 | 48.5 | 47.9 | 47.3 | 46.8 | 46.3 | 45.8 | 45.4 | 44.9 | 44.5 | 44.2 | 43.8 |
| 45 | 51.5 | 50.7 | 50.0 | 49.4 | 48.7 | 48.1 | 47.5 | 46.9 | 46.3 | 45.8 | 45.3 | 44.8 | 44.4 | 44.0 | 43.6 | 43.2 |
| 46 | 51.2 | 50.5 | 49.8 | 49.1 | 48.4 | 47.7 | 47.1 | 46.5 | 45.9 | 45.4 | 44.8 | 44.3 | 43.9 | 43.4 | 43.0 | 42.6 |
| 47 | 51.0 | 50.2 | 49.5 | 48.8 | 48.1 | 47.4 | 46.7 | 46.1 | 45.5 | 44.9 | 44.4 | 43.9 | 43.4 | 42.9 | 42.4 | 42.0 |
| 48 | 50.8 | 50.0 | 49.2 | 48.5 | 47.8 | 47.1 | 46.4 | 45.8 | 45.1 | 44.5 | 44.0 | 43.4 | 42.9 | 42.4 | 41.9 | 41.5 |
| 49 | 50.6 | 49.8 | 49.0 | 48.2 | 47.5 | 46.8 | 46.1 | 45.4 | 44.8 | 44.2 | 43.6 | 43.0 | 42.4 | 41.9 | 41.4 | 40.9 |
| 50 | 50.4 | 49.6 | 48.8 | 48.0 | 47.3 | 46.5 | 45.8 | 45.1 | 44.4 | 43.8 | 43.2 | 42.6 | 42.0 | 41.5 | 40.9 | 40.4 |
| 51 | 50.2 | 49.4 | 48.6 | 47.8 | 47.0 | 46.3 | 45.5 | 44.8 | 44.1 | 43.5 | 42.8 | 42.2 | 41.6 | 41.0 | 40.5 | 40.0 |
| 52 | 50.0 | 49.2 | 48.4 | 47.6 | 46.8 | 46.0 | 45.3 | 44.6 | 43.8 | 43.2 | 42.5 | 41.8 | 41.2 | 40.6 | 40.1 | 39.5 |
| 53 | 49.9 | 49.1 | 48.2 | 47.4 | 46.6 | 45.8 | 45.1 | 44.3 | 43.6 | 42.9 | 42.2 | 41.5 | 40.9 | 40.3 | 39.7 | 39.1 |
| 54 | 49.8 | 48.9 | 48.1 | 47.2 | 46.4 | 45.6 | 44.8 | 44.1 | 43.3 | 42.6 | 41.9 | 41.2 | 40.5 | 39.9 | 39.3 | 38.7 |
| 55 | 49.7 | 48.8 | 47.9 | 47.1 | 46.3 | 45.5 | 44.7 | 43.9 | 43.1 | 42.4 | 41.6 | 40.9 | 40.2 | 39.6 | 38.9 | 38.3 |
| 56 | 49.5 | 48.7 | 47.8 | 47.0 | 46.1 | 45.3 | 44.5 | 43.7 | 42.9 | 42.1 | 41.4 | 40.7 | 40.0 | 39.3 | 38.6 | 38.0 |
| 57 | 49.4 | 48.6 | 47.7 | 46.8 | 46.0 | 45.1 | 44.3 | 43.5 | 42.7 | 41.9 | 41.2 | 40.4 | 39.7 | 39.0 | 38.3 | 37.6 |
| 58 | 49.4 | 48.5 | 47.6 | 46.7 | 45.8 | 45.0 | 44.2 | 43.3 | 42.5 | 41.7 | 40.9 | 40.2 | 39.4 | 38.7 | 38.0 | 37.3 |
| 59 | 49.3 | 48.4 | 47.5 | 46.6 | 45.7 | 44.9 | 44.0 | 43.2 | 42.4 | 41.5 | 40.7 | 40.0 | 39.2 | 38.5 | 37.8 | 37.1 |
| 60 | 49.2 | 48.3 | 47.4 | 46.5 | 45.6 | 44.7 | 43.9 | 43.0 | 42.2 | 41.4 | 40.6 | 39.8 | 39.0 | 38.2 | 37.5 | 36.8 |
| 61 | 49.1 | 48.2 | 47.3 | 46.4 | 45.5 | 44.6 | 43.8 | 42.9 | 42.1 | 41.2 | 40.4 | 39.6 | 38.8 | 38.0 | 37.3 | 36.6 |
| 62 | 49.1 | 48.1 | 47.2 | 46.3 | 45.4 | 44.5 | 43.7 | 42.8 | 41.9 | 41.1 | 40.3 | 39.4 | 38.6 | 37.8 | 37.1 | 36.3 |
| 63 | 49.0 | 48.1 | 47.2 | 46.3 | 45.3 | 44.5 | 43.6 | 42.7 | 41.8 | 41.0 | 40.1 | 39.3 | 38.5 | 37.7 | 36.9 | 36.1 |
| 64 | 48.9 | 48.0 | 47.1 | 46.2 | 45.3 | 44.4 | 43.5 | 42.6 | 41.7 | 40.8 | 40.0 | 39.2 | 38.3 | 37.5 | 36.7 | 35.9 |
| 65 | 48.9 | 48.0 | 47.0 | 46.1 | 45.2 | 44.3 | 43.4 | 42.5 | 41.6 | 40.7 | 39.9 | 39.0 | 38.2 | 37.4 | 36.6 | 35.8 |
| 66 | 48.9 | 47.9 | 47.0 | 46.1 | 45.1 | 44.2 | 43.3 | 42.4 | 41.5 | 40.6 | 39.8 | 38.9 | 38.1 | 37.2 | 36.4 | 35.6 |
| 67 | 48.8 | 47.9 | 46.9 | 46.0 | 45.1 | 44.2 | 43.3 | 42.3 | 41.4 | 40.6 | 39.7 | 38.8 | 38.0 | 37.1 | 36.3 | 35.5 |
| 68 | 48.8 | 47.8 | 46.9 | 46.0 | 45.0 | 44.1 | 43.2 | 42.3 | 41.4 | 40.5 | 39.6 | 38.7 | 37.9 | 37.0 | 36.2 | 35.3 |
| 69 | 48.7 | 47.8 | 46.9 | 45.9 | 45.0 | 44.1 | 43.1 | 42.2 | 41.3 | 40.4 | 39.5 | 38.6 | 37.8 | 36.9 | 36.0 | 35.2 |
| 70 | 48.7 | 47.8 | 46.8 | 45.9 | 44.9 | 44.0 | 43.1 | 42.2 | 41.3 | 40.3 | 39.4 | 38.6 | 37.7 | 36.8 | 35.9 | 35.1 |
| 71 | 48.7 | 47.7 | 46.8 | 45.9 | 44.9 | 44.0 | 43.0 | 42.1 | 41.2 | 40.3 | 39.4 | 38.5 | 37.6 | 36.7 | 35.9 | 35.0 |
| 72 | 48.7 | 47.7 | 46.8 | 45.8 | 44.9 | 43.9 | 43.0 | 42.1 | 41.1 | 40.2 | 39.3 | 38.4 | 37.5 | 36.6 | 35.8 | 34.9 |
| 73 | 48.6 | 47.7 | 46.7 | 45.8 | 44.8 | 43.9 | 43.0 | 42.0 | 41.1 | 40.2 | 39.3 | 38.4 | 37.5 | 36.6 | 35.7 | 34.8 |
| 74 | 48.6 | 47.7 | 46.7 | 45.8 | 44.8 | 43.9 | 42.9 | 42.0 | 41.1 | 40.1 | 39.2 | 38.3 | 37.4 | 36.5 | 35.6 | 34.8 |
| 75 | 48.6 | 47.7 | 46.7 | 45.7 | 44.8 | 43.8 | 42.9 | 42.0 | 41.0 | 40.1 | 39.2 | 38.3 | 37.4 | 36.5 | 35.6 | 34.7 |
| 76 | 48.6 | 47.6 | 46.7 | 45.7 | 44.8 | 43.8 | 42.9 | 41.9 | 41.0 | 40.1 | 39.1 | 38.2 | 37.3 | 36.4 | 35.5 | 34.6 |
| 77 | 48.6 | 47.6 | 46.7 | 45.7 | 44.8 | 43.8 | 42.9 | 41.9 | 41.0 | 40.0 | 39.1 | 38.2 | 37.3 | 36.4 | 35.5 | 34.6 |
| 78 | 48.6 | 47.6 | 46.6 | 45.7 | 44.7 | 43.8 | 42.8 | 41.9 | 40.9 | 40.0 | 39.1 | 38.2 | 37.2 | 36.3 | 35.4 | 34.5 |
| 79 | 48.6 | 47.6 | 46.6 | 45.7 | 44.7 | 43.8 | 42.8 | 41.9 | 40.9 | 40.0 | 39.1 | 38.1 | 37.2 | 36.3 | 35.4 | 34.5 |
| 80 | 48.5 | 47.6 | 46.6 | 45.7 | 44.7 | 43.7 | 42.8 | 41.8 | 40.9 | 40.0 | 39.0 | 38.1 | 37.2 | 36.3 | 35.4 | 34.5 |
| 81 | 48.5 | 47.6 | 46.6 | 45.7 | 44.7 | 43.7 | 42.8 | 41.8 | 40.9 | 39.9 | 39.0 | 38.1 | 37.2 | 36.2 | 35.3 | 34.4 |
| 82 | 48.5 | 47.6 | 46.6 | 45.6 | 44.7 | 43.7 | 42.8 | 41.8 | 40.9 | 39.9 | 39.0 | 38.1 | 37.1 | 36.2 | 35.3 | 34.4 |
| 83 | 48.5 | 47.6 | 46.6 | 45.6 | 44.7 | 43.7 | 42.8 | 41.8 | 40.9 | 39.9 | 39.0 | 38.0 | 37.1 | 36.2 | 35.3 | 34.4 |
| 84 | 48.5 | 47.6 | 46.6 | 45.6 | 44.7 | 43.7 | 42.7 | 41.8 | 40.8 | 39.9 | 39.0 | 38.0 | 37.1 | 36.2 | 35.3 | 34.3 |
| 85 | 48.5 | 47.5 | 46.6 | 45.6 | 44.7 | 43.7 | 42.7 | 41.8 | 40.8 | 39.9 | 38.9 | 38.0 | 37.1 | 36.2 | 35.2 | 34.3 |
| 86 | 48.5 | 47.5 | 46.6 | 45.6 | 44.6 | 43.7 | 42.7 | 41.8 | 40.8 | 39.9 | 38.9 | 38.0 | 37.1 | 36.1 | 35.2 | 34.3 |
| 87 | 48.5 | 47.5 | 46.6 | 45.6 | 44.6 | 43.7 | 42.7 | 41.8 | 40.8 | 39.9 | 38.9 | 38.0 | 37.0 | 36.1 | 35.2 | 34.3 |
| 88 | 48.5 | 47.5 | 46.6 | 45.6 | 44.6 | 43.7 | 42.7 | 41.8 | 40.8 | 39.9 | 38.9 | 38.0 | 37.0 | 36.1 | 35.2 | 34.3 |
| 89 | 48.5 | 47.5 | 46.6 | 45.6 | 44.6 | 43.7 | 42.7 | 41.7 | 40.8 | 39.8 | 38.9 | 38.0 | 37.0 | 36.1 | 35.2 | 34.3 |
| 90 | 48.5 | 47.5 | 46.6 | 45.6 | 44.6 | 43.7 | 42.7 | 41.7 | 40.8 | 39.8 | 38.9 | 38.0 | 37.0 | 36.1 | 35.2 | 34.2 |

## Joint and Last Survivor Table - Life Expectancy (continued)

| Ages | 51 | 52 | 53 | 54 | 55 | 56 | 57 | 58 | 59 | 60 | 61 | 62 | 63 | 64 | 65 | 66 |
|------|------|------|------|------|------|------|------|------|------|------|------|------|------|------|------|------|
| 51 | 39.5 | 39.0 | 38.5 | 38.1 | 37.7 | 37.4 | 37.0 | 36.7 | 36.4 | 36.1 | 35.8 | 35.6 | 35.4 | 35.2 | 35.0 | 34.8 |
| 52 | 39.0 | 38.5 | 38.0 | 37.6 | 37.2 | 36.8 | 36.4 | 36.0 | 35.7 | 35.4 | 35.1 | 34.9 | 34.6 | 34.4 | 34.2 | 34.0 |
| 53 | 38.5 | 38.0 | 37.5 | 37.1 | 36.6 | 36.2 | 35.8 | 35.4 | 35.1 | 34.8 | 34.5 | 34.2 | 33.9 | 33.7 | 33.5 | 33.3 |
| 54 | 38.1 | 37.6 | 37.1 | 36.6 | 36.1 | 35.7 | 35.2 | 34.8 | 34.5 | 34.1 | 33.8 | 33.5 | 33.2 | 33.0 | 32.7 | 32.5 |
| 55 | 37.7 | 37.2 | 36.6 | 36.1 | 35.6 | 35.1 | 34.7 | 34.3 | 33.9 | 33.5 | 33.2 | 32.9 | 32.6 | 32.3 | 32.0 | 31.8 |
| 56 | 37.4 | 36.8 | 36.2 | 35.7 | 35.1 | 34.7 | 34.2 | 33.7 | 33.3 | 32.9 | 32.6 | 32.2 | 31.9 | 31.6 | 31.4 | 31.1 |
| 57 | 37.0 | 36.4 | 35.8 | 35.2 | 34.7 | 34.2 | 33.7 | 33.2 | 32.8 | 32.4 | 32.0 | 31.6 | 31.3 | 31.0 | 30.7 | 30.4 |
| 58 | 36.7 | 36.0 | 35.4 | 34.8 | 34.3 | 33.7 | 33.2 | 32.8 | 32.3 | 31.9 | 31.4 | 31.1 | 30.7 | 30.4 | 30.0 | 29.8 |
| 59 | 36.4 | 35.7 | 35.1 | 34.5 | 33.9 | 33.3 | 32.8 | 32.3 | 31.8 | 31.3 | 30.9 | 30.5 | 30.1 | 29.8 | 29.4 | 29.1 |
| 60 | 36.1 | 35.4 | 34.8 | 34.1 | 33.5 | 32.9 | 32.4 | 31.9 | 31.3 | 30.9 | 30.4 | 30.0 | 29.6 | 29.2 | 28.8 | 28.5 |
| 61 | 35.8 | 35.1 | 34.5 | 33.8 | 33.2 | 32.6 | 32.0 | 31.4 | 30.9 | 30.4 | 29.9 | 29.5 | 29.0 | 28.6 | 28.3 | 27.9 |
| 62 | 35.6 | 34.9 | 34.2 | 33.5 | 32.9 | 32.2 | 31.6 | 31.1 | 30.5 | 30.0 | 29.5 | 29.0 | 28.5 | 28.1 | 27.7 | 27.3 |
| 63 | 35.4 | 34.6 | 33.9 | 33.2 | 32.6 | 31.9 | 31.3 | 30.7 | 30.1 | 29.6 | 29.0 | 28.5 | 28.1 | 27.6 | 27.2 | 26.8 |
| 64 | 35.2 | 34.4 | 33.7 | 33.0 | 32.3 | 31.6 | 31.0 | 30.4 | 29.8 | 29.2 | 28.6 | 28.1 | 27.6 | 27.1 | 26.7 | 26.3 |
| 65 | 35.0 | 34.2 | 33.5 | 32.7 | 32.0 | 31.4 | 30.7 | 30.0 | 29.4 | 28.8 | 28.3 | 27.7 | 27.2 | 26.7 | 26.2 | 25.8 |
| 66 | 34.8 | 34.0 | 33.3 | 32.5 | 31.8 | 31.1 | 30.4 | 29.8 | 29.1 | 28.5 | 27.9 | 27.3 | 26.8 | 26.3 | 25.8 | 25.3 |
| 67 | 34.7 | 33.9 | 33.1 | 32.3 | 31.6 | 30.9 | 30.2 | 29.5 | 28.8 | 28.2 | 27.6 | 27.0 | 26.4 | 25.9 | 25.4 | 24.9 |
| 68 | 34.5 | 33.7 | 32.9 | 32.1 | 31.4 | 30.7 | 29.9 | 29.2 | 28.6 | 27.9 | 27.3 | 26.7 | 26.1 | 25.5 | 25.0 | 24.5 |
| 69 | 34.4 | 33.6 | 32.8 | 32.0 | 31.2 | 30.5 | 29.7 | 29.0 | 28.3 | 27.6 | 27.0 | 26.4 | 25.7 | 25.2 | 24.6 | 24.1 |
| 70 | 34.3 | 33.4 | 32.6 | 31.8 | 31.1 | 30.3 | 29.5 | 28.8 | 28.1 | 27.4 | 26.7 | 26.1 | 25.4 | 24.8 | 24.3 | 23.7 |
| 71 | 34.2 | 33.3 | 32.5 | 31.7 | 30.9 | 30.1 | 29.4 | 28.6 | 27.9 | 27.2 | 26.5 | 25.8 | 25.2 | 24.5 | 23.9 | 23.4 |
| 72 | 34.1 | 33.2 | 32.4 | 31.6 | 30.8 | 30.0 | 29.2 | 28.4 | 27.7 | 27.0 | 26.3 | 25.6 | 24.9 | 24.3 | 23.7 | 23.1 |
| 73 | 34.0 | 33.1 | 32.3 | 31.5 | 30.6 | 29.8 | 29.1 | 28.3 | 27.5 | 26.8 | 26.1 | 25.4 | 24.7 | 24.0 | 23.4 | 22.8 |
| 74 | 33.9 | 33.0 | 32.2 | 31.4 | 30.5 | 29.7 | 28.9 | 28.1 | 27.4 | 26.6 | 25.9 | 25.2 | 24.5 | 23.8 | 23.1 | 22.5 |
| 75 | 33.8 | 33.0 | 32.1 | 31.3 | 30.4 | 29.6 | 28.8 | 28.0 | 27.2 | 26.5 | 25.7 | 25.0 | 24.3 | 23.6 | 22.9 | 22.3 |
| 76 | 33.8 | 32.9 | 32.0 | 31.2 | 30.3 | 29.5 | 28.7 | 27.9 | 27.1 | 26.3 | 25.6 | 24.8 | 24.1 | 23.4 | 22.7 | 22.0 |
| 77 | 33.7 | 32.8 | 32.0 | 31.1 | 30.3 | 29.4 | 28.6 | 27.8 | 27.0 | 26.2 | 25.4 | 24.7 | 23.9 | 23.2 | 22.5 | 21.8 |
| 78 | 33.6 | 32.8 | 31.9 | 31.0 | 30.2 | 29.3 | 28.5 | 27.7 | 26.9 | 26.1 | 25.3 | 24.6 | 23.8 | 23.1 | 22.4 | 21.7 |
| 79 | 33.6 | 32.7 | 31.8 | 31.0 | 30.1 | 29.3 | 28.4 | 27.6 | 26.8 | 26.0 | 25.2 | 24.4 | 23.7 | 22.9 | 22.2 | 21.5 |
| 80 | 33.6 | 32.7 | 31.8 | 30.9 | 30.1 | 29.2 | 28.4 | 27.5 | 26.7 | 25.9 | 25.1 | 24.3 | 23.6 | 22.8 | 22.1 | 21.3 |
| 81 | 33.5 | 32.6 | 31.8 | 30.9 | 30.0 | 29.2 | 28.3 | 27.5 | 26.6 | 25.8 | 25.0 | 24.2 | 23.4 | 22.7 | 21.9 | 21.2 |
| 82 | 33.5 | 32.6 | 31.7 | 30.8 | 30.0 | 29.1 | 28.3 | 27.4 | 26.6 | 25.8 | 24.9 | 24.1 | 23.4 | 22.6 | 21.8 | 21.1 |
| 83 | 33.5 | 32.6 | 31.7 | 30.8 | 29.9 | 29.1 | 28.2 | 27.4 | 26.5 | 25.7 | 24.9 | 24.1 | 23.3 | 22.5 | 21.7 | 21.0 |
| 84 | 33.4 | 32.5 | 31.7 | 30.8 | 29.9 | 29.0 | 28.2 | 27.3 | 26.5 | 25.6 | 24.8 | 24.0 | 23.2 | 22.4 | 21.6 | 20.9 |
| 85 | 33.4 | 32.5 | 31.6 | 30.7 | 29.9 | 29.0 | 28.1 | 27.3 | 26.4 | 25.6 | 24.8 | 23.9 | 23.1 | 22.3 | 21.6 | 20.8 |
| 86 | 33.4 | 32.5 | 31.6 | 30.7 | 29.8 | 29.0 | 28.1 | 27.2 | 26.4 | 25.5 | 24.7 | 23.9 | 23.1 | 22.3 | 21.5 | 20.7 |
| 87 | 33.4 | 32.5 | 31.6 | 30.7 | 29.8 | 28.9 | 28.1 | 27.2 | 26.4 | 25.5 | 24.7 | 23.8 | 23.0 | 22.2 | 21.4 | 20.7 |
| 88 | 33.4 | 32.5 | 31.6 | 30.7 | 29.8 | 28.9 | 28.0 | 27.2 | 26.3 | 25.5 | 24.6 | 23.8 | 23.0 | 22.2 | 21.4 | 20.6 |
| 89 | 33.3 | 32.4 | 31.5 | 30.7 | 29.8 | 28.9 | 28.0 | 27.2 | 26.3 | 25.4 | 24.6 | 23.8 | 22.9 | 22.1 | 21.3 | 20.5 |
| 90 | 33.3 | 32.4 | 31.5 | 30.6 | 29.8 | 28.9 | 28.0 | 27.1 | 26.3 | 25.4 | 24.6 | 23.7 | 22.9 | 22.1 | 21.3 | 20.5 |

## Joint and Last Survivor Table - Life Expectancy (continued)

| Ages | 67 | 68 | 69 | 70 | 71 | 72 | 73 | 74 | 75 | 76 | 77 | 78 | 79 | 80 | 81 | 82 |
|------|----|----|----|----|----|----|----|----|----|----|----|----|----|----|----|----|
| 67 | 24.4 | 24.0 | 23.6 | 23.2 | 22.8 | 22.5 | 22.2 | 21.9 | 21.6 | 21.4 | 21.2 | 21.0 | 20.8 | 20.6 | 20.5 | 20.4 |
| 68 | 24.0 | 23.5 | 23.1 | 22.7 | 22.3 | 22.0 | 21.6 | 21.3 | 21.0 | 20.8 | 20.6 | 20.3 | 20.1 | 20.0 | 19.8 | 19.7 |
| 69 | 23.6 | 23.1 | 22.6 | 22.2 | 21.8 | 21.4 | 21.1 | 20.8 | 20.5 | 20.2 | 19.9 | 19.7 | 19.5 | 19.3 | 19.1 | 19.0 |
| 70 | 23.2 | 22.7 | 22.2 | 21.8 | 21.3 | 20.9 | 20.6 | 20.2 | 19.9 | 19.6 | 19.4 | 19.1 | 18.9 | 18.7 | 18.5 | 18.3 |
| 71 | 22.8 | 22.3 | 21.8 | 21.3 | 20.9 | 20.5 | 20.1 | 19.7 | 19.4 | 19.1 | 18.8 | 18.5 | 18.3 | 18.1 | 17.9 | 17.7 |
| 72 | 22.5 | 22.0 | 21.4 | 20.9 | 20.5 | 20.0 | 19.6 | 19.3 | 18.9 | 18.6 | 18.3 | 18.0 | 17.7 | 17.5 | 17.3 | 17.1 |
| 73 | 22.2 | 21.6 | 21.1 | 20.6 | 20.1 | 19.6 | 19.2 | 18.8 | 18.4 | 18.1 | 17.8 | 17.5 | 17.2 | 16.9 | 16.7 | 16.5 |
| 74 | 21.9 | 21.3 | 20.8 | 20.2 | 19.7 | 19.3 | 18.8 | 18.4 | 18.0 | 17.6 | 17.3 | 17.0 | 16.7 | 16.4 | 16.2 | 15.9 |
| 75 | 21.6 | 21.0 | 20.5 | 19.9 | 19.4 | 18.9 | 18.4 | 18.0 | 17.6 | 17.2 | 16.8 | 16.5 | 16.2 | 15.9 | 15.6 | 15.4 |
| 76 | 21.4 | 20.8 | 20.2 | 19.6 | 19.1 | 18.6 | 18.1 | 17.6 | 17.2 | 16.8 | 16.4 | 16.0 | 15.7 | 15.4 | 15.1 | 14.9 |
| 77 | 21.2 | 20.6 | 19.9 | 19.4 | 18.8 | 18.3 | 17.8 | 17.3 | 16.8 | 16.4 | 16.0 | 15.6 | 15.3 | 15.0 | 14.7 | 14.4 |
| 78 | 21.0 | 20.3 | 19.7 | 19.1 | 18.5 | 18.0 | 17.5 | 17.0 | 16.5 | 16.0 | 15.6 | 15.2 | 14.9 | 14.5 | 14.2 | 13.9 |
| 79 | 20.8 | 20.1 | 19.5 | 18.9 | 18.3 | 17.7 | 17.2 | 16.7 | 16.2 | 15.7 | 15.3 | 14.9 | 14.5 | 14.1 | 13.8 | 13.5 |
| 80 | 20.6 | 20.0 | 19.3 | 18.7 | 18.1 | 17.5 | 16.9 | 16.4 | 15.9 | 15.4 | 15.0 | 14.5 | 14.1 | 13.8 | 13.4 | 13.1 |
| 81 | 20.5 | 19.8 | 19.1 | 18.5 | 17.9 | 17.3 | 16.7 | 16.2 | 15.6 | 15.1 | 14.7 | 14.2 | 13.8 | 13.4 | 13.1 | 12.7 |
| 82 | 20.4 | 19.7 | 19.0 | 18.3 | 17.7 | 17.1 | 16.5 | 15.9 | 15.4 | 14.9 | 14.4 | 13.9 | 13.5 | 13.1 | 12.7 | 12.4 |
| 83 | 20.2 | 19.5 | 18.8 | 18.2 | 17.5 | 16.9 | 16.3 | 15.7 | 15.2 | 14.7 | 14.2 | 13.7 | 13.2 | 12.8 | 12.4 | 12.1 |
| 84 | 20.1 | 19.4 | 18.7 | 18.0 | 17.4 | 16.7 | 16.1 | 15.5 | 15.0 | 14.4 | 13.9 | 13.4 | 13.0 | 12.6 | 12.2 | 11.8 |
| 85 | 20.1 | 19.3 | 18.6 | 17.9 | 17.3 | 16.6 | 16.0 | 15.4 | 14.8 | 14.3 | 13.7 | 13.2 | 12.8 | 12.3 | 11.9 | 11.5 |
| 86 | 20.0 | 19.2 | 18.5 | 17.8 | 17.1 | 16.5 | 15.8 | 15.2 | 14.6 | 14.1 | 13.5 | 13.0 | 12.5 | 12.1 | 11.7 | 11.3 |
| 87 | 19.9 | 19.2 | 18.4 | 17.7 | 17.0 | 16.4 | 15.7 | 15.1 | 14.5 | 13.9 | 13.4 | 12.9 | 12.4 | 11.9 | 11.4 | 11.0 |
| 88 | 19.8 | 19.1 | 18.3 | 17.6 | 16.9 | 16.3 | 15.6 | 15.0 | 14.4 | 13.8 | 13.2 | 12.7 | 12.2 | 11.7 | 11.3 | 10.8 |
| 89 | 19.8 | 19.0 | 18.3 | 17.6 | 16.9 | 16.2 | 15.5 | 14.9 | 14.3 | 13.7 | 13.1 | 12.6 | 12.0 | 11.5 | 11.1 | 10.6 |
| 90 | 19.7 | 19.0 | 18.2 | 17.5 | 16.8 | 16.1 | 15.4 | 14.8 | 14.2 | 13.6 | 13.0 | 12.4 | 11.9 | 11.4 | 10.9 | 10.5 |

## Joint and Last Survivor Table - Life Expectancy (continued)

| Ages | 83 | 84 | 85 | 86 | 87 | 88 | 89 | 90 |
|------|----|----|----|----|----|----|----|----|
| 83 | 11.7 | 11.4 | 11.1 | 10.9 | 10.6 | 10.4 | 10.2 | 10.1 |
| 84 | 11.4 | 11.1 | 10.8 | 10.5 | 10.3 | 10.1 | 9.9 | 9.7 |
| 85 | 11.1 | 10.8 | 10.5 | 10.2 | 9.9 | 9.7 | 9.5 | 9.3 |
| 86 | 10.9 | 10.5 | 10.2 | 9.9 | 9.6 | 9.4 | 9.2 | 9.0 |
| 87 | 10.6 | 10.3 | 9.9 | 9.6 | 9.4 | 9.1 | 8.9 | 8.6 |
| 88 | 10.4 | 10.1 | 9.7 | 9.4 | 9.1 | 8.8 | 8.6 | 8.3 |
| 89 | 10.2 | 9.9 | 9.5 | 9.2 | 8.9 | 8.6 | 8.3 | 8.1 |
| 90 | 10.1 | 9.7 | 9.3 | 9.0 | 8.6 | 8.3 | 8.1 | 7.8 |

# INDEX

## TOOLS & TECHNIQUES

In Print • Online • CE Filed

The *Tools & Techniques Online Library* covers the following printed titles:

*Charitable Planning*
*Employee Benefit & Retirement Planning*
*Estate Planning*
*Financial Planning*
*Life Insurance Planning*

The *Tools & Techniques Online Library* provides you with immediate access to information across the financial services titles - increasing your ability to plan for your clients' needs. Other features of this annual service include advanced searching, cross-title analysis, results ranked as needed, and more.

The *Tools & Techniques* titles are CE Filed for credit in most states. Go to www.nationalunder-writer.com/educationservices to sign up today.

**PAYMENT INFORMATION AND GUARANTEE**
Add shipping & handling charges to all orders as indicated. If your order exceeds total amount listed in chart, or for overseas rates, call 1-800-543-0874. Any order of 10 or more items or $250.00 and over will be billed for shipping by actual weight, plus a handling fee. Any discounts do not apply to shipping and handling.
Unconditional 30-day guarantee. Product(s) damaged in shipping will be replace at no cost to you. Claims must be made within 30 days from the invoice date.
Price, information, and availability subject to change

| SHIPPING & HANDLING | | | |
|---|---|---|---|
| ORDER TOTAL | | | S&H |
| $10.00 | TO | $19.99 | $5.00 |
| $20.00 | TO | $39.99 | $6.00 |
| $40.00 | TO | $59.99 | $7.00 |
| $60.00 | TO | $79.99 | $9.00 |
| $80.00 | TO | $109.99 | $10.00 |
| $110.00 | TO | $149.99 | $12.00 |
| $150.00 | TO | $199.99 | $13.00 |
| $200.00 | TO | $249.99 | $15.50 |

**SALES TAX** (Additional)
Sales tax is required for residents of the following states: CA, DC, FL, GA, IL, KY, NJ, NY, OH, PA, and WA.

The
**NATIONAL UNDERWRITER Company**
PROFESSIONAL PUBLISHING GROUP

---

The
**NATIONAL UNDERWRITER Company**
PROFESSIONAL PUBLISHING GROUP

**Please send me the following :** *(please indicate quantity)*

The Tools & Techniques of Employee Benefit and Retirement Planning _____ Book (#2710008) $52.95
The Tools & Techniques of Estate Planning _____ Book (#2850012) $49.95
The Tools & Techniques of Financial Planning _____ Book (#2770006) $49.95
The Tools & Techniques of Life Insurance Planning _____ Book (#2700002) $44.95
The Tools & Techniques of Charitable Planning _____ Book (#2500000) $49.95
The Tools & Techniques Online Library _____ 1 Year Subscription (TTLIB) $140.00

❏ Check enclosed*       Charge My ❏ VISA ❏ MC ❏ AmEx (check one)       ❏ Bill me

*Make check payable to The National Underwriter Company. Please include the appropriate shipping & handling and any applicable sales tax.

Card #_____ CVV#**_____ Exp. Date _____
Signature_____
Name_____ Title_____
Company_____
Address_____
City_____ State_____ Zip+4_____
Business Phone (_____)_____
E-mail _____

**For Visa/Mastercard, the three-digit CVV number is printed on the signature panel on the back of the card immediately after the card's account number. For American Express, the four-digit CVV number is printed on the front of the card above the card account number.

**2-BB**

---

The
**NATIONAL UNDERWRITER Company**
PROFESSIONAL PUBLISHING GROUP

**Please send me the following :** *(please indicate quantity)*

The Tools & Techniques of Employee Benefit and Retirement Planning _____ Book (#2710008) $52.95
The Tools & Techniques of Estate Planning _____ Book (#2850012) $49.95
The Tools & Techniques of Financial Planning _____ Book (#2770006) $49.95
The Tools & Techniques of Life Insurance Planning _____ Book (#2700002) $44.95
The Tools & Techniques of Charitable Planning _____ Book (#2500000) $49.95
The Tools & Techniques Online Library _____ 1 Year Subscription (TTLIB) $140.00

❏ Check enclosed*       Charge My ❏ VISA ❏ MC ❏ AmEx (check one)       ❏ Bill me

*Make check payable to The National Underwriter Company. Please include the appropriate shipping & handling and any applicable sales tax.

Card #_____ CVV#**_____ Exp. Date _____
Signature_____
Name_____ Title_____
Company_____
Address_____
City_____ State_____ Zip+4_____
Business Phone (_____)_____
E-mail _____

**For Visa/Mastercard, the three-digit CVV number is printed on the signature panel on the back of the card immediately after the card's account number. For American Express, the four-digit CVV number is printed on the front of the card above the card account number.

**2-BB**

---

Order the *Tools & Techniques Series* and other The National Underwriter Company titles.

**4 Ways To Order:**
1. Call 1-800-543-0874
2. Fax your completed order card to 1-800-874-1916
3. Return your completed prepaid postage order card
4. Go online to www.NationalUnderwriterStore.com

# BUSINESS REPLY MAIL
FIRST-CLASS MAIL     PERMIT NO 68     CINCINNATI OH

POSTAGE WILL BE PAID BY ADDRESSEE

**ORDERS DEPARTMENT**
**THE NATIONAL UNDERWRITER COMPANY**
**PO BOX 14448**
**CINCINNATI OH 45250-9786**

NO POSTAGE
NECESSARY
IF MAILED
IN THE
UNITED STATES

# BUSINESS REPLY MAIL
FIRST-CLASS MAIL     PERMIT NO 68     CINCINNATI OH

POSTAGE WILL BE PAID BY ADDRESSEE

**ORDERS DEPARTMENT**
**THE NATIONAL UNDERWRITER COMPANY**
**PO BOX 14448**
**CINCINNATI OH 45250-9786**